Women Veterans

Women who fight in wars also have to fight for their right to do so. But what are the obstacles impeding their progress in achieving equal status as both active service members and as veterans? This book, written by a team of female veterans and military scholars, demonstrates the ways in which women service members and veterans experience a unique set of challenges when attempting both to serve their country honorably and reintegrate into civilian society following military service. These challenges include – but are not limited to – discrimination, staggering rates of suicide, and barriers to obtaining treatment for military sexual trauma and other critical benefits through the U.S. Department of Veterans Affairs.

Women Veterans: Lifting the Veil of Invisibility examines current service-related policies and gender in the military's hierarchical power structure. Here, a confluence of white male privilege and entitlement, the culture of domination, and the effeminization of the enemy manifest themselves as a backlash against women, calling into question a woman's agency and her very status as a citizen. Special attention in the book is paid to the civil–military divide, representative bureaucracy, and the function of the military and civilian justice systems. Moreover, the need for appropriate healthcare policies and structures is examined within a 'wicked problems' framework. The authors conclude that the responsibility for women veterans, and all veterans for that matter, must become a matter of compelling government interest. This ground-breaking book is required reading for practitioners of public policy and administration with an interest in military and veterans affairs, public health, nongovernmental organizations and activist groups, as well as scholars of gender and public service, public personnel management, and nonprofit management.

G.L.A. Harris is a Professor of Public Administration in the Mark O. Hatfield School of Government at Portland State University, Portland, Oregon. A two time named Fulbright Commission distinguished scholar as Research Chair in North American Integration and as NATO Chair in Security Studies, Dr. Harris is also a Commissioned Officer in the U.S. Air Force Reserve and formerly served on active duty in the U.S. Air Force. She is also a graduate of the U.S. Air Force's junior, intermediate and senior service schools, including Air War College.

R. Finn Sumner is Assistant Professor of Public Administration at Portland State University, U.S.

M.C. González-Prats served in the Army from 1998 to 2004 as an enlisted reservist, and later, as an active duty supply and logistics officer. She is currently pursuing a Ph.D. in Social Work at Portland State University (PSU), and is a TL1 fellow at the Oregon Health Sciences University (OHSU) Clinical and Translational Research Institute.

"There is no other book that addresses the challenges women face in the military as the authors have done in *Women Veterans: Lifting the Veil of Invisibility*. This book represents a comprehensive, systematic examination of the uphill battles that women are forced to endure by the white-male, hierarchical power structure of the military. The authors should be celebrated for their candid and accessible treatment of this significant, formidable topic."

Norma M. Riccucci, *Rutgers University, USA*

Women Veterans
Lifting the Veil of Invisibility

G.L.A. Harris, R. Finn Sumner, and
M.C. González-Prats

NEW YORK AND LONDON

First published 2018
by Routledge
711 Third Avenue, New York, NY 10017

and by Routledge
2 Park Square, Milton Park, Abingdon, Oxon OX14 4RN

Routledge is an imprint of the Taylor & Francis Group, an informa business

© 2018 Taylor & Francis

The right of G.L.A. Harris, R. Finn Sumner, and Maria Carolina González-Prats to be identified as authors of this work has been asserted by them in accordance with sections 77 and 78 of the Copyright, Designs and Patents Act 1988.

All rights reserved. No part of this book may be reprinted or reproduced or utilised in any form or by any electronic, mechanical, or other means, now known or hereafter invented, including photocopying and recording, or in any information storage or retrieval system, without permission in writing from the publishers.

Trademark notice: Product or corporate names may be trademarks or registered trademarks, and are used only for identification and explanation without intent to infringe.

Library of Congress Cataloging-in-Publication Data
A catalog record for this book has been requested

ISBN: 978-1-4987-2760-0 (hbk)
ISBN: 978-1-351-20115-5 (ebk)

Typeset in Times New Roman
by Taylor & Francis Books

Contents

List of illustrations   viii

PART I
Preface   1

PART II
Intersectionality   11

  1 Women as Warriors   20

  2 Women as Other   33

  3 Women as Supporters and Caregivers   49

  4 Women as Sex Objects   65

  5 Women as Marginalized   74

PART III
On Citizenship   89

  6 Agency and Second-Class Status   91

  7 Who Is a Veteran?   103

  8 The Selective Service Act   118

  9 The Equal Rights Amendment: At the Crossroads of Defining Women's Citizenship   133

  10 The Combat Exclusion Policy   143

PART IV
Military Culture   171

11 White Male Privilege   173

12 A Culture of Domination   185

13 The Effeminization of the Enemy   198

14 Backlash against Women   208

PART V
Women and Power   221

15 Women in Power   223

16 Women as Tokens   231

17 Women as Proxies for Men   244

18 The Role of Equalizers   260

PART VI
The Civil–Military Divide   277

19 Who Serves in the Military?   278

20 The Notion of Representative Bureaucracy   284

21 Legal Frameworks Apart: The Military v. Civilian Justice Systems   291

PART VII
Confronting Wicked Problems: The Role of Health and Violence   303

22 Determinants of Health   305

23 Impact of Military Sexual Trauma   343

24 The Military's Response to Military Sexual Trauma   361

25 Biological, Psychological, and Sociological Outcomes   376

26 The Ethics of Responsibility 400

PART VIII
Conclusion **411**

Index 428

Illustrations

Figures

 7.1 Women veterans by period of service, 2013 annual averages — 107
18.1a Unemployed women veterans by period of service, 2013 annual averages — 266
18.1b Unemployed women veterans by age, 2013 annual averages — 267
18.2a Employed women veterans and nonveterans by sector, 2013 annual averages — 270
18.2b Employed women veterans and nonveterans by occupation, 2013 annual averages — 270
23.1 Total military sexual assaults per fiscal year, 2007–14 — 352
24.1 Gender disparity in MST claims — 368
25.1 The social-ecological model — 380

Tables

22.1 Extracted select data, employment situation of veterans, summary table: Gender comparison, 2015–16 — 314
22.2 Employment statistics of civilian population 18 years and over by veteran status, period of service and sex (not seasonally adjusted), unemployment rates in percentage — 315

Part I
Preface

Even as a majority in American society, women are routinely marginalized in multiple venues and especially so where they become the default and underclass in predominantly male institutions like the military. As Kanter (1977) notes, for women to become streamlined as an accepted part of the milieu, on one hand, they must comprise at least 15 percent of the organization for a critical mass and within an occupation. Yet, on the other hand, Kanter admits that achieving critical mass becomes a conundrum for women as it in no way guarantees their acceptance by men in certain facets of organizational life. In fact, as Kanter continues, for women, this critical mass may bring about a degree of unwanted hypervisibility simply because they are women. Thus, women's existence in society, and as the overwhelming research suggests, is predicated on and is one of invisibility even where women represent the majority, and in the process brings unwarranted visibility to them as a group (Kanter 1977, Harris 2012, Vojdik 2002, Firor Scott 1984). Harris (2009) cites the case of Sergeant (Sgt.) Leigh Ann Hester, who, during the initial stages of Operation Iraqi Freedom, was awarded the Silver Star for valor. Hester was also only the second woman recipient of this medal since World War II. When asked by a reporter how she felt about receiving the medal as a woman, Sgt. Hester deliberately sidestepped the question in an attempt to deflect attention from herself. She simply invoked that the receipt of the medal was about her performance as a soldier and was not to be attributed to her gender (Lumpkin 2005, Harris 2009). Sgt. Hester's response, though appropriate, signals the lengths to which women veterans, and notably those in non-traditional jobs, will go to avoid bringing attention to themselves, given gender. Yet, such acts only serve to reinforce their invisibility.

Gardam (1997) describes acts of violence against women, including as combatants, during times of armed conflict when their concerns are routinely subordinated to those of men despite the fact that such matters are legally protected, though rarely enforced, under the Geneva Convention. Making things worse, men are the ones who collect the data that should facilitate the case for prosecution but which only intensifies the dilemma for women. Accordingly, it was only the increased presence of female reporters at the

Yugoslavian conflict, as one example, that brought the plight of women's issues to light. Though it is generally acknowledged that women routinely become the spoils of war, their concerns remain hidden from view. To McElrath (1992), these affairs, or those that are perceived to be only within the purview of women, then do not become the concern of others, who are men. This entrenched silence only fuels women's cumulative invisibility.

All too often women are relegated and/or forced to self-relegate to second-class citizenship. However, truth be told, one modern-day manifestation, especially for military women, is the attempt to negotiate the need for recognition. Together with the cry for agency, women's invisibility is progressively being morphed, albeit destructively, into the collective taking of one's life. This disquieting trend for military women is rearing its ugly head. Military women, particularly those below the age of 25, are successfully carrying out their suicides (Kime 2015). Two longitudinal studies show the alarming suicide rates committed by women veterans. The first, a report by the Department of Veterans Affairs (VA) of women veterans between the ages of 18 and 29, revealed the chasm between veterans and nonveterans (Disabled American Veterans (DAV) 2014). Women veterans are 12 times more likely than women nonveterans to commit suicide. The second study exposed the suicide rate of female veterans to be six times more likely than women within the general civilian population (Hoffmire et al. 2015). A third, but earlier study, the first such large-scale study of its kind about female veterans between the ages of 18 through 34 in 16 states, found that female veterans were three times more likely than civilian women to commit suicide (McFarland et al. 2010). In the more recent study by the DAV, one woman veteran aptly summed up the rationale for this trauma by saying that, "[e]veryone assumes that my husband is the veteran and he has never served in the military. I feel invisible" (DAV 2014, p.9).

In view of these findings, we, the authors of this book, have made what we believe to be a compelling observation, even if anecdotal at this juncture, although the frequency with which such anecdotes are being supported by empirical data has increased. As such, we argue that women veterans of the U.S. military either deliberately do not self-identify, at least publicly, or make it known to others, chiefly in the presence of civilian men and/or male veterans that they, too, are veterans. Moreover, a book by one of us, has unearthed this very disturbing theme from a series of interviews conducted with women veterans (Harris 2015). Even when women veterans do acknowledge their status to others by unequivocally proclaiming themselves as veterans, there is frequently a struggle for credibility of sorts in that they are not taken seriously or, worse yet, are dismissed altogether as falsifying such information.

As women veterans ourselves, we are uniquely aware of this maltreatment all too well in that we, too, identify as not being taken seriously at times, though none of us has ever shied away from proudly declaring ourselves as veterans. Yet, if anything, our personal experiences have taught us that, in many ways, it is these lived experiences that have cumulatively and collectively allowed us to justifiably affirm who we are, despite the naysayers and onslaught of negativity that society consistently hurls at us but which we are forced to confront. For instance, one of us, upon securing her first academic appointment, was informed, although with somewhat of a sleight of hand and so indirectly, that conducting military research was not in the best interest of her career. While she took these cues seriously – even though at the outset and during her series of interviews with this one institution she was candid about her research interest given the dissertation research that she presented as part of the interviews – because she was then in the formative stage of a fledgling career, her obstinate streak enabled her to straddle the fence, so to speak, by delving into other venues of research while still doggedly pursuing her first love: military research.

Another one of us, as one of the first cohorts of women navigators in the Air Force, a coveted position that earned her a place as one of the women featured in Harris's 2015 book about repealing the combat exclusion policy, suffered the degradation of blatant sexism and second-class citizenship in uniform while stationed overseas. She was forced as the only U.S. military woman officer stationed in Saudi Arabia at the time not only to don the traditional hijab, the cultural garb for women in that region, over her military uniform, but was also subjected to sitting in the back of the vehicle and behind male military personnel who were subordinate in rank. This practice, the U.S. military rationalized, was to avoid offending the cultural mores of the host nation. Yet, ironically, this author's own military had no reservations about offending her by serving her up as an expedient sacrificial lamb. The third author, upon returning to the continental U.S. following deployment from Operation Iraqi Freedom, struggled in secret to reintegrate into civilian society in the quest to reclaim some sense of meaning to her life. While these experiences are divergent in kind, we offer ourselves as exemplars of ways in which invisibility as women veterans can be manifested. Still, we know that there are so many others with like experiences and believe that both the evidence and time are ripe enough to bring these urgent issues to the fore.

For these reasons, the impetus for this groundbreaking work lies in the consequence of our experiences as women veterans, the accumulated body of research about women in the military by one of us and the no longer budding but overwhelming research on something which strikes women in the military and women veterans disproportionately, military sexual trauma (MST), a derivative of post-traumatic stress disorder (PTSD) that afflicts veterans. As stated at the outset, the more recent epidemic of the staggering rates of suicides among female veterans is perhaps the most profound indicator of a cry for help by women veterans that can no longer be ignored. In response, we have consciously cast part of the title of the book as *Lifting the Veil of Invisibility* to mean an attempt to unmask its triple denotation of invisibility.

First, we intend to highlight *veil* as sometimes defined by others to mean that, while seen, in that women veterans are indeed visible, their treatment, both inside and outside the military, proves otherwise. As one of many such examples, according to Wagner DeCrew (1995), a form of cultural amnesia by the military and civilian leadership takes hold following each national crisis or major conflict in which military women were instrumental to the successful execution and achievement of the mission. Yet for all their remarkable performance during each campaign, during peacetime, women's performance is all but forgotten. In effect, women's progress in the military has been characterized by stops and starts, never one of linear growth, for women in the military are only perceived as a convenient resource, to be used and disposed of at will (Wechsler Segal 1995).

Second, given this abuse, women veterans themselves either intentionally or unintentionally reinforce this notion of invisibility by slipping under the cover of darkness of a self-imposed veil, if you will, for the purpose of self-protection. Here, conceivably, the justification for such actions is to hold one's credibility and/or identity intact, never to be exposed or questioned because the female veteran does not cavalierly disclose this information for fear of retribution. When she does disclose this information as to her veteran status, she does so primarily to only those whom she trusts or with those within her closest sphere of influence such as family and friends. A recent survey by Gould and Obicheta (2015) underscores the extent to which women veterans experience this invisibility (also see Shane 2015). The researchers uncovered that while women constitute 16 percent of the now post-September 11, 2001 veterans, the largest such number reported in the military's ourstory (her/history), and who unlike their predecessors are more likely to encounter combat, they are disproportionately more likely than male veterans to endure the onslaught of very different challenges with reintegrating into civilian society following military service (Gould and Obicheta 2015). Accompanying many of these challenges while in the military, and which has undoubtedly exacerbated their adjustment as civilians, is that at least 50 percent have experienced some form of harassment, bias or sidelining. Some 70 percent of the women reported feeling stifled given limited career opportunities in the military, 82 percent had reintegration issues as civilians, and only 37 percent felt that they were appreciated and regarded as veterans. The study concluded that collectively women veterans were being forced to continue fighting another war, this time for recognition as veterans following military service.

Third, and directly related to the aforementioned, particularly following deactivation from military service, many women veterans complain of experiencing indifference from those who are most entrusted to serve them when they visit such institutions as the Veterans Administration (VA) to apply for earned benefits. Not only is there a grave divergence in the manner in which both female and male veterans are treated at these institutions, but paradoxically and more insidious is that many of these acts of ignorance and discrimination are often committed by civilian women within the VA. According to Harris 2015 many female veterans, to their detriment, then deliberately do not return or utilize the services of the VA in order to bypass this abuse. Unlike their male veteran counterparts, female veterans suffer the embarrassment of being ignored; not believed as to the credibility of their status as military veterans or combat veterans; and should they be given any attention, the assumption is that their presence must be on behalf of either their fathers or husbands who are veterans, and not themselves.

Even after exiting the physical battlefield, women veterans are compelled to fight, once again, against this invisibility. Fed up, many choose to save face by disappearing off the grid or don another self-imposed veil through self-denial of claiming who they are and what is rightfully theirs. The film *Lioness* and its companion report about the state of women veterans (*Lioness Report* 2012) were integral in bringing to light many issues in the VA that have long dogged women veterans by preventing them from receiving their entitled programs, services and benefits. More important, is that such initiatives be delivered in a manner in terms of access that is on par with those of male veterans. Hence, in light of the above, we see these occurrences as a tripartite conspiracy and hypothesize that it is these very confounding phenomena independently and jointly that keep women veterans invisible and thus veiled.

Therefore, the objective of this book is to address the gulf within the extant literature, and as of this writing, we are pleased to finally see the bevy of research activity that has been dedicated to women veterans. If anything, we believe that this additional attention only strengthens our call to action and cutting-edge work on such gnawing issues. That said, we aim to confront head on those issues or factors that not only contribute to or facilitate women's invisibility but specifically those that impact women veterans.

Admittedly, while there has been an increased flurry of research published about women in the military, much of which speaks to the treatment of military women and, by extension, women veterans, little, if any, contains discourse dedicated to the invisibility of military women and certainly none to date broaches the subject of the invisibility of women veterans. We see our work, then, as an ambitious undertaking. Yet, we are motivated, even compelled, in our zeal to complete this work not simply because of our own experiences but more so for the many women veterans who for multiple reasons choose not to identify themselves as such. We find this to be a frightening and regrettable trend, for women veterans, like men veterans, have served their country valiantly and deserve to be recognized equally for their service, not to mention the cadre of benefits to which they are entitled but which they have neither applied for nor sought because of the ill-conceived stigma of being a woman veteran. The topic for this research, debate and book is long overdue and we speculate stems not just from the marginalized roles which women are often relegated to playing in society, but the invisibility associated with these roles. Consequently, we endeavor to shed much light on this perplexing problem and in the process hope to educate others as to the reasons for its existence and prevalence.

Given what we believe to be the multi-dimensional nature of women's invisibility, and the untapped, yet rich study of the subject as it pertains to women veterans, our approach to the book is comprehensive in scope. We hope that this all-encompassing method will present as much as possible every variable that may conceivably play a role in providing some logic to account for this anomaly for women veterans, notwithstanding a role that women are routinely often expected to conform to in civilian society. As a result, this book is divided into eight distinct parts.

Part I, the Preface, establishes the basis for the book and outlines the format in which the book will proceed. Part II ruminates about the multiple roles and intersecting identities that have been attributed to women veterans – be it as warriors, other, supporters, caregivers, sex objects or as marginalized. Here, we engage in discourse that provides a foundation for these nomenclatures, how they came to be and how they continue to contribute to and/or detract from women's enduring invisibility in the military, as veterans, and in society as a whole. However, it is the underlying intersectionality of these roles that must also become an integral part of the discussion.

In Part III, we delve into the concept of citizenship and how its definition is applied to women in terms of agency and as second-class citizens; who is idealized in society as a veteran; and as a consequence, who is obligated to register and participate in the Selective Service System. The yet to be ratified Equal Rights Amendment (ERA) at both the state and federal levels may indeed have a fundamental role in the framing of the combat exclusion policy, which, although in theory has been repealed, may still be at odds with how women, primarily military women, are viewed by the larger society.

Part IV confronts the intractability of the military's culture where privilege and entitlement are presumed as the rites of passage of men. This ingrained way of thinking and in turn behaving has no doubt bolstered traditional norms of the culture of domination and where the enemy is deliberately effeminized, all as a backlash against the inclusion of women in those venues that are branded off-limits to the so-called sacred grove that is for men only.

In Women and Power, Part V, we examine how modern society has managed to upend the definitions and so the symbolic significance of the language to make them diametric opposites when the ourstory shows that nothing could be further from the truth. Harris (2015), Grant DePauw (1998) and Goldstein (2003), among others, have demonstrated how since the beginning of time, women have skillfully leveraged their prowess and positions as powerbrokers in society and on multiple levels as warrior queens who conquered and amassed territories for economic power, to the more contemporary representation of women as political leaders on the world stage who do so with quintessential finesse.

Women have long established themselves as powerful and so the modern manifestations of women in power, while more constrained in light of contemporary mores, serve as exemplars. Unfortunately, while we do not specifically know when women as a collective began to be identified as a subordinate specie to that of men and began to act in kind, Grant DePauw (1998) offers some insight as to the possible origin. Using the work of scholars like Kanter (1977), Yoder (1991), Goldin (1995) and even Blalock (1967), we show how women have devolved in organizations and where given their dearth in representation, they have come to lack critical mass. However, as Yoder (1991) contends, it is not just about the numbers. Women then may well serve in key positions but only as proxies for men. The 400,000 plus women who were galvanized during World War II come to mind. What factors then may best function to help level the playing field for women in society? It is believed that securing such societal equalizers as money and education can be instrumental not only in increasing the socioeconomic status of women but also become critical components for building wealth, influence, access and ultimately power.

Part VI of the book tackles the civil–military divide, often couched as a rift between the constituents, yet where the relationship is symbiotic in that each depends upon the other for its very existence. This then begs the question, who deserves to serve in the military? If a volunteer military like that of the U.S. is open to all citizens, then is it not a double standard, and in the process a violation of one of the basic tenets of representative bureaucracy within a democracy, that women be excluded from full participation by way of the combat exclusion policy in the military as one such example? Though in theory the policy has been repealed, its very existence in the military simply extends women's continued marginalization as veterans in the larger civilian society. At best, this maltreatment underpins the duplicity with which women must contend. Besides, within a democratic society, if nothing else, the principle of social justice must be upheld. We deliberate the legal frameworks of the military and civilian society and how both maintain their respective modes of operation in sustaining this civil–military divide.

Part VII analyzes the ordeals of wicked problems, some of which comprise the incalculable biological, psychological and sociological costs to society. Consequently, wicked problems characterize those deep-seated, interconnected and complex afflictions such as poor health and violence for which there are no simple solutions (Rittel and Webber 1973). Given their inherent complexity, one can only hope to "tame" wicked problems rather than actually solve them (Rittel and Webber 1973, p.160). Together, over time, these seemingly intractable maladies become physical manifestations and a measure of the degree to which women veterans have access to basic services like healthcare, for example. Other forms of wicked problems include dealing with the conundrum of violent acts like MST. Alas, though, not only does the military's overall response form the outgrowth of the associated biological, psychological and sociological outcomes, but the apathetic and so-called long-term strategies may only compound and lead to unintended consequences like the astounding rates of suicide among women veterans. We believe that it is the confluence of these disparities (i.e., health and healthcare), the conditions that promote them and the circle of violence against women veterans that eventually push them to the precipice of this cry for help. According to Kaplan et al. (2009), not only are the high rates of women veteran suicides disturbing especially as compared to those of nonveteran women in civilian society, but even more alarming is what has become women veterans' weapon of choice for ending their lives – namely, firearms. The researchers warned that in light of these findings it is incumbent upon mental health professionals, including those from such organizations as the VA, to not simply limit their outreach to women veterans of more recent wars such as Operations Enduring and Iraqi Freedom. Such investigations should be extended to women veterans of prior campaigns. In a longitudinal study encompassing 23 states and 173,969 veterans from 2000 through 2010, the VA concluded that the obscene rates of suicide by women veterans may be compounded by not only those who have been raped but those who might have experienced some form of unwelcome sexual contact (Kemp and Bossarte 2012).

Based upon our comprehensive review of these myriad topics in the book, and in view of how we have operationalized the term *veiled invisibility* within the larger context, we then begin to explore the independent, moderating, intersecting and overriding effects of such variables as violence, health, economics and sociology of women veterans, together with the fallout in accession, advancement and attrition rates of women in the military and the overall implications for women veterans. Similarly, as the kink of implementing the repeal of the combat exclusion policy plays itself out in practice, we revisit its implications for various legislations, including the Selective Service Act, military service and the Feres Doctrine for conscripted force v. a voluntary force, the unratified ERA, and the conundrum of attempts to mitigate the aforementioned wicked problems which, because they are rooted, ambiguous and dynamic in nature, and are endemic to society, no amount of legislation can ever eradicate them.

Finally, we scrutinize the ethics of responsibility for women veterans by both the military and civilian society in Part VIII. When all is said and done, we conclude that the responsibility for the state of affairs that befalls women veterans – as for men veterans and all veterans, for that matter – lies with the military and civilian society. Such responsibility must become a matter of compelling government interest, which if nothing else, is paramount for the sake of national security.

Bibliography

Blalock, H.M. (1967). *Toward a Theory of Minority Group Relations*. New York, NY: John Wiley and Sons.

Disabled American Veterans (DAV). (2014). *Women Veterans: The Long Journey Home*. Cold Spring, KY and Washington, DC: Disabled American Veterans.

Firor Scott, A. (1984). On Seeing and Not Seeing: A Case of Historical Invisibility. *The Journal of American History*, 71, 1, 7–21.

Gardam, J. (1997). Women and the Law of Armed Conflict: Why the Silence? *The International and Comparative Law Quarterly*, 46, 1, 55–80.

Goldin, C. (1995). *Career and Family: College Women Look to the Past* (Working Paper, No. 5188). Cambridge, MA: National Bureau of Economic Research.

Goldstein, J.S. (2003). *War and Gender: How Gender Shapes the War System and Vice Versa*. New York, NY: Cambridge University Press.

Gould, O., and Obicheta, O. (2015). *Her Mission Continues: Service and Reintegration Amongst Post-9/11 Women Veterans*. The Mission Continues Research and Evaluation Team.

Grant DePauw, L. (1998). *Battle Cries and Lullabies. Women in War from Prehistory to the Present*. Norman, OK: University of Oklahoma Press.

Harris, G.L.A. (2009). The Multi-faceted Nature of White Female Attrition in the Military. *Journal of Public Management and Social Policy*, 15, 1, 71–93.

Harris, G.L.A. (2012). Multiple Marginality: How the Disproportionate Assignment of Women and Minorities to Manage Diversity Programs Reinforces and Multiplies Their Marginality. *Administration and Society*, 20, 10, 1–34.

Harris, G.L.A. (2015). *Living Legends and Full Agency: Implications of Repealing the Combat Exclusion Policy*. New York, NY: Taylor & Francis Group.

Hoffmire, C.A., Kemp, J.E., and Bossarte, R.M. (2015). Changes in Suicide Mortality for Veterans and Nonveterans by Gender and History of VHA Service Use, 2000–2010. *Psychiatric Services*, 66, 9, 959–965.

Kanter, R.M. (1977). *Men and Women of the Corporation*. New York, NY: Basic Books, Inc.

Kaplan, M., McFarland, B., and Huguet, N. (2009). Firearm Suicide Among Veterans in the General Population: Findings from the National Violent Death Reporting System. *Journal of Trauma-Injury and Critical Care*, 67, 3, 503–507.

Kemp, J., and Bossarte, R. (2012). *Suicide Data Report*. Department of Veterans Affairs, Mental Health Services, Suicide Prevention Program.

Kime, P. (2015). Study: Junior Troops, Women More Likely to Try Suicide. *Military Times*. July 8.

Lioness Report. (2012). *Cultivating Change: Lioness Impact Report*. Based on *Lioness*, a feature documentary directed by M. McLagan and D. Sommers. U.S.: Room 11 Productions.

Lumpkin, J.T. (2005). Woman Earns Silver Star for Duty in Iraq. AOL News. June 16.

McElrath, K. (1992). Gender, Career Disruption and Academic Rewards. *Journal of Higher Education*, 63, 3, 269–281.

McFarland, B.H., Kaplan, M.S., and Huguet, N. (2010). Self-Inflicted Deaths Among Women with United States Military Service: A Hidden Epidemic? *Psychiatric Services*, 61, 12, 1177.

Rittel, H., and Webber, M. (1973). Dilemmas in a General Theory of Planning. *Policy Sciences*, 4, 155–169.

Shane, L. (2015). Survey: Women Struggle to Be Seen as 'Real' Veterans. *Military Times*. June 9.

Vojdik, V.K. (2002). The Invisibility of Gender in War. *Duke Journal of Gender, Law and Policy*, 9, 261–270.

Wagner DeCrew, J. (1995). The Combat Exclusion Policy and the Role of Women in the Military. *Hypatia*, 10, 1, 56–73.

Wechsler Segal, M. (1995). Women's Military Roles Cross-Nationally, Past, Present, and Future. *Gender and Society*, 9, 6, 757–775.

Yoder, J.D. (1991). Rethinking Tokenism: Looking Beyond the Numbers. *Women's Studies*, 5, 2, 178–192.

Part II
Intersectionality

The dual struggles of black women in the U.S., given their marginalization and subjugation along racial and gender lines, gave rise to the conceptualization of the term intersectionality. Coined by Crenshaw (1989, 1991) to rile against the deliberate exclusion of and to highlight the lived routine experiences of race and gender discrimination of African American women and thus their invisibility, the term intersectionality over time has come to symbolize the modern-day oppression of women of all hues and persuasions (Crenshaw 1989, 1991, 2001). Most notably, what is befitting is that contemporary intersectionality owes its origins to and can be traced as far back as that 1851 speech at the Women's Rights Convention in Alknow, Ohio by none other than Sojourner Truth, in which she challenged the essentialist notion of what purportedly the attributes of women ought to be, in 'Ain't I a Woman?' (Brah 2004).

Truth, born in enslavement, was illiterate yet erudite in many ways in that she brazenly defied the conventions of the time. She knew instinctively that as a slave woman, which was implicit and synonymous with subordination, her rights as a human being, and in this case as a black woman, were inherently not a part of the discourse, much less to be debated. Nevertheless, she deliberately inserted herself by giving voice to the following:

> Well children, where there is so much racket there must be something out of kilter, I think between Negroes of the South and the women of the North – all talking about rights – the white men will be in a fix pretty soon. But what's all this talking about? That man over there says that women need to be helped into carriages, and lifted over ditches, and have the best place everywhere. Nobody helps me any best place. And ain't I a woman? Look at me! Look at my arm. I have plowed, I have planted and I have gathered into barns. And no man could head me. And ain't I a woman? I would work as much, and eat as much as any man – when I could get it – and bear the lash as well! And ain't I a woman? I have borne children and have seen most of them sold into

slavery, and when I cried out with a mother's grief, none by Jesus heard me. And ain't I a woman?

(Brah 2004, p.77)

Despite the hellish circumstances under which Sojourner Truth was forced to exist, she exercised free will by asserting control when she contrived the name for which she later became famous, refusing to accept the colonialist-imposed name of Isabella by her white owner (Brah 2004). Sojourner Truth became the forerunner of today's intersectionality movement in that she was a staunch feminist even by modern standards. Intersectionality gained steam over 100 years later with the Combahee River Collective during the late 1970s through 1980s as a conduit for dispelling the singularity of thought, again in how black women were perceived and to not only cross boundaries based upon race and gender but those of heterosexuality and class as well (Brah 2004, Combahee River Collective 1977, Choo and Marx Ferree 2010). Thus, the present-day characterization of intersectionality has assumed a multi-dimensional heft that encompasses a boundary-spanning fluidity of what it means to be a woman, a view that is anti-essentialist in its makeup.

So, it is understood that the premise behind intersectionality is to be inclusive of all categories and without categorizations. Yet, what binds the intersectionality of women is the commonality among them, however that commonality may be defined (Spelman 2007). Women are akin to pebbles on a beach per se (Spelman 1988, Grillo 2013). They are all pebbles but come in varied shapes, sizes and colors. This universality, according to Crenshaw (1989, 1991), and in this case for black women, deliberately resists keeping them at the margins of society that are bound less by sexual and racial foci to which they are often circumscribed. Black women are therefore multifaceted in nature (Geerts and van der Tuin 2013).

Military women and hence women veterans are of the same, though different, mosaic as are all women. What unites them first as women is not just their marginalized status in society but, given such marginalization, the ensuing invisibility that accompanies this status. Moreover, as military women, they reflect an ilk, a special breed, if you will, that still by contemporary norms are to be leveraged as a convenient resource (Wagner DeCrew 1995) despite their consistent, cumulative and formidable performance whenever, wherever and however the nation is called to arms. Likewise, following the termination of each major campaign, unlike other groups – notably men, who ride the euphoria and benefits attributed to their perceived stunning performance – military women instead routinely experience a 'do over' period of consideration as to their capability each and every time their utilization as a resource is ruminated. Consequently, military women never experience a linear growth of recognition by either the institution or the country, for that matter, for especially during peacetime the stops and starts of consideration and reconsideration are once again revisited for the umpteenth time (Wechsler Segal 1995). Accordingly, a collective amnesia both by the civilian and military leadership sets in and the level of women's patriotism is repeatedly deliberated in response to each national crisis. Stated simply, women's participation, presence and function in the military become conditions of the country's involvement in major crises.

This invisibility of military women which only calls for their use when convenient, speaks to another dimension of intersectionality and, by extension, is an affliction that women veterans share with all women: that is the notion of an otherness. Women represent an otherness in society in that though some are white, they are still precluded because they are not white men and are therefore not considered mainstream in American society (DeMello Patterson 2000, Frankenberg 1993). Because their otherness connotes marginalization, subordination and differentness, women are basically deviants (Ellefson 1998) like all nonwhite groups (Law 1999). However, these intersectional domains only compound women's invisibility.

At 16.5 percent of the military, or those who are currently serving on active duty and in the reserve and National Guard components, women still constitute a minority of the institution (Office of the Assistant Secretary of Defense 2013). This minority status for women veterans also comports with their representation as veterans as a whole, either actively serving or who have already separated from the military. Of the reported almost 23 million living veterans which includes those who are still serving in the military (National Center for Veterans Analysis and Statistics (NCVAS) 2016), 2.2 million, or 9.9 percent, are women (Walker and Borbely 2014). Of these, over 50 percent are veterans of what are categorized as Gulf Wars I (August 1990–2001) and II (September 2001 and on), and 17 percent together are veterans of World War II and the Korean and Vietnam Conflicts, with 30 percent having served during other major campaigns from the Vietnam Conflict through Gulf War I.

An interesting finding is that more than in previous campaigns, women were more likely to have served during Operations Desert Shield and Desert Storm (Gulf War I) and Enduring and Iraqi Freedom (Gulf War II) (Walker and Borbely 2014, Rivera and Johnson 2014). Even more revealing is that as the female veteran population gradually increases, or 8 percent of all veterans in 2009 (NCVAS 2011), that figure is projected to grow by 2035 to 15 percent (NCVAS 2011). Of particular interest is that underrepresented minority women who are black and Hispanic surpass their male counterparts in representation who are also veterans (NCVAS 2015). Given this rise in the number of underrepresented minority (URM) (Native American, black and Hispanic) women as compared to their male URM counterparts, of note is the traditional dual, triple and even quadruple marginalization that URM women experience (Moore 1991, 1996). This is especially true for black women given race and gender.

Women, and more pointedly women veterans, have been forced to navigate the seeming minefield of obstacles, all for the purpose of securing their earned entitlements, hurdles which male veterans and especially white male veterans, have never had to tackle. As the first known African American woman to be promoted to the rank of general officer and subsequently to a two-star general in the Air National Guard, Dr. Irene Trowell Harris upon retirement, and even as she accepted her selection as the U.S. Department of Veterans Affairs Center for Women Veterans inaugural director, blasted the institution for its despicable treatment of women veterans. She said that '[t]he VA was basically designed for men. When they started to get more women veterans coming in, they were not treated the same way. They were not treated with dignity and respect' (Women in Military Service for America (WIMSA) n.d.). Despite their growing presence, in light of expanded roles in the military and as an increasing percentage of the overall veteran population, women continue to be burdened with untoward challenges during and following service. Many of these challenges, as Dolsen (2015) describes, are not a female veteran problem but largely owing to the misconceptions about female veterans.

Organizations like the Service Women's Action Network (SWAN) and the Disabled American Veterans (DAV) (*Lioness Report* 2012), which marked the culmination of the groundbreaking documentary on sexual assault within the ranks, together with the work of such researchers as Kaplan et al. (2009) and Gould and Obicheta (2015), have collectively sounded the alarm about the unique hardships that women veterans encounter, particularly in their efforts at transitioning back to civilian life following military service. While the transition process is a feat for all veterans, for women veterans, it is especially worrisome, notwithstanding the myriad other tribulations that plague them. Anna Bhagwati, former executive director of the SWAN (n.d.), delineated some of the most pressing issues of the day for women veterans. They include, but are not limited to, the epidemic rates of military sexual trauma (MST) that continue disproportionately and adversely to plague the lives of military women, and where 5 percent of women on active duty sustain lifelong impact (see Dolsen 2015). According to Bhagwati (SWAN n.d.), in 2009 alone, an increase of 11 percent in MST was reported over the previous year which still represents less than 20 percent of actual sexual cases that were reported. Yet only 8 percent of offenders are prosecuted for these crimes.

During this same period (SWAN n.d.), while there was a whopping 64 percent increase in the reporting of sexual assaults overall, this number only represented 10 percent of sexual assaults that were actually committed. It is believed that the failure to report the offense has more to do with the culture of the military than perhaps anything else, with up to 85 percent of women and approximately 79 percent of men admitting that such maladies did not warrant reporting. Factors that any efforts to report perpetrators include the military culture, inaccurate reporting and procedures for reporting and levying prosecution. The toll of MST manifests in incalculable ways such as problems with health, negative economic outcomes, sabotage of careers, and the threatening of military retention and its state of readiness. Ironically, though, under the Don't Ask, Don't Tell and Don't Pursue (DADT) policy, which was repealed in 2010 under the Obama Administration (SWAN n.d.), women and minorities represented a disproportionate number of those who were discharged (O'Keefe 2010). For instance, in 2009, although women's makeup of the all-volunteer force then stood at 14 percent, data showed that from 30 percent to 39 percent received discharges under the guise of DADT (Gates 2010). That percentage only increased during the 1997 through 2009 period when the rate climbed to 39 percent. For the Army alone, for 2009, its discharges recorded an astounding 48 percent for women (O'Keefe 2010, Shanker 2008). In essence, women were more likely than men to be discharged under the DADT policy. For minorities, the rate was even higher and was especially so for black women according to data from the Pentagon, in that black women were three times more likely than any demographic in the military to have been discharged for violations under the policy (Holloway 2010).

Damiano (1999) points to the military's tactic of 'lesbian baiting' (p.501) as an often employed tool of sexual harassment to reinforce its patriarchal structure of power that serves to keep women in line and thus in their perceived place. In fact, in many ways, the DADT policy only exacerbated the rates at which women were being discharged from the military, while simultaneously silencing them from coming forward with their complaints about sexual-related offenses. 'Women, straight and gay, are accused as lesbians, when they rebuff the advances by men or report sexual abuse. Women who are top performers in nontraditional fields also face perpetual speculation and rumors that they are lesbians' (Damiano 1999, p.501). Lesbian baiting then becomes an effective identifier aimed at discrediting violators who buck the trend of tradition by speaking up (McClintock 1996). In effect, comply or be silenced: this is the undergirding of any power structure that seeks to maintain the status quo for the benefit of one group to the detriment of another group by undermining the latter.

Yet, even as women are forced into silence in an effort to make them invisible, the sheer numbers are such that in still nontraditional career fields, the military was forced to turn to this very group that is being repeatedly shunned. Take the Navy's unprecedented decision to recruit women into one, if not the last, bastion of holdouts for men that is the infamous silent service of the submarines. The move, as Iskra (2012) contends, was not out of benevolence in that for principled reasons the Navy believed that it is simply the right thing to do. Truth be told, the twofold rationale for this decision was one of necessity: one, the traditional rate at which the Naval Academy graduates men with the required degrees for the career field has precipitously declined; and two, fortuitously for the Navy, women entering the Academy are pursuing more technical degrees that call for submariners than ever before. However, once again it is this categorization as a convenient resource (Wagner DeCrew 1995), given the scarcity of another preferred resource, which provides women as a group with the unforeseen opportunity to repeatedly prove their worth. African Americans have long experienced this blatant insult. Painstakingly, they have strategically used the military as a path to legitimacy and citizenship, even as the military not only rebuffed them by repeatedly questioning their patriotism but betrayed them in the process through failure time and time again to recognize their service to the country, until contemporary times (Harris and Lewis, forthcoming).

As with women, African American men in particular were continually only utilized as a convenient resource when it suited the U.S. military (Harris and Lewis, forthcoming). Herein, though, lies the complexity of intersectionality. Inasmuch as its multidimensionality creates opportunities from opposing forces and conflicts, it nonetheless finds its origins in subordination and oppression (Hutchinson 2001). This identity crisis helps fuel the efforts to move black women from the margins of society and invisibility (Pursue-Vaugh and Eibach 2008) to the center (Choo and Feree 2010). Further, women of color viewed their lived experiences as fundamentally different from those of white women (Espiritu 2000). As such, the various categories, be they race, gender and/or class, only serve to confirm one another. It is this robustness, though, that speaks to the staying power and wide application of this theory of intersectionality, which has withstood the test of time (Geerts and van der Tuin 2013). Although the very premise under which intersectionality was devised was to dispel the notion of categories, nevertheless it is this multidimensionality of roles that has come to define women through the prism of multiple identities. For this purpose, this multidimensionality is equally suitable for the discourse about women in the military and by extension women veterans. Women are either positively, albeit less positively, portrayed as warriors or are more likely to be relegated to such subordinate or estranged roles as 'other,' supporters, caregivers and sex objects, making them all the more prone to fit the composite categorization of marginalized.

The following chapters set out to explicate the many and often invoked identifiers that have been used to describe women in the military: first we connote the most positive image as warriors, followed by 'other,' supporters and caregivers, sex fiends or sex objects (Harris 2009), and marginalized.

Bibliography

Brah, A. (2004). Ain't I a Woman? Revisiting Intersectionality. *Journal of International Women's Studies*, 5, 3, 75–86.

Choo, H.Y., and Marx Ferree, M. (2010). Practicing Intersectionality in Sociological Research: A Critical Analysis of Inclusions, Interactions, and Institutions in the Study of Inequalities. *Sociological Theory*, 28, 2, 129–149.

Combahee River Collective. (1997 [1977]). A Black Feminist Statement. In L. Nicolson (Ed.), *The Second Wave: A Reader in Feminist Theory*. New York: Routledge.

Crenshaw, K.W. (1989). Demarginalizing the Intersection of Race and Gender: A Black Feminist Critique of Antidiscrimination Doctrine, Feminist Theory and Antiracist Politics. *University of Chicago Legal Forum*, 1, Article 8, 139–167.

Crenshaw, K.W. (1991). Mapping the Margins: Intersectionality, Identity Politics, and Violence Against Women of Color. *Stanford Law Review*, 43, 6, 1241–1299.

Crenshaw, K.W. (2001). The Intersectionality of Gender and Race Discrimination. Paper presented at World Conference Against Racism, Durban, South Africa, September 2001.

Damiano, C.M. (1999). Lesbian Baiting in the Military: Institutionalized Sexual Harassment Under Don't Ask, Don't Tell, Don't Pursue. *Journal of Gender, Social Policy and the Law*, 7, 3, 499–503.

DeMello Patterson, M.B. (2000). America's Racial Unconscious: The Invisibility of Whiteness. In J.L. Kincheloe, S.R. Steinberg, N.M. Rodriguez, and R.E. Chennault (Eds.), *White Reign: Deploying Whiteness in America* (p. 103–121). New York, NY: St. Martin's Press.

Dolsen, J. (2015). The Mistreatment of Female Veterans Is Not Just a Woman's Issue. *Task and Purpose*. http://taskandpurpose.com/mistreatment-female-veterans-not-just-womens-issue/. Retrieved January 23, 2017.

Ellefson, K.G. (1998). *Advancing Army Women as Senior Leaders – Understanding the Obstacles*. Carlisle Barracks, PA: Army War College.

Espiritu, Yen L. (2000). *Asian American Women and Men*. Walnut Creek, CA: Altamira Press.

Frankenberg, R. (1993). *The Social Construction of Whiteness: White Women, Race Matters*. Minneapolis: University of Minnesota Press.

Gates, G.J. (2010). *Discharges Under Don't Ask, Don't Tell Policy: Women and Racial/Ethnic Minorities*. The Williams Institute, School of Law. University of California at Los Angeles. https://williamsinstitute.law.ucla.edu/research/military-related/discharges-under-the-dont-ask-dont-tell-policy-women-and-racialethnic-minorities-2/. Retrieved February 23, 2017.

Geerts, E., and van der Tuin, I. (2013). From Intersectionality to Interference: Feminist Onto-Epistemological Reflections on the Politics of Representation. *Women's Studies International Forum*, 41, 3, 171–178.

Gould, O., and Obicheta, O. (2015). *Her Mission Continues: Service and Reintegration Amongst Post-9/11 Women Veterans*. The Mission Continues Research and Evaluation Team.

Grillo, T. (2013). Anti-Essentialism and Intersectionality: Tools to Dismantle the Master's House. *Berkeley Journal of Gender, Law and Justice*, 10, 1, 16–30.

Harris, G.L.A. (2009). The Multifaceted Nature of White Female Attrition in the Military. *Journal of Public Management and Social Policy*, 71–93.

Harris, G.L.A., and Lewis, E.L. (Forthcoming). *Blacks in the Military and Beyond*. Lanham, MD: Lexington Books/Rowman and Littlefield.

Holloway, L. (2010). Don't Ask, Don't Tell Hurts African American Women the Most. *The Root*. October 6. www.theroot.com/dont-ask-dont-tell-hurts-african-american-women-the-mo-1790881142. Retrieved January 23, 2017.

Hutchinson, D.L. (2001). *Identity Crisis: 'Intersectionality,' 'Multidimensionality,' and the Development of Adequate Theory Subordination*. University of Florida Law Scholarship Repository.

Iskra, D. (2012). More Navy Women Joining the Silent Service. October 3. http://nation.time.com/2012/10/03/more-navy-women-joining-the-silent-service. Retrieved February 21, 2013.

Kaplan, M., McFarland, B., and Huguet, N. (2009). Firearm Suicide Among Veterans in the General Population: Findings from the National Violent Death Reporting System. *Journal of Trauma-Injury and Critical Care*, 67, 3, 503–507.

Law, S.A. (1999). White Privilege and Affirmative Action. *Akron Law Review*, 32, 603–621.

Lioness Report. (2012). *Cultivating Change: Lioness Impact Report*. Based on *Lioness*, a feature documentary directed by M. McLagan and D. Sommers. U.S.: Room 11 Productions.

McClintock, M. (1996). Lesbian Baiting Hurts All Women. *Women's Voices in Experimental Education*. U.S. Department of Education, Office of Educational Research and Improvement, Educational Resource Information Center (ERIC). files.eric.ed.gov/fulltext/ED412049.pdf. Retrieved February 2, 2017.

Moore, B.L. (1991). African-American Women in the U.S. Military. *Armed Forces and Society*, 17, 3, 363–384.

Moore, B.L. (1996). *To Serve My Country, To Serve My Race*. New York: New York University Press.

National Center for Veterans Analysis and Statistics (NCVAS). (2011). *America's Women Veterans: Military Service History and VA Benefits Utilization Statistics*. U.S. Department of Veterans Affairs. November 23. www.va.gov/vetdata/docs/SpecialReports/Final_W. Retrieved February 22, 2017.

National Center for Veterans Analysis and Statistics (NCVAS). (2015). *Profile of Women Veterans: 2013*. U.S. Department of Veterans Affairs. www.va.gov/vetdata/docs/SpecialReports/Women_Veteran. June. Retrieved February 22, 2017.

National Center for Veterans Analysis and Statistics (NCVAS). (2016). *Profile of Women Veterans: 2014*. U.S. Department of Veterans Affairs. www.va.gov/vetdata/. Retrieved March 24, 2017.

Office of the Assistant Secretary of Defense (Military Community and Family Policy). (2013). *2013 Demographics. Profile of the Military Community*. http://download.militaryonesource.mil/12038/MOS/Reports/2013-Demographics-Report.pdf. Retrieved March 7, 2017.

O'Keefe, E. (2010). Minorities Disproportionately Discharged for Don't Ask, Don't Tell Violations. *Washington Post*. August 17. www.washingtonpost.com/wp-dyn/content/article/2010/08/16/AR2010081605153.html. Retrieved January 23, 2017.

Population Representation in the Military Services. (2015). Office of the Under Secretary of Defense, Personnel and Readiness. www.cna.org/pop-rep/2015/index.html. Retrieved April 12, 2017.

Pursue-Vaugh, V., and Eibach, R.P. (2008). Intersectional Invisibility: The Distinctive Advantages and Disadvantages of Multiple Subordinate-Group Dynamics. *Sex Roles*, DOI doi:10.1007/s11199-11008-9424-9424.

Rivera, J.C. and Johnson, A.E. (2014). Female Veterans of Operations Enduring and Iraqi Freedom: Status and Future Directions. *Military Medicine*, 179, 2, 133–136.

Service Women's Action Network (SWAN). (n.d.). *Military Sexual Trauma: The Facts.* www.pritzkermilitary.org/files/7114/4120/8474/SWAN-MST-fact-sheet1.pdf. Retrieved March 24, 2017.

Shanker, T. (2008). Don't Ask, Don't Tell Hits Women Much More. *New York Times.* June 23. www.nytimes.com/2008/06/23/washington/23pentagon.html. Retrieved February 2, 2017.

Spelman, E. (1988). *Inessential Woman: Problems of Exclusion in Feminist Thought.* Boston, MA: Beacon Press.

Spelman, E. (2007). *Inclusive Feminism: A Third Wave Theory of Women's Commonality.* A Review. N. Zack, Rowman and Littlefield, 2005. *Hypatia*, 22, 3, 201–204.

Wagner DeCrew, J. (1995). The Combat Exclusion and the Role of Women in the Military. *Hypatia*, 10, 1, 56–73.

Walker, J.A., and Borbely, J.M. (2014). *Women Veterans in the Labor Force. Spotlight on Statistics.* U.S. Bureau of Labor Statistics. U.S. Department of Labor. www.bls.gov/spotlight/2014/women-vets/. Retrieved April 8, 2017.

Wechsler Segal, M.W. (1995). Women's Military Roles Cross-Nationally, Past, Present, and Future. *Gender and Society*, 9, 6, 757–775.

Women in Military Service for America Memorial (WIMSA). (n.d.). www.womensmemorial.org. Retrieved January 27, 2017.

1 Women as Warriors

Contrary to contemporary rhetoric, women have always been warriors, so much so that Harris (2015) refers to them as 'Warriors to the Core' (p.27). Researchers like Grant DePauw (1998), Goldstein (2003), Jones (1997), Newark (1989) and Alpern (1998), to name a few, have managed to effectively capture the exploits of female warriors during ourstory, despite the deliberate and calculated attempts by many to do otherwise by destroying any positive record that is to be attributed to women of notable reputation. If anything, says Grant DePauw (1998), it is impossible at best to disentangle such impressive feats by women who have been warriors since the beginning of time and through modern day. Mazur (1998) points to the more contemporary preoccupation with the conception of women as novel participants in this venue – that is, in the military – as if they have never been so before, all for the sake of casting doubt on their presence. Adams (1983) admits that there are other forces at play that may help to explain women's perceived absence from this milieu. Perhaps one of the earliest known inquiries as to the reasons for women's virtual nonexistence in the theater of war (i.e., Lorenz 1966) was spurred by the belief of women's perceived lack of an innate or biological predisposition to aggression. Adams (1983) has debunked these speculations as owing more to cultural proclivities than to biology.

For instance, other researchers, namely, Ember and Ember (1971, 1974), attest to the robust links between marital residency and warfare trends. Most notably, warfare was more likely to occur where the wife resides with either her husband or near his family (patrilocal marital residency) and an existing warfare with another similarly cultural group, or between matrilocal marital residency where the husband resides with his wife or near her family, or warfare with cultures that are outside one's own or the use of different languages. However, especially for the former, that is warfare with patrilocal residency, women faced the possibility of conflicts in interests since wars could endure between their husbands and male relatives in nearby towns. When this occurs, Meggitt (1977) has found that the Mae Enge people, for instance, deliberately barred its women from meetings in which the men make war decisions. Yet, despite these practices, there is no evidence to conclude that the absence of women in war is a consequence of any biological differences toward aggression (Adams 1983). Instead, data suggest more cross-cultural mores related to where both the husband and the wife reside, how close in geographic proximity they reside to familial relations, and whether or not those communities with whom they engage in warfare either share cultural or language characteristics.

Adams does not dispute the preponderance of intersectionality between biology and culture that tend to reinforce one another towards the belief that men, more than women, partake in hunter-gatherer and warlike behaviors. However, he suggests that although some of these behaviors may be biologically predisposed, such as the need for men to serve as hunter-gatherers and warriors during women's pregnancy periods which would inevitably exclude them from such activities, in no way does men's overwhelming presence mean that men have the monopoly or excel in this regard or are therefore more prone to warfare as a result.

Harris (2015) cites as one example the American military's adaptation of Karl von Clausewitz to discredit women as warriors and to exclude them from the discourse. While, as Harris notes, Clausewitz is uni-dimensionally credited for the epic piece *On War* for all things involving the principles of warfare, it is Elshtain (1987) who questions the veracity of whether or not this should be the case. It was Marie von Clausewitz, the wife, not Karl von Clausewitz, the husband, who actually published the now-famous work upon the latter's death. It was Marie, not Karl, who developed the preface for this masterpiece. Then is it not conceivable, as Elshtain (1987) suggests, that Marie, not Karl, could have authored the entire piece as an ode or parting gift, if you will, to both honor and preserve her beloved husband's legacy? In what by all indications could very well have been a function of the times, while Marie von Clausewitz appeared publicly content to play the role of the compliant and submissive wife, she nevertheless tipped her cover following her husband's death stating that 'their publication called for a good deal of work, arranging of materials and consultation and I am profoundly grateful to several loyal friends for their assistance in these tasks' (Elshtain 1987, p.65–67, cited from the preface of *On War*). Unbeknownst to Marie, she revealed her impeccable reservoir of talents to capitalize on the bevy of resources at her disposal. Yet, at no time did Marie directly ascribe this writing to her own handiwork, in keeping with protocol. While *On War* will forever be considered a masterpiece on military principles, Elshtain (1987) has essentially inserted doubt as to which Clausewitz actually deserves credit for its authorship.

While Marie von Clausewitz is evidence of a gentile woman who deliberately subsumed her aspirations to those of her husband, the scant ourstory is nevertheless replete with women with the gravitas to intimidate any man who was considered a warlord of his time. Throughout ourstory, women warriors as heads of state have exercised vision, strategy and political savvy in executing various exploits, all for the purpose of territorial expansion; wielding influence, including embroiling their countries in justifiable wars; and concentrating power. Shammuramat (Semiramis) of Assyria was an unrivalled match to any male ruler during the ninth century BC (Grant DePauw 1998). Her prowess led to her capturing many territories in the quest for empire expansion. She commemorated a bronze statue to herself in celebration of her countless expeditions, with the inscription as follows:

> Nature made me a woman yet I have raised myself to rival the greatest men. I swayed the scepter of Ninos; I extended my dominions to the river Hinamenes Eastward; to the Southward to the land of Frankincense and Myrrh; Northward to Saccae and the Scythians. No Assyrian before me had seen an ocean, but I have seen four. I have built dams and fertilized the barren lands with my rivers. I have built impregnable walls and roads to far places and with iron cut passages through mountains where previously even wild animals could not pass. Various as were my deeds, I have yet found leisure hours to indulge myself with friends.
>
> (Herodotus 4.118, in Grant DePauw 1998, p.41–42)

Similarly, the battle-ready chariot leading men on horseback during the reign of Ramses II of Egypt of the 13th century seemed too effeminate in their pursuit of their targets (Goldstein 2003). It is widely speculated that women were more likely to be employed in these roles for their skillset for accuracy in light of the costs of these activities. So, such choices were not gender-based but more a matter of prudent calculations based upon cost-benefit analysis assessments. However, Egypt's use of women on chariots was not unique for the time. Queen Shammuramat of Assyria and other notable heads of states in North Africa engaged in the same ploy where women served in battle as chariot drivers (Goldstein 2003, Grant DePauw 1998). Other Egyptian queens who preceded those of Assyrian royalty were equally adept as warriors. Take the Egyptian Queen Hatshepsut who was reputed to be a warrior queen and consummate businesswoman (Grant DePauw 1998). Her primary focus was on the seizure of land for territorial expansion, as was often the goal during the period and for economic security. She is also famous in ourstory, among other things, as being the first woman queen to don a beard in battle as part of her identity. Ironically, such practice of taking on male physical characteristics became explicit expressions of possessing the wisdom of pharaohs.

Allen (2006) attributes these exploits in and to Africa, the 'Mother of All Nations,' from which all countries of the world originate. While the Amazons have been reduced in contemporary times to mythical unknowns as characterized in the popular media, these were known warrior women in North Africa and the Sahara who predated their Greek descendants, the Scythian Amazons (Grant DePauw 1998, Goldstein 2003). Essentially, the Amazons are not to be romanticized as mere fictions of the imagination for they were genuine human beings who existed (Grant DePauw 1998). Herodotus, the Greek philosopher, who is believed to be the first ourstorian, depicted the Scythians as deriving their ancestry from the original African Amazons. The Scythian Amazons were primarily a steppe or nomadic people who inter-married Scythian men and evolved into a matriarchal society where women freely assumed roles that were on par with those of men (Grant DePauw 1998, Goldstein 2003). Herodotus wrote that the Scythian Amazon women were observed 'riding to the hunt on horseback, sometimes with, sometimes without their menfolk, taking part in war, and wearing the same sort of clothes as men' (Herodotus 4.117, in Grant DePauw 1998, p.47). Multiple excavations of graves of women during the 1950s unearthed a treasure trove of war tools which included armor, swords, arrowheads, daggers and spears (Davis-Kimball 1997). Many such graves showed women with bowed legs, a reflection of their lifestyle on horseback, whereas other graves contained bent arrowheads, a sign of how the women met their demise in combat.

Kentakes, or Candace, in a long line of Ethiopian queens, who ruled such territories now known as Ethiopia, Sudan, South Sudan and parts of Egypt, became a matter of record following Alexander the Great's miscalculated attempt at conquest to enrich his empire (Jones 1997). Black Queen Candace of Ethiopia, as she was known, proved to be unsurpassed in her ability to rival Alexander's army, the likes of which he had never seen before. Candace's expertise at strategy and skill in the military execution of her forces so overwhelmed those of Alexander that he could not help but admire her strength – one that forced him to retreat for fear of defeat. One hundred and fifty years later, Petronius, then governor of Egypt, was again no match for Queen Amenirenas. Her forces not only held fast in securing her empire but succeeded in its expansion by seizing parts of Petronius's territory (Jones 1997).

Also reputed for their battle-ready superiority are the Yoruba women of West Africa and their neighbors, the Hausa women, who were equally adroit in their skill as commanders (Jones 1997). Albeit several centuries later, Queen Arninatu reigned over the Hausa empire as only one in a sequence of 17 such queens. In one instance, as the oldest female child, the Queen of Zazzau re-designated the territory as Zaire, which in today's terms translates into the Democratic Republic of the Congo. For three years, the queen was notorious for her iron-clad form of rule. During her reign, she was credited with bringing economic prosperity to the region by forging business ventures across other regions of the continent and for bringing the kola nut to the area. The queen is adored by her followers in modern-day Nigeria, and a statue was erected to memorialize her numerous exploits. In the National Theatre in Lagos, in the square, the queen is mounted on horseback, brandishing a sword.

There have been innumerable warrior queens throughout the African continent who are worthy of mention, but nonetheless rendered impractical for discussion in this monograph, including those of Carthage and Mauritania's Dahia 'the sorceress' (Jones 1997, p.85), and Queen of the Falashes, Judith who is most deserving for her reputation, having killed several relatives of King Solomon, and the feats of the Queen of Sheba, also including Solomon. Jones (1997) characterizes Zinga Mbandi, daughter of the King of Ngongo, as the most renowned. During the early 17th century, the territory of Ngongo was seized by the Portuguese (Jones 1997). In an effort to negotiate her territory's independence, Queen Mbandi found herself unable to fully negotiate with the governor at eye level. Accustomed to a position of authority, and judging herself on par, if not at a higher level than the Portuguese governor owing to her royal lineage, the queen found herself without a seat from which to negotiate. She abruptly ordered one of the governor's servants to his knees, sat on him to establish eye-level contact with the governor and proceeded with the negotiations.

The Greeks, like their African ancestors, honed the ability for success in battle. Harpalyce was cultivated by her father King Lycungus of Thrace in the principles of war (Grant DePauw 1998). She assumed the helm following her father's overthrow and led the forces for his recapture. Atalanta was as resourceful in her exploits (Grant DePauw 1998). In addition, Greek art celebrated its warrior women such as those represented on the Parthenon (Goldstein 2003).

Still, many find war to be incompatible with the contrived and fictionalized persona of being female and consider the aforementioned tales, especially those of the African and Greek Amazons, to be inconvenient truths. Some go as far as to mythologize that Amazon women nimbly wielded the bow and arrow in battle by dismembering their breasts for this purpose, or that the term Amazon means without breasts (Goldstein 2003, Grant DePauw 1998). Further, as Grant DePauw (1998) points out, of all the procedures, mastectomy proves ineffective at building muscles of the chest. While she does not dispute this practice by some cultures of the world, she is unequivocal about the Amazons either condoning or executing this practice. The term 'Amazon' is believed to have its origins in the Persian word 'harmozyn,' or warrior (Grant DePauw 1998, p.52), to which the Libyans subscribed. In fact, Libya's Moammar Gadhafi routinely used an entourage of 40 women bodyguards as part of his protection detail (Gombaya 2012). The bodyguards were dubbed Amazon Guards but were allegedly raped as a consequence of this selection, although these allegations were disputed (Squires 2011). The women were reportedly selected for their height of an average of at least six feet (Gombaya 2012, Squires 2011). It was believed that during the rise of the Amazons, the traditional female-male roles, at least as we understand them today, were reversed in these societies (Crim 2000). Men's primary role was that of protector while women were the influencers and holders of power in society. Purportedly, the Greeks held an ambivalent yet revered relationship with the Amazons. The Greeks overthrew the Amazons as a means of preserving masculinity and thus patriarchy in society, yet mythologized Amazons as warriors.

The ourstory books are further filled with warrior queens like Cleopatra of Egypt, who exercised her influence and charisma to wield power against and over the Romans who had captured part of Egypt (Grant 1972). This was a time when the Romans viewed the African continent as one rich in natural wealth and ripe for the taking, yet considered its people to be barbaric (Grant DePauw 1998). Under Roman rule, Cleopatra's father merely served at the occupiers' convenience. It is surmised that this is one among many humiliations that moved Cleopatra to forge an alliance with Mark Antony to avenge her father's fall from power. However, Cleopatra's brother-in-law suspected this alliance was simply a scheme by Cleopatra to concentrate power by returning it to Alexandria. Desperate, Cleopatra turned to Octavia, who balked at her request to now establish a debunked agreement with him. To save face, the queen committed suicide rather than be humiliated by capture and paraded through Rome to symbolize her defeat. Not surprisingly, the ourstory as portrayed by the Romans has not been kind to Queen Cleopatra. Yet, Queen Septima Zenobia, whose reign included such territories as Palmyra in Syria or the modern-day region that encompasses Saudi Arabia, Egypt, Iran, Armenia and Syria, is revered by the Romans (Grant DePauw 1998, Carr Vaughan 1967).

Said of Queen Zenobia:

> Her face was dark and of a swarthy hue. Her eyes were black and powerful, her spirit genuinely great, and her beauty incredible ... Her voice was clear and like that of a man. Her sternness, when necessity demanded, was that of a tyrant; her clemency when her sense of right called for it, that of a god emperor.
>
> (Grant DePauw 1998, p.103)

During her rule, Queen Zenobia repeatedly and successfully fought off incursions into her land by successive rulers, including Claudeus and Aurelian (Grant DePauw 1998). She was known for her fierce fighting in defense of her expansive territories. Aurelian soon realized that he had more than met his match in Queen Zenobia's 70,000-strong force. It moved him to take pause of the situation, realizing that he risked defeat. Aurelian's writings are but a snapshot of his mental angst in coming up against the queen. 'There are Romans who say that I am waging a war against a mere woman, but there is as great as an array before me as though I were fighting a man. I cannot tell you what a great store of arrows, spears and stones is here, what great preparation they have made. There is no section of the wall that is not held by two or three engines of war. Their machines even hurl fire' (Newark 1989, p.64). Worried, Aurelian engaged in letter writing to the queen in an attempt to make her acquiesce to his overtures. However, Queen Zenobia would have none of it as she found his tone to be off-putting. She escaped at night by way of a female camel instead of on horseback as a more expeditious means of travel (Grant DePauw 1998, Carr Vaughan 1967). However, her trip was cut short after making her way into then Persia. Once captured, unlike Queen Cleopatra, Queen Zenobia did not resort to suicide. Instead, she was as eloquent as she was candid in her resolve for not resisting by saying, 'You, I accept as an Emperor because you win victories. But your predecessors I have never regarded as worthy of Emperorship. I desire to come as a partner in the royal power should there be enough land' (Newark 1989, p.73).

Aurelian's victory gave way to the Romans' reputation for celebration (Grant DePauw 1998). Queen Zenobia successfully settled in Rome through remarriage and sealed her influence in the society even as defeated royalty. Her sons grew in stature as did her daughter through marriage. However, Newark's (1989) conjecture is that Queen Zenobia's favorable treatment in Roman literature was more a condition of Aurelian's awestruck opinion of her than anything else. Said Aurelian of the queen: '... what manner of woman she is, how wise in counsel, how steadfast in plans, how firm toward soldiers, how generous when necessity calls, and how stern when discipline demands' (Newark 1989, p.73).

With the demise of the Roman Empire came the prominence of religion, namely Christianity, in Europe. Following his conquest of the Scandinavians in 878 AD, Alfred the Great engaged in multiple alliances to regain swaths of his previously lost territory (Grant DePauw 1998). Aethelflaed, his daughter, also married to establish partnerships with other royalty, including her brother, to consolidate the family's estate. Known by the Church as the Lady of Mercians owing to her refrain from sexual relations with her elderly husband just for the fun of it, Aethelflaed was a force to be reckoned with in that, according to William of Malmesbury, she was 'a woman who protected men at home and intimidated them abroad' (Newark 1989, p.94). Aethelflaed widened her reach and influence through land expansion, including into territories held by the Welsh and the Viking military. Her brother fulfilled her aspirations by capturing Danelaw, a territory that the family had mistakenly relinquished as part of negotiations.

Italy's Matilda lived a life of stark contradictions (Eads 1986, Grant DePauw 1998). As a military woman, she was an aggressive commander of troops in Europe yet was reared to appreciate the much finer things in life such as embroidery although her mother intentionally immersed her daughter in all things that dealt with the principles of war. Matilda was a veteran of multiple battles at the behest of Pope Alexander II. Moreover, 'Now there appeared in Lombardy at the head of her numerous squadrons, the young maid Matilda armed like a warrior, and with such bravery, that she made known to the world that courage and valor in mankind is not indeed a matter of sex, but of heart and spirit' (Grant DePauw 1998, p.85). The queens in feudal Europe were similarly situated. Not satisfied to function as merely wives on the sidelines, they actively participated in debating the affairs of the day, including those of military matters that many may have otherwise considered to be the primacy of men (Crim 2000). It was thus believed that the prominence of bloodline more so than other factors such as gender, gave impetus to this line of thinking. As such, the royal women of the time sought increasing legitimacy and authority by becoming conversant with the important issues of the day and inserting themselves into such discourse with their husbands.

France's Eleanor of Aquitaine was both strategic and political in positioning her every move (Newark 1989). Marriage to Henry II of England and Louis VI of France only brought increasing power and influence. As she and her forces rode through Jerusalem, many of them also women:

> Females were among them, riding horseback in the manner of men, not ... sidesaddle, but unashamedly astride, bearing lances and weapons as men do. Dressed in masculine garb, they conveyed a wholly martial appearance, more mannish than the Amazons. One [Eleanor] stood out from the rest ... and from the embroidered gold which ran around the hem and fringes of her garments was called the Gold Foot.
>
> (Newark 1989, p.107–108)

Eleanor was both reviled and admired for her ability to amass power but it was her feats that endeared the allegiance of her followers (Crim 2000). Christine de Pisan, also of Italy, was influential but in a very different way from all of the warrior women who preceded her. She never physically participated in battle yet was accepted and widely sought after by leaders of the time for her shrewd theoretical knowledge about the principles of war. Likewise, de Pisan took pride in schooling women from all levels of the caste system about warfare. The topics in which she held intellectual discourse such as the military and politics could be considered domains of men even by modern standards. For women, though, she viewed her role as helping them to improve the lives of other women by educating them about the urgent subjects of the time and completed such literary works as *Treasure of the City of Ladies* for this very purpose. *Feats of Armies and Chivalry* was another publication designed to cultivate soldiers and commanders alike (Grant DePauw 1998). However, de Pisan held contradictory ideologies about women and men. Even as she educated women in the ways of warfare, for instance, she not only believed that women should never bear arms but that they were not on equal footing with men. De Pisan instead counseled women on the purpose of arming themselves with such knowledge as cited below:

> The proper role of a good, wise queen or princess is to maintain peace and concord and to avoid wars and their resulting disasters. Women particularly should concern themselves with peace because men by

nature are more foolhardy and headstrong, and that overwhelming desire to avenge themselves prevents them from foreseeing the resulting danger of terrors of war. But woman by nature is more gentle and circumspect.

(Christine de Pisan, as cited by Crim 2000, p.23–24)

De Pisan saw women as playing instrumental roles in maintaining peace and good in the state (Crim 2000). Women were therefore encouraged to occupy themselves with martial arts. Her 1410 publication, *Book of the Deeds of Arms and Chivalry*, appeals to the hearts of princes not to solely strive for war but for that which is in the best interest of the state (Crim 2000).

During the onset of the Muslim religion and the First Crusade from the 11th through 15th centuries in North Africa in the region now considered as the Middle East and Turkey, many women took up arms in defense of Jerusalem (Grant DePauw 1998). Dressed as men, women accompanied male soldiers for this journey. Yet, it is important to note that it was this period to denounce Muslims by inserting Christianity that sparked the indisposition to accept any other religion but Christianity and particularly the presence of women in roles deemed to be the entitlement of men. This was also an era that marked radical contradictions and even falsehoods about women. As previously stated, the Greeks revered yet vilified women for their participation in war (Goldstein 2003), while the Romans regarded women's presence as having an adverse effect of rendering men timid before battle (Grant DePauw 1998).

In the Arab world and during the seventh century that predates Islam, prominent women like Maoria of Syria engaged in territorial expansion through Palestine, Egypt and Phoenicia (Fraser 1990). Others like Hindal-Hinud fought with Mohammed in the battle of Badr and utilized a known trick of deliberately inserting a compromised position in battle all for the purpose of motivating male soldiers to fight ever more gallantly. Still another, Salayan Bint Malhan, was clearly with child when she engaged in combat alongside Mohammed equipped with swords and daggers around her protruding waistline (Miles 1988), while one of Mohammed's wives, Aishah, his last, and other women fought in the Battles of Camel and Yermonks, respectively. Fierce fighters like Kevalah were known to urge men on through chastisement. After being captured, she famously shouted: 'Do you accept these men as your masters? Are you willing for your children to be slaves? Where is your famed courage and skill that have become the talk of Arab tribes as well as in the cities?' (Miles 1988, p.66). Imade ad-Din, an Islamic author, recorded the escapades of Muslim and Christian women who could only be distinguished by the jewelry on their feet. The Second and Third Crusades saw such women of prominence as France's Eleanor of Aquitaine and other women, together with her husband, on horseback with axes and knives in hand for battle, while King Henry II and Richard the Lionheart, his son, employed poor women to travel with foot soldiers as laundresses.

The ourstory books have been kind to one of France's most famous sheroes, Joan of Arc, who encouraged Charles VII to lead forces to invade England allegedly owing to an epiphany from God (Crim 2000). But, despite Joan of Arc's laudable feats in battle, she was disgraced as an apostate who was against the religious norms and teachings of the time. Joan of Arc was executed by burning, an oft-used technique at the time to punish women who committed heresy.

Any account of women warriors of an earlier era would be rendered incomplete without mentioning the contributions of the Amazon women of Dahomey or modern-day Benin. Employed first by King Agadya to create the illusion of an emboldened army to any adversary, the tactic exceeded the king's expectations (Alpern 1998, Goldstein 2003, Grant DePauw 1998). The women soldiers were reputed to be even more loyal than their male peers to the extent that those who were captured to serve the king's army later remained of their own volition, even though they had the opportunity to return home (Goldstein 2003, Alpern 1998, Grant DePauw 1998). In fact, male soldiers routinely deserted their posts, while there were no such reports about female soldiers. The Dahomey Amazons were not only exceptional fighters but were equally proficient in speed and displayed an unswerving commitment to the king (Alpern 1998). However, like Queen Cleopatra, when they anticipated potential defeat by the French, rather than surrender, they destroyed the city with nothing for the French to claim as a symbol of victory.

Women Warriors and the U.S. Military

By all accounts throughout America's relatively short ourstory as compared to other parts of the world, women have a warrior core in which men have no monopoly (Harris 2015; American Civil Liberties Union (ACLU) n.d.). It is this spirit that has been a steadfast trait evident in the U.S. military. The ourstory of women's journey in the American military begins in 1778, it is believed, at the Battle of Monmouth with Molly Pitcher, during which time she took up arms in the defense of her husband's unit, the 7th Pennsylvania Regiment (Holm 1992, Grant DePauw 1998). The true identity of Molly Pitcher has been disputed throughout the years, in that she might have been John Hays's wife, whose regiment she defended after he and others in the unit succumbed to the assault (Holm 1992). Or she is speculated to have been either Mary Ludwig Hays McCauley, or even Margaret in 1776 at the Battle of Fort Washington. Grant DePauw (1998) bemoans that for such a prominent figure, Molly Pitcher has been relegated to a namesake for a New Jersey Turnpike rest stop, and that had Molly Pitcher been a man, this most certainly would not have been the case. However, Holm (1992) struck a more sanguine note. Whatever Molly

Pitcher's true identity is, she was nevertheless the epitome of American ourstory who is worthy of recognition and praise for outstanding military service in the Continental Army, and for which she must be memorialized as emblematic of the country's founding.

Lucy Brewer, who served as a man named George Baker aboard the U.S.S. *Constitution* in the Marine Corps during the War of 1812, was named the first woman Marine (Holm 1992). Another was Sarah Borginis, whose gallantry in guarding the troops at Fort Brown in 1846 during the Mexican offensive, won her the symbolic promotion to the commissioned rank of Colonel by General Zachary Taylor, who was awestruck by her selflessness (Grant DePauw 1998). Rose O'Neal was imprisoned during the First Battle of Bull Run by the Confederate Army for whom she was accused of spying (Holm 1992). Pauline and Sarah Emma Edmonds were both spies for the Union Army (Holm 1992, Grant DePauw 1998, Goldstein 2003). Loreta Janeta Velasquez's zeal to remain in the Confederate Army led her not only to dress in the Confederate Army uniform but to don a beard and mustache to be perceived as an authentically male member of the infantry and cavalry (Grant DePauw 1998, Holm 1992). Clara Barton, the nurse, is credited with the founding of the National Cemetery in Arlington, Virginia, as well as becoming inaugural president of the American Red Cross (Grant DePauw 1998).

During the American Civil War, christened the 'Moses of her People' by Sarah Bradford (1869/1961, as cited by Grant DePauw 1998), was none other than Harriet Tubman who served as a spy for the Union Army and single-handedly and repeatedly led the Army to free hundreds of slaves from their desperate straits, a situation that she intimately understood having absconded from a similar inhumane existence (Allen 2006). Tubman led even more slaves to freedom by way of the Underground Railroad (Hall 1994). Following at least two attempts appealing to the U.S. federal government for the remuneration of wartime military service, Tubman eventually secured a lifetime compensation of $20 per month. Said of Harriet Tubman by Hall (1994), she 'was an extraordinary human being, possibly the most underrated and underappreciated person of either sex or any race, from the Civil War period' (Hall 1994, in Harris 2015, p.39). In 2013, President Barack Obama, America's first known black American president, on behalf of a grateful nation, paid homage to Harriet Tubman on what would have been the 100th anniversary of her death, by allocating 480 acres of land in Dorchester County, Maryland, the place of Tubman's birth, in her honor and in recognition of the monumental role that she played in American ourstory. Most of the women traveling with the military during this period functioned as cooks, laundresses and nurses to bring the troops back to health (Dann 1980). Many, along with their children, traveled with their husbands in the military on whom they depended for subsistence. Fittingly, these women were referred to as 'women of the army' (Kerber 1993, p.110), although they neither received recognition nor compensation for their services to the troops.

While the aforementioned examples represent early American women in the fledgling military, World Wars I and II and onward through Operations Enduring and Iraqi Freedom and New Dawn, expanded women's roles in the military, albeit out of necessity, to women's positions today. Yet, despite this remarkable progress, it has been an ourstory filled with stops and starts, never one of uni-linear growth (Wechsler Segal 1995, Harris 2015). Today, even immediately before the termination of the Don't Ask, Don't Tell and Don't Pursue policy, with the symbolic expansion in or opening-up of occupations, positions and critical assignments as called for by the combat exclusion policy's repeal, it appears that military women, and by extension women veterans, stand no closer to achieving full agency and thus the path to full citizenship by way of either the passage of the Equal Rights Amendment as restitution for omissions in the U.S. Constitution and/or inclusion in the Selective Service System. The fact that Congress has yet again introduced, but only as a matter of necessity, women's potential inclusion in the Selective Service System, only to table such discussions to July 2017, a date that has since passed, is yet again the long-held indication of women's traditional status as simply a convenient resource only to be exploited as the civilian and military leadership deem fit to.

Bibliography

Adams, D.B. (1983). Why There Are So Few Women Warriors. *Behavior Science Research*, 18, 3, 196–212.

Allen, T.B. (2006). *Harriet Tubman, Secret Agent: How Daring Slaves and Freed Blacks Spied for the Union During the Civil War.* Des Moines, IA: National Geographic Children's Books, Scholastic Book Club Edition.

Alpern, S.B. (1998). *Amazon of Black Sparta: The Women Warriors of Dahomey.* New York, NY: New York University Press.

American Civil Liberties Union (ACLU). (n.d.). *Women in the Military.* www.aclu.org/issues/womens-rights/womens-rights-workplace/women-military. Retrieved April 4, 2017.

Carr Vaughan, A. (1967). *Zenobia of Palmyra.* New York: Doubleday.

Crim, B. (2000). Silent Partners: Women and Warfare in Early Modern Europe. In G.J. DeGroot and C.M. Peniston-Bird (Eds.), *A Soldier and a Woman: Sexual Integration in the Military.* Essex, UK: Pearson Publishing.

Dann, J.C. (1980). *The Revolution Remembered: Eyewitness Accounts of the War for Independence.* In J.C. Dann (Ed.) (p. 240–250). Chicago, IL: University of Chicago Press.

Davis-Kimball, J. (1997). Warrior Women of the Eurasian Steppes. *Archeology*, 50, 1, 44–48.

Eads, V. (1986). The Campaigns of Matilda of Tuscany. *MINERVA: Quarterly Report on Women and the Military*, 4, 1, 167–181. Spring.

Elshtain, J.B. (1987). *Women and War.* New York: Basic Books, Inc. Publishers.

Ember, M., and Ember, C.R. (1971). The Conditions Favoring Matrilocal Versus Patrilocal Residence. *American Anthropologist*, 73, 571–594.

Ember, M., and Ember, C.R. (1974). On the Development of Unilineal Descent. *Journal of Anthropological Research*, 30, 69–94.

Fraser, A. (1990). *The Warrior Queens: The Legends and the Lives of Women Who Have Led Their Nations in War*. New York: Vintage Books.

Fritze, J. (2013). Obama to Sign Off on Tubman Monument on Eastern Shore. *Baltimore Sun*. March 22. http://articles.baltimoresun.com/2013-03-22/news/bs-md-tubman-monument-20130322_1_tubman-monument-designation-eastern-shore. Retrieved March 24, 2017.

Goldstein, J.S. (2003). *War and Gender. How Gender Shapes the War System and Vice Versa*. New York: Cambridge University Press.

Gombaya, H.D. (2012). Gaddafi's Bodyguard Reveals Rape, Torture and Murder by NTC. April 14. *The London Evening Post*. www.thelondoneveningpost.com/gaddafis-bodyguard-reveals-rape-torture-and-murder-by-ntc/. Retrieved February 23, 2017.

Grant, M. (1972). *Cleopatra: A Biography*. New York: Barnes and Noble.

Grant DePauw, L. (1998). *Battle Cries and Lullabies. Women in War from Prehistory to the Present*. Norman, OK: University of Oklahoma Press.

Hall, R. (1994). *Patriots in Disguise. Women Warriors in the Civil War*. New York: Marlowe and Company.

Harris, G.L.A. (2015). *Living Legends and Full Agency: Implications of Repealing the Combat Exclusion Policy*. New York, NY: Taylor & Francis Group, a Division of CRC Press.

Holm, J. (1992). *Women in the Military. An Unfinished Revolution*. Revised Edition. Novato, CA: Presidio Press.

Jones, D.E. (1997). *Women Warriors. A History*. Washington, DC: Potomac Books, Inc.

Kerber, L.K. (1993). 'A Constitutional Right to be Treated Like … Ladies': Women, Civic Obligations and Military Service. *The University of Chicago Law School Roundtable*, 1, 1, Article 15, 95–128.

Lorenz, K.Z. (1966). Evolution of Ritualization in the Biological and Cultural Spheres. *Biological Sciences*, 251, 772, 273–284.

Mazur, D.H. (1998). Women, Responsibility and the Military. *Notre Dame Law Review*, 74, 1–45.

Meggitt, B. (1977). *Blood Is their Argument: Warfare Among the Mae Enga Tribesmen*. Palo Alto, CA: Mayfield.

Miles, R. (1988). *The Women's History of the World*. New York: Harper and Row Press.

Newark, T. (1989). *Women Warlords: An Illustrated History of Female Warriors*. London: Blandford Press.

Squires, N. (2011). Gaddafi and His Sons Raped Female Bodyguards. *The Telegraph*. August 29. www.telegraph.co.uk/news/worldnews/africaandindianocean/libya/8729685/Gaddafi-and-his-sons-raped-female-bodyguards.html. Retrieved February 23, 2017.

Wechsler Segal, M.W. (1995). Women's Military Roles Cross-Nationally, Past, Present, and Future. *Gender and Society*, 9, 6, 757–775.

2 Women as Other

Based upon their formidable presence on the battlefield during ancient times and especially so as warrior queens first in Africa, it appears that women's relegation to a subordinate status did not begin until the African descendants, the Greeks, sought to place them in their perceived secondary place. Yet, even as the Greeks agitated over women's subservience by imposing a system of patriarchy, they mythologized women like Athena by making a direct nexus between women and war (Goldstein 2003, Grant DePauw 1998). It appeared, though, that it was the rise of Christianity that accelerated the period of bigotry and chauvinism, beginning with the First Crusade from the 11th century up to the 15th century that witnessed a purposeful and systematic diminution of women's status (Grant DePauw 1998). For women to participate alongside their brethren and not necessarily in battle, they were reduced to merely accompanying men as pseudo-men to render support and comfort when the men were in need and even as they themselves were attired in men's clothing (Grant DePauw 1998). Women of the early American republic similarly engaged in acts all for the purpose of reaping the rewards, if only the psychological satisfaction, of serving one's country by doing so on the battlefield. From Lucy Brewer during the War of 1812 disguised as George Baker, the Marine (Holm 1992); and Sarah Borginis at Fort Brown during the Mexican Offensive whose impressive performance in staving off the onslaught of the enemy by protecting American troops earned her the honorary promotion to the rank of Army Colonel; to Rosie O'Neal Greenhow, the Confederate spy in the Battle of Bull Run during the American Civil War (Holm 1992); and Clara Barton whose service as a nurse led to the establishment of both the National Cemetery in Arlington and who served as the American Red Cross inaugural president (Holm 1992, Grant DePauw 1998).

Like many women in Europe who yearned to contribute to their respective countries as patriots, they did so in disguise as men, with some going as far as evading hospitals when injured to decrease the likelihood of revealing their identity (Grant DePauw 1998). The most celebrated of these early American feminists were of course Molly Pitcher during the Battle of Monmouth in 1778 (Holm 1992, Grant DePauw 1998), and

Harriet Tubman, who, during the Civil War, served as a spy for the Union Army and single-handedly led hundreds of slaves from the South to freedom via the Underground Railroad (Allen 2006). While World Wars I and II and subsequent conflicts witnessed many women breaking barriers, including paying the ultimate sacrifice, it was not until the 2013 symbolic repeal of the combat exclusion policy that the impetus was provided to open up to women many occupations that were formerly barred, along with the revelation of the pandemic levels of sexual assault in the military, primarily against women, and the airing of documentaries like *Lioness* which together functioned as catalysts to reveal the plight of military women and, by extension, women veterans.

This 'othering' or 'others' as Frankenberg (1993) terms it, albeit in the form of hostility, that women in the military and as veterans experience, connotes abnormality or being outside the mainstream. Whereas to be white and male signals the norm and what it means to be white in American society or in a position of supremacy and privilege (DeMello Patterson 2000). Anyone whose disposition is beyond this definition signals deviance. This is the dilemma for minorities (Law 1999) and women (Ellefson 1998). Specifically for minorities and particularly so for black women, the situation shows a lack of forgiveness over which they have no desire or control, for that matter. More regrettable is that these relationships that are borne of a colonial past still persist by playing themselves out in contemporary society. While the military, perhaps better than many institutions within the civilian sector, at least is perceived as having developed solutions to address inequity, especially in terms of race (Kleykamp 2007, Harris and Lewis, forthcoming), Dansby and Landis (1998) revealed that, unlike any other demographic, female minority officers in the military were the least prone to hold a favorable perception of the institution. Pazy and Oron's (2001) study reinforces this view but for a different reason. The study speculated that when women officers have not achieved a critical mass or are in the minority at predominantly male institutions, in this case in the Israeli Defense Force (IDF), their male superiors will routinely underevaluate their performance.

Kanter (1977) theorizes that recognition by the perceived minority group, in this case women, although a majority in the general civilian population of American society (U.S. Census Bureau 2010), in organizations and/or occupations where their presence is in the minority, women must achieve at least a 15 percent representation of either the total organization or occupation within the workforce to be taken seriously by the majority culture (white male), or to deflect unwarranted attention towards themselves as a group. Any amount below this threshold, says Kanter, will sabotage women's efforts to not be perceived as tokens and therefore deviants. Yet, Kanter cautions that even when women attain this 15 percent threshold for critical mass it will not guarantee that they will not be perceived as such. More troubling is that women themselves may not perceive one another favorably. According to Konrad et al. (1992), an increase in women, chiefly of other racial and/or ethnic groups, may not necessarily increase the affinity with women of other similarly situated groups. Equally disturbing is that women self-sabotage by failure to accept one another, even those of the same racial and/or ethnic groups. Rosen et al.'s (1996) research demonstrates this conundrum and in turn the vicious cycle that women create for themselves while seeming to set themselves apart for both the acceptance and attention of the majority group (white males) and at each other's expense. Rosen et al. found that while military women accepted one another as qualified as their representation increased in military units, they were less apt to desire to work with the new female personnel. In the same vein, the experience of the men in the same military units was different. As the number of women increased, the men became more accepting of them yet considered them less competent than themselves. This minority proportion discrimination hypothesis sets in motion an untenable and no-win situation in which women find that even as their numbers increased, in the quest for acceptance by the majority group, they experience alienation by their very group all the while craving acceptance by military men given the perception of incompetence. However, their status as women and thus deviants prevents their acceptance as qualified and therefore on par with the majority group who are white men. In effect, even as women work against themselves and their collective interests, because of group identification, to individually gain acceptance by white men, women self-sabotage in the process by putting the status of all women in peril.

These self-perpetuating and destructive behaviors by women are owing to sex segregation in laws and society that through repeated direct and indirect reinforcement in education, employment, the military and religion, render organizational life self-reinforcing and hence resistant to change (Cohen 2010). The messages become implicit and explicit forms of social control and to women's detriment. Sex segregation then ultimately serves as a system to define the attributes of manhood and the power ascribed to patriarchy. Modes of behavior for each group are normalized and proselytized in society, law, sex and hierarchical gender relationships. Any group, in this case women, is ostracized and/or punished for failure to conform. Proponents of sex segregation are strident about the advantages of this form of control in that it reinforces what defines an individual as masculine and feminine (Cohen 2010). For these individuals, especially boys must become immersed in all things masculine, else they are susceptible to becoming effeminate. Chodrow (1971) cites the rationale for such hegemonic masculinity. Women are perceived as being inherently incapable of performing certain functions and as such are excluded from certain milieus. This includes ensuring that, for instance, ground combat remains the sole province of men in the military. Yet, this exclusion connotes that only men can fully participate in the affairs of the military. As a result, women are implicitly perceived as compromised as this is a domain from which they are to be excluded, and despite the repeal of the combat exclusion policy, they may still be barred from full participation.

Vojdik (2005) invokes two such examples that reify the belief about women and the need for their exclusion from combat. In a testimony to Congress, a female Air Force pilot advised that a male colleague, another pilot, said to her, 'Look, I can handle anything, but I can't handle being worse than you' (Bird Francke 1997, p.260). In the second example, a male sergeant in Special Operations said that 'the warrior mentality will crumble if women are placed in combat positions ... There needs to be, that belief that "I can do this" because nobody else can' (Vojdik 2005, p.343). Both examples convey that because combat is viewed as inherently male, to place women in these occupations that comprise placing them in to combat, is to violate the fundamental premise by introducing a woman, a deviant, who will pollute the domain's prestige by rendering it soft and effeminate. This schema is akin to Goldin's (2002) pollution theory in which she argues that men methodically keep women out of certain occupations like firefighting, as one example, as a way of retaining the prestige of the occupation. To do otherwise, or to allow anyone into the occupation uncensored, is to pollute the occupation because of non-exclusivity. What is interesting, though, about this belief is that even in everyday life, this mode of thinking propagates such as in the conception of men requiring a 'man cave' to the exclusivity of women so as not to have the same right to require on par respite. Accordingly, men need these exclusive territories as sanctuaries from women to remind them that they are men (Cohen 2010) and without the infiltration of deviants who are women.

Prentice and Carranza (2002), and Burgess and Borgida (1999) categorize these normative ways in how women should behave in terms of descriptive and prescriptive stereotypes. Descriptive behaviors are, based on gender stereotypes, the traits that women are believed to possess such as being nurturing, frail and subordinate (Prentice and Carranza 2002, Burgess and Borgida 1999). Prescriptive stereotypes, on the other hand, are those characteristics that women should possess, such as women should not pursue certain occupations that are deemed to be masculine. Either way, though, women become vulnerable to violating both when they function beyond described and prescribed behaviors. While descriptive stereotypes almost certainly result in sex discrimination and thereby exclusion because women are viewed as lacking certain attributes or qualifications within male-dominated organizations like the military, in prescriptive stereotypes, women who violate norms of expected behavior become prey to sex discrimination in such forms as sexual harassment and assault (Case 1995, Schultz 1998, Franke 1997).

Given the undue demands of family, for example, Harris (2009) describes the unconventional strategies that women who are commissioned military officers and academics are forced to contrive, all in an effort to successfully meet the excessive claims on them for the institutions by which they are employed on one hand and their families on the other hand. Consequently, the employers and families are both dubbed greedy institutions given the simultaneous ultimatums that they exact on the professional woman as she aspires to advance her career. According to Harris (2009), few men have these competing priorities and obligations. Nevertheless, the professional woman must work harder than her white male peers, and even when she succeeds against all odds, she is beholden to outmoded standards of behavior against which she is judged. For example, once the professional woman assumes the role of motherhood, a status characteristic (Ridgeway and Correll 2004), she is no longer considered as competent despite her level of performance. Why? Because motherhood and by extension gender are also status characteristics that reinforce one another and both dictate women's treatment in society. However, while society considers the role of motherhood important, it is nonetheless a role for which the woman is never compensated as it is also a descriptive stereotype (Prentice and Carranza 2002, Burgess and Borgida 1999). The professional woman is also engaging in behaviors that violate perceived cultural norms or prescriptive stereotypes (Prentice and Carranza 2002, Burgess and Borgida 1999), for which she is punished.

Says Snitow (1990), women have no place in predominantly male organizations unless they are prepared to be perceived as 'conceptual men' (p.26). Jorgenson (2000) believes that women only exacerbate this conflict by choosing to pursue both a profession within a male-dominated organization while attempting to raise a family because the roles are incongruent. Like their civilian counterparts, military women, in this case commissioned officers, employ similar strategies to stave off the perception of weakness and particularly so when they become mothers (Harris 2009). Military women are thus forced to walk this line to purposely deflect any appearance of weakness. This is the case, declares Ellefson (1998), because it is men's behaviors, not women's behaviors that are valued by the military. Moreover, military women are considered deviants. According to Harris (2009), notwithstanding the progress that women have made in society, traditional customs of behavior expected of women remain deeply ingrained. Where women enter organizations and/or occupations that are still perceived as the dominion of men, they are persecuted for doing so. Essentially, the demands and expectations are such that a woman can either have a career or a family, but not both. Should she defy conventional wisdom by not only pursuing a career but one that is male-dominated and within a like male-dominated organization, she is persecuted for being as similarly ambitious as a man.

Like military women, women athletes and especially those in sports like basketball and hockey that are perceived to be particularly masculine, are unmercifully scrutinized, prompting those most capable, as in the military, to be labeled as lesbians (Blinde and Taube 1992, Damiano 1999), and where Damiano (1999) refers to the targeting of women in the military as 'lesbian baiting' (p.501). McClintock (1996) blames the need for power structures to keep perceived violations of organizational norms in line. Ignoring the rampant violations of these norms can become a credible threat to the organizational culture (Blinde and Taube 1992), for it is this gendering system and composition of groups in organizations that maintain the hierarchies and the extent to which groups will relate (Reskin et al. 1999). This is a form of social control. Becker (1964) identifies those who are in positions of power, privilege and control as deviance definers who are incentivized to act to maintain their power, privilege and control. In Harris's (2012) theory of multiple marginality, she regards this undermining strategy as one of containment. The label lesbian, whether true or perceived, is one such strategy in keeping potential violators in check. Military women and female athletes therefore challenge traditional norms of gender and are subject to a variety of marginalization attempts that come in the forms of devaluation and stigmatization as other.

Because the majority of such lesbian labeling is designed to undermine the targets, Klemke and Tiedman (1990) point to the fundamental reasons for these accusations, which at their root may be false. The pure error signifies accusations that, while unintended, may come as a result of false information. Accusations may also be an outgrowth of a person's association and/or over-exposure with persons perceived to be of a certain sexual orientation (Klemke and Tiedman 1990). The second, intentional error arises as a method of subjugation to advantage those who are making the accusation. For example, women in the military, especially those who may be perceived as holding occupations of power which are believed to be the purview of men, are pursued as a way of either discouraging them to continue along this path or dissuade others from doing so. In so doing, the prospect functions as a way of preserving the natural order of things. The third, or legitimized error occurs when entrenched cultural beliefs do not allow for contradictory views about the subject matter at hand. In this instance, an athlete who discloses her sexual orientation as that of a lesbian is used to reinforce the legitimacy of the accusation that all female athletes are of this sexual orientation. Finally, victim-based error may in fact be erroneous. This is where the target actively solicits this label owing to their manner of attire and appearance. In research by Klemke and Tiedman (1990), some respondents blame other female athletes for encouraging such labels because of the way in which they are perceived to conduct themselves.

Yet, these categories are forms of labeling that serve to stigmatize in order to discredit the targets which may be perceived or real (Klemke and Tiedman 1990). As such, the targets of these accusations respond with coping mechanisms of their own. One such mechanism is one of concealment through self-segregation (Blinde and Taube 1992). Here again, like military women and by extension women veterans, they turn only to each other for mutual support and by doing so self-segregate with only the like-minded or those who validate them. However, with self-segregation come other impediments. The targets become isolated from the general population of veterans, for instance, or worse yet, from the general civilian population at large (Adler and Adler 1987). So, to control the degree to which information is disclosed about them, targets may participate in passing as a camouflage for their true identities (Elliott et al. 1990). One way of doing so is to speak disparagingly about a group to divert negativity about oneself and association with this very group. Others involve themselves in behaviors that become dis-identifiers or distractions, particularly about lesbianism, by dressing very effeminately and associating themselves with those of the opposite sex under the guise that they are heterosexual (Goffman 1963). To further dissociate themselves from perceived contamination, targets do all that they can to ensure that they are never seen with the discredited group. This is also another form of deflection from stigmatization.

There are cases, however, where due to the target's status, the aforementioned tactics may be pointless or moot. Many targets choose to take the high road, so to speak, by attempting to educate the population about different points of view. Elliott et al. (1990) call this a form of normalization. One strategy to advance is that the competence of the athletes should be at issue, not the person's sexual orientation, as Snyder (2003) notes for military women that gender should be an irrelevant consideration. Foremost must be how the individual who happens to be a woman performs to achieve military effectiveness. Still, Elliott et al. (1990) believe that these efforts may be for naught, for the objective of the target should be to refute these stereotypes, not simply explain them away, re-educate and/or redefine the stigmatization. An interesting finding from the Blinde and Taube (1992) study on female athletes revealed a somewhat unintentional consequence. Some of the athletes were actually emboldened by such labels, that is of lesbianism, viewing them as a mark of strength and pushing the targets to simply shrug off or not care about what others think about them. In essence, being perceived as deviants only strengthened their resolve to be independent and proud of what they do. Nevertheless, Blinde and Taube (1992) find that the extent to which women must rely on stigma management does nothing to mitigate the challenges of being female athletes. Regrettably, the strategies employed are just seen as ways to make the stereotypes more prominent and the associated stigmatization enduring.

In the case of the military, the othering of women by the institution is legendary. Jeffreys (2007) describes this ploy as one of masculine domination through such exploits as prostitution and pornography. Such tactics are basic to gearing men up for the hunt in many militaries around the world. Brownmiller (1975) cites the Pakistani Army's use of pornography as one way of getting the men pumped up for war. Pakistani troops raped several Bangladeshi women as the ultimate weapon of war. *The Rape of Nanking* details how Japanese soldiers carried out myriad atrocities, one of which included the rape of Chinese women where 65 percent experienced the denigration at least once while others were gang raped, many of whom were left for dead (Chang 1997). Particularly brutal, at least in more contemporary times, was the en masse rape of female civilians during the Bosnia-Herzegovina Conflict. Seifert (1994) recounts the systematic rape of women that manifested the total disdain or perhaps more appropriately the hatred that the othering of women and of their bodies engendered. Following each rape, not only were women's breasts dismembered from their bodies but their stomachs were impaled. As Seifert (1994) suggests, the act was not just one perpetrated against a perceived foe but was far more sinister. The systematic rape of civilian women represented a loathing so vile that it embodies an instinctive sense of entitlement which is not only pervasive in the culture but to which men ascribe.

This violent act against women is intensified during times of crisis. However, this hatred against women which increases during times of war is not uncommon, as depicted in the mass rape of Chinese women and men in *The Rape of Nanking* (Chang 1997). Similar acts by U.S. soldiers in Vietnam highlight this pattern, as with the rape of a Vietnamese woman described by this soldier:

> When we got up to her she was asking for water. And the lieutenant said to kill her. So, he ripped off her clothes, they stabbed her in both breasts, they spread her eagle and shoved an E-tool up her vagina, an entrenching tool, and she was still asking for water. And then they took that out and they used a tree limb and then she was shot.
> (Brownmiller 1975, p.109)

Seifert (1994) dubs these and similar violent acts against women as 'the elevation of masculinity that accompanies war in Western cultures' (Seifert 1994, p.65, in Jeffreys 2007). Particularly for the U.S. military, and more so during the Vietnam Conflict, most such assaults do not occur during high emotion or in the heat of battle per se. Some 60 percent of these exploits were carried out as an occupational army, not as a combat force (Brownmiller 1975). Seifert (1994) explicates this behavior in that men are prepared for committing these acts as part of the acculturation in society even before they are indoctrinated into the military. Boys over time are taught to hate other women at home via such media as pornography. Pornography becomes normalized during peacetime and is collectively extolled at home as a symbol of men's power over women. Kelly (2000), like Brownmiller (1975), goes further by saying that sexual violence against women cannot be simply explained away as behavior that is induced during the heat of battle but constitutes a behavior that is cultivated in men not only to be manifested with greater intensity during times of war.

Operations Enduring and Iraqi Freedom exposed the extent to which sexual assault can play itself out, and the hatred with which such acts are executed. More importantly, the mindset and attitudes of the perpetrators are likely ingrained well before the onset of these incidents. The findings by Monahan and Neidel-Greenlee (2010) speak to this pattern in the U.S. military, already at epidemic levels. The Army's Lieutenant General Ricardo Sanchez, then the Commander of the Coalition Ground Forces in Iraq, labeled the environments of both wars a 360 degree combat zone where the stress was so overwhelming that the level gave birth to rampant sexual assault (Sanchez and Phillips 2008), but Monahan and Neidel-Greenlee (2010) call attention to the fact that this kind of behavior can only occur with either the implicit or explicit consent of commanders. The military could rid the institution of this affliction by not only holding its leaders accountable for its occurrence but leveling the appropriate penalties at the culprits. Four such incidents of sexual assault during Operations Enduring and Iraqi Freedom are noteworthy, yet so contemptible that collectively they signal a disease that not only must be rooted out as a matter of safety for the military's workforce, but which is a risk to military readiness.

The case of Private First Class (PFC) LaVena Johnson signals the lengths to which the U.S. Army was willing to go to conceal the facts surrounding the circumstances that resulted in her demise. PFC Johnson's death was immediately ruled as a suicide due to suspected self-inflicted wounds from an M-16 rifle (Monahan and Neidel-Greenlee 2010). Captain David Woods, her commanding officer, corroborated the soldier's sound state of mind at the time that immediately preceded her death. However, Dr. Johnson and Mrs. Johnson, her parents, became suspicious of the Army's conclusion and once PFC Johnson's body was returned to them, Dr. Johnson examined the body and instantly noticed inconsistencies with the Army's findings that evidenced that their daughter died of self-inflicted injuries. Following much stonewalling by the Army and with the intervention of the Congressional Office, the Army conceded that PFC Johnson was raped and then murdered (Monahan and Neidel-Greenlee 2010). The substantiated proof, consisting of planting an M-16 rifle across her chest, the injuries to her face and body and glued white gloves to her hands were all attempts by the attackers to mask the crime (Wright 2008). PFC Johnson's body was then hauled from one contractor's tent to another, where a caustic fluid was poured over her genitals to camouflage any signs of rape. More wicked is that fully clothed, her body was then burned. What is incomprehensible, though, is the Army's refusal to reopen the case for reinvestigation and to simply re-label PFC Johnson's death as a noncombat-related homicide.

In the second case, that of PFC Tina Priest, also of the U.S. Army, she was raped and subsequently killed by a soldier in Iraq; like PFC Johnson, an M-16 rifle was placed across her body and the death was labeled a suicide (Monahan and Neidel-Greenlee 2010). Also like PFC Johnson's parents, Mrs. Priest, PFC Priest's mother, took the Army to task for ruling her daughter's death a suicide, for even following the rape, as Mrs. Priest insisted, her daughter was in no way at the precipice of suicide. What is despicable and certainly shocks the conscience is that even following the sperm taken from PFC Priest that inconclusively tied her rape to that of a fellow soldier, without explanation, the indictment against the soldier was dropped (Wright 2008), although the soldier was charged with insubordination, loss of pay for two consecutive months, confinement to military quarters for 30 days, and 45 days of extra duty.

In the third case, also involving the U.S. Army, for PFC Duerksen, like the previous cases, death was judged as a suicide after being raped (Jones 2006, Wright 2008). PFC Duerksen's diary identified her rapist and the rape that occurred during training after consuming a drink spiked with a date rape drug, and even though the evidence pointed otherwise that she could not have committed suicide and following the arrest of the offender, the Army insisted on ruling the case as a suicide and denied a reinvestigation to accurately reflect the position of the case as a homicide (Jones 2006).

In the fourth case, and prior to Operations Enduring and Iraqi Freedom, the U.S. Army's Captain Jennifer Machmer was repeatedly raped before separating from the military in 2004 (Jeffreys 2007). It was in Poland, where she was a platoon leader, where she was first assaulted in 2001. Ironically, her attacker was a subordinate whom she had transferred. More egregious, though, was that after seeking counseling from a military chaplain for marital difficulties, she was raped by the chaplain. This time, however, Captain Machmer did not report the incident. While in Kuwait one month later in 2003, she was again sexually assaulted, this time again by a subordinate, a senior enlisted member with whom she was well acquainted. While Captain Machmer reported the violation, she was forced to relive her terrifying experience with her credibility in question, as to whether or not the incident that occurred was actually rape. In this case, Jeffreys (2007) believes that in the military, neither a woman's status as a commissioned officer nor rank as an officer commanding enlisted subordinates protects her from sexual assault. Even high-ranking women at the general officer rank are not necessarily immune from such exploits. In fact, the literature is rife with research citing the multiple rationale of the sexual harassment of so-called uppity women.

Take the case of Lieutenant General Claudia J. Kennedy. At the time, in 1996, she was the highest ranking woman in the Army, when she accused her subordinate, Major General Larry G. Smith, of sexual harassment (Marquis 2000). The incident allegedly occurred four years earlier when Kennedy and Smith were at the same rank. Lieutenant General Kennedy claimed that she was now motivated to lodge a complaint against Major General Larry G. Smith because as the Army's new Deputy Inspector General, he would be in a position to investigate misconduct that he himself perpetrated. In essence, it is those women who violate the prescriptive stereotypes (the shoulds) of gender ideals or of what men believe are those traits that define women, who are more likely to be sexually harassed (Berdahl 2007), than women who meet or reinforce those characteristics (descriptive stereotypes) (Berdahl et al. 1996, Maass et al. 2003).

Especially from the four sexual assault cases cited in the Army, it appears then that the shocking yet deplorable message from the military is that sexual assault in its various machinations, such as even prostitution, is for the taking and thus the debasement of women as being within the purview of men (Harris 2015), much of which is seen as a prize of sorts for serving in the military. At the time of Moon's (1997) study, 84 percent of men in the military reported that they had had at least one such sexual experience in the military. According to Moon, prostitution largely serves as a form of satisfaction for military men. Yet, more recently, as Hunter (2007) notes, there are no considerations for the consequences of such decisions. The military has in effect rationalized the use of such abhorrent tools, all for the sake of combat readiness, not for the repercussions on military women and women as veterans in general. Reportedly, nations like South Korea, although maybe not as much today, used to sing the praises of prostitution for the satisfaction of the U.S. military for the business contributed to the growth of the South Korean economy (Moon 1997). The South Korean International Tourism Association is said to have enthusiastically promoted such initiatives on behalf of its government to support this industry and did so by training comfort women or prostitutes for this purpose. These acts, yet again, only reinforce military men's belief that sex is a man's birthright and the more often one can have it, the better (Hunter 2007). More grotesque, says Hunter (2007), is the notion that, should one be deprived of this perceived entitlement, they will be more likely to indulge in wayward behaviors like sexual assault. By extension, host nations calculatingly engage in this behavior to provide certain segments of their female population to reduce the likelihood that U.S. military men will violate the decorum of the perceived more honorable women in their own population. Yet, this is exactly what has occurred. Two cases bear mentioning.

In the first, in 1995, three U.S. Navy men were found guilty of raping a Japanese girl in a rental car (Enloe 1996). What is beyond any decency and fairness was the response to the incident by the Navy's leadership, represented by the then Commander of the Pacific Fleet, Admiral Richard Macke. He joked, 'I think it was absolutely stupid as I've said several times. For the price they paid to rent a car, they could have a girl prostitute' (Enloe 1996, p.15).

In the second incident, two U.S. Navy sailors were convicted, receiving ten-year and nine-year sentences, respectively, for the rape of a Japanese woman in 2012 (Watkatsuki and Shaughnessy 2013). In some cases, the U.S. military has claimed innocence for its implication of personnel involvement in soliciting prostitutes by rationalizing that it is not its place to meddle in the domestic matters of its host nations since the issues are not those of the U.S. military (Hunter 2007). Moreover, it is not the U.S.'s place to impose its standards on its host nations. However, the U.S. military has repeatedly demonstrated that when it believed its personnel were at risk of compromise, it instituted protocols, as necessary, to protect them, it was only when U.S. military men began marrying prostitutes from the English-speaking countries where they were stationed and retaining them as legal wives in the U.S., did the U.S. see the need to curb the practice for fear of compromising U.S. secrets (Hunter 2007).

Ironically, in 1997, the U.S. Army mounted efforts to curtail its men's use of child prostitutes, referring to the infringement of U.S. interests, the need to protect its soldiers and the safety of the children (Hunter 2007). Yet, as Seifert (1994) argues, where men are made to believe that as warriors, women's sole purpose is for their recreation, and where military men only interact with women as prostitutes, the situations establish the pretext for sexual assault. Besides, the prostitutes with whom many of these military men interacted were primarily from the Pacific Rim, such as the Philippines, where many were socio-economically disadvantaged (Moon 1997), thus the military men will learn to carry out these behaviors not only without repercussions but to see women as for their own gratification and for the taking, and come to view military women in kind. As Harris (2015) states, then undoubtedly this makes military women increasingly vulnerable to sexual assault by military men. Enloe (1992) demonstrates the impact of the military's use of prostitution and how in turn these abuses embolden the masculinity of abusers:

> Among these different men there may be diverse masculinities. Women in Okinawa, Korea and the Philippines describe how they had to learn what made American men manly during sex; it was not always what they had learned made their Korean, Japanese or Filipino sexual partners feel manly ... Tourists, colonial officials, international technocrats and businessmen and soldiers have long been internationalizers of sexualized masculinity.
>
> (Enloe 1992, p.25)

Says Jeffreys (2007), the above speaks to the othering of women, and at the expense of women as a way of toughening men. Still, in light of the above, Jeffreys also poses such points as to the presence of women in the military as if anything provoking these attitudes of misogyny and the intense hatred of women. She contends that it may be the very presence of women that is spurring the prevalence of sexual assault in the military. Jeffreys bemoans that if the military requires aggressiveness in the form of masculinity to kill an enemy with whom one has no personal quarrel, is the military then a place for women? If so, given this sense of patriarchy, can women serve as equals in the institution that is the military?

Bibliography

Adler, P.A., and Adler, P. (1987). *Member Roles in Field Research*. Qualitative Research Methods, 6. Thousand Oaks, CA: Sage Publications.
Allen, T.B. (2006). *Harriet Tubman, Secret Agent: How Daring Slaves and Freed Blacks Spied for the Union During the Civil War*. Des Moines, IA: National Geographic Children's Books, Scholastic Book Club Edition.
Becker, G.S. (1964). *Human Capital*. New York: National Bureau of Economic Research (NBER).
Berdahl, J.L. (2007). The Sexual Harassment of Uppity Women. *Journal of Applied Psychology*, 92, 2, 425–437.
Berdahl, J.L., Magley, V.J., and Waldo, C.R. (1996). The Sexual Harassment of Men: Exploring the Concept with Theory and Data. *Psychology of Women Quarterly*, 20, 527–547.
Bird Francke, L. (1997). *Ground Zero. The Gender Wars in the Military*. New York, NY: Simon and Schuster.
Blinde, E.M., and Taube, D.E. (1992). Women Athletes as Falsely Accused Deviants: Managing the Lesbian Stigma. *The Sociological Quarterly*, 33, 521–533.
Brownmiller, S. (1975). *Against Our Will. Men, Women, and Rape*. London: Secker and Warburg.
Burgess, D., and Borgida, E. (1999). Who Women Are, Who Women Should Be. Descriptive and Prescriptive Gender Stereotyping in Sex Discrimination. *Psychology, Public Policy and Law*, 5, 3, 665–692.
Case, M.A.C. (1995). Disaggregating Gender from Sex and Sexual 'Orientation': The Effeminate Man in the Law and Feminist Jurisprudence. *Yale Law Journal*, 105, 9–18.
Chang, I. (1997). *The Rape of Nanking. The Forgotten Holocaust of World War II*. New York, NY: Penguin Books.
Chodrow, N. (1971). Being and Doing: A Cross-Cultural Examination of the Socialization of Males and Females. In V. Gornick and B.K. Moran (Eds.), *Sexist Society: Studies in Power and Powerlessness* (p.173–186). New York, NY: Basic Books.
Cohen, D.S. (2010). Keeping Men 'Men' and Women Down: Sex Segregation, Anti-Essentialism, and Masculinity. *Harvard Journal of Law and Gender*, 33, 509–553.
Damiano, C.M. (1999). Lesbian Baiting in the Military: Institutional Sexual Harassment under 'Don't Ask, Don't Tell, Don't Pursue.' *The American University Journal of Gender, Social Policy, and the Law*, 7, 3, 49–522.
Dansby, M.R., and Landis, D. (1998). Race, Gender, and Representation Index as Predictors of an Equal Opportunity Climate in Military Organizations. *Military Psychology*, 10, 87–105.
DeMello Patterson, M.B. (2000). America's Racial Unconscious: The Invisibility of Whiteness. In J.L. Kincheloe, S.R. Steinberg, N.M. Rodriguez, and R.E. Chennault (Eds.), *White Reign: Deploying Whiteness in America* (p. 103–121). New York, NY: St. Martin's Press.
Ellefson, K.G. (1998). *Advancing Army Women as Senior Leaders – Understanding the Obstacles*. Carlisle Barracks, PA: U.S. Army War College.
Elliott, G.C., Ziegler, B.L., Altman, B.M., and Scott, D.R. (1990). Under Stigma: Dimensions of Deviance and Coping. In C.D. Bryant (Ed.), *Deviant Behavior* (p.423–443). New York, NY: Hemisphere Press.

Enloe, C. (1992). It Takes Two. In S. Pollack Sturdevant and B. Stoltzfus (Eds.), *Let the Good Times Roll. Prostitution and the U.S. Military in Asia.* New York, NY: New Press.

Enloe, C.C. (1996). Spoils of War. *Ms. Magazine.* March/April, 15.

Franke, K.M. (1997). What's Wrong with Sexual Harassment? *Stanford Law Review*, 49, 691–772.

Frankenberg, R. (1993). *The Social Construction of Whiteness: White Women, Race Matters.* Minneapolis, MN: University of Minnesota Press.

Goffman, E. (1963). *Stigmas: Notes on the Management of Spoiled Identity.* New York, NY: Simon and Schuster.

Goldin, C. (2002). *A Pollution Theory of Discrimination: Male and Female Differences in Occupations and Earning.* National Bureau of Economic Research (NBER) Working Series. Working Paper 8985. www.nber.org/papers/w8985. Retrieved February 21, 2017.

Goldstein, J.S. (2003). *War and Gender. How Gender Shapes the War System and Vice Versa.* New York, NY: Cambridge University Press.

Grant DePauw, L. (1998). *Battle Cries and Lullabies. Women in War from Prehistory to the Present.* Norman, OK: University of Oklahoma Press.

Harris, G.L.A. (2009). Women, the Military and Academe: Navigating the Family Track in an Up or Out System. *Administration and Society*, 41, 4, 391–422.

Harris, G.L.A. (2012). Multiple Marginality: How the Disproportionate Assignment of Women and Minorities to Manage Diversity Programs Reinforces and Multiplies Their Marginality. *Administration and Society*, 20, 10, 1–34.

Harris, G.L.A. (2015). *Living Legends and Full Agency: Implications of Repealing the Combat Exclusion Policy.* New York, NY: Taylor & Francis.

Harris, G.L.A., and Lewis, E.L. (Forthcoming). *Blacks in the Military and Beyond.* Lanham, MD: Rowman & Littlefield.

Holm, J. (1992). *Women in the Military. An Unfinished Revolution.* Revised Edition. Novato, CA: Presidio Press.

Hunter, M. (2007). *Honor Betrayed. Sexual Abuse in America's Military.* Ft. Lee, NJ: Barricade Press.

Jeffreys, S. (2007). Double Jeopardy: Women, the U.S. Military and the War in Iraq. *Women's Studies International Forum*, 30, 16–25.

Jones, K. (2006). Fort Hood-Based Soldier 'Loved People, and They Knew It.' *Associated Press/Temple Daily Telegram.* March 21.

Jorgenson, J. (2000). Interpreting the Intersections of Work and Family: Frame Conflicts in Women's Work. *Electronic Journal of Communication*, 10, 3–4.

Kanter, R.M. (1977). *Men and Women of the Corporation.* New York, NY: Basic Books.

Kelly, L. (2000). Wars Against Women: Sexual Violence, Sexual Politics, and the Militarised State. In S. Jacobs, R. Jacobson and J. Marchbank (Eds.), *States of Conflict, Gender, Violence and Resistance* (p.45–65). London: Zed Books.

Klemke, L.W., and Tiedman, G.H. (1990). Toward an Understanding of False Accusation: The Pure Case of Deviant Labeling. In *Deviant Behavior: Readings in the Sociology of Norm Violations.* New York, NY: Hemisphere Publishing Corporation.

Kleykamp, M. (2007). Military Service as a Labor Market Outcome. *Race, Gender, and Class*, 14, 3–4, 65–76.

Konrad, A.M., Winter, S., and Gutek, B.A. (1992). Diversity in Work Group Sex Composition: Implications for Majority and Minority Workers. *Research in the Sociology of Organizations*, 10, 115–140.

Law, S.A. (1999). White Privilege and Affirmative Action. *Akron Law Review*, 32, 603–621.

Maass, A., Cadinu, M., Guarnieri, G., and Grasselli, A. (2003). Sexual Harassment under Social Identity Threat: The Computer Harassment Paradigm. *Journal of Personality and Social Psychology*, 85, 853–870.

Marquis, C. (2000). Army Confirms Officer's Claim of Harassment. *New York Times*. May 11. www.nytimes.com/2000/05/11/us/army-confirms-officer-s-claim-of-harassment.html. Retrieved March 23, 2013.

McClintock, M. (1996). Lesbian Baiting Hurts All Women. In K. Warren (Ed.), *Women's Voices in Experimental Education* (p.241–250). Dubuque, IA: Kendall Hunt.

Monahan, E.M., and Neidel-Greenlee, R. (2010). *A Few Good Women. America's Military Women from World War I to the Wars in Iraq and Afghanistan*. New York: Anchor Books.

Moon, K. (1997). *Sex Among Allies: Military Prostitution in U.S.-Korean Relations*. New York, NY: Columbia University Press.

Pazy, A., and Oron, I. (2001). Sex Proportion and Performance Evaluation Among High Ranking Military Officers. *Journal of Organizational Behavior*, 22, 689–702.

Prentice, D.A., and Carranza, E. (2002). What Women and Men Should Be, Shouldn't Be Are Allowed to Be, and Don't Have to Be: The Contents of Prescriptive Gender Stereotypes. *Psychology of Women Quarterly*, 26, 269–281.

Reskin, B.F., McBrier, D.B., and Kmec, J.A. (1999). The Determinants and Consequences of Workplace Sex and Race Composition. *American Review of Sociology*, 25, 335–361.

Ridgeway, C.L., and Correll, S.J. (2004). Motherhood as a Status Characteristic. *Journal of Social Issues*, 60, 4, 6, 83–700.

Rosen, L.N., Durand, D.B., Blieses, P.D., Halverson, R.R., Rothberg, J.M., and Harrison, N.L. (1996). Cohesion and Readiness in Gender-Integrated Combat Service Support Units: The Impact of Acceptance of Women and Gender Ratio. *Armed Forces & Society*, 22, 537–553.

Sanchez, R., with Phillips, D.T. (2008). *Wiser in Battle: A Soldier's Story*. New York: Harper Collins e-books, Kindle Edition.

Schultz, V. (1998). Reconstructing Sexual Harassment. *Yale Law Journal*, 107, 1683–1796.

Seifert, R. (1994). War and Rape: A Preliminary Analysis. In A. Stiglmayer (Ed.), *Mass: The War Against Women in Bosnia-Herzegovina*. Lincoln, NE: University of Nebraska Press.

Snitow, A. (1990). A Gender Diary. In M. Hirsch and E.F. Keller (Eds.), *Conflicts in Feminism* (p. 9–43). New York: Routledge.

Snyder, R. Claire. (2003). The Citizen-Soldier Tradition and Gender Integration of the U.S. Military. *Armed Forces and Society*, 29, 2, 185–204.

U.S. Census Bureau. (2010). Quick Facts. www.u.s.census.gov. Retrieved February 9, 2017.

Vojdik, V.K. (2005). Beyond Stereotyping in Equal Protection Doctrine: Reframing the Exclusion of Women from Combat. *Alabama Law Review*, 57, 2, 303–350.

Watkatsuki, Y., and Shaughnessy, L. (2013). Two U.S. Servicemen Imprisoned for Rape in Japan. *CNN*. March 1. www.cnn.com/2013/03/01/world/asia/japan-u-s-rape-sentencing/index.html. Retrieved April 2, 2013.

Wright, A. (2008). Is There an Army Cover-up of Rape and Murder of Women Soldiers? *Common Dreams News Center*. April 28. www.commondreams.org/archive/2008/04/28/8564. Retrieved March 23, 2013.

3 Women as Supporters and Caregivers

Many believe in the biological argument that women are predisposed to be caregivers or in the primary role as supporters, with a fragile nature which requires that they be protected. Therefore, they have no business in that which is the prerogative of men. Those who espouse this opposition view to women's inclusion in the military and, worse yet, women's integration into combat roles, are of this mindset. They contend that women's skeletal frame and stature render them unfit for combat duty (Maninger 2008). Further, purportedly, women's vulnerability to all things dangerous mandates that they be protected (Nantais and Lee 1999), because they are victims who function best and are more appropriately suited as the caregivers, nurturers and supporters of men in society (Kennedy-Pipe 2000). Jeffreys (2007) goes as far as to say that women may be asking for abuse when they subject themselves to environments like the military which are inherently places of masculine hegemony and domination and where women become the pawns of sexual subjugation by both friend and foe alike. In effect, women's presence in these milieus is thought to instinctively make them open to becoming the spoils of war, say the opponents. Others, like Kennedy-Pipe (2000) and Hicks Stiehm (1988), describe the military as no place for a lady.

Other staunch opponents of women in the military, like van Crevald (2016), question women's pervasive presence in the military, particularly in combat roles which they believe should be preserved for men only. Van Crevald (2002), though, does not question the capability and indeed the performance of some women in the military. However, what he finds to be most officious is placing women into combat for more reasons than one. First, van Crevald (2000) says that women's presence would harbor the resentment of men who view it as their right to take these positions. Second, because joining the military for many men is a conduit through which to prove their masculinity, women's presence make it all the more challenging for them to do so. Third, integrating women into this hypermasculine environment only b̶ ̶ ̶ ̶such ̶ ̶ ̶ ̶ties as sexual harassment and the like against them. S̶ ̶ ̶ ̶ ̶ ̶ ̶ ̶ ̶ ̶elihood of these occurrences, van Crevald recom̶ ̶ ̶ ̶ ̶ ̶ ̶ ̶ ̶ ̶cap women's overall presence in the institution at 10 percent, eliminate co-educational training as such arrangements only function to humiliate men, abolish the practice of integrating women altogether into direct ground combat positions, to include placing a moratorium on how far women can ascend in the rank structure, and reform the military to be segregated along gender lines where women can only command women and men can only command men. Fourth, one must lament that van Crevald believes that the condition known as post-traumatic stress disorder (PTSD) has become one for the pity party. He interprets the prevalence of the condition as owing to the military's reward for having the malady. van Crevald sees this pattern as prevalent and one that encourages veterans' claims to have the condition. Finally, while van Crevald acknowledges war as unspeakable, he simply recommends its acceptance as coming with a reframing of America's attitude towards it. Can van Crevald's views actually be seriously contemplated given contemporary times? He proposes a radical shift to the pre-1973 U.S. military when the institution was not only of a conscripted force but when all of his propositions were then common practice and a reality for military women.

Even military women like the Marine Corps Captain Kate Petronio (2012) has bought into the belief that women constitute a compromised sex, even as she herself has demonstrated her prowess in advising commanders during both Operations Enduring and Iraqi Freedom on how best to integrate Team Lioness, the all-female military combat teams, into meeting the military's mission. Captain Petronio's provocative article entitled 'Get Over It! We Are Not Created Equal,' perhaps unintentionally sparked divisive debates on both sides of the aisle on the issue about women in combat (Petronio 2012). However, even Petronio does not disagree with women's capabilities in combat, having seen what the likes of such initiatives like Team Lioness can achieve, not just in integrating women into combat but the same conditions which these women were forced to endure and without the protection afforded to male troops under a combat exclusion policy environment. Petronio's concern apparently arises from whether or not women possess what it takes over time to withstand and sustain the rigors of war. However, if Captain Petronio had witnessed the women in Team Lioness having been provided with the same training, equipment and protection that their male peers received, would she have advocated this biologically compromised argument as most opponents of women in the military do when she herself stands as an exemplar of the hellish duress under which any human being can survive?

Harris's (2015) portrayal of Sergeant Michelle Wilmot, an Army reservist and combat medic who was drafted impromptu and without the benefit of the training, equipment or protection, rites of passage that are automatically granted to her peers serving in Iraq and one which grew out of the need for his capacity, is a case in point. Wilmot was duly qu c and combat stress control non-commissioned officer (NCO) and even with the additional duties in the combat theater as the retention NCO for her unit. No one dared to accuse this woman of not exceeding the expectations, particularly because she was ill-equipped, untrained for this role and without the necessary protection as her male comrades. Sergeant Wilmot's part in Team Lioness became one of necessity. Still, with all of the minefields in her path that left her vulnerable to unforeseen conditions, again, conditions for which her male counterparts were trained, adequately equipped and protected, this NCO improvised, defied the odds, as did her fellow Team Lioness members, and proved to be hell on wheels.

Supporters of women's full integration into the military, still most controversially into occupations designated as combat, have essentially blunted especially the biological argument that women should not serve in these roles. Wechsler Segal (1982) observes the allegation that women lack upper-body strength. She asks then should all men be excluded from certain careers in the military simply because some of them lack upper-body strength? To the misconception that women's physique makes them unsuitable for military duty (Maninger 2008), research by Hosek et al. (2001) highlights the disproportionate number of women recruits who are discharged due to poor physical preparation and medically related problems. However, studies by Wilson (1995) and the U.S. Army (2002) itself prove otherwise. As well, what makes many of these results neither ones about sub-par physical conditioning nor medical injuries per se and thus not credible is that a 2012 report by the Defense Advisory Committee on Women in the Services (DACOWITS) found that the many reasons why military women sustain inordinate medical woes in the forms of back, knee, hip pain and other maladies are not out of any biological incapacity to complete any related combat training but more because the equipment is not designed for women, but for men. Consequently, as one of its recommendations, DACOWITS indicated that the Department of Defense (DoD), and by extension the military branches, must cooperate on the analysis, development and purchase of products and designs of gear that is suitable for women (DACOWITS 2012).

Other proponents of women's full integration into the military dispel the arguments as to women's physical acumen in the field. Former Congresswoman Patricia Schroeder disputed this allegation by identifying training as a key component for optimizing performance (Schroeder 1991). She cites such sporting greats as Kathy Aremdsen, known for her 96-mile-per-hour pitches underhand, and running star Florence Griffith Joyner who can run faster than O.J. Simpson could ever do while he was an athlete at the University of Southern California. However, the Congresswoman evolved. Congresswoman Schroeder, even as she earlier described herself as a feminist, was a staunch opponent of women's inclusion in the Selective Service System, primarily because of the risk of combat duty (Kerber 1993). The U.S. Army's (2002) research showed that it is commitment to one's ability in training that determines one's performance in the field. Gender was a moot variable.

Pregnancy, advanced as another argument to bar women from serving in combat (Maninger 2008), is an often-cited myth held by opponents of women in combat. Similar to the upper-body strength argument in barring all men because some men lack it, Wechsler Segal (1982) said it is just as hollow as the pregnancy argument in that women are not perpetually pregnant. Such conditions only occur during given times of a woman's life (Wagner DeCrew 1995). Plus, as Wechsler Segal (1982) noted, men, too, are not continuously in combat. Men are only in combat during limited periods of their careers in the military. She continued this theme in showing how nonsensical this line of thinking is in that because certain people within given groups have a greater propensity to contract the flu, it is equally as ludicrous to prevent all members of these same groups from enjoying certain activities for risk that the flu may become a contagion. Harrell and Miller (1997) and Hosek et al. (2001) also debunk this assertion. In actuality, due to the associated weaknesses that are perceived to come with pregnancy and the fear of compromising the mission, many women do everything in their power to avert any such perceptions.

Titunik (2000, 2008) challenges the notion that women in the military only serve as distractors to military men. She believes that the military has been unfairly characterized as hyper-masculine. Likewise, some argue that it is cultural socialization that leads people to hold these biases about women (Goldstein 2003, Snyder 2003, Wagner DeCrew 1995, Ellefson 1998). More importantly, like men, women must be socialized as warriors as the traits are not innate in either sex (Goldstein 2003, Snyder 2003). Wechsler Segal (1995) laments that it has been these unsubstantiated beliefs about women in the military that prevent their uni-linear progress since their status has been one of stops and starts given the 'cultural amnesia' (p.761), a convenient practice by the civilian and military leadership during peacetime following women's collective service to the country. Proponents of women in the military declare that the combat exclusion for women was deliberately put in place. Military leadership emanates from those who have served in combat (Putko 2008, Kennedy-Pipe 2000). Before, unlike men, only women were sanctioned as noncombatants even though the military's crafting of what defines direct ground combat has been fluid and changed over time (Wilson 1995).

The military's more recent use of the all-female engagement teams, Team Lioness, is not that novel in the sense that while this was the first such known embedding of women in combat, women in the U.S. military have always served in combat, sanctioned or not, and without the recognition of having done so. The women featured in Harris's (2015) research make clear that this practice has long been the case. Take Chief Warrant Officer 5 Trish Thompson, an Army helicopter pilot, now retired, who served front and center in 1985 in El Salvador and Honduras during the height of Manuel Ortega and the Sandinista National Liberation and the Contras supported by the U.S. Central Intelligence Agency (CIA). Thompson received a combat patch for this mission, itself an acknowledgement that she had indeed served under conditions defined as combat and was therefore a combatant. Commander (Dr.) Darlene Iskra, the first woman in the U.S. military to command a ship in the Navy, described an accidental situation in the Western Pacific in 1981 aboard the U.S.S. *Hector* (Harris 2015). As one of only six women among a crew of 800 men, the ship found itself navigating into territory that was considered a combat zone, in support of the hostages in Iran. The captain of the ship was ordered to remove the women on board but deliberately disobeyed, citing that the women's skills as divers, engineers, deck officers and supply officers were critical to the immediate mission.

Even as late as 2012, in a report based on the documentary *Lioness* that showcased many of the women in the Army and Marine Corps all-female engagement teams during Operations Enduring and Iraqi Freedom, the women's DD Forms 214 inaccurately omitted their service as one of combat (*Lioness Report* 2012). What is more tragic is that as a result of this calculated oversight, many of the women were deprived of their earned and deserved veterans' benefits, an obvious betrayal of their military service. Burrelli (2012) admits that Operations Enduring and Iraqi Freedom have been irregular and nonlinear in nature in the sense that there were no lines of demarcation on the battlefield to distinguish which areas constituted direct ground combat and which did not. The Army's own research findings indicated that, despite opponents of women in combat, mixed-gendered units, that is with women and men, outperformed segregated or single-gendered ones (U.S. Army 2002). Claims Harris (2015), in light of the then theoretical repeal of the combat exclusion policy, women have already been performing in the military as combatants. Thus the evidence in light of both the reality and research could no longer be ignored and notably so during guerrilla-style warfare environments like those of Operations Enduring and Iraqi Freedom.

What has been even more remarkable is that the calls for the combat exclusion policy's repeal have been internal to the military (Putko and Johnson 2008, Grosskruger 2008, Twitchell 2008), with many commanders with women within their commands as some of the staunchest supporters of women in combat (Grosskruger 2008, Twitchell 2008). In 2009, DACOWITS issued a report that included the uniformed assurance that commanders had female personnel within their commands during Operations Enduring and Iraqi Freedom (DACOWITS 2009). Although most of the women deployed were found in support occupations, given their capabilities, mounting calls for their service frequently brought them into harm's way and thus into direct ground combat in the infantry, gunnery crew and seamanship, despite their designation as noncombatants.

The opponents inside and outside the military are strident about the biological argument or the very nature of women that renders them unfit for military service and more so for combat. In an emotional testimony by General Robert Barrow, then Commandant of the Marine Corps, he was almost pleading with Congress to protect women from a battlefield environment so brutal that to place women into these theaters of operations that are essentially killing fields, would be barbaric. Barrow said:

> Exposure to danger is not combat. Being shot at being killed, is not combat. Combat is finding ... closing with ... and killing or capturing the enemy. It's KILLING! And it's done in an environment that is often as difficult as you can possibly imagine. Extremes of climate. Brutality. Death. Dying. It's ... uncivilized! And, WOMEN CAN'T DO IT! Nor should they even be thought of as doing it. The requirements of strength and endurance render them UNFIT to do it. And I may be old-fashioned, but I think the very nature of women disqualifies them from doing it. Women give life. Sustain life. Nurture life. They don't take it.
>
> (Holm 1992, p.482)

In Harris's (2015) series of interviews with pioneering women veterans about their views on women in combat, Major General Marcelite Harris, a woman with multiple firsts to her credit while in the Air Force, briefly pondered the question and reached the conclusion that it appears that the worth of a woman's life, at least in American society, is dictated by the fact that it is women, not men, who possess the unique capability of giving life through childbirth. Captain Troy Devine's case reflects the level of animus, not simply against women, but the extent to which the military was willing to go to remind women who dared to challenge conventional wisdom that, even if they succeeded in overcoming the barriers to acceptance in certain career disciplines, there were those disciplines that were off limits to them, and advancing the biological argument was the weapon of choice.

As a graduate of the Air Force Academy in 1985, all indications were that Captain Devine's career trajectory was that of a fighter pilot (Holm 1992). Unfortunately for her, she was made a woman, not a man. Captain Devine was subjected to pregnancy tests every two weeks under the compulsory waiver that she signed promising not to get pregnant during her assignment at Beale Air Force Base's Ninth Strategic Reconnaissance Wing, an assignment which proved not to be her preference because, given her sex, it was limited and by extension so was her choice of occupation. Indignities like the purportedly 39 women sailors who became pregnant during the debut of the voyage of the U.S.S. *Dwight Eisenhower* to the Adriatic Sea, the Arabian Gulf and the Mediterranean with 415 sailors on board, dominated the news (Garrison 1995). This would have never happened if an equally scandalous situation involving sailors occurred, as Bird Francke (1997) declared, because of the military's 'white male culture' (p.259).

Admittedly, while some of these pregnancies do occur for sinister reasons – to avoid military duty, for instance – some are unintentional and are therefore not deemed as a credible issue for opponents of women in combat to advance (Solaro 2006). One soldier who found out that she was pregnant was so despondent at the discovery that after disclosing the news to her commander, she returned to the U.S. for the expressed purpose of undergoing an abortion and with every intention of returning to Iraq to be with her comrades. Additionally, the notion that women are to be protected from combat has been repeatedly discredited (Holm 1992, Monahan and Neidel-Greenlee 2010, Fenner 2001, Bird Francke 1997, Goldstein 2003, Herbert 1998, Eltshain 1987, Grant DePauw 1998). As Holm (1992) argues, the enemy does not distinguish between male and female targets in combat. Further, women on the front lines, at least in American ourstory, can be traced as far back as Molly Pitcher taking up arms during the American Revolution in the protection of others (Grant DePauw 1998), and most recently embedded as all-female engagement teams by the Army and Marine Corps during Operations Enduring and Iraqi Freedom (McLagan and Sommers 2010, Alvarez 2009, *Lioness Report* 2012). To be clear, these are only the recorded exploits of which the American public is aware.

Another myth about women in the military, much less in combat, speaks to that of former Marine Corps Commandant and Captain Petronio's assertions, also of the Marine Corps, that women are too fragile and therefore cannot prevail in the harsh environment of combat (Holm 1992, Petronio 2012). Moreover, the argument is made that American women have become too acculturated to the 'creature comforts' (p.462) of civilian life (Holm 1992). Holm (1992) concedes, though, that while the latter point is true given the high standard of living in the U.S., nurses during the Vietnam Conflict, as one example, demonstrated that they were as skilled as the men, if not better, in surveying the battlefield, adapting to its ruggedness and doing whatever the situation called for in meeting or exceeding the mission. Besides, nurses, even as caregivers, are notorious for surviving in insurgency-plagued environments. Another widely held myth is that the American public is not emotionally prepared to witness women returning home in body bags or being captured as prisoners of war (POW) (Holm 1992). This myth has some degree of truth in it, given the American public's low threshold for stomaching the signs of dead Americans, male or female. Still, the public's level of recall about such incidents is fleeting (Fenner 2001). Yet, this myth persists under the belief that, should a military woman become a POW, military men would become overwhelmed by the need to protect her. However, contradictory evidence shows that this is simply not the case. Fenner (2001) mentions that during World War II women successfully penetrated the enemy's intelligence. During the Vietnam

Conflict's Tet Offensive, women were on their own (Fenner 2001, Saywell 1985, Breuer 1997). No male soldiers ever came to their defense, nor were the women waiting around to be protected by the men because, like male soldiers, they simply moved on to safer zones.

The Air Force's survival, escape, resistance and evasion training (SERE), yielded some vital information about POW behaviors. While the belief held was that in the case of the capture of female pilots by the enemy, male pilots would relent, no such hypothesis was borne out (Fenner 2001, Bird Francke 1997). The opposite was true and the training simply confirmed what military women had known all along. In fact, should male POWs emotionally react to the beating of their female comrades by surrendering, this would only aggravate the situation for their female colleagues in that the women may become subjected to greater levels of mistreatment. Similarly, yet more enlightening, was that men were no more likely to react to the ill-treatment of women over the ill-treatment of men. Monahan and Neidel-Greenlee (2010) attribute this unsubstantiated belief to the frenzy created by those in Congress, the military and military ourstorians. Also the skewed coverage of information is conveniently opted for proselytizing as truth. Additionally, the incessant presentation of the same information over time by various forms of the media, establishes and reinforces this perception as truth.

Still another myth about military women that has been perpetuated is that because they are primarily caregivers, their role as mothers is imperiled (Holm 1992). Propaganda in the form of such headlines as 'Mommies Going to War' during Operation Desert Storm and that the military is becoming a place reputed for unwed mothers only reinforces the myth that women do not belong in the military (Fenner 2001, Holm 1992, Bird Francke 1997). It is true that Operation Desert Storm did expose post-Vietnam the extent to which parenthood and family challenges became overriding concerns for the military given the personnel impacted by especially overseas deployment (Fenner 2001, Holm 1992, Bird Francke 1997). However, Bird Francke (1997) blames these conditions on the military culture and environment. Interestingly enough, the all-volunteer force perhaps unintentionally created new challenges that only played out during the lead-up to Operation Desert Storm. Because deployments were now extended, a greater number of technically trained personnel were required. Likewise, unlike conscription during the Vietnam Conflict and for prior campaigns, an all-volunteer force now required two-year, four-year and six-year enlistment contracts. While the longer deployments required more technically competent personnel and longer enlistments altogether encouraged a more family-oriented and stable workforce for the military, these variables also resulted in unintended consequences.

During the Vietnam Conflict, the average age of a recruit was 19, whereas during Operation Desert Storm it had increased to almost 27 (Bird Francke 1997). Adding to this complication was that over

50 percent of the enlisted corps was married. This not only lent to a more stable force but a family-oriented environment that reduced the likelihood of problems with discipline, especially those that were drug related. A stable workforce and family-oriented environment facilitated re-enlistments for the military. Benefits such as housing, medical and other incentives became attractive following the Vietnam Conflict. Many of these benefits were equally attractive to single fathers who represented a disproportionate segment of the military. Yet, as cultural mores would have it, it was not the single fathers but the single mothers who were allegedly the group of ill repute for the military. For example, the Navy instituted a policy barring recruits from securing custody of their children, with violators subject to discharge under the guise of 'fraudulent enlistment' (Bird Francke 1997, p.140).

The Navy survey, however, discovered that most children were actually residing with their parents (Thomas and Thomas 1992). Nevertheless, it was the single mothers, not the single fathers, whom the Navy detailers avoided, citing that every transgression including pregnancy and single mothers but, conveniently, not single fathers, would prove to be taxing for the Navy, especially in deployment. Thomas and Thomas (1992) point to the Navy expending excessive time locating assignments for dual military married couples at the expense of single mothers. The Navy treated single mothers as exiles who were relegated to unskilled jobs for the most part, even though they were more qualified to perform skilled ones (Bird Francke 1997). One single mother remarked: 'This guy in my unit takes time off to take his kid to the doctor and everyone says "Oh, isn't he wonderful?" I take my kid to the doctor and my supervisor marks it down as time lost off the job' (Bird Francke 1997, p.140). What is also noteworthy is that single fathers were more likely than single mothers to have several children in tow, which correspondingly translated into higher costs for the military. Yet, it was the single mothers who were blamed for all things that went awry. Both the Navy and Army were unwelcoming to single mothers and did whatever was necessary to keep them out of their units. Sadly, it was the single mothers who conveniently provided the media with the rationale needed to spin the truth. Operation Desert Storm came to be known for single mothers with problems pursuing a career in the military. Holm (1992) took issue with this designation and countered that this was not the case; the consequence was primarily a condition of an all-volunteer force. And despite Holm's (1992) counterargument, four journalists cast the military as a repository for unwed mothers (Reed 1999). Even with the Pentagon's findings that of its 67,000 single parents, 66 percent were men (Holm 1992), journalists inaccurately reported that the majority of single parents in the military were women (Reed 1999). Such rhetoric was also in keeping with the knowledge that after World War II, Operation Desert Storm represented the largest number of women, this time all military women, ever to be mobilized for a war effort (Holm

1992). Oddly enough, less than 0.5 percent of single parents and couples during Operation Desert Storm were unable to deploy because of family-related reasons.

Another well-advanced myth is that by bringing women into the military, the institution's standards would be compromised (Holm 1992). Major General Marcelite Harris addressed this very point during her interview with Harris (2015). According to Major General Harris, it appeared that the military did not even establish standards until it began recruiting women. If anything, because the military's requirements for women's entrance were far more stringent than those for men's entrance, it resulted in a more educated workforce of women for the military. The military even admitted that its female workforce was more educated than its male workforce (Holm 1992). Moreover, research by the DoD confirmed these findings as early as the 1970s, when some 90 percent of women in the military possessed at least a high school diploma compared to 63 percent of the men recruits (Bird Francke 1997). A more educated female workforce also proved positive for the military in the long term. The retention rates for women were higher than those for men, and the military experienced fewer disciplinary problems with them. Further, women officers, on average, outscored men officers by an average of ten points on the Air Force Officer Qualifying Test (Fenner 2001). This tradition of having a more educated female workforce as well as more educated women veterans has not changed.

However, aside from having a female workforce that is more educated than the male workforce in the military, women have increasingly recognized that the path to financial and economic security is through an advanced education (Goldin 2009, Bailey and Dynarski 2011, Lee and Freeman 2012, DiPrete and Buchanan 2013, Pew Research Center 2013, Schow 2016, Lam 2017). By age 22, women's educational attainment is higher than men's in the same cohort (Entwisle et al. 2005). Women veterans, for instance, at far greater rates than men veterans, take advantage of the educational benefits offered through the GI Bill (Walker and Borbely 2014, U.S. Department of Veterans Affairs 2015, Women's Bureau n.d.).

There is also the unsubstantiated myth that women and men cannot work together because doing so will only increase the likelihood of sexual relations between them (Holm 1992). It is believed that these situations will invariably produce compromising effects for the military in the way of its mission. However, this myth has been disproven. Research on earlier campaigns such as Operation Desert Storm yields the effectiveness of performance in mix-gendered units (Bird Francke 1997, Moskos 1998), and in training situations these rumors have been discredited (U.S. Army 2002), including by research on the Marine Corps (Gereben Schaefer et al. 2015). The later research by Gereben Schaefer et al. (2015) of RAND Corporation for the Marine Corps had its spinners cast the findings as conclusive that single-gendered units that are all-male consistently exceeded the performance of mix-gendered units. This is not the case. The researchers for the Marine Corps study were careful to highlight that, for instance, the performance of unit members is contingent upon leadership. Because performance has a far greater effect on the cohesion of a unit than cohesion has on the performance of the unit, it is the culture and hence the leadership of the units that makes the difference in the gender integration of those units and how receptive or how hostile the culture is towards this integration that ultimately matters in unit performance.

It is also worth noting that, because women do not perform well in groups where they are token members or the few women in groups, their performance will likely decline (Lord and Saenz 1985, Sekaquaptewa and Thompson 2003). The researchers of the Marine Corps study were equally thoughtful in recommending to the Marine Corps the importance of implementing cohesion-building strategies for the integration, assimilation and increase in the cohesion of female and male unit members over time (Gereben Schaefer et al. 2015). This is not to say, however, that the integration of men and women into the same unit will not at times result in sexual relations and social relations (Holm 1992). However, negative accounts, if any, have been minimized and unit members, especially as related to unit cohesion, were never negatively impacted (Harrell and Miller 1997, Harrell et al. 2002). It is also of note that it was Army commanders from Operations Enduring and Iraqi Freedom, who, with first-hand knowledge of the performance of their subordinate female commanders and other women under their commands, were moved to support the integration of women into combat occupations (Putko and Johnson 2008, Grosskruger 2008, Twitchell 2008).

The above also immediately speaks to the next myth that women's presence jeopardizes unit cohesion (Holm 1992). As previously indicated, studies by Harrell and Miller (1997), Harrell et al. (2002) and others (i.e., Rosen et al. 1996, 1999) have undermined this myth. Say Harrell and Miller (1997), for example, one's gender is of minor consideration in the event of unit conflicts. Researchers like Gereben Schaefer et al. (2015) pointed to leadership as foremost in mitigating these skirmishes (Harrell and Miller 1997). Studies by Rosen et al. (1996, 1999) also found gender to be a negligible variable in units, although for the latter study, a meta-analysis of five Army units, the nexus between unit cohesion and gender was unfounded (Rosen et al. 1999).

In another myth, women are purported to be an unreliable source for the military when every campaign, small and large, has shown otherwise (Holm 1992). Wechsler Segal (1995) continues to attribute this preposterous myth to a case of 'cultural amnesia' (p.720) that conveniently afflicts the civilian and military leadership during peacetime once women have been demobilized. Fears of women getting pregnant and/or using pregnancy as a rationale to leave the military have been invalidated. Harrell and Miller (1997) found that, because military women recognize this perceived weakness for the mission, they do whatever is necessary to keep this untoward perception at bay (Harris 2009), and appear to have succeeded because the study indicated that pregnancies are not perceived as hindering the mission (Harrell and Miller 1997). Solaro (2006) invokes the military's treatment of its female workforce as that of how a married man treats his mistress, by using her talents whenever and however he deems fit and only making her public when doing so suits his purpose.

The final myth that also feeds into the notion that women's roles should only be those of supporters and caregivers is the biological reason that they are the fairer and weaker sex, if only to suggest that women do not have what it takes to be in the military and certainly lack the attributes for combat (Holm 1992). This myth also appeals to American women's inability to live without the 'creature comforts' (p.462) to which they have grown accustomed. Holm provides the ability especially of nurses during such guerrilla warfare environments like Vietnam as clear evidence that this is not the case. In the harsh conditions of the Persian Gulf during Operation Desert Storm, women, unlike men who secured their regular supply of shaving cream, did without basic sanitation products by improvising and finding creative ways to adjust to the austere environment. Monahan and Neidel-Greenlee (2010) speak of situations where black women, like all military women, were not only having to contend with incidents of rampant sexual assault and restrictions owing to the cultural mores of the region, but with race discrimination as well. Together these untoward behaviors potentially endangered women's unit performance and that of the military's overriding mission in the region. Likewise, as noncombatants women were devoid of training, equipment and protection, where especially in the Army and below the brigade level they were routinely placed into combat positions that unnecessarily imperiled their lives (Solaro 2006). The military employed these tactics given conditions on the ground by attaching the women rather than assigning them to units. Accordingly, here 'in the military, if you're not assigned to a unit, you are an orphan' (Solaro 2006, p.70).

Harris's (2015) interviews with primarily Army women confirm this practice. In one case, one of the interviewees not only objected to the assignment of a less experienced male soldier whom she had trained but who was elected over her for a particular post. The members of other units also protested this assignment solely on the basis of gender and because the more experienced female soldier was a noncombatant even though she obviously possessed combatant skillsets. In the end, while the more experienced female soldier was selected for the post, she was never credited with the designation as a combatant.

Advanced as a collective, these myths are designed to fit a preconceived notion of women by deliberately using the narrative that women are innately compromised for the military and undoubtedly so for combat duty (Holm 1992, Eltshain 1987, Grant DePauw 1998, Fenner 2001, Bird Francke 1997, Herbert 1998, Goldstein 2003, Monahan and Neidel-Greenlee 2010). This serves the agenda of opponents that women do not belong in the military (Gutmann 2000, Mitchell 1997, van Crevald 2000, 2002,

Maninger 2008). However, as Holm (1992) so accurately states, for the enemy to discern whether or not the target on the ground is male or female in order to annihilate them is simply impractical, for a target, regardless of gender, is just a target to the enemy. Suffice it to say, altogether, these myths do nothing more than speak to the intransigence of opponents in their desire to turn back the hands of time by denying the country in leveraging the talents of a key resource for its national defense. These regressive beliefs only manage to willfully subordinate the inalienable rights and contributions of more than one-half of the country's citizenry, who are women, while undermining America's standing as the leader of the free world.

Bibliography

Alvarez, L. (2009). G.I. Jane Breaks the Combat Barrier. *New York Times*. August 16, AI.
Bailey, M.J., and Dynarski, S.M. (2011). *Gains and Gaps: Changing Inequality in U.S. College Entry and Completion*. National Bureau of Economic Research (NBER). http://users.nber.org/~dynarski/Bailey_Dynarski_Final.pdf. Retrieved March 23, 2017.
Bird Francke, L. (1997). *Ground Zero. The Gender Wars in the Military*. New York, NY: Simon and Schuster.
Breuer, W.B. (1997). *War and American Women: Heroism, Deeds, and Country*. Westport, CT: Praeger Publishing.
Burrelli, D.D. (2012). *Women in Combat: Issues for Congress*. April 5. Washington, DC: Congressional Research Service (CRS). www.dtic.mil/get-tr-doc/pdf?AD=ADA584292. Retrieved March 24, 2017.
Cohn, M. (2006). The Fear That Kills. Appalling New Evidence Reveals That Female Soldiers Serving in Iraq Made Fatal Decisions in Their Attempts to Avoid Rape. January 31. www.alternet.org/story/31584/the_fear_that_kills. Retrieved March 24, 2017.
Defense Advisory Committee on Women in the Services (DACOWITS). (2009). *Status Report*. http://dacowits.defense.gov/Portals/48/Documents/Reports/2011/Documents/DACOWITS%20September%202011%20Committee%20Meeting/16%20USMC%20WISR%20DACOWITS%20Brief.pdf. Retrieved March 13, 2017.
Defense Advisory Committee on Women in the Services (DACOWITS). (2012). *Status Report*. http://dacowits.defense.gov/Portals/48/Documents/Reports/2012/Annual%20Report/dacowits2012report.pdf. Retrieved May 25, 2017.
DiPrete, T.A., and Buchanan, C. (2013). *The Rise of Women*. New York, NY: Russell Sage Foundation.
Ellefson, K.G. (1998). *Advancing Army Women as Senior Leaders – Understanding the Obstacles*. Carlisle, PA: U.S. Army War College. AD A344984.
Eltshain, J.B. (1987). *Women and War*. New York: Basic Books, Inc.
Entwisle, D.A., Alexander, K.L., and Olson, L.S. (2005). First Grade and Emotional Attainment by Age 22: A New Story. *American Journal of Sociology*, 110, 5, 1458–1502.
Fenner, L.M. (2001). Moving Targets: Women's Roles in the U.S. Military in the 21st Century. In L.M. Fenner and M.E. deYoung (Eds.), *Women in Combat. Civic Duty or Military Liability?* Washington, DC: Georgetown University Press.

Garrison, B. (1995). Deployed and Pregnant. *Navy Times*, April 3, 6.

Gereben Schaefer, A., Wenger, J.W., Kavanagh, J., Wong, J.P., Oak, G.S., Trail, T.E., and Nichols, T. (2015). *The Implications of Integrating Women into the Marine Corps Infantry*. Santa Monica, CA: RAND Publications.

Goldin, C. (2009). The Rising (and Then Declining) Significance of Gender. In F.D. Blau, M.B. Brinton and D.B. Grusky (Eds.), *The Declining Significance of Gender?* (p.67–101). New York, NY: Russell Sage Press.

Goldstein, J.S. (2003). *War and Gender. How Gender Shapes the War System and Vice Versa*. New York: Cambridge University Press.

Grant DePauw, L. (1998). *Battle Cries and Lullabies. Women in War from Prehistory to the Present*. Norman: University of Oklahoma Press.

Grosskruger, P.L. (2008). Women Leaders in Combat: One Commander's Perspective. In M. Putko and D.V. Johnson III (Eds.), *Women in Combat Compendium*. Carlisle, PA: U.S. Army War College.

Gutmann, S. (2000). *A Kinder, Gentler Military: Can America's Gender-Neutral Fighting Force Still Win Wars?* New York and London: A Lisa Drew Book.

Harrell, M.C., Chiayang Chien, S., Beckett, M.K., and Sollinger, J.M. (2002). *The Status of Gender Integration in the Military: Analysis of Selected Occupations*. Santa Monica, CA: RAND Publications.

Harrell, M.C., and Miller, L. (1997). *New Opportunities for Military. Effects Upon Readiness, Cohesion, and Morale*. National Defense Research Institute (NDRI). Santa Monica, CA: RAND Publications.

Harris, G.L.A. (2009). The Multifaceted Nature of White Female Attrition in the Military. *Journal of Public Management and Social Policy*, 15, 1, 71–93.

Harris, G.L.A. (2015). *Living Legends and Full Agency: Implications of Repealing the Combat Exclusion Policy*. New York, NY: Taylor & Francis Group, a division of CRC Press.

Herbert, M.S. (1998). *Camouflage Isn't Only for Combat. Gender, Sexuality, and Women in the Military*. New York and London: New York University Press.

Hicks Stiehm, J. (1988). The Effects of Myths about Military Women on the Waging of War. In E. Isaksson (Ed.), *Women and the Military System*. New York, NY: Simon and Schuster.

Holm, J. (1992). *Women in the Military. An Unfinished Revolution*. Revised Edition. Novato, CA: Presidio Press.

Hosek, S.D., Tiemeyer, P., Kilburn, R., Strong, D.A., Ducksworth, S., and Ray, R. (2001). *Minority and Gender Differences in Officer Career Progression*. Santa Monica, CA: RAND Publications.

Jeffreys, S. (2007). Double Jeopardy: Women, the U.S. Military and the War in Iraq. *Women's Studies International Forum*, 30, 16–25.

Kennedy-Pipe, C. (2000). Women and the Military. *Journal of Strategic Studies*, 23, 4, 32–50.

Kerber, L.K. (1993). 'A Constitutional Right to Be Treated Like Ladies': Women, Civic Obligations and Military Service. *The University of Chicago Law School Roundtable*, 1, 1, Article 15, 95–128.

Lam, J. (2017). Battle of the Sexes: Why Women Have More Debt Than Men. May 10. *Credit Sesame*. www.creditsesame.com/blog/debt/battle-of-the-sexes-why-women-have-more-debt-than-men/. Retrieved March 1, 2017.

Lee, W.Y., and Freeman, K. (2012). *From Diplomas to Doctorates: The Success of Black Women in Higher Education and Its Implications for Equal Educational Opportunities for All.* Sterling, VA: Stylus Publishing.

Lioness Report. (2012). *Cultivating Change: Lioness Impact Report.* Based on *Lioness,* A Feature Documentary directed by M. McLagan and D. Sommers. U.S.: Room 11 Productions.

Lord, C.G., and Saenz, D.S. (1985). Memory Deficits and Memory Surfeits: Differential Cognitive Consequents of Tokenism for Tokens and Observers. *Journal of Personality and Social Psychology,* 9, 4, 918–926.

Maninger, S. (2008). Women in Combat: Reconsidering the Case Against Deployment of Women in Combat-Support and Combat Units. In H. Carreiras and G. Kummel (Eds.), *Women in the Military and Armed Conflict* (p.9–27). VS Verlang fur Sozialwissenschaften.

McLagan, M., and Sommers, D. (2010). Introductions: How We Came to Make 'Lioness.' July. www.pbs.org/pov/regardingwar/conversations/women-at-war/introductions-how-we-came-to-make-lioness.php. Retrieved May 21, 2017.

Mitchell, B. (1997). *Women in the Military: Flirting with Disaster.* Washington, DC: Regnery Publishing, Inc.

Monahan, E.M., and Neidel-Greenlee, R. (2010). *A Few Good Women: America's Military Women from World War I to the Wars in Iraq and Afghanistan.* New York: Anchor Books.

Moskos, C. (1998). The Folly of Comparing Race and Gender in the Army. *Washington Post,* C1. January 4.

Nantais, C., and Lee, M.F. (1999). Women in the United States Military: Protectors or Protected? The Case of Prisoner of War Melissa Rathburn-Nealy. *Journal of Gender Studies,* 8, 2, 181–191.

Petronio, K. (2012). Get Over It! We're Not All Created Equal. *Marine Corps Gazette.* www.mca-marines.org/gazette/article/get-over-it-we-are-not-all-created-equal. Retrieved May 25, 2017.

Pew Research Center. (2013). In Educational Attainment, Millennial Women Outpace Men. December 10. www.pewsocialtrends.org/2013/12/11/on-pay-gap-millennial-women-near-parity-for-now/sdt-gender-and-work-12-2013-0-04/. Retrieved February 23, 2017.

Putko, M. (2008). The Combat Exclusion Policy in the Modern Security Environment. In M.M. Putko and D.V. Johnson III (Eds.), *Women in Combat Compendium.* Carlisle Barracks, PA: U.S. Army War College. January.

Putko, M.M. and Johnson, D.V. (2008). *Women in Combat Compendium.* M.M. Putko and D.V. Johnson III (Eds.). Carlisle Barracks, PA: U.S. Army War College. January.

Reed, F. (1999). Recruiting and Gender. *Armed Forces News.* November 18. www.armedforcesnews.com. Retrieved January 2017.

Rosen, L.N., Bliese, P.D., Wright, K.A., and Gifford, R.K. (1999). Gender Composition and Group Cohesion in U.S. Army Units: A Comparison across Five Studies. *Armed Forces and Society,* 25, 3, 365–386.

Rosen, L.N., Durand, D.B., Bliese, P.D., Halverson, R.R., Rothberg, J.M., and Harrison, N.L. (1996). Cohesion and Readiness in Gender-Integrated Combat Service Support Units: The Impact of Acceptance of Women and Gender Ratio. *Armed Forces and Society,* 22, 4, 537–553.

Saywell, S. (1985). *Women in War.* New York: Viking Press.

Schow, A. (2016). Women Earning More Doctoral and Masters Degrees Than Men. *Washington Examiner.* July 1. www.washingtonexaminer.com/women-earning-more-doctoral-and-masters-degrees-than-men/article/2602223. Retrieved March 20, 2017.

Schroeder, P. (1991). The Combat Exclusion Law Should Be Repealed. In C. Wekesser and M. Polesetsky (Eds.), *Women in the Military.* Farmington Hills, MI: Greenhaven Press.

Sekaquaptewa, D., and Thompson, M. (2003). Solo Status, Stereotype Threat and Performance Expectancies: Their Effects on Work Performance. *Journal of Experimental and Social Psychology,* 39, 1, 68–74.

Snyder, R.C. (2003). The Citizen-Soldier Tradition and Gender Integration of the U.S. Military. *Armed Forces and Society,* 29, 2, 185–204.

Solaro, E. (2006). *Women in the Line of Fire. What You Should Know About Women in the Military.* Emeryville, CA: Seal Press.

Thomas, P.J., and Thomas, M.D. (1992). *Impact of Pregnant Women and Single Parents Upon Navy Personnel Systems.* San Diego, CA: Navy Personnel Research and Development Center, Women and Multicultural Research Office [Report TN-92-87]. February.

Titunik, R.F. (2000). The First Wave: Gender Integration and Military Culture. *Armed Forces and Society,* 26, 2, 229–257.

Titunik, R.F. (2008). The Myth of the Macho Military. *Polity,* 40, 2, 137–163.

Twitchell, R.E. (2008). The 95th Military Police Battalion Deployment to Iraq – Operation Iraqi Freedom II. In M.M. Putko and D.V. Johnson III (Eds.), *Women in Combat Compendium.* Carlisle Barracks, PA: U.S. Army War College. January.

U.S. Army. (2002). *Women in the Army: An Annotated Bibliography.* U.S. Army Research Institute for the Behavioral and Social Sciences. Special Report 48. May.

U.S. Department of Veterans Affairs. (2015). *Veteran Economic Opportunity Report.* www.benefits-va.gov/benefits/docs. Retrieved December 6, 2016.

Van Crevald, M. (2000). The Great Illusion: Women in the Military. *Millennium – Journal of International Studies,* 29, 2, 429–442.

Van Crevald, M. (2002). *Men, Women and War: Do Women Belong in the Front Line?* New York, NY: Cassell Publishing, a division of Barnes and Noble.

Van Crevald, M. (2016). *Why the Rest Keeps Beating the West.* Seattle, WA: CreateSpace Independent Publishing.

Wagner DeCrew, J. (1995). The Combat Exclusion and the Role of Women in the Military. *Hypatia,* 10, 1, 56–73.

Walker, J.A., and Borbely, J.M. (2014). *Women Veterans in the Labor Force. Spotlight on Statistics.* U.S. Bureau of Labor Statistics. U.S. Department of Labor. www.bls.gov/spotlight/2014/women-vets/. Retrieved April 8, 2017.

Wechsler Segal, M. (1982). The Argument for Female Combatants. In N. Loring Goldman (Ed.), *Female Soldiers: Combatants or Noncombatants?* Farmington Hills, MI: Greenwood Press.

Wechsler Segal, M.W. (1995). Women's Military Roles Cross-Nationally, Past, Present, and Future. *Gender and Society,* 9, 6, 757–775.

Wilson, B.A. (1995). Women in Combat – Why Not? http://userpages.aug.com/captbarb/combat.html. Retrieved March 27, 2017.

Women's Bureau. (n.d.). Veterans Profile. Issue Brief. U.S. Department of Labor. www.dol.gov/wb/resources/women_veterans_profile.pdf. Retrieved March 2, 2017.

4 Women as Sex Objects

In the theory of attrition, Harris (2009) postulates multiple reasons for white women's premature exodus from the military. One such reason includes being cast as sexual fiends whose sole role is to serve as appendages, all for the purpose of derailing the battle-ready objectives of men. Black women, who have to straddle the dual minefields of gender and race, have been leered at and vilified for their curvaceous anatomy, not their intellect (Nalty 1986, Harris and Lewis, forthcoming). Moore (1991) counsels that the military has taken liberty with African American women by relegating them to primarily menial tasks, and disproportionately to support and administrative positions. Accordingly, these occupations not only keep black women in their perceived place as a consequence but owing to the additional burden of race, they endure greater hardships than their white female counterparts. Says Harris (2009), these beliefs only function to diminish the value altogether of women as assets to the military either by preferring to stereotype them as damsels in distress by minimizing their repeated stellar military performance (Harris 2009), or that women have no place in male bastions like the military as it will only bring about the effeminization of the institution (Titunik 2000). Moreover, the military should be devoid of such experiments.

No wonder, as Harris (2009, 2015) contends, the military has become a haven for maladies like sexual harassment and, worse yet, sexual assault. In an effort to inculcate the warrior spirit, demeaning and sexual expletives are routinely hurled at male recruits during basic training for the purpose of male bonding and socialization. Such terms as 'girlie' (Snyder 2003, p.192) or 'You wuss, you baby, you goddam female' (Bird Francke 1997, p.155) are designed to further humiliate. According to Snyder (2003), '[t]here can be few soldiers in the English-speaking world who have not, at sometime or another, been called the bluntest of all Anglo-Saxon synonyms for what any dictionary terms "the female pudenda"' (Holmes in *Acts of War*, p.47, as cited by Snyder 2003, p.192). Taking this matter further, this objectification of women is a problem of acculturation of men throughout the military. Hunter (2007) sees the raunchiness of military language that is sexually laced as one such depiction, where multiple examples abound. The beginning of the academic year at the Army's U.S. Military Academy at West Point is known to all as 'reorganization week' (Hunter 2007, p.17). Yet, frequently, the period has been dubbed 'reorgy week' (Hunter 2007, p.17). In the dining hall, after the dessert has been sliced ready to be eaten, the custom goes that the dessert corporal announces that 'Sir, the dessert has been raped and I did it!' (Hunter 2007, p.17; Janda 2002, p.88). Similarly, cadence calls are permeated with sex and violence. Again, as Hunter (2007) continues, these rituals are not about sex per se but a call to bring about violence, hurt and degradation to one's target. Terms like 'cunt' and 'faggot' are par for the course, for the message to female cadets at West Point is that you are not normalized as other women like mothers, wives and girlfriends (Hunter 2007, p.20). As women in the military, Hunter says that you are to be objectified and must therefore function as sexual objects. Rape is the work and form of objectification and the ultimate toll of dishonor. The implicit understanding is that because men are warriors, women serve at their pleasure as recreation (Seifert 1994), essentially denigrating the female as a gender and person, and this becomes the deliberate pretext for instilling the warrior ethos in military men at her expense.

Chodrow (1971) alleges that such behaviors are the norm even for boys, who must prove at an early age that they are ready to delve into all things that are identified as masculine while renouncing any participation in activities that are identified as feminine or effeminate in nature. Chodrow even calls upon the Freudian theory of the Oedipus complex and the need for boys to dis-identify or separate from their mothers for fear of becoming effeminate. Another behavior is to reinforce the notion of patriarchy, which acknowledges that it is women, not men, who are subordinate. Still yet another reason for this pressure at the earliest age for boys is to disavow any perception of weakness in the presence of other boys and men. Chodrow refers to these strategies as hegemonic masculinity, which includes the need to maintain policies like combat exclusion for the posterity of masculinity in the military at least to preserve those occupations that are designated as ground combat. Sex segregation is one manner of such preservation. Another is rebuffing homosexuality. However, now that both policies, meaning those of Don't Ask, Don't Tell and Don't Pursue and of combat exclusion have been repealed, will the level of sexual assault, already at epidemic levels, be exacerbated?

Ironically, many military men, too, have been victims of sexual assault as borne out by lawsuits filed on behalf of primarily women veterans but which include a number of male veterans in *Cioca v. Rumsfeld et al., 2013* (Goldstein 2013), *Marquet and Kendzior v. Gates et al., 2012* (Katz 2012), and *Klay and Hellmer v. Panetta et al., 2013* (Tucker 2012). While the first lawsuit was dismissed under what many view as the convenient pretext that it is inappropriate for the civilian courts to insert themselves into the affairs of the military, Harris (2015) convincingly demonstrates how the civilian courts have customarily done so when deemed appropriate and with at least three women veterans who are the subject of her research as the primary and named litigants in legal precedent-setting actions against the Department of Defense (DoD) for sex discrimination. In these more recent lawsuits, in the first case of *Cioca v. Rumsfeld et al., 2013*, Judge Liam O'Grady still found cause, however, to comment that even as he dismissed the case, he found it to be 'troubling' (Harris 2015, p.96). In *Klay and Hellmer v. Panetta et al., 2013*, the allegations are stark in that the military has been lambasted as having a '[h]igh tolerance for sexual predators in its ranks' (Tucker 2012, Harris 2015, p.96). With the lawsuits also came allegations that the military retaliated against those who dared to report any infraction or incident of sexual assault. More damning, says Nancy Parrish of the organization Protect Our Defenders, who was unapologetic in her excoriations of the military, 'the Pentagon is camouflaging the truth about rape in the military' (Parrish 2012). Strite Murnane (2007) adds that even when any form of sexual misconduct has been proven, there is no level playing field on which these cases are handled for women and men. She goes as far as to point out that military leaders often dismiss such cases while upholding others.

All the more despicable, though, is where senior military female leaders take the side of the accused against the word of the female victim, not to mention going against legal counsel to preserve the career of the accused male. This happened in the case of Lieutenant General Susan Helms, then Vice Commander of the Air Force's Space Command, and the first woman to travel into space on the *Endeavor* space shuttle, who overturned the conviction of a male Air Force captain, despite evidence against him (Whitlock 2013). Senator Claire McCaskill (D-MO), the former attorney general for her state and a member of the Senate Armed Services Committee, was unflinching in her chastisement of the general, saying that '[i]t looks like somebody taking care of one of their guys' (Whitlock 2013, Harris 2015, p.112). The senator continued that '[w]ith her action, Lieutenant General Helms sent a damaging message to survivors of sexual assault,' in that '[t]hey can take the difficult and painful step of reporting the crime, they can endure the agony involved in being subjected to intense questioning often aimed at putting the blame on them, and they can experience a momentary sense of justice in knowing that they were believed when their attacker is convicted and sentenced, only to have that justice ripped away with the stroke of a pen' (Whitlock 2013).

To Hunter (2007), these verdicts come as no surprise. All too often in the military culture the implicit and sometimes explicit message is that because men are trained as warriors, a woman's place is to serve at their pleasure (Seifert 1994). Throughout American culture, women are routinely sexualized in every corner of the media. This sexualized nature of portraying women in the media also conjures up an in kind and disturbing depiction of them as victims, powerless and seemingly out of control

(Stankiewicz and Rosselli 2008). These negative images of women are rampant in American society and this speaks to the general view of how women are perceived by men and all the more so by some women. As a matter of fact, women and girls use these routine portrayals to make evaluations about themselves and their own behaviors (Groesz et al. 2002, Field et al. 1999, Levine et al. 1994), and whether or not their physical attributes and behaviors comport with those that are deemed attractive by society. This objectification theory, as described by Fredrickson and Roberts (1997), moves women to assess themselves only from the perspective of an outsider, typically a male and never from their own point of view. Consequently, women become bound to the constant monitoring of themselves. We see this self-objectification by women as a relentless pursuit in American society which appears in two forms. Trait self-objectification is characterized by an acute measure by someone of what others think about their bodies while state self-objectification is marked by a more transitory condition of one's body. This latter form can come about as a result of stares on the target within a certain moment in time.

In today's society, particularly adolescent women fall prey sometimes to these unrealistic images of beauty, and chiefly when such behaviors are modeled by perceived icons of beauty. Kim Kardashian and Amber Rose come to mind. It appears that their every movement in scanty attire is the preoccupation and subject of consistent commentary in the media. Like their perception as deviants, women themselves become the sources for the perpetuation of the very behaviors that treat them as sex objects.

Studies of print, television and the Internet media also found that women are customarily depicted in demeaning, powerless and sexualized ways as objects. In print advertisements, for instance, the majority of men's magazines represented women as victims and sex objects (Stankiewicz and Rosselli 2008). Even women's magazines disproportionately present women as sex objects (Lindner 2004), although in men's magazines women were more likely to appear as decorative accessories at greater rates (Baker 2005). Farrid and Braun (2006) found that even girls' magazines were targeted for men's pleasure. Women appeared no less as either sex objects or victims on television. Levine et al. (1999) found that women's exposure to sexist television advertisements caused them to perceive themselves as heavier in weight and hence more unattractive than women shown on television. However, the degree of discrepancy between the images depicted on television and the women's actual body types varied according to the feminist viewpoint that the women held. The more staunch the level of feminism of the women, the more negatively they viewed the images of women portrayed in contrast with their own image. The researchers also infer that women's dissatisfaction was heightened when they viewed sexist images of other women owing to both depression and low self-esteem, and that such conditions would be exacerbated as a result.

More recent work on the effects of exposure to sexually explicit material via the Internet has shown an increase in the degree to which women are perceived by adolescent male viewers as sex objects (Peter and Valkenburg 2007). Likewise, the attitudes and mental reasoning of male adolescents are similarly impacted (Peter and Valkenburg 2009). What is surprising, though, is that women may hold these same beliefs about women (Peter and Valkenburg 2007). Also, increased exposure to such images reinforced these beliefs. However, only male adolescents were more likely to indulge in increased exposure to such materials. In a more up-to-date study, while there were no differences between the likelihood of exposure to sexually explicit material on the Internet between male and female adolescents who would in turn perceive the women as sex objects, as revealed in previous studies, exposure to this material only led the male adolescents to crave increased exposure to it (Peter and Valkenburg 2009).

Using information from a major Canadian newspaper for personal advertisements by women seeking male partners and men seeking female partners, Davis (1990) found that, consistent with the traditional stereotypes held about each gender, the women and men emphasized those very attributes that are desirous in a mate. For example, far more women than men expressed the importance of attributes around financial status, professional standing, intelligence, employment, commitment and emotions, whereas men were far more likely than women to prioritise attributes surrounding attractiveness, physique, having a photograph of a prospective partner which speaks to the significance of physical traits and sex. In keeping with findings by Farrell (1986, in Davis 1990), these results are not surprising given the manner in which each gender is depicted in the media. Women, more than men, will seek out financial security, personal attributes like personality (Deaux and Hanna 1984) and commitment to a long-term relationship (Basow 1986). More men, on the other hand, sought the conventional homebound wife as the ideal mate (Basow 1986). Farrell (1986) and Davis (1990) concluded that women are illustrated in the media as sex objects while men are illustrated as success objects. In an earlier study which may partly be a reflection of the times yet the findings still resonate in contemporary society as they did when the study was conducted, as a way of attracting prospective partners, female respondents simulated their intellectual inferiority (Braito 1981), while in the more current study by Davis (1990), male respondents were more likely than not to seek out women who were intellectually inept.

A study by Furia and Bielby (2009) is particularly relevant to the military but more importantly, given the period captured, how women were represented in film, in this case, by Hollywood, as exemplifying its ideals of military life. The researchers analyzed 42 films about the military from World War I through the more recent campaigns of Operations Enduring and Iraqi Freedom. Not surprisingly, how women were depicted in military films was a condition of the time period reflected in the films. Of the films sampled, 7 percent of them did not contain female characters, and while the remaining films included women, at 93 percent, 19 percent of them included no women with speaking roles. However, 25 percent of the 39 films in which women had speaking roles were of limited substance and 16 percent of the 39 included women with several speaking parts, although most of the women in uniform were nurses. What was interesting is that of those movies that were produced during the Vietnam era (1960–79) – which marked a time when the U.S. was rocked by protests over the country's involvement in Vietnam, civil rights, along with the women's movement that challenged archaic notions of race, gender and feminism, a period of unrest and social upheaval – many of the films, with three in particular, *The Dirty Dozen* (1967), *Green Berets* (1978) and *Force 10* (1978), objectified women as either prostitutes or sex objects, although in the latter two, the women functioned as double agents or spies. More poignant was that these portrayals also appeared to serve as a backlash against the movements of the times which included those of women and the American woman's struggle for agency despite their unyielding commitment to building an American society.

To no surprise, all of the films were directed by men (Furia and Bielby (2009). The researchers' analysis is significant in the study's novel representation of genre that only depicted women in film but specifically the roles that women played in military films throughout a 70-year period of military campaigns, both large and small, and the degree to which women's roles in the larger American society were epitomized in film. The researchers say that the art form, film, is no unfiltered expression of life, for at the time that they were produced, they were more of a personification of culture and the mutual experiences within that culture. Although romanticized, film is an expression of commonly held beliefs in life. Film, therefore, becomes a medium through which symbols can become reinforced and be legitimized. Military films then merely strengthen and validate the organization as one of hegemonic masculinity. Still, even during periods of social change, women's roles in military film were restrained, if they were included at all, to proselytize traditional stereotypes. Women experience an 'inclusive exclusion' in that, though they are part of the military, they are seen as the military wishes them to be revealed within the hegemonic masculine context that is in turn authenticated through film (Furia and Bielby 2009, p.222).

Furia and Bielby (2009) conclude that, unlike war films, military films are indecisive about the accurate portrayal of women in the military. This ambivalence 'mirrors a culture that has yet to figure out how a woman can be a soldier without being similarly obliterated' (Linville 2000, p.109). So, the military woman is featured in one of two ways: first, as one that emphasizes her as effeminate yet disparages her stellar performance in the military; or second, to be successful, characterizes her with a masculine hue thus denigrating her feminine aspects as a woman. Neither portrayal does justice to the military woman on film, for as McCracken (2003) notes, to point her out as a woman warrior would prove incongruous with staunchly held stereotypes of what it is to be a woman (Furia and Bielby 2009). Equally so, society is ill-prepared or perhaps more appropriate, unwilling, to see women as warriors because 'women making war shatters quintessential categories of gender and family' (Hanson 2002, p.47). What is striking, though, is that Mrs. Anna Flynn Monkiewicz, the oldest female veteran to be the subject of Harris's (2015) research as a living legend, even as she twice broke barriers for the U.S. military as one of the first women cohorts in the Women Airforce Service Pilots (WASPs) and as a pilot, still a traditionally male-dominated profession, when asked about the combat exclusion policy, was adamant about the limits of women's roles in combat, in that a woman's place is in the home, having children and raising a family, not committing such atrocities as killing others, as she put it. In essence, women do not belong in combat. Yet, even Mrs. Monkiewicz recognizes that she is of a different generation and concedes that young women today would view such treatment, that is being barred from participation in combat, as abhorrent and unfair. So, even as she disagrees, Mrs. Monkiewicz believes that the contemporary military woman, like men, should be equitably treated in terms of the careers that they choose to pursue and, as such, women should not be subjected to a combat exclusion policy.

Yet, admittedly, it is these very ingrained stereotypes about women in general, and specifically those about women in the military, that no doubt have been advanced and reinforced by the likes of the combat exclusion policy, even in its theoretical repeal. For military women, engaging in an endeavor, like men, was simply a reflection of their desire to demonstrate their patriotism. Nevertheless, the backlash against them in the form of sexual assault has reached such epidemic proportions in the military that it will take strong leadership on the military's part to ensure that only through continuous training and intentional acculturation can they root out and dispel these deeply ingrained mindsets to force change over time about the perception of military women.

Bibliography

Baker, C.N. (2005). Images of Women's Sexuality in Advertisements: A Content Analysis Black- and White-Oriented Women's and Men's Magazines. *Sex Roles*, 52, 13–27.

Basow, S. (1986). *Gender Stereotypes: Traditions and Alternatives*. Pacific Grove, CA: Brooks/Cole Publishing Co.

Bird Francke, L. (1997). *Ground Zero: The Gender Wars in the Military*. New York, NY: Simon and Schuster.

Braito, R. (1981). The Inferiority Game: Perceptions and Behavior. *Sex Roles*, 7, 65–72.

Chodrow, N. (1971). Being and Doing: A Cross-Cultural Examination of the Socialization of Males and Females. In V. Gornick and B.K. Moran (Eds.), *Sexist Society: Studies in Power and Powerlessness* (p.173–186). New York, NY: Basic Books.

Cioca v. Rumsfeld et al., 2013.

Davis, S. (1990). Men as Success Objects and Women as Sex Objects: A Study of Personal Advertisements. *Sex Roles*, 23, 43–50.

Deaux, K., and Hanna, R. (1984). Courtship in the Personals Column: The Influence of Gender and Sexual Orientation. *Sex Roles*, 11, 363–375.

Farrell, W. (1986). *Why Men Are the Way They Are*. New York, NY: Berkley Books.

Farrid, P., and Braun, V. (2006). Most of Us Guys Are Raring to Go Anytime, Anyplace, Anywhere: Male and Female Sexuality in *Cleo* and *Cosmo*. *Sex Roles*, 55, 295–310.

Field, A.E., Cheung, L., Wolf, A.M., Herzog, D.B., Gortmaker, S.L., and Colditz, G.A. (1999). Exposure to Mass Media and Weight Concerns Among Girls. *Pediatrics*, 103, 54–60.

Fredrickson, B.L., and Roberts, T. (1997). Objectification Theory: Toward Understanding Women's Lived Experiences and Mental Health Risks. *Psychology of Women Quarterly*, 21, 173–206.

Furia, S.R., and Bielby, D.D. (2009). Bombshells on Film: Women, Military Films, and Hegemonic Gender Ideologies. *Popular Communication*, 7, 4, 208–224.

Goldstein, N. (2013). The Military Can't Handle the Truth. *The American Prospect*. May 10. http://prospect.org/article/military-cant-handle-truth. Retrieved February 18, 2017.

Groesz, L.M., Levine, M.P., and Murnen, S.K. (2002). The Effect of Experimental Presentation of Thin Media Images on Body Satisfaction: A Meta-Analytic Review. *International Journal of Eating Disorders*, 31, 1–16.

Hanson, C. (2002). Women Warriors: How the Press Has Helped – and Hurt – in the Battle for Equality (Women in the U.S. Military). *Columbia Journalism Review*, 41, 1, 46–49.

Harris, G.L.A. (2009). The Multifaceted Nature of White Female Attrition in the Military. *Journal of Public Management and Social Policy*, 15, 1, 71–93.

Harris, G.L.A. (2015). *Living Legends and Full Agency: Implications of Repealing the Combat Exclusion Policy*. New York, NY: Taylor & Francis Group, a division of CRC Press.

Harris, G.L.A., and Lewis, E.L. (n.d., forthcoming). *Blacks in the Military and Beyond*. Lanham, MD: Rowman & Littlefield.

Hunter, M. (2007). *Honor Betrayed. Sexual Abuse in America's Military*. Fort Lee, NJ: Barricade Books.

Janda, L. (2002). *Stronger Than Custom: West Point and the Admission of Women*. Westport, CT: Praeger Publishers.

Katz, E. (2012). Reported Sexual Assaults at Military Academies Continue to Rise. *Government Executive*. December 27. www.govexec.com/defense/2012/12/reported-sexual-assaults-military-academies-continue-rise/60361/. Retrieved February 18, 2017.

Klay and Hellmer v. Panetta et al., 2013.

Levine, M.P., Smolak, L., and Hayden, H. (1994). The Relations of Sociological Factors to Eating Attitudes and Behaviors Among Middle School Girls. *Journal of Early Adolescents*, 14, 471–490.

Levine, M.P., Piran, N.S., and Stoddard, C. (1999). Mission More Probable: Media Literacy, Activism, and Advocacy as Primary Prevention. In N. Piran, M.P. Levine and C. Steiner-Addir (Eds.), *Preventing Eating Disorders for Handbook of Interventions and Special Challenges* (p.1–25). New York, NY: Taylor & Francis Publishers.

Lindner, K. (2004). Images of Women in General Interest and Fashion Magazine Advertisements from 1955 to 2002. *Sex Roles*, 51, 409–421.

Linville, S.E. (2000). The Mother of All Battles: Courage Under Fire and the Gender-Integrated Military. *Cinema Journal*, 39, 2, 100–120.

Marquet and Kendzior v. Gates et al., 2012.

McCracken, P. (2003). The Amenorrhea of War. *Signs*, 28, 2, 625–644.

Moore, B.L. (1991). African American Women in the Military. *Armed Forces and Society*, 17, 3, 363–384.

Nalty, B.C. (1986). *Strength for the Fight: A History of Black Americans in the Military*. New York: Free Press.

Parrish, K. (2012). DoD Opens More Jobs, Assignments to Military Women. *American Forces Press Service*. February 9. U.S. Department of Defense. www.defense.gov/news/newsarticle.aspx?id=67130. Retrieved February 18, 2017.

Peter, J., and Valkenburg, P.M. (2007). Adolescents' Exposure to a Sexualized Media Environment and Their Notions of Women as Sex Objects. *Sex Roles*, 56, 381–385.

Peter, J., and Valkenburg, P.M. (2009). Adolescents' Exposure to Sexually Explicit Internet Material and Notions of Women as Sex Objects: Assessing Causality and Underlying Processes. *Journal of Communication*, 59, 3, 407–433.

Seifert, R. (1994). War and Rape: A Preliminary Analysis. In *Mass Rape: The War Against Women in Bosnia-Herzegovina*. Lincoln, NE: University of Nebraska Press.

Snyder, R.C. (2003). The Citizen-Soldier Tradition and Gender Integration of the U.S. Military. *Armed Forces and Society*, 29, 2, 185–204.

Stankiewicz, J.M., and Rosselli, F. (2008). Women as Sex Objects and Victims in Print Advertisements. *Sex Roles*, 58, 579–589.

Strite Murnane, L. (2007). Legal Impediments to Service: Women in the Military and the Rule of Law. *Duke Journal of Gender Law and Policy*, 14, 1061–1096.

Titunik, R.F. (2000). The First Wave: Gender Integration and Military Culture. *Armed Forces and Society*, 26, 2, 229–257.

Tucker, E. (2012). 8 Women File Lawsuit, Accuse Military of Having 'High Tolerance for Sexual Predators in Their Ranks.' *Huffington Post*. March 6. www.huffingtonpost.com/2012/03/06/military-rape-lawsuit_n_1324899.html. Retrieved February 18, 2017.

Whitlock, C. (2013). General's Promotion Blocked Over Her Dismissal of Sexual-Assault Verdict. *Washington Post*. May 6. http://articles.washingtonpost.com/2013-05-06/world/39060954_1_sexual-assault-jury-commander. Retrieved May 12, 2017.

5   Women as Marginalized

The multiple roles that women play in society, or are relegated to playing in society, are the very roles that reinforce their subordinate status and, through systematic coercion, all function to keep them marginalized as a group. This notwithstanding the further stratification of women as a group by race, for example, which in turn subordinates them even further to the margins of society and determines their pecking order and in-kind treatment. Black women come to mind as being the very last in the food chain or are at least so perceived and reinforced by other groups. While the now infamous adage of the angry black woman has rightly or wrongly come to define how she is personified in society, this portrayal may in some very real way, jest aside, be an accurate portrayal, given the constant cry for recognition for what those groups who are perceived to come before her, including other women, take for granted.

Sojourner Truth's call to be recognized in her now famous speech 'Ain't I a woman?' still epitomizes what it means to be a black woman in American society. Yet, Sojourner Truth instinctively knew that since no one, including her black male partner, who himself at the time was at the margins of society, would come to her aid, it was up to her and her alone in a symbolic cry for all black women who are subordinated by the multiple marginalities of race, gender and class as a slave, to push for equal treatment nonetheless. For after all, is she not a woman like any other woman, including white women? Malcolm X once said that '[t]he most disrespected person in America is the Black woman, the most unprotected person in America is the Black woman. The most neglected person in America is the Black woman' (excerpt from a speech by Malcolm X, 'On Protecting the Black Woman,' May 22, 1962). Little known, though, is that Truth, a staunch abolitionist and feminist by modern standards, had the audacity to legally challenge a white man in court for illegally selling and transferring one of her children, a son, into slavery in the deep South (Biography.com). By then New York had become one of the first states in the country to abolish the institution of slavery but not its practice. Against all odds, Truth won the case and was reunited with her son soon afterwards, becoming the first black woman ever recorded in America to win a legal case against a white man. Lightning struck twice when Truth won a second lawsuit, accusing the miscreants of slander that she was implicated in the murder of a close associate. Sojourner Truth, given the times, demonstrated that indomitable spirit alone made her a force to be reckoned with.

It is hence ironic, yet a tribute to an icon like Sojourner Truth and the struggles of black women, that white feminists should now see fit to couch their own survival and struggle and that of women as a group through the lens of a former slave and black woman, and to use the work of one of her descendants, Kimberle Crenshaw, who coined the term intersectionality to draw attention to black women's collective experiences (Crenshaw 1989, 1991). It is this intersectionality that has largely come to define the modern feminist movement.

Despite their ourstories as leaders in ancient and now contemporary societies, in many ways, women continue to lose their footing in modern-day America. This inequity permeates society and has been the subject of a wealth of research. For instance, Goldin's (2014) and England's (2005) analyses of women's status in the labor markets show them as consistently being penalized as a consequence of both gender and status – in this case, motherhood. Ridgeway and Correll (2004) describe motherhood as a status characteristic that although generally prized by society, women are routinely punished for in organizational life. A similarly situated man and father, both status characteristics, is not similarly treated. In fact, because a man is perceived as the breadwinner and as a father or the protector of his family, he derives benefits from these two designations and thus enjoys a higher status in society as a result (Deutsch and Saxton 1998), and is additionally rewarded in the way of higher earnings. Single women do enjoy a modicum of perception that they are competent (Fiske et al. 2002) and are more likely not to have children (Goldin 1995). However, once they become mothers, a low status characteristic, they are penalized (Ridgeway and Correll 2004).

A study conducted by Meulders et al. (2010) actually shows that women are making great strides in closing the gap in those occupations under the broad category of the sciences, technology, engineering and mathematics. Yet, despite this progress, it is the segregation across certain economic sectors and along gender lines as well as segregation within the disciplines and vertically that stymie any across-the-board progress for women. According to Kanter (1977), it is the failure to achieve a critical mass, which she determines should be at least 15 percent, that prevents women from being accepted into certain organizations. Any number below 15 percent would increase the likelihood that women are perceived as tokens. Reskin et al. (1999) support this finding that it is the gender and race composition of an organization that dictates how groups are treated. However, Yoder (1991) sees it differently and, like Blalock (1967), believes that it is the status not the number in terms of representation that is attributed to groups which governs how the respective groups are treated by the majority (white men) within organizations. Others like Etzkowitz et al. (2000) agree that it is not the critical mass of the groups that matters but the perceived status of the groups that shape their treatment (in Harris 2009a). Nkomo (1992) and Zimmer (1988) see sexism as one way of reinforcing these group distinctions.

As Harris (2012) asserts, women are so treated and relegated to insignificant jobs in predominantly white male institutions because of the multiple lines of marginality along which they are judged and assigned. These lines of demarcation include being perceived as tokens and employing these tools by organizations to ultimately function as a strategy for containment of this group. Given women's otherness (p.6), the power structures must be maintained in organizations to encourage the diminution of any power that they may hope to amass as a group (Harris 2012). For example, where minority women are selected to manage the organization's diversity program, carrying out these functions by an organization is taken as a matter of symbolism in that organizations are doing something admirable for women and minorities. Yet this tactic serves only as a tool to silence critics, especially for public organizations where the overriding goal is for the benefit of the public good and thereby representative bureaucracy. To do otherwise would invite public outcry. These jobs are perceived, though, as women's and minorities' jobs and thus within the purview of these groups alone for throwing limited resources at these diversity programs is by design to fail by starving the programs. Yet, if these programs fail, critics cannot say that resources were never provided, even if those resources were so scantily allocated that it inherently triggers a lack of commitment by the organization's leadership for the success of diversity programs. This move in turn absolves the organization's leadership, that is primarily white male, should the diversity programs fail. In the end, according to Harris (2012), all such ploys by the organization's leadership serve as calculated ways to reinforce women's marginality, including the status of minority groups.

For women, the situation in the U.S. military is particularly onerous. Here, the combat exclusion policy was originally established to control the status of women by keeping them in check and consequently marginalized. As Harris (2015) also contends, women face a double-edged sword in that, even as they are deliberately being marginalized as a group by the military, they are still being held accountable for circumstances owing to essentially an unjust policy over which the women have neither control nor say. Silva (2008) highlights the extent to which the most junior women in the military as cadets encounter as citizen-soldiers the no-win situation of being taken seriously as a military person while simultaneously negotiating to maintain or perhaps hold fast to society's notion of their femininity in the process. In the study, the women in the Reserve Officers Training Corps (ROTC), upon graduation, like the male cadets, were commissioned as officers to serve for four years in one of the branches of the U.S. military. Despite their youth, as Silva (2008) notes, the primarily homogeneous group of white middle-class women was using the ROTC as a medium to prove their strength as women and to dispel traditional notions of femininity. Yet, while not conscious of these contradictions, the interviews revealed the straddling of the fence where the female cadets strove to be taken seriously as cadets based on their performance as individuals but struggled in the process to ensure that they were still being perceived as women. However, the male cadets were oblivious and had no such need to engage in these mind-playing contradictions for, as Silva (2008) points out, 'they never distinguished between manhood and personhood, either in the university setting or in the military' (p.45). The women, however, even if unaware, employed an endless back-and-forth maneuver in gender neutrality as military cadets, and as manifested by an ever-present mindfulness of themselves as women and persons. Male cadets held no such need to constantly negotiate their identity as societal and military organizational standards made it unnecessary to engage in mind games (Silva 2008).

As Bird Francke (1997), Harris (2015), Snyder (2003) and Harris (2009b) have made clear, enlisted male recruits are subjected to an onslaught of denigrating labels about women, all designed for male bonding and exuding the warrior spirit but at the expense of female recruits with whom they are called to serve once they graduate from basic training. Harris (2009b) then questions, how can an organization inculcate such hostility against and towards women as part of the male socialization process in the military where women are perceived as inferior to men and not anticipate the backlash in the form of sexual assault and other sex-related offenses that are perpetrated against female peers? Harris (2009b, 2015) continues that such behaviors should then come as no surprise, 'given the open level of animus toward them [women] which has permeated the American culture in such slights as "You run like a girl" (Harris 2015, p.98).

Certain demands, especially on women, are typical of greedy institutions like the military and the family (Harris 2009a, Wechsler Segal 1986, Coser 1974, Coser and Laub Coser 1974). Harris (2009) asserts that women's marginalization in society and as reinforced in organizations leads women, like the young female cadets identified above, to also straddle the fence, this time between their professional lives and that of their respective families, in an attempt to appease both while ensuring that they are not neglecting their own needs in the process. Harris (2009a) provides contrasts, yet similarities, in the multiple strategies that women as commissioned officers in the military and academic women must contrive to succeed in serving their organizations, their families and themselves. While their expected stereotypical descriptive roles surround the family, in choosing to pursue a profession outside traditional spheres of expected behaviors, they become outliers. Women are then punished for both since they are only expected to pursue one endeavor, the traditional path of the family. Gunter and

Stambach (2003) see this life as of one of a balancing act, for in academia, for instance, it is 'a truth universally acknowledged that a woman might produce books or babies but not both, just as she might organize her life around marriage or a career, but not both' (Ostriker 1998, p.3). Women who pursue professional lives, and especially in predominantly male organizations like academe and the military, pay a steep price as they concurrently strive to maintain a family (Finkel and Olswang 1996), for these institutions were established for men and by men, not women. Where childbearing and the family are concerned, these functions are not within the purview of men. As such, appendages like childbearing and the family that are believed to be the sole province of women become invisible only to those who are not affected by them (McElrath 1992). These are notably men.

Berdahl (2007) and others like Maass et al. (2003) have unearthed some illuminating research about the marginalization of women, chiefly successful and/or uppity and masculine women, who are perceived to have crossed the line; in the case of women who are believed to possess masculine personalities, the punishment by men has been empirically proven to be more severe. Berdahl (2007) distinguishes between sexual harassment in that the target is harassed because they are purported to evoke certain sexual responses, while gender harassment, on the other hand, encompasses a broader swath of characteristics that are considered to be either male or female. For example, the characteristics most likely found to be attributable to men are independence, assertiveness and dominance, whereas those found to be attributable to women are warmth, deference and modesty (Fiske and Stevens 1993, Prentice and Carranza 2002). Berdahl (2007) postulates that since the aforementioned is the case in that more men sexually harass women given biology, status and power, then women who satisfy these ideals of femininity should be sexually harassed the most. In the case of gender harassment, however, those who are harassed the most are women who violate prescriptive modes of behavior (Fiske and Stevens 1993, Maass et al. 2003). Berdahl (2007) cites *Sanchez v. City of Miami Beach, 1989* where a female police officer, who was also a bodybuilder, was exposed to sexually derogatory noises and the like, and discovered vibrators, an apparatus for urinals, a sanitary napkin and a soiled condom in her mailbox. Likewise, in *Price Waterhouse v. Hopkins, 1989*, the litigant sued her employer for sex discrimination when she was denied partnership in the firm despite her stellar performance because she did not fit the prescribed mold of femininity that the partners of the firm believed a female employee should represent. She was subjected to such statements as she needed 'to walk more femininely, wear make-up, have her hair styled and wear jewelry' (Berdahl 2007, p.426).

Many believe that the *Price Waterhouse v. Hopkins, 1989* lawsuit reflected the classic example of sex discrimination based on traditional gender prescriptions of what it allegedly means to be a woman. Maass et al. (2003) and Dall'Ara and Maass (1999) proved that this was indeed the case. In two experiments, the researchers employed a computer through which men communicated electronically with a female partner. Some 50 percent of the men communicated with a woman who stated that she was studying economics in order to pursue a career as a bank manager, was a member of the union and was a women's rights advocate. The remainder of the sample of men corresponded with a woman who stated that, although her original intent was to pursue law, doing so would interfere with the responsibilities to her family and so she had opted to pursue a career as an elementary school teacher instead, which she found to be more appropriate. The study revealed that the woman who stated that she planned to pursue a career in banking received more sexually explicit pornography than the woman who was planning to pursue a profession that was foremost in consideration of her family. What Maass et al. (2003) and Dall'Ara and Maass (1999) discovered was that men who espoused sexist views not only possessed the propensity to gender harass women but to sexually manipulate women as well. Consequently, while such behaviors may have sexual desires at the root, the overall goal is to punish the target by putting her in her perceived place, and specifically so when she was viewed as violating her place. Minkowitz (1994) went even further. A woman who managed to evade attention by passing as a man was raped by two male friends as she was not a man, but a woman who dared to and successfully passed as one. In essence, she was severely punished because she crossed the line.

The Berdahl (2007) study showed that women who were employed in jobs in male-dominated plant environments were more likely to be sexually harassed than either men or women employed in female-dominated customer service centers. Yet, while the study proved that women are punished through sexual harassment when they assume male-dominated jobs in male-dominated environments, exhibiting so-called masculine personalities did not protect them either. Even more nuanced is that Berdahl's (2007) research uncovered that it is the women perceived as having masculine personalities who were sexually harassed and at greater rates than women who were perceived to have feminine personalities. Berdahl (2007) classified the group of women who were more likely to be sexually harassed in male-dominated organizations as 'uppity' (p.434). The researcher concluded that either way, women would be in an unenviable position of being vulnerable to sexual harassment and thus punishment. Worse yet, successful women and/or those who ostensibly assumed male characteristics would attract the greatest wrath. Therefore, women face a double bind, for regardless of what they do, 'they are dismissed and disrespected if feminine but scorned and disliked if masculine' (Berdahl 2007, p.435). Berdahl postulates that these situations place women in an untenable position. For this reason, it is then incumbent upon organizations to develop structures and policies that reduce the likelihood of these negative consequences for women. More importantly, like Schulz (1998), organizations should not be preoccupied with outlawing sexual harassment per se but establish policies that foster respectful workplaces, regardless of gender.

Billing's (2011) work on the use of male norms in defining women's roles in management confirms the extent to which these norms become normalized in delineating how women are expected to behave. Yet, when they do, to survive, women simply serve as another conduit to reinforce the stereotypes in the division of labor and, by doing so, they become further marginalized because, as Billing writes, these masculine and feminine expected modes of behavior are social constructions. Only when activated are these behaviors reproduced and normalized in the process. What is thought provoking, however, is that when men pursue those occupations that are classified as women's jobs, they benefit from bringing masculinity to these jobs (Simpson 2004), while women do not derive any benefits by bringing femininity even to those jobs that are considered to be women's work. Harris (2012) validates this finding whereby women and minorities are assigned to manage diversity programs, which in turn reinforces their marginalization and operates as yet another medium for multiple avenues of marginalization. However, Cheng (1996) disputes some of these findings, in that in bringing masculinity to management positions, for instance, women who do so are considered most successful whereas the converse is true for women who bring femininity to these same positions.

Like the Berdahl (2007) study, Gherardi (1995) concurs that women do experience a double bind and are forced to walk a tightrope to balance any perception of either to the detriment of the other. Hence, in managerial positions, women must be seen as competent (masculine) but not so masculine that being so takes away from their recognition as women (feminine). Say Eagly et al. (1992), either way, 'women pay a price in terms of relative negative evaluation if they intrude on traditional male domains by adopting male stereotypic leadership styles or occupying male dominated leadership positions' (p.18). This is not the case when women pursue feminine occupations. Both women and men contribute to these falsehoods or stereotypes (Butler 2004), and these stereotypes are more likely to exist in traditional organizations. Billing (2011) also found that this may be the case in information technology firms, although more recent data still point to an inhospitable environment for women which has resulted in an exodus and a high attrition of women (Orser et al. 2012, Allen et al. 2006, Kosoff 2016, Lien 2015, Vagianos 2017). A report exposes the marginalization of especially engineering professors at the Massachusetts Institute of Technology (MIT), ironically not in terms of salaries that are found to be on par with male professors in the discipline but a dearth in both the pool and the lack of tenured engineering professionals (Sciencemag.org 2012). The barriers are alleged to be of such persistent bias and exclusion, where women professors are only called upon to substitute for male colleagues on sabbatical, for example. At the time of the report, of the 94 tenured women professors at MIT, only four were women of color and only one was African American.

What is remarkable is that even in democracies like Israel where conscription into the military is compulsory by law for all in the service of country, women are still marginalized. The Israeli Defense Force (IDF) is described as also infused with a masculine culture (Sasson-Levy 2007), a classification, with that of Enloe (1988), as an institution that is characterized by patriarchy. Mandating military service in the IDF for men and women was legislated in 1949, soon after the creation of the sovereign state in 1947 (Sasson-Levy 2007). Although conscripting women was in keeping with the egalitarian ethos of the country's founding, it soon devolved into one of marginalization for women given the associated stigmas both during and following military service. As Berkovitch (1997) explains, conscripting women into the Israeli military was originally aligned with the notion that not only did women deserve the right to do so but existed as a resource in the need to harness the country's human capital that also embraces a liberal discourse view of citizenship. However, the country has devolved into conservative diatribe over the need to maintain its 'demographic balance' in population with its Palestinian rival or a republic discourse of citizenship (Sasson-Levy 2007, p.485).

Women's marginalization in the Israeli Army began with their exemption from military service for parenthood to create a gendered structure of the military where, though women can be found in all occupations, they are disproportionately found in clerical roles and more so in jobs as secretaries (Sasson-Levy 2007). Consequently, this subordination of roles by way of exemption for motherhood has resulted in a limited form of citizenship, says Izraeli (1997), where women are not equal to men. Enloe (1988), Cohen (1997) and Izraeli (1997) deduce that this action construes hierarchical relationships in accordance with gendered divisions of labor that stifle women's advancement in the military as a consequence. Correspondingly, this structure establishes jobs as masculine and feminine while in the process reinforcing a male hegemonic chauvinistic culture. For example, of the 18 percent of women in the Israeli military, 87 percent serve as secretaries while only 1 percent of male soldiers are so designated (Sinai 2006, Yohalan 2006).

To Sasson-Levy (2007), this system creates a double marginality for women soldiers, yet under the façade of egalitarianism and citizenship. Such a practice perpetuates the traditional male construction of stereotypes of women. Hareven (1989) argues that what women in the Israeli military learn disguised as *we* in practical terms operationally translates as men, where women are simply relegated to ancillary functions. Women learn to measure themselves and their achievements through assistance and not by their own actions. Many of the 15 women who were interviewed post-military as part of Sasson-Levy's (2007) research believed that they did not benefit from military service. If anything, they lamented that they felt degraded and demoralized by the military. One former soldier and secretary said: 'I'm punished twice, once because of the stigma about secretaries, and again in the service itself' (Sasson-Levy 2007, p.489). Regrettably, this last statement reflected the general sentiment of the interviewees that their service in the military was, for the most part, a waste of time. Some believed that the time could have been better spent pursuing a university education, and with something tangible to show upon completion. As Snyder (2003) claims, this is the problem when you construct a system that was meant for men and integrate women as an afterthought and without altering the system even when the chasm has been discovered. This is also the case for the U.S. military.

Pershing (2003) explores why women in one of America's elite military academies, the U.S. Naval Academy, rarely, if ever, report incidents of sexually related violations against the institution by male colleagues. Using data obtained from a previous survey conducted by the U.S. General Accountability Office (GAO), 40 graduates, of whom 14 were women from the U.S. Naval Academy who were subsequently commissioned as officers in the Navy and the Marine Corps, were interviewed in 1994. Of the women surveyed by the GAO, almost 97 percent of them admitted that they were sexually harassed at least once from July 1990 to December 1990, and 48 percent had experienced multiple such violations during the same period. Only 11 percent of the men reported ever having any such recurring experiences. The interviews in the Pershing (2003) study not only uncovered the prevalence of hostility in the form of sexually related offenses suffered by women in the Naval Academy but the preponderant reason(s) for their failure to report the offenses to authorities. One documented comment by a male respondent in the survey was instructive as to the hostile environment and the frequency of occurrence of the abuse of the targets at the Naval Academy:

> Women don't belong here. They enter a world that has been dominated for a long time by men and they expect us all to get along. It doesn't work ... I know a great number of women who came here just to have a 10:1 man/woman ratio so they can have sex as often as they'd like ... The last thing we need is more women officers here.
> (U.S. Naval Academy midshipman, GAO, 1994, p.22, as cited in Pershing 2003, p.12)

The female graduates at the Naval Academy were of the mindset that given their experiences, filing complaints was simply a waste of time (Pershing 2003). As the institution's administration was not only seen as complicit but the midshipman chain of command to which such complaints were filed reduced the likelihood that they would ever be taken seriously. Further, the culture of silence or not reporting on one another made the chances of advancing such complaints all the more futile. In one case, the interviewee mentioned that two individuals in her cohort were witness to a sexual harassment incident yet chose to remain silent. It was speculated that the two witnesses' silence, which was the overwhelming general reason for failure to file complaints, was the belief that nothing would be done to punish the perpetrators. Another pressing reason for the failure to report these violations, it is believed, is that the women did not want to bring unwanted attention to themselves. Military women appear to struggle with this decision most as they could unintentionally invite negative repercussions in the form of being ostracized or retaliation against them for 'outing' one of their own.

Says Pershing (2003), because the Naval Academy as an institution is hierarchical in nature, it signifies how the multiple levels within the system must relate to one another. Moreover, the cultural weight attributed to loyalty and male bonding makes departing from established group norms unsanctioned. For these reasons and more, the women are forced to acquiesce to the prevailing culture as individuals to their own detriment in order to preserve the norms of the group (Harris 2012). In the case of holding fast to the values of greedy institutions like the military, as Westwood and Turner (1996) suggest, the problem lies with the fact that 'women don't have wives' (p.46). More directly, Harris (2009a) observes that the barriers that women experience as they attempt to become mainstream in organizations like the military is a lingering ramification that men feel that they are not only being coerced to accept women into their traditional male spheres but they are also being asked to flout long-held rules to accommodate them. Yet, as Harris (2009a) continues, the rules in these hierarchical organizations were never established with women in mind since they 'were developed by men for men' (p.413), and to bring women into these institutions is 'not as a way of compromising standards but to accommodate the unique needs of the disaffected partners who are women' (p.413).

Harris (2009b) recalls during the initial phase of Operation Iraqi Freedom when Sergeant Leigh Ann Hester was conferred the Silver Star for valor, the only woman to receive this recognition since World War II (Lumpkin 2005). When asked by a reporter how she felt about receiving this medal, to deliberately deflect attention from herself, Sergeant Hester ascribed her achievements not to herself, but to her group instead. At the time in the security police, as was the case for many military women during the dual wars of Operations Enduring and Iraqi Freedom, the blurred lines of demarcation on the ground were such that she functioned very much in the role of a combatant, although then by law under the combat exclusion policy, as a woman she was a noncombatant.

Unfortunately, for Captain Linda Bray, this was not the case. Upon returning home from deployment during Operation Just Cause, she suffered the onslaught of media hype that labeled her the first woman in the U.S. military ever to have led troops into combat (Titunik 2000). However, Captain Bray's status was in question because as a woman, even if the reality in the theater of operations dictated her actions, she could not serve under conditions that were designated as combat where she was in harm's way by directly engaging the enemy. So it was illegal for the Army to have placed her in this position and it was far worse that this closely guarded secret was finally disclosed to the American public. Even worse was that, at least as it was perceived, it was Captain Bray the woman, not her group as a whole, who took credit for this unprecedented feat of doing a man's job and doing so single-handedly given the recognition for outstanding performance. Both represented clear violations of protocol given the norms of this hierarchical organization and communal environment.

Harris (2009b) concludes using Mazur's (1998) novelty effect to advance a theory of attrition as to the rationale for white women's premature departure from the military not only owing to their maltreatment but as a struggle for full agency. Captain Bray's situation is reminiscent of women's endless dilemma in the form of at least a double bind, and in many respects, for women of color, a triple bind. At one end of the spectrum, women as a group are perceived as weak and helpless or as 'damsels in distress' (Harris 2009b, p.72), while at the other end they may be celebrated as champions. Yet, in the end, fundamentally, because women lack full agency, under both circumstances they are equally condemned as victims and marginalized in the process.

Bibliography

Berdahl, J.L. (2007). The Sexual Harassment of Uppity Women. *Journal of Applied Psychology*, 92, 2, 425–437.

Berkovitch, N. (1997). Motherhood as a National Mission: The Construction of Womanhood in the Legal Discourse in Israel. *Women Studies International Forum*, 20, 5–6, 605–619.

Billing, Y.D. (2011). Are Women in Management Victims of the Phantom of the Male Norm? *Gender, Work and Organization*, 18, 3, 298–316.

Biography.com. Sojourner Truth. www.biography.com/people. Retrieved February 22, 2017.

Bird Francke, Linda. (1997). *Ground Zero: The Gender Wars in the Military*. New York, NY: Simon and Schuster.

Blalock, H.M. (1967). *Toward a Theory of Minority Group Relations*. New York, NY: John Wiley.

Butler, J. (2004). *Undoing Gender*. London: Routledge Press.

Cheng, C. (1996). (Ed.). *Masculinities in Organizations*. London: Sage Press.

Cohen, S. (1997). Towards a New Portrait of the (New) Israeli Soldier. *Israeli Affairs*, 3, 3–4, 77–117.

Coser, L.A. (1974). *Greedy Institutions. Patterns of Undivided Commitment*. New York, NY: Free Press.

Coser, L.A., and Laub Coser, R. (1974). The Housewife and Her 'Greedy Family.' In *Greedy Institutions. Patterns of Undivided Commitment*. New York: Free Press.

Crenshaw, K. (1989). Demarginalizing the Intersection of Race and Sex: A Black Feminist Critique of Antidiscrimination Doctrine, Feminist Theory and Antiracist Politics. *The University of Chicago Law Forum*, 139–167.

Crenshaw, K. (1991). Mapping the Margins: Intersectionality, Identity Politics, and Violence Against Women of Color. *Stanford Law Review*, 43, 6, 1241–1299.

Dall'Ara, E., and Maass, A. (1999). Studying Sexual Harassment in the Laboratory: Are Egalitarian Women at Higher Risk? *Sex Roles*, 41, 681–704.

Deutsch, F.M., and Saxton, S.E. (1998). Traditional Ideologies, Nontraditional Lives. *Sex Roles*, 38, 331–362.

Eagly, A.H., Makhijini, M.G., and Klonsky, B.G. (1992). Gender and the Evaluation of Leaders: A Meta-Analysis. *Psychological Bulletin*, 111, 3–22.

England, P. (2005). Gender Inequality in Labor Markets: The Role of Motherhood and Segregation. *Social Politics*, 12, 2, 264–288.

Enloe, C. (1988). *Ethnic Soldiers: State Security in Divided Society*. Athens, GA: University of Georgia Press.

Etzkowitz, H., Kemelgor, C., and Uzzi, B. (2000). *Athena Unbound: The Advancement of Women in Science and Technology*. Cambridge, MA: Cambridge University Press.

Finkel, S.K., and Olswang, S.G. (1996). Child Rearing as a Career Impediment to Women Assistant Professors. *The Review of Higher Education*, 19, 2, 123–139.

Fiske, S.T., and Stevens, L.E. (1993). What's So Special about Sex? Gender Stereotyping and Discrimination. In S. Oskamp and M. Costanza (Eds.), Gender Issues in Contemporary Society. Newbury Park, CA: Sage Press.

Fiske, S.T., Cuddy, A.J.C., Glick, P., and Xu, J. (2002). A Model of (Often Mixed) Stereotype Content: Competence and Warmth Respectively Follow from Perceived Status and Competition. *Journal of Personality and Social Psychology*, 82, 878–902.

Gherardi, S. (1995). *Gender, Symbolism and Organizational Cultures*. London: Sage.

Goldin, C. (1995). *Career and Family: College Women Look to the Past* (Working Paper, No. 5188). Cambridge, MA: National Bureau of Economic Research.

Goldin, C. (2014). A Pollution Theory of Discrimination: Male and Female Differences in Occupations and Earnings. In L.P. Boustan, C. Frydman, and R.A. Margo (Eds.), *Human Capital in History: The American Record* (p.313–348). Chicago, IL: The National Bureau of Economic Research (NBER). University of Chicago Press.

Gunter, R., and Stambach, A. (2003). Balancing Act and as Game: How Women and Men Science Faculty Experience the Promotion Process. *Gender Issues*, 21, 2, 24–42.

Hareven, G. (1989). Chic and Sparkle: On Women's Service in the IDF. *Shdemot*. August.

Harris, G.L.A. (2009a). The Multifaceted Nature of White Female Attrition in the Military. *Journal of Public Management and Social Policy*, 15, 1, 71–93.

Harris, G.L.A. (2009b). Women, the Military and Academe: Navigating the Family Track in an Up or Out System. *Administration and Society*, 41, 4, 391–422.

Harris, G.L.A. (2012). Multiple Marginality: How the Disproportionate Assignment of Women and Minorities to Manage Diversity Programs Reinforces and Multiplies Their Marginality. *Administration and Society*, 20, 10, 1–34.

Harris, G.L.A. (2015). *Living Legends and Full Agency: Implications of Repealing the Combat Exclusion Policy*. New York, NY: Taylor & Francis Group, a division of CRC Press.

Izraeli, D. (1997). Gendering Military Service in the Israeli Defense Forces. *Israel Social Service Research*, 12, 129–166.

Kanter, R.M. (1977). *Men and Women of the Corporation*. New York, NY: Basic Books.

Kosoff, M. (2016). Silicon Valley's Exodus Begins. Hot Air Isn't the Only Thing Escaping the Tech Bubble. *Vanity Fair*. March 6. www.vanityfair.com/news/2016/03/silicon-valleys-exodus-begins. Retrieved May 26, 2017.

Lien, T. (2015). Why Are Women Leaving the Tech Industry in Droves? *Los Angeles Times*. April 22. www.latimes.com/business/la-fi-women-tech-20150222-story.html. Retrieved May 26, 2017.

Lumpkin, John T. (2005). Woman Earns Silver Star for Duty in Iraq. *AOL News*, June 16.

Maass, A., Guarnieri, M., and Grasselli, G. (2003). Sexual Harassment Under Social Identity Threat: The Computer Harassment Paradigm. *Journal of Personality and Social Psychology*, 85, 853–870.

Malcolm X. (1962). Excerpt from a speech on May 22. Who Taught You To Hate the Color of Your Skin? On Protecting the Black Woman. AZ Quotes. www.azquotes.com. Retrieved February 22, 2017.

Mazur, D.H. (1998). Women, Responsibility and the Military. *Notre Dame Law Review*, 74, 1, 1–45.

McElrath, K. (1992). Gender, Career Disruption and Academic Rewards. *Journal of Higher Education*, 63, 3, 269–281.

Meulders, D., Plasman, R., Rigo, A., and O'Dorchai, S. (2010). Horizontal and Vertical Segregation. Meta-Analysis of Gender and Science Research. www.genderandscience.org/genport.ouc.edu/sites/default/files/resource_pool/TR1_Segregation.pdf. Retrieved January 24, 2017.

Minkowitz, D. (1994). Love Hurts: Brandon Teena Was a Woman Who Lived and Loved as a Man. She Was Killed for Carrying It Off. *The Village Voice*. April 19.

Nkomo, S. (1992). The Emperor Has No Clothes: Rewriting 'Race in Organizations.' *Academy of Management Review*, 17, 487–513.

Orser, B., Riding, A., and Stanley, J. (2012). Perceived Career Challenges and Response Strategies of Woman in the Advanced Technology Sector. *Entrepreneurship and Regional Development*, 24, 1–2, 73–93.

Ostriker, A. (1998). The Maternal Mind. In C. Coiner and D.H. George (Eds.), *The Family Track: Keeping Your Faculties While You Mentor, Nurture, Teach, and Serve*. Champaign, IL: University of Illinois Press.

Pershing, J.L. (2003). Why Women Don't Report Sexual Harassment: A Case of an Elite Military Institution. *Gender Issues*, 21, 4, 3–20.

Prentice, D.A., and Carranza, E. (2002). What Women and Men Should Be, Shouldn't Be, Are Allowed to Be, and Don't Have to Be: The Contents of Prescriptive Gender Stereotypes. *Psychology of Women Quarterly*, 26, 269–281.

Reskin, B.F., McBrier, D.B., and Kmec, J.A. (1999). The Determinants and Consequences of Workplace Sex and Race Composition. *American Review of Sociology*, 25, 335–361.

Ridgeway, C.L., and Correll, S.J. (2004). Motherhood as a Status Characteristic. *Journal of Social Issues*, 60, 4, 683–700.

Sasson-Levy, O. (2007). Contradictory Consequences of Mandatory Conscription. The Case of Women Secretaries in the Israeli Military. *Gender and Society*, 21, 4, 481–507.

Schulz, V. (1998). Reconceptualizing Sexual Harassment. *Yale Law Journal*, 107, 1683–1796.

Sciencemag.org. (2012). Women in Academia. Engineers Marginalized MIT Report Concludes. March 12. http://andrewlawler.com/website/wp-content/uploads/Science-2002-Lawler-Engineers_Marginalized_MIT_Report_Concludes-2192.pdf. Retrieved May 26, 2017.

Silva, J.M. (2008). A New Generation of Women? How Female ROTC Cadets Negotiate the Tension Between Masculine Military Culture and Traditional Femininity. *Social Forces*, 87, 2, 937–960.

Simpson, R. (2004). Masculinity at Work: The Experience of Men in Female Dominated Occupations. *Work, Employment and Society*, 18, 2, 349–368.

Sinai, R. (2006). Deserving But Still Not Promoted. *Ha'aertz*. December 5.

Snyder, R.C. (2003). The Citizen-Soldier Tradition and Gender Integration of the U.S. Military. *Armed Forces and Society*, 29, 2, 185–204.

Titunik, R.F. (2000). The First Wave: Gender Integration and Military Culture. *Armed Forces and Society*, 26, 2, 229–257.

Vagianos, A. (2017). This CEO Hopes Her Story Can Change Silicon Valley's Culture of Sexual Harassment. Why Cheryl Yeoh Is Speaking Out Now. *Huffington Post*. July 7. Retrieved May 26, 2017.

Watkins Allen, M., Armstrong, D.J., Riemenschneider, C.K. and Reid, M.E. (2006). Making Sense of the Barriers Women Face in the Information Technology Work Force: Standpoint Theory, Self-Disclosure, and Causal Maps. *Sex Roles*, 54, 11–12, 831–844.

Wechsler Segal, M. (1986). The Military and the Family as Greedy Institutions. *Armed Forces and Society*, 13, 1, 9–38.

Westwood, J., and Turner, H. (1996). *Marriage and Children as Impediments to Career Progression of Active Duty Career Women Army Officers*. Carlisle, PA: U.S. Army War College.

Yoder, J.D. (1991). Rethinking Tokenism. Looking Beyond Numbers. *Gender & Society*, 5, 2, 178–192.

Yohalan. (2006). The Revolution of the Secretaries in the IDF. *Electronic Newspaper*, #5. March. www.huffingtonpost.com/entry/this-ceo-is-using-her-story-to-change-silicon-valleys-culture-of-sexual-harassment_us_595eb2bbe4b0d5b458e95adc. Retrieved August 7, 2017.

Zimmer, L. (1988). Tokenism and Women in the Workplace: The Limits of Gender Neutral Theory. *Social Problems*, 35, 64–77.

Part III
On Citizenship

The ideal notion of citizenship confers the rights and responsibilities that come with the designation. To be considered whole, or as satisfying the prerequisites as a citizen, four criteria are employed. First is the requirement for loyalty (Kerber 1993). With loyalty comes the implicit understanding that one will in no way subvert the interests of or commit treasonous acts against the state or that would place one's loyalty into question. Second, one has the duty to contribute to the welfare of the state by paying one's share of taxes for its upkeep. Third, when called upon, one must serve on a jury for the purpose of rendering an impartial legal verdict on a fellow citizen or citizens. Fourth, one is duty bound for the sake of the country to answer the call to military service and to risk one's life in defense of one's country.

While American women have increasingly gained ground towards a desired meaning of citizenship by way of amendments to the U.S. Constitution, it is the fourth responsibility, or the obligation for military service, that remains unrealized. Women have and continue to serve with distinction in the U.S. military. However, until the legal weight of the Equal Rights Amendment (ERA) is brought to bear, together with the compulsion that, like men, women must serve in the military given inclusion into the Selective Service System, even in light of the combat exclusion policy's repeal, American women's journey towards full citizenship and in turn full agency will forever be short-circuited.

Part III of this book is three-fold in exploring women's ourstorical agency and status in both theory and practice, and that of a citizen. One, in accordance with the legal definition along with the associated traditions, customs and treatment, who is a veteran? Two, how, in the absence of ratifying the ERA, and despite the symbolic repeal of the combat exclusion policy, and with women's potential inclusion into the Selective Service System still hanging in the balance, why does women's acceptance as full citizens, particularly with regard to the obligation for military service, continue to be questioned? Three, the rationale for the existence of the combat exclusion policy is discussed, along with its 2013 symbolic repeal along with the opening up of formerly closed occupations, positions and critical assignments as called for by the conditions of the repeal, its uncertain future in light of the ideology of the Trump Administration and the reticence of its Secretary of Defense, himself a former Marine.

Bibliography

Kerber, L.K. (1993). 'A Constitutional Right to be Treated Like ... Ladies': Women, Civic Obligation and Military Service. *The University of Chicago Law School Roundtable*, 1, 1, Article 15, 95–128.

6   Agency and Second-Class Status

Harris's (2015) chronicle of 17 pioneering, prominent and/or elite women veterans signals in all cases that at no time did any of the women profiled seek glory or fame. The women overwhelmingly saw military service as one of the most demonstrable ways in which to exemplify love of country and patriotism. While each woman's journey to this decision was unique and in her own right, none considered themselves subordinate in any way to their male peers in the military even as noncombatants serving under the oppressive and exclusionary regime of the combat exclusion policy. Yet, the combat exclusion policy served nevertheless as a glaring reminder that they were indeed unequal as citizens in the eyes of the law, though equality was conveniently feigned when it suited both the military and society. Now that the combat exclusion policy has been repealed, given the hegemonic masculinity of the military that inherently creates and maintains asymmetric systems to benefit one group to the detriment of another, how long will it require for a cultural shift to take place where military women can be fully accepted as functioning viable members in law, in practice, in culture and in American society?

Mazur (1998) suggests that while it is the military's responsibility to make such cultural and systematic changes, it is equally women's responsibility never to cloak themselves from the robes of victims. While Mazur admits that it is the exclusion of women in certain milieus of the military that depicts them as different or as outliers, it is this notion of not being seen or present in certain venues that classifies women as such. Enter the novelty effect, says Mazur (1998), because women are allegedly absent from combat and combat-related jobs in the military even as they have already served and continue to serve in those capacities, if not so designated. Still, Mazur believes that some of the responsibility in order to be seen to renounce the perception of victimhood lies with women. In accordance with agency theory, to achieve partial agency is also to be perceived as equally compromised. But this middle-of-the-road and tenuous status still makes one not entirely responsible for the oppression that they experience. Either way, women are responsible for remaining as victims and are treated in kind as a novelty by the media. The inference here is that it is women, not men, who are responsible for leading men astray, and taking responsibility for men's participation in untoward behaviors. Mazur challenges this belief system, though, as nothing could be further from the truth, for even in a combat exclusion environment, women have always been on the front lines of combat.

Mazur (1998) highlights women's roles in serving as Air Force missileers or missile officers for the purpose of launching nuclear intercontinental ballistic missiles from remote, underground locations across the U.S. Although never acknowledged, the Cold War era witnessed women on the front lines where they were in direct ground combat should the country be confronted with a nuclear attack by the enemy despite the rhetoric emanating from the Pentagon. Colonel Beverly 'Sam' Stipes of the U.S. Army was not only the first woman to be assigned at the tip of the spear of the Nike Hercules Battery Missile Unit but was also the first woman assigned to a Patriot Battle Missile Unit (Harris 2015). Colonel Stipes held the dubious distinction of serving in these underground bunkers at least twice in her military career. Captain Linda Bray, who served during Operation Just Cause, is another such example (Titunik 2000). Hailed by the media as the first woman to lead troops into combat, Captain Bray was subsequently vilified because she had the temerity not only to perform a job that was essentially that of a man and to do so exceedingly well, but to take credit for that performance as well. Further, she did so by failing to share the attention of the media with her all-male subordinate troops whom she led successfully in executing the mission. Mazur (1998) blames the media's recurring novelty effect in never seeing women in these masculine constructed roles. The criticism that Bray encountered forced her demise and eventual premature departure from the military (Titunik 2000), not as the trailblazer that she was purported to be but because she had outdone herself as a woman, and was punished for doing so. That is why, claims Mazur (1998), women in the military find themselves in a no-win situation. The capture of Private First Class (PFC) Jessica Lynch, the blonde haired, blue-eyed Army soldier, who was allegedly rescued during the early phase of Operation Iraqi Freedom, was all the evidence that opponents of women in the military needed to provide the rationale that the military is no place for a woman and especially in combat (Center for Military Readiness (CMR) 2002). They conveniently chose to ignore the ultimate sacrifice of her colleague PFC Lori Piestawa of the same platoon. This prescribed image of the damsel in distress who is worthy of male protection is preferable to the heroine or 'shero' (Harris 2009).

However, in either role, the military woman falls victim because when all is said and done, she is still being deprived of full agency (Mazur 1998). Titunik (2000) quotes from Plato's *Republic* that in the heat of battle, when the women join in the fight, that force is declared indomitable as a result. Harris (2009) furthered Mazur's (1998) agency theory to develop a theory of attrition as to the rationale for white women's untimely exodus from the military. She speculates following two complete diametrically opposed research studies, which showed that, though white women are the most supportive segment of the military's population of women's full integration into the military, and as such, are also proponents of placing women into all occupations throughout the military, including combat, it is both disturbing yet ironic that white women are also the most likely of any demographic group in the military to prematurely separate from the institution (Moskos 2005). Harris (2009) determines that, because of such variables like multiple and frequent deployments together with menacing behaviors such as sexually related offenses and the like, white women perceive the military as a hostile environment for them. While attrition is a natural occurrence in all segments of the military's population over time, white women's attrition is occurring at such unsustainable rates that it outpaces their rates of recruitment and retention. Still, as troubling as their attrition patterns are, white women's premature exodus from the military, declares Harris (2009), is an exercise in the struggle for full agency. It thus behoves the military not to alienate the very group upon which it depends for its female workforce.

However, given ourstory, the expectation to be in the home, or with family and to be protected, at least in the U.S., has always been the perceived jurisdiction of the white female (Buchanan et al. 2008, Collins 2000, Frankenberg 1993). No such luxuries have been afforded to especially the black female, who has long been perceived, and partly as a consequence of the wholesale enslavement of African Americans, and as a workhorse who, as property, was subjected to repeated debasement in the forms of rape and abuse in the way of beatings and the like (Davis 1998). Besides the double jeopardy of race and gender, black women were and continue to be sexualized today through various imposed stereotypes leveled by the white male culture to describe them (Bell 2004, Collins 2000, West 2004). While the white woman is held to the moral high ground whose chastened character kept her suitable for sex for all the right reasons such as for procreation (Collins 2000, Scully and Bart 2003), the black woman was sexualized as a jezebel (Bell 2004, West 2004), where, unlike the white woman, she purportedly had a sexually unquenchable appetite, and was uninhibited in her behavior because she is immoral (Collins 2000, West 2004). For these reasons, the black woman has not only been sexually exploited but modern depictions of her in various settings reinforce her multiple levels of marginalization. Essentially, these low statuses make the black woman, more so than the white woman, more vulnerable to sexual harassment in the workplace, for instance (Buchanan et al. 2008).

Research by Buchanan et al. (2008) supported the hypothesis that, while white women would experience more sexual harassment and gender harassment, black women were subjected to more vulgar behavior and bullying for sex, though white women did experience a significant amount of obscene sexual behavior as well. While in the military enlisted women experienced more of these untoward behaviors overall, women officers experienced less sexual harassment; yet, the patterns of behavior that the various military personnel experienced both as a condition of race and rank, were borne out by the ourstory of both black women and white women. Buchanan et al. (2008) concluded that, while it is expected even as women, black women are expected to work, so being in the military is not perceived to be inappropriate for them, whereas for white women the opposite is true. Likewise, black women showed greater psychological resilience to these types of indecent behaviors, although the researchers noted that the results may be a matter of expectation. However, as gender harassment increased, black women began to experience similar levels of psychological stress as white women. Enlisted women in both groups were particularly vulnerable.

According to Herbert (1998) and Reskin et al. (1999), gender functions as a predictor in the workplace in not only how power is dispensed and allocated but in the associated ideologies, practices and imagery that are created. The military is about war and as such is equated with manhood (Herbert 1998). Thus, power is dispensed and allocated by the white male structure along the lines of gender roles and occupations in the military. The ideologies, practices and imagery underscore the importance of manhood by demeaning women. In many ways, women in the military serve to strengthen masculinity (Bourke 1996). Goffman (1977) writes that these rituals sort of operate as reminders of what men can do and what women cannot do. In this manner, having women in the military is not the norm since men join the military either to reinforce manhood or attain manhood (Herbert 1998). Gender stereotypes are furthered through segregation of the sexes by occupation, among other domains (Andrews 1992, Pearson 1985). Correspondingly, men and women internalize what are defined as desirable behaviors to display and which align with what Stewart et al. (1990) label as congruency theory, by which men behave as stereotypical men (i.e., dominant and assertive) and women exude those behaviors that are believed to be stereotypical of women (i.e., yielding and compassionate) (Bem 1993, Nadler and Nadler 1990). However, when either gender participates in behaviors that are seemingly inappropriate, they are severely criticized (Stewart et al. 1990).

So, when women pursue careers in male-dominated organizations like the military, they are perceived as being inappropriate by going against the grain and that is culturally improper (Herbert 1998). However, even as women pursue these still perceived traditional male professions, they are expected to behave in ways that are deemed to be culturally appropriate for women. During World War II, Oveta Culp Hobby, director of the Women's Army Corps (WAC), felt the need to qualify women's role in the military to the American public (Holm 1992). She explained that women were neither 'Amazons rushing into battle' nor 'butterflies fluttering freely' (Freedom of Press 1942, in Holm 1992). Additionally, to stave off questions about the possible loss of women's femininity because they were attired in men's garb during the war, the Office of Emergency Management announced that:

> There is an unwholesomely large number of girls who refrain from even contemplating enlistment because of male opinion. An educative program needs to be done among the male population to overcome this problem. Men – both civilian and military personnel – should be more specifically informed that it is fitting for girls to be in service. This would call for copy ... which shows that the services increase, rather than detract from, desirable feminine characteristics.
> (In Honey 1984, p.113)

In this advertisement, the Army was certain to couch even the woman in a flight suit with the feminine allure of makeup (Holm 1992). Similarly, the woman was illustrated below, this time as a civilian, in full feminine regalia and adorned in jewelry such as earrings and a prominent ring on her left hand to denote that she is also married. With her, arm in arm, is a male, perhaps to infer by presence and association as her husband. As Harris (2015) surmised, the purpose of the advertisement was twofold. First, to aid in recruitment by appealing to women for the war effort to enlist in jobs that were traditionally performed by men. Second, to appease potential women recruits by allaying their fears that donning men's attire and performing so-called men's work would make them less feminine. Herbert (1998) calls this tactic 'doing gender' (p.14), to control the perception of what each gender does while making them accountable for remaining women and conducting the work of soldiers who are innately men. So, the assumption and, by association, the definition and redefinition of gender are not only as feminine and masculine but structural as well.

Herbert (1998) speculates that placing women into the military puts the institution on a collision course given these assumptions, associations and definitions. By redefining what constitutes feminine within a male context as necessary, the U.S. military has found a way to conveniently reconcile this conflict to incorporate women yet preserve the institution as fundamentally male. By integrating women then but along segregated lines, the military has essentially satisfied this goal. Though experimental, the Army, for example, pursued integrated basic training of the sexes and found virtually no instances of fraternization as a result; however, the Army still abandoned the training by rationalizing that the presence of women during training produced lowered training standards for men even as the Army's own research finding found otherwise (U.S. Army 2002). In this same vein and preceding the Don't Ask, Don't Tell and Don't Pursue policy and its subsequent repeal, the military invoked a like rationale. The institution deliberately barred the enlistment of homosexuals into the military under the guise that such enlistments would provide disparate entitlements to homosexuals not enjoyed by heterosexual men and women

(Herbert 1998). Hence, maintaining the status quo, that is, barring such enlistments, would preserve order and morale. This fallacy, argues Herbert (1998), is that all the while such policies have never prevented the enlistment of homosexuals into the military. These pronouncements were merely a cloak to uphold traditional cultural norms of what defines men and women.

Yet, Navy Vice Admiral Joseph Donnell's characterization of lesbians in the military as 'hardworking, career-oriented, willing to put in long hours on the job, and among the command's top performers' (Gross 1990, p.24) signaled the military's determination to regulate the conception of gender. Admiral Donnell conceded that the command's findings about these alleged lesbians had resulted in a less-than-committed effort by the Navy to investigate so-called untoward behaviors for the purpose of discharging perpetrators from the military (Herbert 1998). One female drill instructor at Parris Island condensed the conundrum for the military, and in effect, that of its perceived lesbian personnel: 'The qualities and traits that we demand and are supposed to be training our recruits are the same traits that make us look homosexual' (Shilts 1993, p.56). Consequently, more women than men were targeted for these witch hunt investigations and were discharged as a result.

Women then face a double bind in that the very qualities that are judged as preferable to succeed in certain occupations such as those in the military are also the very ones for which they may be penalized as lesbians given their pursuit of these occupations (Herbert 1998). Because the military is the epitome of all such male institutions and professions, men, not women, are the preferred gender. Women thus face this balancing act by not being too much of either in order to be perceived as credible. Consider Bevans's (1960) claims some 40 years earlier: 'A woman in business is supposed to be a woman, not one of the boys. On the other hand, you must avoid being so female that you embarrass your co-workers' (p.69). It is disappointing that such sentiments about the roles and stereotypes of women have not changed even in modern times. Women in the military must then construct organizational schemes for their survival given what Herbert (1998) typifies as a 'hostile terrain' (p.22) in which they must work. However, these burdens are not borne by men, who are not unreasonably tasked to negotiate perceived traits over which one has no control but must display nonetheless as a means of survival. One Navy lieutenant's statement reveals the level of frustration experienced by military women: 'One of the hardest parts of being a military woman is just the constant scrutiny and criticism. Act "too masculine" and you're accused of being a dyke; act "too feminine" and you're either accused of sleeping around, or you're not serious; you're just there to get a man' (Herbert 1998, p.112). Harris's (2015) portrayal of the 17 women veterans revealed the same levels of exasperation, where despite their trailblazing careers, the women were repeatedly taunted by military men to prove themselves. One veteran became so fed up that she purposely short-circuited her promising career by retiring early. Many of these women veterans believe that, especially unlike their white male counterparts, they have fallen short of translating their achievements in the military by parlaying such experiences into the civilian sector.

Says Harris (2015), no legislation – including the U.S. Constitution; the 19th Amendment that bequeathed women the right to vote; attempts universally to enact the Equal Rights Amendment (ERA) that today still fall short since its introduction in 1923 in the quest for the necessary ratification by the individual states in making it the law of the land; the Civil Rights Act of 1964 or its amendment in the way of the Glass Ceiling Act of 1991 – separately or together, have radically altered the entrenched cultural and collective mindset that still afflicts America which falsely touts itself as the world's exemplar of democracy and granted its self-appointed status as the leader of the free world given its self-anointed *exceptionalism*. Even Hillary Clinton – perhaps the best chance at and still the only woman in the U.S. to have come the closest in realizing the quest for full citizenship and by extension full agency – could not break this glass ceiling in her failed and final attempt at achieving the promise of what it really means to be truly equal.

Schwarzenbach (2003) is not taken aback by these outcomes, for neither the word 'woman' nor 'women' is expressly mentioned in the initial iteration of the Constitution. Not to be alarmed, as in keeping with the times, the drafting of the document was conceived by men, for men. Nevertheless, the word 'man' was explicitly mentioned no fewer than 30 times throughout the document. These remain important points for at the time of the Constitution's creation, women did not have universal suffrage, could not own property under the law and were nowhere a part of the public sphere unless as deemed appropriate by their fathers or husbands. Morris (1987), and others like Hoff (1991), Gunderson (1987) and Smith-Rosenberg (1992) concur that it was calculated by the drafters of the Constitution that women were to be excluded from the country's discourse. Kerber (1998) believes that this exclusion from participation on juries and contemporary society in the military in the form of the combat exclusion policy, are schemes to consign women to second-class-citizen status in American society. Even as the 14th Amendment of the U.S. Constitution grants equal protection under the law, through combat exclusion, for instance, the military found a way to legally subordinate the status of women. Moreover, as Horrigan (1992) reminds us, the Navy's over 150 years of tradition is immersed in this custom.

More glaring is the fact that the U.S. Supreme Court apparently chose to address the plight of the enslavement of African Americans over that of the sanctioned discrimination against women. It is important to note here that any discourse or even rumination about the status of black women was not only remote, but moot. However, it is what the High Court said that seems to capture the sentiments of the day: 'The natural and proper timidity and delicacy which belongs to the female sex evidently unfits it for many of the occupations in civil life ... The paramount destiny and mission of the woman are to fulfill the noble and benign offices of wife and mother. This is the law of the Creator' (Horrigan 1992, p.242). Of note again is the reference to 'delicacy,' which reinforces the inconsequential nature of the African American woman who was no doubt then a slave. As enlightening as the Court's citation is, it is undoubtedly suspect in the use of the word 'it' in denoting even the status of the white female's place and role in life as ones preordained by none other than the Creator, according to man.

In the 1973 *Frontierro v. Richardson* ruling that challenged the Air Force's policy of treating female and male spouses who were dependents of its personnel disparately and the 1978 *Owens v. Brown* challenge to the Navy and congruently the Department of Defense's (DoD) combat exclusion policy, in both cases, the U.S. Supreme Court partly came to the defense of women in the military. In *Frontierro v. Richardson*, the High Court ruled in the litigant's favor that the Air Force's benefits policy did indeed discriminate against its female workforce with dependents while in the *Owens v. Brown* case, the Court struck down the DoD's restriction of women's assignments to certain vessels, but it upheld the larger assignment that barred women from combat or combat-related assignments and vessels. In her research, Harris (2015) fortuitously featured both primary litigants in her book as precedent setting, as the cases also represented the first time that the High Court ruled in favor, albeit only partly in the latter, for women in the military.

In the second legal challenge, *Owens v. Brown, 1978* though, while a positive ruling no doubt set the stage for the toppling of other barriers, including the most recent repeal of the combat exclusion policy, it nonetheless conveyed the tepid approach by the U.S. Supreme Court to universally strike down such policies despite gender-based policies that are 'inherently suspect' (Horrigan 1992, p.245). The Court methodically dodged this bullet under the cover that 'classifications by gender must serve important government objectives and must be substantially related to the achievement of these objectives' (Horrigan 1992, p.250) in support of the DoD's combat exclusion policy.

The language in the 14th Amendment is also itself at issue. Had the term 'natural rights' been invoked, both African Americans and women would have been given the right to full citizenship (Buescher n.d.). The framing of the language could have also afforded both groups comprehensive protection under the Constitution for political and practical reasons, and it is believed that the standards of the day would have allowed its passing, especially where women were concerned. However, although the amendment speaks to anyone who is either born or naturalized as being entitled to the same rights of full citizenship, again, given the conventions of the time, the law did not clearly include women as so entitled. Herrmann

(2008) also questions this exclusion since the Constitution goes to great lengths in the 14th Amendment to delineate the benchmarks for representation in the U.S. Congress for 'male citizens' in Section II of the amendment (p.7), without any such declaration for women. Nevertheless, even with the ratification of the 15th Amendment thus giving women the right to pursue suffrage under the pretext of 'All citizens,' women were never explicitly mentioned. And even with the passing of the 14th Amendment for equal protection under the law, the drafting of the yet-to-be-ratified ERA was the justification to close this chasm of seeming neglect to include women as full citizens.

Young (2005) bemoans the ambiguous absence of women in the U.S. Constitution, preferring to explain the purported reason in terms of the good and bad woman. The *good* woman, it is argued, willingly surrenders herself to the safeguard of a man, which, given the times, meant the security of her father or husband, whereas the *bad* woman connotes a person who is forced to fend for herself for she rejects such subordination to the will of men (Young 2005, p.25). In each situation, though, the woman is exposed as a helpless victim who must wait for the protection of a man. In modern-day vernacular, Young sees this treatment as akin to being a *good citizen* or a *bad citizen* in terms which conjure up fear to secure citizens' compliance. However, arguably *subordinate citizenship* is compatible with democracy (Young 2005, p.27). Irrespective of the expressed mention of women in the Constitution, democracy connotes citizenship and the representation by others who must be accountable to the citizenry. It follows, then, that it is this relationship through representation that recognizes all citizens, explicitly stated or not, as equal. Harris (2015) challenges the irony that still at 50.8 percent of the general civilian population (U.S. Census Bureau 2010) or the country's majority, and although a minority at 16 percent in total representation of the military (Population Representation in the Military Services 2015), that by way of the combat exclusion policy, despite its recent repeal, women continue to be denied representation of full citizenship even as the 14th Amendment states otherwise by guaranteeing such rights under the law (Harris 2015).

What is equally alarming, though, is that women like Gutman (1997) remain fervent opponents of women in the military, more so for serving in combat. Such attitudes, claims Harris (2015), are borne of ignorance that serves to sabotage not only women in the military but all women in American society. Titunik (2000) states that '[w]hat no one is publicly saying (but what everyone in the military knows) is that incidents like these (referring to sexual assault at the Army's Aberdeen Proving Ground) are bound to recur. In a military that is dedicated to full integration as best as it can, sex and sexual difference will continue to be a disruptive force' (p.18). Unfortunately, this statement has dual implications that military women will 'insert their ill-mannered selves to thwart the efforts of men off to battle,' but in so doing, 'women's mere presence induces grown rational men to view them as temptresses ready to lead them astray' (Harris 2009, p.71). Harris (2015) rejects such folly.

As Harris (2009) posits through the theory of attrition, the white female's premature exit from the military signals her fight for full agency in light of what she perceives as the military's unwelcoming climate, while Snyder (2003) concurs that to exclude women from full participation throughout the military contradicts the values of a democratic society and the role of the citizen-soldier. To do otherwise is inimical to the exclusion of over 50 percent of the country's citizens and the undermining of women's rights as not having the full prerogative of military service as men. Therefore, to eradicate sexism, the preoccupation for the military should be in maintaining readiness and meeting its mission (Snyder 2003) in the interests of national security. Consideration of gender should have no place in such affairs. The American Civil Liberties Union (ACLU), in its rebuke of the military, says that 'men do not have a monopoly on patriotism, physical ability, desire for adventure, or willingness to risk their lives. Until both the responsibilities and rights of citizenship are shared on a gender-neutral basis, women will continue to be considered less than full-fledged citizens' (ACLU 2013).

Accordingly, in spite of the 14th Amendment and even the 15th Amendment, for that matter, legally excluding women by way of a policy that affords men the right to bear arms denies one-half of the country that same right (Harris 2015). Harris (2015) maintains that while in principle women have been ostensibly granted full citizenship, in practice this is not the case, despite the legislation to fill that void, including by way of other legislation such as the Civil Rights Act of 1964, the Voting Rights Act of 1965, and the 14th and 15th Amendments passed for this very purpose to shore up the intrinsic shortcomings of the Constitution. Paraphrasing the late Major General Jeanne Holm, the first woman in the military to achieve this rank, women's fight in the military is about securing the rights and responsibilities of full citizenship (GenderGap.com 2000). Likewise, women deserve the right to full citizenship. Says Harris (2009), simply put, women's struggle in the military is about realizing full agency. The combat exclusion policy's repeal is only one step in myriad actions towards this fundamental goal (Harris 2015).

Bibliography

American Civil Liberties Union (ACLU). (2013). Combat Exclusion Policy for Women. www.aclu.org/combat-exclusion-policy-women. Retrieved March 27, 2017.

Andrews, P.H. (1992). Sex and Gender Differences in Group Communication: Impact on the Facilitation Process. *Small Group Research*, 23, 1, 74–94.

Bell, E.L. (2004). Myths, Stereotypes, and Realities of Black Women: A Personal Reflection. *The Journal of Applied Behavioral Science*, 40, 146–159.

Bem, S.L. (1993). *The Lens of Gender: Transforming the Debate on Sexual Inequality.* New Haven, CT: Yale University Press.
Bevans, M. (1960). *McCall's Book of Everyday Etiquette.* New York: Golden Press.
Bourke, J. (1996). *Dismembering the MALE. Men's Bodies, Britain and the Great War.* Chicago, IL: University of Chicago Press.
Buchanan, N.T., Settles, I.H., and Woods, K.C. (2008). Comparing Sexual Harassment Subtypes Among Black and White Women by Military Rank: Double Jeopardy, the Jezebel, and the Cult of True Womanhood. *Psychology of Women Quarterly,* 32, 347–361.
Buescher, J. (n.d.). Voting Rights and the 14th Amendment. http://teachinghistory.org/history-content/ask-a-historian/23652. Retrieved January 12, 2017.
Center for Military Readiness (CMR). (2002). Demise of the DACOWITS. http://cmrlinl.org/dacowits.asp?docID=142. Retrieved February 20, 2017.
Collins, P.H. (2000). *Black Feminist Thought: Knowledge, Consciousness, and the Politics of Empowerment.* 2nd Edition. New York, NY: Routledge.
Davis, A.Y. (1998). Reflections on the Black Woman's Role in the Community of Slaves. In J. James (Ed.), *The Angela Y. Davis Reader* (p.111–128). Malden, MA: Blackwell Publishing.
Frankenberg, R. (1993). *White Women, Race Matters: The Social Construction of Whiteness.* Minneapolis, MN: University of Minnesota Press.
GenderGap.com. (2000). Women and the Military. July 4. www.gendergap.com/military.htm. Retrieved December 16, 2016.
Goffman, E. (1977). The Arrangement Between the Sexes. *Theory and Society,* 4, 301–331.
Gross, J. (1990). Navy Is Urged to Root Out Lesbians Despite Abilities. *New York Times.* September 2, 24.
Gunderson, J.R. (1987). Independence, Citizenship, and the American Revolution. *Signs,* 13, 1, 59–77.
Gutman, S. (1997). Sex and the Soldier. *New Republic.* February 24, 18–22.
Harris, G.L.A. (2009). The Multifaceted Nature of White Female Attrition in the Military. *Journal of Public Management and Social Policy,* 15, 1, 71–93.
Harris, G.L.A. (2015). *Living Legends and Full Agency: Implications of Repealing the Combat Exclusion Policy.* New York, NY: Taylor & Francis Group, a division of CRC Press.
Herbert, M.S. (1998). *Camouflage Isn't Only for Combat. Gender, Sexuality, and Women in the Military.* New York and London: New York University Press.
Herrmann, J. (2008). *The National Organization for Women and the Fight for the Equal Rights Amendment.* Frankfurt and Munich: GRIN Verlag Publishers.
Hoff, J. (1991). *Law, Gender, and Injustice: A Legal History of U.S. Women.* New York: New York University Press.
Holm, J. (1992). *Women in the Military: An Unfinished Revolution.* Revised Edition. Novato, CA: Presidio Press.
Honey, M. (1984). *Creating Rosie the Riveter: Class, Gender, and Propaganda During World War II.* Amherst, MA: University of Massachusetts Press.
Horrigan, C. (1992). The Combat Exclusion Rule and Equal Protection. *Santa Clara Law Review,* 32, 1, 229–263.
Kerber, L.K. (1998). The Paradox of Women's Citizenship in the Early Republic: The Case of Martin V. Massachusetts, 1805. *American Historical Review,* April, 349–378.

Mazur, D.H. (1998). Women, Responsibility and the Military. *Notre Dame Law Review*, 74, 1, 1–45.

Morris, R.B. (1987). *The Forging of the Union, 1781–1789*. New York: New American Nation Series/HarperCollins Children's Books.

Moskos, C. (2005). Author communication via e-mail. January 7.

Nadler, L.B., and Nadler, M.K. (1990). Perceptions of Sex Differences in Classroom Communication. *Women's Studies in Communication*, 13, 46–65.

Pearson, J.C. (1985). *Gender and Communication*. Dubuque, IA: William C. Brown Press.

Population Representation in the Military Services. (2015). *Population Report*. Center for Naval Analyses. www.cna.org. Retrieved March 27, 2017.

Reskin, B.F., McBrier, D.B., and Kmec, J.A. (1999). The Determinants and Consequences of Workplace Sex and Race Composition. *American Review of Sociology*, 25, 335–361.

Schwarzenbach, S.A. (2003). Women and Constitutional Interpretation: The Forgotten Value of Civic Friendship. In S.A. Schwarzenbach and P. Smith (Eds.), *Women and the United States Constitution. History, Interpretation, and Practice*. New York: Columbia University Press.

Scully, D., and Bart, P. (2003). A Funny Thing Happened on the Way to the Orifice. *Women in Gynaecology, Feminism and Psychology*, 13, 11–16.

Shilts, R. (1993). *Conduct Unbecoming: Gays and Lesbians in the U.S. Military*. New York: St Martin's Press.

Smith-Rosenberg, C. (1992). Dis-covering the Subject of the 'Great Constitutional Discussion,' 1786–1789. *Journal of American History*, 79, 3, 841–873.

Snyder, R.C. (2003). The Citizen-Soldier Tradition and Gender Integration of the U.S. Military. *Armed Forces and Society*, 29, 2, 185–204.

Stewart, L.P., Stewart, A.D., Friedley, S.A., and Cooper, P.J. (1990). *Communication between the Sexes: Sex Differences and Sex-Role Stereotypes*. 2nd Edition. Scottsdale, AZ: Gorsuch Scarisbrick Publishers.

Titunik, R.F. (2000). The First Wave: Gender Integration and Military Culture. *Armed Forces and Society*, 26, 2, 229–257.

U.S. Army. (2002). *Women in the Army: An Annotated Bibliography*. U.S. Army Research Institute for the Behavioral and Social Sciences. Special Report 48. May.

U.S. Census Bureau. (2010). Demographic Profile. www.census.gov/popfinder/. Retrieved February 12, 2017.

West, C. (2004). Mammy, Jezebel, and Sapphire: Developing an 'Oppositional Gaze' toward the Image of Black Women. In J.C. Chrisler, C. Golden, and P.D. Rozzee (Eds.), *Lectures on the Psychology of Women* (p.20–233). New York, NY: McGraw Hill.

Young, I.M. (2005). The Logic of Masculine Protection: Reflections on the Current Security State. In M. Friedman (Ed.), *Women and Citizenship*. New York, NY: Oxford University Press.

7 Who Is a Veteran?

In accordance with Title 38 of the Federal Code of Regulations, a veteran is defined as anyone who has served in the military, and did so through any branches of the service and was honorably discharged (Veterans Authority (VA) n.d.). Veterans then may have served in the military under the designation of one or more of the following. Active duty service signifies that the member once served as a full-time employee, albeit on a 24 hours, seven days per week cycle barring vacation periods and/or other authorized leave. As such, while assigned as a member of a specific branch of the military, the member falls under the authority of the Department of Defense (DoD). The military branches under its jurisdiction include the Army, Navy, Air Force, Marine Corps and Coast Guard, although the latter now falls under the jurisdiction of the U.S. Department of Homeland Security (Baldinelli 2002).

Veterans also may have served within various time designations, usually considered part time, although many may have served in a full-time capacity (VA n.d.). Military members might have either continued their active service via one of these alternative time designations or may have solely served in any one or all of these alternative designations in the forms of either or both active duty training (i.e., two weeks or 14 days of annual tour) or individual duty training (IDT) (i.e., one weekend per month) in the reserve and/or National Guard components of the respective services. The Army, Navy, Air Force, Marine Corps and Coast Guard all have reserve components that complement their active duty mission and forces. These reserve components are federalized and therefore fall under the federal government. Selected military branches through state-controlled means also possess National Guard components. This additional categorization is only offered through the Army and the Air Force.

The National Guard may too limit its members to a two-week active duty annual tour and at least a one weekend per month requirement (VA n.d.). State governors primarily control their respective National Guard components and are employed and deployed for active duty in the service of the state (Title 10) or federal service (Title 38). Additional designations under the reserve and National Guard components include active guard reserve (AGR) whereby reserve and National Guard members work routinely on active duty in support of daily operations. AGR members function as active duty personnel and are extended the same such benefits as veterans. A final categorization, or that of the individual ready reserve (IRR), must enlist in a contract with the military for at least eight years. Despite this obligation, which usually follows active duty or reserve service, the member neither participates on active military pursuits, say, for two weeks of active duty training and/or IDT, nor is compensated for such participation. However, these inactive duty members can be recalled as necessary to support military missions.

There are also additional designations of what or who is defined as a veteran, which correspondingly determine what benefits one is entitled to receive. Further designations such as war veteran v. combat veteran are invoked. War veteran connotes any person or government issue (GI) who was sent by the military to serve in harm's way (Coleman 1973). A combat veteran is any person or GI who sustains hostility for any time as a result of an offensive, defensive or friendly fire in operations involving the enemy under combat or war conditions. These designations also determine the benefits to which one is entitled. Yet this designation and associated eligibility requirements as to what or who is defined as a veteran have evolved over time. There are length of service restrictions (Moulta-Ali 2015). For example, until September 1980, there was no such restriction regarding length of service in order to be considered a veteran for one's eligibility for a cadre of benefits. Since then, a length of two years of active duty service or the entire time of active duty is considered the criterion for eligibility. However, there are exceptions. Service-connected disability may make a service member eligible for benefits if it is demonstrated that the member incurred the condition as a result of military service. Hardship discharges or those who retired or left the military as a result of service-connected disability may be exempt from such length of service restrictions. As well, women who served as pilots under the Women Airforce Service Pilots (WASPs) were neither designated as military personnel nor were they even considered veterans, making them ineligible for a time for veteran benefits. It was not until the GI Improvement Act (P.L.95–202) in 1977 that these women's active duty service to their country was recognized (Moulta-Ali 2015).

One veteran, 94 years young at the time of her interview, Mrs. Anna Flynn Monkiewicz, said that it took almost 40 years before the federal government saw fit to confer such a designation and accompanying benefits, and over 60 years before she was officially honored for her service, for which she and other women each received the Congressional Gold Medal (Harris 2015). At the discretion of the Secretary of Defense, other designations could be bestowed upon deserving civilians and contractors who have served their country honorably in some capacity and are offered entitlement for VA benefits. These groups may include those who served during World War I in the Signal Corps Female Telephone Operators Unit,

Engineering Field Clerks, Male Civilian Ferry Pilots during World War II, and civilians who were involved in war-connected occupations. While the eligibility for veteran benefits is also limited to only military personnel who were honorably discharged, the exception for the collection of veteran benefits may even apply to some veterans who received a bad conduct discharge under other than honorable conditions. In this case, the VA will review the circumstances under which the military member was discharged from service and determine accordingly whether the member is to be afforded any veteran benefits (Moulta-Ali 2015). Despite the law, even dishonorable discharge does not totally preclude a service member from securing VA benefits. Veteran benefits may even be given to incarcerated veterans and those on parole. Additionally, should someone be discharged under the condition of insanity, that person may be eligible for VA benefits. Here, the nexus between the person's insanity and offense need not be made to secure benefits.

Securing benefits may also be a condition of when and how the service member's military service was classified (Moulta-Ali 2015). Because VA benefits are classified as either wartime or peacetime, the veteran might be entitled to certain wartime benefits, for instance, even if the person has never served in a combat zone but served during a period that was designated by Congress as wartime. Occasionally, however, members of the Reserve and National Guard may encounter opposition when they attempt to claim benefits for not having met the legal standards for benefits such as the federal active duty and/or length of service requirements for eligibility. Yet, certain programs under the post-September 11, 2001 (9/11) GI Bill may render individuals eligible for certain VA benefits which may vary with each veteran.

In *Monk v. Mabus, 2014*, a group of Vietnam-era veterans sued the secretaries of the respective services (Army, Navy, Air Force) for violating the Administrative Procedure Act in the review of their military records for an upgrade to their discharge status (Moulta-Ali and Panangala 2015). The group sought an upgrade to establish eligibility for some basic VA benefits. In response, then Secretary of Defense Chuck Hagel, by way of a memorandum to the military branches, gave those branches the authority to make 'liberal considerations' (Moulta-Ali and Panangala 2015, p.1) in appeals for modification in discharge status as well as help the Boards for Correction of Military Records to reach equitable outcomes for the aggrieved. This was particularly cogent for post-traumatic stress disorder (PTSD) and related cases. Though the VA was never the subject of this legal action, it was nevertheless implicated under the 'character of service' (p.1) in making benefits determination based on the type of discharge that a service member received. It is this veterans' status after meeting certain eligibility requirements that the VA utilizes for this process. Under certain circumstances, even if the service member's discharge status is in question, an established prima facie eligibility may show eligibility for benefits.

Exceptions are also made for service members who have experienced military sexual trauma (MST). As a result, the Veterans Access, Choice and Accountability Act of 2014 was amended to include service members with such experiences during inactive duty training as reservists and members of the National Guard.

Of the more than 23 million people today classified as military veterans, 21.2 million or 9 percent of them are veterans (Zoli et al. 2015, U.S. Census Bureau 2016, Walker and Borbely 2014, Women's Bureau n.d.), and 2.1 million or 1 percent are actively serving in the military on either active duty, as reservists or in the National Guard (Zoli et al. 2015). Women constitute approximately 10 percent of the total veteran population (Women's Bureau 2015), or an estimated 2 million veterans (U.S. Department of Veterans Affairs (VA) 2017, Walker and Borbely 2014), although these data vary slightly according to the source. For example, data from the VA estimate that women veterans represent 8 percent of the overall veteran population (National Center for Veterans Analysis and Statistics (NCVAS) 2017), whereas data from the U.S. Bureau of Labor Statistics (BLS) state that figure at 13 percent for 2014 (BLS 2015, Council on Veterans Employment Women Veterans Initiative 2015), while still others assess this figure at 8.5 percent or 1.6 million of an 18.8 million veteran population for 2015 (U.S. Census Bureau 2016).

The largest group of women veterans hails from the Gulf I (Operations Desert Shield/Storm) and Gulf II (post-9/11 and Operations Enduring and Iraqi Freedom) eras combined (Walker and Borbely 2014, Zoli et al. 2015, Women's Bureau n.d., NCVAS 2016a), followed by those who served prior to the Gulf Wars during the Vietnam and Korean Conflicts and World War II. Perhaps as a condition of the size of the respective military branches, women veterans disproportionately served in the Army (48.6 percent), Air Force (22.7 percent), Navy (19.7 percent), Marine Corps (5.8 percent) and Coast Guard (0.7 percent) (Nanda et al. 2016). Women are also more likely than men to have served in the commissioned corps than the enlisted corps (Women's Bureau n.d.). These data may also help to explain the overall higher education rate for women veterans as well as women veterans' propensity, also at a higher rate than their male cohort, to pursue higher education upon separation from the military (Walker and Borbely 2014). It is also of note that, while more current data starkly contrast the trend where female veterans on average are younger than male veterans (NCVAS 2016a), as compared to past data of especially those on active duty as older (Holm 1992), the current data confirm the higher educational attainment of women veterans in general (Walker and Borbely 2014). Whether intentional or not, these findings also confirm the ourstorical requirement for a more intelligent female workforce in the military given the initially more stringent entry requirements for women from the general civilian population during the conscripted period (Holm 1992), though women have never been subject

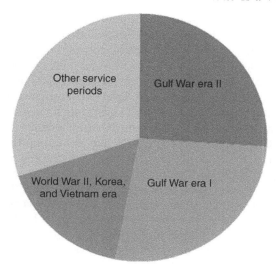

Figure 7.1 Women veterans by period of service, 2013 annual averages
Source: Walker and Borbely 2014, U.S. Bureau of Labor Statistics 2015.

to the draft. Figure 7.1 is a representation of women veterans by period of service.

Texas (183,597), California (163,332) and Florida (154,820), in that order, are the states where women veterans are most populous (U.S. Department of Veterans Affairs 2016). While the largest proportion of both women and men veterans self-report as white, women veterans are more racially diverse than their male counterparts (NCVAS 2016a, Women's Bureau n.d., Nanda et al. 2016, Walker and Borbely 2014). Again, these data vary according to the sources but outside those respondents who self-identify as white (66 percent and 74 percent), between 12 percent and 19 percent described themselves as black; 2.4 percent to 5.8 percent as Asians to include such groups as Native Hawaiians and Pacific Islanders; 0.9 percent as Native Americans or Alaska Native; 2.6 percent from two or more races; and 7.8 percent to 9.1 percent as Hispanics (Nanda et al. 2016, NCVAS 2016a, Women's Bureau n.d.). Today, women veterans are more likely to be Hispanic, regardless of race (Women's Bureau n.d.) (because the designation as Hispanic is an ethnicity, it applies and crosses all races).

The age range of women veterans is across the spectrum, with the largest cohort between 45 years and 55 years, with a median age of 50 years (Nanda et al. 2016, NCVAS 2016a, Walker and Borbely 2014), although on average, women veterans are more likely to be younger than male veterans but older than women nonveterans (Women's Bureau n.d.). As previously noted, women veterans are also more likely to outpace their male veteran peers in educational attainment beyond high school as well as nonveteran female cohorts within the general civilian population (Nanda et al. 2016, Women's Bureau n.d.). An interesting finding, though, by Walker and Borbely (2014) is that, despite this higher level of educational attainment, or women veterans armed with at least an undergraduate degree in 2013, those 25 years and older experienced higher rates of unemployment than women nonveterans with the same level of education (5.9 percent v. 3.7 percent). Also, incidentally, the unemployment rate for the largest group of women veterans, or from the Gulf I and II eras combined, showed similar patterns to male veterans, although male veterans during the latter period (Gulf II) had a lower unemployment rate (9.6 percent v. 8.8 percent) (Walker and Borbely 2014). Compared to male veterans at about 65 percent, women veterans are less likely to be married (45 percent v. 47 percent) and are far more likely than their male veteran counterparts either to be divorced or to never have been married (Nanda et al. 2016, NCVAS 2016a).

Surprisingly, women veterans more than men veterans 54 years of age and younger have higher rates of disability (Nanda et al. 2016, NCVAS 2016a), even though inexplicably as age increases, or at 65 years and older, it is men veterans who experience higher rates of disability than women veterans of the same age group (Nanda et al. 2016). Although these data have not been disaggregated to further delineate whether or not disability rates are service connected and/or are a condition of age, women veterans are more likely than men veterans and at higher rates to utilize the health services of the VA (NCVAS 2016a). When service-connected disability is disaggregated, women veterans more than men veterans have higher overall rates (Nanda et al. 2016), although in 2011, these rates were reflected as virtually equal (Women's Bureau n.d.). Whilst, as stated, women veterans experience higher employment rates than men veterans even with the higher education advantage, their median annual household income is still lower than that of men veterans. For example, women veterans for all age groups out-earn their nonveteran female peers, yet earned between $5,000 to $7,000 less per annum than both men veterans and nonveteran men in general, for all age groups (NCVAS 2016a). Also, while more women veterans than men veterans secure employment in positions that are categorized as management, professional, sales and office, they did so disproportionately in the federal, state and local governments (Women's Bureau n.d., Walker and Borbely 2014, Council on Veterans Employment Women Veterans Initiative 2015). Many, however, have pursued such careers at even higher rates in the private sector (Walker and Borbely 2014).

What remains troubling, however, is the rate at which veterans find themselves in poverty, which may spiral out of control resulting in one of the many wicked problems: homelessness. Unfortunately, data for 2014 show that veterans overall, and women veterans in particular, are far more likely than male and female nonveterans to be in poverty, regardless of age (NCVAS 2016b, U.S. Department of Veterans Affairs 2016b). An anomaly, though, appears to be in the Midwest, where women veterans are more likely to fall into poverty than women veterans in other regions of the U.S. Although generally, men veterans have lower rates of poverty than women veterans (6.7 percent v. 9.4 percent), the greatest disparities between the groups occur among the very young (17 years–34 years: 10.5 percent v. 13.1 percent), and the oldest (65 years and older: 4.9 percent v. 7.9 percent). This is primarily so among veterans who are considered disabled (9.4 percent v. 15.3 percent). Equally egregious is the fact that Native American women veterans more than any other racial and/or ethnic group stand the highest chance of being in poverty and at an astonishing rate of 21 percent. Veterans, male or female in Puerto, also show a particularly high rate of poverty at 20 percent, followed by those in Washington, D.C. (11.6 percent).

Between 2009 and 2015, the homeless rate for veterans witnessed a precipitous decline to 47,725, or 35 percent less, including a 46 percent reduction in the number of street homeless veterans (National Coalition for Homeless Veterans 2015). Women veterans constitute about 9 percent of the total homeless veteran population, or 4,338 (National Center on Homelessness Among Veterans 2016). However, there are a number of risk factors that lend themselves to making women veterans susceptible to homelessness and three times more likely to fall prey as a result: such variables as being in poverty, of a young age, being single and unemployed, suffering from a service-connected disability, self-reporting as African American and residing in the Northeast. Factors exacerbating these risks for homelessness include substance abuse and/or mental health disorders as a condition of diagnoses like schizophrenia, depression and alcohol or drug abuse. Adding to this already precarious mix are PTSD and MST, which diagnoses compound the likelihood of exposure to homelessness. The VA describes a latent class analysis (LCA) that distinguishes certain dominant characteristics of the typical female veteran who is most predisposed to homelessness: age 40; low patrons of healthcare yet have a high need for such services; and served an average of 8.5 years or less during Operations Enduring and/or Iraqi Freedom. While both men and women are likely to have experienced some level of abuse as children prior to military service, that rate of abuse is much higher for women who join the military (Collins 2016, Zinzow et al. 2008).

A comprehensive study by Zoli et al. (2015) yielded some thought-provoking findings about veterans overall, as many transition from the military into the civilian sector. The sample of more than 8,500 veterans of whom 63 percent, 17 percent and 20 percent, respectively, identified as active in all components of the military (active duty, reserve, National Guard) and who served during Operations Enduring and Iraqi Freedom (Gulf II era/post-9/11), Operation Desert Shield/Storm (Gulf I era) and pre-Gulf Wars (Vietnam and Korean Conflicts and World War II), is considered as encompassing one of the most far-reaching datasets to date based on the experiences of veterans and their families. Some 53 percent and 52 percent of the respondents were primarily motivated to join the military in order to secure a higher education and did so because of patriotism, while 88 percent and 87 percent believed that joining the military was not only the right thing to do but that the decision has positively impacted their lives, with generally 92 percent who trust that their higher educational attainment obtained in the military has had or will play a significant role in their post-service transition. Over one-third (36 percent), however, voluntarily separated from the military due to a loss of faith in the military and/or civilian leadership, another 32 percent did so to pursue educational and training opportunities beyond the military, with less than one-third (31 percent) leaving the military because of family obligations.

It is important to note that of those sampled, less than half have capitalized on taking advantage of their GI benefits (Zoli et al. 2015). What is preventing these veterans from doing so may be the degree to which they are able to access these benefits. For example, 60 percent of the respondents indicated that navigating the VA system is particularly onerous, followed by securing civilian employment (55 percent), re-acclimating to the civilian culture (41 percent), coping with financial issues (40 percent) and translating those skills acquired in the military to civilian practice (39 percent). Disabled veterans, or 59 percent of respondents with a service-connected disability, encountered more daunting challenges in transitioning to civilian life. Some 79 percent found their disability to be an impediment to the process, which invariably and adversely impacts their personal lives (87 percent), securing (37 percent) and maintaining employment (40 percent), as well as pursuing (12 percent) and realizing (28 percent) their higher educational pursuits.

Although the Zoli et al. (2015) study constitutes the most extensive information on the transitional experiences of veterans as a group, these data were not disaggregated to reflect the unique and lived experiences of women veterans. Stories abound about women veterans' invisibility and not being taken seriously by those at the VA – typically women, ironically, often being the gatekeepers of making benefits determination due for their military veteran kinfolk. Harris's (2015) chronicling of at least four women veterans in her research is chiefly indicative of this debilitating experience. As with all of the women captured in the book, Colonel Pamela Rodriguez encountered such challenges in and out of the military. However, Colonel Rodriguez's experience was particularly distinctive as she did so as an aviator, a discipline that is still the stronghold of white men. So much so that upon retirement, Colonel Rodriguez seldom mentions, if ever, that she was a pilot, and much less that she was so in the military. Putting up with what she regarded as wanton harassment, when it came to her beloved flying, Colonel Rodriguez, without flinching, said that 'they [the military] beat the love of it' out of her (Harris 2015, p.156).

The feisty and resolute Sergeant Michelle Wilmot, one of the women from the now famous female engagement teams dubbed Team Lioness during Operations Enduring and Iraqi Freedom, cited a memorable but teachable moment when she visited a VA facility all for the purpose of applying for and claiming her well-earned benefits as a combat veteran, only to be rebuffed by none other than a female benefits counselor because Sergeant Wilmot's DD Form 214 inaccurately did not reflect this information; worse yet, because she is a woman this information was not only deliberately and conveniently missing owing to the combat exclusion policy, but also because she was not found to be credible as a result (Harris 2015). As a consequence, unlike her male counterparts, Sergeant Wilmot was not treated in kind because of her gender. Shrewdly, Sergeant Wilmot used the occasion as a teaching moment to educate the VA counselor. Yet, when she also applied to the Federal Bureau of Investigation (FBI), she was again reminded of her invisibility as a woman veteran and was not taken seriously as especially a combat veteran. During her final interview for a position with the FBI, the man conducting the polygraph phase of the process, albeit inappropriately, attempted to delve deeply into Sergeant Wilmot's experiences in Iraq by implying that such experiences would not make for good morale in the office environment. Sergeant Wilmot correctly suspected that this line of questioning was gender based. If anything, as she thought, had she been a man, and given the position for which she was applying, this experience would have been branded an invaluable asset to the FBI. However, the razor-sharp sergeant settled the score and in no uncertain terms, even at the risk of jeopardizing the opportunity of advancing to the next level of the employment process, by declaring, 'So, I'm good enough to die on the battlefield but I'm not good enough to work in one of your offices' (Harris 2015, p.236).

Notwithstanding her experiences both on and off the battlefield, there were multiple reminders that even though she had repeatedly demonstrated that she could not only match but outdo her male peers, the problem with Mrs. Tiffany Kravec-Kelly was that she was a woman, plain and simple (Harris 2015). Luckily for her, her husband, himself a veteran of the Special Forces, seizes every opportunity in public when he is acknowledged as a veteran to also remind others that his wife is a fellow veteran. Still, understandably, Chief Warrant Officer 5 (CWO5) Trish Thompson's initial experience in visiting a VA facility proved so demoralizing that she never returned. Another woman veteran, this time in North Carolina, was reportedly shamed when a passer-by in a parking lot unwittingly placed a note on the windshield of her car criticizing her temerity to park in a spot that was reserved for veterans (Fox News 2015).

Justifiably, the research landscape is no longer confined to the study of male veterans or veterans with limited study about the experiences of women, and the VA and other entities and scholars are now increasingly seeing fit to dedicate a growing amount of resources to the study of women veterans. One need only to review the literature, which appears to be now teeming with such research. Besides, researchers like Pollard et al. (2015), Zoli et al. (2015) and Resnick et al. (2012) predict an uptick in the number of women veterans within the general civilian population. Only now, more than ever, this new attention to research on women in the military and women veterans reveals that being a woman and a woman veteran are actually idiosyncratic. Many of these symptoms are also borne of the cumulative burden of simultaneous wars (Operations Enduring and Iraqi Freedom) that unduly placed women in combat situations for which they were ill prepared in terms of specific training, equipment and protection, for at the time while women were legally designated as noncombatants, nevertheless, many found themselves as either illegally placed in combatant situations, or due to the fluid nature of the war zones, in roles as combatants.

As Resnick et al. (2012) note, in a combat exclusion environment, many women were inappropriately placed in combat situations as either attached or assigned and in direct harm's way. The lack of training and access to equipment rendered women then designated as noncombatants even more vulnerable in the line of fire because they were not equally protected as their male counterparts (Di Leone et al. 2013). Adding to an already volatile concoction, women were also battling a war on dual fronts – on the physical battlefield and against sexual predators in their respective units and civilian contractors employed by the U.S. military (Harris 2015, Monahan and Neidel-Greenlee 2010, Haskell et al. 2010). Consequently, the transition period to civilian life following military service was inevitably expected to present complex and unique challenges for the women who served (Cohen et al. 2012).

Owens et al. (2009) cite the ignorance surrounding the woman veteran's plight upon return from these wars, including by healthcare professionals, family, friends and the women themselves. Dutra et al. (2011) analyzed following these deployments the stressors that were invariably the resultant mental health outcomes. Moreover, Taft et al. (2008) see the invaluable contributions to the literature of examining the effects of the exposure to war for women veterans following their return to civilian life. Further, addressing the gap in the extant literature will yield fruitful lessons in helping women veterans' readjustment to civilian life as well as in understanding those issues that are most challenging for them. Resnik et al. (2009) concur in promoting such research as a mechanism for supporting female veterans with reintegration challenges as well as to educate healthcare professionals and those in the community about them (Resnick et al. 2012). Robinson's (2016) study further delineates the importance of this kind of research by filling a significant gap in these lived experiences.

For example, unlike their peers in the civilian sector, female veterans face a six-times-greater likelihood of committing suicide, and those between the ages of 18 and 29 encounter an even greater rate of being 12 times more likely than their civilian cohort to do so (Collins 2016). Deployment from combat zones like those of Operations Enduring and Iraqi Freedom had a tripling effect on women veterans' susceptibility to suicide. Such cumulative stressors while in the theater of operations in the forms of self-imposed pressure to prove to male counterparts that they are as capable, result in unintended consequences like injuries and heatstroke (Collins 2016). Compounding these stressors is the invisibility factor of not being recognized for one's contribution and in connecting with likeminded women in their communities. Still added to these challenges is the invalidation of women's primary role as the caregiver in their families. During deployment, this mental pressure increases exponentially.

The higher divorce rate for military women as compared to their male counterparts is equally telling (Collins 2016). The divorce rate for men in the Army is 2.9 percent, whereas the rate for their female counterparts is almost triple, at 8.5 percent. Those in the Marine Corps reflect a similarly disturbing trend. For men, the divorce rate is 3.3 percent, while for women that rate is significantly higher at 9.2 percent. A process of self-selection where women segregate themselves for fear of taking on the stigma of other women in their respective units unwittingly results in self-isolation. MST, where, of those reported, 37 percent were violated multiple times while 14 percent were gang raped, only intensifies both the magnitude and complexity of these already convoluted situations.

What the preceding information clearly demonstrates is the almost vicious cycle of seemingly unending challenges for women veterans. Some deliberately initially seek out the military to escape their dismal circumstances, only to confront more of the same and worse in the military. For many, separating from the military also brings no solace or relief. If anything, this new status or the attempt at reintegrating into civilian life amplifies the need for help yet simultaneously reeks of isolation. Thus the invisibility becomes self-imposed as a means of self-protection, and women deny their status as veterans in the process.

It is undetermined as to whether or not this self-concept, as manifested in attitudes and behaviors, has a positive effect on women's identity as a group as veterans (Di Leone et al. 2013). However, a report suggests that women veterans' failure to identify as such may itself pose a barrier in seeking out and receiving earned services (U.S. Department of Labor 2015). This makes outreach to women veterans as a group all the more problematic to mitigate the challenges. Second, the literature implies that women veterans may unknowingly engage in stereotype threat (Steele 1997, Danaher et al. 2008), a form of self-sabotage that results in them succumbing to the very negative stereotypes of their group that they are attempting to overcome as individuals. Examining the degree to which women veterans are exposed to negative messaging may well yield invaluable research in readjusting image or self-esteem in how women veterans may present themselves, for instance, to prospective employers (U.S. Department of Labor 2015). Third, Kay and Simpson (2014) invoke what they call a confidence gap between men and women, which even professional women inadvertently impose upon themselves, although as

Bensahel et al. (2015) discovered that women in the military, unlike their civilian peers, contend less with. Conversely, the distinction as a military woman versus that of a woman veteran warrants the highlighting of some of the unique challenges that women veterans encounter in readjustment to civilian life. As such, more research in this area is necessary in determining the degree to which such a mindset impacts women veterans' ability to successfully adjust to civilian life, one element of which includes securing desired employment in the civilian sector (U.S. Department of Labor 2015).

Empirical evidence shows that women veterans' frustration emanates from lived experiences in the form of biases by prospective employers (Thom and Bassuk 2012), although such perceptions of female veterans may simultaneously be both pessimistic and optimistic (Abt Associates, Inc. 2008). Kleykamp's (2010) study indicates a higher rate of callback for women veterans than nonveteran women, but alludes that the bias against women veterans is more likely to take place during the actual interviews than the preliminary phase of the employment process. Studies by Heilman and Okimoto (2007) and Heilman et al. (2004) reveal a strong and positive correlation for men's likability and success over that of women's likability and success (see U.S. Department of Labor 2015). Further research may then determine whether or not likability and success are correlated for women veterans, especially for still perceived nontraditional jobs for women and employers' propensity to bias against women veterans based on these attributes (U.S. Department of Labor 2015).

Finally, research intimates that women's reintegration into civilian life is complex and multidimensional in scope (Business and Professional Women's Foundation 2008). This process may even continue long after female veterans have been successfully placed with employers. A longitudinal study might be in order to analyze these long-term effects and the associated induced duration between job placement and the onset of such challenges (U.S. Department of Labor 2015). A comparative study of a nonveteran female group may also produce some interesting results.

Bibliography

Abt Associates, Inc. (2008). *Employment Histories Report: Final Compilation Report*. www1.va.gov/VETDATA/docs. Retrieved January 27, 2017.

Baldinelli, D.C. (2002). The U.S. Coast Guard's Assignment to the Department of Homeland Security: Entering Uncharted Waters or Just a Course Correction? December 9. www.uscg.mil. Retrieved May 26, 2017.

Bensahel, N., Barno, D., Kidder, K., and Sayler, K. (2015). *Battlefields and Boardrooms: Women's Leadership in the Military and the Private Sector*. Center for New American Security. www.cnas.org. Retrieved February 5, 2017.

Business and Professional Women's Foundation. (2008). Understanding the Complexity of Women Veterans Career Transitions. http://bpwfoundation.org/wp-con

tent/uploads/2015/03/FINAL10.19LaunchReportWomenVeteransinTransition.pdf. Retrieved February 27, 2017.
Cohen, B.E., Maguen, S., Bertenthal, D., and Yi Shi, V. (2012). Reproductive and Other Health Outcomes in Iraq and Afghanistan Women Veterans Using VA Health Care: Association with Mental Diagnoses. *Women's Health Issues*, 22, 5, 461–471.
Coleman, P. (1973). What Is a Veteran?www.americanwarlibrary.com. Retrieved May 26, 2017.
Collins, J. (2016). Challenges Facing Today's Female Warriors and Veterans. April 21. www.va.gov/GPDTm.Challenges_Facing_Todays_Female_Warriors_Veterans_4-21-2016.pdf. Retrieved May 26, 2017.
Council on Veterans Employment Women Veterans Initiative. (2015). Employment of Women Veterans in the Federal Government. March. www.va.gov.reports. Retrieved March 23, 2017.
Danaher, K., and Crandall, C.S. (2008). Stereotype Threat in Applied Settings Re-examined. *Journal of Applied Social Psychology*, 38, 6, 1639–1655.
Di Leone, B.A.L., Vogt, D., Gradus, J.L., and Resnick, P.E. (2013). Predictors of Mental Health Care Use among Male and Female Veterans Deployed in Support of the Wars in Afghanistan and Iraq. *Psychological Services*, 10, 2, 145–151.
Dutra, L., Grubbs, K., Greene, C., Trego, L.L., McCartin, T.L., and Kloezeman, K. (2011). Women at War: Implications for Mental Health. *Journal of Trauma and Dissociation*, 12, 1, 25–37.
Fox News. (2015). Female Vet Reportedly Gets Shamed for Parking in Veteran-Reserved Spot. June 22. www.foxnews.com. Retrieved February 6, 2017.
Harris, G.L.A. (2015). *Living Legends and Full Agency: Implications of Repealing the Combat Exclusion Policy.* New York, NY: Taylor & Francis Group, a division of CRC Press.
Haskell, S.G., Gordon, K.S., Mattocks, K., Duggal, M., Erdos, J., Justice, A., and Brandt, C.A. (2010). Gender Differences in Rate of Depression, PTSD, Pain, Obesity, and Military Sexual Trauma among Connecticut War Veterans of Iraq and Afghanistan. *Journal of Women's Health*, 19, 2, 267–271.
Heilman, M.E., and Okimoto, T.G. (2007). Why Are Women Penalized for Success at Male Tasks? *Journal of Applied Psychology*, 92, 1, 81–92.
Heilman, M.E., Fuchs, D., Tamkins, M.M., and Wallen, A.S. (2004). Penalties for Success: Reactions to Women Who Succeed at Male Gender-Typed Tasks. *Journal of Applied Psychology*, 89, 3, 416–427.
Holm, J. (1992). *Women in the Military: An Unfinished Revolution.* Revised Edition. Novato, CA: Presidio Press.
Kay, K., and Simpson, C. (2014). *The Confidence Code: The Science and Art of Self-Assurance – What Women Should Know.* New York, NY: HarperCollins Publishers.
Kleykamp, M.A. (2010). Women's Work After War. Working Paper, No. 10–169. Upjohn Institute. http://research.upjohn.org/up_working papers/169. Retrieved May 23, 2017.
Monahan, E.M., and Neidel-Greenlee, R. (2010). *A Few Good Women. America's Military Women from World War I to the Wars in Iraq and Afghanistan.* New York: Anchor Books, Division of Random House, Inc.
Moulta-Ali, U. (2015). Who Is a 'Veteran'? – Basic Eligibility for Veterans Benefits. February 13. Congressional Research Service (CRS). https://fas.orf/R42324.pdf. Retrieved March 23, 2017.

Moulta-Ali, U., and Panangala, S.D. (2015). *Veterans' Benefits: The Impact of Military Discharges on Basic Eligibility*. Congressional Research Service (CRS). March 6. https://fas.org/R43928.pdf. Retrieved March 23, 2017.

Nanda, N., Shetty, S., Ampaabeng, S., Techapaisarnjaroenkij, T., Patterson, and Garsky, S. (2016). Women Veteran Economic and Employment Characteristics. Contract Number DOL13RQ21724. February. www.dol.gov/WomenVeteranEconomicandEmploymentCharacteristics.pdf. Retrieved January 21, 2017.

National Center for Veterans Analysis and Statistics (NCVAS). (2016a). Profile of Women Veterans: 2015. December 22. www.va.gov/Veterans_Profile_12_22_2016.pdf. Retrieved March 23, 2017.

National Center for Veterans Analysis and Statistics (NCVAS). (2016b). Profile of Veterans in Poverty. March 2016. www.va.gov/Profile_of_Veterans_in_Poverty_2014.pdf. Retrieved February 23, 2017.

National Center for Veterans Analysis and Statistics (NCVAS). (2017). Profile of Veterans: 2015. Data from the American Community Survey. March. U.S. Department of Veterans Affairs. www.va.gov. Retrieved March 23, 2017.

National Center on Homelessness among Veterans. (2016). Women Veterans and Homelessness. July. www.v.gov/HERS-Womens-Proceedings.pdf. Retrieved May 26, 2017.

National Coalition for Homeless Veterans. (2015). *FY2015 Annual Report*. www.nchv.org. Retrieved May 26, 2017.

Owens, G.P., Herrera, C.J., and Whitesell, A.A. (2009). A Preliminary Investigation of Mental Health Needs and Barriers to Mental Health Care for Female Veterans of Iraq and Afghanistan. *Traumatology*, 15, 31–37.

Pollard, M.S., Amaral, E.F.L., Mendelson, J., Cefalu, M., Kress, A., and Ross, R. (2015). Current and Future Demographics of the Veteran Population, 2014–2024. Paper 7602. https://paa.confex.com/2015-09-Veteran-projection_paper_reduced.pdf. Retrieved January 6, 2017.

Resnick, E.M., Mallampalli, M., and Carter, C.L. (2012). Current Challenges in Female Veterans' Health. *Journal of Women's Health*, 21, 9, 895–900.

Resnik, L., Plow, M., and Jette, A. (2009). Development of CRIS: Measure of Community Reintegration of Injured Service Members. *Journal of Rehabilitation Research and Development*, 46, 4, 469–480.

Robinson, M.N. (2016). Exploring Transition Factors among Female Veterans of Operation Enduring/Operation Iraqi Freedom (OEF/OIF). Walden Dissertation Abstracts and Doctoral Studies. Walden University. http://scholarworks.walden.edu/dissertations. Retrieved May 26, 2017.

Steele, C.S. (1997). A Threat in the Air: How Stereotypes Shape Intellectual Identity and Performance. *American Psychologist*, 52, 613–629.

Taft, C.T., Schuman, J.A., Panuzio, J., and Proctor, S.P. (2008). *An Examination of Family Adjustment among Operation Desert Storm Veterans*. Fort Dietrick, MD: U.S. Army Research and Material Command.

Thom, K., and Bassuk, F. (2012). *Chicagoland Female Veterans: A Qualitative Study of Attachment to the Labor Force*. National Center on Family Homelessness. www.familyhomelessness.org/media/391.pdf. Retrieved January 20, 2017.

U.S. Bureau of Labor Statistics. (2015). *Women in the Labor Force: A Databook*. BLS Reports. www.bls.gov. Retrieved March 23, 2017.

U.S. Census Bureau. (2016). FFF: Veterans Day: Nov 11. Release Number: CB16-FF.21.October 25. www.census.gov. Retrieved March 28, 2017.

U.S. Department of Labor. (2015). *Women Veterans and Employment Opportunities for Future Research*. Veterans Employment and Training Service. www.dol.gov/WVRGMay2015.pdf. Retrieved May 24, 2017.

U.S. Department of Veterans Affairs (VA). (2016). Women Veterans Population Fact Sheet. October 20. www.gov/WomenVeteransPopulationFactSheet.pdf. Retrieved March 26, 2017.

U.S. Department of Veterans Affairs (VA). (2016b). *Women Veterans and Homelessness*. Homeless Evidence and Research Roundtable Serves VA National Center on Homelessness Among Veterans. July. www.va.gov/HOMELESS/nchav/docs/HERS-Womens-Proceedings.pdf. Retrieved February 6, 2017.

U.S. Department of Veterans Affairs (VA). (2017). *VA Report: The Past, Present and Future of Women Veterans*. Women Veterans Report. February. www.womenvetsusa.org. Retrieved March 25, 2017.

Veterans Authority (VA). (n.d.). Who Is a Veteran? The Legal Definition. www.va.org. Retrieved May 26, 2017.

Walker, J.A., and Borbely, J.M. (2014). *BLS Spotlight on Statistics: Women Veterans in the Labor Force*. Washington, DC: U.S. Department of Labor, Bureau of Labor Statistics.

Women's Bureau. (n.d.). *Women Veterans Profile*. Issue Brief. U.S. Department of Labor. www.dol.gov/women_veterans_profile.pdf. Retrieved March 23, 2017.

Women's Bureau. (2015). *Women Veterans Profile for 2013*. U.S. Department of Labor. www.dol.gov/women_veterans_profile.pdf. Retrieved February 24, 2017.

Zinzow, H.M., Grubaugh, A.L., Fruch, B.C., and Magruder, K.M. (2008). Sexual Assault, Mental Health and Service Use among Male and Female Veterans Seen in Veterans Affairs Primary Care Clinics: A Multi-Site Study. *Psychiatry Research*, 159, 226–236.

Zoli, C., Maury, D., and Fay, D. (2015). *Missing Perspectives: Servicemembers' Transition from Service to Civilian Life*. Institute for Veterans and Military Families, Syracuse University. https://surface.syr.edu/ivmf. Retrieved March 28, 2017.

8 The Selective Service Act

It is estimated that less than 1 percent of the population has served in the military (Miles 2011, Office of the Deputy Assistant Secretary of Defense 2014, Pew Research Center 2011). As a result, the military experience is far removed from the average American citizen. One of the chief reasons for this civilian–military divide is the inception of the All-Volunteer Force (AVF) and the Selective Service System, which replaced the conscription or draft of the military force in 1973 (Rostker 2006a, 2006b). Although the AVF has played a significant role in increasing the professionalism of its service members, and in modernizing the U.S. fighting force, several constraints have been placed upon the equal and full participation of citizens (Fenner 1998).

During the spring of 2016, the topic of the nation's conscription and Selective Service System was revisited by both houses of the Congressional Armed Services Committees when the question of including women in the Selective Service System was discussed (Demirijan 2016, Kheel 2016b). Although there were numerous Congressional representatives and senators who supported this move, that is for women's inclusion into the Selective Service System like their male peers, the issue drew strident opposition from several elected officials and others in socially conservative constituencies and grassroots organizations (Center for Military Readiness 2016, Concerned Women for America (CWA) 2016, Family Research Council 2016).

Given this controversy, the issue was tabled for discussion at a later date as per the National Defense Authorization Act (NDAA) for fiscal year 2017 (Shane 2016, 114th Congress 2016a, 2016b). The Secretary of Defense was due to present to both Congressional committees on July 1, 2017 about the merits of the current Selective Service System as well as a prospective National Service Program whereby every citizen would be expected to serve a compulsory term in some component of the public sector: the U.S. government, military, public agency or nongovernmental organization (NGO) (114th Congress 2016b).

This part of the chapter essentially provides an overview of the current Selective Service System as well as the AVF system in place, exploring some of the enablers and barriers to the success of both programs in terms of full and equitable inclusion and participation of all American citizens. The discussion then concludes with the most recent debate in the U.S. Senate about sustaining the Selective Service System.

Current Selective Service System

Currently, the U.S. law of conscription gives the president the power to draft male citizens during a time of war (Rostker 2006b). The law mandates that men living in the U.S. between the ages of 18 and 25, born on or after January 1, 1960, must register for selective service. In addition to natural born male U.S. citizens, those required to register include, but are not limited to, permanent residents (green card holders), refugees, asylum seekers, dual citizens, undocumented immigrants, physically or mentally handicapped individuals who are able to function with or without assistance, and U.S. citizens or immigrants who are born male but changed their gender to female (Selective Service System 2017b). The *exceptions* to selective service registration include, but are not limited to (Selective Service System 2017b, 2017c):

a   Men over 26 years old (born 1960 and after)
b   Men 18–25 who are:
    i   Active duty military
    ii Cadets/Midshipmen at military service/Coast Guard academies
    iii Seasonal agricultural workers (H-2A Visa)
    iv Incarcerated, hospitalized (medical reasons), or institutionalized in a residence
c   Women
d   Transgender individuals who were born female and have changed their gender to male

According to the Selective Service System, eligible males who fail to register are unable to access state and federal benefits, and opportunities such as financial aid for school, federal and state employment, federal job security clearances for contractors, and U.S. citizenship for immigrants. Failure to register or noncompliance with the Military Selective Service Act is considered a felony with a fine of up to $250,000, or a prison term of up to five years (Selective Service System 2017b). In an effort to mainstream the selective service registration, some states have used the driver licensing process as a way to facilitate this process (Selective Service System 2017c).

Civic Responsibility, Conscription and the Evolution of the All-Volunteer Force

Of the four-pronged prerequisites for citizenship, it is the last, or the obligation for military service, that has been the most contentious in leveling the playing field for women. This service involves risking one's life in the service of one's country but this requirement has proven to be illusive for women (Kerber 1993). Consequently, the brunt of this responsibility has been an uneven burden for American men, although this is not to say, though not an obligation, that women have not served, many succumbing to the same risk of life as men. Yet, it is this very distinction that makes clear that given this exemption, the obligation for military service has varied according to gender, thus depriving women, like men, of the full panoply of what it means as citizens to serve their country. It is within the context of this gendering and the rationale for and where the Equal Rights Amendment (ERA) would further address the limitations for women in meeting the full and ultimate prerequisite for citizenship and also leveraging women's inclusion into the Selective Service System as one of the mechanisms for doing so. As Kerber (1993) put it, women were never part of the discourse by the founding generations of the American public. If anything, a woman's identity was tied through marriage to that of her husband. For this union, it was implicit that for protection, the woman accepted that any presumed liberty, including her identity as a citizen, was to be subordinated to control by her husband. Consider that this was a time when women could not even own property. Women lacked independent and free will over their affairs, including their own bodies to which their husbands had full access for both sex and punishment (Tapping et al. 1998). Using this concept, exclaims Pateman (1988), men became free agents while women entered into a social contract for their husbands to represent them in all affairs given marriage. Since women, through their husbands, for example, functioned in a secondary role, the right to bear arms was not theirs and neither was the responsibility of citizenship. The Second Amendment's reference to people and citizens is deliberately vague with respect to gender (Kerber 1993).

The subject of a woman's right to bear arms was never raised, nor was it much of a subject of discourse until the U.S. Supreme Court's decision in *United States v. Schwimmer, 1928*. A pacifist, Rosika Schwimmer applied for naturalization of citizenship for the U.S. (Kerber 1993). To the question '[i]f necessary, are you willing to take up arms in defense of this country?' (Kerber 1993, p.108), Schwimmer replied 'no.' It did not matter to the Court that at the time of her application Schwimmer was already 50 years old; even if she had responded affirmatively, the matter would have been moot. Still, the High Court denied her citizenship, reasoning that 'it is the duty of citizens by force of arms to defend our government against all enemies whenever necessity arises as a fundamental principle of the Constitution' (Kerber 1993, p.95). Subsequently, during the Vietnam Conflict, anti-war sentiments, together with those who dodged the draft, those who requested and were granted deferments, and those who joined the National Guard to avoid serving in Vietnam, rendered loyalty to country and the willingness to die for it a misplaced federal policy (Janowitz 1983). Further, not long after that not only did the conscription of citizens for military duty end but it marked the advent of the AVF in 1973. Nevertheless, women have always been part of the military landscape (Kerber 1980, Holm 1992, Grant DePauw 1998, Harris 2015).

President Woodrow Wilson became an ardent proponent of American conscription during World War I since at the time the country only had a small army of approximately 100,000 men. Consequently, Congress passed the Selective Service Act, requiring that all men in the U.S. between 21 years and 30 years of age register for military service (History Channel 2017, Yockelson 1998). Of the 24 million registered under the Selective Service Act, almost 60 percent of the 4.8 million who served in World War I were drafted for military service (History Channel 2017, Yockelson 1998).

However, it was not until World War II and with the passing of the Women's Armed Services Integration Act in 1948 that women were legally accepted into and seen to have a place in the U.S. military (Holm 1992), even as the War Department debated how to restructure the Selective Service System. The exemplary performance of military women so moved President Dwight Eisenhower that he predicted that it would only take another war before women would be a conscripted force in the military as men were (Kerber 1993).

Despite this bold prediction by the president, it was understood then and regrettably this conviction still prevails, that to have women in the military is to 'profoundly disturb the sexual order' (Kerber 1993, p.109), as reservations remain about women and their obligation for military service. Women were not only exempt from combat duty, but they were restricted in the number who could be recruited and the rank that could be achieved. It was not until 1967 that a woman was placed into a command position and women secured fewer benefits than men of equal and lower ranks in the military. Even the female pilots of the Women Airforce Service Pilots (WASPs) could neither ferry men as passengers nor share the cockpit of an airplane with a man (Hartmann 1982). Likewise, women could not supervise men, although the Marine Corps concocted a brilliant scheme to circumvent this requirement by using the rationale that as long as the orders for duty originated from a male supervisor, which was invariably the case, then the rule did not apply.

Up until the 1960s, the system and practice of conscription was regarded as socially acceptable (Rostker 2006a). However, the draft became increasingly controversial and polarizing for the following five reasons: 1) increased and ongoing discipline problems from draftees in Vietnam; 2) growing unpopularity of the Vietnam Conflict; 3) the draft selection was viewed as inequitable (lower-income individuals have less access to deferments than their more privileged counterparts); 4) using volunteers could be cost effective; and 5) the draft was becoming less 'universal' as there were more draft-aged men available who surpassed the military needs at the time (Rostker 2006a).

Following demobilization from the Vietnam Conflict, the Central All-Volunteer Task Force was charged with examining the impact of an all-voluntary force (Kerber 1993). The task force anticipated severe shortfalls in male recruitment for up to five years but, coupled with the passing of the ERA, it recommended a robust recruitment of women into the new military along with providing female personnel in the military with the same complement of benefits enjoyed by men in the military. Nontraditional jobs and assignments that were previously held by men were also extended to women. It was generally understood that, unlike previous wars, women would no longer be considered back fills to enable men to do their jobs but that they themselves would be performing the jobs just as men in the service of the military. The military also viewed the female recruit as an asset. Women were less inclined than their male counterparts to engage in aberrant behaviors that were anti-authoritarian, for instance (Holm 1992). They were less likely to go AWOL (absent without leave) and were not violent (Kerber 1993). Women were also more cost effective to recruit and remained longer in the military (Holm 1992). A holdover from previous wars for the stringent entrance requirements for women resulted in a more educated female workforce who performed well in their jobs.

As early as 1981, the Department of Defense (DoD) requested Congress render the combat exclusion policy invalid (Kerber 1993). However, Congress rejected this request. Further, what constituted the combat exclusion policy and in turn those positions that were defined as combat became fluid and arbitrary, leading Major General Jeanne Holm, then the highest-ranking woman in the military, to observe that '[i]f all the women were discharged tomorrow, most of the distinctions would be abandoned the day after' (Stiehm 1989). In other words, these subjective and moving markers were not only ways of keeping women out of combat by establishing an illogical rationale for this purpose but such justifications were now only being proffered because the military found itself in the enviable position of having a healthy workforce of women. Should the situation change, as Major General Holm pointed out, all bets would have been off, leading to the immediate repeal of the combat exclusion policy.

In 1980, President Jimmy Carter offered a universal draft registration that women, like men, would register into the system by age 18 (Kerber 1993). It is important to note here that in many ways President Carter might have been a man ahead of his time as he was a fervent opponent of doing gender (Kerber 1993) – that is, holding fast to prescribed roles in organizations according to gender. The president was astute in recognizing what he characterized as an inordinate doling out of veteran benefits at all levels of the federal government and even by the states, as well as the use of various preferences for veterans in not only civil service examinations but the rewarding of as much as ten points on such examinations which provided veterans with an unfair advantage over other applicants. However, more importantly, veterans were disproportionately men, which also provided them with vast economic advantages. Accordingly, given the uneven allocation of benefits, men as veterans had economic leverage over the few women veterans – that is, if they were brave enough to go against the conventions of the time by claiming their benefits as veterans. The president felt strongly that the shifting society warranted women's inclusion into the Selective Service System. Further, said the president:

> My decision to register women is a recognition of the reality that both women and men are working members of our society. It confirms what is already obvious ... that women are now providing all types of skills in every profession. The military should be no exception. In fact, there are already 150,000 women serving in our armed forces today ... There is no distinction possible, on the basis of ability or performance, that would allow me to exclude women from an obligation to register.
> (Kerber 1993, p.116)

However, in light of Congress's reluctance to recognize women, like men, as combatants, President Carter compromised by succumbing to women's exemption from combat. What was illuminating about the president's proposal though was his desire to provide women with all of the benefits of citizenship by ensuring that legally, through the Selective Service System, women accepted the responsibility of citizenship. However, the president went even further by making the case for passing the ERA as yet another medium to guarantee not just the responsibility of citizenship to women but their rights thereof that would translate into women's equal standing for obligation to military service just like men. Said President Carter, 'Equal obligations deserve equal rights' (Kerber 1993). Notwithstanding the perceived risks of full citizenship and Congress's reticence to grant women the susceptibility to the risks of combat, the president was measured, even careful, in making the nexus between women's inclusion into a universal draft and women's equity, yet exemption from combat, which he equated to women's utility by the military as the institution saw fit owing to its changing needs (Kerber 1993). Additionally, the president argued that even men's registration into the Selective Service System does not guarantee that they would ever see combat. He utilized a similar compelling argument for women's inclusion in that in doing so, it provided the military and by extension the country, with an invaluable resource that need not mean that women would ever witness combat duty. In fact, the president reasoned that such consideration could be tabled later for future discussions.

Siding with the president but unlike the president by taking an all or none stance, Senator Nancy Kassenbaum (R-KS) took to the Senate floor to urge through a resolution for women's compulsory registration into the Selective Service System and without exemption from combat duty (Kerber 1993). However, opponents remained unconvinced and with the ERA on the brink of passing, legislators on both sides of the aisle succumbed to the most visceral appeal to human emotion with such fear-mongering as that 'innocent young girls' (Kerber 1993, p.118) were to become pawns of the military only to be brutalized. Senator Sam Ervin (D-NC), following the Senate's passage of the ERA, read a letter aloud from one of his constituents, a mother, who said: 'I am ashamed and terrified at what the future holds for my three little girls. Will my shy, sweet Tommy be drafted in six years? So modest I can't even see her undress. Oh God! I can't stand it. I just can't bear it' (Kerber 1999, p.283). The word 'sex' was effectively sprinkled throughout the debate to conjure up images of innocent 'girls,' not women, being manhandled or robbed of their innocence or without the protection of their parents to save them from such brutality. Opponents essentially laced these disturbing, albeit false images, throughout the narrative about women's lost innocence should the ERA be passed and, moreover, women's inclusion into the Selective Service System would only magnify the likelihood of this being realized. Even then an unevolved self-described feminist, Congresswoman Patricia Schroeder (D-CO), balked at the idea of drafting women by cynically likening such overtures to the squandering of money that could be more suitably earmarked for fighting the Russians (Kerber 1993).

Judy Goldsmith of the National Organization for Women (NOW) made an impassioned plea for women's inclusion into the Selective Service System within conditions such as exemption from combat:

> Now believes they must include women. As a matter of fairness and equity ... Any registration or draft that excluded females would be challenged as an unconstitutional denial of rights under the Fifth Amendment.
> (Testimony of Judy Goldsmith, in Kerber 1993, p.120)

Foremost, NOW and Goldsmith were focused on the economic benefits as veterans that women's inclusion into the Selective Service System would afford them (Kerber, 1993). Goldsmith believed that the coupling of the women's draft into military service but more importantly to secure the status as veterans was key to women's first-class citizenship, for as veterans, preferences were implicit. This designation alone would open up so many doors for women by putting them on the same playing field as men. Again, the economic component of this classification as veterans was crucial in procuring pay parity for women and by association a more stable financial footing with men. Even more critical, Goldsmith implored, was that an exemption from the Selective Service System would rob women, unlike men, of sharing in the decision making of the country's standing and future. Besides, continued Goldsmith,

> Discrimination against women in the military depresses opportunities, career paths, training, and benefits for women. The military provides thousands of jobs, training programs, and educational opportunities

which are, for the most part, presently closed to women. Military pay, which is on the average some 40 percent higher than female civilian pay could be the only way out of poverty for countless young women. Restrictions on women in the military, far from protecting them, serve to continue their second class citizenship, pay and opportunity. And this discrimination exercised by the military affects women's lives, and employment opportunities and wages throughout their entire work lives because of veterans preferences.

(Kerber 1993, p.120)

Goldsmith's argument for women's inclusion into the Selective Service System was a powerful one, but perhaps even more evocative were the social implications for its denial, as her plea applied directly, oddly enough, to the rampant sexual assault against women in the military today, if not the repercussions for the larger American society. Goldsmith maintained that women's inclusion in combat would be far reaching as such training would provide them with the confidence that women as a group need without awaiting the protection of men (Kerber 1993). Further, the knowledge by men that women were equally trained for combat would render women less vulnerable as targets for sexual assault. Goldsmith invoked the training of a woman Marine as the ultimate exemplar – the imprimatur, if you will – of the implications for women, society and the country.

However, partly owing to the times and partly or perhaps overwhelmingly to the influences of the Judeo-Christian ethos, the entrenched prescribed roles for women resonated most with Congress, along with such justifications as that of Kathleen Teague as to the fungibility of these roles in that they are not one and the same and are therefore not fungible (Kerber 1993). Quintessentially, women are not fungible with men. Teague encapsulated the overriding attitude of the anti-ERA and thus the anti-Selective Service System for women's inclusion when she derided the advocates of these policies by concluding that 'just because a handful of women, unhappy with their gender, want to be treated like men' (Kerber 1993, p.122) does not provide a reasonable case that all women are similarly situated, nor should they be similarly treated.

What is interesting, though, is that following President Carter's proposal that women should be included into the Selective Service System under a universal draft in 1980 and Congress's failure to approve the president's proposal thereby validating the male-only draft system, *Goldberg v. Rostker et al., 1980* was in litigation. Bernard Rostker was the director of the Military Selective Service System and Robert Goldberg, the litigant, challenged the federal government's male-only draft registration system as unconstitutional and in violation of the Equal Protection Clause of the Fifth Amendment of the U.S. Constitution (Oyez.com n.d.). The federal district court concurred with the litigants that the policy was illegal, for as per the court, 'classifications based upon gender, not unlike those based upon race, have traditionally been the touchstone for pervasive and subtle discrimination' (Kerber 1993, *Goldberg v. Rostker et al.* 1980). More importantly, the district court based the burden on the federal government to justify that women's exclusion from the Selective Service System fulfills an important government interest. As per the court, it was in no mood to accept archaic definitions of gender roles that amounted to an expedient tool to discriminate against one group given gender (Oyez.com n.d.). The court was explicit in its ruling that such decisions should not deliberately consign women to a subordinate status. Said the court:

> It is incongruous that Congress believes on the one hand that it substantially enhances national defense to constantly expand the utilization of women in the military, and on the other hand endorses legislation excluding women from the pool of registrants available for induction. Congress allocates funds so that the military can use and actively seek more female recruits but nonetheless asserts that there is justification for excluding females from selective service.
> (Kerber 1993, p.123)

In essence, according to the court, Congress was speaking from both sides of its mouth and wanted to have it both ways. The court was explicit in its ruling when it declared that the Military Selective Service System for male-only registration for the draft was in clear violation of the Fifth Amendment (Kerber 1993). However, upon appeal, the U.S. Supreme Court, in a 6–3 ruling, reversed the lower court's decision by upholding that such a policy 'was not "the accidental by-product" of a traditional way of thinking about females' (Oyez.com n.d.). Therefore, the male-only draft policy was not in violation of the Fifth Amendment's Due Process Clause. Moreover, said the Court, men and women are not 'similarly situated' with respect to the draft registration.

It is of significance that this ruling was rendered at a time when the High Court was all-male. Yet more striking, was that of the three dissenting justices, the only African American, Thurgood Marshall, saw it fitting to submit a stinging indictment of the Court that the decision in itself was offensive to the Constitution (Kerber 1993). Justice Marshall assailed the ruling as a rebuke against women's civic responsibility and, more troubling, that the Court skirted its obligation of upholding its responsibility to the Constitution. Justice Marshall concluded that preserving a male-only draft registration system was tantamount to 'categorically exclud[ing] women from a fundamental civic obligation' (Kerber 1993, p.124).

Consequently, the Selective Service System was implemented in tandem with the creation of the AVF, which was signed into law by President Richard Nixon in 1971, and included a two-year transition period (Rostker 2006a). The AVF can be considered successful in that it attracted a higher quality of recruits (IQ scores and number of high school graduates), and promoted the concept of military service careerists.

Today, careerists make up over 50 percent of the active duty military, as opposed to 40 percent during the draft (Rostker 2006b). In turn, this move increased the overall professionalization of the armed forces which has sustained the defense of the U.S. for almost 45 years in both peacetime and wartime (Rostker 2006a).

The past and continued success of the conscription system has been contingent upon four factors: 1) support from the president and Secretary of Defense; 2) robust marketing program development to attract quality military recruits; 3) financial resources to keep the military as a competitive employer; and 4) use of empirical and evidence-based data in policy and decision making to continuously evaluate and adapt AVF policies (Rostker 2006a).

Barriers to Full Citizen Participation

Through the transition from a conscripted military to a combined AVF and supplementary selective service system, the military has significantly improved the nation's defense and the quality of its personnel (Rostker 2006a, 2006b). However, five major policies have served as barriers to true universal participation and citizen engagement (Allsep 2013, Belkin 2012, Cheh 1993, Evans 2003, Fenner 1998). They are: 1) racial segregation; 2) the combat exclusion policy; 3) Don't Ask, Don't Tell, Don't Pursue; 4) women's equality; and 5) selective service exceptions to registration. The common thread that links these four legislative policies is that the military service archetype has been rooted in identifying white, heterosexual males as the warrior standard, while women, homosexuals and other minorities are relegated to a secondary, 'other' status (Allsep 2013, Belkin 2012, Cheh 1993, Evans 2003, Fenner 1998).

A key element that has been missing in the countless debates over the suitability of 'the other' is defining what the expectations and responsibilities of a fully engaged U.S. citizen look like, and who is worthy of being called a citizen (Cheh 1993, Fenner 1998). Consider the following questions. Is there one social demographic or group more worthy of earning their right to be a fully engaged citizen than others? Is there one group that has the monopoly on the desire to defend their country? If so, then who (Fenner 1998)? This discussion and its ensuing questions are what should have been at the heart of every discussion behind increasing the quality of our national defense (Fenner 1998).

Current State of the Selective Service System

Despite the multiple deployments and increased operational tempo of our service members since September 11, 2001, retention in the military has remained ourstorically high, although overall military enlistments have decreased (Rostker 2006b). The nation's preference is still to maintain an AVF, and the future of the volunteer military is being tested by the ongoing war on terror in Southwest Asia (Demirijan 2016, Rostker 2006a). As such, a debate revisiting the current Selective Service System, its effectiveness, and its value to our nation's defense is underway (Demirijan 2016, Kheel 2016a, Shane 2016, 114th Congress 2016b).

Last year the Senate Armed Forces Committee voted to include women into the selective service registration (Demirijan 2016). HR 4478, the amendment proposed by Congressman Hunter Duncan (R-CA 50th District), called for women to be included into the Selective Service System as a cynical attempt to initiate a debate about women (and oppose them) in combat roles. The plan backfired as the amendment was passed by the House and Senate Armed Services Committees as there was no longer being any justification for excluding women from the mandatory Military Selective Service Act registry as their male peers (Demirijan 2016).

There still remains resistance to women being included in the draft (114th Congress 2016a) by many elected officials who are opposed to women's formal inclusion into combat arms role, and conservative grassroots and legislative advocacy organizations like the CWA, Family Research Council, Heritage Action, and the Center for Military Readiness (CWA 2016, Family Research Council 2016, Kheel 2016a, Shane 2016, 114th Congress 2016a, 2016b, Center for Military Readiness 2016). The provision of the NDAA, including women's inclusion into the Selective Service System, had been part of earlier drafts which passed the Congressional Armed Services Committees (Shane 2016). However, strong conservative opposition to the provision resulted in its exclusion from the final draft. Instead, a review of the entire Selective Service System has been called for cost effectiveness and efficacy of future military draft (Kheel 2016a, Shane 2016). Currently, this legislation, to include women in the draft, is under review as per Section 553 of the 2017 NDAA (Kheel 2016a, 114th Congress 2016a, 2016b).

As per the NDAA, the Secretary of Defense is tasked with submitting a report no later than July 1, 2017 to the Congressional Armed Services Committees and to the National Commission on Military, National and Public Service, to evaluate the merits or benefits of the current Selective Service System, specifically in the areas of: 1) aiding military recruiting; 2) serving as a deterrent to potential U.S. enemies; 3) expanding the system to include women, and its impact; and 4) eliminating focus on mass mobilization for primarily combat troops to a system that focuses on mobilization of all military occupational specialties (and the extent to which such change would impact the need for both male and female inductees), as well as an analysis of the DoD's personnel needs in the event of an emergency requiring mass mobilization, to include critical skills that would be needed (e.g., medical and engineering) (114th Congress 2016b, Section 553).

Additionally, in Section 553, an analysis is called for to evaluate National Service as an option for the mobilization of all citizens in the event of a national emergency. This would include not only military but civilian jobs in critical occupations in government, public agencies, and nongovernmental organizations (114th Congress 2016b, Section 553). Finally, the comptroller general was scheduled to submit to the Congressional Armed Services Committees to review DoD procedures evaluating selective service requirements by December 2017 (114th Congress 2016b, Section 552).

Conclusion

For 35 years of America's 241 years as a republic, the country has had a system of military conscription in place (Rostker 2006a). The 1973 transition from a conscripted military to an all-volunteer force was one of the most ourstorical milestones to positively impact the quality of military recruits and the overall professionalization of the armed forces (Rostker 2006b). The supplementary Selective Service System currently in existence provides a viable contingency plan for a national emergency.

However, the operational effectiveness of the Selective Service System has been questioned and widely criticized for not being authentically equitable by favoring the conscripted service of lower-income men from marginalized communities who have fewer opportunities for deferment over their privileged peers from wealthier communities (Rostker 2006b). As well, women have been deliberately excluded from the Selective Service System given the condition for combat duty. The combat exclusion policy was to further codify this exclusion. While the combat exclusion policy was repealed in early 2013 to allow women to serve in all military occupations, including in direct combat, doing so has revived the debate about whether or not to include women in the Selective Service System registration, as is the case for men (Demirijan 2016, Shane 2016). As a result, the DoD is tasked with preparing an assessment of the continued viability of the Selective Service System, to include, but not be limited to, weighing the benefits of drafting women, by July 2017 (114th Congress 2016a). The DoD is also tasked with preparing a triadic system of universal national service (military, government or public agency) for development and consideration in the event of a national emergency (114th Congress 2016b).

This is a déjà vu where during peacetime, this time following two simultaneous wars, the country once again deliberates as to whether or not to build upon women's previous gains in the quest to bear arms as part of military service, a fundamental right and obligation of citizenship. This remains a perpetual source of contention for the country and one that calls into question women's citizenship. Only when women, as called for by the conditions of the repeal of the combat exclusion policy along with their inclusion into the Selective Service System, are given the right and obligation to bear arms as do men, will they be able to claim full citizenship and in turn full agency into this democratic society.

Bibliography

114th Congress, 2nd session. (2016a, February 4). H.R. 4478, 'Draft America's Daughters Act of 2016', Committee on Armed Services. United States Congress. www.congress.gov/bill/114th-congress/house-bill/4478. Retrieved March 19, 2017.

114th Congress, 2nd session. (2016b, April 12). Sec 552. Preliminary Report on Purpose and Utility of Registration System Under Military Selective Service Act. H.R.2943 -National Defense Authorization Act for Fiscal Year 2017. www.congress.gov/bill/114th-congress/senate-bill/2943. Retrieved March 19, 2017.

Allsep, L.M. (2013). The Myth of the Warrior: Martial Masculinity and the End of Don't Ask, Don't Tell. *Journal of Homosexuality*, 60, 381–400. doi: doi:10.1080/00918369.2013.744928.

Belkin, A. (2012). *Bring Me Men: Military Masculinity and the Benign Facade of American Empire, 1898–2001*. New York, NY: Columbia University Press.

Center for Military Readiness (CMR). (2016). McCain Establishes National Commission Likely to Promote His Goals: 'Draft American's Daughters' Registration and Mandatory Military, National, or Public Service. December 14. www.cmrlink.org/content/home/37780/mccain_establishes_national commission_likely_to_promote_his_goals_draft_america_s_daughters_registration_and_mandatory_military_national_or_public_service. Retrieved March 19, 2017.

Cheh, M.M. (1993). Essay on VMI and Military Service: Yes, We Do Have to Be Equal Together. *Wash. & Lee L. Rev.*, 50, 49.

Concerned Women for America (CWA). (2016). Don't Draft Our Daughters! August 15. http://concernedwomen.org/dont-draft-our-daughters/. Retrieved March 19, 2017.

Demirijan, K. (2016). Key Senate Panel Endorses Women in the Draft, Making Policy Change More Likely. *Washington Post*. May 14. Washington, DC. www.washingtonpost.com/news/powerpost/wp/2016/05/14/key-senate-panel-endorses-women-in-the-draft-making-policy-change-more-likely/. Retrieved June 2, 2016.

Evans, R. (2003). *A History of the Service of Ethnic Minorities in the U.S. Armed Forces*. Santa Barbara, California. http://archive.palmcenter.org/files/active/0/Evans_MinorityInt_200306.pdf. Retrieved July 5, 2016.

Family Research Council (FRC). (2016). These Boots Are Made for ... Fighting? May 24. www.frc.org/updatearticle/20160524/boots-fighting. March 19, 2017.

Fenner, L. (1998). EitherYou Need These Women or You Do Not: Informing the Debate on Military Service and Citizenship. *Gender Issues*, 16, 3, 5. doi:10.1007/s12147-998-0020-2.

Grant DePauw, L. (1998). *Battle Cries and Lullabies. Women in War from Prehistory to the Present*. Norman, OK: University of Oklahoma Press.

Harris, G.L.A. (2015). *Living Legends and Full Agency: Implications of Repealing the Combat Exclusion Policy*. New York, NY: Taylor & Francis Group, a division of CRC Press.

Hartmann, S.M. (1982). *The Homefront and Beyond: American Women in the 1940s*. Woodbridge, CT: Twayne Publishers.

History Channel. (2017). This Day in History: May 18, 1917: U.S. Congress Passes Selective Service Act. www.history.com/this-day-in-history/u-s-congress-passes-selective-service-act. Retrieved March 19, 2017.

Holm, J. (1992). *Women in the Military. An Unfinished Revolution*. Revised Edition. Novato, CA: Presidio Press.

Janowitz, M. (1983). *The Reconstruction of Patriotism: Education for Civic Consciousness*. Chicago, IL: University of Chicago Press.

Kerber, L.K. (1980). *Women of the Republic: Intellect and Ideology in Revolutionary America*. Chapel Hill, NC: University of North Carolina Press.

Kerber, L.K. (1993). 'A Constitutional Right to Be Treated Like Ladies': Women, Civic Obligations and Military Service. *The University of Chicago Law School Roundtable*, 1, 1, Article 15, 95–128.

Kerber, L.K. (1999). *No Constitutional Right to Be Ladies: Women and the Obligation of Citizenship*. New York, NY: Hill and Wang Publishers, a division of Farrar, Strauss and Giroux.

Kheel, R. (2016a, November 29). House, Senate Finalize Annual Defense Policy Bill. *Hill*. http://thehill.com/policy/defense/307968-house-senate-finalize-annual-defense-policy-bill. Retrieved March 19, 2017.

Kheel, R. (2016b, November 29). Congress Drops Plans to Make Women Register for the Draft. *Hill*. http://thehill.com/policy/defense/308014-congress-drops-plans-to-make-women-register-for-draft. Retrieved March 19, 2017.

Miles, D. (2011). *Survey Shows Growing Gap between Civilians, Military*. Washington, DC: American Forces Press Service. http://archive.defense.gov/news/newsarticle.aspx?id=66253. Retrieved November 24, 2015.

Office of the Deputy Assistant Secretary of Defense. (2014). 2014 Demographics: Profile of the Military Community. http://download.militaryonesource.mil/12038/MOS/Reports/2014-Demographics-Report.pdf. Retrieved March 19, 2017.

Oyez.com. (n.d.). *Rostker v. Goldberg 1981*. www.oyez.org/cases/1980/80-251. Retrieved July 22, 2017.

Pateman, C. (1988). *The Sexual Contract*. Stanford, CA: Stanford University Press.

Pew Research Center Social and Demographic Trends. (2011). *The Military-Civilian Gap: War and Sacrifice in the Post-9/11 Era*. Washington, DC. www.pewsocialtrends.org/2011/10/05/war-and-sacrifice-in-the-post-911-era/. Retrieved March 19, 2017.

Rostker, B. (2006a). *The Evolution of the All-Volunteer Force*. Santa Monica, CA: RAND Corporation. www.rand.org/pubs/research_briefs/RB9195.html. Retrieved December 28, 2016.

Rostker, B. (2006b). *I Want You! The Evolution of the All-Volunteer Force*. Santa Monica, CA: RAND Corporation. www.rand.org/pubs/monographs/MG265.html. Retrieved December 28, 2016.

Selective Service System (2017a). Benefits and Penalties. www.sss.gov/Registration-Info/Who-Registration and www.sss.gov/Portals/0/PDFs/WhoMustRegisterChart.pdf. Retrieved March 19, 2017.

Selective Service System (2017b). Who Must Register? www.sss.gov/Registration-Info/Who-Registration. Retrieved March 19, 2017.

Selective Service System (2017c). State/Commonwealth and Territory Legislation. www.sss.gov/Registration/State-Commonwealth-Legislation. Retrieved March 19, 2017.

Selective Service System (2017d). Women and the Draft. www.sss.gov/Registration/Women-And-Draft. Retrieved March 19, 2017.

Shane, L. (2016). Congress Drops Plans to Make Women Register for the Draft. *Military Times*, November 29. www.militarytimes.com/articles/ndaa-final-draft-pay-end-strength. Retrieved July 3, 2016.

Stiehm, J. (1989). *Arms and the Enlisted Woman*. Philadelphia, PA: Temple University Press.

Tapping, R., Parker, A.J., and Baldwin, C.E. (1998). *The Law of Baron and Femme, Of Parent and Child, Guardian and Ward*. 3rd Edition. Clark, NJ: Reprinted by the Law Book Exchange, Ltd.

Yockelson, M. (1998). They Answered the Call: Military Service During World War One, 1917–1919. *National Archives*, 30, 3. www.archives.gov/publications/prologue/1998/fall/military-service-in-world-war-one.html. Retrieved March 19, 2017.

9 The Equal Rights Amendment
At the Crossroads of Defining Women's Citizenship

Whether or not the country is willing to acknowledge it, in its original form the framers of the U.S. Constitution deliberately set out to exclude certain demographic groups within the new republic's population as unworthy of the recognition of citizenship. Debate on this point is at best naïve or woefully ignorant and at worst dubious, given that these groups were absent from the original version of the document. Yet, these exclusions were nonetheless the reality and revealed much about the mores of the time, albeit from the unilateral perspective of rich white male colonialists. After all, these so-called founding fathers were of self-appointed privileged blue blood who had derived their material wealth upon the backs of the less privileged, notably through the systematic exploitation and enslavement of one group, the Africans and their descendants, while committing genocide on another group, the Native Peoples, the first Americans and the wholesale pilfering of their lands. One can only then speculate that these predatory behaviors undoubtedly resulted in the likelihood that most, if not all, of the framers were themselves slave owners. One, Thomas Jefferson, the chief architect of the Declaration of Independence (Pratkanis and Turner 1999, Harris 2010), owned approximately 200 human beings even as he hypocritically spouted the rhetoric of liberty and equality for all, all the while repeatedly and sexually violating one of his slaves, Sally Hemmings, then a child, who bore at least seven children as a result of these molestations (History.com n.d., Harris 2010). Jefferson defiled Hemmings continuously for some 37 years whilst simultaneously decrying the act as not only immoral but as he found the Negro to be subhuman (Pratkanis and Turner 1999). Publicly, Jefferson cloaked his true sentiments by denouncing slavery as inherently racist yet the institution represented the very source from which he derived his stolen wealth.

At the time black women were collectively at the margins of American society at multiple levels, given race, gender and class as slaves. No wonder, as Jefferson wrote that while on one hand 'All men are created equal' (excerpt from the Declaration of Independence as cited in Held et al. 1997, p.113), 'were our state a pure democracy, there would still be excluded from our deliberations ... women, who, to prevent depravation of morals and ambiguity of issues, should not mix promiscuously in gatherings of men.' In essence, the republic's founding and principles by way of the U.S. Constitution codified from the beginning and conferred on even white women a second-class status or that which is subordinate to white men. The Equal Rights Amendment (ERA), as was the 19th Amendment in granting women suffrage, is yet another legal attempt to close the chasm caused by the ill considerations of the white male framers of the Constitution, to remedy for past omissions.

As a result, both African Americans and women have had a fundamentally different and tenuous relationship with the sovereign because that relationship was both a condition and function of race and gender (Kerber 1993). For example, while the famous adage 'taxation without representation' (p.96) is frequently invoked, blacks were deliberately disenfranchised through the outright denial of representation even as they were compelled to pay taxes (Kerber 1992). They were also not called upon to serve on juries although they had already achieved the right to vote by way of the 15th Amendment. It was not until 1966, or following the passing of the Jury Reform Act, that African Americans were allowed to serve on juries, given blatant race discrimination. Similarly, women were not granted universal suffrage until the 19th Amendment. Still, women were exempt from jury duty, considered an obligation of citizenship for men but a privilege to serve for women (Alschuler 1989). Finally, in 1975, women's names were added as an obligation, yet were not a privilege of service or even citizenship at this point.

This chapter introduces a current status report about women in the U.S. and their place on the world stage as it pertains to equality, and provides an overview of the ERA, including the obstacles to its passage, and strategies in place to pass the amendment. In addition, the chapter discusses the nexus between the ERA and the Selective Service Act and in turn the Selective Service System, together with the contentious debates that ensued in advancing the narrative for women's citizenship via military service but in the end without the benefit of full citizenship. The chapter closes with the implications of not passing the ERA and women's continued exclusion from the Selective Service System.

The passage of Title VII of the Civil Rights Act of 1964, the 2009 Lilly Ledbetter Act and the 2013 lifting of the combat exclusion policy for women in the military, represent examples of ourstorically significant events in the advancement of women's equality in the U.S. (U.S. Equal Employment Opportunity Commission n.d., Wire Reporters 2015). However, progressive milestones such as these remain unsustainable in that they remain vulnerable to being reversed or even eradicated without an ERA in place to protect the rights and protection of women as equal citizens in American society (Alice Paul Institute n.d.a, Ginsburg 1977). This is especially so in the workplace as well as in decisions regarding women's healthcare and family planning.

For over 45 years, there has been a push by feminists, social justice advocates, jurists, and legislators alike to pass the ERA to the U.S. Constitution, to guarantee the equal rights and protection of women (Alice Paul Institute n.d.a, Ginsburg 1977). Stalwarts like Betty Friedan, author of the provocative bestseller *The Feminine Mystique* (1963), Gloria Steinem and Shirley Chisholm, the first known African American woman to seek the office of the president of the United States, joined forces to advance and pass the ERA (Quinn 2013). Unfortunately, the opposition, led by the likes of Phyllis Schafly and Karen Teague of the Eagle Forum and Stop Taking Our Privileges (STOP), prevailed (Kerber 1993, Davis 2008).

In 2007, the late Senator Edward Kennedy (D-MA) reignited the debate about the ERA by pointing to the disproportionate fiscal inequities borne by women and the national urgency to resolve them (Davis 2008). In the House of Representatives, a co-sponsor of the bill, Congresswoman Carolyn Maloney (D-NY), coincidentally a distant relative by marriage of Alice Paul who first crafted the ERA, was more specific when she said that women were clearly disadvantaged in wages in both the public and private sectors, and twice as likely as men to become poor as a result during their golden years. This echoes the findings of a similar report that very year by the U.S. General Accountability Office (GAO) citing that women are losing out economically during their most productive working years (GAO 2007). The report found that women find themselves on the losing end as they see the ramifications of earlier decisions too late, when they retire to face reduced standards of living of 70 percent of the lifetime earnings of white men, at a time in their lives when they are least able to recover from this cumulative economic loss (Harris 2011).

U.S. Supreme Court Justice Ruth Bader Ginsburg, the co-founder and former head of the Women's Rights Project of the American Civil Liberties Union (ACLU) (Biography.com n.d.), who has spent her career as a staunch women's advocate in defending women's rights, has strategically utilized her position on the High Court to add a woman's voice to her dissent. In *Gonzales v. Carhart, 2007*, the majority carried the day, with fellow Justice Anthony Kennedy opining that a woman's right to an abortion should be legally abridged on the basis that because some women regret terminating their late-term pregnancies, therefore all women should be subjected to the same legal fate. Said Justice Ginsburg in her dissent, this ruling 'deprives women of the right to make an autonomous choice, even at the risk of safety' (Findlaw.com n.d.). In her dissent in *Ledbetter v. Goodyear Tire and Rubber Co., 2007*, where the majority ruled in favor of the defendant based simply on the statute of limitations that requires the filing of a disparate pay complaint, Justice Ginsburg again used the occasion to shed light on the hypocrisy of the Court's ruling in that the litigant could not have brought legal action against her former employer as she could not have known that she was being underpaid solely on the basis of her sex (Cornell.edu n.d.). Despite the loss, Justice Ginsburg conveyed a veiled message to the incoming administration of the need to redress the injustice of this ruling. Newly elected President Barack Obama symbolized his ourstoric win by signing the Lilly Ledbetter Fair Pay Act in 2009, the first major legislation of his presidency to essentially revoke the High Court's ruling, making null and void the time limitation for filing a disparate pay complaint (Houchins 2015).

More recently, Nevada became the 36th state to pass the ERA in its legislature, but the ERA still remains two states short of completing the ratification process to add an amendment to the Constitution (Editorial Board 2017, Alice Paul Institute n.d.a, Ginsburg 1977).

Ourstorically, issues of gender-based discrimination have relied on the 14th Amendment of the Equal Protection Clause of the Constitution, which was originally intended to address racial discrimination. Consequently, the text of the 14th Amendment lacks the explicit legal foundation and clarity to serve as the basis of judicial decisions (Ginsburg 1977). Additionally, there are long-term policy implications for the U.S. in not having an ERA, including a significant pay gap that continues unabated today between men and women. This is especially the case for women of color and their lack of representation in executive leadership positions in all sectors of American society, including the military, which altogether have relegated the U.S. to a number 45 ranking worldwide (Editorial Board 2017, Hess et al. 2017, World Economic Forum 2016).

This 2016 Global Gender Gap ranking for the U.S. (Editorial Board 2017), with a score of 0.722 out of a possible 1.0 (World Economic Forum 2016), assesses each country on the basis of four categories (p.4):

1) Economic participation and opportunity: e.g., wage equality between men and women for comparable employment, ratio of female legislators, senior officials over male counterparts.
2) Educational attainment: e.g., ratio of female literacy over male literacy, ratio of net number of female primary/secondary/tertiary enrollment over male enrollment.
3) Health and survival: e.g., ratio of female life expectancy over male expectancy.
4) Political empowerment: e.g., ratio of female seats in national legislature over male seats, number of years with female head of state in last 50 years over male head of state.

In terms of U.S. economic participation and opportunity, there still exists a substantial gender gap in the rate of pay between women and men, which is not expected to close until 2058 (Editorial Board 2017, Hess et al. 2017). This pay gap varies from state to state in the U.S., from a high of 87.6 cents that on average a woman earns for every dollar earned by a white male (New York), to a low of 66.7 cents on average for women per every dollar earned by a white male (Louisiana) (Hess et al. 2017).

There is an even greater pay disparity for women of color, who earn less than their white female counterparts' rate of 76.9 percent to that of every dollar earned by a white male (Hess et al. 2017). Hispanic women are at the lowest end of earning potential at 46.2 percent, then Native American women at 59.6 percent, followed by black women at 65.4 percent, concluding with Asian Pacific Islander women at the higher end of the earning scale for women of color, or at 88.5 percent (Hess et al. 2017), thus on average outpacing her white female counterpart. This disparity in gender pay rates has also contributed to the increase of women living in poverty, resulting in an increase from 12.1 percent in 2002 to 14.5 percent in 2013 (Hess et al. 2017).

Although women in the U.S. represent nearly half of the workforce, barely 40 percent are represented in management, 23 percent in senior organizational leadership roles, and 5.8 percent as chief executive officers (CEOs) in Fortune 500 companies (Catalyst 2017, Editorial Board 2017). This is in stark contrast to the near one-third of U.S. businesses that have zero women in senior roles (Catalyst 2017). Women have also made significant advances at the local, state and federal government levels with increasing representation in politics, although as measured by the consistent languishing pace since 1960, it would take until 2117 to achieve parity with their male counterparts (Hess et al. 2017).

The aforementioned examples of women's underrepresentation in the senior and executive levels of management and leadership across the various sectors of American society play an important role in perpetuating women's continued secondary, if not 'invisible,' status as citizens and participants. These findings underscore the crucial imperative to pass equal rights legislation for the protection of women, to be institutionalized in the form of the ERA to establish the legal foundation for protecting advancements made so far and serve as a catalyst in facilitating future progress.

The ERA was written in 1923 by Alice Paul, a prominent leader in the women's suffrage movement, shortly after the right to vote was passed and added to the Constitution by the 19th Amendment (Alice Paul Institute n.d. a, National Council of Women's Organizations 2016). The text of the ERA reads as follows (National Council of Women's Organizations 2016, p.1):

- Section 1: Equality of rights under the law shall not be denied or abridged by the United States or by any state on account of sex.
- Section 2: The Congress shall have the power to enforce, by appropriate legislation, the provisions of this article.
- Section 3: This amendment shall take effect two years after the date of ratification.

As per Section V of the Constitution, the ratification process requires that the proposed ERA must be passed with a two-thirds majority in

Congress in 1972 before ratification by the individual states, and within seven years (Alice Paul Institute n.d.c). However, by 1982, the vote fell short of the 38 state votes needed to ratify the proposed ERA, which has been repeatedly introduced into every Congressional session since (Alice Paul Institute n.d.c).

There were significant changes made to the proposed amendment which included removing the timeline attached to the ratification process as well as revising the text (Alice Paul Institute n.d.b). By making the language more explicit so that it specifically used the word 'woman' in the first section, and included 'and the several states' in the second section, the wording reinforced the notion that sex-based discrimination is unconstitutional, and that the responsibility for enforcement of the amendment is expected at the state and federal levels of government (National Council of Women's Organizations 2016).

Much of the opposition to the passage of the ERA was rooted in the same campaign of fear and sexism that was communicated during the women's suffrage movement, which would purportedly threaten the institution of family and the patriarchal structure that dominated the institutions in the U.S. (Alice Paul Institute n.d.d). Other groups, including the business community, opposed the measure, as they were concerned that the change would incur additional costs, while those in local government were worried that states' rights would be usurped by a federal mandate like the ERA (Alice Paul Institute n.d.d).

An estimated 45 years later, the same anachronistic arguments can be found opposing the ERA in the state of Nevada (Editorial Board 2017). The concerns about its passage ranges from the belief that doing so would promote abortions, compel women into combat roles, and damage the institution of family as a whole, to the opinion that a formal amendment was unnecessary because of the numerous advances by women since the 1970s (Editorial Board 2017).

According to Mansbridge (1986), the anti-ERA movement was successful because it fueled the public's fears particularly with regard to the ERA's potential impact on military service, privacy and marriage. The U.S. Supreme Court's decision in *Roe v. Wade, 1973* only strengthened the opposition's resolve to block its passage. Primarily Schafly was especially shrewd in shaping and advancing the narrative by highlighting the vices of the trinity – ERA, abortion and homosexuality – as unholy (Siegel 2006). As if in a cruel throwback, in early 2017, two North Dakota legislators voted to uphold that state's blue laws requiring some businesses to be opened on Sundays while others should be closed (Hatch 2017). Representatives Bernie Satrom and Vernon Laning stated their wish to roll back the hands of time to the 1950s in their quest for women to remain home on Sundays for the purpose of providing their husbands with breakfast in bed. While North Dakota ratified the ERA in early 1975 (Equal Rights Amendment n.d.) and these legislators' views were clearly in the minority, it nevertheless proved the frightening reality that in the 21st century these sexist mindsets about a woman's role as subservient to a man still persist.

As such, legislators, advocates, and organizations like the Alice Paul Institute and the National Organization for Women (NOW), have identified two concurrent strategies to finally bring the passage of the ERA to fruition, almost 100 years following the granting of women's suffrage (Alice Paul Institute n.d.a, National Council of Women's Organizations 2016).

The first strategy is to continue to secure the last two states of the 38 states required to move the ERA to be ratified and written into the Constitution as per the traditional ratification process. The states of Illinois and Virginia have been identified by NOW as the most amenable to the passage of the ERA in their state legislatures (Alice Paul Institute n.d.a, National Council of Women's Organizations 2016).

The second strategy involves removing the time constraints from the original ratification process *ex post facto*, as well as securing the passage of the ERA in an additional three states so as to ensure the ratification goes through in case there are questions about the constitutionality of the ratification and time limits (National Council of Women's Organizations 2016, National Council of Women's Organizations and Alice Paul Institute 2016).

Since the founding of the American republic, women have had a fundamentally different relationship with the sovereign, all due to the founding fathers' expressed intent to exclude them as citizens. To atone for these deliberate slights, women successfully lobbied and secured legislation as the 19th Amendment giving them universal suffrage. However, despite the numerous advances that they have gained since the passage of the 19th Amendment, the ERA, another attempt to secure rights as full citizens, remains elusive and ensures that whatever progress has been made to date, will be short-lived, unsustainable and without the institutionalized backing of legal protection to protect and enforce against gender-based discrimination in American society. Moreover, the lack of an ERA to guarantee the rights and protection of women, and men, has additional implications for closing the pay gap between women and men, improving women's representation in management, and senior/executive roles in the public, private and governmental sectors (state and federal), and securing the freedom to make one's own health-related and family-planning decisions. This is especially important for women of color who are often the most disadvantaged in all aspects of American society, including in pay and limited opportunities in the workplace such as underrepresentation in government (Hess et al. 2017).

In the absence of the ERA, the Equal Protection Clause of the 14th Amendment has been used in its place since 1971 for the judicial review of discrimination cases pertaining to sex and gender. However, gender-based discrimination claims are provided more limited review and scrutiny than the original purpose of the 14th Amendment, which was to deal with matters of race discrimination (Emerson et al. 1971, National Council of Women's Organizations and Alice Paul Institute 2016).

The passage of the Equal Rights Amendment would provide a constitutional guarantee of equal rights for men and women, and a solid foundation of protection and judicial clarity for the courts.

> The amendment would have symbolic importance. It would serve as a forthright statement of our moral and legal commitment to a system in which neither sons nor daughters are pigeonholed by government because of their sex. Rather, so far as laws and officialdom are concerned, males and females will be free to grow, develop, and aspire in accordance with their individual talents, preferences, and capacities.
> (Ginsburg 1977, p.73)

Bibliography

Alice Paul Institute. (n.d.a). *Equal Rights Amendment: Unfinished Business for the Constitution.* www.equalrightsamendment.org/index.htm. Retrieved March 19, 2017.

Alice Paul Institute. (n.d.b). *ERA Ratification Bills in the 115th Congress (2017–2018).* www.equalrightsamendment.org/congress.htm. Retrieved March 19, 2017.

Alice Paul Institute. (n.d.c). *Constitutional Ratification Process (Article V).* www.equalrightsamendment.org/ratification.htm. Retrieved March 19, 2017.

Alice Paul Institute. (n.d.d). *The History Behind the Equal Rights Amendment.* www.equalrightsamendment.org/history.htm. Retrieved March 19, 2017.

Alschuler, A. (1989). The Supreme Court and the Jury: Voir Dire, Peremptory Challenges, and the Review of Jury Verdicts. *The University of Chicago Law Review,* 56, 1, 153–233.

Biography.com. (n.d.). Ruth Bader Ginsburg. www.biography.com/people/ruth-bader-ginsburg-9312041#!. Retrieved July 23, 2017.

Catalyst. (2017). Women in Management. Knowledge Center. February 17. www.catalyst.org/knowledge/women-management. Retrieved March 19, 2017.

Cornell.edu. (n.d.). *Ledbetter v. Goodyear Tire and Rubber Co., 2007.* www.law.cornell.edu/supct/html/05-1074.ZS.html. Retrieved July 23, 2017.

Davis, M.F. (2008). The Equal Rights Amendment: Then and Now. *Columbia Journal of Gender and Law,* 17, 3, 419–460.

Editorial Board. (2017). Pumping Life into the Equal Rights Amendment. *The New York Times,* March 25. www.nytimes.com/2017/03/25/opinion/sunday/pumping-life-into-the-equal-rights-amendment.html. Retrieved March 19, 2017.

Emerson, T.I., Brown, B.A., Falk, G., and Freedman, A.E. (1971). The Equal Rights Amendment: A Constitutional Basis for Equal Rights for Women. *Faculty Scholarship Series.* Paper 2799. http://digitalcommons.law.yale.edu/fss_papers/2799.

Equal Rights Amendment. (n.d.). Equal Rights Amendment. Unfinished Business for the Constitution. www.equalrightsamendment.org/states.htm. Retrieved July 22, 2017.

Findlaw.com. (n.d.). *Gonzales v. Carhart, 2007.* http://caselaw.findlaw.com/us-supreme-court/550/124.html. Retrieved July 22, 2017.

Ginsburg, R.B. (1977). Let's Have E.R.A. as a Signal. *American Bar Association Journal*, 63, 1, 70.

Harris, G.L.A. (2010). The Unintended Consequences of the Stigmatization of Affirmative Action for Beneficiaries: A Review of the Literature. *Journal of Public Management and Social Policy*, 16, 2, 75–96.

Harris, G.L.A. (2011). The Quest for Equity. Book Review of *The Declining Significance of Gender?* In F.D. Blau, M.B. Brinton, and D.B. Grusky (Eds.). 2009. Russell Sage Foundation. New York, NY. *Public Administration Review*, 71, 1, 123–126.

Hatch, J. (2017). Lawmaker Wants Women to Spend Sundays Making Husbands Breakfast in Bed. February 6. *Huffington Post.* www.huffingtonpost.com/entry/lawmaker-wants-women-to-spend-sundays-making-husbands-breakfast-in-bed_us_5898816ce4b040613137c57c. Retrieved July 23, 2017.

Held, A.L., Herndon, S.L., and Stager, D.M. (1997). The Equal Rights Amendment: Why the ERA Remains Legally Viable and Properly Before the States. *William and Mary Journal of Women and the Law*, 3, 1, Article 5, 113–136.

Hess, C., Milli, J., Hayes, J., Hegewisch, A., Mayayeva, Y., Román, S., Anderson, J., Augeri, J. (2017). The Status of Women in the States: 2015, Executive Summary. Institute for Women's Policy Research. http://statusofwomendata.org/wp-content/uploads/2015/02/SWS-Exec-Summary-final.pdf.

History.com. (n.d.). Sally Hemmings: Facts and Summary. www.history.com/topics/sally-hemings. Retrieved July 22, 2017.

Houchins, M. (2015). This Day in History: Equal Pay Trailblazer Lilly Ledbetter Turns 77. The White House (President Barack Obama). April 14. https://obamawhitehouse.archives.gov/blog/2015/04/14/day-history-equal-pay-trailblazer-lilly-ledbetter-turns-77. Retrieved July 22, 2017.

Kerber, L.K. (1992). The Paradox of Women's Citizenship in the Early Republic: The Case of Martin v. Commonwealth of Massachusetts, 1805. *American Historical Review*, 97, 2, 349–378.

Kerber, L.K. (1993). 'A Constitutional Right to Be Treated Like Ladies': Women, Civic Obligations and Military Service. *The University of Chicago Law School Roundtable*, 1, 1, Article 15, 95–128.

Mansbridge, J.J. (1986). *Why We Lost the ERA (Equal Rights Amendment)*. Chicago, IL: University of Chicago Press.

National Council of Women's Organizations (2016). The Equal Rights Amendment: Frequently Asked Questions. ERA Task Force. May. www.equalrightsamendment.org/misc/faq.pdf.

National Council of Women's Organizations and Alice Paul Institute (2016). The Equal Rights Amendment: Simple Justice, Long Overdue. May. www.equalrightsamendment.org/misc/ERA_presentation.pptx.

Pratkanis, A.R., and Turner, M.E. (1999). The Significance of Affirmative Action for the Souls of White Folks: Further Implications of a Helping Model. *Journal of Social Issues*, 55, 4, 787–815.

Quinn, S. (2013). Once Again, Feminist Take U Fight We Shouldn't Have. March 14. *The Washington Post.* www.washingtonpost.com/lifestyle/style/once-again-feminists-take-up-fight-we-shouldnt-have/2013/03/14/bed436cc-8ce4-11e2-9f54-f3fdd70acad2_story.html?utm_term=.d3e74ab4fd32. Retrieved July 23, 2017.

Siegel, R. (2006). Constitutional Culture, Social Movement Conflict and Constitutional Change: The Case of the De Facto ERA. *Yale Law School Legal Scholarship Repository*, Paper 1097. http://digitalcommons.law.yale.edu/fss_papers/1097?utm_source=digitalcommons.law.yale.edu%2Ffss_papers%2F1097&utm_medium=PDF&utm_campaign=PDFCoverPages. Retrieved July 23, 2017.

U.S. Equal Employment Opportunity Commission. (n.d.). *Equal Pay Act of 1963 and Lilly Ledbetter Fair Pay Act of 2009.* www.eeoc.gov/eeoc/publications/brochure-equal_pay_and_ledbetter_act.cfm.

U.S. General Accountability Office (GAO). (2007). *Retirement Security. Women Face Challenges in Ensuring Financial Security in Retirement.* GAO-08-105. October.

U.S. National Archives and Records Administration. (n.d.). *19th Amendment to the U.S. Constitution: Women's Right to Vote.* www.archives.gov/historical-docs/19th-amendment.

Wire Reporters. (2015). Defense Secretary Tells Military to Open All Combat Jobs to Women. *Chicago Tribune.* December 3. www.chicagotribune.com/news/nationworld/ct-military-combat-jobs-women-20151203-story.html. Retrieved January 24, 2016.

World Economic Forum. (2016). Global Gender Gap Index. http://reports.weforum.org/global-gender-gap-report-2016/rankings/. Retrieved March 19, 2017.

10 The Combat Exclusion Policy

The contemporary depiction of women as Amazons, Carreiras (2006) submits, is a disturbing and unnatural persona of women as warriors. This portrayal is far from one of admiration and perhaps one of disgust in that it implies that women are aggressive deviants because they are suspected to exude masculine traits. Such allusions, as Kirk (1988) and Hardwick (1996) argue, only serve to marginalize the modern-day woman given what many have come to accept as stereotypical descriptions of what it means to be a woman. Besides, as Kirk (1988) describes, Amazon women represented outliers, not the binary nature in society as either men or women, and Amazons 'were the opposite of the ideal Athenian women: they did not marry, they controlled their own offspring, they were warriors and they lived outside ... on the borders of the known world; they desired men but did not want male babies' (p.31).

So, while women's presence has always been part of the battlefield, it is their present-day role of being disarmed that reduces them to invisibility (Hacker 1981). With the rise of the professional military, the institution became increasingly and exclusively for men. As a matter of fact, the disappearance of women from military roles had a domino effect in the larger society where:

> like the women healers who had vanished from the history of medicine or who were recalled only as witches, the female camp followers of early modern armies vanished from military history or were recalled only as whores. And just as the loss of the history of women healers made the rise of professional nursing and of limited places for women doctors in the nineteenth century seem novel, so the loss of army women made the rise of military nursing and the opening of restricted careers for uniformed women's auxiliaries appear as something new.
> (Hacker 1981, p.671)

An exception in modern times occurred when women reverted to the positions of days of old during World War I. The Soviet Union mobilized in excess of 1 million women because of a dearth of available male recruits for the military (Carreiras 2006). The women served in all capacities including in antiaircraft defense, the infantry and artillery and armored vehicles, and while the practice in modern militaries is to demobilize women from their positions during peacetime, the Soviets did no such thing and retained women even in those functions following the war. As a result, Mazur (1998) would probably surmise that women might not have experienced the novelty effect like American military woman since women's presence in the Soviet military was throughout the institution, thus declaring gender inconsequential. Wechsler Segal (1995) cites the routine and repeated modern societies' mobilization of women as a convenient resource and in the process negating their ourstorical contributions during prior campaigns. Wechsler Segal blames the collective cultural amnesia and the failure of these societies to recollect women's performance in the crises in which they are repeatedly engaged, and for which they receive no credit. Up until recently, the U.S. employed an exclusion policy from combat for women whereas other countries invoke an omission policy for women in the military during peacetime (Carreiras 2006). The question then raised by Carreiras (2006) and advanced years later by Harris (2015) is why, then, have women not exploited these wartime crises to their own benefit to correspondingly reap the collective agency for the group despite the stereotypical gender customs? While military women like Holm (1992) and underscored by Harris (2015) frame the need for transformation of the military in the form of a revolution, so to speak, others like van Crevald (2001) and Mitchell (1997) perceive the movement as a danger to the military. What Brownmiller (1993), though, sees as clear is that women are no longer content to be passively sidelined. Women are demanding change, for as Higonnet and Higonnet (1987) note, although women have secured the right to vote and have assumed new employment roles in society, such gains influenced neither their political nor social power, and as a group they bear the reprisals against and because of gender. Women's deployment by the military was always only for the duration of each immediate crisis when for the love of country, all resources, including human resources, are to be marshaled for the war effort. Mothers and wives were therefore expected to participate in unconventional undertakings temporarily and as it suited the military but were also expected to resume traditional modes of behavior once demobilized after the crisis had passed.

Specifically for the American experience, Harris (2015) convincingly captures the absurdity of the logic behind the U.S. military's combat exclusion policy even as supporters of the policy themselves fail to articulate it effectively. Take this nonsensical exchange between then Senator William Cohen (R-ME) and former Air Force Chief of Staff General Merrill McPeak:

COHEN: Suppose you had a woman pilot ... of superior intelligence, great physical conditioning in every way she was superior to a male

counterpart vying for a combat position. Would ... [you personally] because you would not want to see the risk of her life increased ... pick the male over the female under these circumstances?
MCPEAK: That is correct.
COHEN: So in other words you would have a militarily less effective situation because of a personal view.
MCPEAK: Well, I admit, it doesn't make much sense, but that's the way I feel about it.
>(in Goldstein 2003, p.101; Holm 1992, p.484; Testimony, June 18, 1991)

What is even more inexplicable is that General McPeak himself admits that the policy does openly discriminate against women in the military solely on the basis of gender (Goldstein 2003, Holm 1992). Remarkably, he also admitted that women pilots are unquestionably more advanced than their male counterparts in pulling gravitational forces. Still, General McPeak rationalized that it was not at his discretion to make such decisions and these are decisions that are left to the Air Force. In an embellishment of sorts even verging on the hysterical, General Robert Barrow, then Commandant of the Marine Corps, was far more emotional in his testimony to Congress when he said that:

> exposure to danger is not combat. Being shot at, even being killed, is not combat. Combat is finding ... closing with ... and killing or capturing the enemy. It's KILLING. And it's done in an environment that is often as difficult as you can possibly imagine. Extremes of climate. Brutality. Death. Dying. It's ... uncivilized. And, WOMEN CAN'T DO IT! Nor should they ever be thought of as doing it. The requirements of strength and endurance render [them] UNFIT to do it. And I may be old fashioned, but I think the very nature of women disqualifies them from doing it. Women give life. Nurture life. They don't take it.
> (Holm 1992, p.483)

Moreover, General Barrow continued that having women in combat would 'destroy the Marine Corps ... something no enemy has been able to do in 200 years' (Holm 1992, p.483). Then the chief of naval operations went as far as to say that there is general agreement among military women that they do not aspire to combat roles, without any proof that such statements had been made by any woman.

Holm (1992), like Mazur (1998), deftly countered such arguments about women in the military neither serving or having never served in combat. They both provide examples of the Air Force's placement of women missileers underground and in remote locations across the country, who are armed with intercontinental ballistic missiles (ICBMs) to thwart the enemy's nuclear power capability. Operation Desert Storm witnessed first-hand women's performance in pursuing and dismantling Saddam Hussein's Patriot missiles (Holm 1992), and women's assignments to all female engagement teams (FETs) by the Army and Marine Corps during Operations Enduring and Iraqi Freedom solidified already irrefutable arguments about women's abilities and capabilities on the front line in compromising the enemy (Harris 2015). Holm (1992) classifies these assignments as clearly defensive in nature, although some might also argue that the FETs constituted offensive tactics. So, the rationale surrounding the combat exclusion policy, as Holm (1992) points out, is analogous and as nonsensical as the *Alice's Adventures in Wonderland* sequel, *Through the Looking-Glass*, where Alice rebukes Humpty Dumpty for speaking in illogical language by imposing the same terms for dissimilar meanings. However, the language that was originally crafted in the 1948 Women's Armed Services Integration Act was inherently designed for women's diminution to second-class status, subjected to the dictates and whims of men under whose command they served (Harris 2015). In effect, the legislation was purposeful that, irrespective of women's performance during any crisis, their essential function in the military and to the military was not only limited but skillsets were to be employed and deployed as necessary (Monahan and Neidel-Greenlee 2010, Harris 2015).

Solaro (2006) equates this abuse in the relationship to that of a married man's convenient use of his mistress, who, for his own purpose, remains a secret for the married man and is only taken out, if at all, and placed on display as needed. Here, the mistress operates as symbolic of women in the military and how they are mistreated by the institution. In contrast to the married man's spouse, the mistress has no legitimate rights unless as recognized by a court of law. Like women in the military, when the mistress once again has repeatedly fulfilled her obligations and attempts for the umpteenth time to advance her case for recognition, she is again struck down by her lover under the cover that he will again mull over the evidence before making a decision when he knows full well that this is yet another stall tactic (Solaro 2006). Even after the lover has divorced and become a single man, his mistress once again attempts to go forward in citing her rationale for recognition, this time for marriage, when she is yet again struck down. It was never her lover's intent in the first place to acknowledge her as his mistress but only to use her as a convenient resource, however often, for his purpose alone.

Harris (2015) employs Goldin's (2006) pollution theory to explicate the military's effective use of ensuring the convenient exclusion of women from combat occupations even as the military has always conveniently utilized women in these very roles. Pollution theory, like the military's combat exclusion policy, seeks to exclude women from entering the most prized occupations. Goldin (2006) equates the occupation of firefighters as one such example where women are intentionally kept out of the occupation to ensure that it remains exclusively male, for to allow women into this sacred domain would be to pollute both its prestige and exclusivity. It is believed that the pandemic, that is the prevalence of sexual assault in the military and disproportionately so against its female workforce, represents a similar credible threat. This backlash is not just to prevent women's entrance and ascendance into the military but, more importantly, to obstruct any attempt for their perceived entrance into certain prized occupations such as those in combat, which were once the sole purview of men in the military. While the military has politically framed the precipitous increase in sexually related offenses as a mark of success in terms of awareness and reporting, regrettably, as Cassata (2013) also reports, commanders continue to play a broad discretionary role despite the efforts of Senator Kirsten Gillibrand (D-NY) (Whitlock 2013, Harris 2015) and the Defense Advisory Committee on Women in the Services (DACOWITS 2012, Harris 2015) to extricate them from the adjudicatory process of such cases altogether as well as to hold them accountable for such incidents via climate surveys as one gauge of their performance. Further, removing commanders from influencing the process, it is believed, would go far in not only changing the military culture that fosters sexually related offenses but increase the prosecution of such crimes, as commanders would no longer be able to upend such verdicts (Lawrence and Penaloza 2013, Montagne and Lawrence 2013, Harris 2015).

Many remain irked at the level of tolerance attributed to the culture that enables sexual assault and like behavior to thrive in the military. More disconcerting, though, is the belief that the highest level of federal government, in this case Commander-in-Chief President Donald Trump has himself been implicated in views that he is alleged to hold about women in general and an ourstory of denigrating remarks about them. Women overall, and women veterans in particular, see the election of this president as a credible threat to, and a retrenchment of, women's rights (Cahn 2017). This fear rises to the level of the unforeseen and irreparable damage that the Trump Administration poses for women's progress in the country, including women's health (Farokhmanesh 2016). For instance, Vice President Mike Pence is believed to have said that he will ensure that the 1973 *Roe v. Wade* decision on a woman's right to an abortion is sent 'to the ash heap of history' (Crockett 2016). In fact, the vice president is viewed as no less of a threat to women than President Trump (Crockett 2016). For women in the military, the Trump Administration may represent a literal rolling back of gains made under the combat exclusion policy's repeal and then Secretary of Defense Ashton Carter's acceleration of women's integration as combatants into occupations formerly closed to them because denying such opportunities to one half of the nation's population, as the then secretary stated, is simply 'crazy' (Bennett 2015).

Launched in late 2016 with a report of its findings in late 2017, the Service Women's Action Network (SWAN) survey of active military and women veterans, revealed the overriding concerns for women who are actively serving in the military and women veterans (SWAN 2016). The survey further reduced these findings as perceived by respondents into two categories: personnel challenges and challenges within the community. For women who are currently serving in the military, job assignment (40.8 percent) and gender bias (30 percent) remain primary challenges for them. While gender bias (36.2 percent) was a close secondary personal challenge, sexual assault and harassment (39.66 percent) remained one of the top concerns within their respective communities. Understandably, neither the combat exclusion policy nor its repeal were cited as paramount concerns, but issues perhaps owing to simply being treated as an anomaly both by the system that is designed to provide them with care and problems that are being created within the communities as a consequence became challenges for women veterans. Yet, at the root of these problems has been one of exclusion, with the combat exclusion policy as the legal basis of this. Women veterans perceived mental health (34.46 percent), financial stability (32.64 percent) and networking with other women veterans (31.61 percent) as personally challenging for them. Community challenges came in the forms of the ability to secure healthcare that is specifically targeted to women veterans (39.12 percent), mental health (37.05 percent) and problems in navigating the Department of Veterans Affairs (VA) system for claiming benefits, the top three issues for women veterans. All women's groups surveyed overwhelmingly pointed to three key issues in educating the public to change the perception about women in the military and namely women's lived experiences, women's contributions and leadership in the military, together with the trials and tribulations that women veterans must encounter and endure. Respondents cite gender bias as a major issue that continues to plague women in the military and women veterans of the military. Sexual assault and military sexual trauma (MST) they say remain rampant and, moreover, the military fails to provide even adequate transition services for women for reintegration into civilian life.

Said the chief operating officer of SWAN, Kate Germano, prior to President Trump's inauguration: 'Here we have a soon-to-be commander-in-chief who has a pattern of groping women, who has a pattern of judging women based solely on their looks and on their physical attributes and he's going to be in charge of the military' (De Luce and McLeary 2016). Likewise, Secretary of Defense Marine Corps General James Mattis opposes the overturn of the combat exclusion policy (De Luce and McLeary 2016). A forthcoming book by the secretary cites the policy's repeal as in keeping with a 'progressive agenda' that is designed to compromise the military. Then candidate Donald Trump tweeted, a practice for which he is now infamously known, that '26,000 unreported sexual harassments in the military – only 238 convictions. What did these geniuses expect when they put men and women together' (cited in Smith and Keneally 2016). This glimpse into the psyche as to the president's view about the situation and his view of women in the military is telling.

At the root of the combat exclusion policy and still today are the myths that provide such perverted thinking and irrational staying power that support them. As a consequence, the popular mantra 'Be All That You Can Be' at least for the Army and specifically as it applies to women, conveniently assumed the meaning of 'Be All We'll Let You Be' (Holm 1992, p.400). As Harris (2009a) sees it, the conundrum lies in men's desire to forever place women into preconceived notions of what they believe that women ought to be and what Abramovitz (1996) defines as suitable, in that women unquestionably adopt the subordinated functions of wife and mother. Both are respectful roles but women are made to believe that should they markedly depart from these straight-jackets, then they are less than women. This appears to be the case, for despite the so-called progress that women have made as a group, they continue to be disproportionately found in jobs deemed traditional for women, at 80 percent (Faludi 2006). This speaks to the continual advancement of those well-honed myths and men's agenda for, while untrue, these myths prevail and dictate the choices that are made for women including the very choices that women make for themselves. So deep-seated is this agenda that women appear to be in a self-perpetuating spiral of control that is in itself out of control. Essentially, '[t]he American woman is trapped on this asymptomatic spiral, turning endlessly through the generations, drawing ever nearer to her destination without ever arriving' (Faludi 2006, p.62).

These myths thus entrap military women without realizing that it was never part of the original equation for their sanctioned inclusion into combat. It was not until 1989 or during Operation Just Cause in Panama that the magnitude of women's roles played itself out for the public (Holm 1992), and for which Captain Linda Bray was sacrificed for having dared to go where other women had gone before her but had never been allowed to engage the enemy in combat even though all the while or ad infinitum women have always been part of this landscape. It was the arbitrary nature of how the combat exclusion policy was applied or used capriciously that gave the different military branches their license for misuse. To the first myth, women are to be protected from engaging in combat (Holm 1992). To Holm (1992), the enemy does not discriminate who it will target and who it will not. More preposterous is that although civilian women journalists as early as World War I were on the front lines reporting about the war and where even military nurses often found themselves, military women at large were formally barred from being at the tip of the spear (Goldstein 2003, Monahan and Neidel-Greenlee 2010, Holm 1992, Grant DePauw 1998, Elshtain 1987). Studies were repeatedly conducted by the Army, for instance, to obstruct any advancement of its female workforce. According to Major General Mary Clarke, who at the time of her retirement was the Army's highest-ranking female in 1987, penned a letter to Army women but which was a direct rebuke to its leadership saying that '[t]he duty performance of the average soldier is a solid, quality performance – too good ever to return to an all-male force with only a few token women' (Holm 1992, p.402). What was more counterintuitive at the time was that in the midst of the Army's resistance, its own research revealed positive findings about its female workforce's performance at the unit level and specifically in its Women Content in Units Force Development Test (MAXWAC) and REFORGER 77 (REFWAC) Women's Army Corps studies. Further, said the findings of the studies, any negative results between male and female soldiers were of no significance. Moreover, research on women soldiers in co-educational units yielded even more impressive results than those found in uni-gendered units (U.S. Army 2002).

Other series of studies during the Ronald Reagan Administration, coined WITA or Women in the Army, appeared to be another attempt not only to justify delaying women's advancement into closed occupations that were designated as combat related but also as a way of control by reducing the degree to which women were assigned to such noncombatant occupations even as electricians and plumbers (Holm 1992). Dr. Mary Huey, then DACOWITS chair, fired off a letter to Defense Secretary Casper Weinberger that such undermining tactics by the Army amounted to a reinvestigation of already known information about women's performance in these jobs and that these studies were no more than a witch hunt to locate obstacles to women soldiers' performance that did not exist.

While initially the Navy appeared more cooperative in its agreement to increase both the number of women and the occupations in which they were placed for ship assignments, no such expansion took place (Holm 1992). In fact, the Navy employed such tactics in ensuring that women were not only barred from seafaring assignments but continued to present these assignments as all-male. In 2002, Harrell et al. confirmed the Navy's underhanded scheme all along to prevent women from entering such occupations under the pretext of recoding those positions to ensure that no women could ever be assigned to them. This study additionally exposed that these maneuvers were not limited to the Navy but represented the ploys to which the leadership of the respective military branches were willing to stoop to circumvent civilian orders and even the law. More pointedly, Harrell et al. (2002) highlighted the dubious practices in which the services have long engaged to keep and deter women from the prized combat positions by even invoking variables that women were not interested in certain occupations given the physical rigor and drudgery associated with such work. The researchers proved once and for all that these allegations and the myth about women remained unsupported and were at best farfetched. Still, more mind boggling was that more than three decades earlier, in 1981, the Navy was exuberant about the performance of its women with commanders even preferring the hard work and discipline of its female workforce over that of its male workforce (Holm 1992).

For the Marine Corps, with then only a 2 percent female workforce, the decision was to initially commission studies on both its enlisted and commissioned corps to determine what its overall female end strength should be and where to assign them to be most effective (Holm 1992). While the approach was contrary to what Holm (1992) sees as the branch of the military most likely to depict the call for 'A Few Good Men' (p.414), as it was the epitome of 'the last bastion of the classic fighting man' (p.414), the Marine Corps reckoned that to fully capture all of the characteristics of what it means to be a Marine, this would necessitate that its women's workforce be integrated into all occupations, including those considered as combat such as artillery, infantry and the like. Conveniently, though, using this broad definition meant that women would be effectively barred from all such occupations under the combat exclusion policy. However, the Marine Corps also concluded that as Marine women could potentially confront conditions that might be considered combat, consequently its female workforce should undergo weapons training, a requirement for its male workforce. Incidentally, women Marines surpassed such prospects for qualifications by 98 percent (Jones 1986).

Nevertheless, a task force commissioned by the then Marine Corps Commandant Alfred Gray found a disquieting pessimism among male Marines as to the increased presence of women Marines (Holm 1992). These deleterious attitudes appear to permeate all levels of command. More deplorable is that even as Commandant Gray chided his fellow male Marines for failure to regard their female colleagues respectfully, he, himself, engaged in behavior that was incongruent with his rhetoric. The commandant flatly rejected proposals by his veteran officers that women be integrated into such occupations and assignments as pilots, embassy guards units or security forces, or participate in assault or offensive combat training despite the agreement for women's defensive basic warrior training (Moore 1988). Fortunately, then Secretary of Defense Frank Carlucci vetoed the commandant's decision by assigning women Marines as guards to American embassies in Germany, France and Switzerland (Holm 1992). However, the Marine Corps still found ways to undercut and thereby reduce the assignment of women to coveted positions designated as combat by refilling many of these positions with men. In doing so, the Marine Corps not only managed to surreptitiously regulate where its female workforce was assigned but restricted the recruitment of women as well. Some 30 years later, following the employment of these puerile tactics, the Marine Corps in early 2017 is now being forced to come to terms with its culture that remains antithetical to women in its ranks.

In early 2017, it came to light that on an underground Facebook page dubbed Marines United, approximately 30,000 Marines evidently shared and commented on the unauthorized and nude photographs of 12 fellow female Marines (Kheel 2017, Brennan 2017). Many of the photographs elicited obscene sexual comments about the anatomy of female Marines.

Interestingly enough, the scandal came at a time when the Marine Corps was intentionally attempting to increase its recruitment of women (Brennan 2017). Reportedly, the page was restricted to men only of the U.S. Marines and Navy and the British Royal Marines, and allegedly upholding the motto 'no discussing Marines United; no threats, harm or harassment; and no racists and illegal posts' (Brennan 2017, p.4). The salacious content of the page was primed at the outset with the following disturbing and racy verbiage that is obviously intended to titillate the appetite of its followers: 'Here you go, you thirsty fucks ... this is just the tip of the iceberg. There is more coming' (Brennan 2017, p.5). This website was unearthed by a Marine, turned journalist, James LaPorte, who became aware of the site upon invitation by a fellow Marine (McLaughlin and Stapleton 2017), although the Marine Corps credits another veteran, Thomas Brennan, creator of The War Horse, a military news site, with reporting the information to the Marine Corps and the Naval Criminal Investigative Service (NCIS) (McLaughlin and Stapleton 2017).

While the originator of the page is identified as a veteran Marine, who, according to the Marine Corps, is a government subcontractor and has reportedly been terminated from his employment, more recent coverage contradicts that of the Department of Defense (DoD) that the page is still in operation, albeit under a new name (McLaughlin and Stapleton 2017). Apparently, the members are now being redirected to a new webpage, Marines United 2 (MU2), which assures that it will do a better job of monitoring the site for infiltration. Even worse, the proselytizers of the page are content to go further by suggesting that, '[i]t would be hilarious if one of these FBI or NCIS f.s found their wife on here,' as one member of Marines United quipped. Some of the site members are basically giving the middle finger to the investigating agencies because they believe that they are above the law.

Psychiatrist Dr. Frank Ochberg, once associate director of the National Institute of Mental Health, a board member of the International Society for Traumatic Stress Studies and the innovator of the diagnosis of post-traumatic stress disorder (PTSD), says that the military's sexual assault scandal endangers the mental health of victims (Brennan 2017). In addition, he said that '[i]t impairs the ideal of brotherhood and sisterhood, being able to count on somebody.' He continued that '[w]ithin the military, this is a violation of family ... Therefore, few organizations hold to such esteem as the Marine Corps. They stand for honor, courage and commitment. This destroys honor ... This is sadistic ... This is disloyalty' (Brennan 2017, p.5).

However, disloyalty appears to come from all directions for military women, and in this case for Marine Corps women, from their own. Marine Corps Lieutenant Colonel Kate Germano, who was tapped to command the institution's all-women boot camp, was relieved of duty because she was accused of being at odds with her male commanding officer as well as her female subordinates (Phillips 2015). By all indications, it appears that

Lieutenant Colonel Germano drew the ire of her superiors and subordinates when she pushed the envelope in her zeal to prove to the Marine Corps that women were as capable as men to overcome the rigors of the rugged terrain of what it means to be a Marine. In her own words when she assumed command, and at a time when women failed the obstacle course at three times the rate of men on the rifle range, 'the thinking was girls can't shoot, so why bother?' (Phillips 2015). While Lieutenant Colonel Germano's training style was questionable, she nevertheless surpassed the training pass rates of women at 95 percent, rivaling those of male Marines on the range by working with trainers in delivering more effective training to the women Marines. The results for strength tests and retention were equally impressive despite declines in written tests.

Lieutenant Colonel Germano was described by her admirers and critics alike as strong-willed and demanding, qualities that would otherwise have earned her high marks if not for the complaints and subsequent investigation that resulted in her removal from command (Phillips 2015). Yet, the Marine Corps disagreed with this characterization of the rationale for her removal, citing the insubordination and rebuke of subordinates instead. Allegedly, Lieutenant Colonel Germano had usurped her commander's advice by appealing to higher command in an effort to muster the support that she felt was necessary for the women recruits to succeed in training. Supposedly, '[o]nce we showed the recruits and the coaches and drill instructors it was possible, it filled them with so much confidence' (Phillips 2015). She persisted that '[t]hey knew they were as good as every other recruit and my hope was the Marines saw it too.'

Yet, to proponents of women's full integration into the military, Lieutenant Colonel Germano's relief from command basically reinforced questions about the Marine Corps' compliance with the policy (Phillips 2015). This suspicion is also supported by the institution's reputation as not only the most male dominated of the military branches but having the smallest workforce of women at 7 percent. Notwithstanding the most recent sexually explicit scandal involving the Marine Corps, the institution is said to also yield the highest rates of sexual assault among the services. Former Marine Corps infantry officer turned policy director of the SWAN, Greg Jacob, admits that of all the services, the Marine Corps has long struggled with integrating women due to an outdated system of indoctrinating recruits by gender (Phillips 2015). Paradoxically, the Marine Corps' own experience demonstrates otherwise or that the morale of mix-gendered units is not adversely impacted. Its Ground Command Element Integrated Task Force study that was mandated by the Barack Obama Administration essentially debunked the Marine Corps' basis for continuing to exclude women from combat jobs. However, most disturbing and despite the repeal of the combat exclusion policy, Marine Corps officers at the Parris Island training facility advised that they have been instructed by commanders to halt any additional efforts toward training women recruits as no mandate to do so exists despite the combat exclusion policy's repeal. By employing such instructions, the Marine Corps is deliberately and knowingly flouting an existing law and failing to accede to the orders of its civilian superiors.

Says Holm (1992), the Air Force was the least impacted by the combat exclusion policy as most combat positions dealt with working on aircraft. However, as Holm points out, this exclusionary behavior of women by the military leadership did not mean that the Air Force was not equally culpable. In fact, like its sister services, the Air Force's leadership found ways of excluding its female workforce from positions that were distantly related to combat missions or those with a 'high probability' (Holm 1992, p.419) of engaging in 'direct combat or exposure to hostile fire or capture.' The Air Force concocted sophisticated mathematical models to make such determinations in addition to artificially imposing thresholds on the recruitment of women into the service. However, these manipulations were short term. Through the National Defense Authorization Act, Congress mandated that the Air Force must bolster its recruitment of women to 22 percent over its 1987 level of 19 percent, and in 1989 forbade the service from levying any restrictions on women's recruitment outside of those explicitly expressed under the combat exclusion policy (Holm 1992). DACOWITS' involvement also resulted in the opening up of an unprecedented 97 percent of occupations in the Air Force to women, although this was still in theory but not in practice.

Of all the services, then still under the auspices of the U.S. Department of the Navy in the event of war, the Coast Guard has been most responsive to integrating women throughout its ranks, and unlike the other branches of the military, was never part of the Women's Armed Services Integration Act of 1948 (Holm 1992, Bird Francke 1997). As well, the Coast Guard has never restricted its female workforce to the combat exclusion policy (Holm 1992). As early as 1978, the Coast Guard was explicitly clear in both policy and practice that there would be no such restrictions on its female workforce on the grounds of gender (Bird Francke 1997, Holm 1992). In 1982, Admiral James Carey, then Coast Guard commandant, declared, '[m]y view on the performance of women in the Coast Guard is that they are Class A! They are great! They have performed up to all expectations and beyond most people's expectations' (Holm 1992, p.421). Unlike the Navy, the Coast Guard was already navigating uncharted territory by having its female workforce command ships, among other functions. The Coast Guard's nondiscriminatory assignments by gender were effectively undermined by the Navy's gender-based assignments in accordance with the combat exclusion policy (Bird Francke 1997). However, even then, despite the Coast Guard's assertions, the empirical data demonstrated otherwise (Holm 1992). The service was only employing its female workforce at 7.8 percent. The report spurred a 20 percent increase in the accession rate of women to the Coast Guard as a result. The Coast Guard went even further by instituting a two-year sabbatical leave for all of its personnel, regardless of gender or corps, to serve a two fold purpose: one, for neonatal care; and two, to improve the retention rate of incumbents in critical career fields.

Commanding at sea represented the Navy's sacred grove, from which women were barred; the aviation community for all of the services was similarly held, even as the U.S. military provided such training to the military women of fellow members of the North Atlantic Treaty Organization (NATO) as early as the 1980s while hypocritically barring its own women from such assignments (Bird Francke 1997, Holm 1992). However, during this period, the U.S. military experienced the exodus of qualified female pilots fed up with the mandatory caps that had been placed on their careers solely on the basis of gender. One memorable simulation underscored women's flying prowess all along as well as proved that, for at least American male pilots, despite the evidence, yielding such ground to women would be a fight to the end and with only one victor or gender standing. Take Canadian fighter pilot Captain Jane Foster, then one of only two women to be endowed with this accolade (Holm 1992). She beat a U.S. Marine pilot in simulation with a missile from her CF-18 Hornet, annihilating his AV-8B Harrier in the process (Bird Francke 1997). However, for the U.S. Marine fighter pilot, it was not the loss per se that induced his disgust. It was the fact that he had lost the dogfight to a woman. A Canadian Armed Forces flight safety officer said, '[w]e like to think [flying] is a man's job, but it's not' (Holm 1992, p.429). Another, this time a Norwegian F-18 pilot, weighed in that '[i]t's more a matter of women entering the ranks. Fighter pilot has been male territory up until now' (Holm 1992, p.429). Such machismo permeates the U.S. military aviation community.

In 1988, the then U.S. General Accountability Office (GAO) showed the plots that the Air Force devised to prevent these prized assignments from being given to women (Holm 1992). Further, for the few women who were fortunate enough to enter these hallowed halls, it is inconceivable to imagine the lengths to which the Air Force was willing to go to protect these positions. Troy Devine, an Air Force captain and graduate of the Air Force Academy learned this first-hand. Devine received her silver wings as a pilot in 1985 and was not only consigned to second-class status to the Ninth Strategic Reconnaissance Wing at Beale Air Force Base in California, but a condition of her assignment was having to sign a waiver that for at least one year she would not get pregnant and be subjected to biweekly pregnancy tests (Holm 1992). This practice had two aims: one, to ensure that any woman who entered the discipline knew her place; and two, to keep her in line should she think otherwise.

Holm (1992) considered the Air Force's unscrupulous interpretation of the combat exclusion policy even more limiting than that of the Navy. Paradoxically, though, while the Navy's interpretation of the policy was in keeping with the law and in accordance with its mission, not aircraft type, thus affording Navy women the perception of the prospects for more of such assignments, this was far from its actual practice. As Holm recounts, women in the Navy flew high-performance jet aircrafts in 1975, and Lieutenant Junior Grade Rosemary Conaster comes to mind as also becoming the first woman, in 1990, to assume command of a tactical electronics warfare squadron. Many women as early as 1985 flew combat aircraft from which Air Force women were barred. Yet, because Navy carriers embodied the service's holy grail, Navy women were never designated to squadrons on these vessels but to the U.S.S. *Lexington*, although Navy women aviators frequently launched from and around them. Because carriers comprised combat aircraft and ships, this was in effect a dual exclusion for Navy women pilots, hence restricting Navy women pilots and navigators at the time to 1.8 percent and 1.2 percent, respectively.

The Army's direct combat probability coding (DCPC) system was so designed for its capricious adjustment of the combat exclusion policy to represent the institution's fancy at any given time to guarantee women's exclusion from coveted combat missions that would involve the Apache Attack helicopters and even those for support missions such as the Chinook and Black Hawk helicopters (Holm 1992). No decisions were ever to be rendered based on its female workforce's exemplary performance during such excursions as Operations Just Cause and Desert Storm. Even the transportation of troops and supplies to and from the theater of operations by female pilots was targeted as combat-related missions. True to form, the Marine Corps convincingly made the argument that since all of its missions were combat related, all women were barred. What is remarkable, though, is that the Marine Corps commandant successfully advanced this argument despite an internal task force's recommendation to do otherwise and without any objections from civilian superiors. Even as the DoD's risk rule took effect, an effort to reconcile the divergence between each service's interpretation of the combat exclusion policy, and given DACOWITS' counsel to establish unambiguous benchmarks that determined women's exclusion from so-called combat jobs, was in itself unclear (Holm 1992). Holm (1992), Solaro (2006) and Bird Francke (1997) question the concern that women should fall prey to 'direct combat, hostile fire, or capture' (Holm 1992, p.433, Harrell et al. 2002, p.2), when all along women have been assigned to discharge ICBMs with nuclear warheads to destroy those of the enemy, even as they were prevented from employing conventional weapons (Holm 1992). Holm (1992) further characterized this folly as a case of 'misplaced chivalry' (p.433) to keep the irrationality of such exclusions in place and one which flies in the face of established wisdom when measured against the backdrop of the following testimony to Congress in 1990. Air Force Chief Personnel Officer Lieutenant General Thomas Hickey attested to the performance of Air Force women by stating that:

They can fly fighters, they pull Gs, they can do all those things. They are physically [and] emotionally capable ... the issue is if you want us to put them there, just change the law and the Air Force will do that.
(Holm 1992, p.432)

Irrespective of each service's rationale for barring women from their cherished combat missions, what it comes down to, says Holm (1992), is that these myths about women are so ingrained that they are self-reinforcing as expressed by the likes of van Crevald (2000, 2001), Maninger (2008) and Mitchell (1997). However, the challenges faced under the combat exclusion policy are only real to those who are adversely impacted by it (McElrath 1992). The myth then that women need to be protected from combat, according to Holm (1992), is a delusion because on the battlefield the enemy does not pursue its objective with respect to gender. Holm again cites the case where military nurses, though not sanctioned, have routinely served on the battlefield and civilian female journalists were often found on the front lines of war reporting the news (Holm 1992, Monahan and Neidel-Greenlee 2010, Goldstein 2003, Grant DePauw 1998, Elshtain 1987). Women have even done inhumane things like the murdering of Native Americans and lynching of African Americans (Grant DePauw 1998). Molly Pitcher was believed to have been the first American woman to take up arms during the American Revolution (Grant DePauw 1998); women camouflaged as men fought with their brethren on the battlefield during the Civil War, Harriet Tubman led the Union Army as a spy and to her own peril to liberate hundreds of slaves also during the Civil War (Allen 2006); and military nurses have notoriously sustained injuries and made the ultimate sacrifice on behalf of the nation (Holm 1992). Says Harris (2015), the dynamics of modern warfare are such that even the military medic must assume arms in the defense of patients. The now famous stories about the Army and Marines FET, christened Team Lioness, represent one of the multiple yet vital ways in which the military has employed its female workforce (McLagan and Sommers 2010, *Lioness Report* 2012, Alvarez 2009), even as the institution has repeatedly done so by treating this invaluable resource as one of convenience. Harris's (2015) portrayal of one such FET member was in itself an inexplicable profile in courage of all that the women endured and devoid of the proper equipment, training and protection to their own detriment for the sake of a country with some who, miraculously, live to tell about their experiences.

There is another unfounded myth about military women which remains a myth, of course, but continues to stoke fear by proselytizers who are hell-bent on advancing the narrative that women cannot be a reliable resource, and it contradicts the irrefutable evidence that has already discredited it (Holm 1992). As stated, from the beginning of the American republic and through every major campaign and war, military women have been involved and without them none of these crises could have been overcome. Nevertheless, this cultural amnesia, as Wechsler Segal (1995, p.761) calls it, rears its ugly head every time to question women's gallantry and readiness for war despite countless corroborations. For example, studies by Harrell and Miller (1997) and Harrell et al. (2002) refute pregnancy as a variable for negatively affecting the mission. As a matter of fact, these studies point out that the military women do all that they can to overcome such perceptions that they undermine the mission (Harris 2009a).

Women's perceived vulnerabilities call into question a third myth, that they lack the right stuff to function under the arduous conditions of war (Holm 1992). What is disconcerting is that there are women (e.g., Elaine Donnelly at the Center for Military Readiness, April 2002), and including military women like Captain Kate Petronio of the Marine Corps, who believe that men, not women, should serve in combat (Petronio 2012), even as Petronio herself amassed an impressive record during Operation Enduring Freedom. Harris (2015) hopes that the repeal of the combat exclusion policy will level the playing field for women in the military in not just the occupations that women pursue and the assignments in which they are placed but ultimately in how women are perceived as equal to their male partners in every sense of the word. Be that as it may and even as women make ourstoric strides in shattering that seemingly impervious glass ceiling in military jobs formerly closed to them, as earlier invoked, the Trump Administration's stance, also mirrored through an equally reticent Secretary of Defense as to the role of women in the military, portends a treading in place, if not a rolling back altogether, despite the public rhetoric about not undoing the gains previously made. This, in essence, means that as Harris (2015) predicted, while repealed, the combat exclusion policy stands to remain merely in theory for the foreseeable future.

Another myth's intransigence that shares much with the aforementioned is that military women lack the attributes to perform under the less than ideal conditions that are combat, in that women's innate makeup as the fairer sex makes them compromised for the role (Holm 1992). In this view, the American woman's propensity for certain 'creature comforts' owing to her associated high standard of living (Holm 1992, p.462). Actually, Holm (1992) does not deny this existence but nonetheless looks to the experiences of nurses in Vietnam (Holm 1992) and more recently during Operations Enduring and Iraqi Freedom as evidence that this is simply not the case (Harris 2015). Even the DoD's own data state otherwise (U.S. Army 2002). This evidence not only speaks to women's superior ability to adapt when they have repeatedly served as unsanctioned combatants and without the commensurate training, equipment or protection to succeed that their male counterparts routinely receive to survive in such harsh conditions. Holm (1992) points to women being deprived of basic sanitation supplies during Operation Desert Storm, while the menfolk received their regular supplies of shaving cream, as only one such example. Harris (2015), Monahan and Neidel-Greenlee (2010) and Solaro (2006) validate women's clear disadvantage given accompanying cultural mores in the forward deploying regions about gender and roles yet the illegal placement of women as combatants on the ground as commanders saw fit to employ them. Worse yet, military women's lives were further imperiled when as the needs existed, they found themselves as singular American personnel patrolling enemy territory – assignments for which they received no credit because such placements were in violation of the combat exclusion policy.

To add insult to injury, upon return to the U.S., in an effort to claim earned benefits through the VA as combat veterans, women veterans were more often than not to meet with the obstructionist attitudes of VA claims personnel, ironically women for the most part, who were only too quick to dismiss them as being not credible benefit claimants (*Lioness Report* 2012, p.18, Harris 2015). Harris's (2015) interviews with women veterans reveal the extremes, and in a war zone no less that women went to convince superiors not to place less experienced men into certain assignments when they were better equipped to do so. In one case, during Operation Iraqi Freedom, one soldier incurred wrath in the process and never received credit for a combat designation simply because she was a woman. As Solaro (2006) insists, these routine assignments where women are attached but not assigned to units cloak their actual combat assignments, rendering them orphans.

Another myth that continues unabated about women in the military is that their presence will adversely impact the morale and cohesion of a unit (Holm 1992). Still worse, their presence will destroy male bonding. Countless studies, including by the military, have refuted such preposterous claims. While Rosen et al. (1996) describe unit cohesiveness as a crucial component for military readiness and morale, Harrell and Miller (1997), Harrell et al. (2002) and Rosen et al. (1996, 1999) have all found that single-gendered units do not perform as well as mixed-gendered ones. Studies by the U.S. Army (2002, U.S. GAO 1997) concur with this finding. Harrell and Miller (1997) also confirm that gender is of secondary importance in a unit and functions in the same way as would rank, for instance. In fact, Holm (1992) cites that unit cohesion experiences the highest levels when the unit is under duress such as when attacked. Here, mixed-gendered units bonded to collectively overcome the adversity. Said the Army's Captain Mosely: 'When the action starts every soldier does what they are trained to do. Nobody cares whether you're male or female. It's just: can you do the job' (Holm 1992, p.463).

Myth number six comes in the form of what Harris (2009a) characterizes as a misconstrued dual and general overriding belief about women that on one hand they are inherent detractors to military men, a view espoused by the most conservative in ideology, while on the other hand, another belief held by the more liberal wing can be seen an effort to dismiss the military as a bastion of maleness that subordinates women not only as inferior but objectifies them as sexual evil doers (Harris 2009a). Rosen et al. (2003)

made an explicit nexus between a certain level of masculinity and the number of men within a military unit. However, this correlation was proven counterproductive to a unit's morale and readiness but only at the individual level; the findings were contrary for the group. Yet, while individual unit members derided the presence of hypermasculinity, the actions in which they engaged as a group indicated otherwise. Solaro (2006) understands this conundrum that individual male unit members face as a strategy for organizational survival as not being viewed and negatively so as an outlier by other male unit members. However, Solaro (2006) condemns this behavior as that of 'scumbags' (p.311), for male members contribute to these undertakings, even as they consider them to be juvenile in nature, as a way of thwarting any suspicion by fellow male unit members as feminine in kind. Solaro postulates that the infusion of women into these units will potentially make participation in these behaviors not as appealing to men. Another interesting development is that when women are rejected by their male counterparts, the same acute psychological trauma levels that are suffered by them are also manifested by male members as depression and loneliness that signals an empathy for female unit members (Solaro 2006). Yet, Solaro interprets these findings as male unit members not agonizing enough to move them to openly support their female comrades given their internal angst of divided allegiance.

Harris (2015) raises a third view that was proffered by one of the women portrayed in her research on women veterans. For those military women who are not trivialized as whores, then they can only be lesbians when they refuse sexual affairs with male unit members (Firestone and Harris 2008). This deliberate division of sex by the military was to circumvent such situations as well as to steer clear of allowing anyone access to the military who was suspected of homosexuality (Herbert 1998). The rationale? Homosexuals must be deprived of the same liberties as those of heterosexuals. Despite innumerable examples to prove otherwise, more recently during Operations Desert Storm, Enduring Freedom, and Iraqi Freedom, that military men and women can work productively together without the possibility of sexual relations ever occurring between them (Holm 1992, Solaro 2006, Monahan and Neidel-Greenlee 2010), the myth still resonates as truth. This is not to say that relationships do not develop as a result of men and women working together. And even if should sexual relationships occur between unit members, the research bears out that there is no adverse effect on the unit's readiness or mission (Bird Francke 1997, Moskos 1994), although in some cases morale was negatively impacted (Moskos 1994). Studies by Randal (1981) and Randal and Yanz (1995) on women in the Nicaraguan Sandinista guerrilla army signify the lengths to which the women were willing to go to be with their comrades. In one example, an injured female soldier was hospitalized only to clandestinely return to be with her fellow soldiers.

Finally, another myth holds that Americans have no stomach for seeing their women die or be captured as prisoners of war (POWs) (Holm 1992).

To be fair, it is theorized that such sensitivities do not necessarily arise from the myth to avert female casualties per se but the need to avoid any perceived untoward casualties who are American (Sigmund Gartner 2008). Apparently, female casualty rates only become problematic when the overall casualty rate is anticipated to be unacceptable. Further, as Devine (1997) contends, America's tolerance for casualties during wartime is a misunderstood phenomenon. Yet, this sensitivity has become part and parcel of military strategy and doctrine due to the need to wage limited wars (i.e., Korean Conflict, Vietnam Conflict, Operation Desert Storm) and the broad use of air power not only to reduce American casualties but to maintain public support. However, doing so is unrealistic for it is such factors as the public's cost-benefit analyses of going to war, the degree of political consensus to conduct war, the actual on-the-ground progress of war and the accompanying changing expectations which all together serve as barometers influencing America's sensitivity toward casualties. However, Americans are also known to have short memories (Fenner 2001), and more disturbing is that this so-called sensitivity level appeals to the notion that women are victims (Holm 1992). Likewise, while the sight of any American returning in a body bag is disquieting, it is purportedly so when the contents of these body bags are women. The line is that military men would concede the mission if this was to occur. The same reaction is speculated should women become POWs.

According to Fenner (2001), Breuer (1997) and Saywell (1985), however, this is simply not the case and they cite the Tet Offensive during the Vietnam Conflict where every man and woman each retreated to safety to protect themselves. Even the travails of women during Operation Desert Storm and especially so during Operations Enduring and Iraqi Freedom, have not dispelled this myth, despite the fact that there was no negative public reaction to these experiences. Multiple studies concur that American women's capture and casualty do not garner any more public objection than those of men (Solaro 2006, Fenner 2001, Monahan and Neidel-Greenlee 2010, Bird Francke 1997, Holm 1992). The Air Force discovered during its survival, escape, resistance and evasion (SERE) training that male pilots would not compromise their own safety for that of female pilots whose planes were downed in enemy territory (Bird Francke 1997, Fenner 2001). The training discredited long-known information that male soldiers would risk further ill treatment should their female counterparts be beaten. Besides, the men reacted no more to the mistreatment of female associates than mistreated male associates. Monahan and Niedel-Greenlee (2010) ascribe such sensationalism to the media, the U.S. military, Congress and the skewed nature of this reporting to ourstorians. Harris (2015) explains that it is the constant repetition through the various media that makes this myth so ingrained into the American psyche.

In addition to the aforementioned myths presented by Holm (1992), other myths about women in general are utilized as more justification for regulating women's behaviors (Abramovitz 1996), and for the purpose of this book, the behaviors of military women, in that the American military should not be used for social experiments (Fenner 2001), an argument that was similarly employed to derail the integration of African Americans into the military. For women, an analogous argument has been continually advanced as that of radical feminists (Solaro 2006, Fenner 2001, Bird Francke 1997, Holm 1992). This distraction comes in framing the false yet effectively couched narrative that by bringing women into combat occupations, the military will only succeed in lowering its standards (Fenner 2001). Yet, for all intents and purposes and as declared by the highest-ranking interviewee in Harris's (2015) publication about the combat exclusion policy, Major General Marcelite Harris, the U.S. appeared to summon the use of standards only when women began to join the military. In reality, women's call by the U.S. government during World War II came with the caveat of much more rigorous recruiting standards for women entering the military than for men entering the military (Holm 1992), in keeping with Major General Harris's quip that it was women who actually became the impetus for the military to establish criteria for recruitment.

Fundamentally, the military had a more intelligent workforce after the integration of women than if it had remained all-male. Too, an argument can be made that in repealing the combat exclusion policy, the military can only realize its talents best by not only integrating women throughout all of its occupations but in doing so leveraging the intelligence of its women for a more effective workforce. For example, of the women who were admitted into the military between 1971 and 1976, 90 percent secured high school diplomas whereas only 63 percent of the men held the same credentials (Bird Francke 1997). As well, women were more likely to outperform their male peers by an average of 10 points on entrance examinations (Holm 1992). The retention rates of women also exceeded those of men, an average of 70 percent of women recruits in 1973 were still in the military in 1976 compared to 64 percent for men (Bird Francke 1997). For the commissioned corps in 1979 and 1980, respectively, women outscored men on the Air Force Officer Qualifying Test (Fenner 2001). What is interesting to note is that unlike male recruits, the military only recruited women who scored in the highest quartiles of its entrance examinations, not those in the lowest quartiles or Category IV (Fenner 2001). The DoD eventually admitted that its female workforce was more intelligent than its male workforce (Bird Francke 1997), but rationalized that such compromises were necessary owing to a more intelligent woman being less prone to disciplinary challenges but also not as physically equipped as her less intelligent male counterpart.

The Army in its quest to meet recruitment goals even recruited low-intelligence men, because it was never successful at recruiting more educated men (Holm 1992), but instituted a routine strategy to bolster its recruitment levels. Approximately 5 percent to 10 percent of its recruits lack a high school diploma (Harris 2003). Appallingly, the practice gave way to expand the degree of dumbing down the intelligence of the Army even further (Inkeep and Bowman 2008, Kaplan 2008), which manifested itself in unforeseen yet expected ways. Monahan and Neidel-Greenlee (2010) cited the horrific account of the Army's Private First Class Green, whose criminal record even as a child should have given recruiters much cause for pause. During Operation Iraqi Freedom Green, as the ringleader, convinced fellow soldiers to rape, pillage and kill an Iraqi teenager and her family in retaliation for killing one of their own. It was only because one of the miscreants, who by then was already discharged, disclosed the details about the act to his father that ultimately light was shed on the situation. Monahan and Neidel-Greenlee (2010) put the blame strictly on the Army and the DoD because '[i]t is that military hierarchy that sets the tone for all military situations and environments' (p.404). In essence, only with the military's and by extension the DoD's explicit and/or implicit consent can such atrocities occur. The conclusion is that only by integration of women throughout the military can the DoD expect to have an intelligent, agile and responsive workforce to prevent the penetration of the country's national defense.

In the long line of contrived myths, the sole responsibility for parenting is yet another one that has been advanced, that military women and military women in society have to live down. According to Fenner (2001) and others (Holm 1992, Bird Francke 1997), it was Operation Desert Storm that illuminated the extent to which military women were largely being blamed for neglecting their responsibilities as parents. The wrath was particularly poignant for single mothers in that the military was becoming an arsenal for unwed mothers (Holm 1992). However, it was the military, blames Bird Francke (1997), that facilitated this state of affairs. An outcome of the modern-day military has been extended deployments coupled with the need for a more technically competent workforce. This fact coincided with its workforce's family-bearing years. Additionally, the gone by conscription years of the Vietnam Conflict and prior which expected shorter enlistment contracts gave way to an all-volunteer military with as long as six-year contracts. The typical enlistee during the Vietnam Conflict was 19 years old whereas by contrast, the average enlistee during Operation Desert Storm was 26.7 years old (Bird Francke 1997). Complicating matters, more than 50 percent of the military's population were now married even as the institution considered marital status to not only have a stabilizing effect on its workforce, reducing the associated untoward behaviors such as alcohol and drugs challenges, but facilitating more re-enlistments in the process. The military's goal was to foster a family environment.

Consequently, families and even single parents found the programs offered by the military to be attractive (Bird Francke 1997). This was especially true for single fathers. Thus together these groups represented a disproportionate segment of the military's population. Yet, during Operation Desert Storm it was the single mothers, not the single fathers, who took the heat for being ill prepared for the challenges ahead. For instance, while the Navy barred newly minted recruits by upholding sole guardian for their children (Bird Francke 1997), a survey in 1992 revealed that most children were living with their parents (Thomas and Thomas 1992). Again, it was the single mothers who paid the price. Navy detailers avoided them at all costs, preferring to assign dual and married military couples instead. Single mothers, even if technically competent, were relegated to unskilled tasks.

Ironically, unlike single mothers, single fathers incurred greater expense for the military, for, on average, they had more children than single mothers (Bird Francke 1997). Still, it was the single mothers who bore the brunt of all blame, for the Navy leadership did not want them. The bias against single mothers was such that especially the media framed the information to the American public as if it was that of the single mothers alone, with no single fathers ever implicated who could not simultaneously juggle the obligations of parenthood and the military (Holm 1992). Implicit in this message to the public as 'mommies going to war' (Fenner 2001, Holm 1992, Bird Francke 1997) was that women were inherently incapable of managing these dual responsibilities. This harks back to the archaic notion as per Harris's (2009b) research on the travails of academic women and women as commissioned officers in the military that at least in the academy it is 'a truth universally acknowledged that a woman might produce books or babies, but not both, just as she might organize her life around marriage or a career, but not both' (Ostriker 1998, p.3). Inciting the public with such incendiary language as that of journalist Fred Reed, that the military has become a stronghold for 'unwed mothers' (Holm 1992), only reifies the myth.

The Pentagon's own reporting during Operation Desert Storm that more than two-thirds of single parents in the military were men did not dissuade the likes of Reed from pronouncing this propaganda as a problem of single mothers. Even more erroneous is that these uncorroborated myths never adversely affected the deployment of troops during this period (Bird Francke 1997). If anything, an indiscernible less than 0.5 percent of personnel were not deployed because of family-related issues (Sagawa and Duff Campbell 1992). At this time, the military's challenge was a consequence of moving from a conscripted force to an all-volunteer one (Holm 1992).

As Harris (2015) sees it, notwithstanding then the existing combat exclusion policy, while progress towards the repeal has been exceedingly slow, there is hope that the likes of groups like DACOWITS will hold the military accountable for implementing the conditions of its repeal. The committee was so troubled that it saw fit to intervene to ensure that the DoD's drawdown from Operations Enduring and Iraqi Freedom to Operation New Dawn, at least in Iraq, would retain 'highly qualified women' (DACOWITS 2012, Executive Summary). This intervention and finding were due in part to earlier troubling findings by the Military Leadership Diversity Commission (MLDC 2011) that the military stands to lose a disproportionate pool of qualified women if the institution failed to put measures into place. DACOWITS (2012) responded by imploring the DoD to take heed when instituting the following. One, that the military must be proactive in not only staving off the loss of critically qualified women as part of the overall drawdown, but must do so in a manner that preserves both the diversity and talents of the force. Two, and prior to the repeal of the combat exclusion policy, the committee realized the detriment to the military because of the potential loss of highly qualified women. As such, DACOWITS urged the military to remove the combat exclusion that prevented women from serving in combat and the associated critical assignments. Three, for this purpose, the committee asked that closed occupations, training and assignments that are designated as combat be opened to women and in so doing establish *gender-neutral standards* as one of an array of approaches to meet this goal. Therefore, like men, women should be placed in these assignments based on their qualifications, not gender. As Harris (2015) counsels, the weight of the earlier repeal of the Don't Ask, Don't Tell and Don't Pursue policy and the epidemic levels of sexual assault and related offenses in the military have separately and collectively dealt the final blow for the eventual collapse of the combat exclusion policy.

Still, it remains to be seen, in light of the combat exclusion policy's repeal and a call for the full integration of women into the military and specifically into combat and combat-related occupations, positions and assignments, how implementation will play out given the ideology, it is believed, of the Trump Administration. This is coupled with a reticent Secretary of Defense whose acculturation has been that of a lifer in the Marine Corps, the most chauvinistic vestige of outdated mores about women and the most resistant to the acceptance of women in the military, particularly in combat.

Bibliography

Abramovitz, M. (1996). *Regulating the Lives of Women. Social Welfare Policy from Colonial Times to the Present*. Revised Edition. Boston, MA: South End Press.

Allen, T.B. (2006). *Harriet Tubman, Secret Agent: How Daring Slaves and Freed Blacks Spied for the Union During the Civil War*. Des Moines, IA: National Geographic Children's Books, Scholastic Book Club Edition.

Alvarez, L. (2009). G.I. Jane Breaks the Combat Barrier. *New York Times*, August 16, A1.

Bennett, J. (2015). Ash Carter Sounds Like He's Already Come to a Decision on Women in Combat. *Daily Caller*. www.dailycaller.com. Retrieved February 27, 2017.

Bird Francke, L. (1997). *Ground Zero. The Gender Wars in the Military*. New York, NY: Simon and Schuster.

166   On Citizenship

Brennan, T.J. (2017). Hundreds of Marines Investigated for Sharing Photos of Naked Colleagues. March 4. *Reveal.* www.revealnews.com. Retrieved May 12, 2017.

Breuer, W.B. (1997). *War and American Women: Heroism, Deeds, and Country.* Westport, CT: Praeger Publishing.

Brownmiller, S. (1993). *Against Our Will: Men, Women, and Rape.* New York, NY: Ballantine Books.

Cahn, D. (2017). Some Vets Will Join Women's March to Protest after Trump Inauguration. *Stars and Stripes.* January 20. www.military.com. Retrieved January 30, 2017.

Carreiras, H. (2006). *Gender and the Military. Women and the Armed Forces of Western Democracies.* London and New York: Routledge.

Cassata, D. (2013). Kirsten Gillibrand Targets Military Sexual Assault Law. *Huffington Post Politics,* July 29. www.huffingtonpost.com/2013/07/29/kirsten-gillibrand-military-sexual-assault_n_3669914.html. Retrieved March 22, 2017.

Crockett, E. (2016). Mike Pence Is No Less of a Threat to Women than Donald Trump. October 8. *Vox.* www.vox.com. Retrieved February 27, 2017.

De Luce, D., and McLeary, P. (2016). Female and Transgender Troops Fear Combat Exclusion in Trump's Pentagon. *Foreign Policy.* www.foreignpolicy.com. Retrieved February 27, 2017.

Defense Advisory Committee on Women in the Services (DACOWITS). (2012). *Status Report.* http://dacowits.defense.gov/Portals/48/Documents/Reports/2012/Annual%20Report/dacowits2012report.pdf. Retrieved February 24, 2017.

Devine, T.E. (1997). *The Influence of America's Casualty Sensitivity on Military Strategy and Doctrine.* School of Advanced Airpower Studies. Air University, Maxwell AFB, AL.

Elshtain, J.B. (1987). *Women and War.* New York: Basic Books, Inc. Publishers.

Faludi, S. (2006). *Backlash. The Undeclared War Against American Women.* Revised Edition. New York, NY: Three Rivers Press.

Farokhmanesh, M. (2016). How a Trump Administration Threatens Women's Health. December 12. *The Verge.* www.theverge.com. Retrieved February 27, 2017.

Fenner, L.M. (2001). Moving Targets: Women's Roles in the U.S. Military in the 21st Century. In L.M. Fenner and M.E. deYoung (Eds.), *Women in Combat. Civic Duty or Military Liability?.* Washington, DC: Georgetown University Press.

Firestone, J.M., and Harris, R.J. (2008). Sexual Harassment in the U.S. Military Reserve Component. A Preliminary Analysis. *Armed Forces and Society,* 36, 1, 86–102.

Goldin, C. (2006). The Rising (and Then Declining) Significance of Gender. In F. D. Blau, M.C. Brinton, and D.B. Grusky (Eds.), *The Declining Significance of Gender?* New York, NY: Russell Sage Foundation.

Goldstein, J.S. (2003). *War and Gender. How Gender Shapes the War System and Vice Versa.* New York, NY: Cambridge University Press.

Grant DePauw, L. (1998). *Battle Cries and Lullabies. Women in War from Prehistory to the Present.* Norman, OK: University of Oklahoma Press.

Hacker, B.C. (1981). Women and Military Institutions in Early Modern Europe: A Renaissance. *Signs,* 6, 4, 643–671.

Hardwick, L. (1996). Ancient Amazons: Heroes, Outsiders, or Women? In I. Mac Auslan and P. Walcot (Eds.), *Women in Antiquity* (p.156–176). Oxford: Oxford University Press.

Harrell, Margaret C., and Laura L. Miller. (1997). *New Opportunities for Military Women: Effects upon Readiness, Cohesion, and Morale.* Washington, DC: National Defense Research Institute. Santa Monica, CA: RAND Publications.

Harrell, M.C., Beckett, M.K., Chien, C.S., and Sollinger, J.M. (2002). *The Status of Gender Integration in the Military: Analysis of Selected Occupations.* Santa Monica, CA: RAND Publications.

Harris, G.L.A. (2003). The Impact of Monetary Strategies on Organizational Commitment in the Military. Unpublished dissertation. Rutgers University. May.

Harris, G.L.A. (2009a). The Multifaceted Nature of White Female Attrition in the Military. *Journal of Public Management and Social Policy*, 15, 1, 71–93.

Harris, G.L.A. (2009b). Women, the Military and Academe: Navigating the Family Track in an Up or Out System. *Administration and Society*, 41, 4, 391–422.

Harris, G.L.A. (2015). *Living Legends and Full Agency: Implications of Repealing the Combat Exclusion Policy.* New York, NY: Taylor & Francis Group, a division of CRC Press.

Herbert, M.S. (1998). *Camouflage Isn't Only for Combat. Gender, Sexuality, and Women in the Military.* New York and London: New York University Press.

Higonnet, M.R., and Higonnet, L.R. (1987). The Double Helix. In *Behind the Lines: Gender and the Two World Wars.* New Haven, CT: Yale University Press.

Holm, J. (1992). *Women in the Military. An Unfinished Revolution.* Revised Edition. Novato, CA: Presidio Press.

Inkeep, S., and Bowman, T. (2008). Army Documents Show Lower Recruiting Standards. National Public Radio (NPR), April 17.

Jones, M. (1986). Women Marines Doing Better Than Expected on Rifle Range. *Navy Times*, January 27, 3. Unavailable. Originally retrieved March 7, 2012.

Kaplan, F. (2008). Dumb and Dumber. The U.S. Army Lowers Recruitment Standards ... Again. *Slate.* January 24. www.slate.com/articles/news_and_politics/war_stories/2008/01/dumb_and_dumber.html. Retrieved October 21, 2017.

Kheel, R. (2017). Armed Services Chair; Military Doesn't Fully Grasp Nude Photo Sharing Scandal. March 16. MSN. www.msn.com. Retrieved May 12, 2017.

Kirk, I. (1988). Images of Amazons: Marriage and Matriarchy. In S. McDonald, P. Holden and S. Ardener (Eds.), *Images of Women in Peace and War: Cultural and Historical Perspectives* (p.27–39). London: Macmillan Education.

Lawrence, Q., and Penaloza, M. (2013). Sexual Violence Victims Say Military Justice System is 'Broken.' National Public Radio. March 21. www.npr.org/2013/03/21/174840895/sexual-violence-victims-say-military-justice-system-is-broken. Retrieved February 26, 2017.

Lioness Report. (2012). *Cultivating Change: Lioness Impact Report.* Based on *Lioness*, A Feature Documentary directed by M. McLagan and D. Sommers. Room 11 Productions.

Maninger, S. (2008). Women in Combat: Reconsidering the Case Against Deployment of Women in Combat-Support and Combat Units. In H. Carreiras and G. Kummel (Eds.), *Women in the Military and Armed Conflict.* Wiesbaden: VS Verlag fur Sozialwissenschaften.

Mazur, D.H. (1998). Women, Responsibility and the Military. *Notre Dame Law Review*, 74, 1, 1–45.

McElrath, K. (1992). Gender, Career Disruption and Academic Rewards. *Journal of Higher Education*, 63, 3, 269–281.

McLagan, M., and Sommers, D. (2010). Introductions: How We Came to Make 'Lioness.' July. www.pbs.org/pov/regardingwar/conversations/women-at-war/introductions-how-we-came-to-make-lioness.php. Retrieved May 2, 2017.

McLaughlin, E.C., and Stapleton, A.C. (2017). Secret Marines Group Is Still Sharing Nude Photos Amid Scandal. March 9. *CNN Politics.* www.cnn.com. Retrieved May 12, 2017.

Military Leadership Diversity Commission (MLDC). (2011). From Representation to Inclusion: Diversity Leadership for the 21st-Century. March 15. www.hsdl.org/?view&did=715693. Retrieved May 2, 2017.

Mitchell, B. (1997). *Women in the Military: Flirting with Disaster.* Washington, DC: Regnery Publishing, Inc.

Monahan, E.M., and Neidel-Greenlee, R. (2010). *A Few Good Women. America's Military Women from World War I to the Wars in Iraq and Afghanistan.* New York: Anchor Books.

Montagne, R., and Lawrence, Q. (2013). What Does It Mean To Be a Woman in the U.S. Military? *National Public Radio.* March 22. www.npr.org/2013/03/22/175014364/what-does-it-mean-to-be-a-woman-in-the-u-s-military. Retrieved February 26, 2017.

Moore, M. (1988). Top Marine Bars Widening Women's Roles. *Washington Post,* April 26, 1.

Moskos, C. (1994). From Citizens' Army to Social Laboratory. In W.J. Scott and S.C. Stanley (Eds.), *Gays and Lesbians in the Military: Issues, Concerns and Constraints* (p.83–94). Hawthorne, NY: Walter de Gruyter Publishers.

Ostriker, A. (1998). The Maternal Mind. In C. Coiner and D.H. George (Eds.), *The Family Track: Keeping Your Faculties While You Mentor, Nurture, Teach, and Serve.* Champaign: University of Illinois Press.

Petronio, K. (2012). Get Over It! We're Not All Created Equal. *Marine Corps Gazette.* www.mca-marines.org/gazette/article/get-over-it-we-are-not-all-created-equal. Retrieved May 12, 2017.

Phillips, D. (2015). Marine Commander's Firing Stirs Debate on Integration of Women in Corps. July 12. *New York Times.* https://mobile.nytimes.com. Retrieved May 12, 2017.

Randal, M. (1981). *Sandino's Daughter: Testimonies of Nicaraguan Women in Struggle.* Vancouver: Star Books.

Randal, M., and Yanz, L. (1995). *Sandino's Daughters: Testimonies of Nicaraguan Women in Struggle.* New Brunswick, NJ: Rutgers University Press.

Rosen, L.N., Durand, D.B., Bliese, P.D., Halverson, R.R., Rothberg, J.M., and Harrison, N.L. (1996). Cohesion and Readiness in Gender-Integrated Combat Service Support Units: The Impact of Acceptance of Women and Gender Ratio. *Armed Forces and Society,* 22, 4, 537–553.

Rosen, L.N., Bliese, P.D., Wright, K.A., and Gifford, R.K. (1999). Gender Composition and Group Cohesion in U.S. Army Units: A Comparison across Five Studies. *Armed Forces and Society,* 25, 3, 365–386.

Rosen, L.N., Knudson, K.H., and Fencher, P. (2003). Cohesion and the Culture of Hypermasculinity in U.S. Army Units. *Armed Forces and Society,* 29, 3, 325–351.

Sagawa, S., and Duff Campbell, N. (1992). *Recommendation in the Presidential Commission on the Assignment of Women in the Armed Forces Regarding Parents in Military Service.* Washington, DC: National Women's Law Center. November 14.

Saywell, S. (1985). *Women in War.* New York: Viking Press.
Service Women's Action Network (SWAN). (2016). Annual Survey of Service Women and Women Veterans. www.servicewomen.org. Retrieved February 28, 2017.
Sigmund Gartner, S. (2008). Secondary Casualty Information: Casualty Uncertainty, Female Casualties, and Wartime Support. *Conflict Management and Peace Management*, 25, 2, 98–111.
Smith, C., and Keneally, M. (2016). Trump Stands By Controversial Tweet about Military Sex Assaults. September 7. *ABC News.* www.abcnews.com. Retrieved February 26, 2017.
Solaro, E. (2006). *Women in the Line of Fire. What You Should Know About Women in the Military.* Emeryville, CA: Seal Press.
Thomas, P.J., and Thomas, M.D. (1992). *Impact of Pregnant Women and Single Parents Upon Navy Personnel Systems.* San Diego, CA: Navy Personnel Research and Development Center, Women and Multicultural Research Office [Report TN-92-87]. February.
U.S. Army. (2002). Women in the Army: An Annotated Bibliography. U.S. Army Research Institute for the Behavioral and Social Sciences. Special Report 48. May.
U.S. General Accountability Office (GAO). (1997). Gender Integration in Basic Training: The Services are Using a Variety of Approaches. June 5. GAO/T-NSAFD-97-174.
Van Crevald, M. (2000). The Great Illusion: Women in the Military. *Millennium – Journal of International Studies*, 29, 2, 429–442.
Van Crevald, M. (2001). *Men, Women and War: Do Women Belong in the Front Line?* New York, NY: Cassell Publishing.
Wechsler Segal, M.W. (1993). Women in the Armed Forces. In R. Howes and M. Stevenson (Eds.), *Women and the Use of Military Force.* Boulder, CO: Lynne and Rienner.
Wechsler Segal, M. (1995). Women's Military Roles Cross-Nationally, Past, Present, and Future. *Gender and Society*, 9, 6, 757–775.
Whitlock, C. (2013). General's Promotion Blocked Over Her Dismissal of Sexual-Assault Verdict. *Washington Post.* May 6. http://articles.washingtonpost.com/2013-05-06/world/39060954_1_sexual-assault-jury-commander. Retrieved May 12, 2017.

Part IV
Military Culture

Lest we forget, the recent scandal involving men, primarily from the Marine Corps, uploading unauthorized nude photographs of their female colleagues to the Internet for the sole purpose of illicit, and unbridled sexual entertainment, need only serve as a reminder that while of this writing it is the year 2017, and the 2013 repeal of the combat exclusion policy only called for full implementation in 2016, the military culture has still far to go in integrating women and branding its sisters-in-arms as equal partners in the fight for national security. As Faludi (2006) notes, this culture, that is of male domination, is a problem of American society. The military is simply a subset of this larger society from which the institution recruits to populate its workforce. Thus, the military is a reflection of American culture.

Shere Hite in 1987, according to Faludi (2006), was admonished for her presumed biased appraisal of American women's desires in the face of ever demanding male partners as they do all that they can to gain an equal footing with men. Allegedly, Hite's 922-page report based on a sample of 4,500 women, revealed that 80 percent of them bemoaned not being treated as equals, with only 20 percent of them feeling that they have achieved equal footing at home. The dissatisfied 80 percent believed that their pursuit of autonomy has generated a backlash for which they were ill-prepared. However, as Faludi notes, Hite's report was recollected more for the controversy that it engendered than the fundamental message of her findings. Around the same time, in 1985, a book by Scully Blotnick, a male psychologist, offered a diametrically opposed conclusion: that the career woman was doing a disservice to her family since her career 'poisons both the professional and personal lives of women' (Faludi 2006, p.22). In his 25-year study of 3,466 women, Blotnick noted that women were only destined for a life devoid of love despite having held successful careers. However, the façade of Blotnick's book became apparent in light of his criticisms of the feminist movement, which he described as a 'smoke screen behind which most of those who were afraid of being labeled ego manically grasping and ambitious hid' (Faludi 2006, p.22). Interestingly enough, though, unlike the reception to Shere Hite's conclusion, Blotnick's findings were favorably embraced, even encouraging more of such studies. What is even more appalling, says Faludi (2006), is that Blotnick's methodology was dubious at best, yet no one questioned it.

It is of note that, for starters, Shere Hite is a woman who was roundly criticized by the media as utilizing jaundiced methodology (Faludi 2006). No such criticism was ever leveled against Blotnick, the man. However, as Faludi implores, the statistics that were employed by Blotnick to yield his incredible findings, are the very ones that people should have been the most cynical about. Further, Faludi describes that the period during which these data were erroneously collected was during the Reagan Administration, and they served as gauges or points of significance in women's lives to the extent that the Administration became part of the problem in producing similar data to reinforce these already spurious findings. Faludi (2006) dubbed this period 'a war against women's independence' (p.24). This mindset is akin to Abramovitz's (1996) regulation of women's lives, of which the combat exclusion policy is one such ploy as the military's version that is borne of military culture and male dominance.

This preamble highlights the contents of Part IV of the book, which delves into such foci as white male privilege and entitlement, the military as a culture of male domination, the effeminization and thus degradation of the enemy, women as a proxy for men, and the backlash against women in their quest for full agency and success.

Bibliography

Abramovitz, M. (1996). *Regulating the Lives of Women: Social Welfare Policy from Colonial Times to the Present*. Brooklyn, NY: South End Press.

Faludi, S. (2006). *Backlash. The Undeclared War Against American Women*. New York, NY: Three Rivers Press.

11 White Male Privilege

Some years back, the lead author of this book had an interesting exchange with a senior ranking officer and retired pilot of one of the reserve components of the U.S. military, who at one time had also served on active duty. At the time, in 2012, I advised this retired officer that I was in the process of collecting data for a study on pioneering, prominent and/or elite women veterans in light of the combat exclusion policy for my subsequent 2015 book publication. He remarked that 'you women need to wait your turn,' to which I immediately replied by stating that when one (women) has been waiting on the other side for men to do the right thing, yesterday for this change to occur is not soon enough. While I am certain that the retired officer took offense at my retort, that was the point, or at least to get him thinking about the consequences of his selfish remark. In other words, military women were no longer, if ever, content to wait and need not wait until military men or the civilian leadership decided when it was time to do that which is in the best interest of the military and the country, not themselves, by leveraging the talents of all in the military, including women, to have equal access to all career assignments as military men.

That said, women should no longer endure discomfort for the sole purpose of having to needlessly prop up the insecurity and creature comforts of their male counterparts. It is from this privileged stance that no doubt this retired military officer, a white male pilot, spoke without regard to the adverse impact on the morale of the military's female workforce, and by doing so, was showing how the military was depriving the institution and the country, for that matter, of the full complement of the talents and skillsets of its female workforce. While, in theory, the combat exclusion policy no longer exists, regrettably, the regressive mindsets of the institution and the accompanying attitudes and behaviors still persist.

Such destructive belief systems, pronounces Abramovitz (1996), view women as the property of men while contributing to women's subjugation. Being white and male confers an implicit legitimacy that requires no explanation (Bourdieu 2001). Faludi (2006) speaks of the wrath against American women by the likes of academic Michael Levin, also during the late 1980s, who rails against what he believes is wrong with feminism. In fact, Levin classifies the movement as antidemocratic and totalitarian in its premise and goes on to prescribe what are the natural inclinations of women and men: that women pursue successful, professional vocations to the detriment of engaging in conjugal relations and parenthood, that the division of labor duties for men and women are misunderstood for women are innately domesticated while men excel in mathematics, for instance. Paradoxically, despite what Levin spewed in his public writings, he was bound to the opposite lifestyle at home. Levin's wife, a Yeshiva University professor, was not only like her other half a philosophy scholar, but her specialty is no other than 'the philosophy of math' (Faludi 2006, p.308). Additionally, the responsibility of childrearing in his household is divided equally between the parents. Needless to say, what Levin was espousing as a public figure was far from the reality in his personal life. Nevertheless, these bouts of ill-will against women by a perceived notable scholar, in this case in the public domain no less, again do nothing but reinforce the existing rancor toward American women.

The American military is similarly plagued. The institution is infused throughout with notions of masculinity where such perceived disruptions as the women's movement and the demand for the full integration of women throughout the military, especially in combat, challenge the status quo or what is understood to be the domain of white men. The termination of conscription and the advent of the all-volunteer force represented a turning point, a crisis of sorts in masculinity, or at least a time of change for what defined masculinity, for as Brown (2012) alludes, it is this very prodigy upon which military recruitment rests. Without it, or the lure of transforming boys into men, what could the military now utilize to entice the same group for the service of country? For this reason, each military branch was compelled to create its own conception or varying forms of masculinity to meet its own mission (Brown 2012). Many have criticized the military as a result for moving away from traditional notions of masculinity to the disadvantage of masculinity in the quest to achieve a more balanced strategy by appealing to women in the process, although arguably, the Marine Corps has successfully adhered to its warrior spirit, that is combat. However, times are changing.

Owing to contemporary times and the need to adjust to the demands of societal realities at hand, the Marine Corps is being forced to change its tune as it now actively deploys a campaign in the pursuit of attracting more women to the institution using the rationale of good citizens and under the umbrella of 'Battle Won' (Fox News 2017). Some have already disparaged the campaign as a diluted version to diversify the institution. The move has been made all the more challenging as the Marine Corps, the smallest of the military branches with a considerably smaller female workforce, works to overcome the sex-laced scandal that is dogging the institution and hampering its potential recruitment of millennial women in the process.

In Western vernacular, gender or sex is defined in binary terms, as one or the other (Brown 2012). Masculine becomes diametrically opposed to feminine as is light to dark. Using this definition, as Scott (1986) asserts, masculine and feminine are the principal terms to denote power. Power conveys the privileges and entitlements that men subliminally enjoy and directly and indirectly express over women. However, the taxonomies are more complex than this. To be masculine or hegemonic masculinity confers several levels of authority and control over others, including women (Connell and Messerschmidt 2005, Connell 1987). For example, Harris's (2012) theory of marginality holds that such groups as minorities and women are routinely assigned to manage so-called diversity programs as a 'strategy of containment' (p.6), which merely succeeds in further marginalizing these already marginalized groups. Even affirmative action programs that are codified into law to advance the status of these same marginalized groups should then not be scrutinized for their minimal gains for, in actuality, these programs were designed by white males as yet another strategy of containment (Aguirre 2000, Law 1999). Frankenberg (1993) also speaks to the Eurocentric view of whiteness to denote what is conceived in America as the norm. Essentially, to be white in America signifies 'dominance' and 'economic superiority' (DeMello Patterson 2000, p.104), whereas being nonwhite implies subordination and marginalization, and because women and minorities, at least in America, are perceived as outliers in the population, they are considered to be deviants (Ellefson 1998, Law 1999). Likewise, as Grimes (2002) claims, unlike other groups in America and by inference white men, white men need not prove their citizenship for they are the 'true' (p.398) Americans while nonwhite groups and women are suspect.

Mindful of any threat to their economic and/or political power, white men will not cede control to other groups, at least in any meaningful way. So, power determines the social ordering of groups (Kanter 1977, Reskin et al. 1999) and is another way by which to distribute resources to minorities and women (Reskin et al. 1999). This is especially true in austere times when resources are scarce. On top of the heap in America sits the white male whose self-appointment helps him to control the movement and maintain the power balance and distribution of resources between the perceived ingroup (white men) and outgroups (women and minorities) (Reskin et al. 1999) as ways of reinforcing political and economic prowess (Renfro et al. 2006, Frederico and Sidanius 2002a, 2002b, Kravitz et al. 2000). However, with these delineations comes an increase in discrimination against perceived outgroups as defined by the ingroup (Renfro et al. 2006). Kanter (1977) recommends that to offset these shortcomings that result in increased discrimination against outgroups, these groups should increase their critical mass or size in the organization to at least 15 percent for representation. Yet, even Kanter (1977) concedes, and Etzkowitz et al. (2000) concur, that this increase might be for naught given the conspicuous nature of such groups. Groups like African Americans are especially vulnerable. Plus these divisions purposefully exist to preserve gender and race distinctions (Nkomo 1992, Zimmer 1988). Hence, this nuanced existence or what Thomas (1991) calls assimilated diversity, is only superficial in nature to ensure that all groups adhere to the implicit rules to which they were neither party in developing nor solicited for input, but which have been nonetheless concocted by white men (Hall and Stevenson 2007).

Tokens are sometimes elevated by the ingroup to serve as exemplars of their respective groups (Kanter 1977), albeit through asymmetric lens (Harris 2012). However, an unintended consequence of such selection moves members of these perceived outgroups to self-sabotage. Members of these outgroups respond through the calculated diversion of any unique accolades toward themselves even as they engage in Herculean bids to prove to the bestowers of these inauthentic honors that they are worthy of them while taking on more of such responsibilities that are necessary tactics that no one from the ingroup would even contemplate (Kanter 1986).

We see multiple examples of this practice where military women minimize achievements that have been conferred on them. The move by Sergeant Leigh Ann Hester, highlighted in a previous section of this book, is a typical tactic when she deliberately deflected a compliment from the media upon receiving the Silver Star for valor, the first woman to be so decorated since World War II, during the initial phase of Operation Iraqi Freedom, for sheroic action (Lumpkin 2005). Sergeant Hester, in an answer to questions about the award and attention, was restrained in her response by stating: 'I am honored to even be considered much less awarded the medal. It really doesn't have anything to do with being female. It's about the duties that I performed that day as a soldier' (Lumpkin 2005, p.1, Harris 2009, p.84–85). Technically, Sergeant Hester was correct, for it was her outstanding performance that earned her the award. Nevertheless, at least for the press, what eclipsed the award was her role as a woman and noncombatant performing the duties of a combatant and a man.

Take the demise of Captain Linda Bray, also earlier mentioned, when during Operation Just Cause she allegedly became the first woman at the helm to take soldiers into combat (Titunik 2000). Captain Bray incurred such ire in the Army's pursuit to downplay her role as a combatant, much less as a woman leading troops into combat, that she became a casualty of her own success and one whom the Army willingly scapegoated to advance its own agenda. Both women, as Harris (2009, 2015) hypothesized, were in a struggle for full agency. While Sergeant Hester astutely deflected attention from herself in light of her humble response to the media, Captain Bray suffered the onslaught of the secret finally being disclosed to the American public that the military had been employing women as combatants all along, a fact confirmed by one of the women in Harris's (2015) research who was deployed to Central America around the same period as Captain Bray.

Both Hester and Bray as military women bore the awesome burden of representing all women in and out of the military. Both women were also acutely aware of the potential backlash of being singled out as women by the media for commendation for performance in the line of duty but with the military's expectation that such achievements should be shared, although Sergeant Hester expertly played her hand by modulating any such criticisms.

For some tokens, in the quest to overcome the very reputed stereotypes for their groups, they bow to the pressure by reinforcing the stereotypes (Steele 1997). These behaviors inadvertently spiral out of control as tokens virtually establish themselves on stage to satisfy every unimaginable role to be conceived by the white male establishment. In effect, tokens become overachievers. Still, this self-destruction may yield even more unintended costs as tokens may never fully realize their aspirations for accordingly their elevation in the organization is strictly monitored by their sponsors or those within the ingroup (Elliott and Smith 2004). As a consequence, it is alleged that women and minorities, at least in America, cannot themselves become sponsors and yet it is this sponsorship that purportedly gives them the opportunity to ascend in an organization. Formal and informal networks also become the go-to establishments for invaluable information about such opportunities but it is the latter that takes precedence over the former (Bridges and Villemez 1986, Podolny and Baron 1997). While women and minorities naively cling to formal organizational networks as the primary modes for access to information and organizational resources, it is the informal networks that will invariably bear more fruit and produce a bounty of information and resources for those with access (McGuirre 2002). This access to informal networks is also tightly controlled by the ingroup through a form of rank ordering of individuals from various groups. Consequently, such qualifications as education and experience through formal networks and upon which women and minorities tend to depend are so designed to take those who aspire to greater organizational heights only so far. In the end, it is the informal networking that eventually determines if, when and where one is elevated within the organization.

For tokens, there is still another barrier to overcome, and one which stifles women and minorities in organizations. Kanter (1977) refers to this phenomenon as homosocial reproduction. At this point, it is the prestige of the position that dictates who goes where and when. The greater the stature and significance that the position holds, the greater the likelihood that women and minorities will be discounted as candidates. Yet, again, by using this strategy, the ingroup (white men) selects his own to represent, solidify and advance his interests. Should the ingroup depart from this time-honored norm by selecting someone from the outgroup, the selection, token or otherwise, comes with the understanding as to who lies where on the organizational food chain. Even so, some of the selections for women and minorities come with little to no authority (Kanter 1979), which in turn serves only to undermine and reinforce their marginalization (Harris 2012). This practice where the white male or ingroup is more likely to choose his own is known as attraction selection attrition (Schneider 1987). This practice also operates to dissuade women and minorities from applying for certain positions and creates a double jeopardy, where for women, no man or even woman will risk political or economic capital to sponsor another woman. When women succeed, they are only believed to have done so because of familial relationships, for example. Harris's (2012) theory of multiple marginality holds that in effect, women and minorities are caught in an interminable state of marginality because they are bereft of any power.

So, by invoking this European culture and by extension a sense of American culture as representative of the majority or ingroup (white men), the U.S. military perpetuates hegemonic masculinity, a culture of entitlement (Connell 1995) that is valued as one with the warrior spirit. This warrior spirit is promoted at the expense of emotion. Some have portrayed the military as gendered owing to emphases on violence, hazing and the vilification of women (Burke 1999, Bird Francke 1997), and that this nexus is *historical* in the founding of the American republic and its subsequent wars (Dubbert 1979, Jarvis 2004). Moreover, war and hence the military, are one and the same with masculinity. Hunter (2007) describes the military like any other culture in that there are norms and rules, spoken and unspoken, written and unwritten, and where it is both the unspoken and unwritten rules that in many ways dictate the manner in which the culture plays out. For the military, as Hunter notes, violence, via one such means as sexual assault or the objectification of the enemy or other human beings, is endemic in the military. Hypermasculinity is at the heart of military culture. It is infused in basic training whereby culture change for the civilian recruit includes the deprecation of women as part and parcel of the indoctrination process (Bird Francke 1997, Hunter 2007). In this view, hypermasculinity is about competition, not competition with women but competition with other men (Hunter 2007). After all, competition is about who wins and who loses. Therefore, losing to a woman is rendered meaningless for, after all, 'she is only a woman' (Hunter 2007, p.37), and because innately a man is simply better than a woman in every meaningful endeavor.

A Naval Academy tradition for departing first year students at the culmination of the academic year includes forming a human pyramid with the goal of reaching atop a 21-foot obelisk to confiscate the sailor's hat (Hunter 2007). The intent here is neither to merely climb the obelisk nor retrieve the sailor's hat but to do so by improving upon the previous class's record. Legend has it that the person who successfully retrieves the sailor's hat is likely to make it to the rank of admiral unless the member who retrieves the sailor's hat is a woman. As tradition has it, no male cadet would want to be disgraced by being remembered as ever being part of this class when a woman prevails in retrieving the sailor's hat. Similarly, power and emotional control, characteristics of the warrior spirit, are aligned with this notion of manhood. Yet, having these characteristics comes at a price, where, when given to exasperation, such forms of violence as sexual assault become one of myriad ways to vent, including at women colleagues (Hunter 2007). Even so, to engage in this kind of violence or specifically sexual assault or some sex act is envisaged as a rite of passage, an entitlement for men in the military as it is to endure pain (Hunter 2007). 'Pain is weakness leaving the body' (Hunter 2007, p.38). A deplorable component of enduring this pain is the right to inflict one's frustration sexually on those who have consented, or not, to engage in such behaviors. In this way, in the military, the release of this sexually is not only an expectation of military men but one that has become synonymous with violence (Hunter 2007).

Truth be told, the higher one's rank in the military, the more the incumbent white male is afforded this privilege or entitlement. This becomes more perverse as it is believed that one is entitled to such rewards as one demands them. This mindset aligns with misogyny or the debasement of women. No wonder the military orients particularly its most vulnerable and newest recruits by denigrating them as if they were women as in when a drill sergeant seeks to offend his subordinates by referring to them as a 'bunch of girls' or 'ladies' (Hunter 2007, p.40).

When Sally Millett, a World War II prisoner of war (POW) was asked by the media to comment about the fate and the detainment of Specialist Melissa Rathbun-Nealy by the Iraqis during Operation Desert Storm, she sneered by saying that '[t]hey [the Iraqis] don't hate women any more or as much as American men hate women' (in Hunter 2007, p.40). Or, as with the indoctrination of recruits, one military member recalled it as:

> The lessons on mankind ... focus lies on creating what the Army wanted than defining what the Army did not want. This is why calling recruits faggots, sissies, pussies and girls had been a time honored stratagem for drill instructors through the Armed Forces. The context was clear: There is not much worse you could call a man.
> (In Hunter 2007, p.41)

It is no irony, claims Hunter (2007), that the Marine Corps, the branch of the military with the highest incidence of sexual assault, refers to its coequal branches of the military as 'the sister services' (Hunter 2007, p.41). This is a deliberate form of insult.

Yet, in spite of this boorish bravado, on the opposite side of hypermasculinity lies a feeble being. When confronted by women, this is especially the case (Hunter 2007). Specifically, hypermasculinity is threatened in the presence of capable women, gay men and lesbians. Testifying at a Congressional hearing, former Chairman of the Joint Chiefs of Staff General

John Vessey, Jr., said that bringing women into the military had essentially traumatized the all-male institution. What was profound, questioned Major General Jeanne Holm at the time, was how the limited presence of women into the military could so impact the psyche of a force that was overwhelmingly male. More alarming, as Major General Holm saw it, was, though never directly acknowledged, the women's collective ability to successfully perform those tasks that were previously the purview of men. Even more telling, asserts Hunter (2007), was that the initial class of 100 women at the Army's U.S. Military Academy at West Point, literally terrified the 4,000 men in the student body. Translating this state of affairs to one of combat could then mean that 'how tough a force would have to be to intimidate an enemy 40-times their number' (Hunter 2007, p.44).

However, contemporary times demand contemporary action, even at the risk of bucking tradition. The fact that the Marine Corps of all the military branches is now looking to women, ostensibly the enemy, to shore up its fighting prowess even as the institution attempts to explain away the current scandal as one that is not representative of its workforce, speaks volumes. Brown (2012) sees this quandary as illustrative of hypermasculinity in crisis. However, Kimmel (1996) explains that this so-called crisis is not new.

As social transformations have taken place, such as with the family and the economy, institutions like the military that are defined by masculinity have been forced to respond in kind (Kimmel 1996). Each period has been described as a critical juncture for men, given these shifts. Nevertheless, following each reputed crisis, there has been a corresponding state of calm. To Kimmel, American men personify the need for control: when they experience undue urgency, they redirect this vulnerability onto others; and when they are unable to cope with this perceived pressure, they seek refuge by running away. Joining the military was by all means a way then to reassert manhood. World War I exemplified a time of moral exceptionalism while the post-Vietnam Conflict years were a blow to America's collective distinctiveness (Gibson 1991). The social actions in turn proved a crisis of conscience for the nation and the military, and questioned what it means to be a man and a warrior. For it was the military, says Gibson (1991), to which men looked for their reaffirmation of manhood, 'to restore the nation's cultural heritage as the land of good men who always win' (p.183). In case we are inclined to forget, these notions and aspirations of men and country are for white men only. For, as Herbert (1998) reminds us, a woman cannot be feminine and still be a soldier – at least, not an acceptable one. If she is deemed a soldier, she jeopardizes her identity and risks being maligned as a lesbian.

In late 1994, Navy Lieutenant Kara Hultgreen, one of the few women to qualify to fly the F-14, lost an engine during a training exercise in the Pacific and went down as a result (*Minerva Bulletin*, Fall/Winter 1994; Herbert 1998). She died upon impact. The rumor mill had it that Hultgreen was unqualified to fly the fighter jet (Herbert 1998). An investigation following the crash proved otherwise. The president of the Women Military Aviators, Commander Trish Beckman, noted that a combination of factors contributed to Lieutenant Hultgreen's loss of control of the aircraft, a confluence that no pilot could have corrected for, given the reaction time necessary. In similar incidents with male pilots, no such defamation of the victim's character ever took place, let alone so publicly. No similar accusation of ineptitude ensued later that year when two male Navy pilots crashed a helicopter over North Korea's demilitarized zone causing the death of one of the pilots and the internment of the other, nor were there any questions about their capability to fly the plane.

States Herbert (1998), women in the military must walk this treacherous tightrope; invoking their femininity risks being perceived as incompetent while the very perception of competence risks being labeled as enacting masculinity. Either way, military women are caught in a catch-22 situation or no-win phenomenon in doing gender where women are perpetually marginalized and hence maligned as a group no matter what they do as individuals and/or as a group. Apparently, in light of this phenomenon, there are rare exceptions. During Operation Desert Storm, despite this unwarranted reputation as a group in the military as not possessing the killer instinct unless they are to be *outed* as lesbians, Major Rhonda Cornum rose to the enviable position of being granted this distinction. She was taken as a POW with Sergeant Troy Dunlap, who said, during an interview with the media: 'I was really amazed ... I was overwhelmed by the way she [Major Cornum] handled herself' (Herbert 1998, p.121). He continued: 'She can go to combat with me anytime.' In response to these statements of affirmation about her performance and acceptance as worthy of praise by a male who was subordinate in rank, Cornum said: 'I don't think that I'll ever change his mind that says that women as a category of people shouldn't go to combat, but I think that I did change his mind that this one individual person who happens to be female can go' (Herbert 1998, p.121).

Be that as it may, and now even in an environment where both the Don't Ask, Don't Tell and Don't Pursue and combat exclusion policies have been repealed, not much has changed. However, in a recent interview, Senator Elizabeth Warren (D-MA) said that she was emboldened to continue her fight for women during the record Women's Day March after noticing a handwritten sign carried by a young girl that read, 'I fight like a girl' (Christopher 2017).

Bibliography

Abramovitz, M. (1996). *Regulating the Lives of Women. Social Welfare Policy from Colonial Times to the Present.* Revised Edition. Boston, MA: South End Press.

Aguirre, A. (2000). Academic Storytelling: A Critical Race Theory of Affirmative Action. *Sociological Perspectives*, 43, 319–339.

Bird Francke, L. (1997). *Ground Zero. The Gender Wars in the Military.* New York, NY: Simon and Schuster.
Bourdieu, P. (2001). *Masculine Domination.* Stanford, CA: Stanford University Press.
Bridges, W.P., and Villemez, W.J. (1986). Informal Hiring and Income in the Labor Market. *American Sociological Review,* 51, 574–582.
Brown, M.T. (2012). *Enlisting Masculinity. The Construction of Gender in U.S. Military Recruiting Advertising During the All-Volunteer Force.* London and New York: Oxford University Press.
Burke, C. (1999). Military Folk Culture. In M.F. Katsenstein and J. Reppy (Eds.), *Beyond Zero Tolerance: Discrimination in Military Culture.* Lanham, MD: Rowman & Littlefield.
Christopher, T. (2017). Elizabeth Warren to the Resistance: 'Fight Like A Girl.' April 1. *Shareblue.* www.shareblue.com.
Connell, R.W. (1987). *Gender and Power: Society, the Person and Sexual Politics.* Stanford, CA: Stanford University Press.
Connell, R.W. (1995). *Masculinities.* Cambridge: Polity Press.
Connell, R.W., and Messerschmidt, J.W. (2005). Hegemonic Masculinity: Re-thinking the Concept. *Gender and Society,* 19, 6, 829–859.
DeMello Patterson, M.B. (2000). America's Racial Unconscious: The Invisibility of Whiteness. In J.L. Kincheloe, S.R. Steinberg, N.M. Rodriguez, and R.E. Chennault (Eds.), *White Reign: Deploying Whiteness in America* (p. 103–121). New York, NY: St. Martin's Press.
Dubbert, J. (1979). *A Man's Place: Masculinity in Transition.* Englewood Cliffs, NJ: Prentice-Hall Press.
Ellefson, K.G. (1998). *Advancing Army Women as Senior Leaders – Understanding the Obstacles.* Carlisle Barracks, PA: Army War College.
Elliott, J.R., and Smith, R.A. (2004). Race, Gender, and Workplace Power. *American Sociological Review,* 69, 365–386.
Etzkowitz, H., Kemelgor, C., and Uzzi, B. (2000). *Athena Unbound: The Advancement of Women in Science and Technology.* Cambridge, MA: Cambridge University Press.
Faludi, S. (2006). *Backlash. The Undeclared War Against American Women.* Revised Edition. New York, NY: Three Rivers Press.
Fox News. (2017). Marines Launch New Ad Campaign: 'Battles Won.' March 17. www.foxnews.com. Retrieved April 27, 2017.
Frankenberg, R. (1993). *The Social Construction of Whiteness: White Women, Race Matters.* Minneapolis, MN: University of Minnesota Press.
Frederico, C.M., and Sidanius, J. (2002a). Racism, Ideology, and Affirmative Action, Revisited: The Antecedents and Consequences of 'Principled Objections' to Affirmative Action. *Journal of Personality and Social Psychology,* 82, 488–502.
Frederico, C.M., and Sidanius, J. (2002b). Sophistication and the Antecedents of White's Racial Policy Attitudes: Racism, Ideology and Affirmative Action in America. *Public Opinion Quarterly,* 66, 145–176.
Gibson, J.W. (1991). Redeeming Vietnam: Techno-Thriller Novels of the 1980s. *Cultural Critique,* Fall, 179–202.
Grimes, D.S. (2002). Challenging the Status Quo? Whiteness in the Diversity Management Literature. *Management Communication Quarterly,* 15, 381–409.

Hall, D.M., and Stevenson, H. (2007). Double Jeopardy: Being African-American and 'Doing Diversity' in Independent Schools. *Teachers College Record*, 109, 1–23.

Harris, G.L.A. (2009). The Multifaceted Nature of White Female Attrition in the Military. *Journal of Public Management and Social Policy*, 15, 1, 1–34.

Harris, G.L.A. (2012). Multiple Marginality: How the Disproportionate Assignment of Women and Minorities to Manage Diversity Programs Reinforces and Multiplies Their Marginality. *Administration and Society*, 20, 10, 1–34.

Harris, G.L.A. (2015). *Living Legends and Full Agency: Implications of Repealing the Combat Exclusion Policy.* New York, NY: Taylor & Francis Group, a division of CRC Press.

Herbert, M.S. (1998). *Camouflage Isn't Only for Combat. Gender, Sexuality, and Women in the Military.* New York and London: New York University Press.

Hunter, M. (2007). *Honor Betrayed. Sexual Abuse in America's Military.* Ft. Lee, NJ: Barricade Press.

Jarvis, C.S. (2004). *The Male Body at War: American Masculinity During World War II.* Dekalb, IL: Northern Illinois University Press.

Kanter, R.M. (1977). *Men and Women of the Corporation.* New York, NY: Basic Books.

Kanter, R.M. (1979). Power Failure in Management Circuits. *Harvard Business Review*, 57, 4, 65–75.

Kanter, R.M. (with Stein, B.). (1986). *A tale of 'O': On Being Different in an Organization.* New York, NY: Harper Torchbooks.

Kimmel, M.S. (1996). *Manhood in America: A Cultural History.* New York, NY: Free Press.

Kravitz, D.A., Klineberg, S.L., Avery, D.R., Nguyen, A.K., Lund, C., and Fu, E.J. (2000). Attitudes toward Affirmative Action: Correlations with Demographic Variables and with Beliefs about Targets, Actions, and Economic Effects. *Journal of Applied Social Psychology*, 30, 1109–1136.

Law, S.A. (1999). White Privilege and Affirmative Action. *Akron Law Review*, 32, 603–621.

Lumpkin, John T. (2005). Woman Earns Silver Star for Duty in Iraq. *AOL News*, June 16.

McGuirre, G.M. (2002). Gender, Race, and the Shadow Structure: A Study of Informal Networks and Inequality in a Work Organization. *Gender & Society*, 16, 303–322.

Nkomo, S. (1992). The Emperor Has No Clothes: Rewriting 'Race in Organizations.' *Academy of Management Review*, 17, 487–513.

Podolny, J.M., and Baron, J.N. (1997). Resources and Relationships: Social Networks and Mobility in the Workplace. *American Sociological Review*, 62, 673–603.

Renfro, C.L., Duran, A., Stephan, W.G., and Clason, D.L. (2006). The Role of Threat in Attitudes toward Affirmative Action and Its Beneficiaries. *Journal of Applied Social Psychology*, 36, 41–74.

Reskin, B.F., McBrier, D.B., and Kmec, J.A. (1999). The Determinants and Consequences of Workplace Sex and Race Composition. *American Review of Sociology*, 25, 335–361.

Schneider, B. (1987). The People Make the Place. *Personnel Psychology*, 40, 437–453.

Scott, J.W. (1986). Gender: A Useful Category of Historical Analysis. *American Historical Review*, 91, 5, 1053–1075.

Steele, C.S. (1997). A Threat in the Air: How Stereotypes Shape Intellectual Identity and Performance. *American Psychologist*, 52, 613–629.

Thomas, R.R. (1991). *Beyond Race and Gender: Unleashing the Power of Your Total Workforce by Managing Diversity.* New York, NY: AMACOM.

Titunik, Regina F. (2000). The First Wave: Gender Integration and Military Culture. *Armed Forces and Society*, 26, 2, 229–257.

Zimmer, L. (1988). Tokenism and Women in the Workplace: The Limits of Gender Neutral Theory. *Social Problems*, 35, 64–77.

12 A Culture of Domination

Brown (2012), among others (Bird Francke 1997, Holm 1992, Herbert 1998, Hunter 2007, Solaro 2006), have identified what the military has effectively constructed as a culture of domination for its call to arms, even as the institution finds itself at odds with the needs of the modern military. For example, and as stated elsewhere in this book, the military has repeatedly utilized the recruitment of women into its ranks as a convenient resource, not only to simply backfill men off to war as it did en masse prior, during and following World War II (Wechsler Segal 1995), but including most recently in Operations Enduring and Iraqi Freedom. However, there have been a series of notable high-profile and unprecedented elevations of women in the military since the Army's Ann Dunwoody was the U.S. military's first woman four star general (Burnes 2008). In 2012, the Air Force's Colonel Jeannie Leavitt became was the first female to be appointed to the helm of a combat fighter wing (Associated Press 2012). The Air Force followed that same year with the promotion of Janet Wolfenbarger, its first four star woman general (Coleman 2012, Dawley 2012). In January 2013, the Air Force selected Major General Michelle Johnson to head the Air Force Academy (Rodgers 2013), and the Navy followed suit by promoting its first woman, Michelle Howard, an African American, to the rank of Admiral (Rafferty 2016).

As early as 2009, the Navy found itself pondering assignment to the silent service of the submarines, something that it had vowed that it would never do (Bynum and Jelinek 2009). The truth is that in coming to this decision, the Navy did not suddenly come to its senses out of a crisis of conscience per se. The decision was borne of an overriding urgency to stave off a dual problem, yet opportunity. In other words, yet another crisis was at hand that moved the military to seek out women as its consummate convenient resource in light of the scarcity of its preferred and primary resource, men. First, the number of male graduates in the U.S. Naval Academy who traditionally pursued technical disciplines for the submariner careers precipitously declined (Iskra 2012). Second, women in the U.S. Naval Academy coincidentally and fortuitously for the Navy began pursuing these same technical disciplines at a faster rate than ever before. Since then and as early as 2012, the Navy graduated its first all-woman cohort of submariners (Friedrich 2012). Since the repeal of the combat exclusion policy, there have been unprecedented improvements to legitimately move military women ever closer to realizing full agency, or at least for now, to narrow the gaping chasm of inequity through critical occupations, positions and assignments as combatants.

In August 2015, two years following the announcement of the repeal of combat exclusion policy and one year before its full integration of women into the military was to be implemented (Christensen 2013, Migdal 2013, Evans 2013), with the exception of any services that could demonstrate that this was not the case and what positions women were not yet prepared to shoulder (Sutton 2013), two female junior officers made ourstory by successfully completing Army Ranger School (Sanchez and Smith-Spark 2015). However, these authors offer two important observations. First, it is not that women have never before performed these now recognized feats. Only one knows. Second, the military has made it routine and the go-to tactic of choice by perpetually studying women's propensity to perform in these positions. Therefore, for all we know, women might have already covertly or overtly successfully performed in these capacities in the past. It is only now that the military can legally utilize their talents and publicly so in these roles. On December 3, 2015, with then Secretary of Defense Ashton Carter's announcement, the Army opened up 220,000 positions that were previously closed to women (Lamothe 2015). These occupations are in combat arms (infantry, armor, special operations). According to the secretary:

> There will be no exceptions. This means that as long as they qualify and meet the standards, women will now be able to contribute to our mission in ways they never could before. They'll be allowed to drive tanks, fire mortars, and lead infantry soldiers into combat. They'll be able to serve as Army Rangers and Green Berets, Navy SEALS, Marine Corps infantry, Air Force parajumpers, and everything else that previously was open only to men.
>
> (Tan 2015)

In April 2016, the Army produced its first known female infantry officer (Tan 2016) with the first class of women in combat arms (infantry and armor) expected for deployment to their respective units by early 2017. The record surge in the number of women enlisting into these occupations illustrates the level of interest in the desire to make a difference (Knodell 2017).

Yet, in spite of these laudable improvements, the reality exists that, as expected, all is not well. Groups like the Service Women's Action Network (SWAN), the American Civil Liberties Union (ACLU), the National Women's Law Center, and Women in International Security, say that while the Army has done a better job of integrating women into occupations that were previously closed to them, the Marine Corps has been exceedingly slow to respond to calls to do so (Cahn 2017). This is not surprising, say critics, as the service has been the most obstructionist in changing its culture. In fact, in 2015, Commandant of the Marine Corps General Joseph Munford was unambiguous in his recommendations to Navy Secretary Ray Mabus that the Corps was against integrating women into combat positions, especially those in infantry and reconnaissance (Kovach 2015).

The spokesman for the Marines United Facebook page, which faced a backlash over the viewing and sharing of unauthorized nude photographs of women in the military, used the salacious postings as the rationale for why women should not be in the military (LaPorta 2017). According to Harris (2015), the repeal of the combat exclusion policy in 2013 signified a confluence of events, namely: the onslaught of legal challenges against the military by especially women veterans and the ACLU alleging a military culture that is rife with sexual assault and where the perpetrators are rewarded with promotions and who 'openly mocked and flouted the modest Congressionally-mandated reforms' that despite the public posture about the need for such reforms, the military is an environment of 'zero tolerance in leadership, period' (Parker 2011); the repeal of the Don't Ask, Don't Tell and Don't Pursue policy in 2011 (Garamone 2011); the release of the documentary *Invisible War* that exposed the depth of sexual assault in the military, the adverse impact on victims and the military's refusal either to take seriously and/or acknowledge the prevalence of the malady; then Secretary of Defense Leon Panetta's desire to stave off the avalanche of direct and concomitant dilemmas and the growing calls to resolve them along with the need to preserve his otherwise pristine reputation in public service (Harris 2015); and the dual and complementary roles of the Military Leadership Diversity Commission (MLDC) and the Defense Advisory Committee on Women in the Services (DACOWITS) in making the compelling case for repealing the combat exclusion policy. Harris (2015) suspects that it might have been these last one-two knockout punches by two formidable players that resulted in the ultimate demise of the combat exclusion policy and led to its symbolic repeal.

Nevertheless, even as Senators Kirsten Gillibrand (D-NY) and Barbara Boxer (D-CA) were united in their push to amass a bipartisan force through the Senate (Tilghman 2013) with 46 senators (Sohn 2013), including the likes of Senator Ted Cruz (R-TX) and Rand Paul (R-KY) (Delmore 2013), to hold commanders accountable and remove them from any discretionary role in the process to adjudicate complaints by deferring sexual assault-related cases to a cadre of impartial senior military attorneys who are unaffiliated with these commanders (Tilghman 2013), the military still prevailed. This stark but lamentable outcome bespeaks the deep-rooted military culture and influence despite its subordinate role to civilian leadership. The indoctrination of new recruits by way of breaking them down 'to build them up our way' (Hunter 2007, p.15) is a time-honored tradition of military socialization process that 'involves forms of discipline and domination that border on humiliation. The bodies of new recruits in basic training are putty in the hands of their commanders' (Hunter 2007, p.16). With this frame of mind comes the instinct for preservation in 'kill or be killed' (Hunter 2007, p.18–19).

However, when this inculcation knows no boundaries, and is perceived as legitimate, including as a course of reaction towards comrades, it is dangerous. Sexual assault in its myriad forms is one such strategy to induce violence, pain, humiliation and fear in the target (Hunter 2007). Objectifying the target helps to negate the fact that the person is another human being because to experience compassion and/or any kind of identification is to render blunt an instrument for killing, which defeats the very purpose of invoking violence (Hunter 2007). This involves a level of psychological distancing and impersonalizing *the other* as subhuman to enable both the execution and achievement of one's goal. Psychological distancing in turn masks the perception of especially women in the military as comrades who are thinking and feeling human beings like the perpetrator.

Fellow male cadets at the U.S. Military Academy at West Point who violated their female colleagues viewed them as different from other women in that they did not represent mainstream American women like their wives, sisters, mothers and girlfriends (Hunter 2007). Good women deserve to be protected and respected. This is not the same defense for female cadets. They are not like average American women and so warrant ill treatment, offensive designations like 'cunt' and 'faggots,' terms that reinforce *the other* or subhuman nature of women to justify the abuse. This is especially an effective tactic post-war when the population of the conquered nation is more likely to continue to endure rampant sexual degradation because of an intransigent negative perception by the victor. This was evident throughout and following World War II and the Korean and Vietnam Conflicts. War is notably a time that is most ripe for these atrocities. Psychological distancing leads to social distancing, which is itself implicit throughout the military by way of rank and in the manner of relating between members of the enlisted and commissioned corps (Hunter 2007). This social construction along certain lines of demarcation invites the likes of sexual assault against certain groups. Another type of distancing or stance on moral and/or religious grounds justifies the case for the mistreatment of women who are viewed as either amoral or immoral. Together, these perspectives of psychological, moral, social and even cultural distancing led to such scourge of the earth acts as that chronicled in *The Rape of Nanking*. Here, as earlier indicated, Chang (1997) unleashes a captivating description of the wholesale, multiple gang rape of Chinese civilian women and some civilian men by Japanese soldiers who viewed them as culturally, morally and socially inferior to them and vindicated the purpose of their actions on behalf of the emperor, a god-like figure. As one Japanese soldier elucidated, the fact that he was an agent of the emperor in carrying out this charge then absolved him of the crime. Likewise, to mistreat women and/or others viewed as inferior, subordinate or *other* rationalizes the abuse (Hunter 2007).

Bourdieu (2001) implies, though, that attempting to parse out masculine domination will itself produce more masculine domination since structurally it is *historically* a system in both how it is viewed and understood. Therefore, masculine domination is one of masculine order that is self-producing and self-reinforcing in nature. The American military is perhaps the closest personification of masculine domination or hypermasculinity. Says Hunter (2007), this is the context in which sexual assault thrives. In this culture, doing gender results in clear lines of demarcation in what constitutes masculinity and femininity, and by all accounts what delineates masculinity always trumps that which defines femininity.

The traits that categorize each are opposing forces where the twain will never meet. The implicit and explicit ways of expressing this polarization that men are rational and strong-willed while women are demonstratively sensitive and weak (Hunter 2007) may serve to reinforce the military's acculturation of male dominance and the marginalization of women (Bird Francke 1997). It is then no accident that drill instructors pepper their language during the indoctrination process of basic training with insulting taunts at male recruits that reflect what are understood as feminine traits, as in 'crybabies' (Bird Francke 1997, p.155). Even female recruits are brutally reminded of their subordinate status during these exercises, that to be female means to be compromised or, as Ellefson (1998) and Law (1999) note, that they are deviants by using such demeaning verbiage as 'You wuss, you baby, you goddam female' (Bird Francke 1997, p.155).

To demonstrate the depth of this acculturation, one woman commander at a Naval recruiting station yelled at one female recruit, 'You boy!' which according to Bird Francke (1997) should have been more of a compliment given the derogatory comments that are hurled at male recruits to instill the warrior spirit in them (p.155).

Military aviators are supposedly exemplars of manliness (Bird Francke 1997). So much so that as one example, a whopping 97 percent of Air Force recruits exist to maintain 3 percent of its force of aviators, whereas in the Navy, aviators on carriers are sustained by some 5,000 crew members. World War II ace Chuck Yeager perhaps best evokes the ideal image of this aura of manliness. In effect, this hegemony calls for the collective supremacy of men at the expense of the collective subordination of women (Bird Francke 1997).

However, especially in the Marine Corps, says Bird Francke (1997), the military uniform is another sign of manliness and is meant to visibly bring attention to each man by giving weight to the male body. The only exception is in prison. The male physique is highlighted by virtue of a fastidiousness to the various parts of the male anatomy and is by design.

This egotism that is perceived to come with maleness is one of self-admiration, self-centeredness and self-absorption. In one encounter in 1992, a retired general cavalierly commented to an Air Force officer who was summoned to a hearing that, 'I can see why the Defense Department sent you. You're so handsome' (Bird Francke 1997, p.154). However, this self-aggrandizement and vanity breed an inherent sense of superiority, with the uniform as one of man's symbols of power and a passport to inflict violence. This perceived moral high ground transcends the way that men in the military project themselves as apart and as exceptional from even men in the general civilian population. As such, the implicitly understood but protected tradition is to maintain this image of hyper-masculinity. While these same traditions are more understated in the other branches of the military, this pride in the male body and its physicality is there nevertheless, but, deplorably, the way to keep this maleness in check is to visibly tear down all that is female.

Stoltenberg (1984) writes that schemes like pornography function to promote and institutionalize the domination of men over women, just as segregation was a tool for racism and the fortification of whites as supreme. Studies on gang rapes appear to bear this out. Twenty-six gang rapes that were committed during a ten-year period, or from 1980 to 1990, showed that the participants had already been acculturated to such activities in male groups (Bird Francke 1997).

More revealing is that gang rapes committed between 1989 and 1990 by college athletes involved those in single-oriented sports like tennis or swimming. All of the gang rapes were committed by men who took part in a team sport like basketball or football. These studies suggest that this group mentality is prevalent in the military. Correspondingly, time spent together as a group is considered critical to the bonding and eventual success of the unit. Each unit member depends on the others such that the needs of any one unit member become subordinate to the needs of the unit. Says Brownmiller (1975), men who would not rape as an individual did so as group members as if carrying out the act was not for themselves but for each other. The director of the Rape Treatment Center at California's Santa Monica Hospital stated that '[i]t's more important to be part of the group than to be the person who does what's right' (Bird Francke 1997, p.160).

During the now infamous 1991 Navy Tailhook Association convention incidents, women were perceived as mere trophies that came with t-shirts emblazoned with the likes of 'Women Are Property,' as evidence of the winnings (Bird Francke 1997). The Vietnam Conflict exposed both the disgust and the manner in which the antipathy manifested itself. The abandoned body of a woman following a sexual assault was found with her legs extended and a brigade patch inserted between her legs as a deliberate indication of the identity of the perpetrators of her defilement (Hunter 2007, Bird Francke 1997), while others were posed in similar positions but their vaginas were blocked with grease guns, grenades, and entrenching tools. While it has been an established fact that rape is a tool of war, the crime was not so designated until 1996 by the International Criminal Tribunal in The Hague (Simons 1996).

In the military, the benign use of expletive-laced language is one form of subordination (Bird Francke 1997, Hunter 2007). For instance, the U.S. Naval Academy's WUBA, or Working Uniform Blue Alpha, conveniently devolved to 'women used by all' (Bird Francke 1997, p.161). In other words, hypermasculinity or masculine dominance is perpetuated throughout and women are forever reminded of their marginalized status as essentially pawns to be used for the sole enjoyment of men. Yet, to survive, women in the military are caught in a double bind. Being feminine connotes certain attributes, roles and ways of behaving. With these expectations come positive and negative consequences (Herbert 1998). Herbert ascribes these sometimes mixed messages for women as having their origins in women's sanctioned entrance into the military when, in the absence of men to perform those functions, women were called to arms and successfully fulfilled these needs. While in a time of need the skills that women possess are valued, during peacetime they are derided for filling these very roles. Herbert claims that when these needs exist during times of crisis and women fulfill them, they now become 'good women' (Herbert 1998, p.33). Ordinarily, being perceived as feminine is ideal except when there is a legitimate sense of urgency as determined by men to do otherwise. Some believe that these gender roles were created by God for the purpose of division of labor (Hunter 2007). Women in the military and particularly so in combat strictly depart from their endowed roles and morally infringe upon those of men who vow to protect them.

Dominance theory commands that women be submissive and men have dominion over them (Leszkay 2003). In American society, it is men, not women, who should have this obligation of completing military service as a responsibility of citizenship. This is the duty of the virtuous citizen (Hunter 2007). Because a woman is considered not meant for military service, she is thus excluded from being a virtuous citizen. Allowing women into the military and worse yet into combat then calls dominance theory into question, as doing so would require a reform of the military as an institution as we know it. The repeal of the combat exclusion policy and thus the requirement for women's full integration throughout the military goes against this tradition thus warranting the redefinition of what it means to be a citizen (Leszkay 2003).

The incomprehensible exchange between former Senator Cohen (R-ME) and then Air Force Chief of Staff General McPeak on why he would not select a female pilot whose skills were clearly superior to those of her male counterpart signals the irrationality of this mindset, says Harris (2015), even at the risk of compromising the mission owing to stanch sexism. When pressed, the general capitulated that his rationale for this decision is illogical but nevertheless that it was simply how he felt about the issue (Holm 1992, Hunter 2007, Harris 2015), making it the more illogical for invoking his own personal feelings into the equation. The events in the Abu Ghraib prison during the initial phase of Operation Iraqi Freedom highlight how military woman are effectively used as instruments to humiliate a culture where the preeminence of women is not only denounced but their authority, especially over men, is not condoned (Hunter 2007, Monahan and Neidel-Greenlee 2010).

So, for the military to become devoid of cultural sensitivity where military women were not only placed in compromising positions, that is, having authority over male prisoners and engaging in immoral acts that violated the cultural mores of the country that the U.S. military occupied, shocked the conscience of even culturally prescribed roles for American women. To Hunter (2007), while these actions might have violated even Western norms for women, like men, are capable of such barbarism. This is reminiscent of Irma Grese, who at only 21 years old was placed in charge of the SS squads at the Nazi Belsen concentration camp, whose acts of inhumane treatment of prisoners included having dogs feed on live prisoners and tying together the feet of pregnant women prisoners in labor and watching as the women and their babies died (Hunter 2007). A total of 28 women from that camp alone were indicted for such crimes. In other words, women, like men, are as capable of behaviors that abuse their power over others, including the control and denigration of men.

Still, the perception and expectation of women and in this case those in the military to act according to prescribed roles, persist. Military women walk a tightrope in this regard. To be perceived as too feminine is subject to securing high-profile positions as in an appointment to the staff of general officers (Herbert 1998). At the same time, women are pilloried for being incompetent for their sole purpose is that of a sex object. For those women who are competent and/or possess such traits as aggressiveness or being direct and thereby viewed as masculine, they too suffer the contradiction of this double standard. Such derogatory terms as 'castrating bitch' are leveled against them (Herbert 1998, p.33). Masculine domination also entails competition which is considered no activity for a woman (Hunter 2007). Further, to engage a woman into competition with a man, the outcomes are believed to prove futile either way for the man. If the woman wins, the victory is hollow or not taken seriously by the man for, 'after all, she is only a woman' (Hunter 2007, p.37), whereas should the man lose, he is less of a man for having lost to a mere woman.

The experience of one of the women veterans in Harris's (2015) research points to this very dilemma for military women. Darlene Iskra was the first woman in the Navy to command a ship (Harris 2015). Yet, for all of her achievements, she was routinely subjected by male subordinates' desire to engage her in puerile activities, all for the purpose of the opportunity to prove that they were better than her. While she never resorted to such tactics, the experience proved over time to be burdensome and the cumulative effect resulted in her constructive and premature discharge from the military. Herbert (1998) asserts that for every advancement that women have made in the military, there has been an equal backlash. Thus Harris's (2015) hypothesis that should women achieve full agency by way of repealing the combat exclusion policy not only in principle but in practice, and should it mark one of the many mechanisms to level the playing field for women, the most intransigent of male-dominated institutions will have moved the needle forward thereby increasing the likelihood that civilian organizations, including other male-dominated ones, and traditional male-dominated disciplines and occupations, will follow suit. No doubt for now, though, with the combat exclusion policy's repeal, there may come some repercussions. Again, owing to the issue of gender appropriateness, how can women progress in the military yet still be recognized as women? Or should women even care how they are being perceived, for either way they will be maligned?

Herbert (1998) contends that the military has a stake in maintaining these masculine and feminine distinctions separate and intact, for it is in the military's interest not only to retain the image as an inherently masculine institution but to keep the conceptions about gender appropriateness in check. This polarization of men versus women is key in preserving masculine domination. Harris (2015) points to the rationale behind the combat exclusion policy and the relegation of women to second-class status as primarily responsible for maintaining this systemic asymmetry. Herbert (1998) admits, though, that if the business of the military is masculinity and women are allowed to partake in some of these roles, then irrespective of gender, military personnel will be expected to manifest the attributes of both genders. So, by repealing the combat exclusion policy, while the expectation will be for military women to display some masculine traits, the same notion may not hold for military men in that they will now be expected to exhibit feminine traits for the military is fundamentally a masculine institution. This misogyny, exclaims Hunter (2007), is what must distinguish masculine from feminine in rendering women the inferior of the sexes. Even when men pronounce that they do not hate women, should these women, i.e., military women, depart from prescribed roles, they are spurned and penalized for not holding fast to these norms, even by men who would not self-describe as misogynistic.

Hypermasculinity has been found to correlate with enmity and violence towards women (Hunter 2007). For example, men who are prone to rape, nurse a deep misogyny for women and find them to be intrinsically suspect. In fact, many identify women as what Harris (2009) calls 'sex fiends' or 'temptresses,' whose sole purpose is to manipulate and dominate men by way of sexual favors (p.72). These men view women as sexual teases or pariahs to be forcibly taken and dealt with sexually (Hunter 2007). Seifert (1994) argues that many military men are guided by the misconception that a woman's sole purpose is for their recreation for they, the men, are the only warriors. This mindset is especially common among military men who have had sexual encounters with prostitutes, most of whom, if not all, are socio-economically disadvantaged. As despicable as it may sound, this depraved behavior is seen as legitimate for it ultimately serves the objective for the dominance of men through subordination by sexualizing women.

Studies conflate this deep-rooted hatred of women by men with a propensity for rape and violence against women (Hunter 2007). Studies of rape-prone cultures, including in the U.S., signal similar findings. Many such societies have a high incidence of domestic violence with hypermasculinity as the root cause. Another study reports that men's position on feminism is the single most reliable predictor of their views about rape, and that they are inclined to espouse the following views about women and gender roles: hold stereotypical roles about gender; are homophobic; see women as the possessions of men; are proponents of domestic violence; believe that women like to engage in aggressive sex or like to be roughed up during the act; are combative in personal relationships; and have a dismal view of feminism (Hunter 2007).

Nevertheless, despite the overriding need to propagate hypermasculinity, all for the sake of male domination, it is a phenomenon that is descried as fragile (Brown 2012, Hunter 2007). The emotional testimony to Congress by then Marine Corps Commandant General Robert Barrow as to why women should not be in combat, not only because it constitutes killing but because women's purpose in life is to give life itself, not take it (Holm 1992), signals the length to which military men will go to protect their perceived turf. Further, to bring women into combat roles is to violate the most sacred ground of the warrior and what it means to be a man (Harris 2015). A first sergeant, in his testimony to the Presidential Commission, described it best that '[t]he warrior mentality will crumble if women are placed in combat positions' (Hunter 2007, p.43). As a matter of fact, there is a group of factors, a tripartite effect, if you will, that is purported to threaten men's standing and existence in the U.S. military: capable women, homosexual women and homosexual men (Hunter 2007). To the degree that these threats are perceived as credible, former Chairman of the Joint Chiefs of Staff General John Vessey, in his testimony at a Congressional hearing which is also mentioned elsewhere in this book, said that the increase of women in the military has essentially morphed an otherwise masculine institution into one that is co-educational and as a result has brought trauma to men in the military. Major General Jeanne Holm was taken aback, even amused, in terms of how the presence of a few military women could have such a debilitating effect on the much larger body of military men. Yet, as perceived by military men, this threat was credible in that women's increased presence represented an encroachment on their alleged territory. To Hunter (2007), if this is a concern, then what would have been the response by military men in the heat of combat to military women's presence? Brown (2012) couches this malaise as a crisis in masculinity. Kimmel (1987) recalls its occurrence as synonymous with the response to social upheavals or social changes occurring in the country at any given time.

With respect to the repeal of both the Don't Ask, Don't Tell and Don't Pursue and combat exclusion policies, this real and present danger is manifesting itself into the likes of a predicted and collective cry for help by military men who are lashing out en masse. No wonder this resentment is manifesting itself into the most recent scandal to plague the Marine Corps involving the unauthorized downloading and sharing of sexually compromising photographs of female colleagues. Besides, the Marine Corps represents the most patriarchal of the services (Hunter 2007, Bird Francke 1997, Herbert 1998), and the most likely to adhere to the perceived manly ways of behaving, and the most persistently opposed to women in the military, especially in combat. For all the pomp and circumstance about hypermasculinity and masculine domination, the body of research to date clearly demonstrates the fragility of the male ego and self, and that this bravado may simply be, to invoke an oft-used American colloquialism, all bark and no bite, although in the form of sexually related offenses, this bite is a clear and present danger for victims and a credible threat to military readiness.

Bibliography

Associated Press. (2012). Air Force Picks 1st Woman to Command Fighter Wing. *Air Force Times.* May 23. www.airforcetimes.com/article/20120523/NEWS/205230328/AF-picks-1st-woman-command-fighter-wing. Retrieved March 23, 2017.

Bird Francke, Linda. (1997). *Ground Zero: The Gender Wars in the Military.* New York, NY: Simon and Schuster.

Bourdieu, P. (2001). *Masculine Domination.* Stanford, CA: Stanford University Press.

Brown, M.T. (2012). *Enlisting Masculinity. The Construction of Gender in U.S. Military Recruiting Advertising during the All-Volunteer Force.* London and New York: Oxford University Press.

Brownmiller, S. (1975). *Against Our Will: Men, Women and Rape.* New York, NY: Simon and Schuster.

Burnes, T. (2008). *Contributions of Women to U.S. Combat Operations.* Strategy Research Project. Carisle Barracks, PA: U.S. Army War College. March 15.

Bynum, R., and Jelinek, P. (2009). Navy Moves to Put Women on Submarines. *Associated Press.* October 13. www.msnbc.msn.com/id/33297422/ns/38027577. Retrieved March 22, 2017.

Cahn, D. (2017). Groups Say Marines Slow in Integrating Women into Combat Arms Jobs. April 5. *Stars and Stripes.* www.stripes.com. Retrieved May 26, 2017.

Chang, I. (1997). *The Rape of Nanking: The Forgotten Holocaust of World War II.* New York: Basic Books.

Christensen, S. (2013). Ban on Women in Combat Ends. *My San Antonio.* January 24. www.mysanantonio.com/news/article/Ban-on-women-in-combat-ends-4218940.php. Retrieved March 22, 2017.

Coleman, K. (2012). President Obama Nominates First Woman as Four-Star U.S. Air Force General. National Public Radio (NPR). February 7. www.npr.org/blogs/thetwo-way/2012/02/07/146518211/president-obama-nominates-first-woman-as-four-star-u-s-air-force-general. Retrieved March 23, 2017.

Dawley, K. (2012). Gen, Wolfenbarger Receives Fourth Star, Assumes Leadership of AFMC. *Aerotech News/Desert Wings*. June 8. www.aerotechnews.com/edwardsafb/2012/06/08/gen-wolfenbarger-receives-fourth-star-assumes-leadership-of-afmc/. Retrieved March 8, 2017.

Delmore, E. (2013). Senator Gillibrand's Sexual Assault Bill Gets Tea Party Backing. MSNBC. July 16. http://tv.msnbc.com/2013/07/16/sen-gillibrands-military-sex-assault-bill-gets-tea-party-backing/. Retrieved May 22, 2017.

Ellefson, K.G. (1998). *Advancing Army Women as Senior Leaders – Understanding the Obstacles*. Carlisle Barracks, PA: Army War College (AD A344 984).

Evans, B. (2013). Defense Department to Remove Female Combat Exclusion Policy. January 28. www.ivn.us/2013/01/28/military-to-remove-female-combat-exclusion-policy/. Retrieved March 22, 2017.

Friedrich, E. (2012). Navy Pins First Nuclear-Qualified Female Submariners. December 5. www.kitsapsun.com/news/2012/dec/05/navy-pins-first-nuclear-qualified-female/#axzz21.ay2FBLh. Retrieved March 22, 2017.

Garamone, J. (2011). Don't Ask, Don't Tell Repeal Certified by President Obama. July 22. www.defense.gov/news/newsarticle.aspx?id=64780. Retrieved May 22, 2017.

Harris, G.L.A. (2009). The Multifaceted Nature of White Female Attrition in the Military. *Journal of Public Management and Social Policy*, 15, 1, 71–93.

Harris, G.L.A. (2015). *Living Legends and Full Agency: Implications of Repealing the Combat Exclusion Policy*. New York, NY: Taylor & Francis Group, a division of CRC Press.

Herbert, M.S. (1998). *Camouflage Isn't Only for Combat. Gender, Sexuality, and Women in the Military*. New York and London: New York University Press.

Holm, J. (1992). *Women in the Military. An Unfinished Revolution*. Revised Edition. Novato, CA: Presidio Press.

Hunter, M. (2007). *Honor Betrayed. Sexual Abuse in America's Military*. Ft. Lee, NJ: Barricade Press.

Iskra, D. (2012). More Navy Women Joining the Silent Service. October 3. http://nation.time.com/2012/10/03/more-navy-women-joining-the-silent-service. Retrieved March 23, 2017.

Kimmel, M.S. (1987). The Contemporary Crisis of Masculinity in Hierarchical Perspective. In H. Brod (Ed.), *The Making of Masculinities: The New Men's Studies*. Boston, MA: Allen and Unwin.

Knodell, K. (2017). American Women Are Signing Up for Combat in Unexpected Numbers. www.medium.com. Retrieved May 26, 2017.

Kovach, G.C. (2015). Exclusive: Marines Found Benefits to Women in Combat, Significant Risks. *The San Diego Union-Tribune*. www.sandiegotribune.com. Retrieved March 23, 2017.

Lamothe, D. (2015). Pentagon: Opening Combat Jobs to Women Alters Factual Backdrop in Keeping Them Out of the Draft. December 7. www.washingtonpost.com. Retrieved March 27, 2017.

LaPorta, J. (2017). Marines United Spokesman: Nude Photo Scandal Shows Why Women Shouldn't Serve. March 16. *Daily Beast*. www.thedailyeast.com. Retrieved May 26, 2017.

Law, S.A. (1999). White Privilege and Affirmative Action. *Akron Law Review*, 32, 603–621.
Leszkay, B. (2003). Feminism on the Front Lines. *Hastings Women's Law Journal*, 14, 2, 133–170.
Migdal, A. (2013). *Women in Combat: Policy, Meet Reality*. American Civil Liberties Union (ACLU) Women's Rights Project. January 24. www.aclu.org/blog/womens rights/women-combat-policy-meet-reality. Retrieved March 23, 2017.
Monahan, E.M., and Neidel-Greenlee, R. (2010). *A Few Good Women. America's Military Women from World War I to the Wars in Iraq and Afghanistan*. New York: Anchor Books.
Parker, A. (2011). Lawsuit Says Military Is Rife With Sexual Assault. February 15. www.nytimes.com/2011/02/16/us/16military.html?_r=0. Retrieved May 22, 2017.
Rafferty, J.P. (2016). Michelle Howard. United States Admiral. In *Encyclopedia Britannica*. www.britannica.com. Retrieved May 26, 2017.
Rodgers, J. (2013). Major General Michelle Johnson First Woman to Lead Air Force Academy. *Denver Post*. March 1. www.denverpost.com/breakingnews/ci_22698627/air-force-ac. Retrieved March 23, 2017.
Sanchez, R., and Smith-Spark, L. (2015). Two Women Make Army Ranger History. *CNN*. www.cn.com. Retrieved May 27, 2017.
Seifert, R. (1994). War and Rape: A Preliminary Analysis. In *Mass Rape: The War Against Women in Bosnia-Herzegovina*. Lincoln, NE: University of Nebraska Press.
Simons, M. (1996). For First Time, Court Defines Rape as War Crime. June 28. *New York Times*.
Sohn, D.S. (2013). Kirsten Gillibrand Gains on Chain of Command Changes. *Politico Pro*. August 13. www.politico.com/story/2013/09/kirsten-gillibrand-sexual-assault-military-reforms-97530.html. Retrieved May 22, 2017.
Solaro, E. (2006). *Women in the Line of Fire. What You Should Know About Women in the Military*. Emeryville, CA: Seal Press.
Stoltenberg, J. (1984). Pornography and Freedom. In *Men's Lives* (p.485). London: Pearson.
Sutton, J. (2013). Ending U.S. Combat Ban Will Even Career Playing Field, Servicewomen Say. January 23. *Reuters* and the *Chicago Tribune*. www.chicatribune.com/news/politics/sns-rt-us-usa-military-women-reactionbre90n046-20130123,0,6408329.story. Retrieved March 28, 2017.
Tan, M. (2015). Army Infantry, Armor, Spec Ops Units Open to Women in 2016. December 26. *Army Times*. www.armytimes.com. Retrieved March 22, 2017.
Tan, M. (2016). Meet the Army's First Female Infantry Officer. *Army Times*. April 27. www.armytimes.com. Retrieved March 22, 2017.
Tilghman, A. (2013). Pentagon Advisory Panel: Strip Commanders' Ability to Prosecute Sexual Assaults. September 30. www.armytimes.com/article/20130930/NEWS06/309300029/Pentagon-advisory-panel-Strip-commanders-ability-prosecute-sexual-assaults. Retrieved May 22, 2017.
Truman, D.M., David, T.M., and Fischer, A.R. (1996). Dimensions of Masculinity: Relations to Date Rape Supportive Attitudes and Sexual Aggression in Dating Situations. *Journal of Counseling and Development*, 74, 555–562.
Wechsler Segal, M.W. (1995). Women's Military Roles Cross-Nationally, Past, Present, and Future. *Gender and Society*, 9, 6, 757–775.

13 The Effeminization of the Enemy

The literature is rife with the various forms of denigration that are leveled against recruits during the indoctrination phases of boot camp as part of the military's overall initial acculturation of its workforce (Hunter 2007, Bird Francke 1997, Herbert 1998, Snyder 2003). The use of derogatory terms is par for the course in describing the enemy, including women, on and off the battlefield of the U.S. military. The outright disparagement of women hence becomes the rallying cry for the vilification and effeminization of the enemy. One only need to review the research containing the sexually explicit language – not as explicitly blatant in today's military, perhaps, as once condoned, but which nevertheless remains entrenched in this culture. This misogyny is so endemic among military men that, as earlier mentioned, when World War II prisoner of war Sally Millett was questioned by a reporter as to her views about the capture of Specialist Melissa Rathbun-Nealy by the Iraqis during Operation Desert Storm, she offered up her candid assessment as to the likelihood of the soldier's mistreatment by the Iraqis. Millett intimated that because the Americans hate women even more than the Iraqis, perhaps the soldier stood a better chance of not being mistreated (Hunter 2007). This damning indictment speaks to the intensity of the animus that American men in the military are believed to harbor towards their female counterparts, and while many would argue otherwise, notwithstanding the existing level of sexually related incidents that continue to haunt the U.S. military, the more recent Marine Corps scandal when male Marines illegally shared illicit photographs of their female comrades serves as yet another reminder of this clear and ever-present danger to the institution and that owing to acculturation, not much has changed in the mindset of this male-dominated workforce.

Hunter's (2007) allegations are even more apt in that there are three things that most terrify men in the U.S. military: capable women, homosexual women (lesbians) and homosexual men (gays). Strangely enough, the one prevailing theme that is common in these three variables is femininity, or at least those perceived as having effeminate traits, and even as the U.S. military has become more reliant on women as more than an outwardly convenient resource given the nature of how war has changed over time

(Titunik 2008). The Marine Corps' quest to increase its female workforce while downplaying the recent scandal is a prime example of the dilemma in which the military finds itself particularly in light of an all-volunteer force. Yet, what is suspected to be one of the most effective tools in keeping a fighting force at its peak readiness is to demonize the enemy by hurling slanderous and effeminate vernacular at him all for the glorification of self as superior. 'You wuss, you baby, you goddam female' (Bird Francke 1997, p.155).

During Operation Enduring Freedom in 2005, as an insult to the Taliban and by extension to Islam, the U.S. military exterminated the bodies of Taliban fighters by burning them (Sturcke 2005). Islam prohibits disposal of the body by cremation. To add insult to injury, the U.S. military positioned the bodies facing west as another way of flouting the prescriptions of Islam that such observances must be carried out while facing east to Mecca. One of the American sergeants shouted in the native dialect: 'You allowed your fighters to be laid down facing west and burned. You are too scared to come down and retrieve the bodies. This proves you are the lady boys we always believed you to be' (Schmitt 2005). Another soldier said sarcastically: 'You attack and run away like women.' Similarly, and from basic training onward, male recruits are inculcated to associate their weaponry with either genitalia as in, '[t]his is my rifle, this is my gun; one is for fighting, the other's for fun' (Snyder 2003, p.192). Or when defeated one has been 'pussy whipped' (Hunter 2007, p.35).

The U.S. military academies, the most challenging period of indoctrination for many in the quest to become officers in the commissioned corps, have been depicted by the Defense Advisory Committee on Women in the Services (DACOWITS) as 'vestiges of resistance' (U.S. General Accounting Office (GAO) 1994, p.52). One of the many incidents that became typical of hypermasculine behaviors in the manner in which male students treated their female compatriots was at the Naval Academy. In 1989, second-year midshipperson Gwen Dreyer was accosted by two male peers. They blasted into her room and took her forcibly into the men's bathroom (Bird Francke 1997). At first Dreyer mistook the act for a prank and retaliation for an earlier snowballs rough housing during which time one of her snowballs successfully landed on one of the miscreants. However, this was not the case. Instead, Dreyer was handcuffed to one of the urinals in the bathroom. Dreyer became the fodder for gyrating male onlookers while others photographed her. One of the onlookers who provided the handcuffs was none other than one of the members of the Academy's Human Relations Council. While Dreyer never reported the incident, an expectation of all female students, she confided in her parents, who did. Not only did the Naval Academy procrastinate on following up with an investigation of the incident, but the two main perpetrators spent the time engaging in intimidation whenever they had a chance encounter with Dreyer. The Naval Academy determined that the offenses that comprised the incident amounted to no more than to be dismissed since none rose to the level of either premeditation or hazing. While the main perpetrators received demerits for general misconduct and one month's forfeiture for each offense, the remaining co-conspirators were never reprimanded.

Not surprisingly, not long after, similar incidents were found to be prevalent at the U.S. Military Academy at West Point and the Air Force Academy as well (Bird Francke 1997). While the Dreyers kept out of the public view in deference to their daughter, a tip galvanized a reporter to contact them based upon information about similar incidents. It turned out that the Dreyer incident was not an isolated one. In fact, the problem was widespread to the point where the matter came to the attention of Congress. It was well known, at least at the Naval Academy, that the male students not only routinely exposed themselves to their female peers and showed pornographic materials in the co-educational recreation room, but referred to the female students as 'cunsters' (Bird Francke 1997, p.184). Women naval officers who had braved the four-year obstacle course admitted to the hostile environment for female students. Still, in an inexplicable turn of events that some would argue is reminiscent of the condition dubbed Stockholm Syndrome, when the protesters from the National Organization for Women (NOW) visibly showed their disgust at the rampant acts of sexism, they were snubbed by the female students at the Naval Academy. The female students claimed that they willingly engaged in these rituals, including the same acts of urinal handcuffing of a male cadet at the Army's West Point. The rationale, said one female student, was that these acts have nothing to do with gender but the rituals simply represented a way of life. Further, NOW's presence would prove damaging for them (Bird Francke 1997).

The contradictory evidence unearthed by the Naval Academy's Women Midshipmen Study Group proved how complex the issue was. The findings of the study revealed that 45 percent of the first year female students felt that they were not welcomed by their male peers at the institution (Bird Francke 1997). More than one-third of male graduates echoed the disdain at the women's presence. Apparently, as late as 2005, these sentiments remained as ingrained, as per the study by the Department of Defense's inspector general (Harris 2009). Many found the behaviors of male Naval Academy students as tantamount to chauvinism (Bird Francke 1997) – so much so that an officer at the Army's West Point referred to them as 'hormones with legs' (Bird Francke 1997, p.190). One alarming ritual involved the Naval Academy's male students wearing Dole banana stickers on their hats as evidence of their sexual liaisons and trysts with female students, dubbed 'scores' (Bird Francke 1997, p.190). Accordingly, the Naval Academy's culture of the subservience of women was so institutionalized that the male students, particularly those in aviation, would revel en route to various events. These 'brown wings' and 'The S and M Man' songs became legendary. At the Army's West Point, part of the students' indoctrination process included similar rituals at the start of every academic year or reorganization week which is sexualized and referred to as re-orgy week (Hunter 2007, Bird Francke 1997). Each table in the dining hall has an assigned dessert corporal who after apportioning the prescribed amount to each classmate at their respective tables, announces the completion of this task by shouting, 'Sir, the dessert has been raped and I did it' (Hunter 2007, p.17).

Interestingly enough, unlike the early days of women's sanctioned entrance to the military, the qualifications of the women cadets at West Point disproportionately exceeded those of their male counterparts (Bird Francke 1997), as they generally did in the military (Holm 1992). There were more Rhodes and Marshall scholars as well as many women who were either members of the National Honor Society or the valedictorians or salutatorians of their high schools. In spite of these achievements, the bottom line for the Army was about physical prowess. Yet, Rebecca Marier in 1995, managed to excel at both academics and fitness (Bird Francke 1997). Finishing first in her class, the first female to do so, she achieved a 3.95 grade point average along with a record six-minute mile, 70 push-ups and 100 sit-ups. Still, the environment at West Point remained unwelcoming to women, but this did not bother its leadership. In truth, the leadership was mindful of it but merely chalked it up to fate. A whopping 48 percent to 71 percent of the male cadets surveyed said that women were not accepted at the academy (testimony by Colonel Patrick Toffler 1991, see Bird Francke 1997, p.200). Despite these disquieting results, the Army's leadership was unmoved (Bird Francke 1997).

Jodies and cadences, as they are called, are part of the military's indoctrination process for both the enlisted and commissioned corps, and that is instilled throughout military culture by becoming a way of life for its personnel (Hunter 2007, Bird Francke 1997, Snyder 2003). As disturbing as they may be, they are designed to build and continuously reinforce the warrior spirit. Yet, many of these mechanisms are purposely infused with sex and violence (Hunter 2007), and deriding epithets about women as the brunt of this inculcation (Jeffreys 2007, Bird Francke 1997). Prostitution and pornography as part of the othering of women and by extension the enemy become natural outlets (Hunter 2007, Jeffreys 2007, Brownmiller 1975, Enloe 1992). Women in Asia, for instance, came to understand what American men desired during sexual intercourse to bolster their manliness (Enloe 1992). Seifert (1994) cites rape as a weapon of hatred for men that is 'actualized in times of crises' (Seifert 1994, p.65). It is a hatred of the enemy through violence and pornography during peacetime that increases in intensity during times of armed conflict (Kelly 2000). This weapon of war, as Brownmiller (1975) terms it, becomes such a weapon when men discover that their genitalia can also function as a tool of terror (Buss 2009). Rape then serves a dual purpose: for violence against women and violence against the enemy (Brownmiller 1975), who are both effeminized and couched as women. Elshtain (1987) goes further by stating that women are representative of a nation's body politic or ideology (Buss 2009). Women then inevitably become the targets of violence because they are the collective consciousness of a nation-state.

However, when individuals using violence and aggression lose sight of the context in which they occur to carry out such behaviors on their own, that is against military women, it is not only problematic but becomes destructive for the institution itself. Sexual assault is not about sex (Hunter 2007). The premise behind its use is to inflict pain, humiliation and violence against the enemy. The Navy's Tailhook and Army's Aberdeen Proving Ground sexual harassment claims (Harris 2009) in no way insulate other branches of the military. In 2003, the leadership of the Air Force Academy not only admitted to investigating at least 54 such assaults but that the actual occurrence was probably higher owing to underreporting by victims and the perceived retribution for their careers (Schmitt and Moss 2003). Even so, when the Office of Special Investigation (OSI) inserted a confidential informant into the ranks of the Academy which resulted in the conviction of cadets, the first such convictions in 15 years, it resulted in the doubling of these complaints in the Academy, which eventually led to the resignation of the institution's superintendent (Hess 2014). While admirable, Eric Thomas, a cadet at the Academy, who was recruited by the OSI and who for two years assisted the agency as an informant while managing his own academic and other commitments, found himself the repeated target of retaliation not only at the hands of the Air Force Academy but also the very agency for which he sacrificed his career, the OSI (Jenkins 2016).

Despite the number of convictions in Operation Gridiron that came about as a result of Thomas's work, the perceived environment that his work created to enable victims to come forward and to lodge complaints, and the multiple awards that the OSI received because of his work, Thomas was dis-enrolled from the Academy, received six months of probation, but was placed on an 18-month probation altogether for failure to report his work to his superiors, and was restricted to 400 hours in a 10-foot by 10-foot room for his good deeds (Jenkins 2016). The former cadet was also stripped of his rank, his class privileges and confined to the military installation. Before his demise, Eric Thomas was the epitome of what it means to be an Air Force Academy cadet. He was responsible for the supervision of 400 other cadets, one group and ten squadrons. Moreover, he was pilot-qualified and awarded his top pick of a pilot slot that more than 300 other cadets had failed to achieve, and was repeatedly cited for exemplary work by the Sexual Assault Response coordinator and colonel of the Academic Department for the 'highest level of character, diligence, honor, integrity and fortitude.' Yet, for all of Thomas's achievements, his career aspirations have been dashed. Says Senator Kirsten Gillibrand (D-NY), '[i]t's a case of retaliation for people whose job is to root out and prosecute sexual assault cases.' Branson Enos, the former OSI agent who enlisted

Eric Thomas, but was directed not to address the issue for Thomas prior to his dis-enrollment, said: 'I don't think what the Air Force realizes, that when they actually punished Eric Thomas, they sent a very, very bad message to all cadets. You don't talk about sexual assault, as a victim or witness, because you will not graduate.'

So much for being the perceived most women-friendly of the military branches, that is the Air Force. Consequently, the Air Force is hell-bent on suppressing the facts that are meant to illuminate the prevalence of sexual assault at the Air Force Academy (Jenkins 2016), even if its actions go against its Honor Code: 'We will not lie, steal, or cheat, nor tolerate among us anyone who does.' Eric Thomas's treatment by the Air Force Academy is both implicitly and explicitly clear in its message. The level of shaming and punishment inflicted is designed to be punitive enough to deter anyone who would even contemplate, much less dare to challenge the organization's unwritten rules of conduct. Further, given Thomas's position at the time, even as a cadet, he had reached a degree of access to the sanctioned leadership that is only afforded a few cadets. His insertion into the sanctity of the institution by way of his access is perhaps believed to be a perceived breach of confidence. Eric Thomas was perceived to have crossed the line by exposing the inner sanctum of the sacred grove. In response, or as perhaps the Air Force Academy saw it, a line in the sand had to be drawn. The penalty therefore brings to bear the might of the organization for having violated that trust.

In 2013, then Secretary of Defense Chuck Hagel nominated Major General Michelle Johnson as the first woman to head the 57-year-old Air Force Academy (Rodgers 2013). Of all the military academies, however, the Air Force Academy remains the highest for sexual assault prevalence despite a one-third decline (Roeder 2017). So, essentially, has having a woman at the helm of this traditional male institution made a positive difference for a female cadet's quality of life at the institution? The jury is still out, for only time will tell as the ourstory surrounding the opening of the military academies was initially met with the very resistance that provided the rationale for the combat exclusion policy, that the purpose of the military and in turn its academies, is to produce combat officers, from which women were excluded (Bird Francke 1997). Of course, relying on the outmoded adage that the military is no place for social experiments, which is the very foundation for women's exclusion from combat, '[t]hat we not experiment in this direction with the future defense of the nation' pleaded the then superintendent of the Air Force Academy, Lieutenant General A.P. Clark, a graduate of the Army's U.S. Military Academy at West Point (Bird Francke 1997, p.192).

The challenge is not only with hatred of the enemy but the effeminization of the enemy in the process, though the deprecation used during times of war, should the victor prevail, continues even during peacetime (Hunter 2007). Sexual assault is one such manifestation. Throughout World War II and the Korean Conflict, the U.S. military put to death personnel who were sentenced for rape. However, capturing the cavalier attitude towards the insidious act of rape during the Vietnam Conflict, John Smail, a squad leader commented: 'That's an everyday affair. You can nail just about everybody on that – at least once. The guys are human man' (Hunter 2007, p.20). Yet, it is baffling that this humanity should be called upon for justification for the act of the white male soldier in the U.S. military to callously inflict himself upon while deliberately defiling the rights of women, in this case women of color, who also represented the enemy. While it is seemingly appropriate to be more likely to accept this barbarism during conditions of war, it is wholly inappropriate to do so during peacetime for it has been found that the U.S. military perpetrates 66 percent more acts of rape as an occupational force than during the war itself (Hunter 2007). In keeping with Hunter's (2007) views that the chances for the likelihood of sexual assault are exacerbated during times of war whereby men view the period as authorization for lawlessness to brandish their feelings of supremacy and dominance, some commanders essentially rationalize the utility of rape as an effective conduit for helping to release their troops' stress. The Vietnam Conflict became emblematic of this kind of behavior.

The U.S. Army's 11th Brigade as a posse raped and murdered a woman, and following the assault and murder, strategically inserted the brigade's patch by her vaginal area (Hunter 2007). Says Hunter, the problem here is that the participants all have a mutual interest in keeping this profane act a secret simply out of allegiance to one another. This case suggests both a social and moral distancing, and that the enemy pertains to a woman as a deviant (Ellefson 1998, Law 1999), which warrants her marginalization and subordination (DeMello Patterson 2000) given her otherness, and especially so as a woman of color (Frankenberg 1993), and the perceived moral high ground and superiority of the offender to engage in these illicit acts given the woman's violation of her prescribed roles. Again, the infamous Rape of Nanking comes to mind in prosecuting such atrocities as gang rape on behalf of the god-like figure of the emperor. On the rare occasion that a woman is accepted by her male counterparts, the caveat that '[s]he's not like other women, she's like a guy' (Hunter 2007, p.22) is often invoked.

However, as more women join the U.S. military, Jeffreys (2007) is troubled that this mentality remains unbroken. As Miller (1997) suspects, perhaps military men are resorting to sexual assault because women's increasing presence in the military represents an infringement of their professed male territory. What then will an environment look like where, as called for in the repeal of the combat exclusion policy, women are fully integrated throughout all positions, occupations and assignments in the military? Studies on hypermasculinity, including during basic training, show the derogatory name-calling imposed on all under the guise of getting recruits to 'man up' (Koeszegi et al. 2014, p.230, Snyder 2003, Bird Francke 1997). The implicit message through and through such name-calling is for the deliberate subjugation of all things feminine, including such epithets as 'faggots' (Koeszegi et al. 2014, p. 230) to produce manly men. Rosen et al.'s (1996) study of single-gendered male units manifested the degree to which the defamation of women is thought of as an effective tactic for male bonding and unit cohesion. In such units, the research revealed, even when women become a part of these units, the nature of hypermasculinity remains persistent. Even more inexplicable is women's reaction for the sake of their own survival as well as to the increased presence of other women in these units. Remarkably, though, in this same study, Rosen et al. found that as a matter of distancing themselves from other women who were newcomers into the units, those women already present did not approve of the newcomers' inclusion though they considered them as equally qualified as themselves to perform their respective duties.

Other studies demonstrate how women engage in a form of dissociation from other women as a survival mechanism in order to deflect perceptions of being feminine, to underplay problems of sexism and to assimilate into the rituals of these male-dominated units (Pershing 2003). However, such organizational strategies over time only result in keeping the conventions of hypermasculinity intact. For Pazy and Oron (2001), women officers in the Israeli Defense Force, for example, were routinely under-evaluated by male superiors in male-dominated units. A subsequent meta-analysis, also by Rosen et al. (1996) was inconclusive, though, in determining whether or not gender composition adversely impacted unit cohesion, although studies by the U.S. Army debunked any question that unit effectiveness declined with the inclusion of women (U.S. Army 2002).

Whatever the findings, Snyder (2003) and others like Bird Francke (1997) and Harris (2009) suggest that the wholesale and collective subordination of women in the U.S. military is intolerable and unacceptable. Snyder (2003) says that such treatment and the use of demeaning language to describe women as a strategy for the motivation of male recruits is undemocratic and obfuscates the real issue by damaging the standing of women in the military. Bird Francke (1997) insists that this treatment is tantamount to the collective marginalization of women. While Harris's (2009) theory of attrition particularly by white women as a group from which the military recruits, probes the efficacy of such strategies in debasing one group by another during basic training and especially so at the most developmentally vulnerable phase of maturity for recruits. Further, this exercise does nothing to improve the military's standing among women. Harris (2009, 2015) indicates that white women prematurely separate from the military not only because of this maltreatment but because they are also in search of full agency.

Denigrating the enemy in the context of war then should be appropriately prescribed on the battlefield. Women in the military are not the enemy and therefore military men must be socialized to respect them. Sexism is at the root of this insidious belief system (Snyder 2003), but its use is undemocratic in principle as well as in practice. According to Harris (2009), '[i]f a woman's place in the military is framed in terms of her right to call to arms as a free and full citizen in a democratic society, then indeed she is equal. Anything less would reduce her to that of a second class citizen' (p.74). Military service and the inclusion of more women need not be about gender integration (Snyder 2003). This act simply underscores the citizen-soldier tradition, and in any democratic society, like men, women have the responsibility, including the right to bear arms. Hence the emphasis is moot; only the talents and the performance of the workforce upon which the military must depend for the effective execution of its mission are at stake.

Bibliography

Bird Francke, L. (1997). *Ground Zero. The Gender Wars in the Military.* New York, NY: Simon and Schuster.

Brownmiller, S. (1975). *Against Our Will: Me, Women and Rape.* London: Secker and Warburg.

Buss, D.E. (2009). Rethinking Rape as a Weapon of War. *Feminist Legal Studies,* 17, 2, 145–163.

DeMello Patterson, M.B. (2000). America's Racial Unconscious: The Invisibility of Whiteness. In J.L. Kincheloe, S.R. Steinberg, N.M. Rodriguez and R.E. Chennault (Eds.), *White Reign: Deploying Whiteness in America* (p.103–121). New York, NY: St. Martin's Press.

Ellefson, K.G. (1998). *Advancing Army Women as Senior Leaders – Understanding the Obstacles.* Carlisle Barracks, PA: U.S. Army War College.

Elshtain, J.B. (1987). *Women and War.* New York, NY: Basic Books.

Enloe, C. (1992). It Takes Two. In S. Pollack Sturdevant and B. Stoltzfus (Eds.), *Let the Good Times Roll: Prostitution and the U.S. Military in Asia.* New York, NY: New Press.

Frankenberg, R. (1993). *The Social Construction of Whiteness: White Women, Race Matters.* Minneapolis: University of Minnesota Press.

Harris, G.L.A. (2009). The Multifaceted Nature of White Female Attrition in the Military. *Journal of Public Management and Social Policy,* 15, 1, 74–93.

Harris, G.L.A. (2015). *Living Legends and Full Agency: Implications of Repealing the Combat Exclusion Policy.* New York, NY: Taylor & Francis Group, a division of CRC Press.

Herbert, M.S. (1998). *Camouflage Isn't Only for Combat. Gender, Sexuality, and Women in the Military.* New York and London: New York University Press.

Hess, A. (2014). Sexual Assault, Football, and a Mole Inside the Air Force Academy. *Slate.* www.slate.com. Retrieved February 22, 2017.

Holm, J. (1992). *Women in the Military. An Unfinished Revolution.* Revised Edition. Novato, CA: Presidio Press.

Hunter, M. (2007). *Honor Betrayed. Sexual Abuse in America's Military.* Ft. Lee, NJ: Barricade Press.

Jeffreys, S. (2007). Double Jeopardy: Women, the U.S. Military and the War in Iraq. *Women's Studies International Forum,* 30, 16–25.

Jenkins, D.M. (2016). A Life Sentence for a Former Air Force Academy Cadet Who Helped Expose Sexual Assaults at the Academy? We Can't Let that Happen! June 6. *Huffington Post*. www.huffpost.com. Retrieved May 26, 2017.

Kelly, L. (2000). Wars Against Women: Sexual Violence, Sexual Politics, and the Militarized State. In S. Jacobs, R. Jacobson, and Jennifer Marchbank (Eds.), *State of Conflict, Gender, Violence and Resistance* (p.45–65). London: Zed Books.

Koeszegi, S.T., Zedlacher, E., and Hudribusch, R. (2014). The War against the Female Soldier? The Effects of Masculine Culture on Workplace Aggression. *Armed Forces and Society*, 40, 2, 226–251.

Law, S.A. (1999). White Privilege and Affirmative Action. *Akron Law Review*, 32, 603–621.

Miller, L. (1997). Not Just Weapons of the Weak: Gender Harassment as a Form of Protest for Army Men. *Social Psychology Quarterly*, 60, 1, 32–52.

Pazy, A., and Oron, I. (2001). Sex Proportion and Performance Evaluation among High Ranking Military Officers. *Journal of Organizational Behavior*, 22, 689–702.

Pershing, J.L. (2003). Why Women Don't Report Sexual Harassment: A Case Study of an Elite Military Institution. *Gender Issues*, 21, 4, 3–30.

Rodgers, J. (2013). Major General Michelle Johnson First Woman to Lead Air Force Academy. *Denver Post*. March 1. www.denverpost.com/breakingnews/ci_22698627/air-force-ac. Retrieved March 22, 2017.

Roeder, T. (2017). Sexual Assault Reports Down by a Third at Air Force Academy, but Still Highest Among Services. March 16. *The Gazette*. www.m.gazette.com. Retrieved March 22, 2017.

Rosen, L.N., Durand, D.B., Blieses, P.D., Halverson, R.R., Rothberg, J.M., and Harrison, N.L. (1996). Cohesion and Readiness in Gender-Integrated Combat Service Support Units: The Impact of Acceptance of Women and Gender Ratio. *Armed Forces and Society*, 22, 537–553.

Schmitt, E., and Moss, M. (2003). Air Force Academy Investigated 54 Sexual Assaults in 10 Years. March 7. *New York Times*. www.mobile.nytimes.com. Retrieved March 3, 2017.

Schmitt, J. (2005). Army Opens Inquiry into Treatment of Dead Taliban. October 20. *Star Tribune*.

Seifert, R. (1994). War and Rape: A Preliminary Analysis. In A. Stiglmayer (Ed.), *Mass Rape: The War Against Women in Bosnia-Herzegovina* (p.54–72). Lincoln, NE: University of Nebraska Press.

Snyder, R.C. (2003). The Citizen-Soldier Tradition and Gender Integration of the U.S. Military. *Armed Forces and Society*, 29, 2, 185–204.

Solaro, E. (2006). *Women in the Line of Fire. What You Should Know About Women in the Military*. Emeryville, CA: Seal Press.

Sturcke, J. (2005). U.S. Soldiers Desecrated Taliban Bodies. October 20. *Guardian*. www.theguardian.com. Retrieved March 27, 2017.

Testimony of Colonel Patrick Toffler. (April 19, 1991). Reference 60, chapter 7, p.200. (See L. Bird Francke. (1997). *Ground Zero. The Gender Wars in the Military*. New York, NY: Simon and Schuster.)

Titunik, R.F. (2008). The Myth of the Macho Military. *Polity*, 40, 2, 137–163.

U.S. Army. (2002). *Women in the Army: An Annotated Bibliography*. U.S. Army Research Institute for the Behavioral and Social Sciences. Special Report 48. May.

U.S. General Accounting Office. (1994). *Military Academy: Gender and Racial Disparities*. GAO/NSIAD-94-95. March.

14 Backlash against Women

In her epic book, now in its second edition, chronicling the journey of American feminism, Faludi (2006) unequivocally lambasts what she views as the backlash against women as an undeclared war, the title of which she credits to a movie about a man who entraps his own wife for a crime for which he is responsible. Faludi is unapologetic about the seeds of this backlash in that they are fallacious in both kind and intent. While it is evident in most, if not all, walks of life that the status of chiefly the white American woman has markedly improved, that advancement, Faludi bemoans, has come at a steep price. Women overwhelmingly credit the women's movement for providing the catalyst for this change. However, they complain that their professional and personal lives are still very much unequal to those of men. Throughout her book, Faludi illustrates how the hypocrisy of the American media conveniently filters information according to gender in advancing gender-based arguments. In an earlier chapter, the authors of this book provide examples invoked by Faludi such as the media's skewed representation of the female researcher Shere Hite's work and the onslaught of criticism that she endured, yet male psychologist Srully Blotnick's work, the favored narrative, Faludi describes as being based on dubious at best data.

Abramovitz (1996) sees this backlash as a counterattack by certain standards as a means of regulating women's lives and where women are limited to the domestic roles of marriage, motherhood and raising families. Moreover, by these very conservative principles, many issues that are disproportionately more likely to impact women, especially poor women, are rendered abhorrent in the sense that they should not exist – divorce, immigration, abortion, labor laws and affirmative action. Further, women who move away from these prescribed modes of behavior, unlike men, are punished even as so-called women's work goes without remuneration despite being recognized as important to society, i.e., motherhood (Ridgeway and Correll 2004). Here, the contradiction lies in that, notwithstanding its magnitude in society, motherhood is a status characteristic for which women are also not compensated. It is a diminished role that connotes someone of a lower stature. Thus, the reason why otherwise professional women who are seen as competent, once they assume the status of motherhood, are viewed as compromised as a result. Even men, once they take on the mantle of fatherhood or of caretakers, they too suffer some backlash in the form of under-evaluated performance, although not to the extent that professionals who are mothers in the workplace do (Deutsch and Saxton 1998).

By extension, given motherhood, gender is also a status characteristic (Ridgeway and Correll 2004). Yet, when men become fathers, their societal position as the family protectors helps to ward off any loss in status. Because they are men, another status characteristic, these two designations as father and man not only reinforce one another but help to forestall any presumed losses as well (Deutsch and Saxton 1998). Women who are single and professional retain the allure of competence in the workplace (Fiske et al. 2002) because they are less likely to be mothers (Goldin 2000). When positions are low status or require no more than a high school diploma as the minimum qualification, applicants draw the ire of employers for they are speculated to be more likely female and mothers who will bring nothing but the anticipated challenges of absenteeism granted their status characteristics. Ironically, male applicants do not raise these biases (Kennelly 1999). Female applicants who are black invoke negative and provocative stereotypes as single mothers. Snitow (1990) cautions employers that bring women into occupations and male-dominated ones under the misconception that they are equal and gender neutral. Likewise, professional women who work for these organizations are tagged as 'conceptual men' (Snitow 1990, p.26). However, Jorgenson (2000) believes that eventually women must own up to the veracity of the situation for especially after having children, it is at odds with having a profession.

Harris (2009a) asserts that despite women's progression given the women's movement, for instance, women are still being held to outmoded mores. Wechsler Segal (1986), like Coser and Laub Coser (1974), and Currie et al. (2000), deem male-dominated institutions like academe and the military to be greedy institutions where women are concomitantly duty bound to them. However, the family is itself a greedy institution (Coser and Laub Coser 1974, Wechsler Segal 1986), and the majority of its responsibilities fall on the women in the relationship. This creates an asymmetry where a woman is relegated to a lower status irrespective of her external obligations to her profession. The man or husband in the family does not experience any such conflicts and is considered the head of the household. The relationship between the man and woman and the wife and husband is 'skewed and unequally yoked' (Harris 2009a, p.395). Say Coser and Laub Coser:

> As long as the 'greedy' families could rely in the main on housewives who accepted with equanimity their unequal position of power, it could operate with a minimum of friction, even though it seems often

> to have exerted a high toll in psychic stress and emotional disturbance. But once women began to realize that there existed realistic chances of achieving more nearly equal status with their husbands if and when they involved themselves in the upper reaches of the occupational and professional world and so acquired new resources, the 'greedy' family was in trouble. Once women were no longer as ready as they had once been to support the careers of their husbands by offering auxiliary services, once they were no longer as ready to serve as tension relievers, recharging the emotional batteries of husbands come home to find repose from competitive battles, the terms on which the marital dyad was built began to change.
>
> (Coser and Laub Coser 1974, p. 99)

As evidenced, women's pay continues to lag behind that of white men, and minority women, especially those from underrepresented groups like African Americans, Hispanics and Native Americans, are more likely to bear the brunt of this burden (Harris 2009b). Although women represent 51.9 percent of the general civilian population (U.S. Census Bureau 2010), with 57 percent in the workforce (U.S. Department of Labor (DOL) n.d.), women as a group only earn 80 cents for each dollar that a white male earns (American Association of University Women (AAUW) 2017). For women of color, the rate is most dire. For African American women, the rate is 63 cents; Hispanic women, 54 cents; and for Native American and Alaska Native women, the rate stands at 58 cents for each dollar earned by a white male. Yet, surprisingly, for Asian women, the earnings rate actually trumps that of the white female at 85 cents. Data from the U.S. Department of Labor for 2015 cite comparable figures (U.S. DOL n.d.). Nevertheless, according to the AAUW, at white women's rate of 80 cents for every dollar earned by white men, women are not expected to reach pay parity with white men until 2050. Similar figures have also been reported by Catalyst for women in the U.S. (Catalyst.org 2017). More disturbing is that for every racial and/or ethnic group, women's pay disparity with that of white men and men in their own racial and/or ethnic group increases with age, with married white and Asian men amassing the highest earnings.

More significant is that even though women on average are outpacing men by securing more college degrees than ever before (U.S. Bureau of Labor Statistics (BLS) 2015), men still out-earn women at every educational level, where Asian men out-earn white men at 117 cents and Asian women at an average of 87 cents for every dollar earned by a white man (Pew Research Center 2016).

A 2007 report by the U.S. General Accountability Office (GAO) yielded some troubling findings about the overall and future earnings status for American women. Because, unlike men, women are more likely to interrupt their work lives for the purpose of child rearing and elderly care, for instance, they are less likely than their male counterparts to recapture the rewards necessary for a quality of life in retirement and at a time when they have limited to no time to recover such earnings (GAO 2007, Harris 2011). In the private sector, only 14.2 percent of senior leadership positions for corporations in the Standard & Poor's 500 companies are occupied by women (Egan 2015). Worse, only 24 of the Fortune 500 companies have women as chief executive officers. The prognosis, laments Rita McGrath of Columbia University's Business School, is essentially if you do not have women in the pool as candidates, you do not have women from whom to promote, although women represent 16.5 percent of executives at the level below the chief executive officer.

Harris's (2009a) comparative analysis of female military officers and academic women shows the extent to which women must go in an attempt to please their employers, their families and themselves. However, the conundrum lies in the fact that women's challenges such as the inordinate responsibility for childrearing and the family are invisible to men. As Finkel and Olswang (1996) allege, the problems that impact women for the most part or are seen as within the domain of women go unnoticed or are nonexistent to men. For military women, and specifically those within the commissioned corps, much of the problem stems from the fact that in such male-dominated organizations, it is men's performance that is respected, not women's, for military women do not represent the norm or the mainstream because they are deviants (Ellefson 1998, Law 1999). When women are called out for superior performance, they are identified by gender as the exception, not the rule. Research on women in even the Israeli military shows that when women officers are the minority in their units, their performance is under-evaluated by male superiors (Pazy and Oron 2001). Plus, it is the token status of women (Kanter 1977), their actual identity (Rosen et al. 1999) and subordinate status as a minority group when contrasted with men, the majority group (Yoder 1991), along with the limited resources that are allocated to them (Blalock 1967), which undergirds the maintenance of deep-seated stereotypes about them.

In response to these total claims upon them by their employers and families, women devise survival strategies in an attempt to overcome these obstacles because unlike military men, declare Westwood and Turner (1996), '[w]omen don't have wives' (p.46). Harris's (2015) research of 17 American women veterans bears this out. To navigate the minefield of the combat exclusion policy, the women sought ways to get noticed. Some did so by attaining more education while others confronted the system head on through litigation knowing that they would come up against Goliath in both personal and professional loss, but staunchly believing that all along what is right would triumph. More notable is that even as the women defied this openly disparate system, at no time did they blame the military but instead impugned the unenlightened men who were ordered to implement it. Many of the women's battles resulted in their premature and voluntary attrition from the military for bucking the institution's norms and traditions. Yet, without doing so, many of the developments that have advantaged women in the military, if not for these brave souls, would not have been possible. Even the repeal of the military's Don't Ask, Don't Tell and Don't Pursue policy is to be attributed to one of the women veterans highlighted by Harris (2015), who unknowingly challenged the blatant discriminatory system at a rally as a civilian when she was inadvertently outed. Harris's research therefore underscores the perilous path that military women were forced to walk, but who nevertheless were moved to act despite the obstacles and risks to their own careers.

The fortuitous irony and slight that did not go unnoticed is that military women were never a part of the equation in the women's movement (Holm 1992). More insidious was that the women directors of the military services, even as they fought for women's increased acceptance into the military, were blind to these oversights. Said Chandler (1967), '[i]t behooves every woman to remember she is not going to be asked to put her life at stake as the men are.' This was duplicitous and the height of hypocrisy, according to Holm (1992), in that this message represented the very sentiments of the few women in leadership in the military at the time, as if women basically functioned as more of an appendage than as an integral part of the military. It is therefore worth noting that Harris's (2015) work also draws attention to the fact that the two general officers whom she featured both paid homage to Major General Jeanne Holm, the first woman in the U.S. military to be promoted to this rank and former director of Women in the Air Force (U.S. Air Force), as being instrumental to their own careers.

Major General Holm fought a lonely battle, though, and is to be credited with paving the way for women in leadership positions in the military who followed her (Schudel 2010). Then a colonel, Holm became so frustrated with the male-dominated system and challenges with the likes of then Air Force Chief of Staff General Curtis LeMay, that she submitted her retirement papers in disgust, which paradoxically was followed by a promotion to brigadier general in 1971, a first in the Air Force, and in 1973, promotion to the rank of major general. Of her illustrious career, the general captured it by not mincing words, saying: 'When you were face to face with some of the garbage they were handing out, it just wore you out. One time, in 1971, I handed in my retirement papers. I'd just had it up to the eyeballs' (Schudel 2010). Yet, by all accounts, Major General Holm used her position and influence to open doors for other women in the military, and, despite a great career, it was evident that even in retirement, the wounds of fighting and living within a clearly then even more oppressive system for women in the military had not healed for the general. As difficult as it may seem for today's military women, one dare not imagine the routine obstruction, undermining and the like that Major General Holm must have encountered during her career.

Backlash against Women 213

Gutman (2000) cynically makes light of the extent to which the contemporary military has moved away from its former self, although she cites sociologist Tiger's warning that for the purpose of male bonding, men have a propensity to invent more brutal rituals to outdo one another as proof that they possess what it takes as men to become soldiers. While some believe that the remnants of the Army of the past still exist, the transformation to a more politically correct, more team-oriented Army, for example, is not without its critics. However, one must remember that these now draconian methodologies represented a conscripted military, not an all-volunteer one. According to Mark Thompson, a military reporter for *Time Magazine* in 1997, the new military is unrecognizable compared to its former self from the 1950s and 1960s. In the Army, for example, there is more adherence to regulations, emphasis on teamwork and that a recruit becomes a soldier from day one, many bemoan, without having worked to earn this title. Says one instructor at Fort Jackson, while he understands the need for the military to avoid abusing its personnel, he believes that the institution has moved away from its roots. 'You're not being a soldier, you're being a Mama' (Gutman 2000, p.71). He continued:

> We're setting them up for failure down the road. In reception, recruits got a speech about do's and don't's that the drill sergeants are allowed. They can't do this and they can't do that. It destroys what we call our power base right there. A drill sergeant can't touch you, a drill sergeant can't cuss at you, a drill sergeant can't this, that, or the other and 'you have the right to do this, you have the right to do that,' right down the line. By the time they get down to the basic training company they have this huge attitude.
>
> (Gutman 2000, p.71)

Another drill instructor reminisces about when the limits of recruits were driven to the brink (Gutman 2000), while another gripes: 'You're either making warfighters or you're not. We're making peacekeepers here' (Gutman 2000, p.72). Even then Secretary of Defense William Cohen criticized that under the guise of the 'New Army,' basic training was being compromised (Gutman 2000, p.73). Perhaps another drill sergeant summarized it best following the subpar performance of several women recruits who wanted to know why they had not passed the grenade qualifying course even though they believed that they had done their best. Sergeant Rick Ayala bluntly replied: 'There are some situations in war where your best effort doesn't matter. You either throw a grenade out of bursting range or you get yourself and your buddies killed' (Gutman 2000, p.79).

Others seem to believe that the military has become so sensitized by succumbing to the levers of political whims, and that the institution functions in doublespeak in an effort to obscure its underlying message, especially as it relates to the media. One senior Navy officer stated that such hot topics as gender integration are seemingly a distraction in accomplishing the institution's mission (Gutman 2000). An early 1998 *Navy Times* survey yielded a plethora of findings that largely revealed confusion in the workforce. Many complained about lacking confidence in leaders, not finding their positions as enjoyable, and the Navy's change in culture. Further, those in the lower leadership ranks of the Navy's chain of command found themselves being unnecessarily and overly responsive to a new workforce that was quick to advance their complaints through the chain of command, prompting supervisors to become exceedingly attentive to subordinates. An F-14 pilot who short-circuited his military career said that unlike in the past when one was encouraged to build up and release that frustration in the event that war never materialized, the New Navy did not allow for this energy to be channeled. If anything, the pilot said, this energy is impeded, resulting in a premature attrition of personnel to the civilian sector.

Gutman (2000) goes as far as saying that while the gender norming of the military whereby mothers-to-be are given such considerations as 'bonding breaks' (p.114), the Army was less discerning in doling out citations for Bronze Stars post-Operation Desert Storm, resulting in the receipt of the medal by almost anyone and where the then highest-ranking woman in the Army, Lieutenant General Claudia Kennedy, engaged in consideration of others' sessions with an audience of seasoned non-commissioned officers for the purpose of 'sensing sessions' (Gutman 2000, p.114). Likewise, says Gutman (2000), there are more troubling concerns of this kinder, gentler military – what she calls and described for the Air Force as the 'Reach Out and Bomb Somebody' (p.115) program and general officers' hugging released prisoners of war (POWs) on the tarmac. As one Special Forces officer, now retired, scoffed, if the POWs had been more preoccupied with combat readiness, they would have eluded capture.

Yet, for all of the criticisms about this seemingly new military, Gutman (2000) appears to be oblivious to what she mockingly refers to as the kinder, gentler military. Amid these criticisms, Gutman (2000) clearly misses the point that unlike in the past, when the military could issue dicta given a conscripted workforce, an all-volunteer force was adjusting and responding to a new reality, that is, in order to attract high-quality recruits owing to competition from the civilian sector, and particularly so during a robust economy, it is only prudent that the military adopts new strategies to sustain itself. Illogically, in making her case, Gutman (2000) unwittingly, or perhaps wittingly, exposed her slight of hand through an Amelia Earhart quote from 1930: 'Men would rather vacate the arena [of combat] altogether than share it with women' (as cited in Gutman 2000, p.276). This quote from a woman who at the time managed to break barriers in aviation to become the first known woman to cross the Atlantic and Pacific Oceans solo, and who in 1923 was only one of 16 women in the U.S. to be granted a license as a pilot (Amelia Earhart, Biography.com). Regrettably, too, Gutman (2000), a woman, is a co-conspirator in the backlash against women in the military, if not all women in society, for having dared to aspire to the same wants and desires as military men, if not all men. And in her censure of a more respectful military that is now being told to leverage the talents of all of its workforce for the sake of country. It is important not feed into the insecurities of one group, by joining other likeminded women as Linda Chavez and Elaine Donnelly in decrying women as wholly unfit for military service, thereby reinforcing its nature as a man's prerogative in which women should play no part (Titunik 2008).

In commenting on the debacle about the Abu Ghraib prison during Operation Iraqi Freedom, conservative provocateur Ann Coulter went as far as to characterize the women who participated in violating the Iraqi prisoners' rights as 'too vicious to be in the military' (Cottle 2004, p.28), while Elaine Donnelly impugned the women's behavior to one akin to 'mean girls' who were merely mirroring the collapse in structure and control that had given way to gender-integrated boot camp (Donnelly 2004). Gutman (2000) counsels that the military should institute a number of draconian measures in an effort to restore it to its hallowed image and offer 'rites of passage, powerful male mentors (not "bossy female majors and captains"), and a place in a hierarchy of "elites" who fight real bloodstake battles' (p.277). She not only endorses eradicating quotas for recruiting women and minorities (i.e., blacks and Hispanics), but promotes bringing in more black and Hispanic men from the working class and high school dropouts.

Does this commentary not strike the reading audience as not only incendiary but downright racist in its appeal to the lowest common denominator to abuse the already trampled rights of such traditionally marginalized groups for military service? One can only then speculate that these groups would be sacrificed for the preservation of the country's majority white elite population, since white women would also be saved from recruitment into the military. Among other groups, Gutman (2000) opposes mix-gender basic training and advocates gender-specific training as practised in the Marine Corps and the Israeli Defense Force. Titunik (2008), as these authors, takes issue with Gutman's (2000) perception of the feminization of the U.S. military because the institution has become more 'female friendly' (p.154). Most sinister is that Gutman (2000) admits that her regressive stance will mark the inclusion of fewer women in the military's ranks, but what she deliberately cloaks from the reader yet implies is that by fewer women, she means fewer white women will be asked to put their lives on the line for the country, although as she explicitly states, they need not worry for the price will be paid by black and other minority men and women.

Fortunately, cooler heads prevailed. The Military Leadership Diversity Commission (MLDC 2011b), together with the Defense Advisory Committee on Women in the Services (DACOWITS 2012), moved the Department of Defense to not only repeal the combat exclusion policy that has cumulatively robbed all women of their inalienable rights to contribute as full citizens towards the defense of the country's national security and in doing so, it is hoped, will eventually remove the 'barriers and inconsistencies, to create a level playing field for all qualified servicemembers who meet the qualifications' (MLDC 2011b, Summary, p.xviii). Similarly, in the wake of Operations Enduring and Iraqi Freedom, the drawing down of military personnel and transition into Operation New Dawn, the MLDC (2011a) warned that given the existing dearth of women and minorities in the senior enlisted and commissioned corps, the military needs to be mindful of its attrition strategies for these groups. Of note, and which has been consistently part of the commentary, and thus their repeated employment, commanders have long cited the exemplary performance of their female workforce on the ground and higher-echelon commanders have attested to the competence and leadership abilities of their women commanders (DACOWITS 2009, Grosskruger 2008, Twitchell 2008). Further, it was many of those of the leadership inside the military, who are primarily men, who were most ardent about repealing the combat exclusion policy (Twitchell 2008, Grosskruger 2008). As Titunik (2008) suggests, because the military has come to increasingly rely upon the services of women to bolster its expertise and ranks, it then behooves the institution to not uni-dimensionally adhere to the outmoded and hypermasculine beliefs of the past but to embrace the full integration of women into the military in the interests and benefit of military effectiveness.

Bibliography

Abramovitz, M. (1996). *Regulating Women's Lives. Social Welfare Policy from Colonial Times to the Present*. Brooklyn, NY: South End Press.

Biography.com. (n.d.). Amelia Earhart.

American Association of University Women (AAUW). (2017). The Simple Truth about the Gender Pay Gap. Spring. www.aauw.org/research/the-simple-truth-about-the-gender-pay-gap/. Retrieved May 28, 2017.

Blalock, H.M. (1967). *Toward a Theory of Minority Group Relations*. New York, NY: John Wiley and Sons.

Catalyst.org. (2017). Women's Earnings and Income. *Knowledge Center*. June 21. www.catalyst.org/knowledge/womens-earnings-and-income. Retrieved May 20, 2017.

Chandler, R. (1967). Our Military Women. *Air Force Times*. May 17.

Coser, L.A. (1974). *Greedy Institutions. Patterns of Undivided Commitment*. New York: Free Press.

Coser, L.A., and Laub Coser, R. (1974). The Housewife and Her 'Greedy Family.' In *Greedy Institutions. Patterns of Undivided Commitment*. New York, NY: Free Press.

Cottle, M. (2004). G.I. Jane. *New Republic*. May 24, 38.

Currie, J., Harris, P., and Thiele, B. (2000). Sacrifices in Greedy Universities: Are They Gendered? *Gender and Education*, 12, 3, 269–291.

Defense Advisory Committee on Women in the Services (DACOWITS). (2009). *Status Report.* http://dacowits.defense.gov/Reports-Meetings/. Retrieved May 26, 2017.

Defense Advisory Committee on Women in the Services (DACOWITS). (2012). *Status Report.* http://dacowits.defense.gov/Portals/48/Documents/Reports/2012/Annual%20Report/dacowits2012report.pdf. Retrieved May 26, 2017.

Deutsch, F.M., and Saxton, S.E. (1998). Traditional Ideologies, Nontraditional Lives. *Sex Roles,* 38, 331–362.

Donnelly, E. (2004). Mean Girls in the Military. Center for Military Readiness. May 18. www.cmrlink.org/culture.asp?DocID¼225. Retrieved December 16, 2016.

Egan, M. (2015). Still Missing: Female Business Leaders. March 24. *CNN Money.* http://money.cnn.com/2015/03/24/investing/female-ceo-pipeline-leadership/index.html. Retrieved May 24, 2017.

Ellefson, K.G. (1998). *Advancing Army Women as Senior Leaders – Understanding the Obstacles.* Carlisle, PA: U.S. Army War College.

Faludi, S. (2006). *Backlash. The Undeclared War Against American Women.* Danvers, MA: Broadway Books.

Finkel, S.K., and Olswang, S.G. (1996). Child Rearing as a Career Impediment to Women Assistant Professors. *The Review of Higher Education,* 19, 2, 123–139.

Fiske, S.T., Cuddy, A.J.C., Glick, P., and Xu, J. (2002). A Model of (Often Mixed) Stereotype Content: Competence and Warmth Respectively Follow from Perceived Status and Competition. *Journal of Personality and Social Psychology,* 82, 878–902.

Goldin, C. (2000). *Career and Family: College Women Look to the Past.* Working Paper, No. 5188. Cambridge, MA: National Bureau of Economic Research.

Grosskruger, P.L. (2008). Women Leaders in Combat: One Commander's Perspective. In M. Putko and D.V. Johnson III (Eds.), *Women in Combat Compendium.* U.S. Army War College. January.

Gutman, S. (2000). *The Kinder, Gentler Military. Can America's Neutral Gender Fighting Force Still Win Wars?* Lisa Drew Books Series. New York, NY: Scribner Press.

Harris, G.L.A. (2009a). Women, the Military and Academe: Navigating the Family Track in an Up or Out System. *Administration and Society,* 41, 4, 391–422.

Harris, G.L.A. (2009b). Revisiting Affirmative Action in Leveling the Playing Field. Who Have Been the True Beneficiaries Anyway? *Review of Public Personnel Administration,* 29, 4, 354–382.

Harris, G.L.A. (2011). The Quest for Gender Equity. Book Review of *The Declining Significance of Gender?* F.D. Blau, M.B. Brinton and D.B. Grusky (Eds.), 2009. *Public Administration Review,* 71, 1, 123–126.

Harris, G.L.A. (2015). *Living Legends and Full Agency: Implications of Repealing the Combat Exclusion Policy.* New York, NY: Taylor & Francis Group, a division of CRC Press.

Holm, J. (1992). *Women in the Military. An Unfinished Revolution.* Revised Edition. Novato, CA: Presidio Press.

Jorgenson, J. (2000). Interpreting the Intersections of Work and Family: Frame Conflicts in Women's Work. *Electronic Journal of Communication,* 10, 3–4.

Kanter, R.M. (1977). *Men and Women of the Corporation.* New York, NY: Basic Books.

Kennelly, I. (1999). That Single Mother Element: How White Employers Typify Black Women. *Gender and Society*, 13, 168–192.

Law, S.A. (1999). White Privilege and Affirmative Action. *Akron Law Review*, 32, 603–621.

Military Leadership Diversity Commission (MLDC). (2011a). *Decision Paper #6: Diversity Leadership*. February. http://diversity.defense.gov/Portals/51/Documents/Resources/Commission/docs/Decision%20Papers/Paper%206%20-%20Diversity%20Leadership.pdf. Retrieved January 25, 2017.

Military Leadership Diversity Commission (MLDC). (2011b). *From Representation to Inclusion: Diversity Leadership for the 21st Century Military*. Final Report. www.diversity.defense.gov/Portals/51/Documents/Special%20Feature. Retrieved May 26, 2017.

Pazy, A., and Oron, I. (2001). Sex Proportion and Performance Evaluation among High Ranking Military Officers. *Journal of Organizational Behavior*, 22, 689–702.

Pew Research Center. (2016). Racial, Gender Pay Gaps Persist in U.S. Despite Some Progress. July 1. Fact Tank. www.pewresearch.org/fact-tank/2016/07/01/racial-gender-wage-gaps-persist-in-u-s-despite-some-progress/. Retrieved May 26, 2017.

Ridgeway, C.L., and Correll, S.J. (2004). Motherhood as a Status Characteristic. *Journal of Social Issues*, 60, 4, 683–700.

Rosen, L.N., Bliese, P.D., Wright, K.A., and Gifford, R.K. (1999). Gender Composition and Group Cohesion in U.S. Army Units: A Comparison across Five Studies. *Armed Forces and Society*, 25, 3, 365–386.

Schudel, M. (2010). Jeanne M. Holm, 88, Dies, First Female Air Force General. February 25. *Washington Post*. www.washingtonpost.com/wp-dyn/content/article/2010/02/24/AR2010022405278.html. Retrieved May 26, 2010.

Snitow, A. (1990). A Gender Diary. In M. Hirsch and E.F. Keller (Eds.), *Conflicts in Feminism* (p.9–43). New York, NY: Routledge Press.

Titunik, R.F. (2008). The Myth of the Macho Military. *Polity*, 40, 2, 137–163.

Twitchell, R.E. (2008). The 95th Military Police Battalion Deployment to Iraq – Operation Iraqi Freedom II. In M. Putko and D.V. Johnson III (Eds.), *Women in Combat Compendium*. Carlisle, PA: U.S. Army War College. January.

U.S. Air Force. (n.d.). Biography. Major General Jeanne M. Holm. www.af.mil/About-Us/Biographies/Display/Article/106699/major-general-jeanne-m-holm/. Retrieved February 10, 2017.

U.S. Bureau of Labor Statistics. (2015). Women in the Labor Force: A Data Book. BLS Reports. December. www.bls.gov/opub/reports/womens-databook. Retrieved May 20, 2017.

U.S. Census Bureau. (2010). Quick Facts. www.census.gov/quickfacts/. Retrieved March 28, 2017.

U.S. Department of Labor (DOL) (n.d.a). Data and Statistics. *Women's Bureau*. www.dol.gov/wb/stats/stats_data.htm. Retrieved March 28, 2017.

U.S. Department of Labor (DOL) (n.d.b). Breaking Down the Gender Pay Gap. *Women's Bureau*. www.dol.gov/wb/stats/stats_data.htm. Retrieved March 28, 2017.

U.S. General Accountability Office (GAO). (2007). *Retirement Security. Women Face Challenges in Ensuring Financial Security in Retirement*. GAO-08-105. October.

Wechsler Segal, M. (1986). The Military and the Family as Greedy Institutions. *Armed Forces and Society*, 13, 1, 9–38.

Westwood, J., and Turner, H. (1996). *Marriage and Children as Impediments to Career Progression of Active Duty Career Women Army Officers.* Carlisle, PA: U.S. Army War College.

Yoder, J.D. (1991). Rethinking Tokenism: Looking Beyond Numbers. *Gender and Society,* 5, 178–192.

Part V
Women and Power

Throughout ancient ourstory, women have been the backbone and agitators of countless wars, either waging them for the territorial expansion of their respective economies and/or amassing even greater power through strategic marriages with like-minded leaders and elite families. Many have ruled with impunity and retained their seat of power by staving off seizures of already acquired wealth, keeping their competition in check and at bay, and concentrating even greater power politically through the adoration and commitment of their populations. However, what the literature speculates is that with the coming of age of Christianity and the rise of European powers came a period of presumed enlightenment characterized by intolerance during a 400-year span. This confluence appears to have resulted in the gradual decline and devolution in the power and status of women as a group. These 400 years might be considered a calculated war of sorts against the female as a specie and to which today's undue censuring of women owes its origins.

Part V examines an abbreviated version of the series of women warriors who came to power to the elevation of their contemporary equivalents, who, unlike their male peers, are held to unreasonably high standards to the point of only being chosen as leaders when the states and/or organizations are so troubled and at the precipice of failure that women at the helm are believed to be the only path to success. Here, women are viewed best as crisis leaders. Yet, simultaneously, women leaders are similarly persecuted even when they succeed only to be replaced by men who are asked to lead when organizations are the most stable. Thus, men are believed to be success leaders. These unrealistic standards cumulatively and over time cause women to lose ground when they are most vulnerable, or at the time of retirement. In the process, today's women have been relegated to such positions as tokens or as mere proxies for men. Caught in this double bind, and sometimes triple bind for women of color, women are forced to leverage such perceived equalizers as education, economics and money, all in an effort to level this unfair and uneven playing field. Yet, the literature is clear that even when women outpace the white male at these equalizers, they still fall short as a group. Women veterans are no different in this regard.

15 Women in Power

Even in contemporary society, the terms women and power are still not considered synonymous. Yet, as Harris (2015) chronicles, this modern interpretation of women and power is diametrically opposed to women's stature once upon a time in ourstory. Grant DePauw's (1998) discovery of women's roles during ancient times as the protagonists in war, central in amassing wealth for their respective economies; Jones's (1997) depiction of the ancestors of humankind, the Africans, and Africa as the 'Mother of All Nations' (p.81), as he puts it, and the infamous women Amazons who roamed the continent; and Goldstein's (2003) description of the Greeks who succeeded the Africans all portray a landscape rich with the exploits of great women once upon a time that was not the exception but the rule and norm in society. Grant DePauw's (1998) work extends into Europe and finally into America.

Powerful women like Sudanese Jebl Sahaba, the warrior, in 650 BC was one of the first women to be so recorded (Grant DePauw 1998). Sammuramutar, the Assyrian queen, who ruled during the ninth century BC from 811 to 906, commanded excursions that attacked and seized Babylonia, the Citadel, and accumulated territory by occupying what is now modern Pakistan and India (Grant DePauw 1998).

Maryet-Nit, Khen Kavies, Ashotep, Nefraso-bak and Ahmedse Nofretori all ruled Egypt and its vast territories from the 25th through the 16th centuries (Grant DePauw 1998). The business-minded Queen Hatshepsut, also of Egypt, multiplied her domains through territorial expansion, even donning an artificial beard and other male-oriented accoutrements that signified the wisdom of male pharaohs. Grant DePauw (1998) writes about the works of the Greek writer Herodotus, who declared the Amazon women, the Scythians or Sarmatians, whose direct lineage was from the Africans, distinctive in forging relationships with Scythian men in exchange for enjoying much autonomy in society where they were free to engage in warlike behavior with or without their brethren. Accordingly, these women commanded strong cultures as matriarchs over their dominions (Goldstein 2003, Grant DePauw 1998).

Infamous Queen Candace of Ethiopia, who ruled Ethiopia, Sudan and certain territories in Egypt pre-332 BC, was reputed for her power, adroitness and command in execution and empire expansion (Jones 1997). Alexander the Great had had an encounter with the Black Queen, as she was known, and was forced to retreat given the sheer size of the well-equipped forces that she marshaled, which would have dealt his own forces a damning blow. Whereas Queen Amanirenas not only defeated Petronius, then the Roman governor in Egypt, but redoubled her efforts in holding onto her empire and seizing territories from her adversary, this 150 years after 170 BC and following the rule of warrior queens like Shenakdah Kite, Anamishakhete, Malegereabar and Newidemek. The Yorubas of West Africa were equally endowed with a series of queens who ruled with impunity (Jones 1997). Consider the neighboring Hausa women who were distinguished as commanders. Following hundreds of years, a series of 17 queens, including Queen Arnanatu as late as and beginning in 1536, ruled the Hausa dominion or the modern-day Democratic Republic of the Congo for 34 years. She negotiated agreements for trade with territories from the Sahara to the north of the African continent, and is credited with creating the market for and bringing the kola nut to the area. The country in which Queen Arnanatu is most well regarded is Nigeria where she is memorialized in a statue in Lagos's National Theater.

Says Harris (2015), the African motherland has been blessed with innumerable queens, many of whom were reputed as legendary, albeit for sinister reasons. For example, Judith, Queen of the Falashes, is most renowned for the execution of members of King Solomon's family, and others like the Queen of Sheba and the Sorceress Queen Dahia of Carthage and Mauritania (Jones 1997). Yet, more recently, it was Zinga Mbandi, the King of Ndongo's daughter who is eminently remembered for her political prowess. Upon the capture of her father the King in 1620, Queen Mbandi convinced the Portuguese governor to convene with her. When the queen arrived, and perhaps calculatingly, she found only the governor seated with his attendants standing by his side. Knowing the importance of projecting power and owing to her own upbringing, the queen ordered one of the attendants on all fours, sat on him to ensure an eye-level position and proceeded to negotiate with the governor for her father's release (Jones 1997). The Greeks were equally notorious in following their African ancestors' footsteps. Warrior Queen Harpalyce of Thrace led the army to procure her father's freedom while Atalanta was fierce in battle (Grant DePauw 1998, Goldstein 2003).

Queen Cleopatra III of Egypt rose to power at a period when the Romans governed a portion of the empire (Grant DePauw 1998). Although her father the king ruled as merely a figurehead, Cleopatra was shrewd in exercising sway over the likes of Mark Antony and Julius Caesar – so much so that Antony surrendered his holdings, including land, to her. Suspicious of her ulterior motives, Octavian, Antony's brother-in-law, held Cleopatra to blame for conspiring in an alliance with Antony to move the seat of power from Rome to Alexandria. Rather than endure the humiliation of defeat, Queen Cleopatra committed suicide, and still reviled today for wanting to overthrow Rome (Abbott 1941, as cited in Grant DePauw 1998). Nevertheless, despite the succession of queens in Egypt, and at the behest of Roman authority, it was Queen Zenobia with dominion over Palmyra, a vast region, which included such modern countries as Syria, Saudi Arabia, Egypt, Armenia and Persia (Grant DePauw 1998), in the third century, who is most revered by the Romans (Carr Vaughan 1967). Queen Zenobia was ruthless in remaining on the offensive against any attacks by the Romans. She possessed an army of 70,000-strong and despite repeated attempts by both Claudius and Aurelian, they stood in awe of her power to defeat them. When one of Aurelian's numerous attempts to mount a capture of her land resulted in his retreat, he could not help but comment on the intimidating size of her well-endowed and combat-ready forces (Newark 1989). Aurelian's repeated efforts at talks with the queen were rebuffed. The queen found fault with the caustic tone in which he issued his dicta, each letter prompting her blistering response. Fearing that she would be captured, Queen Zenobia fled in the dead of night on a female camel as opposed to a horse as a more expeditious means of transportation into Persia; but her path was diverted and she was taken before entering Persia (Grant DePauw 1998, Carr Vaughan 1967). However, the queen did not resort to suicide as fellow Queen Cleopatra did, and declared as her rationale when queried that she accepted Aurelian as an emperor, for unlike his predecessors, he was successful in his exploits. This the queen respected, while agreeing to a partnership with him after her defeat (Newark 1989).

Queen Zenobia, including her children, assimilated well into Roman power, having married into the royalty and elite of the society. However, as Harris (2015) surmised, while Queen Zenobia's legacy as a leader is held in high esteem, Queen Cleopatra's was not. She was reviled as having resorted to trickery for personal gain, including toppling Rome as the center of power. Queen Zenobia became a formidable ally. Moreover, she was similarly admired by Aurelian, who was in awe of her steady disposition in the handling of personnel and the state's affairs (Newark 1989).

Europe, as early as 878 AD, witnessed a line of great women including Aethelflaed, also known as Lady of Mercians, who proved to be masterful at territorial expansion, even forcing the Welsh to surrender their holdings thus consolidating the reach and range of her power in the process (Grant DePauw 1998). Italy's Matilda was also a force to be reckoned with. She led armies and was fierce in combat and her valor was renowned (Grant DePauw 1998, Eads 1986). It appeared that during this period of feudal Europe when royalty amassed great wealth while disregarding the economic plight of their respective populations, royal women ensured that they became as erudite as their husbands in such affairs as the military and the economy to position themselves for the assumption of power (Crim 2000). Here, it was thought that lineage, not sex, determined who became heir to the throne.

Christine de Pisan, also of Italy, but unlike the warrior Matilda, personified her expertise in a more refined yet still powerful demeanor. She was intellectual in such matters as politics and diplomacy and schooled a wide range of constituents from military leaders and their soldiers to the various castes of women including aristocrats, the bourgeois and peasants (Crim 2000, Grant DePauw 1998). De Pisan reveled particularly in elevating women in different ways of knowing (Crim 2000). The irony, though, is that despite the influence that she exercised in society, including the legacy imparted in her writings about the military, for instance, *Feats of Arms and Chivalry* (Grant DePauw 1998), especially given her quest to enlighten women, de Pisan did not see women as being on par with men (Crim 2000). More perplexing is her belief that women should never assume arms as a way of validating their parity with men, just as she instructed men to do otherwise. De Pisan advocated instead that women engage in martial arts (Crim 2000). She saw the role of royal women or those of influence as proponents of activities that would advance the affairs of the state.

France's Eleanor of Aquitane forged an economic marriage with Henry II of England for territorial expansion that amplified her already extended influence. This at a time when her detractors disparaged the span of her power, Eleanor only managed to strengthen it through greater land acquisitions and another marriage, this time to France's Louis VI. Said of her exploits: 'Females were among them, riding horseback in the manner of men, not ... sidesaddle, but unashamedly astride, bearing lances and weapons as men do. Dressed in masculine garb, they conveyed a wholly martial appearance, more mannish than the Amazons' (Newark 1989, p.107).

Modern-day women heads of state, like their predecessors, are no less adept and powerful at strategically governing, especially during times of war. Yet, ostensibly, in today's world, unlike their predecessors, women leaders are constrained in that they are forced to navigate not only the wicked problems of contemporary societies but the ideological and political lenses through which they are judged. Further, they must walk a precariously fine line between being judged as a leader, as a woman, and as a leader who happens to be a woman who exudes and executes her authority like that of a man but without being perceived as manlike. As well, to ascend politically as a head of state today, no longer necessary is any royal lineage or even the caste of aristocracy. Still, modern women leaders have ably steered their countries onto the correct path, doing so nimbly during wartime and peacetime. Leaders like India's Indira Gandhi, Israel's Golda Meir and England's Margaret Thatcher come to mind (Goldstein 2003). Pakistan's Benazir Bhutto, the first woman in 1988 to lead a majority Muslim country (Biography.com n.d.a), had a contentious relationship with her country's military that played itself out publicly as she successfully controlled its influence. Interestingly enough, not only was Bhutto elected one month after giving birth to her first child, but following her defeat and exile to Britain and Dubai, but she continued to lead her political party, the People's Party of Pakistan (PPP). Bhutto survived at least one assassination attempt, only to succumb to the second one in 2007. Nevertheless, her survival skills even in death are a testament to what a formidable leader she was in life.

The Philippines' Corazon Aquino, too, had an openly combative relationship with the Filipino military (Goldstein 2003). Aquino was known for her adroitness as a politician and diplomat. She skillfully vacillated between employing bellicose rhetoric and more measured speech to restrain the military in its goal to overthrow the government. She survived seven assassination attempts by the military. Yet, when addressing the population, Aquino was known to deftly invoke a softer language by speaking in her native Tagalog (Boudreau 1995, Harris 2015). Turkey's Tan Su Gillard defeated Kurdish rebels and Sri Lanka's Chandraka Bandaranaika Kumartunga resorted to war in opposition to the Tamil separatists (Goldstein 2003). Violeta Chamorro of Nicaragua forged peace amid a civil war. Ellen Johnson Sirleaf of Liberia, known as the Iron Lady, defeated former ally Charles Taylor in 2006, to rise to the country's presidency following Taylor's removal for treason (Biography.com n.d.a). Says Goldstein (2003), this ourstory is replete with examples showing that women are no less warlike than men in executing whatever actions are necessary for effectively governing their countries. The circumstances dictated the particular strategies or tactics that they employed. As such, and when necessary, women will resort to whatever means necessary to preserve their respective sovereignty, power and territories.

While it cumulatively took 400 years, or the period from approximately the end of the 11th century to the 15th century, the range and reach of women's power and influence emerged to have collectively and inexplicably devolved. Says Grant DePauw (1998), this was a time of the First Crusade when Pope Urban II proclaimed in reaction to a perceived Muslim assault on Christianity, a time, of perhaps the first recorded episode of Islamophobia. Women began to be viewed by the largely Christian elite or of Christendom as merely accessories and not a central part and parcel of military engagements or exploits. With this regression came a level of xenophobia and chauvinism against women together with a narrow-mindedness in all things virtuous and therefore of what women should be. It is also worth noting that while the Greeks were in admiration of women, they nonetheless held conflicting opinions about them as to their natural predilections for war (Goldstein 2003), for example. The Romans held similar beliefs about women notwithstanding the belief that they are purported to compromise military men's ability to effectively prosecute wars (Grant DePauw 1998).

Women, during this so-called period of enlightenment but a retrenchment for the specie, found themselves at odds with the ideologies of intolerance of the day and principally those women, like men, who sought ways to serve their respective sovereigns as patriots through military service (Grant DePauw 1998). Women were then relegated and resorted to attiring themselves in men's clothing just for the opportunity to function in some patriotic capacity. As Harris (2015) contends, though commanders found women to be burdensome to their expeditions, women were equally perceived as 'a moral inconvenience' (p.49). Remarkably, such depraved sentiments persist even in the modern American military, whereby women are viewed as convenient outlets for male sexual frustrations (Hunter 2007, Bird Francke 1997). Even when employed in any meaningful way, women are only to be dismissed as irrelevant once the urgency has passed. In essence, once deployed for the expressed purpose of executing the mission and/or during major campaigns or war, military women are rendered as a convenient resource (Wagner DeCrew 1995), all to be forgotten once the imminent danger or crises have passed, given the collective 'cultural amnesia' (Wechsler Segal 1995, p.761) of the nation's civilian and military leadership that sets in during peacetime. One can then only cautiously and optimistically hope that despite overt signs from the Trump Administration that potentially threaten to derail implementation as called for by the 2013 repeal of the combat exclusion policy, advocacy groups like the Service Woman's Action Network (SWAN) and the American Civil Liberties Union (ACLU) and internal to the Department of Defense, the Defense Advisory Committee on Women in the Services (DACOWITS), will hold the military accountable for meeting these milestones. Although Congress has chief oversight for such matters, it is the coalition of these external groups that may prove more fruitful as catalysts for change.

In addressing women's collective devolution of power and agency, it is equally noteworthy that, even as the U.S. stands as the self-appointed leader of the free world, the model of democracy and a country with the highest economic standard of living in the world, despite women's advancement in the country to hold such high-ranking positions as secretary of state (U.S. Department of State n.d.), Federal Reserve Board chair (Board of Governors of the Federal Reserve System n.d.), and chief executive officers in 27 Fortune 500 companies, including women of color like Ursula Burns, who has led the Xerox Corporation for the past eight years but who will soon be retiring (Zarya 2016), essentially leaving a gaping void in the demographic group, the U.S. has yet to produce a woman as its head of state. There are a total of 79 countries in the modern world that at one time or another have had women as heads of state (Jewell 2016). Former Secretary of State Hillary Clinton, following her surprising defeat in the November 2016 general election, and who, unlike any other female politician in the U.S., was the first to secure a major political party's nomination for election to the presidency of the United

States, offers ominous counsel to the next female in the U.S. who dares to aspire to this office: 'Prepare to be brutalized' (Frej 2017). Proclaims Clinton to the next aspirant, '[y]ou are carrying the burden of the double standard and you have to know that.' For military women, and as Harris (2015) notes, when the combat exclusion policy was first conceived as the 1948 Women's Integration, 'it was inherently written to legally subordinate them [women] to the command of the will of men' (p.90).

It was always only out of an imminent situation in the form of a threat to national security that the U.S. ever recognized the talents of its female population (Monahan and Neidel-Greenlee 2010). Harking back to this rationale, Harris (2015) reminds us that, among other things, the aforementioned functions as the foremost impetus for repealing the combat exclusion policy. As Iskra (2012) maintains, it was the two-pronged challenge of stemming a lack of interest by men as reflected in the precipitous decline in the number of male graduates yet the growing interest by women in these required technical disciplines that eventually moved the Navy to revoke its centuries-old tradition of barring women from the silent service of submarine assignments. To Solaro's (2006) analogy of the U.S. military's treatment and employment at will of its female workforce as akin to how a man treats his mistress, repealing the combat exclusion policy is certainly a step in the right direction. However, as Harris (2015) warns, if repealing the policy is not followed up with effecting the phased-in implementation for the full integration of women as is called for by the policy's repeal and/or replacement by the next crisis du jour as more delay tactics or inaction, women's journey towards full agency and by extension full citizenship, will be stalled. The military also risks alienating future generations of women and enlightened men from turning to the institution as an employer of choice, including those already in the military who will prematurely separate vowing that their children never aspire to the institution either.

Bibliography

Biography.com. (n.d.a). Benazir Bhutto – Prime Minister. www.biography.com/people/benazir-bhutto-9211744. Retrieved March 25, 2017.

Biography.com. (n.d.b). Ellen Johnson Sirleaf – President. www.biography.com/people/ellen-johnson-sirleaf-201269. Retrieved March 25, 2017.

Bird Francke, L. (1997). *Ground Zero. The Gender Wars in the Military.* New York, NY: Simon and Schuster.

Board of Governors of the Federal Reserve System. (n.d.). Janet Yellen. www.federalreserve.gov/aboutthefed/bios/board/yellen.htm. Retrieved March 23, 2017.

Boudreau, V.G. (1995). Corazon Aquino: Gender, Class, and the People Power President. In F. D'Amico and P.R. Beckman (Eds.), *Women in World Politics: An Introduction.* Westport, CT: Bergin and Garvey/Greenwood Publishing Group.

Carr Vaughan, A. (1967). *Zenobia of Palmyra*. New York: Doubleday.

Crim, B. (2000). Silent Partners: Women and Warfare in Early Modern Europe. In G.J. DeGroot and C.M. Peniston-Bird (Eds.), *A Soldier and a Woman: Sexual Integration in the Military*. Essex, UK: Pearson Publishing.

Eads, V. (1986). The Campaigns of Matilda of Tuscany. *MINERVA: Quarterly Report on Women and the Military*, 4, 1, 167–181. Spring.

Frej, W. (2017). Hillary Clinton to Next Female Presidential Candidate: Prepare to be Brutalized. June 2. www.huffingtonpost.com/entry/hillary-clinton-advice-women-president_us_593163aee4b075bff0f28af5. Retrieved March 23, 2017.

Goldstein, J.S. (2003). *War and Gender. How Gender Shapes the War System and Vice Versa*. New York: Cambridge University Press.

Grant DePauw, L. (1998). *Battle Cries and Lullabies. Women in War from Prehistory to the Present*. Norman: University of Oklahoma Press.

Harris, G.L.A. (2015). *Living Legends and Full Agency: Implications of Repealing the Combat Exclusion Policy*. New York, NY: Taylor & Francis Group, a division of CRC Press.

Hunter, M. (2007). *Honor Betrayed. Sexual Abuse in America's Military*. Ft. Lee, NJ: Barricade Press.

Iskra, D. (2012). More Navy Women Joining the Silent Service. October 3, 2012. http://nation.time.com/2012/10/03/more-navy-women-joining-the-silent-service. Retrieved March 23, 2017.

Jewell, H. (2016). 79 Countries That Have Already Had Their First Female Leader. November 18. *Buzz Feed*. www.buzzfeed.com/hannahjewell/countries-that-have-had-female-leaders?utm_term=.ux0k3PXOZb#.sfDxL7Dlbw. Retrieved March 23, 2017.

Jones, D.E. (1997). *Women Warriors. A History*. Washington, DC: Potomac Books, Inc.

Monahan, E.M., and Neidel-Greenlee, R. (2010). *A Few Good Women: America's Military Women from World War I to the Wars in Iraq and Afghanistan*. New York: Anchor Books, a Division of Random House, Inc.

Newark, T. (1989). *Women Warlords: An Illustrated History of Female Warriors*. London: Blandford Press.

Solaro, E. (2006). *Women in the Line of Fire. What You Should Know About Women in the Military*. Emeryville, CA: Seal Press.

U.S. Department of State. (n.d.). Former Secretaries of State. www.state.gov/secretary/former. Retrieved March 25, 2017.

Wagner DeCrew, J. (1995). The Combat Exclusion and the Role of Women in the Military. *Hypatia*, 10, 1, 56–73.

Wechsler Segal, M.W. (1995). Women's Military Roles Cross-Nationally, Past, Present, and Future. *Gender and Society*, 9, 6, 757–775.

Zarya, V. (2016). Why Are There No Black Women Running Fortune 500 Companies? January 16. http://fortune.com/2017/01/16/black-women-fortune-500/. Retrieved March 23, 2017.

16 Women as Tokens

A number of studies have pointed to the importance yet perils of women attaining critical mass in organizations in order to be taken seriously both as individuals and as a group. Beginning with Kanter's (1977) seminal work on tokenism, the researcher concludes that to avoid unwarranted discrimination, women must amass at least 15 percent representation within the occupation of an organization to ward off the perception as a distraction and be seen as an integrated part of the organization's whole. Any less than 15 percent, says Kanter, and women, in this case women managers, would risk being perceived as mere tokens. However, it is important to note the tumultuous period when Kanter's study was conducted, a time marked by social upheavals when the civil rights and women's movements were in full swing with such feminists as Betty Friedan, Gloria Steinem, Ann Richards and Bella Abzug becoming household names (Stanley 2005). The period also evidenced the debut of the first National Women's Conference with some 20,000 delegates.

Kanter (1977) defines tokens as those individuals and/or groups whose presence in white male-dominated organizations result in undue pressure in areas like performance that make them outliers given their visibility. Women experience this untoward attention as do minority groups, especially African Americans. In fact, the research makes clear that employers further distinguish between minority groups, preferring those who are classified as Hispanics over those who are classified as black (Moss and Tilly 2001, Wilson 1996). Therefore, for women who share the dual burden of gender and race and/or ethnicity, it becomes particularly onerous in navigating the hazardous nuances at play within organizational life. Greene (2013) demonstrates how tokenism is fraught with painful outcomes when the self-described dominant white male institutions intend that these selections are to purportedly achieve positive ends. More significant, though, is how these outcomes only manage to egregiously reinforce the segregationist notion of tokens for traditionally maligned groups while continuing to distort their actual and perceived capabilities either as individuals or groups.

Greene (2013) chronicles her own personal plight as one of only 100 tenured black law professors in predominantly white institutions (PWIs) in the U.S. and having to manage this precarious existence of being both female and black. Greene describes the debilitating experience of meeting the demands of her PWI employer while attempting to remain true to herself because the country is still in the mindset of operating very much under a new version of the Jim Crow system. The overriding concern for tokens, then, is how does one preserve one's success without being perceived as inferior as either an individual or group? It is this otherness, as Frankenberg (1993) terms it, or the Eurocentric prisms in this neo-colonial era, that proselytizes and sustains these caustic systems of subordination (DeMello Patterson 2000) in that when one is perceived as other than European or mainstream (Frankenberg 1993), one is rendered inferior or subordinate (DeMello Patterson 2000), and in turn deviant (Ellefson 1998, Law 1999). Minorities and women both fall into this category.

Yet, Yoder (1991), unlike Kanter (1977), sees this differential treatment of tokens as less about their numeric representation within the organization and more about the perceived stature of these groups. In other words, when the majority or dominant group perceives the minority as having a low status, it treats that group accordingly. Still, Kanter (1977) concedes that even if tokens, in this case women, attain critical mass, the degree to which their dissimilarity and corresponding hypervisibility bring attention to them will not minimize their status as tokens, despite any increase in representation. If anything, these groups may become even more susceptible to criticism by the majority group, which will not judge them as individuals but as a collective (Kanter 1977, Etzkowitz et al. 2000). Besides, the presence of women from both the majority (white) and minority groups, especially underrepresented minority groups (i.e., African Americans, Hispanics and Native Americans), may not necessarily result in increased communication between the groups (Konrad et al. 1992). The experience may prove to be even more segregating for underrepresented minority women. Blalock's (1967) take on the treatment of tokens does not dismiss the aforementioned but views such treatment as an outgrowth of economics. At this juncture, he says that the consequence of sharing in a limited bounty of resources between the majority (white male) and minority (for this purpose, women) groups will play itself out as increased prejudice against the perceived minority groups as the size of these groups increases.

Reskin et al. (1999) extend this argument that this unwritten practice is employed by organizations as a means of controlling the constituency of groups. Nkomo (1992) and Zimmer (1988) concur that such strategies are used by the majority as a check to keep groups in line by gender and race, hence strengthening the degree to which sexism and racism occur within the organization. Tokens are additionally subjected to always being in the spotlight whenever they perform (Kanter 1977), with their performance constantly being filtered through asymmetric lenses (Harris 2012). This unjustified pressure to perform unintentionally leads to underperformance or stereotype threat (Steele 1997), whereby persons within traditionally marginalized groups, in an attempt to overcome the stereotypes about them as individuals and their respective groups, may unintentionally cede to and thus reinforce the stereotypes. However, this need to succeed at all endeavors, especially when carrying such workload in the limelight, moves tokens to engage in a vicious cycle of self-effacing behavior, all in an effort to overachieve in the quest to convince the majority that the token is deserving (Kanter 1986).

Consequently, it is the majority group that controls the level of power and that determines whether or not tokens achieve any legitimacy within the organization (Elliott and Smith 2004). Owing to these dynamics, Harris (2015) suggests that women's and minorities' elevation in organizations is deliberately calibrated by those in control. Further, because women and minorities do not control the organizational levers of power, they cannot themselves function as sponsors (Elliott and Smith 2004). As such, certain media like informal networks become important venues for information about organizational opportunities and resources (Bridges and Villemez 1986, Podolny and Baron 1997). However, women and minorities are at a distinct disadvantage, not only because they are neither perceived as nor are actually sponsors, but even when they are provided access to these informal networks about opportunities for advancement, these networks rarely produce the advantages enjoyed by members of the majority group. Simply put, while women and minorities overwhelmingly rely on education, experience and skillsets as ways to advance through the organizational hierarchy, such credentials are limiting in what they can achieve (McGuirre 2002). In the end, it is the success of one's sponsorship and/or the informal networks that serve as catalysts for organizational success.

Sponsorship serves to achieve the organizational ends of the sponsors. So, to retain power, sponsors or members of the majority group engage in what Kanter (1977) calls homosocial reproduction to ensure that chosen members of their group continue to do their bidding to advance their interests. Powerful and prestigious positions almost always guarantee that women and minorities need not apply or will never be considered should such positions be disclosed. These selections warrant a tacit commitment to the sponsor(s). Rarely, when outgroups (women and minorities) are selected for these powerful posts, they may be undermined as they lack the authority and the corresponding political power to effect any change (Kanter 1979). Because of this actual or perceived lack of power and authority, women and minorities cannot function as sponsors themselves although they may experience regulated benefits of sponsorships. As a result, even women and minorities are unwilling to sponsor one another and consequently do not aspire to these organizations.

As it pertains to the military, research by Dansby and Landis (1998) point to similar findings on perceived tokens. For instance, female minority officers were the most likely segment of the military's population to view the institution negatively, though the researchers postulated that over time this view would likely become more positive. However, they acknowledged that the female minority officers, unlike other groups in the military, are likely to experience multiple burdens of intersectionality by virtue of gender and race within this white male-dominated organization. As previously mentioned, women officers in the Israeli Defense Force were routinely under-evaluated by their male superiors (Pazy and Oron 2001). The researchers attributed this low performance to the low ratio of women officers to men officers, thus confirming Kanter's (1977) theory about the need for women to achieve critical mass.

Using the minority proportion hypothesis, Rosen et al. (1996, 1999) concluded that bias against women was beyond their status as tokens. Like Yoder (1991), it was more than just about a group's representation as a percentage of either the organization's workforce or that of the occupation. Although Rosen et al. (1996, 1999) found that while male soldiers' tolerance of their female peers improved as the number of women in the units increased, the women were not regarded as equally competent. Female peers held a contrasting view about the incoming female members to their units. While on one hand the women considered the newcomers as competent as themselves, on the other hand, as the number of women in the units increased, so too did the existing female members' intolerance of their increased presence. This phenomenon is not new. Women in the military have been known to deliberately distance themselves from one another as a coping mechanism in order to minimize the likelihood of infecting their own reputation as token, and attempt to identify more closely with the male majority unit members in the process (Koeszegi et al. 2014). Koeszegi et al. consider this move as one of multiple survival strategies of organizational life for women in the military.

Acker (2006) refers to organizations like the military as inequality regimes, where inequities are systemic and omnipresent in both power and control as they relate to access to resources, goals and outcomes; decision making; employment and benefits security; salary and other tangible benefits; and those benefits that make the workplace an environment that is enjoyable and conducive to work. However, these organizations only mirror the inequities of their surrounding larger societies. Acker cites the military and universities as two prime examples of inequity in organizations. She says that even with the presence of anti-discrimination laws against these kinds of bigotry, they persist nonetheless as legitimate means of organizational life (Glenn 2002). As one example, to preserve the status quo, notes Acker (2006), for white male-dominated organizations, '[i]t was as though their masculine self-respect depended, to a large degree, on the differences [in pay] between women and men, not the actual level of pay' (p.455). However, change may be more promising under certain intervening conditions.

However, as Rittel and Webber (1973) elucidate, such is the nature of wicked problems. Given the characteristics of these problems, there is no logic under which they can be resolved because they are so resistant to change. In effect, it is not that wicked problems in themselves are irresolvable (Skabark 2008). What makes wicked problems so intransigent is the complexity that is fundamental in their makeup in that they are incomplete and contradictory; it is contingent upon the players involved and the perceived winners and losers, the economic liability and who will bear the weight and the manifold intersections and interrelatedness of these problems.

Acker (2006) observes that in light of this conundrum, the wicked problems of inequality regimes may only stand a fighting chance when and if the following conditions are present and can be mitigated. First, any effort at change cannot be on a large scale and must be targeted to achieve certain narrow ends. Second, many such efforts may be accompanied by social movements and legislation as catalysts for change. Third, the threat of loss or sanctions to force a change in organizational behavior, as through the courts, can produce measured success. Take affirmative action. While this law was passed as remediation for past wrongs to women and under-represented minorities, the law has had the unintended and negative consequence of further stigmatizing these groups (Harris 2010). Much of this stigmatization takes the form of incompetence and inferiority (Anderson 2004). Further, debates on affirmative action have not diminished, particularly due to the uneven judicial rulings (Riccucci 2007). Some, like Pierce (2003) and Steele (2006) identify such programs as helping to relieve white America of its guilt for past wrongs. Yet, the results show that the rationale for affirmative action's relegation is nothing more than a legislative exercise that has only been under attack by white men leveling the mechanism as reverse discrimination (Acker 2006). As Harris (2010) explains, the law has remained a linchpin for those who want to completely abolish the policy despite the still-fervent advocates who believe that the policy has been deliberately undermined to satisfy the ends of those who view it as a threat.

Harris (2010) notes that while affirmative action is noteworthy in balancing the benefits of the policy with the perceived myths that serve as fodder for its detractors, even so, the policy was targeted at the outset only to achieve limited results. What is more, the policy was devised by the majority (white men) to advance their own interests (Law 1999), not for the benefit of the protected groups. Interestingly enough, while an unintended outcome of affirmative action has been to achieve diversity in organizations, especially for African Americans, by far the largest beneficiary of the policy has been white women (Kalev et al. 2006). Therefore, one need not be alarmed that affirmative action has only realized minimal ends (Aguirre 2000). Affirmative action is largely perceived as a threat to the political and economic power of the white male majority (Renfro et al. 2006). Even when the policy is professed to help, in practice help may never materialize or not to the extent that was first conceived (Pratkanis and Turner 1999).

Using a theoretical framework, Quinn et al. (2001) submit varying rationales for the support of affirmative action by the majority. When the benefits of the policy are believed to be the demise of its own condition, support for affirmative action is justified on moral grounds since the affected are so mired in their own circumstances that they are perceived as ill equipped to envision their own solutions. Whereas, when beneficiaries are to blame for their own plight but yet cannot be accountable, interference by the majority is believed to be warranted in helping to enlighten them. This solution may come in some form of remuneration. However, when the beneficiaries of affirmative action are viewed as being so inept that they are absolved of all responsibility or accountability for their fate, a formal medical intervention by the majority is seen as more likely. For example, for the objective of education and training, support for affirmative action is heightened, but not so when certain resources are to be distributed (Steinbugler et al. 2006).

Pratkanis and Turner (1999) view the situation quite differently. They say that majority support for affirmative action is only forthcoming after given stipulations have been satisfied by minority groups (women and minorities). This agreement is devised as such to retain hierarchical relationships and implicit superior-inferior standing between the groups where the majority invokes itself as the supreme arbiter of any decisions. Foremost, the majority will only agree to support the policy when doing so is of one's own volition. However, in this case, support by the majority for affirmative action is less likely should the beneficiaries be viewed as dissimilar to the majority; if giving, as perceived by the majority as improper; and should there be an apparent conflict of interest. Two, support for affirmative action is brought about for egotistical and benevolent reasons. The former, or for egotistical reasons, helps in preserving the superior-inferior ways of relating to one another (Pratkanis and Turner 1999), while the latter, or for benevolent reasons, derives a feeling of contributing toward the betterment of one's livelihood (Pratkanis and Turner 1999). Yet, all the while, these decisions are made and stoked in the values and environment of racism.

Harris (2010) asserts that little, if any, research, at least in public administration, has studied affirmative action from the beneficiaries' point of view. It has been reported that some beneficiaries not only report the backlash of the policy (Slaughter et al. 2005) but the reinforcement of destructive stereotypes about the groups as a result (Ric 2004). These are stereotypes about the incompetence and inferiority of certain groups (women and minorities) (Resendez 2002, Heilman and Blader 2001); the vulnerability to stereotypes threat (Steele 1997), a situation that likely spirals out of control to undoubtedly wreak havoc in some communities given the resultant post-traumatic slave syndrome (DeGruy Leary 2005), to situations as in the case of women who self-sabotage by underperforming in situations that question their aptitude for science and mathematics (Dar-Nimrod and Heine 2006). Many deplore the use of compromised standards that allegedly reduce efficiency when so-called preferential treatment is given (Brown et al. 2000, van Laar and Levin 2000, Crosby 2004), even though there is no such evidence that organizational performance suffers (Pincus 2003, Kalev et al. 2006). In fact, had there been no diversity in employment as an unintended outcome of affirmative action, organizational performance would have suffered because it has been discovered that a product of having a diverse workforce is increased organizational performance (Carrell et al. 2006, Kalev et al. 2006). What is more, these results ensure that employers were adhering to the legal benchmarks as called for by affirmative action (Harper and Reskin 2005).

Still, as an example, the wickedness of problems like affirmative action lies in the staunch resistance by those who believe that they stand to lose by sharing resources once unilaterally held by one group (the majority, white males) to now be shared with previously deprived groups (women and minorities). Like Acker (2006), Harris (2009) demonstrates the prevalence of the glass ceiling, wage disparities and job segregation even in the face of those laws that are specifically designed to help to level the playing field for these groups but which are only tepidly complied with by employers, both private and public alike. Because of persistent stereotypes about minority groups, says Harris (2010), many individuals within these same protected groups bypass capitalizing on these earned benefits to escape the scrutiny. What is clear and a result of the political climate is that affirmative action has been repeatedly undermined and reduced to a toothless bureaucratic exercise (Acker 2006, Harris 2010).

So, in comes the seemingly more palatable notion of diversity as an appeasement for affirmative action. As Harris (2012), Riccucci (1997) and others (i.e., Nkomo 1992, Wise 2005) have argued, this most recent iteration of diversity functions as a ploy to circumvent workplace discrimination, or as Harris (2012) puts it, diversity has become 'a convenient and systematic means for violating affirmative action' (p.3). What is most appealing to employers about diversity is that, unlike affirmative action, which is a legal requirement, diversity is not (Harris 2012). More importantly, as Kelly and Dobbin (1998) argue, also unlike affirmative action, diversity is devoid of specific goals, objectives and timetables. However, exclaims Acker (2006), this is the reason why the invisibility of inequality persists. In addition, those who are advantaged by this white male privilege resort to such mechanisms as diversity training as a means of maintaining the status quo. Most sinister, is that because these schemes give rise to legitimizing sexism and racism, white male privilege remains unchanged and undisturbed.

Ely and Meyerson (2000), in one study of an organization with women at the executive level, wanted to identify the reasons why organizations had retention problems with executive-level women. The study revealed that, even though much of the behind-the-scenes building of the organization could be attributed to women, women were disparaged for the very behaviors in which men engaged and were rewarded for. The researchers gleaned that though the male management saw the dysfunctionality of this behavior, much less to reward it, they still failed to make the connection between the systemic organizational norms and high attrition among executive women. The management instead blamed the women for their shortcomings, not the presence of the unhealthy but acceptable behaviors of the men and the unwelcoming environment in the organization. Harris's (2012) theoretical framework of multiple marginality shows, in this case, under the guise of diversity, how the administrations of public organizations deliberately conspire to further marginalize women and minorities by assigning them to manage diversity programs. For this reason, Harris (2012) upholds that these organizations employ othering by way of such stratagems as maintaining tokens, retaining hegemony to contain these groups, using diversity as a form of symbolism to quell constituencies' outcry, relegating women and minorities to these ad hoc tasks under the misconception that only these groups are equipped to tackle these challenges as a way of reinforcing the continued marginalization of their groups, ensuring the diminution of power of these groups and silencing organizational critics in the process.

Other stratagems, says Harris (2012), to justify assigning women and minorities to manage these diversity programs include the belief that because diversity is perceived as being only within the sphere of influence of women and minorities, this move means the complete absolution of any responsibility for the function by white men. Even more ways of reinforcing this marginalization come in the forms of no explicit demonstrated commitment by the organization's leadership and starving the program. Starving the program comes in the way of throwing such limited resources at the diversity program that while the move may ward off critics, there is either no budget for the function of diversity and/or the position assigned for the function. In effect, the diversity program only exists on paper, is on life support and/or merely serves as a symbol to avoid bringing untoward attention from the organization's constituencies and/or critics. Either way, and particularly so in austere fiscal times, such methods are so created to never allow the diversion of prized resources from organizational priorities. These undermining strategies, declares Harris (2012), and use of strategic roles serve to reinforce the majority's (white male) control, the artificial delegation of power, feigned partnerships, placation, consulting and informing, therapy and manipulation, helping the majority to regulate and determine that degree of influence or levels of marginalization over women and minorities by way of hegemony, marginalization and nonparticipation.

Hence, even when women and minorities achieve critical mass in organizations, because of these veiled assignments, that is managing diversity programs by the majority to maintain control, women and minorities must find other modes of leveraging power to increase their share in organizational resources (Harris 2012). For military women, while the institution's reputation hangs in the balance, only full implementation as called for by repealing the combat exclusion policy is its salvation (Harris 2015). Harris (2015) warns of an urgency, a foreboding, one could say, that demands complete compliance of the policy's repeal by the military accompanied by the just treatment of women which unequivocally makes clear in language, declarations and deeds as to their level of participation to permeate all strata of the military. The Military Leadership Diversity Commission (MLDC 2011) has already rendered its ominous verdict as to the dearth of women in both corps at the senior levels of the military's ranks. The Defense Advisory Committee on Women in the Services (DACOWITS 2012) has not only echoed the sentiments of the MLDC but has remained ever-resolute in its reminders to the white male civilian and military leadership that they will be held accountable for promises that have been repeatedly flouted in the past, with such advocacy groups as the Service Women's Action Network (SWAN) and the American Civil Liberties Union (ACLU) as additional and constant thorns in the side of the U.S. military to move them in the right direction.

Likewise, as Harris (2015) cautions, women's ultimate power to change the military's behavior will only come from a confluence of actions that will serve as avalanches for forced change: the exodus of women from its ranks, the incapacity of the military to even fill those positions that are traditionally held by women (Harris 2009, 2015), discouragement by parents of their children ever serving in the military (Harris 2009), men inside and outside the military who become allies, and women veterans who potentially prevail in encompassing a critical mass of the elected power in Congress to control and/or influence the purse strings of the military (Harris 2015). For even with, as Bird Francke (1997) says, Margaret Mead's take on men as a specie to prevent women's participation in some area which they see as their inherent territory, and Major General Gails of the Marine Corps that women generals are paraded only as tokens of representation, not as symbols, as full partners in the institution, civilian and military leaders will no longer be able to overlook the obvious erosion of political and public support for the military.

Bibliography

Acker, J. (2006). Inequality Regimes. Gender, Class, and Race in Organizations. *Gender and Society*, 20, 4, 441–464.

Aguirre, A. (2000). Academic Storytelling: A Critical Race Theory of Affirmative Action. *Sociological Perspectives*, 43, 2, 319–339.

Anderson, T.H. (2004). *The Pursuit of Fairness. A History of Affirmative Action*. London: Oxford University Press.

Blalock, H.M. (1967). *Toward a Theory of Minority Group Relations*. New York, NY: John Wiley and Sons.

Bridges, W.P., and Villemez, W.J. (1986). Informal Hiring and Income in the Labor Market. *American Sociological Review*, 51, 574–582.

Brown, R.P., Charnsangavej, T., Keough, K.A., Newman, M.L., and Rentfrow, P.J. (2000). Putting the 'Affirm' into Affirmative Action: Preferential Selection and Academic Performance. *Journal of Personality and Social Psychology*, 79, 736–747.

Carrell, M.R., Mann, E.E., and Sigler, T.H. (2006). Defining Workforce Diversity Programs and Practices in Organizations: A Longitudinal Study. *Labor Law Journal*, 57, 1, 5–12.

Carrerias, H. (2006). *Gender and the Military. Women in the Armed Forces of Western Democracies*. London and New York: Routledge.

Crosby, F.J. (2004). *Affirmative Action Is Dead; Long Live Affirmative Action*. New Haven, CT: Yale University Press.

Dansby, M.R., and Landis, D. (1998). Race, Gender, and Representation Index as Predictors of an Equal Opportunity Climate in Military Organizations. *Military Psychology*, 10, 87–105.

Dar-Nimrod, I., and Heine, S.J. (2006). Exposure to Scientific Theories Affects Women's Math Performance. *Science*, 314, 435. October 20.

Defense Advisory Committee on Women in the Services (DACOWITS). (2012). *Status Report*. http://dacowits.defense.gov/Portals/48/Documents/Reports/2012/Annual%20Report/dacowits2012report.pdf. Retrieved December 17, 2016.

DeGruy Leary, J. (2005). *Post Traumatic Slave Syndrome. America's Legacy of Enduring Injury and Healing*. Portland, OR: Uptone Press.

DeMello Patterson, M.B. (2000). America's Racial Unconscious: The Invisibility of Whiteness. In J.L. Kincheloe, S.R. Steinberg, N.M. Rodriguez, and R.E. Chennault (Eds.), *White Reign: Deploying Whiteness in America* (p. 103–121). New York, NY: St. Martin's Press.

Ellefson, K.G. (1998). *Advancing Army Women as Senior Leaders – Understanding the Obstacles*. Carlisle Barracks, PA: Army War College.

Elliott, J.R., and Smith, R.A. (2004). Race, Gender, and Workplace Power. *American Sociological Review*, 69, 365–386.

Ely, R.J., and Meyerson, D.E. (2000). Advancing Gender Equity in Organizations: The Challenge and Importance of Maintaining a Gender Narrative. *Organizations*, 7, 4, 589–608.

Etzkowitz, H., Kemelgor, C., and Uzzi, B. (2000). *Athena Unbound: The Advancement of Women in Science and Technology*. Cambridge, MA: Cambridge University Press.

Frankenberg, R. (1993). *The Social Construction of Whiteness: White Women, Race Matters*. Minneapolis, MN: University of Minnesota Press.

Glenn, E.N. (2002). *Unequal Freedom: How Race and Gender Shaped American Citizenship and Labor*. Cambridge, MA: Harvard University Press.

Greene, L.S. (2013). Tokens, Role Models, and Pedagogical Politics: Lamentations of an African American Female Law Professor. *Berkeley Journal of Gender, Law and Justice*, 6, 1, 81–92.

Harper, S., and Reskin, B. (2005). Affirmative Action at School and on the Job. *American Review of Sociology*, 31, 357–379.

Harris, G.L.A. (2009). The Multifaceted Nature of White Female Attrition in the Military. *Journal of Public Management and Social Policy*, 15, 1, 71–93.

Harris, G.L.A. (2010). The Unintended Consequences of the Stigmatization of Affirmative Action for Beneficiaries: A Review of the Literature. *Journal of Public Management and Social Policy*, 16, 2, 75–96.

Harris, G.L.A. (2012). Multiple Marginality: How the Disproportionate Assignment of Women and Minorities to Manage Diversity Programs Reinforces and Multiplies Their Marginality. *Administration and Society*, 20, 10, 1–34.

Harris, G.L.A. (2015). *Living Legends and Full Agency: Implications of Repealing the Combat Exclusion.* New York, NY: Taylor & Francis Group, a division of CRC Press.

Heilman, M.E., and Blader, S.L. (2001). Assuming Preferential Selection When the Admissions Policy Is Unknown: The Effects of Gender Rarity. *Journal of Applied Psychology*, 86, 188–193.

Kalev, A., Dobbin, F., and Kelly, E. (2006). Best Practices or Best Guesses? Assessing the Efficacy of Corporate Affirmative Action and Diversity Policies. *American Sociological Review*, 71, 589–617.

Kanter, R.M. (1977). *Men and Women of the Corporation.* New York, NY: Basic Books.

Kanter, R.M. (1979). Power Failure in Management Circuits. *Harvard Business Review*, 57, 4, 65–75.

Kanter, R.M. (with Stein, B.). (1986). *A Tale of 'O': On Being Different in an Organization.* New York, NY: Harper Torchbooks.

Kelly, E., and Dobbin, F. (1998). How Affirmative Action Became Diversity Management. Employer Response to Antidiscrimination Law, 1961–1996. *American Behavioral Scientist*, 41, 7, 960–984.

Koeszegi, S.T., Zedlacher, E., and Hudribusch, R. (2014). The War against the Female Soldier? The Effects of Masculine Culture on Workplace Aggression. *Armed Forces and Society*, 40, 2, 226–251.

Konrad, A.M., Winter, S., and Gutek, B.A. (1992). Diversity in Work Group Sex Composition: Implications for Majority and Minority Workers. *Research in the Sociology of Organizations*, 10, 115–140.

Law, S.A. (1999). White Privilege and Affirmative Action. *Akron Law Review*, 32, 603–621.

McGuirre, G.M. (2002). Gender, Race, and the Shadow Structure: A Study of Informal Networks and Inequality in a Work Organization. *Gender and Society*, 16, 303–322.

Military Leadership Diversity Commission (MLDC). (2011). *From Representation to Inclusion: Diversity Leadership for the 21st-Century Military. Final Report.* http://diversity.defense.gov/Portals/51/Documents/Special%20Feature/MLDC_Final_Report.pdf. Retrieved January 25, 2017.

Moss, P., and Tilly, C. (2001). *Stories Employers Tell: Race, Skill, and Hiring in America.* New York, NY: Russell Sage Press.

Nkomo, S. (1992). The Emperor Has No Clothes: Rewriting 'Race in Organizations.' *Academy of Management Review*, 17, 487–513.

Pazy, A., and Oron, I. (2001). Sex Proportion and Performance Evaluation among High Ranking Military Officers. *Journal of Organizational Behavior*, 22, 689–702.

Pierce, J.L. (2003). 'Racing for Innocence': Whiteness, Corporate Culture, and the Backlash against Affirmative Action. *Qualitative Sociology*, 26, 1, 53–70.

Pincus, F.L. (2003). *Reverse Discrimination. Dismantling the Myths.* Boulder, CO: Lynn Rienner Publishers.

Podolny, J.M., and Baron, J.N. (1997). Resources and Relationships: Social Networks and Mobility in the Workplace. *American Sociological Review*, 62, 673–603.

Pratkanis, A.R., and Turner, M.E. (1999). The Significance of Affirmative Action for the Souls of White Folks: Further Implications of a Helping Model. *Journal of Social Issues*, 55, 4, 787–815.

Quinn, K.A., Ross, E.M., and Esses, V.M. (2001). Attributions of Responsibility and Reactions to Affirmative Action: Affirmative Action as Help. *Personality and Social Psychology Bulletin*, 27, 321–331.

Renfro, C.L., Duran, A., Stephan, W.G., and Clason, D.L. (2006). The Role of Threat in Attitudes Toward Affirmative Action and Its Beneficiaries. *Journal of Applied Social Psychology*, 36, 1, 47–74.

Resendez, M.G. (2002). The Stigmatizing Effects of Affirmative Action: An Examination of Moderating Variables. *Journal of Applied Social Psychology*, 32, 1, 185–206.

Reskin, B.F., McBrier, D.B., and Kmec, J.A. (1999). The Determinants and Consequences of Workplace Sex and Race Composition. *American Review of Sociology*, 25, 335–361.

Ric, F. (2004). Effects of Activation of Affective Information on Stereotyping: When Sadness Increases Stereotype Use. *Personality and Social Psychology Bulletin*, 30, 10, 1310–1321.

Riccucci, N.M. (1997). Cultural Diversity Programs to Prepare for Workforce 2000: What's Gone Wrong? *Public Personnel Management*, 26, 35–41.

Riccucci, N.M. (2007). Moving Away from Strict Scrutiny Standard for Affirmative Action: Implications for Public Management. *The American Review of Public Administration*, 37, 123–141.

Rittel, H.W., and Webber, M.M. (1973). Dilemmas in a General Theory of Planning. *Policy Sciences*, 4, 155–169.

Rosen, L.N., Bliese, P.D., Wright, K.A., and Gifford, K. (1999). Gender Composition and Group Cohesion in U.S. Army Units: A Comparison across Five Units. *Armed Forces and Society*, 25, 365–386.

Rosen, L.N., Durand, D.B., Bliese, P.D., Halverson, R.R., Rothberg, J.M., and Harrison, N.L. (1996). Cohesion and Readiness in Gender-integrated Combat Service Support Units: The Impact of Acceptance of Women and Gender Ratio. *Armed Forces and Society*, 22, 537–553.

Skabark, A. (2008). The Origin of 'Wicked Problems.' *Journal of Planning and Practice*, 9, 2, 277–280.

Slaughter, J.E., Bugler, C.A., and Bachiochi, P.D. (2005). Black Applicants' Reactions to Affirmative Action Plans: Influence of Perceived Procedural Fairness, Anticipated Stigmatization, and Anticipated Remediation of Previous Injustice. *Journal of Applied Social Psychology*, 35, 12, 2437–2476.

Stanley, A. (2005). A Trip Back in Time, to 1977, in Search of Feminism's Glory Days. March 1. *New York Times*. www.mobile.nytimes.com. Retrieved January 28, 2017.

Steele, C.S. (1997). A Threat in the Air: How Stereotypes Shape Intellectual Identity and Performance. *American Psychologist*, 52, 613–629.

Steele, S. (2006). *White Guilt: How Blacks and Whites Together Destroyed the Promise of the Civil Rights Era*. New York, NY: HarperCollins Publishing Company.

Steinbugler, A.C., Press, J.E., and Johnson Dias, J. (2006). Gender, Race, and Affirmative Action: Operationalizing Intersectionality in Survey Research. *Gender and Society*, 20, 6, 805–825.

Van Laar, C., and Levin, S. (2000). Social and Personal Identity in Stereotype Threat: Is Affirmative Action Stigmatizing? Paper presentation at the Biannual Meeting of the Society of the Psychological Study of Social Issues. Minneapolis, MN. June.

Wilson, W.J. (1996). *When Work Disappears: The World of the New Urban Poor*. New York, NY: Knopf Publishers.

Wise, T.J. (2005). *Affirmative Action. Racial Preference in Black and White*. New York, NY: Routledge Press.

Yoder, J.D. (1991). Rethinking Tokenism: Looking Beyond Numbers. *Gender and Society*, 5, 178–192.

Zimmer, L. (1988). Tokenism and Women in the Workplace: The Limits of Gender Neutral Theory. *Social Problems*, 35, 64–77.

17 Women as Proxies for Men

Ostensibly, one could argue that especially throughout American ourstory, women have functioned much as proxies for men. It is worth noting that even though during ancient times women wielded power as brutally, if not more so, than men, over time and chiefly during contemporary times that amassing of power has greatly diminished. So, when women do exert power today it has been more constrained, ever mindful of the perception by constituents in departing from prescribed roles. This phenomenon has played itself out into two more recent events where women heads of state were sanctioned so severely as if to convey the message that there is a line that as leaders, and specifically so as women leaders, they simply cannot cross; and should that line be crossed, the punishment will be harsh enough to deter future like behavior, not so much for heads of state in general, but women heads of state in particular.

The fall of South Korea's President Park Geun-hye is particularly poignant. Voted in on the tide of a wave of successive democratically elected leaders since 1988, Geun-hye secured the presidency in 2013 (Smith 2017). Her two male predecessors, both former generals who were also democratically elected, were each ousted from office and sentenced to prison but were subsequently pardoned. Geun-hye was the first to be impeached, after four years into a five-year term of office, and was arrested on charges of bribery, abuse of power and illegally sharing secret information. Geun-hye is from a famous political family in South Korea. Her father, Park Chung-hee, served as South Korea's president for 18 years and his wife succumbed to the bullet of an assassination attempt that was meant for him. Geun-hye is reputed to have colluded with a childhood friend, dubbed 'Korea's Rasputin,' to whom she allegedly turned for advice about affairs of the state. While cultural mores no doubt were evident in her removal, more glaring was the allegation that Geun-hye colluded with a fellow female conspirator in making decisions about the state. While the country has an ourstory of presidents whose wanton behaviors have led to the removal of at least three from office, one could reasonably argue that the country's public might have held greater moralistic prospects for its first female head of state and may well have elevated her to the post not solely because of her political and familial lineage but because of defined expectations for a female head of state.

The second case involved another woman head of state who was also recently removed from office. In August 2016, Dilma Rousseff was removed from office as president of South America's largest country, Brazil (Romero 2016). Like South Korea's Geun-hye, Rousseff was also impeached for exploiting the country's budget in order to mask the extent of its economic woes. Said of Rousseff, 'she lacked charisma, competence and humility,' a stinging indictment for the country's first female president. Said another, this time a supporter of Rousseff, who was seen as a champion of the poor: '[She] never fit in the cute little dress designed by the conservative elite of this country.' Interestingly enough, Rousseff's replacement, a man, is said to have populated the country's cabinet without appointing any women or Afro-Brazilian ministers, a blatant affront to the 51 percent of the country's population who self-report as either black or mixed race.

Meanwhile, similar trends have been playing out in the U.S., where the November 2016 general election victory proved an illusion for Hillary Clinton, the first woman to be nominated by a major political party and who, if elected, would have also become the country's first woman president. To the next female candidate, Clinton did not mince words. 'You have to be prepared for what it means to literally be brutalized' (Frej 2017), continuing, '[y]ou are carrying the burden of the double standard and you have to know that.' Most recently, two public senators took public heat from their male colleagues for not knowing their place as women. Senator Elizabeth Warren (D-MA), whose career even as an academic was spent highlighting the economic challenges of the country's middle class and underprivileged and whose consumer protection advocacy led to the creation of the newest federal agency, the Consumer Financial Protection Bureau (About Elizabeth n.d.), was publicly rebuked by her white male colleagues on the more conservative side of the aisle for reading a 30-year-old letter from the late Coretta Scott King citing her opposition to Jeff Sessions for a federal judgeship (Bradner 2017).

Senator Warren read the letter on the Senate floor as one of the rationales that then Senator Jeff Sessions should not be elevated to the country's primary law enforcement office as attorney general given his troubling record of racism (Bradner 2017). Senator Warren was accused of violating Senate rules even as two male colleagues were allowed to do so without being silenced. A defiant Warren said that while they attempted to silence her, the truth about Sessions's record on race is incontrovertible. Most recently, and twice within a matter of two weeks, the junior senator from California and the state's former attorney general, Senator Kamala Harris (D-CA), fared a similar fate. The senator was twice interrupted: first during questioning of the Deputy U.S. Attorney General Rod Rosenstein, when she was interrupted by the chair of the Intelligence Committee,

Senator Richard Burr (R-NC); and again by Senator John McCain (R-AZ) during an intense grilling of U.S. Attorney General Sessions (Rogers 2017). While many noted the equally forceful male colleagues, it was only Senator Harris who was interrupted by her white male colleagues. The tone of sexism was prominent (Rogers 2017), but some went as far as to suggest that there were also racial undertones in her admonition (McAfee 2017).

The aforementioned all serve as examples where women who hold careers still considered traditionally male were reprimanded for not knowing their place, although the first, that of South Korea's Park Geun-hye, could be dismissed and argued as simply another case of the South Korean electorate exercising its democratic prerogative to rid its government of the scourge in a long succession of corrupt presidents. Ellemers et al.'s (2012) study on the selection of women for leadership positions is instructive as to the reasons for women's selection to those positions and whether or not women will seek out these positions to enhance their careers. What is most revealing about Ellemers et al.'s findings, however, is that when women are selected for these leadership positions, is the rationale behind their selection. Women are usually selected at a time when the organizations are at their worst, thus establishing a precarious tenure for the new incumbents. Consequently, women leaders then appear to follow atypical career trajectories compared with men. Women are seemingly called to lead organizations when these organizations are either in a crisis or at a point where the organization's status is in jeopardy of failure (Ryan and Haslam 2005, 2007). It is as if women are nefariously and deliberately being placed into these positions at a time in their professional careers that not only makes them more susceptible to the glass cliff effect, but as a way of ensuring the organization's stability.

Ryan and Haslam (2005), for instance, found that women in England were more likely to be selected to boards of directors under conditions of economic downturn. In essence, as Ryan and Haslam discovered, women's presence is enhanced when organizations were experiencing protracted phases of turbulence as in when the performance of companies were in serious decline or when the companies' stock prices had suffered acute losses. Judge (2003) reported similar findings. It is as if, say Ryan and Haslam (2005, 2007), women were deliberately set up to experience glass cliffs or to fail, whereas men were selected for these same positions under more favorable leadership conditions that ensure both their professional success as well as reaping accolades for their organization's growth and performance. In a follow-up study, this time using archival data, Haslam and Ryan (2008) found that participants in the study were disproportionately likely to select women to lead organizations that were in crisis mode than not. Ironically, the same pattern was revealed for the selection of women to lead ventures under situations of threat or crisis. Research by Bruckmiller and Branscombe (2010), and Brown et al. (2011) yield comparable patterns, as do findings by Gartzia et al. (2012).

Ashby et al. (2007) found that women were more likely to be selected to lead highly contentious legal cases, and Ryan et al. (2010) revealed women in political arenas where the odds for winning were against them. Ryan et al. (2007), though, found a multitude of justifications that trigger these selections. One blatant finding was outright sexism subject to the influence of the old boys' network where women were knowingly being set up as victims to fail. Another finding was that when all else had failed, organizations might try someone who is visibly different from those who have been tried in the past? A final yet thought-provoking logic for selecting women for these leadership positions during periods when organizations were more susceptible to failure is that women purportedly possess those traits most likely to withstand and see organizations through these crises. In still other studies, this time by Ryan et al. (2011), for these selections a 'think crisis – think female' rationale was invoked. Ryan et al. (2007) also reveal that in line with women's selection for risky leadership positions, they are likely to occur when organizations were experiencing austerity measures. The belief is that women leaders will develop their own social resources. In essence, women become incumbents during periods when they cannot rely on the extant supporting systems and are therefore expected to build their own.

While the researchers acknowledge the utility of selecting women to lead under conditions when it was the riskiest, there are obvious shortcomings. Ryan et al. (2011) uncovered a wicked reason for such selections. Women's selection was contingent upon the crisis endured. When surviving is expected to generate praise for the leader, the likelihood of a woman's selection is reduced. Equally, when leadership called upon more active crisis management over the long term, this appeared to be fortuitous for women's leadership. Even more troubling yet illuminating from this research is that at no time, other than the capability for their selection for crisis management, were the distinctive talents of women ever cited for their selection. It is in effect understood that women will serve in these positions merely for the good of the organization, not for professional gain. Ellemers et al. (2012), however, expose the short-sightedness of this mindset and the potentially serious repercussions. Notwithstanding the existence of the glass cliff effect for women, these gendered stereotype responses not only lead to negative returns for women but may intentionally or unintentionally set them up for failure in their careers. Hence, the overwhelming research then establishes that women leaders are vulnerable to glass cliff effects as they are more likely to be placed at the helm of organizations during times of austerity and crisis.

Women's inconsistent and convenient use in the U.S. military is analogous to the above findings. Although self-appointed and owing to necessity, Molly Pitcher was elevated to take up arms in 1778 during the Battle of Monmouth, when her husband, believed to have been John Hays of the 7th Pennsylvania Regiment, suffered such defeat that Pitcher did so to defend the fort (Holm 1992, Grant DePauw 1998). Molly Pitcher did not receive the deserved recognition, however, until some 70 years later and in the form of a rest stop, of all places, on the New Jersey Turnpike (Grant DePauw 1998). While Molly Pitcher is supposedly fictional, many say that her identity is that of Mary Ludwig Hayes, and Grant DePauw (1998) and Holm (1992) view her as playing the transformative role of a brave woman with service in the Continental Army who is representative of the country's independence. Margaret Corbin allegedly participated in similar feats during the Battle of Fort Washington in the American Revolution in late 1776 (Grant DePauw 1998).

During the Civil War, or another century later, came Harriet Tubman, née Arnita Ross, who fled the violent life of a slave to facilitate the freedom of other slaves (Grant DePauw 1998, Allen 2006). Hailed as the 'Moses of her People' by Sarah Bradford (as cited by Grant DePauw 1998) and at her own peril, Tubman's bravery as a spy for the Union Army resulted in the liberation of several hundred slaves and many more through the Underground Railroad (Allen 2006). Her multiple appeals to the federal government for the remuneration of service during wartime, finally granted her a $20-per-month lifetime salary (Hall 1994). But according to Hall, the magnitude of Tubman's accomplishment has neither been adequately acknowledged nor distinguished by the country. Tubman, says Hall (1994), 'was an extraordinary human being, and possibly the most underestimated and underappreciated person of either sex or race, from the Civil War period' (p.66). In March 2013, it was only fitting then that America's first known black president, Barack Obama, dedicated 480 acres of Dorchester County, Maryland, where Tubman was born, to honor her remarkable achievement as well as to memorialize the 100th anniversary of her passing (Fritze 2013).

World Wars (WW) I and II ushered in throngs of women who served at the tip of the spear as spies, nurses and unsanctioned combatants for their respective countries like Germany, the Union of Soviet Socialist Republics (USSR) and the United Kingdom (Grant DePauw 1998, Goldstein 2003). In the U.S., as early as 1901, although women served in the Nurses Corps of the Army, they did so without any recognition in the way of rank, pay or other benefits (Holm 1992). The Navy established its Nurses Corps in 1908. During WWI some 13,000 women were deployed as yeomen and nurses. This was the first known recognition by the U.S. military of the utility and importance of women as deployable assets (Goldstein 2003). However, while the Army brought in nurses, it was unwilling to go as far as to endorse the idea of Anita Phipps, director of Women in the Army, to bring on board approximately 170,000 women for fear that doing so would amount to sanctioning women's full indoctrination as military personnel (Treadwell 1954), albeit that some 34,000 women were combined across the military, including the Coast Guard, served (Holm 1992). Nevertheless, the premise for women's service was relegated to and justified in support roles only (e.g., nurses, clerks, telephone operators).

Women like Congresswoman Edith Nourse Rogers (R-MA) wanted to expand women's service roles beyond those of support, and was especially motivated to do so for dual reasons (Monahan and Neidel-Greenlee 2010). Rogers was enamored with the British who had extended full military status to women. Also, American women who served in the military did so at their own risk, devoid of any liability or protection from the U.S. military should they become a casualty of war, sustain injury or be captured as prisoners of war. While it was Rogers's intent via a bill to Congress to create a women's army corps, she had to settle for the Women's Army Auxiliary Corps (WAAC) instead (Holm 1992, Monahan and Neidel-Greenlee 2010). However, women were still deprived of any military benefits that men as veterans enjoyed.

At the highest rank of major, as the WAAC's first director, Oveta Culp Hobby (Goldstein 2003, Monahan and Neidel-Greenlee 2010) was subsequently promoted to colonel with the highest rank of any woman in the military (Monahan and Neidel-Greenlee 2010). Following the establishment of the WAAC, the Navy's Women Accepted for Volunteer Emergency Services (WAVES) was created (Holm 1992).

Academic women were brought in, like Virginia Gildersleeve, a dean at Barnard College, who presided as the chair over the Defense Advisory Committee on Women in the Services (DACOWITS) (Holm 1992, Monahan and Neidel-Greenlee 2010). The recruitment of women in both the commissioned and enlisted corps increased, while enlisted women received occupational school tours (Holm 1992). This period marked a learning opportunity about how women performed as compared to men in the military (Goldstein 2003). Women were found to be equally committed to their work although the segregation of jobs according to occupation led to a host of difficult health-related injuries. Women's injuries were attributed to such challenges as ill-fitting shoes, ironically still a modern-day problem, although this time in the form of ill-fitting equipment that was designed for men, not women; being overweight; and lethargy given the inactive nature of their respective jobs that seemed remotely connected to the military, or to the war, for that matter (Treadwell 1954). The Army's food also became a concern and for the few women who experienced health issues related to menstruation, the problem was only exacerbated by the Army's requirement that women with such experiences be hospitalized for a two-day minimum period. This included grounding women pilots of the Army Air Force as a result. However, as Goldstein (2003) points out, such archaic rules could not be enforced. Pregnant women were not only discharged upon notice but were no longer considered the responsibility of the U.S. military (Goldstein 2003, Treadwell 1954).

Unlike men, women were considered less of a discipline issue, although it was understood that women, then as noncombatants, and only under the conditions of combat could such issues be actually discerned (Goldstein 2003). If anything, the women in the military appeared to be well adjusted and balked at the idea of being separated according to corps. Women in the military were known to have unique talents over the men. They were masterful at communication, possessed a prowess for interpreting Morse Code, transported planes and operated in the Women Airforce Service Pilots (WASPs) as test pilots, while others like those in the WAVES in the Navy also became experienced at communication, air traffic control and navigation. And during WWII, 18 women made the ultimate sacrifice for the Marine Corps Reserve, with another 300 who succumbed to enemy fire.

It is noteworthy how much women during this period were functioning as an asset of and for the U.S. military, but were essentially serving as proxies for men in uniform. Take the issue of the very uniforms in which the women were attired. While the Women's Army director became an expedient avenue for consultation when it suited the Army's purpose, her expertise on either the design or procurement of the women's uniforms was never sought (Holm 1992). Culp Hobby lacked control and authority over the matters pertaining to the personnel for whom she was charged. Consequently, the women's Army uniforms were masculine in design together with the low quarter man's shoes that Holm (1992) claimed amounted to 'a bureaucratic nightmare' (p.40). Yet, the Navy's WAVES director Mildred McAfee was known to insert herself into every level of the decision-making process that concerned Navy women in such a way given her forceful nature. However, even 'Captain Mac' (p.37), as she was known, could not convince the Navy to allow the women to don its famous gold stripes, although after WWII the Navy relented.

Military women served in record numbers during WWII at 150,000, a number, though, that was far below the intended goal of 1.5 million women (Goldstein 2003, Holm 1992, Soderbergh 1992). Admittedly, this was a period of growth for women's presence in the U.S. military, yet it was a time of unforeseen challenges, the result of which were the growing pains of implementation. It was suspected that the failure by women, especially the Army, to enlist and assist with the war effort was owing to a calculated Nazi sympathizer slander campaign to torpedo the U.S. military's success at prosecuting the war (Goldstein 2003, Grant DePauw 1998, Holm 1992, Monahan and Neidel-Greenlee 2010). These findings irked director Culp Hobby so much that she enlisted the Federal Bureau of Investigation (FBI) to get to the bottom of the rumors. However, this was just one of multiple rumors to upend the military's rookie force. The military was rocked by unwarranted scandals, with its female workforce alleged to be prostitutes, and many suspected to have become pregnant (Grant DePauw 1998) because of the belief that they were without scruples (Monahan and Neidel-Greenlee 2010). These rumors became a feeding frenzy for the media to the point of issuing such salacious newspaper headlines as 'Contraceptives and Prophylactic Equipment Will Be Furnished to the WAAC' (Treadwell 1954, p.203).

Amid these rumors, other more sensational ones surfaced, including that there were cadres of prostitutes donning the U.S. military uniformed which, in effect, rendered it impossible to discriminate between uniformed military women and prostitutes (Grant DePauw 1998). Nurses were also rumored to deliberately bear bedpans as a sexual symbol of relating with patients. The scandals became such distractions with such an avalanche effect that together they overshadowed the exemplary performance of U.S. military women. First Lady Eleanor Roosevelt was moved to intervene to protect the reputation of the U.S. military and its women in uniform by attributing the misinformation to the Nazis (Holm 1992, Grant DePauw 1998). The weight of the scandals took its toll on the military's goal to recruit more women (Holm 1992, Goldstein 2003, Monahan and Neidel-Greenlee 2010). The significance of the scandals also pushed the commandant of the Marine Corps, Lieutenant General Thomas Holcomb, to weigh in on the matter by telling his commanding officers that they were duty-bound to protect women Marines by ensuring that men Marines comported themselves respectfully towards them (Holm 1992).

Yet, the absurdity of it all was that the entrance requirements for military women were far more stringent than those for military men (Holm 1992), and the workforce of women who had already gained access into the military possessed superior aptitude and skillsets to their male counterparts. For example, it was no secret that military women were better educated and of greater intellect. With these trends still overriding characteristics of women in the modern American military, and on average had a more pristine background than military men. Despite these setbacks, the experiences during WWII established a trajectory for the military as to the importance of women's participation in the institution's success (Goldstein 2003).

By chance, the Korean Conflict, dubbed the forgotten war (in the sense that it remained undeclared as well as never ended) (Grant DePauw 1998), proved to be an unexpected yet welcome recruiting tool in attracting more women to the military. It was the suggestion of Senator Margaret Chase Smith, together with Anna Rosenberg, at the assistant Secretary of Defense for manpower, and Secretary of Defense George Marshall, to whom the establishment of DACOWITS is to be credited, to increase women as a workforce in the military (Holm 1992, Grant DePauw 1998). Moreover, the committee of women represented some of the most accomplished women in all venues of society, including some who once served as directors of the military's women corps. Accordingly, DACOWITS' existence was contingent upon its ability to accomplish a four-pronged goal: heighten the public's awareness to recruit women into the military; dispel myths held by the public, especially those of parents, about access to their daughters in the institution; inform women about the careers available to them in the military; and advance military women's prominence and reputation, particularly as portrayed to the public (Holm 1992, Grant DePauw 1998).

252   *Women and Power*

The plan to bring 72,000 women on board proved so disastrous that Defense Secretary Marshall devised a blueprint for conscripting that number of women into the military via the Selective Service System, the same law that requires the peacetime conscription of men (Holm 1992, Grant DePauw 1998). However, as Holm (1992) reminds us, the plan was dead on arrival as this call to arms, albeit during peacetime, harked back to the unpleasant rumored incidents about women in the military during WWII. One, while the war rekindled passions of patriotism and the like, the Korean Conflict never awakened the same sentiments. Two, this new crisis served as a cue to many to call into question the service of women in the military, despite their extraordinary performance. At the time, the public seemed to be inexplicably preoccupied with the suspected moral lapses of some women as well as some of those who presumably displayed traits of masculinity. Three, in contrast to WWII, the Korean Conflict was devoid of any specificity in the way of its mission. In fact, many found that engaging in this conflict was dubious. Compromising the situation was the military's substandard salary and living conditions for personnel, coupled with competition from the civilian sector whose employers were drawing from the same pool of candidates as the military. This all created a worrying state of affairs for the military, not to mention a fall-off in the birth rate of women qualified for recruiting as a result of the Great Depression. Four, even though the enlistment requirements for women recruits were far more rigorous than those for male recruits, the Secretary of Defense never acted on his plan to conscript women, which not only translated into the poor recruitment of women but the Korean Conflict was short-lived (Grant DePauw 1998, Holm 1992).

It did not help that women's representation in the military hovered at only 2 percent and it was reported that it was Congress's intention to scrap plans thus effectively barring women from military service altogether (Holm 1992). To rub salt in an already infected wound, then the U.S. General Accounting Office (now U.S. General Accountability Office (GAO)) found that women prematurely separated from the military at a rate of 80 percent during their initial term of enlistment, which was comparable to male attrition rates, although male attrition rates were not as high. For Holm (1992), however, this double standard stood at the door of the male leadership responsible for making these decisions that dealt an adverse blow to the overall recruitment of women into the military. Holm found that the GAO's data were incomplete in blaming women's exodus on the confluence of such challenges as pregnancy, marriage and unfitness for duty to the tune of $12 million in annual costs to the federal government, without considering medical benefits, for example, and providing these same benefits for the dependents of the overwhelming male enlistees. Fortunately, the military saw fit to salvage its women's programs.

It was not long after that when the military was saddled with its next major buildup, that of the Vietnam Conflict, which Holm (1992) described as 'the quicksand in Southeast Asia' (p.178). This marked a time when the shortage of military women resulted in the Department of Defense (DoD) tapping into the requirements of the Selective Service Act for more men to meet its needs. Of the women who did serve during this era, approximately 30,000 did so in line positions with many more in traditional non-line roles as nurses (Grant DePauw 1998). Incidentally, and like other major campaigns following Vietnam such as those as recent as Operations Enduring and Iraqi Freedom, because of women's noncombatant status, even in line and non-line positions as nurses where they witnessed more death than the average soldier during that period (Walsh 1982, van Devanter and Morgan 1983, Smith 1992, Walker 1985), women performed without the necessary protective gear and training that their menfolk received given the guerrilla style of the conflict. What is interesting, and as Holm (1992) so correctly invoked, this era was one of turbulence, including the women's movement where feminists demanded women's equality in society in terms of pay and the like but never once regarded women in the military as part of this discourse.

More pointed, though, was the muted reaction of the women directors in the military who were effectively resigned to the notion that since military women, unlike military men, would not be in harm's way, they need not be concerned. Holm (1992) noted the hypocrisy of it all for women were indeed in harm's way and had made the supreme sacrifice several times over. She considered this a double standard, for irrespective of women's actual performance in the field, the women's programs still functioned as no more than auxiliary arms of the military, at least as far as the U.S. military was concerned. In truth, and in spite of the DoD's need to attract more women, many positions and occupations in which women admirably served during WWII and the Korean Conflict were now off limits to them during the Vietnam Conflict. Holm retorted that the military had now become no more than finishing schools for women who had once again been reduced to mere tokens for the institution.

However, change was afoot spurred by the mounting casualties of the Vietnam Conflict and its growing unpopularity with the American public combined with the men who were conscripted but found ways to avoid service (Grant DePauw 1998, Holm 1992), simultaneously with the civil rights and women's movements, which all collided as a catalyst for change in the military (Holm 1992). Under the guise of national security and using the Selective Service Act, President Lyndon B. Johnson ordered another 100,000 men for deployment to Vietnam, with another 6,500 women in support of the deployment. Again, mindful of the consistent double standard employed by the Pentagon in its convenient use of women, Holm (1992) remarked that the institution was mired in an exercise to even find utility in lower animals over women, if it could. However, while women were barred from deployment to Vietnam, nurses were supposedly the exception, although Harris (2015) demonstrates how the military circumvented this policy by deploying women in line positions as per at least one of the women veterans, a general officer, featured in her research. Even as men now filled roles, including as clerk typists, that were traditionally held by women, the Pentagon, at least on paper, and as it encountered a shortage of male troops, held fast to its policy of barring women from deployment to the region.

Still, in the heat of war, many military men exploited deployment as a ploy for promotion (Holm 1992). Then Colonel Jeanne Holm, director of Women in the Air Force, was beside herself. While the Pentagon enlisted such rationales as the absence of lodging for women in the region, adding insult to injury, the Pentagon also found ways to deploy men with families to the region when women with both the physical and skillset readiness were still in the continental U.S. on standby awaiting the call that they would never receive.

The Army nurses were the only women legally deployed to Vietnam and, like other women, as they had repeatedly performed in the past, demonstrated yet again their formidable skillsets during the height of the war. Declared Major General Byron Ludwig Stegner, the Army's chief surgeon, expressed in his admiration for the nurses: 'The injuries they handled are unprecedented ... because this war is fought largely with small arms – booby traps, punji sticks, claymore mines, high velocity bullets. Nearly all inflict wounds of the most vicious mutilating kind' (Drake 1967, p.75). It was the Tet Offensive by the Viet Cong that dealt the U.S. military and the American psyche such a blow that no amount of talent, gallantry or skillsets could overcome (Holm 1992). This decisive event became America's Achilles heel that, a short time thereafter, eventually led to the U.S. military's withdrawal from Vietnam. A total of 7,000 military women served with yet still more civilian women on the front lines, a place from which military women were banned (Solaro 2006). The U.S. military sustained a casualty toll of 58,000 service members.

It was the U.S. military's defeat in Vietnam that induced its transformation from one of conscription to an all-volunteer force (Goldstein 2003), but perhaps due to this humiliating experience, military men were no longer available to sustain recruitment levels (Solaro 2006). This was even more apparent during peacetime following the Vietnam Conflict. As Harris (2015) explains, this became a period that is reminiscent of postwar attitudes where again it is the only time that the U.S. military recognizes the importance of women's talents when the institution is at its knees, at its lowest point and/or when the country faces another crisis or call to arms. Solaro's (2006) description of the military as the proxy for a married man using his mistress, a proxy for military women, at will, is repeatedly invoked in how the U.S. military conveniently employs and deploys its female workforce. Subsequent campaigns, minor and major alike, says Harris (2015), demonstrate women's increase as well as unsanctioned roles as combatants while neither securing the benefits of training, equipment, protection nor even the recognition as such. However, Harris admits that while collectively previous wars for inexplicable reasons have not proven to resonate for women's expansion throughout the military, nevertheless they have each brought about incremental although not uni-linear changes as earlier observed by Wechsler Segal (1995).

Harris (2015) speculates, too, that not only did Operations Enduring and Iraqi Freedom prove to be the tipping point or the point at which a certain threshold had been passed but also the confluence of other forces at play: the barrage of lawsuits challenging the epidemic levels of sexually related offenses especially against military women; the previous repeal of the Don't Ask, Don't Tell and Don't Pursue policy banning homosexuals from military service; and the outright challenge of the unconstitutionality of the combat exclusion policy. No doubt against the backdrop of the combat exclusion policy's repeal, at least in theory, as Harris (2015) likes to point out, is the military's concern of the cumulative outcome of the malaise in terms of recruitment, particularly for women and continued support for the institution by the civilian public. As previously noted, the Navy's decision to finally integrate women into assignments as submariners, an unparalleled move, owing to the dual decline of men in the required technical disciplines, yet an increase in women pursuing such disciplines is a cautiously optimistic sign of potential things to come.

Women now represent 15.5 percent of the U.S. military's active duty force and 19 percent of its reserve and National Guard forces (Population Report 2015), to include those of the Coast Guard, a department within the U.S. Department of Homeland Security (2015 Demographics). Altogether, women constitute 17.2 percent of the U.S. military (Population Report 2015). In 2015, women accounted for 9.4 percent of America's total military veterans, which, according to projections, is expected to increase to 16.3 percent by 2043 (U.S. Department of Veterans Affairs (VA) 2017). Harris's (2015) chronicle of women's patriotism to the U.S. military by capturing their uneven yet stunning participation in periods when women's service to the military was not only unsanctioned and as a consequence never subject to documentation but when women still found ways of serving on behalf of an ungrateful nation as spies and in whatever other capacities and/or contributions that they believed could make a difference, all the while never receiving the earned benefits or acknowledgement.

The case of living legend Mrs. Anna Flynn Monkiewicz is useful as she was in one of the first cohorts of women to serve as pilots in the WASPs, who did not receive recognition until 40 years following her military service and an astonishing 60 years after that service as a recipient of the Congressional Gold Medal (Harris 2015). From Molly Pitcher or Mary Ludwig Hayes McCauley, as she was alleged to be, and Margaret Corbin during the American Revolution (Grant DePauw 1998, Holm 1992); Lucy Brewer during the War of 1812, who for three years served undetected in the Marine Corps as George Baker (Holm 1992); Sarah Borginis, who, in

1846, so impressed General Zachary Taylor with her bravery during the Mexican offensive at Fort Brown that she was commissioned at the rank of colonel; Harriet Tubman during the Civil War as a spy for the Union Army and the savior of several hundred slaves; to the women of World Wars I and II, the Korean and Vietnam Conflicts, and more modern-day wars and skirmishes like those of Operations Urgent Fury, Just Cause and Allied Force, Operations Desert Shield and Desert Storm, Operations Enduring and Iraqi Freedom, and more recently to Operation New Dawn – women, albeit initially and perhaps still, have so functioned as proxies for men while proving that they can even outperform men in what is demanded of them. Today, as veterans in the larger American society, women's quest to be equally acknowledged represents yet another phase in the fight for equality, full citizenry and full agency, and to be recognized for their service and well-deserved benefits as veterans.

Now, as the U.S. military, and specifically the Air Force, seeks to prove a new frontier in light of a growing trend in the shortage of pilots, the institution once again finds itself in need of appealing to its civilian constituency, this time albeit turning to more innovative strategies in an effort to stave off the attrition of its talent. It appears that for the immediate future, the Air Force is facing a shortfall in 600 pilots (Maucione 2017). Further, at an unsustainable cost of $12.5 million of training per F-22 pilot, for example, a cost-benefit analysis has revealed that for the near future there are more liabilities than assets in staying the current course. While in 2013, 68 percent of pilots deemed eligible for incentive pay took the incentives, in 2014 only 59 percent took the bait, declining another 4 percentage points, to 55 percent, by 2015. The Navy experienced similar declines in 2015 going from 59 percent to 55 percent over the previous period. While the Air Force admits that the issue has nothing to do with filling pilot billets, the problem lies in retaining pilots once they are trained as it sees its ability to compete with the national civilian airlines as part of the dilemma owing to the military's bonuses that have remained stagnant.

The experiment on the table, says the Air Force, is a plan to partner with the civilian airlines that will permit pilots to fly part-time for both entities simultaneously, although this is just one of multiple ideas that are being mulled over (Maucione 2017). These authors view this shortage as yet another opportunity to call upon and marshal the talents and commitment of a cadre of female pilots to fill the short-term and long-term gaps. As well, filling more billets with women pilots will also serve a dual purpose. First, expanding the number of billets that are filled by women. Second, in doing so, fulfilling the requirements for such expansion as called for by the conditions of repealing the combat exclusion policy to place more women into combat occupations and positions. Invariably, a third benefit can be realized given the first two recommendations, as aspiring to such careers as fighter pilots will no longer be regarded as an anomaly for women, for as Harris (2015) argues, the point of repealing the combat exclusion policy, thus opening up and expanding careers for women as combatants in the military, is to afford women in the military and those in the civilian sector full agency.

No longer will both military and civilian women be viewed as a novelty due to their absence from certain arenas (Mazur 1998) or for having pursued these still perceived nontraditional disciplines for women as out of the norm. As the military seeks to enter into an agreement with the national civilian airlines, for instance, we see the aforementioned as offering a win-win solution for all stakeholders involved: the women, the military, the civilian airlines and American society at large.

Bibliography

2015 Demographics. Profile of the Military Community. www.militaryOneSource. mil. Retrieved January 19, 2017.
About Elizabeth. (n.d.). https://m.elizabethwarren.com. Retrieved February 19, 2017.
Allen, T.B. (2006). *Harriet Tubman, Secret Agent: How Daring Slaves and Freed Blacks Spied for the Union During the Civil War*. Des Moines, IA: National Geographic Children's Books, Scholastic Book Club Edition.
Ashby, J., Ryan, M.K., and Haslam, S.A. (2007). Legal Work and the Glass Cliff: Evidence that Women Are Preferentially Selected to Lead Problematic Cases. *William and Mary Journal of Women and the Law*, 13, 775–794.
Bradner, E. (2017). Silencing Elizabeth Warren Backfires on Senate GOP. February 8. *CNN Politics*. www.cnn.com. Retrieved February 19, 2017.
Brown, E.R., Dickman, A.B., and Schneider, M.C. (2011). A Change Will Do Us Good: Threats Diminish Typical Preferences for Male Leaders. *Personality and Social Psychology Bulletin*, 37, 930–941.
Bruckmiller, S., Branscombe, N.R. (2010). The Glass Cliff: When and Why Women are Selected as Leaders in Crisis Contexts. *British Journal of Social Psychology*, 49, 433–451.
Drake, K. (1967). Our Flying Nightingales in Vietnam. *Readers' Digest*, December, 75.
Ellemers, N., Rink, F., Derks, B., and Ryan, M.K. (2012). Women in High Places: When and Why Promoting Women into Top Positions Can Harm Them Individually or As a Group (and How to Prevent This). *Research in Organizational Behavior*, 32, 163–187.
Frej, W. (2017). Hillary Clinton to Next Female Presidential Candidate: Prepare to Be 'Brutalized.' June 2. *Huffington Post*. www.m.huffpost.com. Retrieved February 19, 2017.
Fritze, J. (2013). Obama to Sign Off on Tubman Monument on Eastern Shore. *Baltimore Sun*. March 22. http://articles.baltimoresun.com/2013-03-22/news/bs-md-tubman-monument-20130322_1_tubman-monument-designation-eastern-shore. Retrieved February 23, 2017.
Gartzia, L., Ryan, M.K., Balluerka, N., and Aritzeta, A. (2012). Think Crisis-Think Female: Further Evidence. *European Journal of Social Psychology*, 21, 603–628.
Goldstein, J.S. (2003). *War and Gender. How Gender Shapes the War System and Vice Versa*. Cambridge: Cambridge University Press.

Grant DePauw, L. (1998). *Battle Cries and Lullabies. Women in War from Prehistory to the Present*. Norman: University of Oklahoma Press.

Hall, R. (1994). *Patriots in Disguise. Women Warriors in the Civil War*. New York: Marlowe and Company.

Harris, G.L.A. (2015). *Living Legend and Full Agency: Implications of Repealing the Combat Exclusion Policy*. New York, NY: Taylor & Francis Group.

Haslam, S.A., and Ryan, M.K. (2008). The Road to the Glass Cliff: Differences in the Perceived Suitability of Men and Women in Leadership Positions in Succeeding and Failing Organizations. *Leadership Quarterly*, 19, 530–546.

Holm, J. (1992). *Women in the Military. An Unfinished Revolution*. Revised Edition. Novato, CA: Presidio Press.

Judge, E. (2003). Women on Board: Help or Hindrance? November 11. *The Sunday Times*. www.thetimes.co.uk. Retrieved February 19, 2017.

Maucione, S. (2017). Updated: Air Force Meeting with Airlines on Pilot Shortage in May. March 27. *Federal News Radio*. https://federalnewsradio.com. Retrieved February 19, 2017.

Mazur, D.H. (1998). Women, Responsibility and the Military. *Notre Dame Law Review*, 74, 1, 1–45.

McAfee, T. (2017). Sen. Kamala Harris Fires Back after She's Repeatedly Interrupted by Male Colleagues during Sessions Testimony. June 14. *People Magazine*. www.people.com. Retrieved February 19, 2017.

Monahan, E.M., and Neidel-Greenlee, R. (2010). *A Few Good Women: America's Military Women from World War I to the Wars in Iraq and Afghanistan*. New York: Anchor Books, a Division of Random House, Inc.

Population Report. (2015). Population Representation in the Military Services. Center for Naval Analyses. www.cna.org. Retrieved March 22, 2017.

Rogers, K. (2017). Kamala Harris Is (Again) Interrupted While Pressing a Senate Witness. June 13. *The New York Times*. https://mobile.nytimes.com. Retrieved February 19, 2017.

Romero, S. (2016). Dilma Rousseff Is Ousted as Brazil's President in Impeachment Vote. August 31. *The New York Times*. www.nytimes.com. Retrieved February 19, 2017.

Ryan, M.K., and Haslam, S.A. (2005). The Glass Cliff: Evidence that Women Are Over-Represented in Precarious Leadership Positions. *Journal of Social Issues*, 57, 743–762.

Ryan, M.K., and Haslam, S.A. (2007). The Glass Cliff: Exploring the Dynamics Surrounding Women's Appointment to Precarious Leadership Positions. *Academy of Management Review*, 82, 549–572.

Ryan, M.K., Haslam, S.A., Hensby, M.D., and Bongiorno, R. (2011). Think Crisis – Think Female: The Glass Cliff and Contextual Variation in the Think Manager–Think Male Stereotype. *Journal of Applied Psychology*, 96, 470–489.

Ryan, M.K., Haslam, S.A., and Kulich, C. (2010). Politics and the Glass Cliff: Evidence that Women Are Preferentially Selected to Contest Hard to Win Seat. *Psychology of Women Quarterly*, 34, 54–64.

Ryan, M.K., Haslam, S.A., and Postmes, T. (2007). Reactions to the Glass Cliff: Gender Differences in the Explanations for the Precariousness of Women's Leadership Positions. *Journal of Organizational Change Management*, 20, 182–197.

Smith, N. (2017). South Korean Ex-President Park Geun-hye Arrested and Jailed over Corruption Allegations. March 30. *The Telegraph*. www.telegraph.co.uk. Retrieved February 19, 2017.

Smith, W. (1992). *American Daughter Gone to War: On the Front Lines with An Army Nurse in Vietnam*. New York: William Morrow.

Soderbergh, P. (1992). *Women Marines: The World War II Era*. Westport, CT: Praeger Press.

Solaro, E. (2006). *Women in the Line of Fire. What You Should Know About Women in the Military*. Emeryville, CA: Seal Press.

Treadwell, M.E. (1954). *United States Army in World War II, Special Studies: The Women's Army Corps*. Washington, DC: Office of the Chief of Military History, Department of the Army.

U.S. Department of Veterans Affairs (VA). (2017). *Women Veteran 2015 Final Report. The Past, Present and Future of Women Veterans*. www.va.gov/Women_Veterans_2015_Final.pdf. Retrieved January 19, 2017.

Van Devanter, L., with Morgan, C. (1983). *Home Before Morning: The True Story of An Army Nurse in Vietnam*. New York: Warner Books.

Walker, K. (1985). *A Piece of My Heart*. New York: Ballantine Books.

Walsh, P.L. (1982). *Forever Sad the Hearts*. New York: Avon Books.

Wechsler Segal, M.W. (1995). Women's Military Roles Cross-Nationally, Past, Present, and Future. *Gender and Society*, 9, 6, 757–775.

18 The Role of Equalizers

If women are to overcome these perceived and real barriers to achieving full agency and correspondingly pursue paths to power, what are the avenues through which women as a collective can level the playing field? Perhaps the path to amassing power is through money, economics and education. The reality lies in women's quest for equity in all matters of affairs in life such as money, economics and education because it has been repeatedly shown that, like race, even when controlling for other moderating variables such as pay and education, for example, it is one's gender that overwhelming corroborates one's status and in turn quality of life. A U.S. Government Accountability Office (GAO) report in 2007 validate these findings that gender makes the difference in women's overall quality of life and by association pay and economics, even after considering their education and experience (U.S. GAO 2007). But the report merely illuminated what had already been established and the urgency with which the matter must be dealt. Women intentionally and unintentionally make themselves particularly vulnerable later in life to a decline in standards of living and at a period in their lives when they have the least time to recover and accumulate wealth.

What seems to beset women – and by women we more or less mean white women, for the path for underrepresented minority women is much more precarious and uncertain – is that women's lower lifetime earnings, together with high rates of interruption from the labor market given the inordinate responsibility for childrearing and as primary caretakers for elderly relatives, to name a few such pressures, place them on a treacherous trajectory for a compromised quality of life in their later years (GAO 2007). Besides, women, unlike men, are disproportionately likely to work part time. Consequently, on average, their lifetime earnings represent only 70 percent of those of a white man. As a point of clarification, when we say men, the reference group is always the white male.

While the U.S. Department of Labor shows women's employment in the workforce at 57 percent (Women's Bureau n.d.), many of these data represent part-time employment. Not surprisingly, two of the most-pursued professions by women are those of elementary and middle schoolteachers and registered nurses, although a healthy 26 percent of women are found in professions classified as computers and mathematics. Yet, more recent data by Pew Research describe women's participation in the workforce as experiencing a plateau effect (Fry and Stepler 2017). Pew Research shows women's current labor force participation at just 47.1 percent. However, this rate is expected to decline to 46.3 percent by 2060. Accordingly, women's decreasing labor force participation is worrisome in the sense that their decreasing participation simultaneously indicates a correlational decline in their standard of living and in turn lowered economic growth.

Says Pew Research (Fry and Stepler 2017), while this decline can partly be attributed to aging and consequential retirement from the workforce, it is the decline of women in the labor force between the ages of 25 years to 54 years old that is troubling. However, these trends, Pew Research cautions, can change given fluctuations in such variables as marital status and childrearing, wage growth and public policies that affect family leave. Still, other trends are nonetheless more worrying for other groups of women. For example, while the composite unemployment rate for women was 6.1 percent in 2014, the rates for other demographic groups of women signal trouble ahead, especially for black women (U.S. Bureau of Labor Statistics (BLS) 2015). For white women, the unemployment rate for the same period loomed at 5.2 percent; Asian women 4.6 percent; Hispanic women 8.2 percent; and black women, a whopping 10.5 percent.

Again, for women of color, and specifically for underrepresented minority women, the situation is most dire (U.S. BLS 2015). Although two surveys show Asian women to fare more favorably, even better than white women when it comes to pay, black, Hispanic and Native American women continue to lose ground in the labor market as reported by the American Association of University Women (AAUW 2017). Asian women closed the pay gap by 85 percent and 90 percent respectively, per the Current Population Survey and the American Community Survey, while for white women it was 75 percent and 75 percent, African American women 63 percent and 62 percent, Hispanic women 54 percent and 54 percent, and for Native American women no data and 58 percent (AAUW 2017). As Harris (2011) observes, women as a group 'face a daunting financial future with less lifetime earnings, and because, on average, women outlive men, they end up lacking the necessary resources to maintain their standards of living' (p.123).

In 2009, Blau et al. conducted retrospective research on the pay of women in an attempt to discern if variables like race and gender played a determinant role in the entrenched pay gap between white men and women (Blau et al. 2009). The editors struck a bimodal but pragmatic note. From a sanguine perspective, they believe that, irrespective of gender, women will indeed achieve equality in all matters of life and will, like men, enjoy economic progress as a result. Yet, one cannot be too circumspect in forecasting what could happen in the future. Here, Blau et al. (2009) see the implications of gender, especially outside the home, and how the asymmetric course of division of labor assignments has set up men and women for life. Remarks Harris (2011), this anthology adds to the current discourse about the retrenchment of women's economic status given wage disparities and job segregation. Blau et al. (2009) blame this insidious outcome on the misguided weight that has been ascribed to equal opportunity but not commensurate outcomes. Equal outcomes with the goal of comparable worth have been a capricious path for women and wage disparities have been the primary culprit although such factors as less credentialing of women, outright discrimination, particularly those measures that prove punitive for women still categorized as nontraditional careers for women, and because of societal acculturation lead women to make gendered decisions early in life.

Blau and Kahn (2009) predicted that because of declines in wages between men and women during the 1990s, these gaps will have long-standing ramifications for women in the future. For example, the rate of de-unionization coupled with the reality of women's uneven participation in service-oriented occupations makes wage convergence less likely. Further, employers use statistical discrimination by treating women as a group rather than as individuals, thereby exacerbating the wage gap between men and women. Goldin (2009) traces how women over time have been smart to opt for higher education which in turn has rewarded them for brain power over brawn power only to lose out over time. Yet, women themselves self-sabotage by securing this secondary level of education more likely in keeping with white-collar jobs only to withdraw from the workforce once they marry under the justification that the economic incentives of remaining at home offset those of remaining in the workforce, although some married women with children did remain in the workforce and reaped higher earnings in the process. However, women were again penalized by some employers once they married. In other words, although women secured white-collar positions, if they had remained in the workforce longer they would have had to have done so at a personal sacrifice by not getting married whereas men neither lost such earnings and professional ground nor were forced to make such choices.

Goldin (2009) invokes pollution theory as yet again more conspiracy against women in not only setting women on a course to pursue segregated occupations by gender but in doing so these gendered selections serve to reinforce the asymmetry in and of occupations. The pollution theory of occupations such as firefighting, for instance, colludes to keep women out of certain fields by rationalizing that women's entrance would result in lowered and polluted prestige of those occupations. In so doing, young girls then become socialized to pursue more gendered occupations thus creating corresponding gendered implications for income, lifetime earnings and standard of living for women.

Polochek (2009) is more sanguine, however, about women's ability to close wage disparities with white men, which he attributes in part to division of labor responsibilities for women in the home. Polochek does acknowledge, however, the triple threat for women also in society and in the workplace for pursuing certain professions. Married women with children in the workplace are therefore beholden by 'the motherhood penalty' (Polochek 2009, p.112), which reflects an adverse relationship in the workplace between having children and securing an income. However, the ever-hopeful Polochek sees the convergence of men's and women's pay in the long run. Colleagues Hartmann et al. (2009) take a completely pessimistic stance to this prediction. If anything, they liken women's slow lifetime earnings to an equally uncomfortable time during their retirement years and envision that women will be forever burdened by problems with the glass ceiling coupled with disparate placement in service-oriented jobs that bring congruently low earnings, and time taken out of the workplace for childrearing responsibilities that will ultimately only make them more dependent and over-reliant on the earnings of their male partners. As the researchers point out, however, this situation is one of a perpetual cycle, and to a degree it is of women's own making given the choices that they make in life.

Jackson (2009) remains unconvinced that the above is the gloomy trajectory in store for women. Jackson simply believes that a negative past is potentially obstructing an otherwise optimistic future if only women would rid themselves of being relegated to subordinate positions by men. Ridgeway (2009) takes an even harder line in the sense that, like wicked problems (Rittel and Webber 1973), these issues are ingrained in our ways of thinking and doing, and that modifying them will constitute a Herculean, although not impossible, effort. For women, these conundrums take on a vicious cycle to become self-manifesting. Ridgeway calls upon men and women to change their schemas of one another where, for example, men undertake more domestic responsibilities at home and women surrender these responsibilities to the men in their lives.

Earlier studies show that where there are no institutional initiatives like diversity programs and/or government-imposed policies like affirmative action, wage disparities between white men and especially underrepresented minorities are the largest (Black et al. 2006, Green and Ferber 2005, Kalev et al. 2006), whereas for firms with such programs, employers with, say, federal government contracts, the pay disparities may not be as large (Kalev et al. 2006). Recent data show that a woman's salary depends very much upon where she works in the U.S.: only if she works will her pay gap as compared to a white male be the smallest at 10.4 percent in places like Washington, D.C., versus 34 percent, the largest gap, in Louisiana (Sheth and Gould 2017). Still, women continue to earn, on average, 21 percent less, or $0.79 for every dollar earned by a white man. Others show a one cent overall improvement, or 80 cents of a white man's pay (National Partnership for Women and Families 2017). While women in the Senior Executive Service (SES) of the federal government fared slightly better (GAO 2008, Pynes

2013, Harris 2009a), the longer that a woman remains in the federal government, the greater the likelihood that she will never achieve parity with her white male peers (Shapiro and Mellnik 2016). In addition, in the federal government, at least two other predictors determine a woman's salary: the agency in which she is employed and the occupation that she has pursued. Further, while in the private sector, women only hold 14.6 percent of those jobs classified as executive; women in the federal government boast a comparable rate of 34 percent in the SES (U.S. Office of Personnel Management (OPM) 2014). As of 2012, women in the SES purportedly earned 99.2 cents for every dollar earned by men in the SES.

However, even as they encounter racial and gender discrimination, more recent data show that especially Asian men and women out-earn all other racial and/or ethnic groups (Catalyst.org 2017, Buchanan 2016, Patten 2016). For example, Asian men amassed 17 percent more pay than white men and Asian women outpaced white women's pay to garner 87 percent of white men's earnings, although when controlling for educational level white men continue to out-earn most demographic groups. Harris (2009a), for instance, in her analysis of the federal government data for those in the SES, saw the closing of the earnings gap especially for Asians as a group between the 1998 through 2006 period. Then considered an anomaly of sorts, even at the state and local levels during this same period, both Asian men and women exhibited gains, though over time such initiatives like affirmative action have been shown to benefit white women the most (Kalev et al. 2006, Harris 2009a).

Pew Research (Patten 2016) seems to attribute these divergences to experience, education, occupation and industry, even though as Catalyst. org concurs, that while these earnings vary with the industry, women overall have not yet achieved wage parity with men (Catalyst.org 2017). However, Asians as a group in the U.S. are not only the fastest growing group, they are also the most educated, even surpassing whites in the number of undergraduate degrees or higher learning (U.S. Census Bureau 2016, Mekouar 2016). First-generation Asian Americans are more likely to pursue careers in science, technology, engineering and mathematics (STEM) owing to the security, stature and high earnings that these disciplines command (Li 2010), even though the career choices of succeeding generations are expected to shift. It is important to note, though, that the Asian community is not monolithic as this level of education and thus success is not typical of all Asian groups such as the Hmong, Cambodian, Laotian and Pacific Islanders (Mekouar 2016), where high school dropout rates are reportedly very high.

Despite the blatant inequities, the military can boast that, unlike the civilian sector and even other government counterparts, structurally it is illegal for there to be pay disparities as a consequence of gender (Sicard 2015). Yet, what adversely impacts women's salaries in the military is the rate at which men are promoted over women. A 2012 study by RAND

Corporation shows that while white men in the military experience higher promotion rates than minorities, for instance, once promoted, the retention rates for minorities are actually higher than for their white male peers (Asch et al. 2012). As well, while women officers experience lower promotion and retention rates than do male officers, black women officers are the exception, even though they secure lower promotion rates to higher ranks. Women, on average, leave the military prematurely at higher rates due in part to the institution's rigid structure and policies (Sicard 2015), but once women separate from the military, the situation invariably changes. For instance, Mehay and Hirsch (1996), Cooney et al. (2003), and Segal and Wechsler Segal (2004) show that military service may actually prove negative in the civilian sector at least for white women veterans (Harris 2009b), even though white women are more likely to support gender equality and women in combat than any other segment of the military (Wilcox 1992). Findings by Prokos and Padavic (2000) are mixed in the sense that using the U.S. Census 1990 data set, they found that female veterans beyond the age of 35 years, when compared to female nonveterans in the same age group, received higher earnings. Young women veterans or those below the age of 35 years, were the most disadvantaged in mean earnings. However, while a 2015 U.S. Department of Labor poster describes women veterans as 'Equally Valued, Equally Qualified and Equally Serviced' (U.S. Department of Labor 2015), how equally treated are women veterans in the civilian sector when it comes to compensation?

Of the 10.7 million veterans, women represent 1.4 million or 13 percent (U.S. BLS 2015), although these data for 2013 by the U.S. Bureau of Labor Statistics markedly differ from the 2014 figures where the data reflect a total of 21.4 million veterans where women represent 2.4 million or 10 percent of the total veteran population (Walker and Borbely 2014). The unemployment rate for women veterans during the same period was 6 percent, or more or less equivalent to that of all women.

Say Walker and Borbely (2014), multiple variables impact women veterans' participation in the civilian workforce, such as age and level of education. Most women veterans served during the Gulf I (Operations Desert Shield and Desert Storm) and Gulf II (Operations Enduring and Iraqi Freedom) eras. While approximately 17 percent served during World War II and the Korean and Vietnam Conflicts combined, with the remaining 30 percent categorized as those who served between the Vietnam and Gulf I eras. In 2013, almost 100,000 or 6 percent of women veterans were unemployed (U.S. BLS 2015, Walker and Borbely 2014), most of whom were between the ages of 45 years through 54 years old (28 percent) (Walker and Borbely 2014). In all age groups, the unemployment rate for women veterans was higher than unemployed nonveteran women in the same age groups. Additionally, at 40 percent, the largest unemployed group of female veterans was those who served during the Gulf II era and between the ages of 18 years and 24 years old. This number is comparable to civilians in the same age groups. An anomaly revealed during 2013 but consistently borne out by research is that college-educated women veterans were penalized post-service. Figures 18.1a and 18.1b show both the periods of service for unemployed women veterans and the accompanying age groups affected.

Research by Kleykamp (2013) shows that women veterans do suffer a penalty in both unemployment and income post-military service following the September 11, 2001 attacks. While black veterans were not as severely penalized as their white counterparts, they nevertheless suffered a loss. An inexplicable finding, though, is that the least-educated veterans, or those with only a high school diploma, witnessed the most gains in post-service incomes and performed even better than their civilian counterparts with the same education levels. As well, this same veterans category out-earned all veteran groups. Another noteworthy finding is that while women veterans were penalized in earnings and employment, black female veterans were not as castigated. However, an earlier study, also by Kleykamp (2010), using data from the American Community Survey, also illustrates a slight penalty for white female veterans in the civilian labor market over their black female veteran counterparts. Presumably, black women are also disadvantaged by military service although overall these data suggest a preference by employers to hire female veterans over nonveteran females.

Even more recent research, this time by Routon (2014), confirms some of the previous findings. Post-military service from Operations Enduring and Iraqi Freedom shows that all groups of veterans are advantaged by

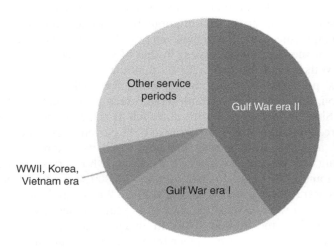

Figure 18.1a Unemployed women veterans by period of service, 2013 annual averages
Source: Walker and Borbely 2014, U.S. Bureau of Labor Statistics 2015

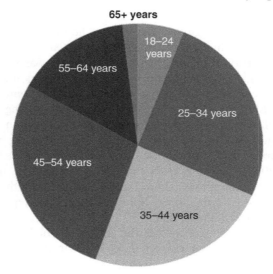

Figure 18.1b Unemployed women veterans by age, 2013 annual averages
Source: Walker and Borbely 2014, U.S. Bureau of Labor Statistics 2015

military service. Still, minorities are more likely to reap the reward of military service in civilian income over white veterans. Similarly, both female and minority veterans are more likely to pursue two-year college degrees over four-year degrees. For women veterans who return home to their rural communities post-service, the road to civilian employment is less certain. Szelwach et al. (2011) discuss a life beset with multiple challenges given geographical locale that result in restricted opportunities for employment coupled with services for childcare. The researchers identified the need to create programs, educate employers and engage in partnerships to meet the needs of this constituency. Another study, by Gottschalck and Holder (2009), found that white and black female veterans between the ages of 25 years through 64 years, out-earned their female nonveteran peers by 20 percent and 9 percent, respectively. Yet, more recent research on women veterans signals an uncertain financial future owing to findings that women veterans who served in the military following 2001 are more likely to have a disability than male veterans and nonveterans (Prokos and Cabage 2015). The authors conclude that disabilities, especially those that are service connected, are primary predictors of unemployment and time spent in the civilian workforce.

Still, another more recent study shows that the median income of a woman veteran is approximately $36,900 – an annual number that is higher than the average earnings for women nonveterans at $27,300 (Nanda et al. 2016). Of note, say the authors, is that, unlike their nonveteran peers, women veterans, on average, worked longer hours during the week as well as longer during the year than women nonveterans. Nevertheless, for all age groups, the median household income for 2014 was higher than for households headed by women veterans, though on average the disparity in income between the groups was not significantly different: women veterans households at $54,993 versus men veterans at $56,995 (U.S. Department of Veterans Affairs, National Center for Veterans Analysis and Statistics (NCVAS) 2016). A previous finding in 2012 also showed women veterans out-earning their female nonveteran counterparts, although slightly behind the earning power of both male veterans and male nonveterans. The study showed that while women veterans' average salary was $30,929 versus $21,071 for nonveteran women, male veterans and male nonveterans earned $36,672 and $31,586 during the same period (U.S. Department of Labor n.d.). Similar figures were reported for 2010 (U.S. Department of Labor 2011).

Women have long recognized the value of higher education in helping them to level the playing field in their professional pursuits. Women in every demographic group are outpacing men in their respective age groups in the attainment of an undergraduate education (Bailey and Dynarski 2011, Lee and Freeman 2012, DiPrete and Buchanan 2013, Pew Research Center 2013, Lam 2017, Schow 2016), even as women continue to earn less than men (West and Curtis 2006, Lam 2017) and are saddled with more debt than men. Women veterans face a similar fate.

Education is reputed to be the great equalizer. Multiple studies identify that outside of patriotism, education is one of the primary reasons for civilians' call to military service (Moore 2014, Moore 1991, Kleykamp 2006, Rumann and Hamrick 2009). Many veterans while serving on active status in any component of the military (active duty, reserve, National Guard) and post-military service have taken advantage of their military benefits whether in the form of the Montgomery GI Bill or that of the Post 9/11 GI Bill (Moore 2014). Veterans in general showed higher educational levels than nonveterans, although the researcher explained this incongruity as a condition of having had a higher education and more training given military service (Moore 2014).

Women, more likely than men, showed higher levels of educational attainment once they reach the age of 22 years (Entwisle et al. 2005). Likewise, as stated, women veterans as a group are better educated than male veterans (Walker and Borbely 2014, Women's Bureau n.d.), even though educated women veterans experience higher unemployment rates than their male cohorts and have a higher propensity for enrollment in institutions of higher learning (Walker and Borbely 2014). Moreover, because veterans' benefits such as the GI Bill are designed to reduce the economic barriers that unnecessarily burden veterans particularly in their transition back and reintegration into civilian life, the fact is that female veterans not only have higher rates of college completion when compared to male veterans as well as a higher use of these educational benefits, but this use actually translates into a 14 percent increase in median income over nonveteran females as a result (U.S. Department of Veterans Affairs 2015).

By all accounts as indicated, women veterans are more likely to enroll into those programs that advance their educational attainment, and as a demographic are better educated and close the salary gap in the process between the earnings of women veterans and men veterans outside of the military. In the military, women are equally remunerated as men according to rank and time in service, and controlling for other variables such as gender and the reduced probability of being promoted in the military also as a consequence of gender. However, once they transition into the civilian sector, what other variables may serve as a disadvantage? Conceivably, women may be unwittingly self-sabotaging these sustained gains and in turn losing ground by virtue of the employment decisions that they make as civilians. Data for 2013 show the majority of women veterans' employment in the private sector followed in succession by the federal, state and local governments and self-employment (Walker and Borbely 2014). Women veterans are also more likely to pursue employment in management, professional and related professions within sales and administrative/ office; service; production, transportation and material moving; and natural resources, construction and maintenance, in that order. The data are similar to those reported for the same period for the employment sectors in which women veterans are most likely to be found (Women's Bureau n.d.). Figures 18.2a and 18.2b reflect the sectors and occupations where women veterans are more likely to be employed.

So, presumably, women veterans' employment patterns appear to mimic those of their male peers in that they are employed at similar rates, or 61 percent versus 63 percent and 59 percent employment rate for nonveteran women (Nanda et al. 2016). Yet, when these data are disaggregated, therein lies a disturbing truth. Like their nonveteran female counterparts (at 37 percent), women leave the workforce 27 percent of the time to take care of their families with disabilities, which is being cited as the second reason for leaving the workforce. Women veterans younger than 54 years of age are more likely than their male peers at the same age to be disabled, but unlike men they have higher service-connected disability rates and are more likely than men to have served in either the reserve or National Guard. In earlier research by Kleykamp (2010), while both black and white women veterans demonstrate strong propensities to remain in the labor market post-military service, black women do so at higher rates than white women. Equally important is that both groups enjoy civilian employers' preference to hire female veterans over nonveteran females.

Women veterans between the ages of 55 years through 64 years old and over are the least likely to be unemployed (Walker and Borbely 2014).

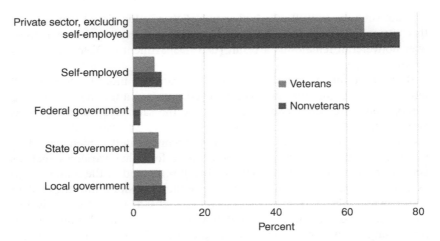

Figure 18.2a Employed women veterans and nonveterans by sector, 2013 annual averages
Source: Walker and Borbely 2014, U.S. Bureau of Labor Statistics 2015

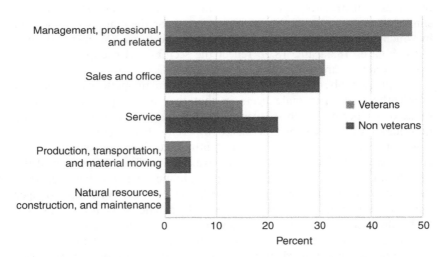

Figure 18.2b Employed women veterans and nonveterans by occupation, 2013 annual averages
Source: Walker and Borbely 2014, U.S. Bureau of Labor Statistics 2015

However, these rates could invariably reflect the critical mass of women veterans in these age groups. While according to the data from 2015, women veterans are more likely than men veterans to be employed, at rates of 55 percent versus 47 percent. Where women veterans lose out, as expected, is that they tend to not only pursue lower-paying occupations than men (U.S. Department of Veterans Affairs 2011), but are also prone to find themselves in minimum-paying jobs and living in poverty as a result. This contradicts the overwhelming research on women veterans who are generally better educated than men veterans. So, yet again, these data do not fully explicate the complete story. However, three subcomponents of the data may help to clarify the conflicting outcomes. Even though women veterans are more likely to be educated as a group than male veterans, they may be found in subpopulations that are more prone to having high unemployment rates given enrollment in school, tend to be under the age of 35 years old, and to have served in the military during the Gulf II era (Council on Veterans Employment Women Veterans Initiative 2015). For example, in 2014 for women between the ages of 18 years through 54 years old, women veterans enrolled in school at higher rates than male veterans (11 percent v. 6 percent), and of those who served in the military during the Gulf II era, 32 percent were found in the civilian workforce compared to 22 percent for men.

The federal government represents a growing proportion of women veterans' employment. For the 2013 and 2014 periods, women veterans made up 14 percent of the federal government as compared to only 2 percent of nonveteran females (Council on Veterans Employment Women Veterans Initiative 2015). In the fiscal year 2013 alone, women veterans' employment in the executive branch of federal agencies was 23 percent of all new employment. Because women on active duty in both the enlisted and commissioned corps tend to be concentrated in certain career fields, these skills in turn are transferrable as critical skills in the federal government.

Women veterans comprise a small but sizeable percentage in those occupations in the federal government that are deemed mission critical. These comprise positions as economists to contracting and human resources (Council on Veterans Employment Women Veterans Initiative 2015). While women do not yet have a critical mass in still nontraditional disciplines such as those in STEM that will no doubt draw higher earnings potential, the federal government's post-9/11 GI Bill serves as a viable conduit for these pursuits. What is encouraging, though, is that in the executive branches of the federal government, women veterans are the most diverse at 44.7 percent compared to male veterans at 31.8 percent.

Admittedly, women's increasing education and remaining in the workforce longer have together contributed to a narrowing of the wage gap. However, this wage gap seems to widen with age. In essence, even Asian women must work on average another seven years to gain parity with white men, black women another 23 years and Hispanic women another 34 years

(Catalyst.org 2017). Paradoxically, women as a group have narrowed the wage gap the most with white men in the construction industry at 98 percent. Today, while women are earning more college degrees than ever before, the path to wage parity with men for women is still by advancing one's education (National Center for Education Statistics 2015, Catalyst.org 2017).

On a tangential yet related issue that incorporates women's uncompensated to minimally compensated roles in the U.S. military as camp followers, cooks and the like, the military consigned them by neither recognizing nor rewarding the sacrifices of these unsung sheros who risked their own lives not only to serve their country but to accompany their husbands in the process (Enloe 1983, 2000). This marginalization has coincidentally set the stage for the meager earnings of military wives in contemporary military life. Both Booth et al. (2000) and Booth (2003) make the claim that military wives are poorly compensated in labor market areas (LMAs) that are within close proximity to military installations, despite the belief that economically, military bases serve as economic lifelines to the surrounding civilian communities (Booth 2003). However, contrary to this belief, these outcomes benefit women, and women who are military spouses, the least. Notwithstanding the frequent relocation with active duty male spouses, military wives suffer on average a 5 percent penalty in earnings given the LMAs, and overall encounter a cumulative disadvantage as a result. Results may also vary with individual characteristics such as race and/or ethnicity, where they reside and the LMAs in which they seek employment.

For women veterans, the lesson then appears to be that the way forward in gaining economic security and financial power lies in pursuing an advanced education, securing a career that is not only viable but in an industry or sector with the most growth and where high earnings can be attained. These factors combined have emerged to constitute the most prudent and likely recipe for success as the route for accumulating wealth, an increase in the quality of life and maintaining a high standard of living that will prove beneficial during one's golden years and particularly at a period in life when one has less time to recover that wealth.

Bibliography

American Association of University Women (AAUW). (2017). The Simple Truth about the Gender Pay Gap. Spring. www.aauw.org/research/the-simple-truth-about-the-gender-pay-gap/. Retrieved February 24, 2017.

Asch, B.J., Miller, T., and Malchiodi, A. (2012). *A New Look at Gender and Minority Differences in Officer Progression in the Military.* Santa Monica, CA: The RAND Corporation. National Defense Research Institute.

Bailey, M.J., and Dynarski, S.M. (2011). *Gains and Gaps: Changing Inequality in U.S. College Entry and Completion.* National Bureau of Economic Research (NBER). http://users.nber.org/~dynarski/Bailey_Dynarski_Final.pdf. Retrieved March 18, 2017.

Black, D., Haviland, A., Sanders, S., and Taylor, L. (2006). Why Do Minority Men Earn Less? A Study of Wage Differentials among the Highly Educated. *Review of Economics and Statistics*, 88, 300–313.

Blau, F.D., Brinton, M.B., and Grusky, D.B. (2009). Introduction. Chapter 1. In F. D. Blau, M.B. Brinton and D.B. Grusky (Eds.), *The Declining Significance of Gender?* (p.3–34). New York, NY: Russell Sage Press.

Blau, F.D., and Kahn, L.M. (2009). Making Sense of Change and Stability in Gender Equity. In F.D. Blau, M.B. Brinton and D.B. Grusky (Eds.), *The Declining Significance of Gender?* (p.37–66). New York, NY: Russell Sage Press.

Booth, B. (2003). Contextual Effects of Military Presence on Women's Earnings. *Armed Forces and Society*, 30, 1, 25–51.

Booth, Bradford, Falk, William W., Segal, David R., and Wechsler Segal, Mady. (2000). The Impact of Military Presence in Local Labor Markets and the Employment of Women. *Gender and Society*, 14, 2, 318–332.

Buchanan, A. (2016). Asian Americans Earn Top Wages Yet Still Face Discrimination. July 12. *Vox*. https://nonprofitquarterly.org/2016/07/12/asian-americans-earn-top-wages-yet-still-face-discrimination/. Retrieved March 22, 2017.

Catalyst.org. (2017). Women's Earnings and Income. Knowledge Center. June 21. www.catalyst.org/knowledge/womens-earnings-and-income. Retrieved March 23, 2017.

Cooney, Richard T., Wechsler Segal, Mady, Segal, David R., and Falk, William W. (2003). Racial Differences in the Impact of Military Service on the Socio-economic Status of Women Veterans. *Armed Forces and Society*, 30, 1, 53–86.

Council on Veterans Employment Women Veterans Initiative. (2015). Employment of Women Veterans in the Federal Government. March. www.blogs.va.gov/VAntage/wp-content/uploads/2015/04/Report.pdf. Retrieved March 2, 2017.

DiPrete, T.A., and Buchanan, C. (2013). *The Rise of Women*. New York, NY: Russell Sage Foundation.

Enloe, C. (1983). *Does Khaki Become You:. The Militarisation of Women's Lives*. Boston, MA: South End Press.

Enloe, C. (2000). *The International Politics of Women's Lives*. Berkeley, Los Angeles and London: University of California Press.

Entwisle, D.A., Alexander, K.L., and Olson, L.S. (2005). First Grade and Emotional Attainment by Age 22: A New Story. *American Journal of Sociology*, 110, 5, 1458–1502.

Fry, R., and Stepler, R. (2017). Women May Never Make Up Half of the U.S. Workforce. January 31. www.pewresearch.org/fact-tank/. Retrieved February 23, 2017.

Goldin, C. (2009). The Rising (and Then Declining) Significance of Gender. In F. D. Blau, M.B. Brinton and D.B. Grusky (Eds.), *The Declining Significance of Gender?* (p.67–101). New York, NY: Russell Sage Press.

Gottschalck, A.O., and Holder, K.A. (2009). *We Want You! The Role of Human Capital in Explaining the Veteran – Non-Veteran Earning Differential*. Washington, DC: U.S. Census Bureau. Housing and Household Economic Statistics Division.

Green, C.A., and Ferber, M.A. (2005). Do Detailed Work Histories Help to Explain Gender and Race/Ethnic Wage Differentials? *Review of Social Economy*, 63, 55–85.

Harris, G.L.A. (2009a). Revisiting Affirmative Action in Leveling the Playing Field. Who Have Been the True Beneficiaries Anyway? *Review of Public Personnel Administration*, 29, 4, 354–372.

Harris, G.L.A. (2009b). The Multifaceted Nature of White Female Attrition in the Military. *Journal of Public Management and Social Policy*, 15, 1, 74–93.

Harris, G.L.A. (2011). The Quest for Gender Equity. Book Review of The Declining Significance of Gender? F.D. Blau, M.B. Brinton and D.B. Grusky (Eds.), 2009. *Public Administration Review*, 71, 1, 123–126.

Hartmann, H., Rose, S.J., and Lovell, V. (2009). How Much Longer in Closing the Earnings Gap? In F.D. Blau, M.B. Brinton and D.B. Grusky (Eds.), *The Declining Significance of Gender?* (p.125–155). New York, NY: Russell Sage Press.

Jackson, R.M. (2009). Opposing Forces: How, Why and When and When Will Gender Inequality Disappear? In F.D. Blau, M.B. Brinton, and D.B. Grusky (Eds.), *The Declining Significance of Gender?* (p.215–244). New York, NY: Russell Sage Press.

Kalev, A., Dobbin, F., and Kelly, E. (2006). Best Practices or Best Guesses? Assessing the Efficacy of Corporate Affirmative Action and Diversity Policies. *American Sociological Review*, 71, 589–617.

Kleykamp, M.A. (2006). College, Jobs or the Military? Enlistment During a Time of War. *Social Science Quarterly*, 87, 2, 272–290.

Kleykamp, M. (2010). *Women's Work After War.* W.E. Upjohn Institute for Employment Research. Working Paper 10-169.

Kleykamp, M. (2013). Unemployment, Earnings and Enrollment among 9–11 Veterans. *Social Sciences Research*, 42, 836–851.

Lam, J. (2017). Battle of the Sexes: Why Women Have More Debt Than Men. May 10. *Credit Sesame*. www.creditsesame.com/blog/debt/battle-of-the-sexes-why-women-have-more-debt-than-men/. Retrieved March 1, 2017.

Lee, W.Y., and Freeman, K. (2012). *From Diplomas to Doctorates: The Success of Black Women in Higher Education and Its Implications for Equal Educational Opportunities for All.* Sterling, VA: Stylus Publishing.

Li, H. (2010). Asian Americans Increasingly Defying the STEM Stereotype. *IB Times*. www.ibtimes.com/asian-americans-increasingly-defying-stem-stereotype-246578. Retrieved February 22, 2017.

Mehay, Stephen L., and Barry T. Hirsch. (1996). The Post Military Earnings of Female Veterans. *Industrial Relations*, 35, 2, 197–217.

Mekouar, D. (2016). Why Asian Americans Are the Most Educated Group in America. *Voice of America*. https://blogs.voanews.com/all-about-america/2016/04/11/why-asian-americans-are-the-most-educated-group-in-america/. Retrieved February 12, 2017.

Moore, B. (1991). African American Women in the Military. *Armed Forces and Society*, 17, 3, 363–384.

Moore, B. (2014). Predictors of Educational Attainment for Veterans. *Academic Exchange Quarterly*, 18, 2, 77–82.

Nanda, N., Shetty, S., Techapaisarnjaroenkij, T., Patterson, L., and Garasky, S. (2016). *Women Veteran Economic and Employment Characteristics.* Contract #DOL131RQ21724. Impaq International.

National Center for Education Statistics. (2015). *Digest of Education Statistics 2015.* https://nces.ed.gov/programs/digest/d15/. Retrieved March 2, 2017.

National Center for Veterans Analysis and Statistics (NCVAS). (2016). *Profile of Women Veterans: 2014.* March. U.S. Department of Veterans Affairs. www.va.gov/vetdata/docs/SpecialReports/Women_Veterans_2016.pdf. Retrieved March 1, 2017.

National Partnership for Women and Families. (2017). America's Women and Wage Gap. April. www.nationalpartnership.org/research-library/workplace-fairness/fair-pay/americas-women-and-the-wage-gap.pdf. Retrieved March 28, 2017.

Patten, E. (2016). *Racial, Gender Wage Gap Persist in U.S. Despite Some Progress.* Pew Research Center, Fact Tank. July 1. www.pewresearch.org/fact-tank/2016/07/01/racial-gender-wage-gaps-persist-in-u-s-despite-some-progress/. Retrieved February 22, 2017.

Pew Research Center. (2013). *In Educational Attainment, Millennial Women Outpace Men.* December 10. www.pewsocialtrends.org/2013/12/11/on-pay-gap-millennial-women-near-parity-for-now/sdt-gender-and-work-12-2013-0-04/. Retrieved February 23, 2017.

Polochek, S.W. (2009). How the Life-Cycle Human-Capital Model Explains Why the Gender Wage Gap Narrowed. In F.D. Blau, M.B. Brinton, and D.B. Grusky (Eds.), *The Declining Significance of Gender?* (p.102–124). New York, NY: Russell Sage Press.

Prokos, A., and Cabage, L.N. (2015). Women Military Veterans, Disability and Employment. *Armed Forces and Society*, 43, 2, 346–367.

Prokos, A., and Padavic, I. (2000). Earn All That You Can: Income Differences Between Women Veterans and Nonveterans. *Journal of Political and Military Psychology*, 28, 1, 60–74.

Pynes, J.E. (2013). *Human Resource Management for Public and Nonprofits Organizations*. 4th Edition. San Francisco, CA: Jossey-Bass Publishers.

Ridgeway, C.L. (2009). Gender as an Organizing Force in Social Relations: Implications for the Future of Inequality. In F.D. Blau, M.B. Brinton and D.B. Grusky (Eds.), *The Declining Significance of Gender?* (p.265–288). New York, NY: Russell Sage Press.

Rittel, H.W., and Webber, M.M. (1973). Dilemmas in a General Theory of Planning. *Policy Sciences*, 4, 2, 155–159.

Routon, W. (2014). The Effect of 21st Century Military Service on Civilian Labor and Education Outcomes. *Journal of Labor Research*, 35, 1, 15–38.

Rumann, C.B., and Hamrick, F.A. (2009). Supporting Student Veterans in Transition: New Directions for Student Services. In R. Ackerman and D. DoRamio (Eds.), *Creating a Veteran-Friendly Campus: Strategies for Transition and Success* (p.25–34). No. 16, Summer. San Francisco, CA: Jossey-Bass.

Schow, A. (2016). Women Earning More Doctoral and Masters Degrees Than Men. *Washington Examiner.* July 1. www.washingtonexaminer.com/women-earning-more-doctoral-and-masters-degrees-than-men/article/2602223. Retrieved March 20, 2017.

Segal, David R., and Wechsler Segal, Mady. (2004). American Military Population. *Population Bulletin*, 59, 4, 1–44.

Shapiro, L., and Mellnik, T. (2016). In the Federal Government, How Likely is it that a Woman Will Make More than a Man? *The Washington Post.* www.washingtonpost.com/graphics/national/women-federal-pay/. Retrieved March 25, 2017.

Sheth, S., and Gould, S. (2017). 5 Charts Show How Much Men Make More than Women. *Business Insider.* March 8. www.businessinsider.com/gender-wage-pay-gap-charts-2017-3. Retrieved March 28, 2017.

Sicard, S. (2015). The U.S. Military Has No Gender Pay Gap. December 15. *Task and Purpose.* http://taskandpurpose.com/us-military-has-no-gender-pay-gap/. Retrieved February 9, 2017.

Szelwach, C.R., Steinkogler, J., Badger, E.R., and Muttukumaru, R. (2011). Transitioning to the Civilian Workforce Issues Impacting the Reentry of Rural Women Veterans. *Journal of Rural Social Sciences*, 26, 3, 83–112.

U.S. Bureau of Labor Statistics (BLS). (2015). *Women in the Labor Force: A Data Book*. Report No. 1059. BLS Reports. www.bls.gov/opub/reports/womens-databook/archive/women-in-the-labor-force-a-databook-2015.pdf. Retrieved February 24, 2017.

U.S. Census Bureau. (2016). More Than Half of Asians in U.S. Have Bachelor's Degree or Higher. March 29. Release No. CB16–56. www.census.gov/newsroom/press-releases/2016/cb16-56.html. Retrieved February 21, 2017.

U.S. Department of Labor. (n.d.). Data and Statistics. Women's Bureau. www.dol.gov/wb/stats/stats_data.htm. Retrieved February 23, 2017.

U.S. Department of Labor. (2011). The Veterans Labor Force in Recovery. November 3. www.dol.gov/_sec/media/reports/VeteransLaborForce/VeteransLaborForce.pdf. Retrieved March 2, 2017.

U.S. Department of Labor. (2015). Women Veterans – Equally Valued, Equally Qualified and Equally Serviced. August 26. https://blog.dol.gov/2015/08/26/women-veterans-%E2%80%93-equally-valued-equally-qualified-equally-served. Retrieved March 20, 2017.

U.S. Department of Veterans Affairs. (2011). *America's Women Veterans. Military Service History and Benefits Utilization Statistics*. November 11. National Center for Veterans Analysis and Statistics. www.va.gov/vetdata/docs/specialreports/final_womens_report_3_2_12_v_7.pdf, Retrieved February 10, 2017.

U.S. Department of Veterans Affairs. (2015). *2015 Veteran Economic Opportunity Report*. www.benefits.va.gov/benefits/docs/veteraneconomicopportunityreport2015.pdf. Retrieved February 19, 2017.

U.S. General Accountability Office (GAO). (2007). *Retirement Security. Women Face Challenges in Ensuring Financial Security in Retirement*. GAO-08-105. October.

U.S. General Accountability Office (GAO). (2008). *Human Capital. Diversity in the Federal SES and Processes for Selecting New Executives*. GAO-09-110. Washington, DC.

U.S. Office of Personnel Management (OPM). (2014). Women in Federal Service. A Seat at Every Table. www.fedview.opm.gov/2014files/2014_Womens_Report.pdf. Retrieved March 25, 2017.

Walker, J.A., and Borbely, J.M. (2014). *Women Veterans in the Labor Force: Spotlight on Statistics*. U.S. Bureau of Labor Statistics, U.S. Department of Labor. www.bls.gov/spotlight/2014/women-vets/. Retrieved May 22, 2017.

West, M.S., and Curtis, J.W. (2006). *AAUP Faculty Gender Equity Indicators 2006*. Washington, DC: American Association of University Professors.

Wilcox, Clyde. (1992). Race, Gender, and Support for Women in the Military. *Social Science Quarterly*, 73, 2, 310–323.

Women's Bureau. (n.d.). Women Veterans Profile. Issue Brief. U.S. Department of Labor. www.dol.gov/wb/resources/women_veterans_profile.pdf. Retrieved March 2, 2017.

Part VI
The Civil–Military Divide

The civil–military divide has been offered up as a condition that exists as a form of tension between the military and the exercise of civilian control over the military. Says Cochran (2013), much of this divide can be attributed to the limits of the bureaucracy and the military's aspiration to assume control over its resources, independence and modes of influence for its survival. For Kohn (1997), in strong and established democracies like the U.S., the challenges lie in the civilian leadership exerting power and authority over policy and decision making as the ultimate and final arbiter while allowing the military to revel in prestige, execute military prowess in meeting its various missions and never question civilian authority.

Part VI takes on such issues as who serves in the military, women serving within a democracy under the notion of representative bureaucracy, that the representation of full citizenry is in peril given the double-edged sword of responsibility without authority that military women needlessly encounter, and the legal frameworks as practised by the military and its civilian leadership in parsing out in the end where women actually belong.

Bibliography

Cochran, S.T. (2013). The Civil-Military Divide in Protracted Small War. An Alternative View of Military Leadership Preferences and War Termination. *Armed Forces and Society*, 40, 1, 71–95.

Kohn, R.H. (1997). How Democracies Control the Military. *Journal of Democracy*, 8, 4, 140–153.

19 Who Serves in the Military?

The concept and actual experiences of military service are far removed from the day-to-day life for the average American (Miles 2011). It has been estimated that only half of 1 percent of the U.S. population has been on active military duty at any given time (Pew Research Center 2011), which combined with the official end of the draft and inception of a volunteer military force in 1973, along with the 16 years of sustained (and controversial) U.S. military operations in Iraq and Afghanistan, has significantly contributed to the civilian–military divide (Gonzalez-Prats 2008). In contrast, 16,000,000 men and women served in World War II, representing about 8 percent of the U.S. population, which increased the likelihood that when military members returned to their communities, they were received by other veterans, or by someone whose immediate family member was serving in the military, or had worn the uniform (Gonzalez-Prats 2008, Mettler 2005).

There exist multiple reasons why people choose to serve in the military: an adulthood rite of passage, continuing a family tradition, adventure, job training, future employment and education opportunities (Kelty et al. 2010). For many, especially ourstorically marginalized populations within American society such as African Americans, Hispanics, Native Americans, homosexuals and women, military service represented the ultimate opportunity to access a meritocracy and opportunity for equal status of citizenship often denied to them in the civilian sector (Belkin 2012, Evans 2003, Fenner 1998).

This chapter discusses the current demographics of the armed forces, with specific focus on the contributions of women across the branches of the military, to include several ourstorical milestones that have significantly impacted their evolving roles of increased leadership and recognition. As well, the chapter concludes with the current state of the military and pending policies that could impact future service requirements for its citizens.

Overview of Military Demographics

According to the U.S. Office of the Deputy Assistant Secretary of Defense (2014), there is an estimated total of 3.5 million men and women serving in the active duty, reserve, and National Guard components of the Army, Navy, Air Force, and Marine Corps. This demographic includes the Coast Guard and Coast Guard Reserve, which currently fall under the U.S. Department of Homeland Security (U.S. Coast Guard 2017). The Army and Navy make up the largest of the active duty forces at 1.3 million. Some 77 percent of service members in the active duty component, and about 60 percent of those in the reserve components are on average 30 years old or younger, and since 1990, the percentage of minorities for both the enlisted and officer corps has risen about 10 percent. Currently, there are less than 31 percent of those on active duty and 25 percent of those in the reserve components who identify as a racial or ethnic minority (Office of the Deputy Assistant Secretary of Defense 2014). Additionally, there has been an increase in the number of women within the enlisted and officer ranks (+1 percent to 2.3 percent, respectively) since 2000, bringing the total percentage of women to 15 percent of the active duty forces and 18 percent of the reserve forces (Office of the Deputy Assistant Secretary of Defense 2014).

Evolution of the Role of Women in the Military

Since the beginning of the American republic, women have always been an integral part of the military. Despite their roles as either unknown or downplayed as 'support' for their male counterparts, women have consistently served with distinction in the U.S. from the Revolutionary War to present day (Danyluk n.d., Solaro 2006). However, due to their *de facto* treatment as second-class citizens, they have remained an afterthought or minimal footnote in history as to their contributions in our nation's defense (Fenner 1998).

Prior to 1948 when the Women's Armed Services Integration Act was enacted, no women were permanently enlisted in the military (Weinstein and White 1997). Women were assigned to special 'women's corps,' auxiliary forces that were temporarily established to meet manpower shortages (Weinstein and White 1997, p.101). Those women who served prior to 1948 did so primarily as nurses and laundresses on the battlefield by caring for their husbands, both during the American Revolutionary War and the Civil War (Stiehm 1996). In addition to more traditional supporting positions, women have served in a variety of roles ranging from infantrymen (disguised in men's clothing) to providing comfort and healing as nurses, to parachuting behind enemy lines during World War II as spies, to pilots flying jets and helicopters (Binney 2002, Stiehm 1996, Weinstein and White 1997).

The issue of defining women's role in combat operations versus support roles has been debated off and on since the 1970s integration of women into the military (Fenner 1998). As a result, women's contributions, although significant, were always in the context of support and subservience, never as a valued entity or with an identity that was separate from the male members of society. This in turn heavily influenced how women were perceived and valued in the military, even as they were integrated and gained entry into the service academies and newly formed all-volunteer force in 1973 (Stiehm 1996). Additionally, women in the military have been brought to the forefront of national attention with the high visibility of those who served in both the wars in Iraq and Afghanistan, especially in unique and emerging roles that their male counterparts are unable to fulfill (Baldor 2011, Dunn 2009).

Given the culturally delicate climate, a backdrop of the wars in Iraq and Afghanistan, there has been a growing need for the military to identify alternative ways to win the 'hearts and minds' of the local population, so to speak, especially with the outreach to and engagement with women and children, a role unable to be effectively filled by male soldiers owing to strict Muslim mores. The Army and Marine Corps filled this need by developing Cultural Support Teams or Female Engagement Teams, also known as 'Team Lioness.' These lionesses are female service members who voluntarily put themselves in harm's way, deploying in two-woman teams as part of larger special operations or infantry units, helping gather information and establish trust and buy-in from villagers (Baldor 2011, Dunn 2009, McLagan et al. 2008).

> They are trained to ferret out critical information not available to their male team members, to identify insurgents disguised as women and figure out when Afghan women are being used to hide weapons ... any day that they're walking into a village and engaging with the population they are at the same risk as those Special Forces, SEALS, or special operators they're detailed to ... they are on the front lines in very austere locations.
>
> (Baldor 2011, para. 9)

Conclusion

Women have continued to significantly contribute to the collective fighting force of the U.S. military, especially after September 11, 2001 and in the global war on terror. To date, over 280,000 servicewomen have been deployed to Iraq or Afghanistan (Myre 2013), with over 1,000 women wounded in action, and over 164 women killed in action since those wars (Defense Manpower Data Center n.d.). Additionally, over 9,000 women have received Army Combat Action Badges for 'actively engaging or being engaged by the enemy,' and over 437 women have earned awards for valor, including, but not limited to, two Silver Stars (the nation's third-highest award for valor), three Distinguished Flying Crosses, 31 Air Medals, and 16 Bronze Stars (Sisk 2015, para.12, Tan 2012).

December 2015 also marked the most ourstorical milestone change since the integration of women into the armed forces in the 1940s: the full and unrestricted inclusion of women into all occupations of the military, to include direct combat roles previously closed to them (Wire Reporters 2015). The repeal of the combat exclusion policy is a significant change for several key reasons. First, combat experience is directly tied to ascension opportunities, especially at the higher echelons of rank and top leadership (Rostker 2006). Second, unrestricted opportunity to all military roles and occupations could prove to be a powerful tool for recruitment and retention purposes in an all-volunteer force (Rostker 2006), as well as serve as a powerful conduit for women to gain critical mass of representation across the military (Schmid 2010). Third, the unrestricted access for women to compete for and in all occupations, positions and critical assignments will help them gain true parity with their male peers in the military (Fenner 1998, Rostker 2006). Finally, the inclusion of opportunities for women in the combat arms profession, it is hoped, will help to eliminate another barrier for equal service and full citizenship – that is the right for women to be included in the Selective Service registration, which, since 1981, has been restricted by the U.S. Supreme Court's decision in *Rostker v. Goldberg* (Cheh 1993, Rostker 2006). Equal service, full citizenship and draft registration will put women on the path to full agency and thereby as partners with men in and out of the military.

The prospect of including women in the Selective Service System has been recently revisited by the Congressional Committees on Armed Services. However, the decision was tabled until July 1, 2017, when the Secretary of Defense was tasked to provide a report to the committees as to the 'merits and benefits' of the current Selective Service System, to include expanding the system to include women, as well as an analysis to evaluate national service as an option in the event of a national emergency (Demirijan 2016, 114th Congress of the U.S. 2016). A recent attempt by lawmakers like Jackie Speier (D-CA 14th District) to introduce explicit language requiring women to equally register for Selective Service like their male counterparts was defeated 33–28 in the House of Representatives, when the recent National Defense Authorization Act (NDAA) for the fiscal year 2018 was passed (Associated Press 2017). Opponents like House Armed Services Committee Chairman Mac Thornberry (R-TX 13th District) cited the reason for not including women in the draft registry as the ongoing (and incomplete) review of the necessity of the Selective Service System, and that any expansion should wait until the study's conclusion (Associated Press 2017, Shane 2017).

Bibliography

Associated Press (2017, June 28). Senate Panel Approves $700 Billion Defense Bill. *The Washington Post.* www.washingtonpost.com/politics/federal_government/

the-latest-house-panel-seeks-pentagon-climate-change-review/2017/06/28/0e6e6868-5c45-11e7-aa69-3964a7d55207_story.html?utm_term=.88e26b6048f4. Retrieved April 6, 2017.

Baldor, L.C. (2011, October 25). Death Highlights Women's Role in Special Ops Teams. Associated Press. www.deseretnews.com/article/700191423/Death-highlights-womens-role-in-Special-Ops-teams.html?pg=1. Retrieved January 31, 2016.

Belkin, A. (2012). *Bring Me Men: Military Masculinity and the Benign Facade of American Empire, 1898–2001*. New York, NY: Columbia University Press.

Binney, M. (2002). *The Women Who Lived for Danger: The Agents of the Special Operations Executive*. First U.S. edition. New York: William Morrow.

Cheh, M.M. (1993). VMI Essays: An Essay On VMI And Military Service: Yes, We Do Have To Be Equal Together. *Washington and Lee Law Review*, 50, 1, 49–61. http://scholarlycommons.law.wlu.edu/cgi/viewcontent.cgi?article=1817&context=wlulr. Retrieved March 19, 2017.

Danyluk, K. (n.d.). Women's Service with the Revolutionary Army. www.history.org/history/teaching/enewsletter/volume7/nov08/women_revarmy.cfm. Retrieved April 29, 2016.

Defense Manpower Data Center (DMDC) (n.d.). Defense Casualty Analysis System. www.dmdc.osd.mil/dcas/pages/about.xhtml. Retrieved April 7, 2016.

Demirijan, K. (2016, May 14). Key Senate Panel Endorses Women in the Draft, Making Policy Change More Likely. *The Washington Post*. Washington, DC. www.washingtonpost.com/news/powerpost/wp/2016/05/14/key-senate-panelendorses-women-in-the-draft-making-policy-change-more-likely/. Retrieved June 2, 2016.

Dunn, N.M. (2009, March 13). Lioness Program 'Pride' of the Corps. Marine Corps Air Ground Command. California: Twentynine Palms. www.29palms.marines.mil/News/NewsArticleDisplay/tabid/3005/Article/498488/lioness-program-pride-of-the-corps.aspx. Retrieved April 7, 2016.

Evans, R. (2003). *A History of the Service of Ethnic Minorities in the U.S. Armed Forces*. Santa Barbara, CA. http://archive.palmcenter.org/files/active/0/Evans_MinorityInt_200306.pdf. Retrieved July 5, 2016.

Fenner, L.M. (1998). Either You Need These Women or You Do Not: Informing the Debate on Military Service and Leadership. *Gender Issues*, 16, 3, 5–32. doi:10.1007/s12147-998-0020-2.

Gonzalez-Prats, M.C. (2008). Through a Veteran's Eyes: The Transition of the Army Leader in the Civilian Workforce. Unpublished Master's culminating paper. Sonoma State University, Rohnert Park, California. http://pdxscholar.library.pdx.edu/studentsymposium/2013/Presentation/14/. Retrieved April 6, 2017.

Kelty, R., Kleykamp, M., and Segal, D.R. (2010). The Military and the Transition to Adulthood. *The Future of Children*, 20, 1, 181–207.

McLagan, M., Sommers, Daria, Room 11 Productions, Chicken & Egg Pictures, and Impact Partners. (2008). *Lioness*. Deluxe educational edition. New York, NY: Room 11 Productions.

Mettler, S. (2005). *Soldiers to Citizens: The G.I. Bill and the Making of the Greatest Generation*. Oxford and New York: Oxford University Press.

Miles, D. (2011, November 28). Survey Shows Growing Gap Between Civilians, Military. *American Forces Press Service*. Washington, DC. http://content.govdelivery.com/accounts/USDOD/bulletins/1e626f. Retrieved November 24, 2015.

Myre, G. (2013). Women in Combat: 5 Key Questions. National Public Radio (NPR). January 24. www.npr.org/sections/thetwo-way/2013/01/24/170161752/women-in-combat-five-key-questions. Retrieved April 7, 2016.

Office of the Deputy Assistant Secretary of Defense. (2014). 2014 Demographics: Profile of the Military Community. http://download.militaryonesource.mil/12038/MOS/Reports/2014-Demographics-Report.pdf. Retrieved April 6, 2017.

Office of the Under Secretary of Defense, Personnel and Readiness. (2016). *Population Representation in the Military Services: Fiscal Year 2015 Summary Report*. www.cna.org/research/pop-rep. Retrieved April 6, 2017.

114th Congress of the U.S. (2016). National Defense Authorization Bill for Fiscal Year 2017. www.congress.gov/114/bills/s2943/BILLS-114s2943enr.pdf. Retrieved December 15, 2016.

Pew Research Center Social and Demographic Trends. (2011). *The Military-Civilian Gap: War and Sacrifice in the Post-9/11 Era*. Washington, DC. www.pewsocialtrends.org/2011/10/05/war-and-sacrifice-in-the-post-911-era/. Retrieved March 19, 2017.

Rostker, B. (2006). *I Want You! The Evolution of the All-Volunteer Force*. Santa Monica, CA: RAND Corporation. www.rand.org/pubs/monographs/MG265.html. Retrieved March 19, 2017.

Schmid, M.N. (2010). Combating a Different Enemy: Proposals to Change the Culture of S-2. *Villanova Law Review*, 55, 475–508.

Shane, III, L. (2017). Lawmakers Reject New Plan to Make Women Register for Military Drafts. *The Military Times*. June 28. www.militarytimes.com/articles/hasc-2018-ndaa-women-draft-fails. Retrieved July 3, 2016.

Sisk, R. (2015, August 31). Women in Combat: Silver Stars, Combat Action Badges and Casualties. *Military.com*. www.military.com/daily-news/2015/08/31/women-in-combat-silver-stars-combat-action-badges-casualties.html. Retrieved April 7, 2016.

Solaro, E. (2006). *Women in the Line of Fire: What You Should Know About Women in the Military*. Emeryville, CA: Seal Press.

Stiehm, J.B. (1996). *It's Our Military Too: Women and the U.S. Military*. Philadelphia: Temple University Press.

Tan, M. (2012, May 12). Women in Combat: Army to Open 14k Jobs, 6 MOSs. *Military Times*. www.militarytimes.com/news/2012/05/army-to-open-14000-jobs-6-mos-women-in-combat-050212/. Retrieved April 6, 2017.

U.S. Coast Guard. (2017). The Coast Guard Today. www.gocoastguard.com/about-the-coast-guard/learn-the-history. Retrieved on October 16, 2017.

Weinstein, L.L., and White, C.C. (1997). *Wives and Warriors: Women and the Military in the United States and Canada*. Westport, CT: Bergin & Garvey.

Wire Reporters (2015, December 3). Defense Secretary tells military to open all combat jobs to women. *Chicago Tribune*. Chicago. www.chicagotribune.com/news/nationworld/ct-military-combat-jobs-women-20151203-story.html. Retrieved January 24, 2016.

20 The Notion of Representative Bureaucracy

Ideally, a democracy leverages all of the talents of its citizenry. This especially becomes evident during a call to arms, crisis or when the nation's civilian leadership unites and encourages its citizens to put seemingly petty individual and group differences aside to marshal its resources in the mission to thwart the immediate threat. For a representative bureaucracy, both in its active and passive forms, its theory and practice imply that, in its purest structure, it strives for the broadest appeal in representing and advancing the interests of those whom it exists to serve (Meier and Bohte 2001). On one hand, active representative bureaucracy connotes the bureaucrat's responsibility to use that discretion toward the equitable access and outcomes given certain demographic composition of the people represented in the ways of gender, race and/or ethnicity, to name a few (Saltzstein 1979). Passive representative bureaucracy, on the other hand, is informed by the values and beliefs of the bureaucrats in the agencies, who, it is hoped, will call upon those very values and beliefs in using their discretion to implement public programs, especially for the underrepresented. However, there are limits to representative bureaucracy (Meier and Bohte 2001). These limits require that the bureaucracy and the bureaucrats within it must translate active representative bureaucracy into passive representative bureaucracy by invoking discretion. In this way, representative bureaucracy becomes more responsive to the people whom it exists to serve (Sowa and Selden 2003).

Originally based on the work of Kingsley (1944, as cited by Sowa and Selden 2003) in keeping with the British Civil Service system, the concept of representative bureaucracy has been morphed and extended by the likes of Levitan (1946, as cited by Sowa and Selden 2003) that the bureaucracy should be representative of the public's demographic composition, and in so doing, the public would be more likely to be receptive to its decisions. With refinement by Krislov and Rosenbloom (1981), the concept began to take shape by assuming those values and beliefs of the public thereby allowing the people to feel some bond or sense of relationship with their government. Sowa and Selden (2003) argue that while the discretion of bureaucrats or administrators is at the heart of agency decision making, it is only one of multiple instruments that must be present to enable the administration of programs for equitable outcomes and which must connect active representative bureaucracy to that of passive representative bureaucracy. However, say Riccucci and Saidel (1997), representative bureaucracy has been too narrowly focused and to the exclusion of certain bureaucratic actors, in this case those at the state level, who are appointed and disaggregated according to race and/or ethnicity and gender. The researchers conclude that the term must be framed and practised in meaningful ways by including those appointed in state governments who reflect those within the general population that they serve. In this regard, according to Riccucci and Saidel (1997), women and people of color are not represented in the top echelons of state government and by extension are also absent to personify the interests of women and people of color in their respective citizenries.

Meier and Nicholson-Crotty (2006) extend and confirm Riccucci and Saidel's (1997) research about the narrow-mindedness of representative bureaucracy as it applies to gender. For instance, Meier and Nicholson-Crotty (2006) conclude that where there is a critical force of female police officers in a department's workforce, there is a more determined concentration in response to sexual charges and taking the aggrieved more seriously.

While the U.S. military emanates from a democracy, it is fundamentally undemocratic in both its structure and policies, it must nevertheless be mindful of its need to be representative of the general civilian population on which the institution not only depends for its workforce but on which it must also depend by way of Congress for its very existence in the way of resources for sustenance. This is explicitly the case in the advent of the all-volunteer military and in light of this era and principally during a robust civilian economy where the military finds itself competing with civilian employers for the best and brightest from American society. The federal civilian leadership, to dismantle such archaic albatrosses as Don't Ask, Don't Tell and Don't Pursue that once banned homosexuals followed by the repeal of the combat exclusion policy barring women from serving as combatants, provides reality checks for a traditional institution that for its sustained survival must respond nimbly to an ever-changing civilian society. Women have always represented an important part of this constituency. Yet, as ourstory has repeatedly shown, women's presence in the U.S. military has always been taken for granted as a convenient resource given the willful collective amnesia of the civilian and military leadership (Wechsler Segal 1995, Wagner DeCrew 1995). Now it appears that the full integration of women throughout the military as is called for in the repeal of the combat exclusion policy also hangs in the balance, if not in a static state, another convenient stall tactic for delaying full implementation.

The U.S. military's expedient need for women as a resource has no doubt led to the expansion, if not uneven growth patterns, of women in the military (Wechsler Segal 1995). However, the military's recruitment patterns for certain groups have waned over time as these same groups no longer view military service as either a pathway or prerequisite to citizenship (Harris and Lewis, forthcoming), or as the only option for a viable career (Harris 2009). For example, Moore (1991) has been particularly critical of black women's steadfast dependence on the military as a training ground and employer, where black women are disproportionately assigned by the military to low-skilled support and administrative roles. However, despite the double burden of racism and sexism, black and Hispanic women, for instance, are primarily attracted to the military for economic opportunities (Phillips et al. 1992), and because the military is at least perceived, more so than employers within the civilian sector, to be 'more racially fair' (Segal and Wechsler Segal 2004, p.19). However, in general and unlike during previous generations, African Americans no longer view the military as an employer of choice. As early as during Operations Desert Shield and Storm, blacks began to turn away from the military, and in Nixon's (1993) words, the military was now perceived instead as 'an employer of last resort' (p.59).

Other studies have indicated a pattern of consistent decline in the recruitment and retention of this demographic group (Kleykamp 2006, Military Leadership Diversity Commission (MLDC) 2010). Moreover, youth surveys point to disturbing rates of black disinterest in the military (Carvalho et al. 2008, MLDC 2010). Some of the declines in black recruitment have also been attributed to guidance by elders within the black community as well as black leaders' concern that blacks will bear the disproportionate burden of the nation's future wars while diluting their talent away from the civilian sector (Armor and Gilroy 2009, Asch et al. 2009). Recruitment proves all the more dire during a robust economy, as acknowledged by the military itself (Population Report 2015). Harris (2009), using unpublished data by Moskos (2005), found that white women were more likely to prematurely separate from the military than other segments of the military's population. This is the pattern for women in the enlisted corps. However, similar patterns are reflected in the commissioned corps. For instance, Hosek et al. (2001) confirm that white female officers were not only less likely to remain in the military, but unlike other groups, were also less likely to do so during promotion cycles and were more prone than white male officers to experience shorter retention cycles as a result. White Female officers experience reduced retention rates overall as well, although the incomplete retention cycles do not necessarily explain this finding.

Jones and Roth-Douquet (2017) attack the military as a system in dire need of reform, citing the civilian–military divide as ever widening. They report an urgency for the military to change course for the betterment of American society and in the interest of national security. The military, the authors say, has essentially remained stagnant since World War II despite the change in 21st-century threats that confront the nation. They call for change upon justification of the fact that only 1 percent of the nation now serves in the military coupled with the knowledge that just 7 percent of the public has ever experienced military service, not to mention the startling rate of 75 percent of young adults who are ill prepared for military service because of subpar education, poor physical fitness and/or possessing compromised backgrounds such as having served in prison. Jones and Roth-Douquet's (2017) call to action for reform of the military includes also amending the Selective Service System that requires the registration of male Americans by a certain age as well as to mandate the completion of the military entrance examination for recruitment. The authors view the operations tempo that imposes multiple deployments on military personnel to be unsustainable. Spreading the burden among Americans, they believe, will keep military families intact. The authors also caution that if the Department of Defense (DoD) fails to act, fewer Americans will aspire to military service and those who are still in the military will be more likely to leave the institution.

Yet, recent research finds not only an increasing presence of women in the military but that this increase is largely being borne by minority women (Patten and Parker 2011, Parker et al. 2017). Without a doubt, says the DoD, the military's recruitment picture has consistently loomed below the pre-Great Recession rates of 2007 and 2008 (Population Report 2015). Further, for the fiscal year (FY) 2015, the overall desirability of military service had declined, with many opting to enter college instead. The DoD is additionally challenged by the reality of the times in that, because its budget is constrained, the growth in military pay has weakened (Population Report 2015). As previously stated, the reality has moved the DoD to explore innovative solutions such as partnering with the nation's largest civilian airlines, for instance, as one way of staving off the premature attrition of pilots, most of whom are leaving the military for greater salaries in the civilian sector in light of the military's stagnant bonuses (Maucione 2017).

However, the military's recruitment cycles are characterized by periods of boom and bust (Population Report 2015), which even during times of bust may present some unanticipated and untapped opportunities for growth. The DoD and its military branches have launched female programs in the hope of attracting more women into their ranks. One such initiative includes deploying more female recruiters, increasing maternity leave time for military mothers and approving leave for as long as 12 weeks. These decisions fortuitously come at a time when the 2013 repeal of the combat exclusion policy for phased-in implementation beginning in 2016 but for which former Defense Secretary Ashton Carter accelerated the timetable by opening up all occupations to military women. Women now represent 19.85 percent of the U.S. military (excluding the U.S. Coast Guard, an arm of the U.S. Department of Homeland Security) (active duty: 16.4 percent, Reserve components (including the National Guard): 23.3 percent)

(Population Report 2015), the largest number on record as a percentage of the total force. These findings are also noteworthy in the sense that although the military's end strength of 1.28 million is noticeably 134,000 lower than its FY 2013 total, coming on the heels of the drawdown from both Operations Enduring and Iraqi Freedom and currently in a post-war operations tempo as Operation New Dawn, there are convincing indications that the military has not only heeded the pre-drawdown warnings of the force by both the Military Leadership Diversity Commission (MLDC) and the Defense Advisory Committee on Women in the Services (DACO-WITS) to retain a sustainable cadre of women, especially at the senior levels of the enlisted and commissioned corps, but is expanding in tandem at the recruitment end and installing those initiatives that are more likely to attract a female workforce.

The likely growth in women as combatants, as women are fully integrated into occupations, positions and assignments that were formerly closed to them, will be expected to extend that reach. Although women have yet to achieve parity with men in the military, with their full integration throughout, if implementation proceeds as a condition of repealing the combat exclusion policy, military women will have achieved an important milestone. That is, even as a minority in the military, women will have the potential to realize full agency over time, no longer subjected to what Mazur (1998) dubs the novelty effect given their absence from mission-critical assignments and occupations and positions classified as combat. The double standard hence lies in women's continued and recurrent utility as a convenient yet invaluable asset for deployment during wartime or as the civilian and military leadership deem fit, only to be sidelined and rendered inconsequential again during peacetime. Should the military lose some of its female workforce, as is expected as a consequence of natural or even premature attrition to the civilian sector, it holds much promise that armed with the belated status of full agency, women will be bestowed all of the rights and privileges of full citizenship within a democratic society.

Yet, there is a cautionary note. While this shift in the military's population will undoubtedly change as a condition of like shifts in the general civilian population, the institution must also take heed to ensure that the nation's future defense will not be disproportionately borne by women of color and especially African American women, as Moore (1991) warned some two decades ago. By regulating its recruitment so that its population is representative of the general civilian population, the military can leverage its position politically for sustained support by the public and correspondingly the resources that are allocated from Congress. Though the military is an undemocratic institution, it nonetheless executes the will for policy on behalf of a democracy. In so doing, women will rise to the call for service and in turn the call to arms as a proviso on how the military treats its female workforce and whether or not the institution has been authentic in carrying out the criteria for the full integration of women as per the repeal of the combat exclusion policy. Any action short of these criteria will justly stoke the ire of the country's female electorate, which in many ways as a collective, is an exercise itself in the rights of full citizenship and full agency. Consequently, forcing the military to change its behavior with respect to its female workforce, it is hoped, will in turn translate to women no longer being reduced to invisibility in either active military service or as veterans once they transition from military service, for women's attainment of full agency and by extension full citizenship, is about upholding the tenets of democracy. These are fundamental to the promise of social justice in all walks of American life, including its military.

Bibliography

Armor, D.J., and Gilroy, C.L. (2009). Changing Minority Representation in the U.S. Military. *Armed Forces and Society*, 20, 10, 1–24.

Asch, B.J., Heaton, P., and Savych, B. (2009). *Recruiting Minorities: What Explains Recent Trends in the Army and Navy?* Santa Monica, CA: RAND Corporation.

Carvalho, R., Turner, S., March, S., Yanosky, T., Zucker, A., and Boehmer, M. (2008). *Department of Defense Youth Poll Wave 15: June 2008 Overview Report*. Arlington, VA: Department of Defense. http://jamrs.defense.gov/Portals/20/Documents/Youth_Poll_15.pdf. Retrieved March 24, 2017.

Harris, G.L.A. (2009). The Multifaceted Nature of White Female Attrition in the Military. *Journal of Public Management and Social Policy*, 15, 1, 71–93.

Harris, G.L.A., and Lewis, E.L. (n.d., forthcoming). *Blacks in the Military and Beyond*. Lanham, MD: Lexington Books/Rowman and Littlefield.

Hosek, S.D., Tiemeyer, P., Kilburn, R., Strong, D.A., Ducksworth, S., and Ray, R. (2001). *Minority and Gender Differences in Officer Career Progression*. Santa Monica, CA: RAND Corporation.

Jones, J., and Roth-Douquet, K. (2017). *Serving Those Who Serve. U.S. News and World Report*. May 26. https://bipartisanpolicy.org/article/serving-those-who-serve/. Retrieved June 18, 2017.

Kleykamp, M. (2006). College, Jobs, or the Military? Enlistment During a Time of War. *Social Science Quarterly*, 87, 2, 272–290.

Krislov, S., and Rosenbloom, D.H. (1981). *Representative Bureaucracy and the American Political System*. New York, NY: Praeger Press.

Maucione, S. (2017). Updated: Air Force Meeting with Airlines on Pilot Shortage in May. March 27. Federal News Radio. https://federalnewsradio.com/air-force/2017/03/air-force-meeting-airlines-pilot-shortage-may/. Retrieved June 18, 2017.

Mazur, D.H. (1998). Women, Responsibility and the Military. *Notre Dame Law Review*, 74, 1, 1–45.

Meier, K.J., and Bohte, J. (2001). Structure and Direction: Missing Links in Representative Bureaucracy. *Journal of Public Administration Research and Theory*, 11, 4, 455–470.

Meier, K.J., and Nicholson-Crotty, J. (2006). Gender, Representative Bureaucracy and Law Enforcement. *Public Administration Review*, 66, 6, 850–860.

Military Leadership Diversity Commission (MLDC). (2010). *Propensity to Serve in the Armed Forces: Racial/Ethnic and Gender Differences, Trends, and Causes.* Issue Paper #12. Arlington, VA. http://diversity.defense.gov/Portals/51/Documents/Resources/Commiss... Retrieved May 27, 2017.

Moore, B.L. (1991). African-American Women in the U.S. Military. *Armed Forces and Society*, 17, 3, 363–384.

Moskos, C. (2005). Author communication via e-mail. January 7.

Nixon, R.L. (1993). *Defense Downsizing and Blacks in the Military.* Monterey, CA: Naval Postgraduate School.

Parker, K., Cilluffo, A., and Stepler, R. (2017). 6 Facts About the U.S. Military and Its Changing Demographics. April 13. Pew Research Center, Fact Tank. www.pewresearch.org/fact-tank/2017/04/13/6-facts-about-the-u-s-military-and-its-changing-demographics/. Retrieved June 18, 2017.

Patten, E., and Parker, K. (2011). Women in the U.S. Military: Growing Share, Distinctive Profile. *Pew Social Trends*. December 22. www.pewsocialtrends.org/2011/12/22/women-in-the-u-s-military-growingshare-disctinctive-profile. Retrieved June 18, 2017.

Phillips, R.L., Andrisani, P.J., Daymont, T., et al. (1992). The Economic Returns to Military Service: Race-ethnic Differences. *Social Science Quarterly*, 75, 2, 340–359.

Population Report. (2015). Population Representation in the Military Services. Center for Naval Analyses (CNA). www.cna.org/research/pop-rep. Retrieved March 28, 2017.

Riccucci, N., and Saidel, J.R. (1997). The Representativeness of State-level Bureaucratic Leaders: A Missing Piece of the Representative Bureaucracy Puzzle. *Public Administration Review*, 57, 5, 423–430.

Saltzstein, G.H. (1979). Representative Bureaucracy and Bureaucratic Responsibility: Problems and Prospects. *Administration and Society*, 10, 4, 464–475.

Segal, D.R., and Wechsler Segal, M. (2004). America's Military Population. *Population Bulletin*, 59, 1, 1–42.

Sowa, J.E., and Selden, S.C. (2003). Administrative Discretion and Active Representation: An Expansion of the Theory of Representative Bureaucracy. *Public Administration Review*, 63, 6, 700–710.

Wagner DeCrew, J. (1995). The Combat Exclusion and the Role of Women in the Military. *Hypatia*, 10, 1, 56–73.

Wechsler Segal, M.W. (1995). Women's Military Roles Cross-Nationally, Past, Present, and Future. *Gender and Society*, 9, 6, 757–775.

21 Legal Frameworks Apart
The Military v. Civilian Justice Systems

In the capacity as commander-in-chief, the president of the United States, under the direction of Congress, is authorized to craft federal directives and laws for the purpose of executing military law (Military.com n.d.) in the form of the Uniform Code of Military Justice (UCMJ) (Sherman 1973, Wadsworth n.d.). By way of executive order, the president issues the *Manual for Courts Martial* (MCM). The manual delineates, for instance, those directives under military law for courts martial, stipulating the ceilings or highest forms of punishment for offenses in accordance with the clauses or articles of the UCMJ. Military courts martial range from the most harsh injunctions for offenses from summary courts martial which are rare but where only personnel within the enlisted corps are adjudicated, to special courts martial for offenses considered as moderate in severity, to general courts martial that are reserved for the most serious offenses, and to non-judicial punishment as in Article 15 that shares similar proceedings in characteristics with those of summary courts martial.

Each level of offense dictates the selection of officers who are charged in adjudicating the case (Sherman 1973, Wadsworth n.d.). For example, for a summary courts martial, a commissioned officer, generally at the senior company grade (O-3) or higher, officiates these cases. Here, no juries are present and while having a defense attorney is not a prerequisite, the accused may have a defense attorney present (the Air Force is the exception). For special courts martial, a military judge, both the prosecutor and defense attorneys, and a jury comprising a minimum of three military personnel, are required. For enlisted personnel who stand as the accused, a jury of enlisted personnel can be requested. The jury can also be comprised of and warrant officers. As well, the defendant has the option of a trial solely by a military judge. At the military member's expense, a civilian attorney can also be present. In the case of general courts martial, a military judge is present along with the prosecutor and defense attorneys plus a jury of a minimum of five members. If the accused is an enlisted member, the request that the jury consist of one-third enlisted members can be made. As in the special courts martial, a defendant can choose to also be tried solely by a military judge. The defendant may also choose to have the representation of a civilian attorney but at his or her own expense. Finally, for offenses to be adjudicated in the form of non-judicial punishment or Article 15, the accused commanding officer functions in both roles as judge and jury. While these proceedings are not criminal in nature, the accused still has the option of requesting adjudication via a court martial in lieu of Article 15.

The UCMJ is described as a three-tiered system that is 'commander convened' (p.1398) and 'command centered' (Sherman 1973). For this reason, the adjudication of all courts martial are the sole province of the military. The only departure is trial by the civilian Court of Military Appeals.

By contrast to the UCMJ, the civilian justice system is codified in the U.S. Constitution's Bill of Rights, the first ten of which are amendments to the Constitution, which outlines the basic rights of American citizens and the limits to the government's power (Bill of Rights Institute n.d.). Constructed by James Madison in 1791, the rationale for the Bill of Rights' creation was to preserve the natural rights of the citizenry from the waywardness and overreach of the federal government. For example, the First Amendment is the right to freedom of association and that these rights must not be abridged by the federal government. Another, under the Fourth Amendment, protects the public from the forcible infringement of one's rights by the federal government through unwarranted searches and seizures. The U.S. Constitution thus arms the federal government with sufficient power to do the business of the country on a national level but without trumping the individual rights of its citizens in the process (The White House n.d.). Article III of the Constitution grants the right that every citizen is entitled to an impartial trial to be presided over by a capable judge and a jury of that person's peers. Judges are selected at the federal level based on a dual court system and may preside over cases from the states, involving federal laws and the constitutional rights of citizens (Findlaw n.d.). A dual-tiered system designates federal courts according to Articles I and II of the Constitution.

State courts also adjudicate cases involving state law and even those not within the purview of the federal courts (Findlaw n.d.). Federal judges are further selected under Article III where federal cases are heard by general trial courts. The courts include the district court, courts of appeals, and the High Court – the U.S. Supreme Court. Federal judges have lifetime appointments. The selection of judges under Article I for such categories as bankruptcies, taxes and even some military courts, have limited times of appointment, or ten years, after which time they can be reappointed. At the state level, state judges are selected under myriad systems: by appointment, as a result of merit, partisan elections and nonpartisan elections.

While both the UCMJ and the civilian court systems are an outgrowth and emanate from federal law, both diverge in significant ways. Military law is so structured in code that it is more restrictive in nature, thus limiting the rights of military personnel (LawGuru.com 2012, Gilley 2012). One stark example of these differences is that while civilian law, under the Fourth Amendment, protects citizens from unwarranted searches and seizures by the federal government, no such protection exists under military law (Gilley 2012). The courts martial system via the UCMJ confers harsher levels of punishment should the accused be convicted (Gilley 2012, LawGuru.com 2012). The selection of judges to convene over cases or trials makes military law distinct from civilian law. Fundamentally, the military selects itself to adjudicate matters concerning its personnel. Even the appeals process for both systems differ. The UCMJ follows its own chain of command where in turn each military branch has its own form of appellate system (LawGuru.com 2012). The civilian justice system affords the accused or litigant independent modes of adjudication where cases can advance through various state and federal jurisdictions up to and including the U.S. Supreme Court. Also, although military attorneys function in a similar role in courts martial as do civilian attorneys in courts of law, their specific training requires them to do so as military personnel within the confines of representatives of the Judge Advocate General (JAG).

While military and civilian laws are equally entrenched and thereby systems apart, military law is hailed as 'unique' (Lederer and Hundley 1994, p.63). The civilian court system, especially at the federal level, given lifetime appointments, enjoys a level of autonomy and impartiality not afforded to military judges, who are not only appointed but exercise little authority for they themselves are subject to the very system within which they operate, and even as they, at first glance, are present to represent and protect the interests of their clients. However, as members of the JAG, the work of military attorneys may be called into question as in the long run, whose interests do they actually represent – those of their clients or those of the military? This is where the military attorneys' autonomy is called into question.

There have been cases where rulings of either the appointed military judge and/or assigned attorney of the accused have been suspected of not being impartial and/or were influenced by the whims of the military rather than allowing the adjudicatory process to simply take its natural course. Military judges have been accused of impropriety and particularly so at the time of sentencing. In one case, the secretary of the Navy, albeit in vain, attempted to usurp the system by influencing the Navy's JAG to terminate the appointed trial judge, himself an officer in the Navy, because the secretary disagreed with the judge's ruling (Lederer and Hundley 1994). Similarly, some JAGs have criticized the nature of their assignments as retaliatory in kind and that may result in non-selection for promotion given those assignments. Consequently, the civilian body, the American Judges Association, concluded that:

> without tenure, a military judge is subject to transfer from the service judiciary should he or she render unpopular evidentiary rulings,

findings or sentences. There is no protection from retaliatory action by dissatisfied supervisors in the chain of command.

(Letter from the American Judges Association to the President of the United States; July 21, 1992, in Lederer and Hundley 1994, p.633)

Likewise, the perception exists that judges who make unpopular rulings within the military hierarchy are endangering their possibilities for promotion because that same hierarchy is the system that makes selections for promotion (Lederer and Hundley 1994). In *Weiss v. United States, 1994*, the U.S. Supreme Court opined that specifically for military trials and to allay concerns, it appears that a satisfactory balance between autonomy and capability has been struck by the military judiciary system. Of course, this is an opinion which the Court of Military Appeals did not deem unsuitable to weigh in on, though its concurrence with Justice Scalia's remarks that this is exactly the goal that the military has achieved given the exemplary performance of its cadre of military lawyers (Lederer and Hundley 1994). Declare Lederer and Hundley (1994), in many respects, the Court of Military Appeals is denying the existence of the bias and undue influence in the UCMJ.

In another but more recent case, also involving the Navy, the Navy's top brass in the JAG were accused of unlawfully scheming to influence the case and the sentencing of a Navy SEAL who was accused of rape (Prime 2017). The unjustified interference by two flag officers who represent the Navy's JAG hierarchy resulted in the Court of Appeals for the armed forces' decision to ban any further adjudication of the case by either Navy or Marine Corps judges. However, nowhere is this systemic bias more evident than in the adjudication of sexually related offenses in the military and the military's wanton influence, despite civilian leadership, in influencing the outcome. Senator Kirsten Gillibrand (D-NY) has marshaled a force of her colleagues across political party lines, all in an effort to remove the discretionary authority of commanders to adjudicate such cases by assigning these cases to an independent body of senior ranking military attorneys who are not in the commanders' respective commands (Tilghman 2013). In the face of the senators' dogged determination, there was even a rare rebuke of the military from Senator John McCain (R-AZ), himself a military man and one of the most ardent supporters of the military (Briggs 2013), that until the institution gets its act together, he would discourage any woman from aspiring to the military pending its resolution of the sexual assault epidemic. Yet, given the military's undue influence, Gillibrand and her colleagues still failed to convince the Senate's body as a whole of the overwhelming need for this independence.

Illustrating the deep-rooted indifference by the military despite its rhetoric of intolerance to the prevalence of sexual assault and related offenses in the military, the Air Force's Lieutenant General Craig

Franklin, then commander of the Third Air Force in Europe, dismissed the indictment of a convicted pilot, Lieutenant Colonel James Wilkerson, of sexual assault (Whitlock 2013). When grilled by especially the women senators as to his rationale for this decision, the commander claimed that the evidence was insufficient to prove the pilot's guilt. An incensed Senator Claire McCaskill (D-MO), a member of the Senate Armed Services Committee and a former prosecutor as her state's attorney general, fired back: 'It looks like somebody taking care of one of their guys.' Another case also involved the Air Force, and this time a female commander no less, who was destined for career greatness but was sabotaged by her own short-sightedness as to the long-term implications of her actions. Like the previous case and against the advice of legal counsel, Air Force Lieutenant General Susan Helms overturned the guilty verdict of an Air Force captain who was convicted of sexual assault (Whitlock 2013). Senator McCaskill was mystified by the commander's reason, which was that the commander considered the testimony of the captain more trustworthy than that of the victim. Unconvinced by this testimony, Senator McCaskill said, 'With her action, Lieutenant General Helms sent a damaging message to survivors of sexual assault.' She continued: 'They can take the difficult and painful step of reporting the crime, they can endure the agony involved in being subjected to intense questioning often aimed at putting the blame on them, and they can experience a momentary sense of justice in knowing that they were believed when their attacker is convicted and sentenced, only to have that justice ripped away with the stroke of a pen' (Whitlock 2013). As Harris (2015) suspects, this decision in the end proved fatal for the commander's career.

Yet, perhaps what former Air Force Chief of Staff General Mark Welsh invoked as evidence of 'a hookup culture' (Clift 2013) was a startling admission and indictment, in this case of the Air Force leadership's take on the epidemic, that is sexual assault, and the corresponding seeming disinterest that no doubt permeates all levels of leadership in the institution. For the military women and some men whose lives have been destroyed by the curse of sexual assault, the UCMJ has brought little comfort, if any relief, that the military will take care of its own.

Over 40 years ago, Sherman (1973) argued that the fledgling UCMJ, he feared, would erode, and the unquestioned yielding of military law to civilian rule supports the divergence of the systems, but admitted that the UCMJ should be free of the control of civilian leadership. Sherman reminds us of multiple instances whereby the civilian courts have unnecessarily inserted themselves where judicial ruling was the purview of the military alone. Another reason for reduced civilian control of military law that Sherman summoned is that military society is distinct from that of civilian society, therefore calling for a separate legal structure altogether from the military. Third, this distinction of the UCMJ that Sherman defines as one part judicial and one part disciplinary, is the reason for a system of courts martial to adjudicate cases. Finally, some Western democracies were then transforming the courts martial system of their respective militaries to civilian court-like procedures hoping to exert impartiality into the process over that of discipline (Sherman 1973).

Another shortcoming of the military justice system is reflected in the Feres Doctrine. Members of the military make enormous sacrifices in defense of the nation that they are sworn to protect and defend, oftentimes at great risk to their health and personal safety. Under the current policy of the Federal Tort Claims Act (FTCA) and Feres Doctrine, the men and women of the military (and their families) have no legal recourse to hold the U.S. government responsible for any injuries that they sustain or death during military service, regardless of whether or not there is evidence of gross negligence or malpractice on the part of the U.S. military (*Feres v. United States, 1950*; U.S. House of Representatives, n.d.).

Outside of the military, American citizens enjoy the right to seek legal redress via tort law in cases where harm is done to them. According to the Cornell University Law School Legal Information Institute (1992a), a tort is defined as 'an act or omission that gives rise to injury or harm to another and amounts to a civil wrong for which courts impose liability ... and the primary aims of tort law are to provide relief to injured parties for harms caused by others, to impose liability on parties responsible for the harm, and to deter others from committing harmful acts' (para.1–2). Tort actions differ from criminal liability in three main ways: 1) torts address private wrongs against citizens (versus public wrongs against larger society); 2) torts do not necessarily have to prove intent (whereas it is required in cases of criminal liability); and 3) tort actions are intended to compensate the victim for damages (versus punishing the wrongdoer), in the forms of monetary compensation, an injunction, or restitution (Legal Information Institute 1992a).

Just as individuals within an organization would be liable in tort actions, so too is the U.S. government. As such, the FTCA of 1948, 'recognizes liability for negligent or wrongful acts or omissions of its employees acting within the scope of their official duties' (U.S. House of Representatives n.d., para.2). Under this statute, the U.S. government would serve as the defendant and be held liable, not individual governmental employees (U.S. House of Representatives n.d.)

The original intent of the FTCA was to transfer the responsibility (and subsequent workload) of examining evidence of tort claims against the government from the legislative branch to the judicial branch (Justia, U.S. Supreme Court 2017b). In cases where private claims of malpractice and negligence are made against military personnel, it was thought that the FTCA would be a redundant system of redress because of the existing system for service members and their dependents, namely the U.S. Department of Veterans Affairs (*Feres v. United States, 1950*).

In order to hold the U.S. government liable in accordance with the FTCA, a claimant must show that the injury or property damage was by a federal government employee acting within the official scope of their duties, and that the employee was acting negligently or wrongfully and that these acts caused the injury or damage (U.S. House of Representatives n.d.).

However, there are 14 exceptions to the FTCA, 28 US Code 2680, one of which exempts 'any claim arising out of the combatant activities of the military or naval forces, or the Coast Guard during a time of war' (Legal Information Institute 1992b, subpara. j), a direct result of the 1950 Feres Doctrine. This has had long-term policy implications for the perception of government accountability, and the legal recourse available to military members.

The Feres Doctrine refers to the landmark 1950 U.S. Supreme Court case, *Feres v. United States*, a collapsing of three separate cases into one decision – *Feres v. United States*, *Jefferson v. the United States*, and *Griggs v. United States*. The common thread in the three cases is that soldiers who suffered injury as a direct result of the negligence and malpractice of the U.S. military, held the federal government as responsible for such actions. The question posed to the Court was whether or not the FTCA was applicable in these cases that occurred during military service (*Feres v. United States, 1950*). The ruling concluded that the federal government was not liable under the FTCA for injuries or death that occurred as a direct result of military service (*Feres v. United States, 1950*).

The U.S. Supreme Court determined that the FTCA was not applicable in the case of incidents that occurred during military service as the original intention of the FTCA was never intended for military matters to be decided by civilian judges outside of the military justice system (Justia, U.S. Supreme Court 2017a). It was thought that doing so would significantly undermine and damage the command and control element of the military, exposing military leaders to personal liability for the injuries or death of the service members under their command (Natelson 2009).

> Without exception, the relationship of military personnel to the Government has been governed exclusively by federal law. We do not think that Congress, in drafting this Act, created a new cause of action dependent on local law for service-connected injuries or death due to negligence. We cannot impute to Congress such a radical departure from established law in the absence of express congressional command.
> (*Feres v. United States, 1950*, Section 146, para.2).

For nearly 70 years, the Feres Doctrine has essentially provided blanket immunity to the military and the federal government by protecting them from tort claims made by military service members (Natelson 2009, National Institute of Military Justice 2001, Veterans Equal Rights Protection Advocacy (VERPA) 2001). Despite the fact that the law has not been reviewed since its ruling in 1950, the Feres Doctrine continues to be used as legal precedent for preventing service members from accessing the same legal redress afforded to them as citizens for damages, charges of liability, negligence or malpractice that they experienced in any other workplace in the U.S., outside of the military (Natelson 2009).

Consequently, the Feres Doctrine and its continued intra-military immunity, have been heavily criticized; jurists and veteran advocacy groups have called for its reform and repeal purporting that its continued use significantly diminishes the human and civil rights of service members, and degrades the accountability of the military to the general public (VERPA 2001). The continued use of the 'incident to military service' standard that the Feres Doctrine employs is problematic for two main reasons. First and foremost, the doctrine has not been reviewed and examined critically for its relevance and application to the modern-day military (National Institute of Military Justice 2001). And second, the doctrine limits valid claims of negligence, liability and malpractice against the military and has little to no relevance to the duties being performed by service members (VERPA 2001, p.1).

Nowhere is this 'incident to service test' in more need of review and reform than in the cases of sexual harassment and sexual assault in the military, which occur in the context of military service, yet in no way can be considered related to the expectation or the performance of military duties (Natelson 2009). As one of many examples, in *Cioca v. Rumsfeld, 2013*, some 28 service members who were sexually assaulted, filed a civil suit against the Department of Defense, seeking compensatory damages for incidents that occurred during military service. The plaintiffs claimed that the Secretary of Defense's failure to provide a military justice system that consistently investigated sexual assaults and rapes, prosecuted perpetrators, enforced military law and complied with Congressionally mandated reforms, directly contributed to a military culture that is tolerant of sexual assault.

However, the case was dismissed by both the U.S. District Court and the U.S. Court of Appeals because the case met the 'incident to service test' that was first articulated in *Feres v. United States, 1950* (*Cioca v. Rumsfeld, 2013*, Section 513). Consequently, the plaintiffs cannot be compensated for damages. The disconnect that occurs in cases of sexual harassment and sexual assault is that this test should not be considered an equivalent and foreseeable consequence of military service (Dick 2012, Hunter 2007), such as the potential loss of 'life, limb, or eyesight' (Department of Defense 2012, p.2).

On the 50th anniversary of the conception of the UCMJ, a formal review was conducted by the Cox Commission (National Institute of Military Justice 2001). Although the UCMJ was reviewed in 1968 and again in 1983, it has never been subject to either public examination or scrutiny outside of the military (National Institute of Military Justice 2001). The underlying goal of the commission was to find areas of opportunity for military justice reform vis-à-vis the creation of recorded testimony, and the identification of specific recommendations for improvement and issues worthy of continued investigation and consideration (National Institute of Military Justice 2001).

One of the significant agenda items of the Cox Commission included a discussion as to the continued use of the Feres Doctrine and its applicability to modern-day tort practice (National Institute of Military Justice 2001). The commission included testimony and participation on behalf of various veteran advocacy groups like the Veterans Equal Rights Protection Advocacy (VERPA), which initiated a nationwide petition to reform or repeal the Feres Doctrine, including other antiquated laws in the UCMJ such as those concerning adultery and fraternization (VERPA 2001). However, the commission concluded that further study of the use of the Feres Doctrine was necessary and that critically reviewing and scrutinizing Feres would show a gesture of good faith to military service members about the government's continued commitment to fair and just accountability practices in matters of military personnel (National Institute of Military Justice 2001).

Next to the UCMJ, the Feres Doctrine has been one of the most significant pieces of policy impacting the military justice system since the 1950s, when both policies were enacted. Continued use of this policy is incongruent with the vast modernization that the U.S. military has undergone in its quest to remain a relevant superpower, especially with the shift in demographics and operations.

Numerous jurists and veteran advocacy groups have called for the reform or repeal of the Feres Doctrine, especially in incidents of sexual harassment and sexual assault, which, despite meeting the 'incident to military service' test, bear no relevance to the expectation of duties performed as a member of the military, and as such, should not be used as legal precedent in providing immunity to the military (*Cioca v. Rumsfeld, 2013*, VERPA 2001). Further, it is imperative that the Feres Doctrine be a significant part of the discussion by the Congressional Armed Services Committees when they convene to weigh the merits of using a Selective Service System versus a National Service model (114th Congress of the U.S. 2016). Applying the Feres Doctrine is problematic in the current all-volunteer military model. However, in a mandated system like National Service or military conscription, the legal implications would be even more complex and nuanced, warranting greater scrutiny for reform prior to its inception.

Interestingly enough, Sherman (1973) cites the military court systems of most European countries, where their militaries have reverted to civilian control and in the end concluded that the conversion from military law to civilian law was beneficial. Why? Because, even the UCMJ as Sherman described, offers an inferior justice system for its military personnel. This is further evidenced by the military's continued use of and reliance on the Feres Doctrine to remain insulated from culpability for such criminal offenses as sexual assault. Surprisingly, Sherman recommended a reform of the UCMJ to more closely resemble either the system of Britain or systems that would structurally remain separate. The military system of using courts martial would survive but, Sherman contends, would provide service members with a more effective form of justice.

As witnessed in the many circumstances that have prompted the U.S. civilian courts' intervention into that of military matters, including two such cases highlighted by Harris (2015) in her interviews with the main litigants as in *Frontierro v. Richardson, 1973* (Air Force) and *Owens v. Brown, 1978* (Navy), and where given the outcome of these cases, one ruling rendered by the High Court and the other ruling at the federal district court level, the lives and status of military women in general have markedly improved as a result. More recently, had it not been for the intervention of civilian advocate groups like the American Civil Liberties Union (ACLU) and the Service Women's Action Network (SWAN), to name a few, the fate of still disenfranchised groups like homosexuals under the Don't Ask, Don't Tell and Don't Pursue policy and women under the oppressive yolk of the combat exclusion policy would have remained unchallenged and constitutional. Incidentally, Harris (2015) also interviewed and captured the circumstances surrounding one woman veteran, then the only homosexual to legally serve in the military pending the clarification of the Don't Ask, Don't Tell and Don't Pursue policy, but whose unwitting defiance as a civilian while still serving in the military helped to move the needle forward to eventually result in the landmark repeal of the unjust policy.

However, it was by invoking the basic tenets of the U.S. Constitution, in this case, specifically the Equal Protection and Citizenship Clauses of the 14th Amendment, that the military justice system was declared insufficient and perhaps ill equipped in its structure to both advance and secure the basic rights of its personnel as called for by the Constitution. The civilian courts' insertion into the affairs of the military as they pertain to its workforce need not mean the undermining of the UCMJ or military justice system, but when appropriate, the civilian courts are necessary to function as the final arbiters in order to preserve and enforce service members' fundamental rights as American citizens when it is believed that they are being abridged.

Bibliography

Bill of Rights Institute. (n.d.). Bill of Rights of the United States of America (1791). www.billofrightsinstitute.org/founding-documents/bill-of-rights/. Retrieved March 24, 2017.

Briggs, B. (2013). McCain Cannot Give 'Unqualified Support' for Women Joining the Military Until Crisis Resolved. *NBC News.* June 4. http://usnews.nbcnews.com/_news/2013/06/04/18729878-mccain-cannot-give-unqualified-support-for-women-joining-the-military-until-crisis-resolved. Retrieved April 4, 2017.

Clift, E. (2013). Air Force Blames Increase in Military Rape Hookup Culture. *U.S. New Report.* May 8. www.thedailybeast.com/articles/2013/05/08/air-force-general-blames-increase-in-military-rape-on-hookup-culture.html. Retrieved April 3, 2017.

Department of Defense. (2012). Instruction: Patient Movement (PM). Number 6000.11. www.dtic.mil/whs/directives/corres/pdf/600011p.pdf

Dick, K. (2012). *The Invisible War (Documentary)*. U.S.: Cinedigm/Docurama.

Feres v. United States, 340 U.S. 135 (1950).

Findlaw. (n.d.). How Are Judges Selected? http://litigation.findlaw.com/legal-system/how-are-judges-selected.html. Retrieved April 2, 2017.

Gilley, C. (2012). How Is Military Law Different from Regular Civilian Law? June 16. *Quora*. www.quora.com/How-is-military-law-different-than-regular-civilian-law. Retrieved April 2, 2017.

Harris, G.L.A. (2015). *Living Legends and Fully Agency: Implications of Repealing the Combat Exclusion Policy.* New York, NY: Taylor & Francis Group, a division of CRC Press.

Hunter, M. (2007). *Honor Betrayed: Sexual Abuse in America's Military.* Fort Lee, NJ: Barricade Books.

Justia, U.S. Supreme Court. (2017a). Chappell v. Wallace, 462 U.S. 296(1983). https://supreme.justia.com/cases/federal/us/462/296/case.html Retrieved March 19, 2017.

Justia, U.S. Supreme Court. (2017b). Feres v. United States, 340 U.S. 135(1950). https://supreme.justia.com/cases/federal/us/340/135/case.html Retrieved March 19, 2017.

LawGuru.com. (2012). Five Major Differences in Military v. Civilian Law. January 18. www.quora.com/How-is-military-law-different-than-regular-civilian-law. Retrieved April 2, 2017.

Lederer, F.I., and Hundley, B.S. (1994). Needed: An Independent Military Judiciary – A Proposal to Amend the Uniform Code of Military Justice. *William and Mary Bill of Rights Journal*, 3, 2, 629–680.

Legal Information Institute. (1992a). *Tort Definition*. Cornell University Law School. www.law.cornell.edu/wex/tort. Retrieved March 19, 2017.

Legal Information Institute. (1992b). *Federal Tort Claims Act, 28 U.S. Code 2680-Exceptions.* Cornell University Law School. www.law.cornell.edu/uscode/text/28/2680. Retrieved March 19, 2017.

Military.com. (n.d.). *The Uniform Code of Military Justice (UCMJ)*.

Natelson, R. (2009). A Case for Federal Oversight of Military Sexual Harassment. *Clearinghouse REVIEW Journal of Poverty Law and Policy*, 277–281.

National Institute of Military Justice. (2001). *Report of the Commission on the 50th Anniversary of the Uniform Code of Military Justice.* www.loc.gov/rr/frd/Military_Law/pdf/Cox-Commission-Report-2001.pdf Retrieved March 16, 2017.

114th Congress of the U.S. (2016). *National Defense Authorization Bill for Fiscal Year 2017.* www.congress.gov/114/bills/s2943/BILLS-114s2943enr.pdf. Retrieved December 15, 2016.

Prime, C. (2017). Did Admirals Illegally Conspire Against Navy SEAL in Rape Case? Court Orders Investigation. June 20. *The San Diego Union Tribune*. www.sandiegouniontribune.com/military/sd-me-seal-case-20170620-story.html. Retrieved April 4, 2017.

Sherman, E.F. (1973). Military Justice Without Military Control. *Indiana University Maurer School of Law*, 1398–1425. Paper 2265.

Tilghman, A. (2013). Pentagon Advisory Panel: Strip Commanders' Ability to Prosecute Sexual Assaults. September 30. www.armytimes.com/article/20130930/NEWS06/309300029/Pentagon-advisory-panel-Strip-commanders-ability-prosecute-sexual-assaults. Retrieved April 4, 2017.

U.S. House of Representatives. (n.d.). *Federal Tort Claims Act*. www.house.gov/content/vendors/leases/tort.php. March 16, 2017.

Veterans Equal Rights Protection Advocacy (VERPA). (2001). Point Paper presented at the Commission on the 50th Anniversary of the Uniform Code of Military Justice, 53–66. www.loc.gov/rr/frd/Military_Law/pdf/Cox-Commission-Report-2001.pdf. March 16, 2017.

Wadsworth, M. (n.d.). How the Military Justice System Works. The Military Justice System in a Nutshell. *NOLO*. www.nolo.com/legal-encyclopedia/how-the-military-justice-system-works.html. Retrieved March 23, 2017.

The White House. (n.d.). *The Constitution*. www.whitehouse.gov/1600/constitution. Retrieved May 26, 2017.

Whitlock, C. (2013). General's Promotion Blocked Over Her Dismissal of Sexual-Assault Verdict. *Washington Post*, May 6. http://articles.washingtonpost.com/2013-05-06/world/39060954_1_sexual-assault-jury-commander. Retrieved April 4, 2017.

Part VII
Confronting Wicked Problems: The Role of Health and Violence

Sarah Emma Edmonds, Lizzie Compton, Catherine Davidson, Mary Galloway, Loreta Janeta Velasquez, and Maria Lewis are just six of the hundreds of women warriors discovered to have assumed male identities to fight during the U.S. Civil War but who remain ghosts of the ourstoric past (Schulte, 2013). The genesis of their common desires and actions held similarities to their male counterparts – to show patriotism, to support their respective causes, for adventure, to leave home for various reasons, and to earn money. These women suffered the same injuries as a result of violent exchanges during conflicts, were captured as enemy combatants, and succumbed to the ravages of human disease as those with whom they fought shoulder to shoulder. Upon discovery of their secret, usually following treatment for an injury or illness, or after giving birth, these sheroic women were either accepted as soldiers, sent home or imprisoned – as determined by the whim of the Confederate or Union male hierarchy. Vocal factions were critical of women seeking a life beyond their male-imposed, Victorian rules determined by a gendered society which either used labels such as 'crazy, whores, or homosexuals' or diminished the stories of women's bravery as hoaxes. Further, ourstory-erasing ideologues who subscribed to Separate Spheres of gender, demeaned their service by discounting their roles as soldiers in order to ridicule, misrepresent and malign them simply as prostitutes. Thus, these courageous women were deprived of the honor and celebration they so rightly deserved.

Part VII opens several lenses in order to magnify and detail the landscape and the complexity of inequality in the U.S. military, its causation and the resulting disequilibrium to military operations and the implications for health. The biopsychosocial lens enables deconstruction of the multifaceted dimensions in characterizing violence in the military context, the arrangement of conditions that precede and enable violent acts, and the health effects. A comprehensive exploration of military sexual trauma characterizes the biological, psychological and social effects of these acts of violence and disregard. Further, a look toward leadership, a rethinking of military culture and policy, and local changes as countervailing and preventive offer hope for disrupting a disturbing trend with implications for diminished quality of life, an undermined military mission, and breached public trust. The social-ecological lens enables the examination of layers of society and interactive effects at the confluence of multiple, embedded layers from individual to societal. Through the establishment of complexity by the use of the previous lenses, gender inequality in the U.S. military is characterized through the lens of wicked problems. The wicked problem framework helps to intellectualize the conundrums encountered while attempting to explicate the uncertainty, risk and social complexity in grappling with an unresolved and ourstorically relevant imbalance.

Bibliography

Schulte, B. (2013). Women soldiers fought, bled and died in the Civil War, then were forgotten. The Washington Post, April 29. https://www.washingtonpost.com/local/women-soldiers-fought-bled-and-died-in-the-civil-war-then-were-forgotten/2013/04/26/fa722dba-a1a2-11e2-82bc-511538ae90a4_story.html?utm_term=.60d9f16c8fa1. Retrieved May 2, 2017.

22 Determinants of Health

Introduction

Both individual readiness and group readiness in an integrated and gender-inclusive military are essential to assure high performance of the U.S. military. Readiness implies that each individual is able to perform at peak physical, psychological, and emotional condition within a cohesive environment (Hopkins-Chadwick 2006). Cohesiveness describes the presence of multi-level bonding and trust-building mechanisms, including an enabling culture – an essential condition for organizational and mission success (Siebold 2007). To meet the mission readiness imperative of the military, significant work must continue toward identifying and removing structural and normalized barriers to peak health for women active duty troops. Likewise, women veterans newly reintegrating to civilian status and already reintegrated women veterans must be assured that military institutions and the institutions of civil society across both the social and physical environments can support and ensure peak physical, psychological, and emotional health through each woman's lifespan (U.S. DHHS n.d.).

The priority for achieving peak health lies in providing the opportunity for women to attain the highest level of health. Health-encouraging strategies include reducing inequities or barriers; reducing or eliminating health disparities where there exists a difference in health status between populations based on gender and other factors; and seeking to achieve health equality by targeting social determinants of health. Social determinants seek to evaluate imbalances that may disadvantage women as the minority gender population in the U.S. military service and veteran contexts (American Public Health Association n.d.). This aggregation of priorities is designed to facilitate action and ensure that women are afforded equal treatment by enlisting the social determinants of health, public health framework in discovery and the elimination of barriers for military women. This continuation of a wicked problem articulation and remedial strategy crafting is intended to help construct and understand the complex web of gender-based and institutionalized hazards encountered in navigating the military service continuum especially for women.

First, this chapter examines the definition, origins and dimensions of social determinants of health, and illuminates the alignment and application of Department of Defense (DoD) peak health strategies and goals with the U.S. Department of Health and Human Services (DHHS) Healthy People 2020 (HP 2020) framework. Second, it elucidates institutional and cultural barriers that are hostile to women in achieving peak health, and projects a vision for overcoming barriers to health equality for women across the military service continuum. Finally, the chapter highlights the importance of access to healthcare for women veterans given the associated mental health issues at play.

Social Determinants of Health

Michael Marmot and Jessica Allen (Marmot and Allen 2014) have been vocal advocates and respected luminaries touting research evidence correlating and prioritizing a variety of upstream factors (as opposed to a sole focus on downstream, behavior-based approaches) that affect individual and population health outcomes. The upstream approach takes into account broader social, economic and environmental risk conditions that determine the choices that individuals can make, and have more influence on health than lifestyle factors per se. Programs that overlook the broader social, economic and environmental context are unlikely to effectively improve health outcomes for an entire population. This macro-level emphasis elevates the criticality of changing institutions, policies, programs and culture to support health outcomes (Raphael 2003). Upstream factors will be a main consideration applied to women's military experience in examining social determinants.

The research evidence on determinants of health has, over time, gained significant traction and policy relevance across various social institutions including the World Health Organization's Commission on Social Determinants of Health, U.S. Health and Human Services Healthy People goals, Centers for Disease Control and Prevention, preventive medicine components of the U.S. military and Veterans Health Administration. The U.S. DHHS posits the definition of social determinants of health as:

> ... conditions in the environments in which people are born, live, learn, work, play, worship, and age that affect a wide range of health, functioning, and quality-of-life outcomes and risks. Conditions (e.g., social, economic, and physical) in these various environments and settings (e.g., school, church, workplace, and neighborhood) have been referred to as 'place.'[1] In addition to the more material attributes of 'place,' the patterns of social engagement and sense of security and wellbeing are also affected by where people live. Resources that enhance quality of life can have a significant influence on population health outcome.
>
> (U.S. DHHS n.d.)

Furthering the scope of objectives for social determinants in the U.S., the Advisory Committee on National Health Promotion and Disease Prevention *Objectives for 2020* has augmented the focus to describe 'societal' determinants of health highlighting that social structure has a significant impact on health of populations. These social structures include the interactions between social and physical environments. This reinforces the complexity of upstream structural conditions that either create barriers or serve as enablers that can lead to either downstream adverse health outcomes or increase health improvement outcomes.

The biopsychosocial model provides an organizing construct for examining the social determinants of health in the military context (Bloeser and McCoy 2012). The authors presented research examining social determinants of health and wellbeing influencing (or most likely to influence) veterans' health across systems and, in addition, articulated multi-level interventions including the notion of policy change when structural conditions were forcing unhealthy choices and, subsequently, poor health outcomes.

Using a biopsychosocial construct applied to military sexual trauma (MST) and sexual trauma pre-enlistment provides a rich example to illustrate the potential for consequential effects for both active duty and veteran women across all dimensions – biological, psychological and social. According to Himmelfarb et al. (2006), as cited in Kintzle et al. (2015), women who enlist in the military have higher rates of childhood sexual trauma than nonmilitary women. Women with pre-military service sexual trauma were also found to have a higher chance of subjection to post-service sexual trauma as veterans. Accumulation of various types of trauma (combat violence compounded by sexual assault trauma) by women in the military has important implications for adverse physical and psychological health going forward. Further, MST (discussed elsewhere in this book) can be an extremely debilitating condition that can lead to a constellation of adverse health outcomes. Psychological effects frequently include post-traumatic stress disorder (PTSD). Additional adverse social effects can be exacerbated through re-victimization by receiving an involuntary discharge on the basis of health concerns and/or lead to a decision not to reenlist after serving, i.e., career derailment (Smith 2015). Further, negative repercussions and social isolation from peers and/or from those higher up in the chain of command after reporting an event might be experienced. Re-victimization can also result during determination of disability for MST, which can be highly subjective. MST confirmations are approved at a much lower rate than those of other service-connected disabilities with inconsistencies of disability acceptance across geographic regions (Smith 2015).

Siegrist and Marmot (2004), as cited in Marmot et al. (2006, location no.2559) define the term *'psychosocial environment'* as the range of opportunities available to an individual to enhance his or her wellbeing, sense of productivity, and positive self-experience. The term is frequently applied to the work environment and socio-structural conditions. Traumatic experiences can exact a toll on an individual's sense of wellbeing, self-esteem, and ability to accomplish tasks. When any service-related trauma is left untreated and credibility of a service member is challenged, there can be a devastating effect on the sense of social cohesion in active duty and post-service treatment, leading to the possibility of substance abuse, homelessness, joblessness, entry into the criminal justice system, and attempted or completed suicide (Stansfeld 2009, U.S. Department of Labor 2010). The effects can be cascading and family members are adversely impacted, with children, if present, more severely. The biological dimension of unregulated stress is intimately integrated across whole-body systems. The adverse effects on the neurobiology of the individual under stress can affect cardiovascular health, metabolic changes, immune function, and abridge life expectancy. Although many of these effects are reversible, an individual in this category can become socially withdrawn, feel alienated, and manifest distrust and aversion to institutions where equality and assuredness of physical, psychological and emotional health and support should be expected (Marmot et al. 2006).

Why are Social Determinants Important to Women in the Military?

Gender inequality and minority status are current issues that have been highlighted within the wicked problem and social determinants of health (SDOH) literature (Mascarenhas 2009, U.S. DHHS n.d.). While the gender inequality discussion is threaded throughout this book, the added layer of minority status escalates complexity for women in the military. Intersectionality has been explicated in Part II of this book. We use that discussion as a platform to examine gender and minority status in the U.S. military and specifically women veterans with many of the complex intricacies of health issues.

U.S. Population Data Based on Sex

Even though the 2010 U.S. Census data reported that the female proportion of the U.S. population was 50.8 percent, women only comprised 15.5 percent of active duty military, 19.0 percent of National Guard and Reserve forces, and 9.4 percent of the total veteran population in 2015, but with a growing presence (Women Veterans Report 2017). The minority status of women in the military and those who are veterans has resulted in a lag in funding priority for and/or interest in gender-specific research, policy focused on gender equality, and access to resources as well as different treatment. For example, an investigative report by Diantonio (2017) found that mammogram access in Department of Veterans Affairs (VA) hospitals has limited availability in some regions, with only 60 out of 168 VA hospitals providing access to the life-saving technology at this time (with more planned in the future). In fact, at the time of the report, the technology was unavailable at any Kansas VA facility within the entire state. Upon inquiry, the Kansas City VA spokesperson responded that the VA had explored adding a mammogram machine on site, but still does not have enough women who need those services to justify the cost, staffing, and space for the machine. This slow response has placed women (as well as men since the American Cancer Society estimates about 2,470 new cases of invasive breast cancer in males and about 460 men will die from breast cancer in 2017)[2] at a health disadvantage.

U.S. Military Personnel Based on Sex

Based on the February 2017 DoD, Defense Manpower Data Center (DMDC) Active Duty Personnel File (updated monthly), including military academies, there are an average of 17.35 percent women officers in all military branches and 15.69 percent of women enlisted personnel (DoD DMDC 2017). The total sum of DoD officer and enlisted active duty personnel is 15.98 percent. This is within a population of 1,278,922. The number of women appointed as military academy cadets and midshipmen is 23.75 percent or a population of 12,895. The grand total of females across both population groups is 16.06 percent of 1,291,817. These data imply that as cadets graduate and move on to active duty, the total percentage of women across all branches should increase over time as well as the future female veteran population.[3]

The gender profile for women in the Reserves includes 19 percent female members or 157,052 women out of 826,106 total personnel (DoD Military OneSource 2015, p.66). The population of female enlisted members is 19 percent or 132,011 women out of 694,977 total personnel. The population of female Reserve officers is 19.1 percent or 24,619 women out of 131,129 total personnel, based on 2015 data (DoD Military OneSource 2015, p.67). Thus, Reserve forces have a slightly higher percentage of women.

It is noteworthy that the percentage of women diminishes with higher rank for both the enlisted and commissioned officer personnel (DoD DMDC 2017). The average percentage of women across all active duty branches as an E-1 is 15.68 percent (DoD DMDC 2017). The average female population at E-9 is 8.8 percent. The officer rank (excluding warrant officers) shows a similar trend, i.e., at O-1 rank at 20.7 percent female that declines to 8.1 percent at O-10 or as rank increases. While warrant officers are not part of the Air Force personnel profile, the percentage of female W-1 at 9.5 percent drops to 6.8 percent at the W-5 grade in the aggregate data including Army, Navy and the Marine Corps. While the military branches may or may not achieve gender parity in the future, it is important to highlight that there appears to be incremental movement toward equality.

As demonstrated, women service members are currently a minority population across the military and veteran populations. Health disparities have been identified in women active duty members and veteran populations. Ourstorically, the male warrior has been esteemed as the benchmark for assessing military readiness and cohesion and post-service care (U.S. Department of Veterans Affairs 2015c). However, more recently, with policy changes toward gender diversity and an increased emphasis on gender parity and identification of health disparities in active duty and veteran populations, new research is illuminating emerging perspectives that challenge the traditional paradigm.

With the increase in diversity within the military as an institution, the importance of examining differences within female gender populations has broadened the need for understanding embedded health disparities. For example, according to Blosnich et al. (2013), sexual minority (lesbian and bisexual) identity is more common among women veterans than among male veterans. Unique health issues have been identified among veteran sexual minority women including a higher degree of mental distress and smoking rates than heterosexual women veterans. Further, sexual minority women veterans have three times the odds of poor physical health than their sexual minority nonveteran peers.

Another embedded minority presented by Hopkins-Chadwick (2006) includes the presence of health disparities within the ranks of junior enlisted military women who have a different racial and/or ethnic profile from male enlistees. A further example of an embedded women service personnel segment (with difficult-to-acquire relevant data) includes noncitizen volunteers who are allowed to serve as enlisted personnel only. Additionally, transfemale service members represent one more, frequently ostracized, group not fitting into the traditional male warrior mythology, and are another population for which ensuring equal treatment to secure peak health is important.

Thorough understanding of disparities across a diversity of gender and minority populations is essential to successfully grapple with upstream elements to ensure health for women (as well as men) across the military service continuum. Further, defining benchmarks that consider emerging evidence of gender disparities, collaborating with stakeholders with diverse and knowledgeable perspectives, and adjusting goals as needed to reduce disparities, increase equality and achieve peak health for all service members, align with wicked problem mitigation practices (Weick 1987, Mascarenhas 2009). Effective leadership execution and the application of optimal organizational change strategies are critical enablers.

DHHS Healthy People 2020: The Overlapping Context for the DoD and VA

Setting national objectives for improving the health of Americans began with the 1979 surgeon general's report and has continued to the present.

The 1979 *Healthy People: The Surgeon General's Report on Health Promotion and Disease Prevention* (U.S. Department of Health, Education, and Welfare 1979) initiated the nation's guidance for encouraging health in America's population. In 1986, the DoD issued a health promotion directive aimed at improving and maintaining military readiness and quality of life (U.S. Department of Defense 1986). The current DoD Health Promotion and Disease Prevention directive No. 1010.10 (effective April 28, 2014, expires April 28, 2024) is an administrative policy designed to create a health-focused culture that proactively seeks to build a value system that embraces health promotion and disease prevention programs to both enhance quality of life and mission readiness. The DoD administrative policy explicitly supports and aligns with HP 2020. Currently, the specific HP 2020 goals articulate prevention, achievement of health equity and the elimination of disparities, arrangement of social and physical conditions to promote health, and enabling health across the lifespan.

As implied by the DoD, the health promotion and disease prevention policy directive with statements of alignment that are congruent with HP 2020 goals allows its application in examining barriers or inequalities that exist for women as both active duty service members and veterans. Using this alignment provides a solid platform for both examining social determinants of health for military women and advancing ideas for achieving gender-based health equity.

As noted in Marmot and Allen (2014), the Veterans Health Administration has a strong commitment to equity. Since 2012, the VA Office of Health Equity is mission-focused to ensure that the healthcare provision for veterans provides equitable care appropriate for the individual's circumstances and irrespective of geography, gender, race and/or ethnicity, age, culture, or sexual orientation. There is importance, too, in incorporating socioeconomic factors into the provision of equitable access and care. The Office of Health Equity also brings an equity focus into the organizational discussions of policy, decision making, resource allocation, practice, and performance plans throughout the Veterans Health Administration. The creation of equity-focused healthcare is essential for reducing barriers for women veterans (and all veteran groups).

Unmasking Friction Within the Military

It is critical to identify barriers to achieving the full complement of equality for women's health across the continuum of military service. As revealed and corroborated in other chapters of this book, the dominance of androcentric-rooted institutions has complicated and compromised the full agency of those viewed as 'other' who do not fit a preset and socially constructed notion of the warrior (Abrams 1993). Underpinning the disparity toward gender and minority status, Dunivin (1997) illuminates philosophical pinch points that tend to wall in opposing mental models or paradigms. The author exposes and describes the opposing ends of a continuum between what she terms Traditionalists (combat, masculine warrior – the CMW paradigm) and Evolutionists (social egalitarian paradigm), and observes that there is an ongoing fundamental social change toward the latter. Dunivin (1997) posits that tribalism, as advanced by Wood (1995), is responsible for the 'entrenched CMW paradigm (and its attendant traditional model of culture) promoting homogeneity, separatism and exclusion' (p.21–23). Tribalism can be problematic because it embraces the repression of minorities where the powerful majority is resistant to accommodate change and diversity (Wood 1995, in Dunivin 1997). The military has fought hard to preserve its dominant CMW paradigm, as evidenced by the painfully slow and incremental status of diversity across its ranks (Dunivin 1997).

While incremental movement along the continuum toward a more egalitarian paradigm appears inevitable, the incremental shift motivates a military culture embracing an ideology of equality, diversity and inclusion (Dunivin 1997). Without this shift the military runs the risk of operating outside the norms of society. Subsequently, its consequent insularity could result in the loss of public confidence, respect and support (Dunivin 1997). Subordinating tribal affiliations (traditionalism) in order to sustain a strong national identity for the common good (evolutionism) is essential to ensure the equality of health across gender and all minority populations within and across the continuum of military service (Wood 1995, in Dunivin 1997).

Policies can either aid in reducing or exacerbating the social roots of inequities. However, as noted, policy change is incremental, and changes occur slowly over time. Further, as a unitary measure, policy cannot achieve desired changes in health improvement and fitness for duty – a characteristic of wicked problems (Rittel and Webber 1973, Mascarenhas 2009). Organizational culture is a significant factor in either enabling a thriving, health-centric environment or further enabling a divisive, caustic power differential between groups by advantaging one while disadvantaging the other(s) (Weick 1987).

The wickedness of gender inequality and the limitations of a policy remedy are each illuminated by Doan and Portillo (2015, 2017) in their Project Diane findings. In the Project Diane study, the authors explored both the benefits and barriers of gender integration of the Special Forces (Green Berets) by examining formal policies that structure gender inequalities and informal operational activities that continue to exclude women from career advancement and leadership in the military. The authors found a high degree of resistance to gender integration. They reported that 84 percent of Special Forces operators (women and men) in the study disagree that women should be allowed to serve in all combat jobs. Traditional stereotypes were uncovered as the dominant belief leading to respondents' reporting, which appear to be invisible to military personnel in their daily routines. The covert stereotyping is termed 'gender oblivion' and uses a means that may not intentionally seek to malign or exclude but the outcome is that both become manifest to the disadvantage of women (Doan and Portillo 2017).

As Doan and Portillo (2017) conclude, the living social culture must be debrided of the stereotypical mythologies and become socially revitalized, a complex of tasks that a distant policy alone cannot accomplish. They advocate for a three-pronged approach including: 1 the creation of an engaged, constructive dialogue about how gender oblivion shapes workplace experiences; 2 training on gender stereotypes and norms because these underscore most obstacles to gender integration; and 3 effective use of mentorship and support networks needs to be cultivated and reinforced along with periodic evaluations to ensure (or course-correct) structural and organizational change.

Dimensions of Social Determinants of Health and Women Warriors

Earlier in the chapter, the five place-based dimensions of social determinants were briefly introduced. The HP 2020 approach to social determinants of health uses a 'place-based' organizing framework that reflects five key areas of SDOH developed to detail the HP 2020 goals. The five key determinants include: 1 economic stability; 2 education; 3 social and community context; 4 health and healthcare; and 5 neighborhood and built environment. Each of the five dimensions has relevance for the discussion on military women's health outcomes and determinants of health. The five dimensions are not isolated, but instead overlap, intersect and reinforce in causes and effects as well as wickedness. Each of these five dimensions contains many complex elements that could be applied to military women. The following are selected elements discussed within each SDOH key area.

Economic Stability

Lack of economic stability is one of the five main domains for identifying disparity among military women. The relevant areas that are based under the economic stability heading include poverty, employment, food insecurity, and housing instability. The discussion focus will concentrate on servicewomen and veteran disparity in veteran employment, and reintegration.

In terms of veteran employment disparity, the U.S. Bureau of Labor Statistics comparative employment data examining 2015 and 2016 compare employment for Gulf War-era II veterans and nonveterans segregated by sex. Extracting selected data from Table 22.1 compares unemployment rates.

As noted in Table 22.1, the unemployment rate, while decreasing over time in veteran categories following the nonveteran rate trend, the unemployment rate for male veterans demonstrates greater convergence with the

314 *Confronting Wicked Problems*

Table 22.1 Extracted select data, employment situation of veterans, summary table: Gender comparison, 2015–16

Unemployment rates	Men 2015	Women 2015	Men 2016	Women 2016
Total veterans	4.5	5.4	4.2	5.0
Gulf War II	5.7	6.4	5.0	5.6
Nonveterans	5.3	5.0	4.8	4.6

Source: U.S. Bureau of Labor Statistics 2017b

Note: Employment status of the civilian noninstitutional population 18 years and over by veteran status, period of service, and sex, 2015–16 annual averages. Veterans are men and women who served on active duty in the U.S. armed forces and were not on active duty at the time of the survey. Gulf War-era II veterans served on active duty anywhere in the world sometime since September 2001. Nonveterans never served on active duty in the U.S. armed forces.

lower nonveteran rates (0.4 percent difference in 2015 and 0.2 percent difference in 2016). An interesting finding is that the veteran women's rate is more divergent from the lower nonveteran comparator in both 2015 and 2016 (i.e., 1.4 percent difference in 2015 and 1.0 percent difference in 2016). Even though the gap between veteran and nonveteran women groups has decreased in 2016, it is still 0.8 percent higher than the rate for men. While not explicitly stated in the data source, one possible contributing factor for the elevated unemployment rate for women veterans may be the fact that women veterans are more likely than their male counterparts to enroll in higher education institutions (Women Veterans Report 2017).

Women veteran data by age group suggest employment disparity among women veterans, especially in certain age groups. The Bureau of Labor Statistics (BLS) Office of Economic Opportunity Veterans Benefits Administration provides veteran unemployment data by sex and age group and nonveteran rates for comparison as well as change. The largest increase in unemployment rates for women veterans was noted in the ages 45 to 54.

Table 22.2 examines data averaged over a one-year period comparing 2016 and 2017 across the population groups by gender, Gulf War-period service, veteran average, and nonveterans to aid in discovering potential employment disparity. While unemployment has dropped across groups, the Gulf War II women veteran population continues to rise above other groups in the table by greater than one full percentage point.

The American Community Survey (ACS) is an ongoing survey that provides annual data on the social and economic characteristics of the U.S. population. The 2015 veterans data were extracted and compiled into a report by the National Center for Veterans Analysis and Statistics. According to the survey, a higher percentage of women veterans work in management, professional, sales and office industries than men veterans. Yet women veterans have a lower median household[4] income across each

Table 22.2 Employment statistics of civilian population 18 years and over by veteran status, period of service and sex (not seasonally adjusted), unemployment rates in percentage

Unemployment rates	Men Apr. 2016	Men Apr. 2017	Women Apr. 2016	Women Apr. 2017
Veteran all	4.0	3.7	3.4	3.6
Gulf War II	3.8	3.8	5.1	5.0
Gulf War I	4.3	3.8	2.2	3.3
Nonveteran	4.7	4.0	4.4	3.9

decade of life than men veterans (U.S. Department of Veterans Affairs, National Center for Veterans Analysis and Statistics 2016). Further, data on gender comparisons of veterans examining individual average income by decades of life demonstrates income disparity across all decades of life for women. The most dramatic gender disparity is for women veterans 65 years and older: income for women 65 years to 74 years was 75 percent of men's average income, and 72 percent for those aged 75 years and older. Not surprisingly, women veteran households are more than twice as likely to receive Supplemental Nutrition Assistance Program (SNAP) food stamps, i.e., 13 percent for women veteran households and 6.3 percent for men veterans (U.S. Department of Veterans Affairs, National Center for Veterans Analysis and Statistics 2016, p.9). The aggregate of these data points suggests an increase in the possibility of both food and housing insecurity or disparity for women veterans as well as income inequality for women across the general civilian population. Further, in a survey by the Service Women's Action Network (SWAN 2016) of active military servicewomen and women veterans, 43 percent of the respondents noted that securing job and assignment opportunities was their top challenge.

Education

Education is the second domain of disparity among military women. The relevant areas typically included under education are high school graduation, enrollment in higher education, language and literacy, and early childhood education and development (American Public Health Association n.d.). The focus of discussion concentrates on active servicewomen and women veteran disparity in access to education. Further, the focus of discussion targets the disparity in the relationship of military women's higher accomplishment in education and economic opportunity.

Even though women have officially served in the military since 1901 following the creation of the Army Nurse Corps, parity in access to benefits including education has been slow in arriving (U.S. Department of Veterans Affairs 2015c). The Serviceman's Readjustment Act of 1944 was signed into law on June 22, 1944. This Act became known as the GI Bill and provided benefits for veterans returning from World War II to help re-assimilate them into civilian life. There were an estimated 350,000 women veterans who served in the armed forces during that time. However, women veterans faced barriers in accessing the GI Bill. Many returning women did not even know that they were eligible for education benefits. This was clearly a gender-based disparity in freely accessing education benefits by women veterans – an unfortunate chapter in ourstory. Rather than actively informing women veterans of their eligibility to advance their education to enable a smoother reintegration, social and cultural norms prevailed. Through the societal lens of the imposed assumption of a woman's role, the duty as wife, mother and homemaker took precedence over the personal option to enter the civilian workforce.

More recent evidence of education disparity has been the slow integration of women cadets into the military services academies. On February 3, 2015, the Veterans Legal Services Clinic at Yale University filed a lawsuit on behalf of the SWAN, American Civil Liberties Union (ACLU), and ACLU-Connecticut to access enrollment data and information about recruiting and admission practices in order to understand why the number of women enrolled in U.S. military service academies remained so low despite the DoD's elimination of gender-based restrictions on women's service in combat units and specialties (*SWAN, ACLU and ACLU-Connecticut v. DoD, 2015*). The plaintiffs contended that even though women first matriculated at the academies in 1976, nearly 40 years later the institutions had 'failed to recruit and admit sufficient numbers of women to foster a healthy environment in which they are accepted and integrated' (p.4). The plaintiffs further argued that the continued gender disparities contribute to a campus climate where gender bias and discrimination have become the norm. This abusive climate has created conditions conducive to victimizing women cadets and midshipmen with acts of sexual harassment and assault. In addition, this gender-demeaning climate has promoted a culture of shunning and ostracizing those who report sexual violence. These persistent disparities promote a misogynistic environment and put women in harm's way, according to the plaintiffs.

Further, there exists a current disparity in women's educational accomplishments successfully translating into economic benefits through employment. Women veterans have higher education attainment and are enrolled in college courses at higher rates than men veterans (U.S. Department of Veterans Affairs, National Center for Veterans Analysis and Statistics 2016). The percentage of women veterans with some college (women 44.3 percent vs. men 36.5 percent), a Bachelor's degree (women 20.7 percent vs. men 15.9 percent), and a higher degree (women 13.8 percent vs. men 10.7 percent) exceeds men veterans' percentages across all higher education levels. In addition, more women enter military service with at least a high school diploma compared to men (U.S. Department of Veterans Affairs, National Center for Veterans Analysis and Statistics 2016). However, while military women surpass their male counterparts across the board in educational achievement, the lagging job opportunities for women veterans relative to men veterans have led to their income inequality within society.

Social and Community Context

Social and community context is the third domain of disparity to examine relative to women in the military. The relevant areas that are typically included in the social and community context heading include social cohesion, civic participation, discrimination, and incarceration (American Public Health Association n.d.). This discussion focuses on social cohesion and social exclusion, the reintegration of women Reserve/Guard troops, and the incarceration of women veterans.

Marmot et al. (2006) note that psychosocial factors in the work environment influence the risk of physical and mental illness. The psychosocial work environment relevant to health can be described by the interaction between cognitions, emotions, and behaviors, and the physical and social context. This implies that both the collective or social and the individual role and response are contributors to organizational, group, and individual wellbeing. Further, the organization of work, degree of social isolation, and sense of control over one's life can contribute to the likelihood of developing and dying from chronic diseases such as diabetes and cardiovascular disease (Marmot et al. 2006). There is good evidence supporting the disruptive effect of stressors such as life events on existing medical conditions including diabetes and rheumatoid arthritis, and for the precipitation of myocardial infarction by emotional trauma (Brunner and Marmot 2006).

Social exclusion contributes to an adverse psychosocial work environment (Marmot et al. 2006). The Marine Corps has lagged behind other military branches in accepting women. In a published public statement on December 8, 2016, Dr. Ellen L. Haring, representing the Defense Advisory Committee on Women in the Services (DACOWITS), expressed concern about the possible repeal or rollback of newly installed policies that allow U.S. servicewomen's access to all military occupations and positions (Pellerin 2015). In questioning the Marine Corps' recruitment practices, two challenges were illuminated. First, in a challenge as to the lack of women entering the officer ranks as Marines, Dr. Haring questioned the justification for the infantry training difference in sustained load carry between Marine enlisted and officer training. Enlistees are required to carry a sustained load of 62 pounds while the officer requirement is a sustained load of 152 pounds for 9.3 miles at a 3-mile-per hour minimum pace. All eight women officers in training failed to meet this requirement when the pack load exceeded 120 pounds. The requirement for officers appeared to be incongruous with the fiscal year (FY) 2015 National Defense Authorization Act (NDAA) standards, which state that the screening must 'accurately predict performance of *actual, regular and recurring* duties of a military occupation' (p.2). This conclusion of incongruity was corroborated by informal comments from previously deployed male Marine Corps officers (Haring 2016). A second challenge promoted by Dr. Haring was directed at the data that revealed that more than 130 enlisted women had successfully completed the Marine Corps infantry training yet only three of the qualified women had been moved to combat arms (Haring 2016).

Both of these stonewalling tactics directed at women seeking the Marine Corps infantry training for active duty as expressed by Haring (2016) may be construed to represent an intentional and continuing practice of gender-based social exclusion. These practices describe the creation of structures and dynamic processes of inequality among or between groups in an organization or society (White 2003). Access to membership in the Marine Corps was either denied or very limited to women volunteers, leading to unequal outcomes. Another characterization of social exclusion is the exclusion from social production, a denial of opportunity to contribute to mission readiness (White 2003).

The characteristics of social exclusion tend to occur in multiple dimensions and are often reinforcing. It is an expression of unequal relations of power among groups in society, which then determine unequal access to economic, social, political, and cultural privilege, or the normalization of certain beliefs (Marmot et al. 2006). In Project Diane, Doan and Portillo (2015, 2017) set out to examine resistance to gender integration of women into the U.S. military. The findings from the series of 24 focus groups with 198 Special Forces men and women led to the emergent discovery of structural barriers and assumptions held about women permeating seemingly gender-neutral policies and practices. The outcome of this legacy cultural arrangement has tended to manifest itself as exclusion from social production and denial of full active participation to women in desired military service activities (White 2003).

With regard to the activation and reintegration of women reservists, Peele (2014) studied reintegrating women Reserve and National Guard members following Operation Iraqi Freedom/Operation Enduring Freedom activation and participation. In the qualitative research the author found that each interviewee had encountered some form of bias, discrimination or harassment during the course of their military careers. Several respondents reported feeling a sense of devaluation based on gender by both male reservist peers and active duty males while in theater.

Women make up a higher proportion of reserve members than active duty members (U.S. Department of Defense 2014b). Research is scarce on women reservists reintegrating into society. As noted by Peele (2014), there are presently few, if any, gender-specific programs that sufficiently meet the needs of this demographic, who tend to be older than active duty personnel and have families, have more developed career paths and possess unique psychosocial needs. Deployments for reservists as citizen soldiers result in different and potentially more stressful experiences than for those on active duty; they straddle and participate in two vastly different worlds (Griffith 2010).

Factors discovered about the women reservists/guard lived experiences include heightened negative emotions upon return from deployment, e.g., hyper-vigilance, symptoms of PTSD and anger, as well as a diverse range of rapidly changing emotions (Peele 2014). While the respondents reported a high level of informal support upon return from deployment (e.g., from family and friends), formal support for women reservists reintegrating was reported to be lacking – especially women-specific guidance and resources. Also noted by Peele (2014), as implied by the respondents, is that during reintegration they experienced disruption to family roles caused by deployment, and subsequent return to their families caused significant friction. In most cases for both active duty and Reserve/Guard troops, the focus for reintegration has been on men who were deployed. The author advocates for more research to help understand the unique ways in which women's interpersonal relationships and their individual and family roles are affected by deployment.

Reservists returning to civilian life lack the supportive military communities of their active duty peers and families (Peele 2014). Even with the expanded deployment for Reserve and Guard troops and the significantly larger population of women after Operation Enduring Freedom/Operation Iraqi Freedom, help for these troops is lacking. Active duty troops have several innovative programs designed to support veterans and their families. However, women-specific Guard/Reserve service members were seemingly neglected in this regard.

Veterans who enter the civilian criminal justice system (e.g., court and corrections) are referred to as justice-involved veterans (National Institute of Corrections n.d.). Criminal diversionary programs for justice-involved veterans have been instrumental in helping and empowering male veterans as they receive treatment for PTSD and mental health issues, and support to reduce recidivism. More recently the need for programs addressing women veterans has been identified, thus acknowledging the gender differences in terms of needs and disparity of treatment for women veterans who become involved in the criminal justice system. Advocates for women veterans (e.g., National Resource Center on Justice Involved Women – NRCJIW) highlight the complex conditions that this population faces in the justice-involved environment (NRCJIW 2013).

In 2004, the U.S. Justice Department estimated that veterans composed approximately 10 percent of those serving time in state and federal prisons, with about 1 percent who are women veterans, i.e., approximately 1,400 women (NRCJIW 2013). Women veterans have gender-specific needs for the development of programs that are both gender-informed and trauma-informed. Specific needs noted in the report include parenting and childcare, unemployment, housing and homelessness, substance abuse, and co-occurring disorders, and trauma exposure. Further explained in the report regarding trauma disorder are life exposures like childhood and/or adult abuse, combat trauma, and trauma from sexual assault while in the military (NRCJIW 2013).

While some U.S. prisons have instituted justice programs for women veterans, the sheriff of Las Colinas Detention Facility near San Diego, California, closed down the program at the jail citing too few recipients to justify the resources at the county's only jail for women (Steele 2016). An all-volunteer staff that had argued against the closure had managed the program. The volunteers had worked with between three and six women veterans at any one time, suggesting the presence of a small but consistent population in need of veteran help. Meanwhile, there is an all-veteran 32-bed detention facility in San Diego County dedicated to serving male veterans. The sheriff at Las Colinas has now aggregated women veterans into a 'special needs' group along with nonmilitary women inmates (Steele 2016). This action no longer differentiates women veterans from nonveteran prisoners, and undermines evidence-based treatment for effects of trauma experienced while on active duty especially during periods of conflict and/or MST. More specifically, this lack of augmented aid for women veterans, in many cases experiencing PTSD and/or MST, undermines the commitment to improving civilian care and reintegration (Biden 2007).

Health and Healthcare

Health and healthcare form the broad disparity lens for examining women in the military. The relevant areas under this heading include access to healthcare, access to primary care, and health literacy (American Public Health Association n.d.). This chapter covers health disparities across the women-specific areas including the slow transition to equality in biomedical research investment and across the continuum of women's service roles including active duty, reentry to civilian status, and veteran.

The Persian Gulf War (1990–91) was the precipitous event that helped prioritize access to healthcare for female veterans (Caroselli 2012). In 1994, Congress provided $40 million (the first of two special appropriations) for biomedical research on issues of importance for military women (Friedl 2005). The intent was to bring protection of the health and performance of military women on a par with men, after more than a century of research based solely on males. Further, in 1994, the risk rule for gender-based job assignments was rescinded and replaced by a policy that only excluded women from units with direct ground combat missions and in a few specialized circumstances (Burrelli 2013, Kamarck 2016). With the anticipation of an increasing female presence, there was also a growing awareness of gender-unique differences and, as discovered, faulty assumptions to overcome about them (Friedl 2005).

Assumptions about women such as high injury rates, psychological fitness as fighters, fragility of reproductive systems, concerns about occupational and environmental exposure hazards that might affect pregnant servicewomen or harm fetuses were concerns expressed (Friedl 2005). The overstated significance of women's menstrual cycles and hormonal fluctuations led to the exclusion of women of child bearing age from use as research subjects. To address the disparity of limiting women in research, the 1993 National Institutes of Health (NIH) Revitalization Act (Public Law 103-43) demanded the inclusion of all women (and minorities, who were also excluded in prior years) in each research project, and human use committees stopped accepting excuses about the inconvenience of assumed menstrual cycle effects (Friedl 2005). By closing the large knowledge gaps in understanding the physiology and psychology of females, more equitable and fair policies and standards for military service in fulfilling the DoD mission, it was anticipated, might better serve the common good.

For women on active duty, the targeted increase in resources dedicated to understanding the sex similarities and differences based on biomedical research signalled a willingness to understand how best to ensure women's success and acceptance in the expanding roles across the U.S. military (Friedl 2005). On January 24, 2013, then-Secretary of Defense Leon Panetta announced that the DoD was rescinding the direct combat exclusion rule on women serving in previously restricted occupations (Kamarck 2016). The policy change was guided by several principles including to preserve unit readiness, cohesion, and morale; ensure success of all men and women; retain public trust; use gender-neutral performance standards; and ensure a sufficient cadre of women across ranks (Kamarck 2016).

Looking closer at unit readiness, availability as a dimension of readiness, and unit cohesion, women's health and performance have served as topics that generate controversy. In counteraction to women's physiological weakness, a one-dimensional argument, as a detractor to readiness, women have proved successful in sensitive operations where it was important to communicate with a local female population (Kamarck 2016). Further, a Marine Corps study on the effectiveness of integrated units found that gender-integrated teams performed better than all-male teams on problem sets that were the most cognitively challenging.

Non-availability of service members has a negative impact on unit readiness. While women have experienced higher musculoskeletal injuries during initial basic combat training and they are also slightly higher in a deployed environment, injury rates are similar for men and women in the operational Army (Kamarck 2016). Further, differences in some behavioral health disorders were noted in Army data with women having slightly higher rates in adjustment, depression and anxiety, while males had higher rates of alcohol disorders (Kamarck 2016). Both men and women had similar rates of PTSD.

There are more than 2 million female veterans (U.S. Department of Veterans Affairs 2016). The VA reports that 447,000 women veterans used the VA health system in 2015 – a 123 percent increase since FY 2003 (U.S. Department of Veterans Affairs 2015c; Duffy 2017). The demographics of women veterans differ from their men counterparts. Women veterans are younger than the average male veteran (U.S. Department of Veterans Affairs 2015c). Women are more likely to have served in Gulf War or post-9/11 eras than in previous conflicts. Female veterans are more likely to come from diverse racial backgrounds. They are also more likely to have a service-connected disability and are more likely to use the VA health system (U.S. Department of Veterans Affairs 2015c).

However, some weaknesses for women veterans' care create opportunities for improvement. One issue noted that infertility and complications during pregnancy have emerged as important issues plaguing women who have deployed to more recent conflicts in combat zones. Duffy (2017) advocated for Congress to fund research into conditions during the Gulf War and the recent conflicts in Iraq and Afghanistan, to provide better care for women veterans.

Another issue centers on mental healthcare. In a Veterans of Foreign Wars (VFW) survey, women veterans voiced concern that there is a lack of gender-specific training for mental healthcare providers (Duffy 2017). Care for conditions such as post-partum depression and conditions that stem from menopause and sexual trauma are neither consistent nor adequate for women seeking treatment at the VA. For survivors of MST who also may have symptoms of PTSD, there is a level of discomfort in group therapy sessions with other veterans who have been diagnosed with PTSD but were not victims of sexual trauma. Duffy (2017) advocated for Congress to expand the VA's telemedicine program that is currently restricted to one where sexual assault patients can have the opportunity to talk comfortably in a virtual group setting of people who endured the same trauma.

A mental health issue critical to women veterans' health is depression. Depression is twice as prevalent in women as in men, and is a leading cause of disease-related disability in the Western world (Schmidt 2000, in Resnick 2012). Depression causes increased risk for osteoporosis, cardiovascular disease, metabolic syndrome, dementia and 50 percent of the cardiovascular mortality in postmenopausal women. Unfortunately, depression remains under-diagnosed and undertreated in women veterans.

The VA has identified a much lower utilization and awareness of benefits among older women veterans compared to their younger counterparts (U.S. Department of Veterans Affairs 2015b). Older women veterans are less likely to report receiving disability compensation, but are equally as likely to have been injured or made ill as a result of their military service. Several older women veteran respondents (55 years and older) commented on the VFW survey that they believed that they did not rate the same benefits as their male counterparts – a health-compromising misperception (Duffy 2017). Continuing to enhance the VA's outreach is essential in reaching this deserving population. Overall, Duffy (2017) advocates on behalf of the VFW and urges Congress to work with the Center for Women Veterans to conduct greater oversight of women veteran programs and address barriers or gaps in care and services for women veterans.

A Women's Bureau (U.S. Department of Labor 2010) focus group series illuminated emerging issues regarding the health of women veterans. Active duty pre-separation medical and/or mental health services were frequently not sought by women veterans because of the potential for delay of separation, or concern that their discharge status could be changed to dishonorable if substance abuse was discovered or treatment was requested. Often, underlying trauma is responsible for substance abuse because of coping difficulties from trauma (war, traumatic brain injuries (TBI), MST, exposure, PTSD, and others).

Subsequent to discharge, the transition to VA care was not a seamless process for women veterans. Challenges that recently returning homeless women veterans identified in the focus groups included not knowing where to turn for help, being unaware of benefits and eligibility, mistrust of authority, shame, pride, lacking transportation, resources and access in rural/nonurban areas, not knowing how to access services not provided by the VA, experiencing judgmental staff at the VA, and a resistance to self-identifying as veterans (U.S. Department of Labor 2010).

Mota et al. (2011) concluded that active duty women had an increased likelihood of developing PTSD over their male counterparts, whereas returning women Guard or Reserve members were more vulnerable than men to depression, panic disorder and anxiety problems. The researchers recommend improved screening for mental disorders in women leaving deployment (Mota et al. 2011, Peele 2014). Based on a higher level of support for active duty women reported by Peele (2014), this recommendation is more likely to become a priority for active duty women than for women who are returning Guard/Reserve troops, thus suggesting the presence of unequal access for Guard/Reserve women (Peele 2014).

Nutrition (including particular supplements) is considered a critical factor in ensuring both general health and enhanced recovery from certain types of trauma. Research suggests that TBI, PTSD and other military trauma-induced mental illness may respond to diet (Institute of Medicine Committee on Nutrition, Trauma, and the Brain 2011). Hibbeln and Gow (2014) have advanced the potential efficacy for the application of diet for reducing psychiatric distress, improving mental ill-health outcomes, including reducing symptoms of depression and aggression and lowering the risk of suicide ideation among the U.S. military. One nutrition strategy showing promise includes raising blood levels of omega-3 highly unsaturated fatty acids (HUFAs) and lowering the omega-6 content of U.S. military diets, which increase force efficiency. Specifically, a Mediterranean diet pattern high in omega-3 HUFAs. Education on nutrition can have far-reaching implications for women and women with children (and all veterans) with an ourstory of experiencing trauma, and for improved general health.

While translational medicine (rapid movement of bench to bedside) can generate timely intervention of new findings to augment other treatment, disparity exists for many military women who do not have, or do not know how to access resources that can ensure the best care and health literacy for self-care and health decisions.

With the rapidly changing demographics in the active duty and veteran populations, Congress and the VA are both moving, albeit slowly and incrementally, toward health parity for women across the spectrum of military service. The VA Office of Health Equity provides outreach to women veterans, and with additional time and continued and expanding support, it could close the gender gap of service in many areas that adversely affects women veterans' health.

Neighborhood and Built Environment

Neighborhood and built environment is the fifth and final disparity lens used to examine women in the military. The relevant areas of concern under the neighborhood and built environment heading include access to foods that support healthy eating patterns, quality of housing, crime and violence, and environmental conditions (American Public Health Association n.d.). The two discussion threads focus on those issues surrounding environmental conditions that are either potentially toxic or austere as well as loss of access to quality housing.

Environmental conditions play a significant role in both individual and population health. Two unique environmental conditions encountered by women in the military include toxic exposure and austere environments (Kang et al. 2000, U.S. Department of Veterans Affairs n.d.b, Ryan-Wenger and Lowe 2000, Foster and Alviar 2013).

Military personnel encounter significant exposures to injury-generating activities in both times of peace and conflict: exposures from military weapons, psychological stress and trauma, infectious disease, industrial tasks, and exposures that are challenging to identify and characterize and which may be associated with a delayed impact (Gaydos 2011). Occupational/ employee health programs provide both a general and specific set of regulations to protect employees from toxic exposure and injury-generating processes in the workplace. The federal rule that created the Occupational Health and Safety Administration (OSHA), which directs employers to provide a safe work environment, was passed in 1970 (Gaydos 2011). Initially, federal employees were exempted from the OSHA rules. The OSH Act was amended in 1980 to require safe working environments and education programs for military and civilian DoD employees. The DoD did not compose a directive for creating programmatic elements until 1984 in DoD Instruction 6055.1 'DoD Occupational Safety Health Program.' During the interim period, piecemeal directives targeted specific health behaviors for improvement.

Following the DoD policy directive in 1984, the Army initiated an Occupational Health Program for Soldiers at Fort Campbell, Kentucky. This program became the model for other military installations (Gaydos 2011). However, despite the military's effort to systematically and effectively address hazards and reduce risk to military personnel, environmental exposures have continued to be both problematic in that injuries and illnesses continued to occur, and wicked because in the case of difficult-to-characterize exposures, technology and science are not sophisticated enough to fully understand the long-term impact on the human body. Two complex military occupational exposure situations and the implications for women veterans are briefly discussed. These include: 1 the use of Agent Orange as a chemical defoliant in Vietnam; and 2 open-air burn pits used for waste disposal in Afghanistan and Iraq.

An example of an exposure that has been challenging to characterize and has generated delayed and long-term health effects occurred during Operation Ranch Hand in the Vietnam Conflict when Agent Orange, a tactical chemical defoliant (i.e., military-designed chemical mixture) with known adverse human effects including cancer, was aerial sprayed to remove dense, tropical jungle vegetation to expose the location of enemy North Vietnam and Viet Cong fighters (Gaydos 1991). It was so named because of the orange identifying stripe on the 55-gallon drums in which it was stored. The dioxin-tainted[5] chemical rained down over troops, thus fully exposing U.S. military personnel on land, waterways, and through air delivery, as well as allies and civilians between the years of 1962 through 1971. More than 19 million gallons of herbicides were sprayed over 4.5 million acres of land in Vietnam. In addition, Agent Orange and other herbicides were used, tested or stored elsewhere, e.g., Korea, Thailand and some military bases in the U.S., exposing additional personnel to the harmful effects (U.S. Department of Veterans Affairs n.d.a).

The U.S. finally acknowledged the possibility of adverse health outcomes related to the exposure to Agent Orange in 1991. The passage of the Agent Orange Act of 1991 (Public Law No: 102-4) by Congress marked a turning point for many veterans reporting illness after returning from serving in the Vietnam Conflict (U.S. Department of Veterans Affairs 1995). This law benefited many (but not all) veterans in terms of compensation and VA medical care. The Public Law directed the VA to assume presumption of service connection disability. PL 102-4 also set in motion a series of actions and benefits.[6] In addition, the Public Law requested the Institute of Medicine (currently named the Health and Medicine Division of the National Academy of Sciences, Engineering, and Medicine) to continue to conduct biennial updates that would review newly published scientific literature regarding statistical associations between health outcomes and exposure to dioxin and other chemical compounds in these herbicides, and to review the VA's progress in addressing veterans' care.

The Veterans and Agent Orange 1996 biennial update concluded that there was limited/suggestive evidence of an association between exposure to herbicides used in Vietnam and birth defects in children of Vietnam veterans. However, later research led to a confirmation of a positive correlation in 2000. The study by Kang et al. (2000) revealed evidence of the presence of the birth defect spina bifida in infants born to women veterans exposed to Agent Orange (U.S. Department of Veterans Affairs n.d.a). Unfortunately, this effect of exposure of women veterans and their offspring was discovered decades beyond their service dates after uncompensated, uninformed, and irreparable harm to both women veterans and their children born with birth defects as a result of Agent Orange had already occurred. Critiques of the VA decisions to exclude other birth defects, add 14 additional health conditions presumed to be linked to exposure, and include other military groups who served during the conflict (Korean demilitarized zone veterans and naval veterans who served off the coast of Vietnam) have been made based on independent investigations (Ornstein 2016) and by the VFW (Duffy 2017). The complexity of these exposures which are difficult to preemptively characterize and assess, and to understand their health impact(s) illuminates the dual challenge of both accomplishing a military mission and protecting service women and men without adding to their level of harm.

The military's use of burn pits in Operation Iraqi Freedom, Operation Enduring Freedom and Operation New Dawn in Iraq and Afghanistan has been referred to in the press as 'the new Agent Orange' (Brunswick 2016). KBR (Kellogg, Brown and Root) provided contractor services and was responsible for setting up at least 230 burn pits and operating them, generally adjacent to in-theater bases housing troops and contractors. Some of these pits were more than 10 acres in size (Hickman 2016). These massive open-air burn pits at U.S. military bases billowed toxic smoke and ash composed of all waste from the bases including (but not limited to) chemicals, paint, medical and human waste, metal/aluminum cans, munitions, and other unexploded ordnance, petroleum and lubricant products, plastics, rubber, wood, and discarded food (U.S. Department of Veterans Affairs n.d.b). Complaints by service members reporting health effects perceived to be associated with the burn pits began in 2003 (U.S. Army Center for Health Promotion & Preventive Medicine (ACHPPM) n.d.).

The use of burn pits by the U.S. military in Iraq and Afghanistan was restricted in 2009. While these pits underwent a phase-out, 197 were still operating in Afghanistan as of January 2011 (Institute of Medicine, Committee on Nutrition, Trauma, and the Brain 2011). The largest and most notorious burn pit was hastily constructed at Balad, Iraq, burned all hours of the day and consumed an estimated 100 to 200 tons of waste per day, affecting the 25,000 troops stationed there at any one time (Brunswick 2016).

According to the U.S. Army, dioxins are mainly formed as an unwanted by-product in combustion processes. As noted, following the April 2008 air-sampling results, separation of wastes prior to burning was initiated and a program to eliminate plastic water bottles from the burn pit began reducing waste volume by 50 percent (U.S. ACHPPM n.d.).

As reported, toxins in burn pit smoke may affect the skin, eyes, respiratory and cardiovascular systems, gastrointestinal tract and internal organs (U.S. Department of Veterans Affairs n.d.b). The examination and categorization of toxic chemicals and other materials along with the products of combustion and the effects on living organisms and the environment represent a complex, wicked and, in this case, speculative scientific process because of the lack of data. It is a highly complex process for characterizing the toxicology of a single chemical. When a mixture of chemicals, or in this case, an uncharacterized chemical cocktail in the form of smoke, is created with uncontrolled, frequently changing composition, the task of acquiring accurate exposure data of individual chemicals as well as characterizing the potential for interactive effects on the human organism through all routes of exposure is difficult to analyze (World Health Organization Health Protection Agency 2006). The assessment is further complicated by the various attributes of individuals exposed, including gender[7] (Westervelt 2015). Neither a tracking system characterizing waste composition that was incinerated so that it could be retrospectively studied, nor adequate comprehensive, real-time air monitoring, including personal exposure, were part of the oversight. Nettleman (2015) has been critical of the lack of record keeping by the DoD to safeguard the health of active duty troops and veterans.

In the biennial Institute of Medicine Committee on Nutrition, Trauma, and the Brain (2011) report assessing the VA, burn pit registry and health data as required by Public Law 112-260, the reviewers cautioned that there were significant limitations and uncertainties in burn pit information for reconstructing actual burn pit smoke emissions and exposure to correlate with adverse health outcomes that were being reported through the registry. Four general categories of limitations and uncertainties noted in the report include: 1 descriptive facts about contents of waste burned; 2 limited or incomplete data of conditions at time of ambient air sampling that was done; 3 limited and incomplete scope of exposure assessment (both area and personal); and 4 insufficient data and subsequent diminished modeling capability for reconstructing exposure (Institute of Medicine 2011).

The epidemiological studies by the DoD did not provide sufficient information for evaluating any association between exposure to burn pit emissions and long-term health effects (Institute of Medicine 2011). The DoD studies did not have sufficient follow-up to identify latent health effects, such as cancer and cardiovascular effects. There has been no assessment of individual or personal exposure. The report (Institute of Medicine 2011) highlighted three categories of combustion products of interest – Polychlorinated Dibenzo-p-dioxins and Polychlorinated Dibenzofurans (PCDDs/Fs-dioxins); volatile organic compounds (VOCs); and polycyclic aromatic hydrocarbons (PAHs) and particulate matter (PM) – and their association with long-term health effects. In addition to limited and sporadic air sampling, other sources of pollution were not distinguished, i.e., traffic and jet emissions and dust storms. The U.S. ACHPPM collected ambient air samples at various times and intermittently beginning August 2004, July 2005, and January, March and August 2006 (U.S. ACHPPM n.d.). Additional sampling was done after collaboration with the U.S. Air Force Preventive Medicine and Public Health unit using a revised strategy including January to April 2007 and in October and November 2007. This sampling strategy included additional toxic pollutants. The earlier sampling results reported 'occasional presence of dioxins, PAHs and VOCs' (p.1), and risks were assessed as low.

The January 10, 2013 Public Law 112-260 was enacted by Congress requiring the secretary of veterans affairs to ensure that the VA establishes an open burn pit registry for veterans who may have been exposed to toxic airborne chemicals and fumes caused by open-air burn pits in Iraq or Afghanistan (Dignified Burial and Other Veterans' Benefits Improvement Act of 2012). The registry initiates the voluntary, passive self-assessment surveillance database so that military personnel could report their claims of illness that may be related to burn pits. The registry serves as a way to generate hypotheses for further study based on symptomology. The law also requires biennial reporting by an independent scientific agency regarding an assessment of effectiveness of actions taken by the VA, and recommendations regarding the most prudent means of addressing the medical needs of eligible individuals with respect to conditions that are likely to result from exposure.

In June 2015, the VA released a summary of data collected from the Veterans Affairs Airborne Hazards and Open Burn Pit Registry (U.S. Department of Veterans Affairs 2015a). Following the enactment of Public Law 112-260, the registry opened for pilot testing on April 25, 2014, and was released nationally on June 19, 2014. As of the report, 28,426 service members had completed the questionnaire. Based on demographic data in the report, 20,996 (89.5 percent) of registry participants were male and 2,472 (10.5 percent) identified as female. Gender data were unavailable for 4,958 participants. Data were collected on both the degree of burn pit exposure and dust storm exposure. Dust storms in Middle East deployments are a significant source of exposure to small particles that can become embedded deep in the lungs (American Academy of Allergy, Asthma & Immunology 2015). These mineralized dust particles carry viral, bacterial and fungal organisms, metals and silica, with the potential for causing a variety of illnesses.

An excess of respiratory disease other than allergies including chronic obstructive pulmonary disease (COPD), emphysema, and chronic bronchitis were reported in the registry (Kime 2015, U.S. Department of Veterans Affairs 2015). Moreover, 365 veterans reported a diagnosis with either constrictive bronchiolitis or idiopathic pulmonary fibrosis – rare, crippling and often fatal diseases. Participants in both the burn pit and dust storm exposure groups reported higher rates of insomnia, liver conditions, chronic multi-symptom illnesses and decreased physical function, i.e., walking, running or climbing stairs. There were no excess rates of cancers reported compared to non-exposed participants (Kime 2015, U.S. Department of Veterans Affairs 2015). However, it is important to note that many cancers take a decade or more to develop. Critical of the response to veterans' health issues and accusing the VA of suppressing the findings from burn pit data, Dr. Steven Coughlin, an ethicist and epidemiologist, resigned from his VA Office of Public Health role as senior epidemiologist in 2012 (Percy 2016). Like the case of Agent Orange exposure in Vietnam, reproductive effects on offspring may emerge in the future as well as in other patterns of disease.

In terms of the series of wicked problems, burning tons of waste, including chemical weapons, even though the products of combustion were uncontrolled, with limited air monitoring and acknowledged by the U.S. Environmental Protection Agency to produce toxic smoke dangerous to human and environmental health, provided a solution to reducing the footprint of the bases through waste stream reduction. However, it also created other wicked problems such as substantial environmental damage in Iraq and Afghanistan, probable health damage to local civilians, long-term illness among troops stationed at co-located bases, with similar illness reported among contractors operating the pits – all add burdens on an already stressed VA health system (American Public Health Association 2015).

Therefore, hanging in the balance are three central questions. First, should preventive health considerations be prioritized and integrated within all policies and actions? Second, should DoD policies and contract language (e.g., with contractors such as KBR – who are held harmless) and implementation lean toward the expendability of warriors as utility (a masculinist ethics frame of independence and autonomy), or the ethics of care (a feminist frame of interdependence and obligation) as the moral imperative (Andre and Velasquez 2015)? Herein lies a possible philosophical gender disparity to discern whether the end justifies the means or whether the means matter. Third, should attention turn toward the debate centered on the strict use of evidence-based research ethics as to whether or not decision making on qualifying exposures as military related be limited to scientific evidence, or is there a reason to count knowledge gained in other ways? (Kalichman 2009).

The Agent Orange Act of 1991 House Bill allows for the inclusion of sound medical and scientific evidence along with the National Academy of Sciences (third-party) oversight. Decades passed before Congress and the

VA acknowledged the adverse health effects in the case of Agent Orange exposure. It is important to note that while the Agent Orange study referenced in the previous section associating women veterans' exposure to the chemical with higher rates of spina bifida, research into teratogenic effects from male occupational and environmental exposures has been well established for decades. For example, as referenced in Trasler and Doerksen (1999), one of many findings correlates paternal exposures to solvents, wood and wood products, and pesticides with offspring with higher incidence of birth defects (Schnitzer et al. 1995). So, it is incumbent on the military leadership to preemptively reduce all types of hazardous exposure to military personnel to levels as low as possible, and engage in additional research to more fully examine the effects of exposure of various materials and chemicals on military women.

With regard to austere and combat environments, women who deploy to combat zones may have higher rates of abnormal PAP smears (Hines 1992, in Sidel 2000). There is evidence to suggest that women combat veterans have a higher rate of infertility and complications during pregnancy. Additionally, women have reported to the VFW that they have trouble finding prosthetic options suitable for them, leaving them no choice but to use uncomfortable products that do not fit properly (Duffy 2017). A similar disparity has been reported in regard to protective personal armaments used to reduce the vulnerability to explosive devices. Further, the male-centric armor had an alarming disadvantage in that it frequently compromised a woman's ability to lift her arm appropriately to fire. Redesigned equipment has only recently started to become fielded for women in combat roles (Tritten 2016).

Women deployed to austere environments require different woman-centric medical services. Ryan-Wenger and Lowe (2000) report that 367,000 women serve in the U.S. military and regularly deploy to austere military environments. A survey of military women's perceptions about available healthcare provider treatment for gynecologic infections during deployment indicated that there are barriers to care. The implications of the findings then suggest the need for specific military provider training, sick call policy development, pre-deployment training, and the development of self-care alternatives under austere conditions.

Typically in austere deployments, medical services are tailored to medical needs based on the healthcare patterns of men, although this is improving. Using data collected from the clinical logs at the Women's Health Clinic at Joint Base Balad Iraq from September 2007 to May 2008, Foster and Alviar (2013) were able to identify problems and educational needs to help military women as well as to inform healthcare providers to help women make informed decisions about their health when deployed to austere environments. During the period of data collection more than 26 percent of all visits were gynecologic or women related. Usually, gynecologic care is not available in deployed settings. Further, even in a gender-diverse setting, women are often hesitant to present concerns or highlight difficulties in the field. One reason noted for this hesitancy is the lack of qualified healthcare providers and the reliance on medical technicians at forward operating bases. Moreover, with menstrual irregularities common in deployed settings, 77 percent of women wanted menstruation and birth control management. The majority of these visits could have been prevented with pre-deployment screening and proper education. Other measures that would benefit military women with enhanced pre-deployment gender-specific education include benefits of contraception for birth control and aid with menstrual irregularities, early education so that women starting medication can have time to adjust before deployment, education on ways to prevent urinary tract infections and vaginitis, and the prevention of sexually transmitted infections and pregnancy through abstinence or condom use.

Women Veterans and Homelessness

In an effort to include the voice of homeless women veterans and their experiences at a grass-roots level to better understand the homelessness issue and help generate ideas to end homelessness for our women warriors and counteract health disparities, the U.S. Department of Labor Women's Bureau sponsored a geographically broad series of focus groups. The Homeless Women Veterans Listening Sessions in 2009 included homeless women veterans and service providers across seven states (U.S. Department of Labor 2010). The series of 28 moderated sessions hosted by the Women's Bureau identified factors that led these veterans to become homeless. Homeless individuals become vulnerable to health degradation because of increased likelihood of violence or rape, illegal drug use, poor access to healthy foods, poor hygiene practices, adverse weather conditions, infectious disease, poor access to medical or reproductive and mental health services, among other contributing factors that can compromise women's health. Additionally, often children are involved, thus exacerbating an already stressful and health-compromising life circumstance. The diverse set of complex issues and behaviors include unemployment (job loss, lack of training/skill set, military-to-civilian skill transfer), lack of veteran benefits (non-eligibility or failure to understand access and availability), legal issues, mental health issues (PTSD, MST, and TBI), divorce or separation, domestic violence, lack of either a family or social support network, and substance abuse (U.S. Department of Labor 2010).

Through the listening sessions, a common theme emerged that pointed to disparities for women veterans. The perception that existing programs or services were more accommodating to men and failed to ensure equality in the level and types of assistance provided was a commonly reported experience. Overall, programs geared toward homeless women veterans including women-specific veteran programs regarding benefits and entitlements were identified as essential but lacking. Women-specific veteran programs may help dispel the lack of trust, and forestall women's reluctance to self-identify as veterans. Intermediary service providers identified structural and financial accommodations as problematic and in need of enhancement in order to aid in longer-term planning. These intermediary agencies propose that with changes they could more effectively help homeless women veterans and ensure their success.

The issue of displacement and homelessness in the civilian community has directly impacted every generation of veterans from the Revolutionary War to the present day. However, the Vietnam War was the most significant generation of war veterans that elevated the issue of homelessness, and its disproportionate impact on the veteran population, in the public eye (Coalition for the Homeless 2003). Ourstorically, veterans, and in turn homeless veterans, have been predominantly male, but the increase of women serving in the armed forces and during times of war has produced an emerging subpopulation within the homeless community who have unique needs from their male counterparts that are often overlooked or unconsidered by policies, programs and initiatives aimed at eradicating veteran homelessness (Coalition for the Homeless 2003, U.S. Department of Veterans Affairs 2017).

Today there is an estimated 3 million people who experience homelessness in a year, with 26 percent of that adult population who are veterans (Coalition for the Homeless 2003; Washington et al. 2010). Women veterans are three to four times more likely to become homeless than their nonveteran women counterparts (Washington et al. 2010). In fact, from 2006–10, the number of homeless women veterans has doubled from 1,380 to 3,328 (National Coalition for Homeless Veterans n.d.).

The common challenges facing homeless veterans are mental health disorders and substance abuse disorders, chief among them being PTSD, which negatively impact seeking and maintaining employment (National Coalition for Homeless Veterans n.d.). Additionally, women veterans face unique challenges that place them at a higher risk for homelessness, such as being the sole caregiver for their children (U.S. Department of Veterans Affairs 2017) and/or having a higher prevalence of MST than their male counterparts (53 percent) (U.S. Department of Veterans Affairs 2017, Washington et al. 2010). A comparative study of homeless women veterans and their housed counterparts identified unemployability and disability as risk factors for homelessness, while being married and graduating college served as protective factors (Washington et al. 2010).

In 2009, the Department of Veterans Affairs under former VA Secretary Eric Shinseki, made ending veteran homelessness a national priority, enlisting the support and collaboration of government agency partners, as well as dozens of major cities nationwide, to eradicate veteran homelessness (National Alliance to End Homelessness 2015, National Coalition for Homeless Veterans n.d., U.S. Department of Veterans Affairs 2017).

Currently, there are five main governmental programs in place to help support homeless veterans (U.S. Department of Veterans Affairs 2017), with an increasing focus paid to the emerging and most vulnerable subpopulation of homeless women veterans (Washington et al. 2010). First, the Homeless Veterans' Reintegration Program is a joint venture between the VA and the Department of Labor, with the goal of connecting homeless veterans with employment in their communities, to include a targeted $4 million in grants to address women veteran homelessness. Second, in the Homelessness Prevention and Rapid Re-Housing Program, veterans and their families who have recently become homeless, or would be without this intervention, are eligible to receive rapid re-housing and homeless prevention assistance from community organizations. Third, HUD-VASH is a collaboration between the Housing and Urban Development (HUD) and the VA. This program provides eligible veterans with VA case management and Section VIII vouchers through the public housing authority, and includes special services for the most vulnerable of the homeless veteran population, such as disabled veterans, women veterans, and recently returned combat veterans. Fourth, the Grant and Per Diem Program provides funding for community-based organizations that provide transitional housing or support services for homeless veterans. Last, the Supportive Services for Veteran Families Program provides grants to private and nonprofit organizations supporting low-income veterans and their families transitioning to permanent housing (National Alliance to End Homelessness 2015, U.S. Department of Veterans Affairs 2017).

Although the aforementioned programs have made a significant contribution to eradicating veteran homelessness, there still remains an increased risk for women veterans becoming and/or remaining homeless due to their unique needs for support in the following areas: 1 housing support/care for dependent children; 2 privacy/safety concerns; 3 gender-related care; and 4 treatment for physical and sexual trauma (Washington et al. 2010). Traditionally, many of the existing facilities housing homeless veterans are male dominated, and fail to address the privacy and security concerns of women, especially those who have histories of trauma and/or have children. In fact, reports and audits from the U.S. Government Accountability Office (GAO) and the VA's Office of the Inspector General reveal that between 31 percent and 66 percent of grant per diem facilities are inadequate for homeless women veterans' needs, chief among them facilities that are safe, secure and segregated, and able to house children (National Coalition for Homeless Veterans n.d.).

Further, many advocates for homeless veterans have called for increased female-only trauma-informed treatment programs, expanding availability of college education, job training, as well as more inclusive transitional housing for homeless women veterans and their children (National Coalition for Homeless Veterans n.d.). Homelessness compromises the health of veterans affected. However, gender-specific and appropriate outreach and resources may better build trust and empower women veterans (U.S. Department of Labor 2010).

Conclusion

Social (and societal) factors that can interact to amplify and disadvantage certain groups can impose significant influence regarding health outcomes for women service members past and present. Preventable adverse health outcomes disadvantage readiness and cohesion for the active duty population and undermine the DoD and VA commitment to those who have served. There are many factors of disadvantage that have been noted as contributing to adverse health outcomes. These upstream factors can affect both individual and population health across biological, psychological and social dimensions. Dunivin (1997) illuminates paradigmatic shifts for creating a cultural landscape to enable tempering the countervailing forces that hamper women's equal status and treatment by blunting the combat warrior paradigm and climbing toward a cultural apex of the social egalitarian paradigm where values of equality, diversity and inclusion are lived components of all aspects of readiness and cohesion. While this is a visionary goal for military institutions, the wicked and embedded nature of legacy gender inequality in civil society exceeds the momentum required to overcome the challenge. Further, the philosophical crossroads of treatment needs to align with prevention and humanist values that support long-term health for women as well as all warriors and veterans.

Notes

1 The Healthy People 2020 approach to social determinants of health uses a 'place-based' organizing framework that reflects five key areas of social determinants of health developed for the Healthy People 2020 goals. The five key determinants include: 1 economic stability; 2 education; 3 social and community context; 4 health and healthcare; and 5 neighborhood and built environment.
2 American Cancer Society 'What are the key statistics about breast cancer in men?' www.cancer.org/cancer/breast-cancer-in-men/about/key-statistics.html
3 See February 2017 'women only file,' www.dmdc.osd.mil/appj/dwp/dwp_reports.jsp
4 Income of Households definition: This includes the income of the householder and all other individuals 15 years old and over in the household, whether they are related to the householder or not. Because many households consist of only one person, average household income is usually less than average family income. The median divides the income distribution into two equal parts: one-half of the cases falling below the median and one-half above the median.
5 Dioxin is a shortened form for the group of chemicals Polychlorinated Dibenzo-p-dioxins (PCDDs). One of these within the group present in Agent Orange is the chemical 2,3,7,8-tetrachlorodibenzodioxin or TCDD, which elicits a disease spectrum of biological effects, including carcinogenicity, immunotoxicity, reproductive/developmental toxicity, hepatotoxicity, neurotoxicity, chloracne, and loss of body weight (Institute of Medicine 1996).

6 The VA presumes that specific disabilities diagnosed in certain veterans were caused by their military service. For Vietnam veterans the service-inclusive dates are 1/9/1962 to 5/7/1975. See VA Benefits, www.benefits.va.gov/BENEFITS/factsheets/serviceconnected/presumption.pdf

7 Women have only recently been performing high-risk jobs where exposure to various toxins is likely to occur and long-term health data are lacking for women in this regard. Physiological gender differences include, e.g., women's higher percentage of body fat where certain chemicals can accumulate, the lower body weight of women can reduce the dose that has a harmful effect, and women have a different hormone profile so the interactive effects with chemical assault can vary by gender (Westervelt 2015).

Bibliography

Abrams, K. (1993). Gender in the Military: Androcentrism and Institutional Reform. *Law and Contemporary Problems.* http://scholarship.law.berkeley.edu/facpubs/1213. Retrieved December 12, 2016.

American Academy of Allergy Asthma & Immunology. (2015). Dust in Middle East Deployment Area Poses Significant Health Risks to Veterans. *AAAAI News Release*, February. www.aaaai.org/about-aaaai/newsroom/news-releases/middle-eastern-deployment Retrieved July 1, 2017.

American Public Health Association. (n.d.). Health Equity. www.apha.org/topics-and-issues/health-equity. Retrieved June 2, 2016.

American Public Health Association. (2015). Cleanup of U.S. Military Burn Pits in Iraq and Afghanistan. (Policy Number: 20155). November 3. www.apha.org/policies-and-advocacy/public-health-policy-statements/policy-database/2015/12/16/08/56/cleanup-of-us-military-burn-pits-in-iraq-and-afghanistan. Retrieved July 1, 2017.

Andre, C. and Velasquez, M. (2015 [1990]). Men & Women: Justice & Compassion. Markkula Center for Applied Ethics. www.scu.edu/ethics/ethics-resources/ethical-decision-making/men-women-justice-compassion/. Retrieved May 15, 2017.

Biden, J. (2007). Biden keeps promise to veterans. Press Release, November 11. The American Presidency Project. www.presidency.ucsb.edu/ws/?pid=116226. Retrieved July 12, 2017.

Bloeser, K., and McCoy, K. (2012). Social Obstacles to Change: The Intersection of Epidemiology, Neurobiology, and Clinical Practice with Veterans. Presentation [PowerPoint slides]. https://webcache.googleusercontent.com/search?q=cache:AFI4wzmdiS8J:https://www.warrelatedillness.va.gov/education/webinars/2012-06-21-kmccoy-kbloeser-social-obstacles-to-change.pptx+&cd=2&hl=en&ct=clnk&gl=usVA War Related Illness and Injury Study Center (WRIISC). Retrieved May 12, 2017.

Blosnich, J., Foynes, M., and Shipherd, J. (2013). Health Disparities Among Sexual Minority Women Veterans. *Journal of Women's Health*, 22, 7, 631–636. doi:10.1089/jwh.2012.4214. http://pubmedcentralcanada.ca/pmcc/articles/PMC3761433/. Retrieved May 20, 2017.

Brunner, E. and Marmot, M. (2006). Social Organization, Stress, and Health. In M. Marmot and R.G. Wilkinson (Eds.), *Social Determinants of Health*, 2nd ed. e-reader version. Retrieved May 4, 2017.

Brunswick, M. (2016). Iraq and Afghanistan Vets May Have Their Own Agent Orange. June 18. *Star Tribune-Minneapolis.* www.startribune.com/iraq-afghan-vets-may-have-their-own-agent-orange/383522481/#1 Retrieved July 5, 2017.

Burrelli, D.F. (2013). Women in Combat: Issues for Congress. Congressional Research Services. www.ncdsv.org/images/CongResearchService_WomenInCombatIssuesForCongress_5-9-2013.pdf. Retrieved June 23, 1917.

Caroselli, C. (2012). The Veterans Administration Health System: An Overview of Major Policy Issues. In D.J. Mason, L.K. Leavitt, and M.W. Chaffee (Eds.), *Policy & Politics in Nursing.* e-Book, 6th ed. (p.182–186). St. Louis, Missouri: Elsevier Saunders.

Cecchine, G., Sloss, E., Nelson, C., Fisher, G., Sama, P., Pathak, A., Adamson, D. (2009). *Foundations for Integrating Employee Health Activities for Active Duty.* Santa Monica: RAND Corporation. www.rand.org/content/dam/rand/pubs/monographs/2009/RAND_MG799.sum.pdf. Retrieved May 24, 2017.

Coalition for the Homeless. (2003). War and Homelessness. How American Wars Create Homelessness among United States Armed Forces Veterans. www.csun.edu/~bashforth/155_PDF/ME2_Fall_SI/AmericanWarsCreateHomelessness.pdf. Retrieved April 17, 2017.

Crosby, C. (2017). Fort McClellan and Toxic Exposures: What Veterans Need to Know. Hill & Ponton Disability Attorneys. www.hillandponton.com/fort-mcclellan-toxic-exposures-veterans-need-know/. Retrieved July 8, 2017.

Diantonio, N. (2017). Fox 4 Investigation Reveals Female Veterans Can't Get Mammograms at Local VA Hospitals. April 27. http://fox4kc.com/2017/04/27/fox-4-investigation-reveals-female-veterans-cant-get-mammograms-at-local-va-hospitals/Fox 4 online, Kansas City. Retrieved June 20, 2017.

Dignified Burial and Other Veterans' Benefits Improvement Act of 2012. (2013). *Pub. L. No. 112-260, Title II – Health Care, Establishment of Open Burn Pit Registry,* 38 USC 527. Government Printing Office. www.gpo.gov/fdsys/pkg/PLAW-112publ260/html/PLAW-112publ260.htm Retrieved July 20, 2017.

Doan, A. and Portillo, S. (2015). *Project Diane: Women's Foundation of Greater Kansas City Final Report.* http://static1.squarespace.com/static/545815dce4b0d75692c341a8/t/5640fc56e4b0ad25ec7dc3d8/1447099478084/PROJECTDIANE Final+Report.pdf. University of Kansas. Retrieved June 30, 2017.

Doan, A. and Portillo, S. (2017). Project Diane: Integrating Military Women in Combat Roles. Updated January 12. Associated Press. www.huffingtonpost.com/alesha-doan/project-diane-integrating_b_8962600.html. Retrieved June 26, 2017.

Duffy, B. (2017). Joint Hearing of The Committees on Veterans' Affairs United States Senate and United States House of Representatives. March 1. www.vfw.org/advocacy/national-legislative-service/congressional-testimony/20170301-congressional-statement-of-vfw-national-commander-brian-duffy. Veterans of Foreign War. Retrieved June 2, 2017.

Dunivin, K.O. (1997). Military Culture: A Paradigm Shift? Air War College, Maxwell Paper No.10. February. www.au.af.mil/au/awc/awcgate/maxwell/mp10.pdf. Retrieved June 6, 2017.

Foster, G.A. and Alviar, A. (2013). Military Women's Health While Deployed: Feminine Hygiene and Health in Austere Environments. *Federal Practitioner.* www.mdedge.com/sites/default/files/issues/articles/030010009.pdf. Retrieved July 2, 2017.

Friedl, K.E. (2005). Biomedical Research on Health and Performance of Military Women: Accomplishments of the Defense Women's Health Research Program (DWHRP). *Journal of Women's Health*, November 14, 9, 764–802. Academic Search Premier. www.ncbi.nlm.nih.gov/pubmed/16313206. Retrieved July 2, 2017.

Galabuzi, G.-E. (2009). Social Exclusion. In *Social Determinants of Health: Canadian Perspectives.* 2nd ed. Dennis Raphael (Ed.) (p. 253–268). Amazon.com. Retrieved June 18, 2017.

Gaydos, J.C. (1991). A Historical Review of the Need for Military Toxicology and the U.S. Army. *Proceedings of the Conference on Chemical Risk Assessment in the DoD.* https://archive.org/stream/DTIC_ADP008724/DTIC_ADP008724_djvu.txt. Retrieved July 8, 2017.

Gaydos, J.C. (2011). Military Occupational and Environmental Health: Challenges for the 21st Century. *Military Medicine*, 176, July, Supp. 5–8. EBSCO Publishing. Retrieved July 3, 2017.

Griffith, J. (2010). Citizens Coping as Soldiers: A Review of Deployment Stress Symptoms Among Reservists. *Military Psychology*, 22, 2, 176–206. doi:10.1080/08995601003638967. Retrieved June 28, 2017.

Haring, E.L. (2016). DACOWITS Public Statement. Women in International Security. December 8. http://dacowits.defense.gov/Portals/48/Documents/General%20Documents/RFI%20Docs/Dec2016/Dr.%20Haring_Public%20Comment.pdf?ver=2016-12-04-233243-803. Retrieved July 1, 2017.

Hibbeln, J.R., and Gow, R.V. (2014). The Potential for Military Diets to Reduce Depression, Suicide, and Impulsive Aggression: A Review of Current Evidence for Omega-3 and Omega-6 Fatty Acids. *Military Medicine*, 179, 11, 117–128. http://militarymedicine.amsus.org/doi/pdf/10.7205/MILMED-D-14-00153. Retrieved July 2, 2017.

Hickman, J. (2016). *The Burn Pits: The Poisoning of America's Soldiers.* New York, NY: Skyhorse Publishing, Inc.

Himmelfarb, N., Yaeger, D., and Mintz, J. (2006). Posttraumatic Stress Disorder in Female Veterans with Military and Civilian Sexual Trauma. *Journal of Traumatic Stress*, 19, 6, 837–846. doi:10.1002/jts.20163. Retrieved July 3, 2017.

Hines, J.F. (1992). Ambulatory Health Care Needs of Women Deployed with a Heavy Armor Division during Persian Gulf War. *Military Medicine*, 157, 219–221.

Hopkins-Chadwick, D.L. (2006). The Health Readiness of Junior Enlisted Military Women: The Social Determinants of Health Model and Research Questions. *Military Medicine*, 171, 6, 544–549. http://militarymedicine.amsus.org/doi/pdf/10.7205/MILMED.171.6.544. Retrieved July 12, 2017.

Institute of Medicine. (1996). Veterans and Agent Orange: Update 1996: Summary and Research Highlights 1997. www.nap.edu/read/9079/chapter/3. Retrieved June 13, 2017.

Institute of Medicine, Committee on Nutrition, Trauma, and the Brain. (2011). Nutrition and Traumatic Brain Injury: Improving Acute and Subacute Health Outcomes in Military Personnel. In J. Erdman, M. Oria, L. Pillsbury (Eds.). In *Understanding Pathophysiological Changes.* www.ncbi.nlm.nih.gov/books/NBK209313/. Retrieved July 1, 2017.

Kalichman, M. (2009). Evidence-Based Research Ethics. *The American Journal of Bioethics: AJOB*, 9, 6–7, 85–87. doi:10.1080/15265160902923457. www.ncbi.nlm.nih.gov/pmc/articles/PMC3586321/. Retrieved May 20, 2017.

Kamarck, K. (2016). Women in Combat: Issues for Congress. December 13. Congressional Research Service. https://fas.org/sgp/crs/natsec/R42075.pdf. Retrieved June 23, 2017.

Kang, H.K., Mahan, C.M., Lee, K.Y., Magee, C.A., Mather, S.H. and Matanoski, G. (2000). Pregnancy Outcomes Among U.S. Women Vietnam Veterans (Abstract). *American Journal of Industrial Medicine*, 38, 4, 447–454. www.ncbi.nlm.nih.gov/pubmed/10982986?ordinalpos=183&itool=EntrezSystem2.PEntrez.Pubmed.Pubmed_ResultsPanel.Pubmed_DefaultReportPanel.Pubmed_RVDocSum. Retrieved July 7, 2017.

Kime, P. (2015). New Burn Pit Report: Lung Disease, High Blood Pressure Common in Exposed Vets. *Military Times*. www.militarytimes.com/pay-benefits/military-benefits/health-care/2015/07/22/new-burn-pit-report-lung-disease-high-blood-pressure-common-in-exposed-vets/. Retrieved July 7, 2017.

Kintzle, S., Schuyler, A.C., Ray-Letourneau, D., Ozuna, S.M., Munch, C., Xintarianos, E., Hasson, A.M., and Castro, C.A. (2015). Sexual Trauma in the Military: Exploring PTSD and Mental Health Care Utilization in Female Veterans. *Psychological Services*, 12, 4, 394–401. www.apa.org/pubs/journals/releases/ser-ser0000054.pdf. Retrieved July 3, 2017.

Marmot, M., and Allen, J.J. (2014). Social Determinants of Health Equity. *American Journal of Public Health*, 104, Suppl 4, S517–S519. doi:10.2105/AJPH.2014.302200. www.ncbi.nlm.nih.gov/pmc/articles/PMC4151898/. Retrieved July 1, 2017.

Marmot, M., Siegrist, J., and Theorell, T. (2006). Health and the Psychological Environment at Work. In Michael Marmot and Richard G. Wilkinson (Eds.), *Social Determinants of Health*. 2nd ed. Kindle version. Retrieved July 1, 2017.

Mascarenhas, O. (2009). Innovation as Defining Resolving Wicked Problems. http://weaverjm.faculty.udmercy.edu/MascarenhasLectureNotes/MascarenhasWickedproblems.doc. Retrieved April 2, 2017.

Mota, N.P., Medved, M., Wang, J., Asmundson, G.J.G., Whitney, D., and Sareen, J. (2011). Stress and Mental Disorders in Female Military Personnel: Comparisons Between the Sexes in a Male Dominated Profession. *Journal of Psychiatric Research*, 30, 1–9. doi:10.1016/j.jpsychires.2011.09.014. Retrieved July 1, 2017.

National Alliance to End Homelessness. (2015). Fact Sheet: Veteran Homelessness. www.endhomelessness.org/library/entry/fact-sheet-veteranhomelessness. Retrieved April 17, 2017.

National Coalition for Homeless Veterans. (n.d.). Homeless Female Veterans. www.nchv.org/images/uploads/HFV%20paper.pdf. Retrieved May 17, 2017.

National Institute of Corrections. (n.d.). Justice-Involved Veterans. https://nicic.gov/veterans. Retrieved July 2, 2017.

National Resource Center on Justice Involved Women (NRCJIW). (2013). Responding to the Needs of Women Veterans Involved in the Criminal Justice System. http://cjinvolvedwomen.org/wpcontent/uploads/2015/09/WomenVeteransREV1-21-14.pdf. Retrieved June 2, 2017.

Nettleman, M. (2015). Gulf War Illness: Challenges Persist. *American Clinical and Climatological Association*, 126, 237–247. ncbi.nlm.nih.gov. Retrieved July 2, 2017.

Ornstein, C. (2016). Reliving Agent Orange: Long List of Agent Orange decisions in 2017. *Pro Publica*. www.propublica.org/article/long-list-of-agent-orange-decisions-awaits-va-in-2017. Retrieved July 20, 2017.

Peele, R.B. (2014). Understanding the Reintegration of Female Reservists Activated After September 11, 2001: A Phenomenological Approach. *ProQuest Dissertations Publishing*3583295. http://search.proquest.com/openview/8a6f72a5596f99f2557e8ab399010341/1?pq-origsite=gscholar&cbl=18750&diss=y. Retrieved July 1, 2017.

Pellerin, C. (2015). Carter Opens All Military Occupations, Positions to Women. DoD U.S Department of Defense. *Defense Media Activity News.* www.defense.gov/News/Article/Article/632536/carter-opens-all-military-occupations-positions-to-women/. Retrieved July 3, 2017.

Percy, J. (2016). The Things They Burned. *New Republic.* https://newrepublic.com/article/138058/things-burned. Retrieved July 20, 2017.

Pietrzak, E., Pullman, S., Cotea, C., and Nasveld, P. (2017). Effects of Deployment on Health Behaviours in Military Forces. *Journal of Military and Veterans' Health: A Review of Longitudinal Studies,* 21, 1. http://jmvh.org/article/effects-of-deployment-on-health-behaviours-in-military-forces-a-review-of-longitudinal-studies/. Retrieved July 20, 2017.

Ramirez, R. and Van Dieten, M. (2013). *Responding to the Needs of Women Veterans in the Criminal Justice System.* National Resource Center on Justice Involved Women. http://cjinvolvedwomen.org/wp-content/uploads/2015/09/WomenVeteransREV1-21-14.pdf. Retrieved July 28, 2017.

Raphael, D. (2003). Barriers to Addressing the Societal Determinants of Health: Public Health Units and Poverty in Ontario Canada. *Health Promotional International.* doi:10.1093/heapro/dag411. https://academic.oup.com/heapro/article/18/4/397/631906/Barriers-to-addressing-the-societal-determinants. Retrieved July 3, 2017.

Resnick, E.M., Mallampalli, M., Carter, C.L. (2012). Current Challenges in Female Veterans' Health. *Journal of Women's Health,* 21, 9. doi:10.1089/jwh.2012.3644. Retrieved July 12, 2017.

Responding to the Needs of Women Veterans Involved in the Criminal Justice System (abstract). (2014). National Resource Center on Justice Involved Women. www.ncjrs.gov/App/Publications/abstract.aspx?ID=270220. Retrieved July 3, 2017.

Rittel, H.W., and Webber, M.M. (1973). Dilemmas in a General Theory of Planning. *Policy Sciences,* 4, 155–169.

Ryan-Wenger, N.A. and Lowe, N.K. (2000). Military Women's Perspectives on Health Care During Deployment. *Women's Health Issues,* 10, 6, 333–343. www.ncbi.nlm.nih.gov/pubmed/11077217. Retrieved July 12, 2017.

Schnitzer, P., Olshan, A., and Erickson, J. (1995). Paternal Occupation and Risk of Birth Defects in Offspring. *Epidemiology,* 6, 6, 577–583. www.jstor.org/stable/3703131. Retrieved October 21, 2017.

Service Women's Action Network (SWAN). (2016). First Annual SWAN Survey of Service Women and Women Veterans. November 14. www.servicewomen.org/uncategorized/swan-releases-1st-annual-survey-of-service-women-women-veterans/. Retrieved July 20, 2017.

Service Women's Action Network (SWAN), American Civil Liberties Union (ACLU), and American Civil Liberties Union of Connecticut v. U.S. Department of Defense, U.S. District Court for the District of Connecticut, 2015. www.clearinghouse.net/chDocs/public/EE-CT-0020-0001.pdf. Retrieved July 20, 2017.

Sidel, V.W. (2000). The Roles and Ethics of Health Professionals in War. In *War and Public Health.* Barry S. Levy and Victor W. Sidel (Eds). Washington, DC: APHA.

Siebold, G.L. (2007). The Essence of Military Group Cohesion. *Armed Forces and Society*, 33, 2. Abstract. http://journals.sagepub.com/doi/pdf/10.1177/0095327X06294173. Retrieved July12, 2017.

Smith, S.E. (2015). Too Often, Military Sexual Assault Survivors Must Fight for Disability Benefits. January 26. *Rewire*. https://rewire.news/article/2015/01/26/often-military-sexual-assault-survivors-must-fight-disability-benefits/. Retrieved July 13, 2017.

Stander, V.A., and Thomsen, C.J. (2016). Sexual Harassment and Assault in the U.S. Military: A Review of Policy and Research Trends. *Military Medicine*, 181, 1S. http://militarymedicine.amsus.org/doi/full/10.7205/MILMED-D-15-00336. Retrieved July, 7, 2017.

Stansfeld, S.A. (2009). Social Support and Social Cohesion. In Michael Marmot and Richard G. Wilkinson (Eds.) *Social Determinants of Health*. 2nd ed. Kindle version.

Steele, J. (2016). Female Vets' Jail Program Ends. *San Diego Union Tribune* online. March 9. www.sandiegouniontribune.com/military/sdut-female-veterans-jail-program-2016mar09-story.html. Retrieved July 17, 2017.

Trasler, J.M., and Doerksen, T. (1999). Teratogen Update: Paternal Exposures – Reproductive Risks. *Teratology*, 60, 161–172. http://teratology.org/updates/60pg161.pdf. Retrieved August 5, 2017.

Tritten, T.J. (2016). Form-fitted Body Armor Rolling Out as Combat Roles Expand for Women. *Stars and Stripes*. www.military.com/daily-news/2016/03/04/form-fitted-body-armor-rolling-out-combat-roles-expand-women.html. Retrieved July 30, 2017.

U.S. Army Center for Health Promotion & Preventive Medicine (ACHPPM). (n.d.). Just the Facts: Balad Burn Pit. www.dpc.senate.gov/hearings/hearing50/chppm_fact_sheet.pdf. Retrieved August 1, 2017.

U.S. Bureau of Labor Statistics. (2017a). Economic News Release. Employment Situation of Veterans 2015–2016 Annual Averages. March 22. www.bls.gov/news.release/vet.a.htm. Retrieved July 8, 2017.

U.S. Bureau of Labor Statistics. (2017b). Veterans Summary Table A. Employment Status of the Civilian Noninstitutional Population 18 years and Over by Veteran Status, Period of Service, and Sex, 2015–2016 Annual Averages. March 22. www.bls.gov/news.release/vet.a.htm. Retrieved July 8, 2017.

U.S. Bureau of Labor Statistics. (2017c). Economic New Release, Household Data. April. www.bls.gov/news.release/empsit.t05.htm. Retrieved July 8, 2017.

U.S. Centers for Disease Control and Prevention. (n.d.). Understanding Social Determinants of Health. www.healthypeople.gov/2020/topics-objectives/topic/social-determinants-of-health. Retrieved May 4, 2017.

U.S. Department of Defense. (1986). Health Promotion and Disease/Injury Prevention Directive 1010.10. https://biotech.law.lsu.edu/blaw/dodd/corres/pdf/d101010_082203/d101010p.pdf. Retrieved August 7, 2017.

U.S. Department of Defense. (2014a). Health Promotion and Disease Prevention. April 28. www.dtic.mil/whs/directives/corres/pdf/101010p.pdf. Retrieved August 1, 2017.

U.S. Department of Defense. (2014b). Profile of Military Community: 2014 Demographics. http://download.militaryonesource.mil/12038/MOS/Reports/2014-Demographics-Report.pdf. Retrieved July 5, 2017.

U.S. Department of Defense, Defense Manpower Data Center (DoD DMDC). (2017). DoD Personnel, Workforce Reports & Publications, Active Duty

Personnel by Service by Rank/Grade, Feb. 2017 (Women only). www.dmdc.osd.mil/appj/dwp/dwp_reports.jsp. Retrieved July 18, 2017.

U.S. Department of Defense, Military OneSource. (2015). 2015 Demographics: Profile of Military Community. http://download.militaryonesource.mil/12038/MOS/Reports/2015-Demographics-Report.pdf. Retrieved July 8, 2017.

U.S. Department of Health, Education, and Welfare. (1979). *Healthy People: The Surgeon General's Report on Health Promotion and Disease Prevention.*

U.S. Department of Health and Human Services (DHHS). (n.d.) *Healthy People 2020: Understanding Determinants.*

U.S. Department of Labor. (2010). Women's Bureau, Homeless Women Veterans Listening Sessions. www.dol.gov/wb/programs/listeningsessions.htm. Retrieved July 10, 2017.

U.S. Department of Veterans Affairs. (1995). Agent Orange Review. www.publichealth.va.gov/docs/agentorange/reviews/ao_newsletter_may95.pdf. Retrieved August 1, 2017.

U.S. Department of Veterans Affairs. (2015a). Report on Data from the Airborne Hazard and Open Burn Pit (AH&OPB) Registry. www.publichealth.va.gov/docs/exposures/va-ahobp-registry-data-report-june2015.pdf. Retrieved August 1, 2017.

U.S. Department of Veterans Affairs. (2015b). *Study of Barriers for Women Veterans to VA Health Care: Final Report.* www.womenshealth.va.gov/docs/Womens%20Health%20Services_Barriers%20to%20Care%20Final%20Report_April2015.pdf. Retrieved July 15, 2017.

U.S. Department of Veterans Affairs. (2015c). Women Veterans Report: The Past, Present, and Future of Women Veterans. www.va.gov/vetdata/docs/SpecialReports/Women_Veterans_2015_Final.pdf. Retrieved June 1, 2017.

U.S. Department of Veterans Affairs. (2016). Fact Sheet: Women Veterans Population. www.va.gov/womenvet/docs/womenveteranspopulationfactsheet.pdf. Retrieved July 20, 2017.

U.S. Department of Veterans Affairs. (2017). *VA Programs to End Homelessness Among Women Veterans.* Homeless Veterans. www.va.gov/HOMELESS/for_women_veterans.asp. Retrieved April 17, 2017.

U.S. Department of Veterans Affairs. (n.d.a). Public Health: Birth Defects in Children of Women Vietnam Veterans. www.publichealth.va.gov/exposures/agentorange/birth-defects/children-women-vietnam-vets.asp. Retrieved August 1, 2017.

U.S. Department of Veterans Affairs. (n.d.b). Public Health: Burn Pits. www.publichealth.va.gov/PUBLICHEALTH/exposures/burnpits/index.asp. Retrieved August 1, 2017.

U.S. Department of Veterans Affairs, National Center for Veterans Analysis and Statistics. (2016). Profile of Women Veterans: 2015. www.va.gov/vetdata/docs/SpecialReports/Women_Veterans_Profile_12_22_2016.pdf. Retrieved July 20, 2017.

U.S. Surgeon General. (1979). Healthy People: The Surgeon General's Report on Health Promotion and Disease Prevention. https://profiles.nlm.nih.gov/NN/B/B/G/K/. Retrieved July 3, 2017.

Veterans of Foreign Wars. (2016). Women Veterans: Evaluating VA Health Care and Veteran Benefits. www.vfw.org/-/media/VFWSite/Files/Misc/InTheirWordsEvaluatingVAHealthCareandBenefitsforWomenVeterans.pdf?la=en. Retrieved August 1, 2017.

Washington, D.L., Yano, E.M., McGuire, J., Hines, V., Lee, M., and Gelberg, L. (2010). Risk Factors for Homelessness Among Women Veterans. *Journal of Health Care for the Poor and Underserved*, 21, 1, 82–91. https://doi.org/10.1353/hpu.0.0237. Retrieved April 17, 2017.

Weick, K.E. (1987). Organizational Culture as a Source of High Reliability. *California Management Review*, 29, 2, 119–127. www.itn.liu.se/mit/education/courses/tnfl05-risk-och-olycksanalys/vecka-48/1.305709/Weick1987.pdf. Retrieved July 28, 2017.

Westervelt, A. (2015). Research Lags on the Health Risks of Women's Exposure to Chemicals. *Guardian* online. www.theguardian.com/lifeandstyle/2015/may/05/osha-health-women-breast-cancer-chemicals-work-safety. Retrieved August 1, 2017.

White, P. (2003 [1998]). Urban Life and Social Stress. In D. Pinder (Ed.), *The New Europe: Economy, Society and Environment*. Chichester, UK: Wiley.

Women Veterans Report. (2017) *2015: The Past, Present, and Future of Women Veterans*. Washington, DC: National Center for Veterans Analysis and Statistics, Department of Veterans Affairs. www.va.gov/vetdata/docs/SpecialReports/Women_Veterans_2015_Final.pdf. Retrieved May 15, 2017.

Wood, R. (1995, December 1). Speech on National Security at Air War College, Maxwell AFB, AL.

World Health Organization. (2003). *Social Determinants of Health: The Solid Facts*. 2nd ed. Eds. Richard Wilkinson and Michael Marmot. www.euro.who.int/__data/assets/pdf_file/0005/98438/e81384.pdf. Retrieved May 5, 2017.

World Health Organization Health Protection Agency. (2006). Products of Combustion-Draft Summary Information. www.who.int/hac/techguidance/tools/products_of_combustion_July2006.pdf?ua=1. Retrieved August 1, 2017.

23 Impact of Military Sexual Trauma

Military sexual trauma (MST) is an often misunderstood health issue that greatly impacts the lives of military personnel, and society as a whole. The continued prevalence of sexual harassment and sexual assault in the military represents a type of institutional or systemic abuse that can be viewed through the lens of a wicked problem, which occurs in 'ambiguous or uncertain settings in which unstructured, multi-causal interdependencies dynamically evolve' (Rittel and Webber 1973, p.2).

Due to the complexity and nuances of wicked problems like MST, their subsequent progress and solutions are meant to be continuously improved upon and 'tamed' or 'coped with,' versus a problem to be solved. The key to 'taming' the problem is building the capacity of the organization to problem solve so that solutions do not exclusively rely on a few actors, but a range and multitude of stakeholders (Burns et al. 2013, Rittel and Webber 1973).

MST has been framed by the military community as a gendered violence issue, where women are primarily the victims (Hoyt et al. 2011, Hunter 2007, Miller and Weinstein-Matthews 2013). Given the severity and continued prevalence of sexual harassment and sexual assault in the military, the field needs to identify, reconcile, and contend with multiple challenges (González-Prats 2017).

First, the current narrative that *only* women are victimized harms *all* service members, regardless of gender, as it undermines efforts to effectively address the problem. Second, women are best served when the prevalence of MST is understood and addressed beyond the conventional binary of male/female and when the full spectrum of gender identity and sexual preference is included. Third, one must consider the dynamics of power when examining MST since acts of sexual harassment and sexual assault are often an assertion of dominance and control. Particular attention needs to be paid to marginalized populations, such as military service members who identify as women; people of color; and members of the lesbian, gay, bisexual, transgender and queer (LGBTQ) community.

Lastly, the military's organizational culture of strict accountability and 'good order and discipline' sharply contradicts with its inability to successfully defeat one of the most recurrent and insidious of enemies that is MST. As such, MST continues to degrade the collective effectiveness of our nation's military (González-Prats 2017).

This chapter provides a basic foundation for understanding MST. It is organized in two sections. The first is a general overview of MST, including how it is defined; who it impacts; its physical, psychological and social effects; and its significance to the general public. The second section describes the prevalence of MST, including a description of how the military measures and tracks MST, military sexual assault (MSA), and military sexual harassment (MSH). For the purpose of continuity, the term 'victim' will be used to refer to both victims and survivors of MST, acknowledging that choosing to identify as either a 'victim' or a 'survivor' is a personal choice for the individual who has been impacted (González-Prats 2017, Hannagan 2016).

What is Military Sexual Trauma?

The U.S. Department of Veterans Affairs (VA) (2016) defines MST as incidents of sexual harassment and sexual assault incurred during military service. MST is a term that is used primarily by the VA to evaluate the healthcare, treatment and service-connected disability needs of its victims (Department of Defense (DoD) 2014c).

The military defines sexual harassment as:

> a form of sex discrimination that involves unwelcome sexual advances, requests for sexual favors, and other verbal or physical conduct of a sexual nature when: a) submission to such conduct is made either explicitly or implicitly a term or condition of a person's job, pay, or career, or b) submission to or rejection of such conduct by a person is used as a basis for career or employment decisions affecting that person, or c) such conduct has the purpose or effect of unreasonably interfering with an individual's work performance or creates an intimidating, hostile, or offensive working environment.
> (Workplace includes conduct on or off duty, 24 hours a day; DoD 2014a, p.1)

The military defines sexual assault as:

> Any person subject to this chapter who causes another person of any age to engage in a sexual act by: 1) using force against that other person 2) causing grievous bodily harm to any person 3) threatening or placing that other person in fear that any person will be subjected to death, grievous bodily harm, or kidnapping 4) rendering another person unconscious or 5) administering to another person by force or threat of force, or without the knowledge or permission of that person,

a drug, intoxicant, or similar substance and thereby substantially impairs the ability of that other person to appraise or control conduct. (Joint Service Committee on Military Justice 2008, section IV-68, p.351)

MST is a term often used interchangeably (and incorrectly) to refer to sexual assault. However, in this book, the terms MSA and MSH will be referred to separately, while the term MST will only be used when referring to incidents of sexual harassment *and* sexual assault.

MST occurs across the service branches and service components of the Army, Navy, Air Force, Marine Corps, and Coast Guard,[1] including the military service academies (DMDC 2012, DoD 2014b, Veterans Healthcare Administration 2013). Until 2014, sexual assault and sexual harassment were discussed and tracked separately as two independent and unrelated offenses. However, the most recent (and significant) shift has been the acknowledgement by the DoD that sexual harassment and sexual assault run along a 'continuum of harm' (DoD 2014c, p. 21) that ranges from gender-focused jokes, sexual comments, and vulgar pictures through physical force, sexual fondling, forcible sodomy, and rape (DoD 2016, 2014c).

A 2014 military workplace study revealed three significant findings that supported the existence of MST as a continuum of harm (Morral et al. 2014). First, the study revealed that service members who were sexually harassed were more likely to have experienced sexual assault in the past year.[2] Second, about two-thirds of the victims[3] were sexually harassed either before or after the sexual assault. Finally, there was a positive correlation between gender discrimination and sexual assault, where service members were more likely to be sexually assaulted in work environments that had higher rates of gender discrimination (DoD 2015a, 2015b). It is then evident that MST significantly impacts all service members, regardless of gender. Therefore, one needs to become aware not only of who is impacted by MST, but what the physiological, psychological and social effects are.

Who Does MST Impact?

It is estimated that one in five women and one in 100 men in the military are sexually assaulted (Department of Veterans Affairs 2016). These rates, at least for women, closely resemble the rates in the civilian community, where one in six women, and one in 33 men have experienced an attempted or completed rape in their lifetime (RAINN 2009). The victims who are at an increased risk for sexual violence are members of the American Indian/Native American[4] (Department of Justice 2004, RAINN 2009) and the LGBTQ communities[5] (Cantor et al. 2015, Walters et al. 2013, Human Rights Watch 2015, RAINN 2009). These military and civilian rates are believed to be conservative estimates, as sexual assault/rape are violent crimes that are significantly underreported (RAINN 2009).

Despite the fact that men make up about 80 percent to 85 percent of the active duty and reserve forces and represent about 54 percent of the total number of victims that screen positively for MSA by the VA, the sexual assault of female service members receives most of the public's attention and media coverage (DoD 2015a, 2015b, Hoyt et al. 2011, Office of the Deputy Assistant Secretary of Defense 2014, Steward 2013).

Four significant empirical studies have: 1) made the connection between the prevalence of sexual assault within sexist and hostile work environments; and 2) identified the demographic variables (gender, race/ethnicity, age, rank and branch of service) associated with MST (Katz et al. 2012, Morral et al. 2014, Sadler et al. 2003, Vogt et al. 2007).

The characteristics of the victims[6] and alleged perpetrators[7] in formal[8] and informal[9] sexual harassment complaints were very similar. Whereas the alleged victims tended to be predominantly female and in the same units as the perpetrators, the alleged perpetrators tended to be predominantly male, in the same units as their victims, and more than half were from the enlisted corps (E5-E9), or were enlisted peers (E1-E4) (DoD 2014a, 2016).

Additionally, a characteristics profile has been developed for the victims[10] and perpetrators[11] in unrestricted reports of sexual assault. Sexual assault victims were predominantly female, found within the junior enlisted ranks (E1-E4), and under the age of 25, while the perpetrators tended to be male, from the junior enlisted ranks (E1-E4), and under the age of 35. The victim characteristics from the sexual assault restricted reports mirrored the gender, rank and age profiles from the unrestricted reports (DoD 2014a, 2016).

Further, in a comparative study of sexual assault prevalence conducted by the RAND Corporation, it concluded that there were no statistical differences between the sexual assault prevalence rates of male and female service members in the Army, Navy and Marine Corps (Morral et al. 2014). However, the same comparative analysis reaffirmed that the prevalence of sexual assault for members of the Air Force was statistically lower than the other services, although the findings are inconclusive as to the reasons why. Controlling for factors such as age, education, pay rate and deployment frequency, military personnel in service branches *other than the Air Force* were at a higher risk for sexual assault, or at a rate of 1.7 times for women, and four to five times for men (Morral et al. 2014). Differences between sexual assault prevalence and the active duty[12] and reserve components[13] were also noted. When compared to their active duty counterparts, reservists had a significantly lower prevalence of sexual assault for fiscal year (FY) 2014 (DoD 2015a). However, it is important to note that the part-time status (less than 180 days a year of service) and unique infrastructure of the reserve and National Guard components make it challenging to track rates of MST which may be reflected in the seemingly lower prevalence rates of sexual harassment and sexual assault for these groups.

The Effects of MST

There is evidence that MST has lasting physiological, psychological, and social effects on its victims (Maguen et al. 2012). Women who have experienced MST have higher self-reported rates of medical symptomatology to include gynecological, urological, neurological, gastrointestinal, pulmonary and cardiovascular conditions (Williams and Bernstein 2011). MST victims are also at higher risk for obesity, smoking, heart attack and hysterectomies before age 40 than those who have not experienced MST (Katz et al. 2007).

The psychological effects of MST have been associated with negative long-term impact on its victims (Caplan 2013, Mattocks et al. 2012). The medical and psychological communities have established a strong connection between MST and the emergence of post-traumatic stress disorder (PTSD)-related symptoms (Steward 2013, Stinson 2013). For example, it was found that female veterans with an ourstory of any type of sexual assault, incurred before or during military service, were five times more likely to meet the Clinical Administered PTSD Scale (CAPS) criteria for PTSD,[14] and were nine times more likely to have PTSD as compared to veterans without sexual assault ourstories (Blake et al. 1998, Suris et al. 2004). Additionally, MST has been strongly associated with PTSD, anxiety, depression and substance abuse for both male and female veterans (Steward 2013, Stinson 2013).

Moreover, Katz et al. (2007) concluded that of the three types of war stressors (e.g., MST, being injured, and/or witnessing others being injured/killed), MST was the only stressor that was significantly associated with symptoms and readjustment problems. 'It was surprising that "witnessing others injured or killed" was not correlated with symptoms or readjustment ... it seems that the women accepted this as part of the conditions of war ... for the most part they stated that "it was just part of doing my job"' (p.247). This finding supports the claim by Williams and Bernstein (2011) that sexual trauma poses a risk for developing into PTSD that is as high or higher than the risk from exposure to combat.

Further research has shown that female veterans with an ourstory of MST were twice as likely to be diagnosed with alcohol-related disorders, three times more likely to be diagnosed with depressive disorders, and five to eight times more likely to have PTSD as compared to female veterans who did not experience MST (Maguen et al. 2012). For Operation Enduring Freedom and Operation Iraqi Freedom[15] veterans diagnosed with PTSD and an ourstory of MST, women tend to display certain symptoms such as comorbid depression, substance abuse, anxiety and eating disorders, while men tend to demonstrate symptoms of comorbid depression and substance abuse (Maguen et al. 2012). Additionally, male and female veterans who are exposed to MST are twice as likely to self-harm and/or attempt suicide than veterans who have not experienced sexual trauma (Kelty et al. 2010).

In addition to the psychological implications of MST, victims of MST are also impacted socially, which poses a threat to an individual's ability to foster strong connections with his or her surroundings (e.g., friends, family, and community) (Katz 2007, Mattocks et al. 2012). PTSD greatly impacts an individual's quality of life, especially in connecting with their families or friends, and engaging in activities outside the home in their respective communities (David et al. 2006). Social factors such as family dynamics, support networks, community, and prior trauma and loss can impact a survivor's sense of connection and support (perceived or actual). The existing strength of the survivor's networks of family, friends, sense of community and connection will ultimately determine if they serve as a risk or protective factor for recovery.

Although MST shares many of the same impacts as sexual harassment and sexual assault in the civilian communities, it is aggravated by the unique dynamics of the military culture (Caplan 2013, Hunter 2007, Lucas 2013, Solaro 2006). These significant abuses of power and authority within the context of revered public institutions like the military are examples of *organizational trauma* (Hope and Eriksen 2009) or *institutional betrayal* (Smith and Freyd 2014). Disbelief, victim-blaming, and social and professional retaliation are just some examples of the compounding harm that the military contributes to the overall trauma (Human Rights Watch 2016, Institute for Veteran Policy 2015, Lucas 2013).

Consequently, the VA community and mental health professionals have drawn the parallel between MST and incest because of the strong familial bond that the military environment engenders (Dick 2012, Steward 2013, Stinson 2013). Survivors of MST are a unique population because when they are abused or assaulted in the context of military service, so multiple identities are impacted. The options for MST victims, like those of incest victims, are limited because the victims live and work alongside their perpetrators.

MST is also a risk factor for homelessness (Washington et al. 2010). It is estimated that women make up about 20 percent of homeless veterans, and when compared to nonveteran women, women veterans are more likely to become homeless (Caplan 2013). In a study of homeless and age-matched housed nonveteran women, 53.3 percent of homeless women reported sexual assault during military service, a prevalence that is significantly higher than the 26.8 percent among housed women (Pavao et al. 2013).

Significance of MST to the General Public

MST extends beyond being a military or female problem. It is a problem that affects American society (Dick 2012, DoD 2014b). As such, MST needs to be addressed by the military, veteran and civilian communities for three main reasons (González-Prats 2017). Chief among these reasons is the matter of *social responsibility*. Service members deserve protection and safety from internal abuse and assault. MST poses a threat to the values of equality, justice and dignity because it dehumanizes service members who have volunteered to protect and defend the country, oftentimes at an enormous risk and personal sacrifice to themselves and their families (Protect Our Defenders n.d., Tsongas and Tardiff n.d.). MST is a risk that can be prevented and mitigated through the consistent implementation of policies of accountability (Caplan 2013, Halloran 2013).

A second reason is that the risk of being a victim of MST poses a *threat to recruitment and retention*, which ultimately impacts our national security (Vanden Brook and Jackson 2013, Tsongas and Tardiff n.d.). The military already faces significant recruiting challenges as it is estimated that less than half of 1 percent of the U.S. population has ever served in the military (Miles 2011). In order to solidify voluntary military service members, ensure proper staffing, and sustain a formidable national defense program, it will be essential for the military to ensure safety from sexual victimization from within its ranks.

Lastly, addressing MST is important as a matter of *public safety*. There is a concern that sexual perpetrators could reoffend given their release from the military into the civilian community (Dick 2012, Horgan 2013, Military Justice International 2015). A meta-analysis shows a positive correlation between the increase of recidivism of sexually based offenses with the increase of time, ranging from a rate of 10 percent to 15 percent after five years, to a recidivism rate of 30 percent to 40 percent after 20 years (Hanson et al. 2003).

The public safety concern becomes even greater because not all perpetrators who commit sexually based offenses in the military are investigated, court martialed, convicted of sexual assault, and/or imprisoned, which increases the likelihood that these perpetrators remain a hidden threat in their communities (Dick 2012, Military Justice International 2015, Service Women's Action Network (SWAN) n.d.). Therefore, improving military efforts to prevent and respond to MST is paramount to protect our civilian communities and keep them safe from sexual perpetrators.

The Prevalence of MST

Measuring and Reporting MST

The method of calculating or quantifying the prevalence of MST has been a source of extensive debate, leading to consternation in the military, veteran and civilian communities alike. In turn, the prevention and response efforts of the military are based on these prevalence rates, raising a classic conundrum. On one hand, the DoD would like to show the public how committed it is to eradicating sexual assault by tracking sexual assault rates (Rosenthal and Miller 2013). On the other hand, the DoD demonstrates a distrust of these same statistics, claiming that it is an overstatement of the problem, and that military reform efforts should not be based on current prevalence rates (Rosenthal and Miller 2013).

Such inconsistencies have posed a barrier for MST advocates in their efforts to effectively champion reforms for the prevention and response to MSH and MSA (Rosenthal and Miller 2013).

It is vitally important to understand how the prevalence data of sexual harassment and sexual assault are measured, why the disparity in the statistics is important, and why accurately capturing the demographics of victims and perpetrators matters.

The existing MST prevalence data are contradictory, vague and unreliable (Belkin 2012, Reinke 2006). Ironically, they are incongruent with the military's operational environment that places a premium on strict protocols of accountability, control and discipline. In short, it becomes difficult to form a complete picture of MST, its continued prevalence and the severity of the problem across the branches of service, and the military as a whole, as well as to strategically develop effective prevention and response efforts (Rosenthal and Miller 2013).

As it currently stands, data reflecting the prevalence of MST in the military are based on four primary sources (DMDC 2012, DoD 2014a, 2015a, 2015b, Morral et al. 2014):

1) Restricted and unrestricted sexual assault reports made to a sexual assault response coordinator (SARC), a sexual assault prevention and response (SAPR) victim advocate, or healthcare provider
2) Formal sexual harassment reports made to the Military Equal Opportunity Office (MEO)
3) Restricted and unrestricted reports entered into the Defense Sexual Assault Incident Database (DSAID) by law enforcement and victim advocates
4) Self-report surveys, which provide estimated prevalence data about service members' experiences with sexual harassment and sexual assault in the military

The DSAID[16] is a tool that victim advocates use to enter data from both restricted and unrestricted reports to improve victim case-management efforts and provide dispositional data to legal officers (DoD 2014b, Namrow et al. 2016).

Additionally, the Survivor Experience Survey (SES), administered by RAND Corporation, extends the opportunity for survivors of sexual assault (regardless of which reporting option they chose) to complete an anonymous online survey as a vehicle to share their experiences, not just about sexual assault but the treatment by their respective chains of command, and how effective the victim believes that the services are. These experiences are then compiled into a database, where various trend analyses are

Impact of Military Sexual Trauma 351

then conducted to determine the areas in sexual assault and prevention/ response efforts in order to maintain and/or improve the situation (DoD 2015a, Namrow et al. 2016).

The year 2014 signified a prominent shift in how data were collected and tracked as the DoD complied with a request from the Senate Armed Services Committee to identify an independent contractor to collect and assess sexual assault prevalence (Morral et al. 2014). The contract was awarded to the RAND Corporation, which replaced the Defense Manpower Data Center (DMDC) Workplace and Gender Relations Survey of Active Duty Members with the RAND Military Workplace Study (RMWS) (DoD 2015a, Morral et al. 2014).

RAND created and disseminated two versions of the survey to minimally disrupt the DMDC's trend analysis from previous years and estimate the past year prevalence of sexual assault in the military (Morral et al. 2014). It was the second version of the survey (RMWS form) that included a new measure of sexual assault. This was more congruent with the sexual offense language and definition found in the Uniform Code of Military Justice[17] (UCMJ) (DoD 2015a, Morral et al. 2014).

Regrettably, in the 20 years since Tailhook[18] and Aberdeen,[19] and the subsequent claims of a 'zero-tolerance environment' (Brennan 2017, Dick 2012, National Center on Domestic and Sexual Violence n.d., Newsweek Staff 2003, Spinner 1997), the military has failed to institute measures to derive clear and accurate outcomes on the prevalence of sexual harassment and sexual assault across the various branches of service. Some military service organizations and victim advocates have argued that the military's complacency with the ambiguity as to the totality of the problem contributed to an institutional culture that excused and promoted sexually predatory behavior (Protect Our Defenders n.d., SWAN n.d.).

Measuring and Reporting MSA

Under Section 1631 of the Ike Skelton National Defense Authorization Act (NDAA) for FY 2011, the DoD is federally required to provide an annual report on the sexual assaults involving military service members (Public Law 111–383, in DoD 2015a, 2015b). These yearly fiscal reports only capture data on the incidents of sexual assault in the active duty military components of the Army, Navy, Marine Corps, Air Force, including the National Guard (DoD 2015a, 2015b).[20] Additionally, the 2007 NDAA expanded the very singular act and definition of rape in Article 120 of the UCMJ to consider multiple acts as criminal under the definition of sexual assault (Joint Service Committee on Military Justice 2008, Solaro 2006): 'from rape to forcible sodomy to abusive sexual contact, as well as attempts to commit these offenses' (DoD 2015a, p.28). Prior to this legislative change, military law neither considered forcible sodomy (oral rape and anal rape) as serious as rape itself, nor did it acknowledge penetration with a hand or an object as rape (Solaro 2006).

Victims of sexual assault currently have two options for reporting: restricted[21] and unrestricted[22] methods. Service members also have the option to report a sexual assault that occurred prior to military service, and receive the same type of services or support as if they were reporting an assault perpetrated by a fellow service member. These types of pre-military incidents accounted for about 9 percent of the total reported cases of MST in FY 2014 (DoD 2014a).

As shown in Figure 23.1 from the *Report to the President of the United States on SAPR*, there was a combined total of 3,604 reports, 5,518 reports and 6,131 reports (restricted and unrestricted) of MSA in FYs 2012, 2013 and 2014, respectively (DoD 2014b).

In contrast, the RMWS found different rates of unwanted sexual contact[23] (USC) (Morral et al. 2014). The study found that the percentage of active duty women who experienced USC decreased from an estimated 6.1 percent in 2012 to 4.3 percent in 2014, which represented a significant decrease compared to the male victims, whose USC estimated prevalence rate only decreased by 0.3 percent (DoD 2015a, Morral et al. 2014). Similar to the active duty component, the military service academies showed an increase in sexual assault reporting, an estimated 30 percent from the 2013/14 and the 2014/15 academic program years (APYs) (DoD 2016). Another area that witnessed decreased reporting in sexual assault in FY 2014 was in the combat areas of interest (CAI), in forward-deployed areas like Iraq and Afghanistan. There were a total of 163 reports of sexual assault in CAIs, which represents a 49 percent report decrease from

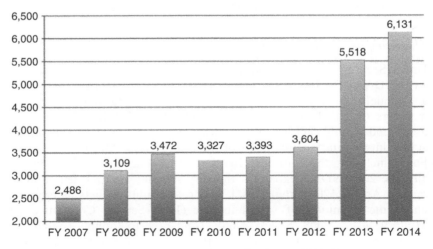

Figure 23.1 Total military sexual assaults per fiscal year, 2007–14
Source: Graph adapted from the Department of Defense 2014b

FY 2013 (DMDC 2012, DoD 2015a, 2015b). This decrease is most likely due to the troop decrease in these deployed areas.

Measuring and Reporting MSH

In FY 2013, the military services and National Guard Bureau reported 1,366 formal and informal sexual harassment complaints, where 59 percent were substantiated, 29.5 percent were unsubstantiated, and 9.2 percent were pending resolution or investigation at the end of the fiscal year (DoD 2014a). It is important to note that the alleged repeat offenders made up 11 percent of formal sexual harassment complaints, of which 72 percent were substantiated. Complaints that involved the same offenders comprised 14 percent of informal sexual harassment complaints, of which cases 35 percent were substantiated (DoD 2014a). Additionally, the military service academies reported an increase from 20 sexual harassment complaints in APY[24] 2013/14 to 28 complaints in APY 2014/15 (DMDC 2016, Roulo 2015).

Similar to the findings from the RMWS, the 2012 DoD Workplace and Gender Relations Survey (WGRS) revealed that 30 percent of women and 19 percent of men who were sexually assaulted, were sexually harassed before and/or after the sexual assault incident (DMDC 2012). Consequently, Section 579(b) of the NDAA for FY 2013 made it a requirement for the Secretary of Defense to report substantiated incidents of sexual harassment involving members of the military, with a special focus on the identification of cases in which a service member is accused of multiple incidents of sexual harassment (DoD 2015a).

Conclusion

The foregoing chapter focused primarily on providing an overview of MST, which includes sexual harassment and sexual assault incurred by military service members. MST occurs across all branches and service components within the U.S. military, including the military service academies, and those serving on active duty and members of the reserve and National Guard components (DMDC 2012, DoD 2014b, Veterans Healthcare Administration 2013).

MST impacts men and women physically, psychologically and socially, and should not be considered a problem that is limited to women or the military. The malaise has larger implications for the general public in terms of the need for social responsibility, national security and public safety. The sustained prevalence of MST continues to be a 'wicked problem' for the military because, ourstorically, it has been treated as: 1) only impacting women; 2) two independent categories of offenses, instead of treating sexual harassment and sexual assault as a form of discriminatory (and criminal) behavior that exists on a continuum of harm; 3) a problem that can only be solved by the military; and 4) a problem that is effectively being addressed by the military.

The next chapter will highlight the military's response to sexual harassment and sexual assault, and explore the continued persistence of MST through the lens of a wicked problem framework. Finally, the opportunities and recommendations for future research will be discussed.

Notes

1. The Coast Guard is not a service branch of the Department of Defense, but is instead part of the Department of Homeland Security. However, the active duty and reserve components, as well as the Coast Guard Academy, maintain a military hierarchical structure and are bound by military law.
2. Fourteen times more likely for female service members and 49 times more likely among male service members.
3. In this chapter the terms victim and survivor will be used interchangeably.
4. Compared to other races, Native Americans are twice as likely to be victims of rape/sexual assault.
5. Bisexual women and transgender college students are disproportionately impacted by sexual violence.
6. The military uses the term 'complainant' to refer to victims in cases of MSH.
7. The military uses the term 'offender' to refer to perpetrators in cases of MSH.
8. A formal complaint is a type of verbal or written MSH complaint made through the military equal opportunity office.
9. An informal complaint is a type of verbal or written MSH complaint usually made through a service member's chain of command or equal opportunity officer.
10. The military uses the term 'victim' to describe service members who have experienced MSA either during their military service or before their military service.
11. The military uses the word 'subject' to refer to perpetrators in MSA cases.
12. Active duty component refers to the service obligation of service members who serve full time in the military.
13. The reserve component refers to part-time status of military service members, usually one weekend a month, two weeks a year. Each branch of service has a reserve component, which is federally funded (versus the National Guard, which is state funded).
14. CAPS is a tool used to measure the frequency and severity of post-traumatic stress disorder (PTSD) symptoms. This particular tool is based on the PTSD criteria listed in the fourth edition of the *Diagnostic Standard Manual* (DSM). CAPS criteria are organized into six sections which include, but are not limited to: exposure to a traumatic event; traumatic event is re-experienced in one or more ways; continuous avoidance of stimuli associated with the trauma; persistent symptoms of hyper-arousal (not present before trauma); duration of disturbing symptoms; and significant distress occurring in social, occupational and other areas of functioning.
15. Operation Enduring Freedom refers to the military campaign that began in October 2011 in response to the terrorist attacks on September 11, 2001, while Operation Iraqi Freedom refers to the military campaign that began with the invasion of Iraq in March 2003, and concluded with the exit of the last combat brigade in August 2010.
16. As of FY 2015, the Coast Guard will be also entering their information for shared used of this database.

17 The UCMJ is the military law that every member is subjected to while serving in the armed forces, to include the Army, Navy, Air Force, Marine Corps, and Coast Guard. Service members of the active duty, reserve, National Guard components and the cadets/midshipmen attending the military service academies are subject to the UCMJ.
18 Tailhook refers to the Naval aviator convention that came into the public spotlight in 1991 as a result of 83 women and seven men who reported being sexually abused at the military-sponsored convention. This was one of the major public scandals that highlighted the issue of the culture of sexual harassment, sexual assault and gender discrimination in the military.
19 Aberdeen Proving Grounds is a training facility in Maryland that came into the spotlight in 1996 when it was found that drill sergeants were sexually abusing Army trainees, some of them acting as part of a ring passing around Army trainees as a game of sexual conquest. There were also commanders/ officers implicated in the sexual abuse scandal. This was one of several sex abuse scandals in the 1990s and early 2000s that brought the issue of military sexual harassment and sexual assault into the mainstream public discourse.
20 Data from the active duty Coast Guard are excluded from the report in accordance with law and are captured separately by the Defense Manpower Data Center (DMDC).
21 The type of sexual assault reporting method that enables the victim to access medical care, counseling and advocacy, without having to make an official report or investigation, and consequently affords the victims the highest level of confidentiality. Victims are also given the option to report sexual assaults that occurred prior to joining the military so they can access the same medical care, counseling and advocacy.
22 The type of sexual assault reporting method in which all of the details of the sexual assault are communicated to the commander and law enforcement, and the victim is not offered any privileged communication either with medical personnel or the chain of command.
23 USC is a term that preceded the 2014 use of 'sexual assault' in self-report surveys, and describes both 'completed and attempted oral, anal, and vaginal penetration with any body part or object, and the unwanted touching of genitalia and other sexually related areas of the body' (Department of Defense 2015a, p.8).
24 The time period when military service academy programs are tracked (usually September through June), like a conventional university, which differs from conventional military components like active duty and reserves, which are on a fiscal year timeline.

Bibliography

Belkin, A. (2012). *Bring Me Men: Military. Masculinity and the Benign Facade of American Empire, 1898–2001*. New York, NY: Columbia University Press.

Blake, D.D., Weathers, F.W., Nagy, L.M., Kaloupek, D.G., Charney, D.S. and Keane, T.M. (1998). *Clinician-Administered PTSD Scale for DSM-IV.* National Center for PTSD. www.clintools.com/victims/resources/assessment/ptsd/protected/CAPSIV.pdf. Retrieved April 17, 2017.

Brennan, T.J. (2017, March 4). Hundreds of Marines investigated for sharing photos of naked colleagues. *Reveal*. www.revealnews.org/blog/hundreds-of-marines-investigated-for-sharing-photos-of-naked-colleagues/. Retrieved March 10, 2017.

Burns, D., Hyde, P., and Killet, A. (2013). Wicked problems or wicked people? Reconceptualising institutional abuse. *Sociology of Health and Illness*, 35, 514–528.

Cantor, D., Fisher, B., Chibnall, S., Townsend, R., Lee, H., Bruce, C., and Thomas, G. (2015, September 21). *Association of American Universities (AAU), Report on the AAU Campus Climate Survey on Sexual Assault and Sexual Misconduct*. www.aau.edu/uploadedFiles/AAU_Publications/AAU_Reports/Sexual_AssaultCampus_Survey/Report%20on%20the%20AAU%20Campus%20Climate%20Survey%20on%20Sexual%20Assault%20and%20Sexual%20Misconduct.pdf. Retrieved April 17, 2017.

Caplan, P.J. (2013). Sexual trauma in the military: Needed changes in policies and procedures. *Women's Policy Journal of Harvard*, 10, 10–21.

David, W.S., Simpson, T.L., and Cotton, A.J. (2006). Taking Charge: A Pilot Curriculum of Self-Defense and Personal Safety Training for Female Veterans With PTSD Because of Military Sexual Trauma. *Journal of Interpersonal Violence*, 21, 4, 555–565.

Defense Manpower Data Center (DMDC). (2012) *Human Resources Strategic Assessment Program. Workplace and Gender Relations Survey of Active Duty Members*. www.sapr.mil/index.php/researchhttp://www.sapr.mil/index.php/research. Retrieved April 12, 2016.

Defense Manpower Data Center (DMDC). (2016). *Annual Report on Sexual Harassment and Violence at the Military Service Academies (Academic Program Year 2014–2015)*. Washington, DC. http://sapr.mil/public/docs/reports/MSA/APY_14-15/APY_14-15_MSA_Full_Report.pdf. Retrieved April 21, 2016

Department of Defense (DoD). (2014a). *Fiscal Year 2013 Department of Defense Report of Substantiated Incidents of Sexual Harassment in the Armed Forces*. Washington, DC. http://diversity.defense.gov/Portals/51/Documents/DoD FINAL_REPORT-FY13IncidentsofSexual_HarassmentReport_15MAY2014.pdf. Retrieved May 12, 2014.

Department of Defense. (2014b). *Provisional Statistical Data on Sexual Assault Fiscal Year 2014*. Report to the President of the United States on SAPR. http://sapr.mil/public/docs/reports/FY14_POTUS/FY14_DoD_Report_to_POTUSAppendix_A.pdf. Retrieved April 16, 2016.

Department of Defense. (2014c). *2014–2016 DOD SAPR Strategic Plan*. Washington, DC. http://sapr.mil/public/docs/reports/SecDef_Memo_and_DoD_SAPR_ Prevention_Strategy_2014-2016.pdf. Retrieved April 16, 2016.

Department of Defense. (2015a). Sexual Assault Prevention and Response Strategic Plan. www.sapr.mil/public/docs/reports/SecDef_SAPR_Memo_Strategy_Atch_20150126.pdf. Retrieved April 16, 2016.

Department of Defense. (2015b). *FY 2014 Department of Defense Fact Sheet*. Washington, DC. www.defense.gov/Portals/1/features/2015/0415_sexual-assault/Fact_Sheet_FY1 DoD_SAPR_Annual_Report.pdf. Retrieved April 16, 2016.

Department of Defense. (2016). *Annual Report on Sexual Harassment and Violence at the Military Service Academies, Academic Program Year 2014–2015*. http://sapr.mil/public/docs/reports/MSA/APY_14-15/APY_14-15_MSA_Report.pdf. Retrieved April 21, 2016.

Department of Justice. (2004). *Office of Justice Programs, Bureau of Justice Statistics, American Indians and Crime, 1992–2002*. www.bjs.gov/content/pub/pdf/aic02.pdf. Retrieved August 22, 2017.

Department of VeteransAffairs (VA). (2016). *Military Sexual Trauma*. www.mentalhealth.va.gov/msthome.asp. Retrieved April 17, 2017.

Dick, K. (2012). *The Invisible War (Documentary)*. U.S.: Cinedigm/Docurama.

González-Prats, M.C. (2017). Accountability, Complacency, or Obfuscation? Analyzing the U.S. Military's Response to MST. *Journal of Public Integrity*. doi:10.1080/10999922.2017.1278668.

Halloran, L. (2013, May 25). Stunned By Military Sex Scandals, Advocates Demand Changes. *NPR*. www.npr.org/2013/05/23/186335999/stunned-by-military-sex-scandals-advocates-demand-changes. Retrieved April 17, 2017.

Hannagan, R.J. (2016). 'I Believe We Are the Fewer, the Prouder'. Women's Agency in Meaning-Making after Military Sexual Assault. *Journal of Contemporary Ethnography*, doi:0891241616636664.

Hanson, R., Morton, K., and Harris, A. (2003). Sexual offender recidivism risk: What we know and what we need to know. *Annals of the New York Academy of Sciences*, 989, 154–166.

Hope, A., and Eriksen, M. (2009). From military sexual trauma to 'organization trauma': practising 'poetics of testimony'. *Culture and Organization*, 15, 1, 109–127.

Horgan, D. (Producer). (2013, May 7). How the military fails miserably to address sexual assault. *All In with Chris Hayes* (TV broadcast). New York, NY: MSNBC.

Hoyt, T., Klosterman Rielage, J., and Williams, L.F. (2011). Military sexual trauma in men: A review of reported rates. *Journal of Trauma & Dissociation*, 12, 3, 244–260.

Human Rights Watch. (2015). *Sexual Assault and the LGBTQ Community.* www.hrc.org/resources/sexual-assault-and-the-lgbt-community. Retrieved April 17, 2017.

Human Rights Watch. (2016). *Booted: Lack of Recourse for Wrongfully Discharged US Military Rape Survivors*. Washington, DC. www.hrw.org/report/2016/05/19/booted/lack-recourse-wrongfully-discharged-us-military-rape-survivors. Retrieved March 16, 2016.

Hunter, M. (2007). *Honor Betrayed: Sexual Abuse in America's Military.* Fort Lee, NJ: Barricade Books.

Institute for Veteran Policy. (2015). *Military Sexual Trauma: Understanding Prevalence, Resources and Considerations to Care*. San Francisco, CA: Swords to Plowshares. www.swords-toplowshares.org/sites/default/files/Military%20Sexual%20Trauma%20-%20Understanding%20(2015).pdf. Retrieved April 17, 2017.

Joint Service Committee on Military Justice. (2008). *Manual for Courts-Martial United States (2008 Edition)*. Department of Defense. www.loc.gov/rr/frd/Military_Law/pdf/MCM-2008.pdf. Retrieved February 22, 2016.

Katz, L.S., Bloor, L.E., Cojucar, G., and Draper, T. (2007). Women who served in Iraq seeking mental health services: Relationships between military sexual trauma, symptoms, and readjustment. *Psychological Services*, 4, 4, 239–249. doi:10.1037/1541-1559.4.4.239.

Katz, L.S., Cojucar, G., Beheshti, S., Nakamura, E., and Murray, M. (2012). Military Sexual Trauma During Deployment to Iraq and Afghanistan: Prevalence, Readjustment, and Gender Differences. *Violence and Victims*, 27, 4, 487–500. doi:10.1891/0886-6708.27.4.487.

Kelty, R., Kleykamp, M., and Segal, D.R. (2010). The military and the transition to adulthood. *Future of Children*, 20, 1, 181–207.

Lucas, M. (2013). *The Brotherhood Will Not Protect You: Mapping (Dis)Empowering Communication in Military Sexual Trauma Narratives* (Master's

Thesis). http://sdsu-dspace.calstate.edu/handle/10211.10/4285. Retrieved April 12, 2015.

Maguen, S., Cohen, B., Ren, L., Bosch, J., Kimerling, R., and Seal, K. (2012). Gender differences in military sexual trauma and mental health diagnoses among Iraq and Afghanistan veterans with posttraumatic stress disorder. *Women's Health Issues.* doi:10.1016/j.whi.2011.07.010.

Mattocks, K.M., Haskell, S.G., Krebs, E.E., Justice, A.C., Yano, E.M., and Brandt, C. (2012). Women at war: Understanding how women veterans cope with combat and military sexual trauma. *Social Science and Medicine.* doi:10.1016/j.socscimed.2011.10.039.

Miles, D. (2011, November 28). *Survey Shows Growing Gap Between Civilians, Military.* Washington, DC: American Forces Press Service. http://content.govdelivery.com/accounts/USDOD/bulletins/1e626f. Retrieved November 24, 2015.

Military Justice International. (2015). Military Justice Guide to Sex Offender Registration Requirements. www.militaryjusticeinternational.com. Retrieved November 28, 2015.

Miller, M. and Weinstein-Matthews, G.L. (2013). *Justice Denied: Military Sexual Trauma, The Men's Stories (Documentary).* U.S.: 9 Point Productions.

Morral, A.R., Gore, K., Schell, T., Bicksler, B., Farris, C., Dastidar, M.G., Jaycox, L.H., Kilpatrick, K., Kistler, S., Street, A., Tanielian, T., and Williams, K.M. (2014). *Sexual Assault and Sexual Harassment in the U.S. Military: Highlights from the 2014 RAND Military Workplace Study.* Santa Monica, CA: RAND Corporation. www.rand.org/pubs/research_briefs/RB9841.html. Retrieved April 27. 2016

Namrow, N.A., Hurley, M.M., Van Winkle, E.P., and De Silva, S. (2016). *Overview Report: 2015 Military Investigation and Justice Experience Survey.* Fort Belvoir, VA. www.sapr.mil/public/docs/reports/FY15_Annual/Annex_3_2015_MIJES_Report.pdf. Retrieved February 4, 2017.

National Center on Domestic and Sexual Violence. (n.d.). *The Military Justice Improvement Act of 2013 S.967: An Overview.* www.ncdsv.org/images/Military-Justice-Improvement-Act-of-2013-an-overview.pdf. Retrieved April 27, 2016.

Newsweek Staff. (2003, March 16). Ghosts of Tailhook. *Newsweek.* www.newsweek.com/ghosts-tailhook-133067. Retrieved December 3, 2016.

Office of the Deputy Assistant Secretary of Defense. (2014). 2014 Demographics: Profile of the Military Community. http://download.militaryonesource.mil/12038/MOS/Reports/2014-DemographicsReport.pdf. Retrieved April 17, 2017.

Office of the Secretary of the Department of Defense. (2013). Department of Defense Fact Sheet: Secretary Hagel Issues New Initiatives to Eliminate Sexual Assault, Updates Prevention Strategy and Releases 2013 Annual Report on Sexual Assault in the Military. www.sapr.mil/public/docs/reports/FY13_DoD_SAPRO_Annual_Report_Fact_Sheet.pdf. Retrieved October 31, 2015.

Pavao, J., Turchik, J.A., Hyun, J.K., Karpenko, J., Saweikis, M., McCutcheon, S., and Kimerling, R. (2013). Military sexual trauma among homeless veterans. *Journal of General Internal Medicine,* 28, 2, 536–541.

Protect Our Defenders. (n.d.). Nine Roadblocks to Justice. www.protectourdefenders.com/roadblocks-to-justice/. Retrieved April 17, 2017.

Rape Abuse Incest National Network (RAINN). (2009). Victims of Sexual Violence: Statistics. www.rainn.org/statistics/victims-sexual-violence. Retrieved April 17, 2017.

Reinke, S. (2006). Abu Ghraib A Case of Moral and Administrative Failure. *Public Integrity*, 8, 2, 135–147. doi:10.2753/PIN1099-9922080202.

Rittel, H. and Webber, M. (1973). Dilemmas in a general theory of planning. *Policy Sciences*, 4, 2, 155–169.

Rosenthal, L., and Miller, K. (2013). *The Data on Military Sexual Assault: What You Need to Know*. http://americanprogress.org/issues/military/news/2013/07/23/70332/the-data-on-military-sexual-assault-what-you-need-to-know/. Retrieved April 12, 2015.

Roulo, C. (2015). Sexual assault rates decrease at military service academies. *DoD News, Defense Media Activity*. February 11. www.defense.gov/News/Article/Article/604087. Retrieved April 29, 2016.

Sadler, A.G., Booth, B.M., Cook, B.L., and Doebbeling, B.N. (2003). Factors associated with women's risk of rape in the military environment. *American Journal of Industrial Medicine*. doi:10.1002/ajim.10202.

Service Women's Action Network (SWAN). (n.d.). Military Sex Offender Registration: Frequently Asked Questions. http://servicewomen.org/wp-content/uploads/2012/08/MilitarySexOffenderRegistryFAQs.pdf . Retrieved November 28, 2015.

Smith, C.P., and Freyd, J.J. (2014). Institutional betrayal. *American Psychologist*, 69, 6, 575–587. doi:10.1037/a0037564.

Solaro, E. (2006). *Women in the Line of Fire: What You Should Know About Women in the Military*. Emeryville, CA: Seal Press.

Spinner, J. (1997, November 7). In the Wake of Sex Scandal, Caution is the Rule at Aberdeen. *Washington Post*. www.washingtonpost.com/wpsrv/local/longterm/library/aberde en/caution.htm. Retrieved April 17, 2017.

Steward, J. (2013, May 3). *Understanding Male Survivors of Military Sexual Trauma*. Portland, OR: V.A. Military Sexual Trauma Conference.

Stinson, E. (2013). Military Sexual Trauma: Impact and Treatment. In *V.A. Military Sexual Trauma Conference*. Portland, OR.

Surís, A., Lind, L., Kashner, T.M., Borman, P.D., and Petty, F. (2004). Sexual assault in women veterans: an examination of PTSD risk, health care utilization, and cost of care. *Psychosomatic Medicine*, 66, 749–756. doi:10.1097/01.psy.0000138117.58559.7b.

Tsongas, N. and Tardiff, R. (n.d.) Silent No More. Blog post. www.notinvisible.org/silent_no_more. Retrieved November 24, 2015.

Vanden Brook, T., and Jackson, D.M. (2013, May 16). Obama says sexual assault crisis hurts national security. *USA Today*. www.usatoday.com/story/news/politics/2013/05/16/obama-hagel-military sexualassaults/2165763/. Retrieved March 20, 2016.

Veterans Healthcare Administration. (2013). Quick Facts about VA's Health Care Services for Military Sexual Trauma. www.uscg.mil/worklife/docs/pdf/sapr_VA_Healthcare_Services.pdf. Retrieved January 31, 2016.

Vogt, D., Bruce, T.A., Street, A.E., and Stafford, J. (2007). Attitudes toward women and tolerance for sexual harassment among reservists. *Violence against Women*, 13, 9, 879–900. doi:10.1177/1077801207305217.

Walters, M.L., Chen, J., and Breiding, M.J. (2013). *The National Intimate Partner and Sexual Violence Survey (NISVS): 2010 Findings on Victimization by Sexual Orientation*. Atlanta, GA: National Center for Injury Prevention and Control, Centers for Disease Control and Prevention. www.cdc.gov/violenceprevention/pdf/nisvs_sofindings.pdf. Retrieved December 3, 2016.

Washington, D.L., Yano, E.M., McGuire, J., Hines, V., Lee, M., and Gelberg, L. (2010). Risk Factors for Homelessness among Women Veterans. *Journal of Health Care for the Poor and Underserved*, 21, 1, 82–91.

Williams, I., and Bernstein, K. (2011). Military Sexual Trauma Among U.S. Female Veterans. *Archives of Psychiatric Nursing*. doi:10.1016/j.apnu.2010.07.00.

24 The Military's Response to Military Sexual Trauma

This chapter builds on the previous chapter on military sexual trauma (MST). It is organized into two sections: the military's response to military sexual harassment (MSH) and military sexual assault (MSA), and a discussion about the opportunities and recommendations for future research and action. Traditionally, military incidents of sexual harassment and sexual assault have been handled by employing a conventional managerial approach typically found in public institutions and hierarchical organizations which are highly compartmentalized, and confined to hierarchical problem solving that is not conducive to taming or coping with wicked problems (Morner and Misgeld 2014). Consequently, the solutions produced tend to be one-dimensional, and exist in a vacuum, separate from other systems that may impact incidents of sexual harassment and sexual assault, leading to short-lived and unsustainable solutions (Morner and Misgeld 2014).

The Military's Prevention and Response Efforts

A common thread that runs through the scandals from the 1990s and early 2000s and the more recently publicized incidents about MST (Brennan 2017, Halloran 2013, Montgomery 2013, Peralta 2013, Seck 2015, Vanden Brook 2011, 2013) is that the military continues to apply the same strategies in dealing with sexual harassment and sexual assault. The military has relied primarily on two tools in its response to sexual harassment and sexual assault: *prevention and response training* and the *military justice system* (Dick 2012, Office of Senator Kirsten Gillibrand 2009, Protect Our Defenders n.d., Service Women's Action Network (SWAN) n.d.). It is important to note that for the purposes of these two MST chapters, the term military justice system is not limited to the laws in the Uniform Code of Military Justice (UCMJ), but refers to the overall infrastructure and key players responsible for carrying out the (equal and consistent) application of these laws, as well as providing support for the victims, such as the military chain of command, law enforcement, and medical personnel.

Additionally, MST-related reform in the areas of commander discretion or jurisdiction (a.k.a. convening authority), sentencing guidelines, the appeals process, and victim services or support, promises to significantly enhance the military's prevention and response efforts to address MST (González-Prats 2017).

MST Prevention and Response Training

In the 15 to 20 years since the sex abuse scandals at the Tailhook Convention, Aberdeen Proving Grounds, and the Air Force Academy (Belkin 2012, Browne 2007, Gutmann 2001, Graham 2003),[1] there have been multiple prevention and response programs and policies designed to eradicate incidents of MST. However, looking at the totality of the statistics from 2005 to present, it is difficult to conclude whether the prevention/ response training has been effective in reversing the trajectory of MSA (González-Prats 2017).

A Department of Defense (DoD)-mandated Sexual Assault Task Force worked in concert with the military branches to implement the sexual assault prevention and response (SAPR) policy, which led to its formal adoption in October 2005 by DoD Directive 6495.01, as well as the emergence of the Sexual Assault Prevention and Response Office (SAPRO) (DoD n.d.). SAPRO ultimately sets policy on all SAPR efforts in the military, to include all of the military service components and military academies, and the Coast Guard Academy (Defense Manpower Data Center 2012, DoD n.d.).

In addition to setting sexual assault policy across the branches of service, SAPRO establishes the guidelines for all of the branches of service in terms of training objectives and deliverables, which are informed by five main lines of effort: 1) prevention; 2) investigation; 3) accountability; 4) advocacy/ victim assistance; and 5) assessment (DoD 2014).

Based on uniform standards and guidelines, each military branch[2] established its own training program primarily aimed at preventing and responding to incidents of sexual assault (DoD n.d.). A strong emphasis has been placed on individual, supervisory and bystander intervention through a variety of media such as print materials (brochures, posters), and mandatory self-paced online training videos, and on-site classes conducted throughout the year. Military service members in leadership and command positions such as non-commissioned officers,[3] warrant officers[4] and commissioned officers,[5] and those in areas of supervisory responsibility, receive additional training that is commensurate with their advancement, promotion and/or change of duties and responsibilities (DoD 2015).

Military units have the opportunity to tailor their programs to their needs and organizational culture as long as they follow the guidelines of the DoD's SAPRO (DoD n.d.). For example, some stateside and overseas/ deployed Army units have added a self-defense pilot to their Sexual Harassment and Assault Response and Prevention program (SHARP) training (Kennedy 2013, Lashleyleidner 2014). However, this specific self-defense training component of SHARP is not necessarily indicative of all of the Army SHARP training, nor the SAPR training offered by other branches of service. Ourstorically, the DoD has focused predominantly prevention and response efforts on female victimization (González-Prats 2017). However, it is worth noting that a recent sexual assault prevention strategy explicitly supported a recommendation to former Secretary of Defense Chuck Hagel to focus on male victims of sexual assault, including outreach strategies for developing enhanced methods to improve assistance and support for male victims (Office of the Secretary of the Department of Defense 2013).

Military Justice System

There have been several significant changes to the military justice system, whose laws for standards and conduct are prescribed by the UCMJ. Recent changes to the UCMJ may help to ameliorate potential bias and conflicts of interest that may exist for unit commanders who may know either the victim or the perpetrator of a sexual assault (Office of Senator Kirsten Gillibrand 2009, Protect Our Defenders n.d.).

First, in 2007, the previous narrowly defined crime of rape in Article 120 was expanded to explicitly include multiple acts as criminal under the broader statute of 'Rape, sexual assault, and other sexual misconduct' (Joint Service Committee on Military Justice 2008, p.351). This change in statute was significant because it finally acknowledged penetration with a hand or an object as rape, as well as equated the seriousness and criminality of forcible sodomy (oral rape and anal rape) with rape itself.

Second, in cases of rape, sexual assault, nonconsensual sodomy, and attempts to commit these crimes, the case is automatically transferred from a lower-level unit commander to a senior-level officer at the rank of O-6: colonel or above in the Army, Air Force and Marine Corps, and captain or above in the Navy and Coast Guard (DoD n.d.).

Changing the special court martial convening authority to an O-6 helps to reduce the possibility that the senior officer either knows the victim or the perpetrator, and increases the likelihood that the senior officer can remain fair and impartial in the adjudication process (Joint Service Committee on Military Justice 2008).

Prior to 2014 the UCMJ designated unit commanders as the convening authority, which granted commanders the discretionary power to decide whether or not to initiate an investigation and/or bring charges against a service member (Joint Service Committee on Military Justice 2008). This former justice protocol was flawed for three main reasons (González-Prats 2017). First, unit commanders lack the specialized legal experience and training to conduct preliminary criminal investigations as law enforcement professionals to determine if a crime has been committed (Dick 2012, Office of Senator Kirsten Gillibrand 2009). Second, convening authorities had the discretion and legal authority to reduce sentences and criminal penalties, and up until 2013, dismissed entire cases (Montgomery 2013). Third, there existed the potential for subjectivity and conflicts of interest, especially in cases where the accused is the unit commander, or if the unit commander has an existing personal or professional relationship with either the victim or the perpetrator (Dick 2012, Office of Senator Kirsten Gillibrand 2009, Protect Our Defenders n.d., SWAN n.d).

Finally, there was also a recent change to the UCMJ that is in the process of being implemented by the DoD, and which will help to remove the subjectivity and potential for bias in the military adjudication process (Miller 2016). The Pentagon will provide military judges with sentencing guidelines for military crimes, replacing the current system where the military juries, made up of service members with limited to no legal experience, were subjectively tasked with carrying out sentencing guidelines. Additionally, the appeals process is being reformed, where convicted service members will have the right to appeal the decision in their cases which, prior to late December 2015, was limited to those who received a sentence of one year or more (Miller 2016).

Despite the recent MST-related reforms and changes to the military justice system, many advocates and leaders are still critical that the reforms for sexual assault do not go far enough in improving the impartiality, fairness and transparency for sexual assault victims (Bhawati et al. 2013, Office of Senator Kirsten Gillibrand 2009, Protect Our Defenders n.d., SWAN n.d.).

Victim Services and Support

In the last five years the most significant improvement to the infrastructure of the military's SAPR program has been in the area of services and support to victims of sexual assault (DoD 2014). There has been an increased professionalization, training, accreditation and deployment of victim assistants and administrators in the SAPR program, which includes an increase in screening and criminal background checks of the SAPR counselors and victim advocates for previous crimes committed (González-Prats 2017). These improvements, in turn, have significantly improved the response services for victims of sexual assault across the military.

Additionally, a measure of protection has been adopted for sexual assault victims to minimize continued contact with the perpetrator. An emergency victim reassignment component to the process was adopted, to expedite a sexual assault victim's request to be approved or disapproved by their commander within a 72-hour period. The reassignment request may result in either the victim or perpetrator being transferred (DoD 2014).

Opportunities for Improvement and Research

It is important to note that a significant part of the challenges of taming or coping with the wicked problem of MST has been applying a singular, *one-size-fits-all* solution like training and/or military justice reform, which gives an inaccurate or false perception of progress, and the completion of problem solving (Morner and Misgeld 2014). Any suggested opportunities for improvement and recommendations for further study should be accompanied by the explicit understanding that the stated wicked problem would be best served by addressing it systematically, that is, through multiple and concurrent points of intervention versus through just one or two independent solutions (Morner and Misgeld 2014).

Despite the military's notable improvements to the MST prevention and response efforts like victim support or services, an increased focus on male victimization, and an expanded UCMJ sexual assault criminal code, there are five areas of opportunity for improvement and further research (González-Prats 2017). These existing areas are:

1) Prioritize the focus on gaps in the prevalence data
2) Analyze the dominant narratives of prevention and response training
3) Alter the discretionary and decision-making authority of military commanders
4) Interrupt and challenge the adverse treatment of sexual assault victims
5) Address the residual effects of the historical second-class/'other' status given to underrepresented populations such as women and members of the lesbian, gay, bisexual, transgender and queer (LGBTQ) community

Gaps in Prevalence Data

First, a review of the existing MST literature underscores the wide variances, if not outright conflicting data about the overall prevalence of MST, as well as the limited amount of comprehensive empirical studies that include sexual harassment and sexual assault, and how they are related. Data collection should include a more consistent definition of MST. The term MST is still being used synonymously (and inaccurately) with MSA, which tends to dominate most of the empirical literature, negatively impacting data collection and, in turn, results about sexual harassment and sexual assault (Kimerling et al. 2010). Additionally, investigators should expand MST research and align it along the 'continuum of harm,' congruent with the military's recent acknowledgement of the correlation between sexual harassment and sexual assault (DoD 2015).

Second, more studies including male and female victims of MST are needed to keep the statistical reality on the forefront that more men are victims of sexual assault than women, despite the underreporting by male victims in the military and civilian communities. The afterthought nature of the 'men are victims too' messaging by the military contradicts the reality of the situation, and further perpetuates the 'male sexual invulnerability' stereotype and female victim-male perpetrator paradigm.

This thwarts any effort to encourage more men to report and makes women who report sexual assault seem weak (González-Prats 2017).

Third, the demographics should expand beyond the conventional and outdated binary of male/female classification to a more inclusive continuum of gender identity, especially in light of the July 2016 DoD policy that lifted the ban on transgender service members in the military (Rosenberg 2016). This improved gender identity continuum would be more congruent with a sophisticated 21st-century profession of arms like our allies in Canada, Australia, and the United Kingdom (Clarke 2014, Frank et al. 2010), but it will also help to engender accurate data for the increased risk for sexual violence that members of the LGBTQ community face (Cantor et al. 2015).

Dominant Narratives of the Prevention/Response Training

Since the widely publicized military sexual abuse scandals of the 1990s, the default response by the military has been to increase mandatory training about sexual harassment and sexual assault, derisively referred to by critics as 'sensitivity training' (Gutmann 2001, p.41). The military's messaging of the prevention and response training continues to focus on upholding the female victim-male perpetrator paradigm and validating the gender stereotype that only women are vulnerable to sexual violence (Hoyt et al. 2011). For example, in one Army unit, as part of the SAPR training for deployed personnel, self-defense courses were exclusively marketed to female soldiers with the goal of decreasing their chances of becoming sexual assault victims (Lashleyleidner 2014).

Rather than addressing the MST problem as an issue of criminality, workplace professionalism, or even a failure of discipline within the ranks, these implicit (and explicit) narratives communicate that women require additional protection and remain unsuited for the rigors of military life (Browne 2007, Dick 2012, Gutmann 2001, Reinke 2006), thus contributing to their secondary status as the 'other' (Okros 2009). This type of messaging is associated with traits of *benevolent sexism*, which on the surface seems like harmless protective behavior and deference towards women, but is instead more about maintaining the status quo of conventional gender roles and the traditional institution of patriarchy (Glick and Fiske 1997).

Discretionary and Decision-Making Authority of Military Commanders

The impartiality (both perceived and actual) of the military justice system has been a source of debate and polarization among the military, veteran and civilian communities. Senior Pentagon officials continue to actively resist efforts for more oversight and accountability. They deem such strategies unnecessary as they feel equipped to deal with the challenges of sexual assault and are actively taking steps to eradicate the problem of MST (Cassata 2014).

However, despite the Pentagon's claim of a 'zero-tolerance' policy for sexual harassment and sexual assault, MST continues unabated at an alarming rate. Consequently, survivors and advocacy groups are seeking to decrease the significant discretionary and decision-making authority that military commanders have when it comes to initiating MST investigations, by supporting the passage of the Military Justice Improvement Act (MJIA) (Bhawati et al. 2013, Office of Senator Kirsten Gillibrand 2009, Protect Our Defenders n.d., SWAN n.d.). This legislation would automatically require moving all sexual offenses (completed and attempted) outside the chain of command to a special military prosecutor, rather than to the current O-6 ranked officer who serves as a convening authority (Office of Senator Kirsten Gillibrand 2009, Protect Our Defenders n.d., SWAN n.d.).

The military's staunch opposition to the MJIA bill has resulted in repeated defeats in multiple legislative sessions (Bhawati et al. 2013, Office of Kirsten Gillibrand 2009). Senior military leaders feel that legislative reforms such as the MJIA, would undermine the commanders' authority and influence, as well as weaken the military overall (Office of Kirsten Gillibrand 2009, Protect Our Defenders n.d., SWAN n.d.). Yet, ironically, by being more focused on maintaining control with minimal to no civilian oversight and accountability than on the outcome for the thousands of service members who have been sexually victimized, the military has damaged its revered 'good order and discipline' (DoD 2014, p.110). This stance has eroded its credibility and the public's confidence and trust in the institution (Dick 2012, Office of Kirsten Gillibrand 2009, Protect Our Defenders n.d.).

The Adverse Treatment of Sexual Assault Victims

Service members who come forward to report sexual assault are often subjected to suspicion, victim blaming and additional stigmatization (Caplan 2013, Dick 2012, Human Rights Watch 2015, Lucas 2013, Office of Senator Kirsten Gillibrand 2009). Oftentimes, the damage from MST is not limited to the incident(s) itself but to the actions (or non-actions) of the unit members, and especially the disbelief and lack of validation from leaders in their chain of command (Caplan 2013, Dick 2012, Hope and Eriksen 2009, Lucas 2013). The disbelief and retaliatory legal military actions taken against victims who make a claim of sexual harassment and/ or sexual assault against another service member, contribute to the institutional betrayal (Smith and Freyd 2014), and organizational trauma (Hope and Eriksen 2009). The victims' overall sense of mistrust and betrayal associated with institutional betrayal and organizational trauma is compounded by their sexual abuse and trauma (Human Rights Watch 2015, Lucas 2013, Morral et al. 2014).

368 *Confronting Wicked Problems*

Additional damage occurs when MST victims are given classifications of mental illness by military therapists (ACLU et al. 2013, Caplan 2013, Subcommittee on Disability Assistance and Memorial Affairs Committee on Veterans' Affairs 2012). In the civilian environment, bipolar disorder and borderline personality disorders are the most common classifications given to women who report MST, at a three-to-one female-to-male ratio (ACLU et al. 2013, Caplan 2013, Subcommittee on Disability Assistance and Memorial Affairs Committee on Veterans' Affairs 2012). These types of diagnoses can negatively impact the servicewomen's opportunities for advancement or promotion as they are considered pre-existing conditions versus service-connected injuries. In turn, the diagnoses can serve as the conduit for their eventual discharge from the military, oftentimes under less than honorable conditions which may negatively impact their ability to receive veteran benefits (ACLU et al. 2013, Caplan 2013, Hoyt et al. 2011, Human Rights Watch 2015, Subcommittee on Disability Assistance and Memorial Affairs Committee on Veterans' Affairs 2012).

This lack of gender parity in the rates of MST-related post-traumatic stress disorder (PTSD) claims was one of the major findings in a 2010 Freedom of Information Act lawsuit against the DoD and the Department of Veterans Affairs (VA) by SWAN, the American Civil Liberties Union (ACLU) of Connecticut, and the ACLU Women's Rights Project (ACLU et al. 2013). It was discovered that there existed a higher evidentiary standard for MST-related PTSD claims than for non-MST-related PTSD claims (Human Rights Watch 2016, Subcommittee on Disability Assistance and Memorial Affairs Committee on Veterans' Affairs 2012).

As shown in Figure 24.1, it is reported that the VA rejects two-thirds of MST claims for rape, sexual assault and sexual harassment, with an additional lower service-connected disability rating for women than men (10–30 percent

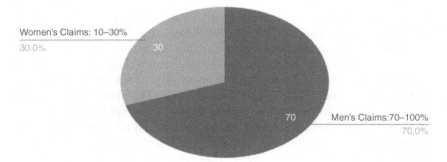

Figure 24.1 Gender disparity in MST claims
Source: Subcommittee on Disability Assistance and Memorial Affairs Committee on Veterans' Affairs, U.S. House of Representatives 2012

vs. 70–100 percent), which translates to lower financial compensation and access to VA benefits.

The Residual Effects of the Ourstorical Second Class/'Other' Status

Finally, an area that has been minimized, if not neglected altogether, in the research, is the impact of previous exclusionary DoD policies like 'Don't Ask, Don't Tell and Don't Pursue' and combat exclusion in institutionalizing the homophobia, sexism and misogyny that have existed in the military (Allsep 2013, DoD 2015, Fenner 1998, Frank 2010, Groves 2013, Standinfer 2012). The integration of women into the American military should include a more comprehensive debate, not just about servicewomen and their evolved roles in the military, but other groups that have been ourstorically marginalized and discriminated against (Fenner 1998).

Conclusion

The recent public attention to MST has increased public awareness and investment about the need for increased research on the prevalence and impact of MST. The military has drawn sharp criticism from the general public, key Congressional leaders and various veteran advocacy groups, who cite safety, quality of life and national security concerns as residual effects of MST. However, what often gets lost in the debates about the prevalence of MSH and MSA is the fact that MST is preventable, and that incidents of sexual harassment and sexual assault should not be considered a foreseeable risk in a modern profession of arms (*Cioca v. Rumsfeld, 2013*), or simply the cost of doing business (Hunter 2007).

Ourstorically, the highly controlled and disciplined environment of the military has institutionalized a culture of strict accountability in terms of personnel, equipment, and overall 'good order and discipline'[6] (DoD 2014, p.110) in one of the most revered institutions in the world. However, the prevention and response efforts to sexual assault and sexual harassment have greatly contrasted to the existing policies of strict accountability and high expectations that have been associated with the military. The military can prevent MST, and bring 'good order and discipline' to this important part of military life.

Despite the fact that the sexual victimization of women in the military is more publicized than that of male victims, men account for a majority of the sexual harassment and sexual assaults that occur in the military (Hoyt et al. 2011, Steward 2013). An increased and specific focus on male victimization across the services has been called for both in prevention and response efforts, as well as in gender-specific medical and mental health treatment (DoD 2015, Hoyt et al. 2011, Office of the Secretary of the Department of Defense 2013).

Victims of MST have been adversely impacted physically, psychologically and socially, which in turn negatively affects their quality of life and overall wellbeing. Victims of MST are at higher risks of developing post-traumatic stress conditions, depression, anxiety, substance abuse disorders, as well as a host of other self-reported rates of medical symptomatology, than service members who have not experienced MST (Hoyt et al. 2011, Williams and Bernstein 2011). The DoD has made positive changes to its prevention and response protocols and military justice system, especially in strengthening its infrastructure for victim services and support. In addition, improvements in data collection and tracking are needed, such as simplifying the prevalence data, and making such data more transparent and consistent to support further progress.

However, the absence of accurate data will render even the best solutions ineffective and unsustainable. The military is ultimately responsible for directly taking steps to eradicate sexual assault and all forms of gender discrimination and sexual harassment, which as stated by the RAND Military Workplace Study, exist on a 'continuum of harm' (Morral et al. 2014). Advocacy groups like Protect Our Defenders and the SWAN are at the forefront of holding our military leaders and public officials accountable. It is incumbent upon all to understand that there is a price to be paid for the privilege of having an all-volunteer military.

There are simple ways that members outside the military can become more involved to bridge the civilian–military divide. Support to eradicate MSA can include advocacy for the MJIA, hosting a screening of *The Invisible War* or *The Silent Truth … the LaVena Johnson Story*, to increase awareness about MST and educate the community, or supporting MST research at the local or national level. MST is an issue that affects us all and should be championed as such (Brooker-Marks 2011, Dick 2012, Protect Our Defenders n.d., SWAN n.d.).

With the 2016 policies lifting the ban on combat exclusion for women and on transgender service members, the military stands at an unprecedented crossroads for increased gender equality, opportunity and inclusion (Rosenberg 2016, Shane 2016, Wire Reporters 2015). As such, it is a crucial time to not only prevent and intervene in MST, but to understand where MST intersects with gender identity, diversity and national security (Catic and von Hlatky 2014, MacIntyre et al. 2004, Okros 2009).

Notes

1 This was one of several sex abuse scandals in the 1990s and early 2000s that brought the issue of military sexual harassment and military sexual assault into the public discourse. This particular scandal occurred in 2003, when 60 female cadets and former cadets reported being sexual assaulted and other abuses at the academy. The independent commission reports found that the Air Force knew about the sexual assaults and failed to respond/investigate the allegations.

2 It is important to note that the Coast Guard (both active duty and reserves) falls under the jurisdiction of the Department of Homeland Security and not the Department of Defense, but they do have their own SAPR program and consequently are subject to the same policies set forth by SAPRO (Department of Defense 2013a, 2013b).
3 Enlisted service members within the ranks of E-5 through E-9 who often serve in positions of supervision and executive leadership are often referred to as the 'backbone of the military.'
4 With the exception of the branch of Aviation, warrant officers hold special positions as technical experts in their field, and are required to have enlisted and been non-commissioned officers before becoming warrant officers. Also nicknamed 'chief.'
5 Commissioned officers hold the ranks of O-1 through O-9 (names of ranks/titles dependent on branch of service).
6 A common term found in the military vernacular used to describe the unwavering obedience, loyalty and unit cohesion, which are often seen as the hallmark of a successful profession of arms. This term has been historically used to push back on socially progressive military policies, to include, but not be limited to, the unrestricted inclusion of African Americans/black Americans, openly gay service members, and women in the military.

Bibliography

Allsep, L.M. (2013). The Myth of the Warrior: Martial Masculinity and the End of Don't Ask, Don't Tell. *Journal of Homosexuality*, 60, 381–400. doi:10.1080/00918369.2013.74492.

American Civil Liberties Union (ACLU), Service Women's Action Network (SWAN), and Veteran Legal Services Clinic: Yale Law School. (2013). *Battle for Benefits: VA Discrimination Against Survivors of Military Sexual Trauma*. New Haven, CT. www.aclu.org/battle-benefits-va-discrimination-against-survivors-military-sexual-trauma. Retrieved March 16, 2016.

Belkin, A. (2012). *Bring Me Men: Military Masculinity and the Benign Facade of American Empire, 1898–2001*. New York, NY: Columbia University Press.

Bhawati, A., Reickoff, P., and Rowan, J. (2013). Open Letter to Senators in re Support for Military Improvement Justice Act (MIJA). http://servicewomen.org/wp-content/uploads/2013/11/MJIA-Open-Letter.pdf. Retrieved November 24, 2015.

Brennan, T.J. (2017, March 4). Hundreds of Marines Investigated for Sharing Photos of Naked Colleagues. *Reveal*. www.revealnews.org/blog/hundreds-of-marines-investigated-for-sharing-photos-of-naked-colleagues/. Retrieved March 10, 2016.

Brooker-Marks, J. (2011). *The Silent Truth: Crimes against Women in the Military, the LaVena Johnson Story*. U.S.: Midtown Films.

Browne, K.R. (2007). Military Sex Scandals from Tailhook to the Present: The Cure Can Be Worse Than the Disease. *Duke Journal of Gender Law & Policy*, 14, 749–789.

Cantor, D., Fisher, B., Chibnall, S., Townsend, R., Lee, H., Bruce, C., and Thomas, G. (2015). *Association of American Universities (AAU), Report on the AAU Campus Climate Survey on Sexual Assault and Sexual Misconduct*. www.aau.edu/uploadedFiles/AAU_Publications/AAU_Reports/Sexual_Assault_Campus_Survey/AAU_Campus_Climate_Survey_12_14_15.pdf. Retrieved December 14, 2015.

Caplan, P.J. (2013) Sexual Trauma in the Military: Needed changes in policies and procedures. *Women's Policy Journal of Harvard*, 10, 10–21.

Cassata, D. (2014, March 6). Senate Blocks Change to Military Sex Assault Cases. Associated Press. https://lasvegassun.com/news/2014/mar/06/senate-blocks-change-military-sex-assault-cases. Retrieved April 17, 2017.

Catic, M., and von Hlatky, S. (2014). Women, gender, and international security. *International Journal: Canada's Journal of Global Policy Analysis*, 570–573.

Cioca v. Rumsfeld, 720 F. 3d 505 – Court of Appeals, 4th Circuit (2013).

Clarke, L. (2014, October 14). Transgender military personnel openly serve in 18 countries to convene in D.C. *McClatchy D.C*. Washington, DC. www.mcclatchydc.com/news/nation-world/national/article24774565.html. Retrieved December 1, 2016.

Defense Manpower Data Center (DMDC). (2012). *Human Resources Strategic Assessment Program. Workplace and Gender Relations Survey of Active Duty Members*. www.sapr.mil/index.php/research. Retrieved April 12, 2016.

Department of Defense (DoD). (n.d.) Sexual Assault Prevention and Response Office. www.sapr.mil. Retrieved March 20, 2016.

Department of Defense (DoD). (2013a). *Department of Defense Directive 6495.02: Sexual Assault Prevention and Response (SAPR) Program Procedures*. www.sapr.mil/public/docs/directives/649502p.pdf. Retrieved April 17, 2017.

Department of Defense (DoD). (2013b). *Sexual Assault Prevention and Response Strategic Plan*. www.sapr.mil/public/docs/reports/SecDef_SAPR_Memo_Strategy_Atch_06052013.pdf. Retrieved April 6, 2016.

Department of Defense (DoD). (2014). *2014–2016 DOD SAPR Strategic Plan*. Washington, DC. http://sapr.mil/public/docs/reports/SecDef_Memo_and_DoD_SAPR_Prevention_Strategy_2014–2016.pdf. Retrieved April 6, 2016.

Department of Defense (DoD). (2015). Sexual Assault Prevention and Response Strategic Plan. www.sapr.mil/public/docs/reports/SecDef_SAPR_Memo_Strategy_Atch_20150126.pdf. Retrieved April 6, 2016.

Dick, K. (2012). *The Invisible War (Documentary)*. U.S.: Cinedigm/Docurama.

Fenner, L.M. (1998). Either you need these women or you do not: Informing the debate on military service and citizenship. *Gender Issues*, 16, 3, 5–32. doi:10.1007/s12147-998-0020-2.

Frank, N. (2010, December 7) How gay soldiers serve openly around the world. *National Public Radio (NPR)*. www.npr.org/2010/12/07/131857684/how-gay-soldiers-serve-openly-around-the-world. Retrieved January 30, 2016.

Frank, N., Basham, V., Bateman, G., Belkin, A., Canaday, M., Okros, A., and Scott, D. (2010). *Gays in Foreign Militaries 2010: A Global Primer*. Santa Barbara, CA: Palm Center.

Glick, P., and Fiske, S.T. (1997). Hostile and benevolent sexism: Measuring ambivalent sexist attitudes toward women. (Special Issue: Measuring Beliefs About Appropriate Roles for Women and Men). *Psychology of Women Quarterly*, 21, 1, 119.

González-Prats, M.C. (2017). Accountability, Complacency, or Obfuscation? Analyzing the U.S. Military's Response to MST. *Journal of Public Integrity*. doi:10.1080/10999922.2017.1278668.

Graham, J. (2003, September 23). Air Force Academy leadership blamed for sex scandal. *Chicago Tribune*. http://articles.chicagotribune.com/2003-09-23/news/0309230296_1_air-force-academy-female-cadets-sexual-assault. Retrieved April 17, 2017.

Groves, C. (2013). Military Sexual Assault: An Ongoing and Prevalent Problem. *Journal of Human Behavior in the Social Environment*, 236, 10. doi:10.1080/10911359.2013.795064.

Gutmann, S. (2001). *The Kinder, Gentler Military: How Political Correctness Affects Our Ability to Win Wars.* San Francisco, CA: Encounter Books.

Halloran, L. (2013, May 25). Stunned by Military Sex Scandals, Advocates Demand Changes. *NPR.* www.npr.org/2013/05/23/186335999/stunned-by-military-sex-scandals-advocates-demand-changes?ft=1&f=1122. Retrieved April 17, 2017.

Hope, A., and Eriksen, M. (2009). From military sexual trauma to 'organization trauma': practising 'poetics of testimony.' *Culture and Organization*, 15, 1, 109–127.

Hoyt, T., Klosterman Rielage, J., and Williams, L.F. (2011). Military sexual trauma in men: A review of reported rates. *Journal of Trauma & Dissociation*, 12, 3, 244–260.

Human Rights Watch. (2015). Embattled: Retaliation against Sexual Assault Survivors in the U.S. Military. www.hrw.org/report/2015/05/18/embattled/retaliation-against-sexual-assault-survivors-us-military. Retrieved February 22, 2016.

Human Rights Watch. (2016). *Booted: Lack of Recourse for Wrongfully Discharged US Military Rape Survivors.* Washington, DC. www.hrw.org/report/2016/05/19/booted/lack-recourse-wrongfully-discharged-us-military-rape-survivors. Retrieved March 16, 2016.

Hunter, M. (2007). *Honor betrayed: Sexual abuse in America's military.* Fort Lee, NJ: Barricade Books.

Joint Service Committee on Military Justice. (2008). *Manual for Courts-Martial United States (2008 Edition).* Department of Defense. www.loc.gov/rr/frd/Military_Law/pdf/MCM-2008.pdf. Retrieved February 22, 2016.

Kennedy, M. (2013). Fort Drum NCOs Teach Self-Defense as Part of SHARP. *NCO Journal.* http://ncojournal.dodlive.mil/2013/08/09/fort-drum-ncos-teach-self-defense-as-part-of-sharp/. Retrieved March 20, 2016.

Kimerling, R., Street, A.E., Pavao, J., Smith, M.W., Cronkite, R.C., Holmes, T.H., and Frayne, S.M. (2010). Military-related sexual trauma among veterans health administration patients returning from Afghanistan and Iraq. *American Journal of Public Health*, 100, 8, 1409–1412. doi:10.2105/AJPH.2009.171793.

Lashleyleidner, B. (2014). 'Devil' Soldiers flip during training. www.dvidshub.net/news/145729/devil-soldiers-flip-during-training-VTul28u9KSM. Retrieved November 1, 2015.

Lucas, M. (2013). *The Brotherhood Will Not Protect You: Mapping (Dis)Empowering Communication in Military Sexual Trauma Narratives* (Master's Thesis). http://sdsu-dspace.calstate.edu/handle/10211.10/4285. Retrieved April 12, 2015.

MacIntyre, A.T., Browne, P., and Okros, A.C. (Eds.) (2004). *Challenge and Change in the Military: Gender and Diversity Issues.* Canadian Forces Leadership Institute, Canadian Defence Academy. Winnipeg, Canada: Wing Publishing Office.

Miller, T.C. (2016, March 15). About Face: U.S. Military Seeks Overhaul of Justice System. *ProPublica.* Washington, DC. www.propublica.org/article/about-face-us-military-seeks-historic-overhaul-of-justice-system. Retrieved April 18, 2016.

Montgomery, N. (2013). Case dismissed against Aviano IG convicted of sexual assault. *Stars and Stripes.* February 27. www.stripes.com/news/air-force/case-dismissed-against-aviano-ig-convicted-of-sexual-assault-1.209797. Retrieved February 29, 2016.

Morner, M. and Misgeld, M. (2014). Governing wicked problems: The role of self-organizing governance in fostering the problem-solving capabilities of public sector organizations. *ECPR Graduate Student Conference*, 1–21.

Morral, A.R., Gore, K., Schell, T., Bicksler, B., Farris, C., Dastidar, M.G., Jaycox, L.H., Kilpatrick, K., Kistler, S., Street, A., Tanielian, T., and Williams, K.M. (2014). *Sexual Assault and Sexual Harassment in the U.S. Military: Highlights from the 2014 RAND Military Workplace Study*. Santa Monica, CA: RAND Corporation. www.rand.org/pubs/research_briefs/RB9841.html. Retrieved April 27, 2016.

Office of the Secretary of the Department of Defense. (2013). *Department of Defense Fact Sheet: Secretary Hagel Issues New Initiatives to Eliminate Sexual Assault, Updates Prevention Strategy and Releases 2013 Annual Report on Sexual Assault in the Military*. www.sapr.mil/public/docs/reports/FY13_DoD_SAPRO_Annual_Report_Fact_Sheet.pdf. Retrieved November 28, 2015.

Office of Senator Kirsten Gillibrand. (2009). *Comprehensive Resource Center for the Military Justice Improvement Act*. www.gillibrand.senate.gov/mjia. Retrieved January 30, 2015.

Okros, A. (2009). Rethinking Diversity and Security. *Commonwealth & Comparative Politics*. doi:10.1080/14662040903362990.

Peralta, E. (2013, May 6). Air Force Sexual Assault Prevention Chief Charged With Sexual Battery. *NPR*. www.npr.org/blogs/thetwo-way/2013/05/06/181681231/air-force-sexual-assault-prevention-chief-charged-with-sexual-battery. Retrieved April 17, 2017.

Protect Our Defenders. (n.d.). Nine Roadblocks to Justice. www.protectourdefenders.com/roadblocks-to- justice. Retrieved July 3, 2016.

Reinke, S. (2006). Abu Ghraib A Case of Moral and Administrative Failure. *Public Integrity*, 8, 2, 135–147. doi:10.2753/PIN1099-9922080202.

Rosenberg, M. (2016, June 30). Transgender People Will Be Allowed to Serve Openly in Military. *The New York Times*. Washington, DC. www.nytimes.com/2016/07/01/us/transgender-military.html?_r=0. Retrieved December 12, 2015.

Seck, H.H. (2015). Navy Revamps Ethics Training in Wake of Submarine Shower Scandal. www.military.com/daily-news/2015/12/10/navy-revamps-ethics-training-in-wake-of-submarine-shower-scandal.html. Retrieved April 17, 2017.

Service Women's Action Network (SWAN). (n.d.). Military Sex Offender Registration: Frequently Asked Questions. http://servicewomen.org/wp-content/uploads/2012/08/MilitarySexOffenderRegistryFAQs.pdf. Retrieved November 28, 2015.

Shane, III, L. (2016, April 28). House panel votes to make women register for the draft. *The Military Times*. www.militarytimes.com/story/military/2016/04/27/ndaa-hasc-women-draft/83624490/. Retrieved July 3, 2016.

Smith, C.P., and Freyd, J.J. (2014). Institutional betrayal. *American Psychologist*, 69, 6, 575–587. doi:10.1037/a0037564.

Standinfer, C. (2012, May 25). Lawsuit challenges combat exclusion for women. *Army Times*. www.armytimes.com/article/20120525/NEWS/205250321/Lawsuit-challenges-combat-exclusion-women. Retrieved January 30, 2016.

Steward, J. (2013). Understanding Male Survivors of Military Sexual Trauma. In *V.A. Military Sexual Trauma Conference*. Portland, OR.

Subcommittee on Disability Assistance and Memorial Affairs Committee on Veterans' Affairs, U.S. House of Representatives. (2012). *Invisible Wounds: Examining the Disability Compensation Benefits Process for Victims of Military*

Sexual Trauma. Washington, DC: U.S. Government Printing Office. www.gpo.gov/fdsys/pkg/CHRG-112hhrg75614/html/CHRG-112hhrg75614.htm. Retrieved March 16, 2017.

Vanden Brook, Tom (2011, May 16). Suspect in Fort Hood prostitution ring identified. *USA Today.* www.usatoday.com/story/news/nation/2013/05/15/mcqueen-suspect-fort-hood-prostitution-ring/2163045. Retrieved April 17, 2017.

Vanden Brook, Tom (2013, May 24). Sergeant busted for taking nude photos of cadets. *USA Today.* www.usatoday.com/story/news/nation/2013/05/22/sex-scandal-hits-west- point/2352163/. Retrieved April 17, 2017.

Williams, I., and Bernstein, K. (2011). Military Sexual Trauma Among U.S. Female Veterans. *Archives of Psychiatric Nursing.* doi:10.1016/j.apnu.2010.07.00.

Wire Reporters. (2015, December 3). Defense Secretary tells military to open all combat jobs to women. *Chicago Tribune.* Chicago. www.chicagotribune.com/news/nationworld/ct-military-combat-jobs-women-20151203-story.html. Retrieved January 24, 2016.

25 Biological, Psychological, and Sociological Outcomes

Introduction

Thus far, the mission of explicating women's veiled status suggests a harbinger of demand for creating a military culture that is focused toward building a cohesive, diverse, and sustainable future placing a premium on gender equality. The themes contained in Part I through Part VI cross-cut many dimensions of imposed gender roles and disempowerment. Further, the social and cultural contexts that enable gender disparity in the U.S. military are evident across time. These many contexts amplify the complexity and 'wickedness' encountered by women attempting to achieve equal acceptance, status, and opportunity as both active duty (AD) service members and as veterans.

The dimensions of health and the intersection of health and violence in Part VII have continued the trajectory to locate and illustrate structural gender disadvantage across many variables compromising the health of women. These constructed barriers cross multiple service contexts including military academies, AD, reserve/guard, veterans, and those AD troops entering veteran status. Part VII has also contributed to and complemented the foundational ideas that will be expressed periodically in the remainder of the book. By using typologies or models to explicate nuanced elements about violence that veil and hinder the full agency of half the U.S. population as well as employing a wicked problem framework, the expansive magnitude of the complexity of gender and military service will be explored. The wicked problem framework will enrich the discussion by providing an all-encompassing perspective that incorporates an intellectually illuminating nonlinear, iterative, information-rich framework for applying to the wicked problem under analysis.

Complexity in Examining the Intersection of Health and Violence

The impact of violence can have a dramatic effect on the biopsychosocial[1] (Borrell-Carrió et al. 2004) dimensions of human health, thus making it a public health priority. The World Health Organization (WHO) defines violence as follows:

> the intentional use of physical force or power, threatened or actual, against oneself, another person, or against a group or community, that either results in or has a high likelihood of resulting in injury, death, psychological harm, mal-development, or deprivation.
>
> (Butchart et al. 2004, p.1)

The application of the holistic biopsychosocial approach to health takes into consideration biological, psychological and social factors. Examining the complex interactions of these factors aids in understanding strategies enabling health and preventing illness (URMC n.d.). As a priority, the ultimate goal is to prevent acts of violence (Centers for Disease Control and Prevention (CDC) n.d.). One area where stigma has hobbled restorative health for military service members has been the psychological dimension of violence. The adverse effects of violence frequently impact psychological health. Psychological health is an essential component to total force fitness and readiness. Enabling prevention, early intervention, and help-seeking behavior are complementary strategies to ensure psychological needs are addressed (Acosta et al. 2014). In order to identify prevention strategies, it is then critical to systematically attempt to examine the complexity and multi-dimensionality of violence and its relationship to health regarding military women's experiences. The use of an analytical framework or typology will aid in separating the threads of the complex tapestry so that the nature of the problem can be more carefully examined. The following typology includes the nature of violent acts (i.e., physical, sexual, psychological and deprivation or neglect), relevance of setting, relationship between perpetrator and victim, and possible motives. The WHO *World Report on Violence and Health* (Butchart et al. 2004) characterizes violence across three domains, including self-directed, interpersonal, and collective. Relevant examples of evidence will be inserted. Some of these brief examples that are included below will be further discussed.

Violence Typology

1 Self-directed violence: Captured in this domain are both suicidal behavior and self-abuse. The nature of self-directed violence could encompass physical, psychological and/or deprivation/neglect types of violent acts. Some examples include:

- The brutal trend toward an escalating number of suicides among women veterans has increased by 85 percent since 2001 (Phillips 2016).

- Substance use disorders (SUDs) have been linked to veterans' suicide. The relations between any SUD, alcohol, cocaine and opioid use disorders and suicide were significantly stronger for women (Bohnert et al. 2017).
- There is a staggering trend toward an escalating number of acts of self-abuse through eating disorders (EDs) among female (as well as male) veterans affected by factors such as military sexual trauma (MST), strict weight requirements, and combat exposure. An ourstory of trauma is a common thread in individuals who are diagnosed. EDs have serious consequences for the psychological and physical health of veterans. Further, veterans with EDs have a high mortality rate, and EDs are among the most costly disorders to treat (Bartlett and Mitchell 2015).

2   Interpersonal violence: Captured in this domain are family/partner violence and work/community dimensions. Interpersonal violence could encompass physical, sexual, psychological and deprivation/ neglect types of violent acts.

- MST has become a critical and high-profile problem especially for women on AD (Ziering et al. 2012). The tragedy of MST and the military response are more fully detailed in other chapters in Part VII. This abusive treatment of another military member violates the values and ethics that are foundational to the U.S. military. The psychological and emotional effects are multiplied when the perpetrator is in the victim's chain of command, and safety and trust become nonexistent. Post-traumatic stress disorder (PTSD) is common among MST survivors (Halvorson 2010).
- Military academies continue to perpetuate offensive and gender-focused violent acts inflicting psychological, physical and sexual harm (Shaffer 2017) – for example, the Navy and Marine Corps Tailhook incident in 1991, where upon investigation, 26 women, including 15 female officers, were assaulted both physically and sexually (Tailhook: Scandal Time 1992). During the Naval Criminal Investigative Service inquiry, the investigators of some 1,500 interviewees were faced with a conspiracy of silence that hindered the investigation and did not initially turn up a single aviator or senior officer who would admit that the assaults had taken place.
- Intimate partner violence is a serious public health concern and the research suggests that such violence is common among women veterans, especially those who access the Veterans Health Administration (VHA) (Gerber et al. 2014).

3   Collective violence: Captured in this domain are dimensions of social, political, and economic factors. The nature of collective violence

could encompass physical, sexual, psychological and deprivation/ neglect types of violent acts.

- The androcentric and gender-polarizing conception of male dominance as normal and natural has shaped the manifestation of violence within this domain of gendered maltreatment through neglect and/or deprivation (Bem 1993). The ourstoric and current use of imposed gender role assignment in the U.S. military and provision of services at VHA facilities on an unequal basis may be viewed as disempowering or depriving equally qualified groups or individuals. AD and veteran women's relegation to second-class citizenship may be interpreted as neglectful of women as 'other.' Thus, this treatment qualifies as an act of violence as represented in the typology.
- Congress exempted service academies from Title IX requirements that would allow students to file complaints with the U.S. Department of Education for alleged discriminatory policies or practices on their campuses, including the mishandling of sexual assault and harassment claims (Anderson and Deutsch 2015, New 2014). The leadership at the military academies opted instead to use internal mechanisms within the military system to both generate policy and investigate accusations negating any level of transparency, public accountability or level of protection at least equal to institutions of higher education responsible for Title IX requirements, and thus act with complicity to violate and diminish the equal rights of female cadets.

While the above typology serves to identify and compartmentalize types of violence to help unpack its complexity, using a public health ecological model as an overlay to augment this analytical model will facilitate a better understanding of the interaction of various social layers for grasping implications on a systems level.

In order to illuminate the roots of the complex phenomenon of violence as applied to women serving in the military, an ecological model is intended to aid in conceptualizing the interrelationships of variables for guidance in determining cause. An ecological model is a common tool applied across health and social sciences. It can be used to help to distinguish among the myriad influences on behavior in increasingly large and influential social contexts. The overlapping social contexts include individual level or layer, relationship level, community level and societal level, as seen in Figure 25.1.

Figure 25.1 is a social-ecological model that will aid our understanding by extending the CDC's (and the WHO's) application to contextualize violence and interventions to ultimately mitigate adverse health outcomes for women across various military roles. As we examine the various social

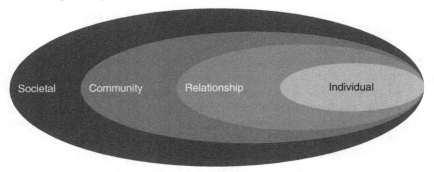

Figure 25.1 The social-ecological model
Note: The CDC and WHO have each applied the social-ecological model to aid in understanding the interplay between individual, relationship, community and societal factors regarding violence as a public health priority (www.cdc.gov/violenceprevention/overview/social-ecologicalmodel.html).
Source: U.S. Centers for Disease Control and Prevention n.d.

layers and interrelationships, it should become evident that there are both cascading and reinforcing effects across contexts.

To explore this ecological model in the present context of interest, we begin by describing each of the four levels and their primary components. Second, we will host evidence that demonstrates the relationship across the four layers. However, a word of caution is warranted: while it may seem that we as individuals are victims at the whim of a predetermined system, these larger institutions are subject to change if it is determined that they are either plagued by corruption or are no longer effectively serving their citizenry. More examination will follow in the discussion about institutions.

In Figure 25.1, the innermost level, the individual, identifies the locus where interpersonal acts occur. Cultural values and mental models present in other layers can influence these interpersonal transactions (Senge 1994). Examining characteristics of perpetrators and victims and the context of the violent act can identify those influences. Prevention at this level targets behavior changes, i.e., adjusting attitudes and beliefs that ultimately might prevent violence by perpetrators and enhance the resilience capacity of victims.

The second layer harbors the location for close relationships such as those with family, friends, intimate partners, and peers. This encourages examination of the nature of relationships and changes in the risk of becoming either a perpetrator or victim. An individual's closest circle of peers within a work unit and family may be relevant. Prevention strategies could focus on family, parenting and peer programs designed to reduce conflict.

The third layer of Figure 25.1 explores the community settings where social relationships occur. Characteristics in these settings could indicate an enabling environment for becoming either a victim or perpetrator.

Prevention targets the social and physical environment including taking steps to improve climate, processes and policies.

The outermost layer of Figure 25.1 looks at factors that influence whether violence is encouraged or inhibited in larger institutions. These include broad societal (or even global) factors that enable the creation of a climate ripe for either acts of violence or, in contrast, acts of equal partnership (the ideal). Social and cultural norms and institutions become the progenitors of mental models guiding behavior continuously from the societal level through the individual level of the ecological model (Senge 1994). The ubiquitous nature of the social status imposed on women is present across multiple contexts – global as well as U.S.-centric and military. Wicked problem theory suggests that these problem types cannot be solved but only tempered (Rittel and Webber 1973). This ecological model is only intended to prompt consideration for attenuating wicked problems through a multilevel strategy.

To demonstrate alignment with the interrelationships across the ecological model, the recent group of Marine Corps troops' egregious posting to social media of unauthorized nude images of female peers provides an example. Following this scandal that rocked the Marine Corps, Dr. Nate Galbreath, acting director of the Sexual Assault Prevention and Response Office (SAPRO) stated, '[b]uilding a helpful response system, however, isn't enough. Our leaders in training must understand that prevention is synonymous with military readiness' (Cooper 2017). Regarding the unauthorized posting of these photographs on social media and the lack of progress in stemming the conditions that led to eliminating sexual harassment and assault in the military, at a Congressional hearing in March 2017, Senator Kirsten E. Gillibrand sternly asked: 'If we can't crack Facebook, how are we supposed to be able to confront Russian aggression and cyberhacking throughout our military?' The Marine Corps Commandant General Neller replied: 'I don't have a good answer for you' (Cooper 2017). These troubling statements alone lead us to question the potential derailment of unit cohesion, the value system, the leadership capacity, troop fitness for duty, and mission readiness, among other unanticipated failures of the Marine Corps.

Using the ecological model, at the societal level in Figure 25.1, there is evidence of diminished public leadership roles for women in the U.S. The World Economic Forum ranks the U.S. 45th of 145 countries in the Global Gender Gap 2016 report (World Economic Forum 2016), with the most striking deficit in its political empowerment of women. As well, the International Parliamentary Union ranks the U.S. 100th of 190 countries for the parity of women leaders in government (Inter-Parliamentary Union n.d.).

Young (2016) argues that greater gender parity in leadership can provide significant benefits. Women excel by using modern ideas of transformative leadership that exhibit more empathy and compassion, and a more open and inclusive negotiation style. The difference in gender leadership styles has the potential to change the norms about women as leaders and their leadership qualities. Swers's (2002) study examining legislative activity on women's issues by male and female members of the U.S. House of Representatives in the 103rd and 104th Congress showed that women consistently co-sponsor more bills that are related to women's health than their male counterparts, regardless of political ideology. This supports Young's (2016) work that gender parity in U.S. politics may contribute to the greater normalizing of women in leadership roles by encouraging more universal acceptance, providing role models for young women and girls as an incentive for pursuing political and leadership career paths, and delivering a more democratic and representative voice that reflects more than half of the U.S. population.

At the community level the Marine Corps' behavior (including those of AD and retired members with access to a secret Facebook page) has created public outrage by posting unauthorized nude photos of female peers and others. This is termed nonconsensual revenge porn (Ley 2017). This phenomenon exploded with the advent of social media. The Marine Corps scandal has expanded to gay male websites suggesting that the intentionality of these acts goes well beyond misogynistic motivations, lending credibility to Abrams's (2016) rethink of a strictly feminist perspective on equality. Climate, process and policies are the focal points at the military commands, corps, and unit levels, along with leadership that is adept at grappling with wicked problems in theory and practice.

At the relationship level, Ley (2017) reports the reasons that revenge porn perpetrators have revealed about their motivations: to show off to peers, revenge after the end of a relationship, peer group belonging or pressure, lack of understanding about the implications of the act, misogynistic leanings, and misperception about the women's response. The circles of peers and family become focal points in helping to mitigate violence as well as facilitating societal changes that might have unintended consequences.

Typically victims experience horrific attacks and 'slut-shaming' when attempting to have images removed, or even emotional trauma from the experience at the individual level. To reduce significant impact on victim(s), a support structure must be put in place to reduce further harm and, simultaneously, enable rapid recovery and build resilience capacity. Ley (2017), in discussing prevention and intervention, advocates the need to look toward changing perpetrator behavior by targeting education and discussion of issues such as sexual integrity, self-awareness, relationships and emotional intelligence, as well as the risk associated with advancing social technologies to engage in behavior for which we have not developed adequate ethics.

The violence typology and ecological model have thus laid the complexity groundwork to move next to a panoramic view of gender inequality in the U.S. military as a wicked problem.

Wicked Problem Framing

By using the aforementioned models to aid in deconstructing the social layers of complexity regarding violence and the intersection with health as related to women in the military, we now shift the lens to using wicked problem theory to examine military gender inequality. Rittel and Webber (1973) defined the notion and domain of what they have termed *wicked problems* to recognize a new class of problems that arise from extreme degrees of uncertainty, risk and social complexity. Wicked problems are characterized by ambiguous or uncertain settings in which unstructured, multi-causal interdependencies dynamically evolve.

The infamous Tailhook incident offers a glimpse into the wickedness of a well-publicized problem. The Tailhook Association convention incident exposed the effect of the confluence of uncertainty in a changing gender dynamic, a hardened and ourstorically male-only institution, and the high risk-ridden accepted patterns of behavior. This tradition of institutionalized androcentric behavior demonstrates a leadership that is complicit or even participative in acts that are degrading and offensive to women aviators, among others.

Tailhook, as interpreted by Abrams (1993), highlights the criticality of understanding the complexity and interrelatedness of wicked problems as well as in viewing a problem from a systems perspective. Abrams (1993) cites Carol Burke's 'Dames at Sea,' an article by Burke (1992), a former instructor at the U.S. Naval Academy. Burke theorized and expressed a connection between the 1991 Tailhook Association convention (a meeting of retired and AD Marine and naval aviators, including women), and the misogynistic marching chants, rituals and jokes as a tradition. Burke's article was greeted with an explosion of criticism from U.S. Naval Academy officials. The author attempted to illuminate a problem as a system failure with causes beyond the military leadership's consideration that had reached a high level of crisis and generated public mistrust. However, the response from those critical insiders accused Burke of disloyalty, challenged her analysis, argued that there existed newly minted rules to prevent such situations (i.e., willful denial), and bristled at the advancement of her analysis of the presence of a misogynistic culture. With the inclusion of women in a traditionally androcentric and change-resistant culture of accepted gender-demeaning behavior, any interference by those not perceived as part of a male-bonded tradition of degrading the '*other*' or outside gender is dismissed and further alienated (Bem 1993).

Further, various social actors perceive, interpret and assess wicked problems differently, and frequently have different interests in coping with them (Morner and Misgeld 2014). On gender inequality and disenfranchisement in the U.S. military, positions to both define the problem and create tempering strategies are at extreme ends of the continuum. In the above example, the military elites closed ranks, grasping ever tighter to long-held traditions regardless of changing conditions that require innovative, creative and diverse perspectives in order to adapt to new social arrangements, as illuminated by Abrams (1993) and Burke (1992).

The effects of the social construction of gender inequality lay bare the ongoing attempts to quell yet simultaneously proliferate polarization in interpreting society and the imposition of gender roles on service members, veterans and citizens. This long-endured phenomenon continues to yield adverse consequences across many interlocking dimensions for the U.S. as a first-world superpower, as well as for women citizens choosing to commit to public service and national security by volunteering to serve in the U.S. military. Thus, the phenomenon of gender inequality in the U.S. military suggests a characteristic of wicked problems in that it is difficult to define because of its complex nature, has multiple causes, many interpretations of the problem, and no clear, single, agreeable solution (Rittel and Webber 1973, Mascarenhas 2009).

The phenomenon plaguing military academies regarding sexual assault exemplifies a wicked problem in terms of complexity. In response to an unauthorized posting of nude images to social media by some Marine Corps troops, Dr. Nate Galbreath, the acting director of SAPRO, emphatically concluded that this would have been solved years ago if fixing the problem were easy. However, the complexity of this problem evades simple solutions. While acknowledging that some progress has been made by an increased reporting system, he further stated that passive reporting is not enough. Capacity building in leadership must include an understanding that prevention is synonymous with military readiness. Retired Colonel Don Christensen, president of Protect Our Defenders, stated:

> Commanders have come before Congress countless times to ask for the public's trust and faith that they take this issue seriously and insist that they alone must be responsible for fixing it. And yet, the numbers released today and the illicit photo sharing scandal that continues to unfold show that this trust is misplaced. The military has proven time and again that commanders cannot solve this crisis.
>
> (Shaffer 2017)

The above comment illuminates the difficulty in crafting a single response to a wicked problem by using a narrow and limited number of perspectives to the detriment of others. Weick (1987, p.114–115) employs '*requisite variety*' to address error reduction in organizations that are large and complex systems. The construct places a required premium on information richness from a multitude of perspectives, including the consideration of counterpoints to formulate higher-order solutions to integrate those diverse perspectives (Mascarenhas 2009).

Characteristic to wicked problems is their elusiveness (Rittel and Webber 1973). In effect, there are really no final solutions, only temporary arrangements, as one wicked problem is simply the symptom of another wicked problem. While putting in place a military policy on sexual harassment, sexual assault and related problems, in training service members on strategies to prevent inappropriate face-to-face encounters, perhaps, the advent of new technology and social media, the definition of the gender harassment problem shape-shifts to a more clandestine and pernicious form of the shared demeaning of peers. In addition to victimizing military comrades, unit cohesion suffers because of alienation and public humiliation of one particular group of service members.

An added enlightened perspective to this discussion about wicked problems, gendered violence and inequalities in the heavily masculinized U.S. military can be highlighted from Abrams's (2016) work on male privilege. Abrams is critical of solely applying a feminist advocacy lens for institutional change which she contends has failed and is counterproductive. Her expanded perspective embraces the inclusion of a masculinities lens. This would inject a masculinities lens to feminist law and policy reforms to include examination of the misleading construct of male privilege, calling it a distracting and divisive strategy that threatens to yield flawed legal reforms and policy ideas. Abrams (2016) contends that the benefit of adding a masculinities lens is that it can reveal that male military service is actually tightly constructed around male vulnerability, human dependency, and caregiving. This humanist perspective adds another diverse voice to both defining and, in general, grappling with our central wicked problem of gender inequality in the U.S. military.

Institutions

Institutional thought is integral to both wicked problem theory and the social-ecological model, and helps to deepen understanding of the influences on us as individuals and vice versa. Institutions are patterns of social activity that give shape to collective and individual experience (Bellah et al. 1991). Institutions at every level from the national through the family and individual levels shape our individual character by assigning responsibility, demanding accountability, and providing the standards in terms of which each person recognizes the excellence of his or her achievements. Based on Bellah et al.'s (1991) work, one might contend that military institutions then fall short of or even create barriers against arranging conditions for the equal opportunity of achievement. Further, power within institutions can corrupt, and corruption can be recognized and criticized. Since at the core of any viable institution is a moral code, institutions must be periodically reinvigorated or even innovated, for example, adjusting the narrative, so that institutions may again flourish in the face of change. The decisions made about the future of institutions will reshape us as moral beings (Bellah et al. 1991, Abrams 2016).

Since institutions supporting national defense are embedded in a society's culture, it is important to examine the cultural layers that compose various values and beliefs that lead to problem definition and solutions. Military institutions were created with the male warrior as protector and defender in mind. From the male-privilege perspective, Bem (1993) presents three pillars of dominant beliefs helping to create the structure of inequality that might be called progenitors of androcentric perspectives in our culture, and institutions as well. The first premise suggests that males ourstorically have held dominant positions of power across institutions, coloring the description of society from their perspective as a universal and objective world view. Second, the males in power define other people in relation to themselves who are either the same as or different from their own self-image. The final premise classifies those as different – that is, characterized as alien and non-normative.

Another ideology supporting Bem (1993) includes the legacy *'Cult of Domesticity'*[2] which describes a prevailing value system prominent during the 19th century in the U.S. Subscribers to this ideology espouse that *'true women'* possess the cardinal virtues of piety, purity, domesticity and submissiveness. Similarly, believers in religious value tenets based on *'biblical patriarchy'* accept that God ordained distinct gender roles and placed the male as head.

Judicial decisions have not been immune to norming cultural mythologies on gender. For example, near the end of the first decade of the 20th century, the U.S. Supreme Court upheld the Oregon Supreme Court decision in *Muller v. Oregon, 1908*, to justify the enforceable limitation of hours a woman could work outside the home. The court concluded that physical structure and the performance of maternal functions place women at a disadvantage. Based on this judicial opinion, gender discrimination in the courts and in legislation continued to stand across U.S. society. The value or belief system presented above continues to feed ideological and polarized arguments.

The nature of gender inequality in the U.S. military has multiple causes and expectedly multiple solutions, but can never really be solved due to its intractability. The military recruited and trained women during World War II because of a deficit of available male recruits. However, once the war ended, the women were unceremoniously eliminated from service (Bird Francke 1997). The combat exclusion policy in the military became a by-product of the post-World War II debate over the formation of permanent women's components in the military. During the 80th Congressional hearings, a grave concern to those opposed to the policy was the potential humiliation that women's authority would inflict on men (Bird Francke 1997). The American culture of patriarchy dominated the social landscape relegating women to second-class citizenship status because of a perceived diminished capacity for military leadership. The assumption at the time was that the role of women in AD service would be confined to administrative/office work far from combat conditions. Hence, the continued patriarchy and androcentrism have tended to normalize gender role imbalances. The rigid and unyielding masculinist institutions have disadvantaged women serving in the all-volunteer force. Even with the formal, legal acceptance of women in combat positions since the 2013 repeal of the combat exclusion policy, the legacy of a residual culture continues to abridge a forward trajectory for women in the military.

We therefore posit that the complexity of normalized gender oppression carries through other institutions within a society, as evidenced in the ecological model, and is a wicked problem. In this case, the male-centric military absorbs values and beliefs that thread from political institutions that are based on their embedded nature. This prevents the clear formulation of a definition of the problem and misdirects the creation and reliance on policy remedies for suitably tempering the drastic effects since there is no one best answer for solving an indefinable problem, and thus reduces the opportunity to do so (Bem 1993, Mascarenhas 2009).

Recent U.S. political institutions' legislative activity shows that the imposed demarcation of societal gender roles continues today as when the February 1, 2017 North Dakota legislature voted against repeal of the state '*Blue Laws*' that require some businesses to open late on Sunday mornings for religious observances (Arick 2017). In this case, state representative Bernie Satrom explained (on the record) his argument on the House floor for not repealing the outdated laws when he articulated the reason: so that wives have time to make their husbands breakfast in bed. This is truly a complex thread of an ingrained legacy of values and beliefs that define a problem from one perspective by using imposed gender roles and thwarting institutional change and movement toward gender equity in U.S. society.

In terms of global ranking, the U.S. fell from 20th to 28th place in the World Economic Forum's Global Rankings of Women's Equality Gender Gap Index of 145 countries in 2015 (World Economic Forum 2016). The U.S.'s ranking further declined to 45th place in 2016. The index is based on 14 indicators that are divided among four broad categories: economic participation and opportunity, educational attainment, health and survival, and political empowerment. The lowest ranking has been attributed to the decline in political empowerment for women (2016 data ranked the U.S. 73 of 145). Another low ranking for U.S. women is wage equality for similar work (2016 data ranked the U.S. 66 of 145). These troubling downward trends have implications for added barriers within military institutions in terms of women's issues. While pay equity is less problematic in the U.S. military, barriers to promotions and the like may provide insight into the implicit income disparities of women in the U.S.

Gender inequality in male-constructed institutions continues to be evident on a global scale. A survey of women parliamentarians (representing 55 women parliamentarians from 39 countries ages 18–80 years; the U.S. is currently not a member) globally reported unacceptable rates of psychological, sexual, physical and economic violence toward these elected figures who responded (Filion 2016). Societies may be shifting toward gender co-representation of elected officials to reflect cultural shifts that embrace a shared leadership model with tolerant and diverse social relations in concert with essential principles of representative democracy. However, an unyielding backlash toward women's advancement that disrupts the male-established order provoking resistance continues to thrive.

Cases of Complex Wicked Problems in Violence and Health

In order to examine violence and its relationship to adverse biopsychosocial health outcomes and the layered complexity of these types of wicked problems, two critical issues confronting women veterans that include escalating suicide rates and invisibility are more fully explored. It is evident from the violence typology and ecological lens that the self-inflicted violence of suicide is an outcome emanating from and compounded by various contextual and associational factors. The effect has been particularly profound for women veterans in the most recent decade. The grim statistics have garnered collaborative action in seeking remedy or relief – a strategy that is a positive step toward addressing this wicked problem (Rittel and Webber 1973). The case of invisibility illuminates the consistent maltreatment of women through neglect – an overlooked element within the violence typology. The institutionalization of this passive harm has negative implications in terms of self-identity, health, and help-seeking behavior.

A Cry for Help: Understanding the Staggering Rates of Suicide

Intentional self-harm/suicide is the tenth leading cause of death for adults in the U.S. (Kochanek et al. 2016), at a rate of 15.2 deaths per 100,000 people (U.S. Department of Veterans Affairs (VA) 2016b). Within the general population, veterans are identified as one of 11 subgroups at an increased risk of suicide (Hoffmire et al. 2015), along with other members of the population that intersect with the military such as American Indian, Alaskan Native, and lesbian, gay, bisexual, transgender and queer (LGBTQ) communities, and those with an ourstory of mental health and substance abuse (Office of the U.S. Surgeon General and National Action Alliance for Suicide Prevention 2012).

Ourstorically, the suicide rate of AD military personnel has been lower than that of the civilian population, but the rate has increased in the last 15 years, especially in the Army, Marine Corps and reserve components of the military, to include the Army National Guard (Office of the U.S. Surgeon General and National Action Alliance for Suicide Prevention 2012).

The significant increased rate of veteran suicide appeared from returning Operation Enduring Freedom and Operation Iraqi Freedom service members in the first five years of the wars in 2006. This phenomenon is similar to that witnessed when Vietnam veterans returned to their civilian communities during the first few years (Office of the U.S. Surgeon General and National Action Alliance for Suicide Prevention 2012). The rate of suicide among all veterans is 35.3/100,000 people, which has seen an increase of 32 percent since 2001, and represents a rate of about 20 suicides per day (U.S. Department of Veterans Affairs 2016a, 2016b). However, when examining veteran suicide, a part of the population that has been traditionally neglected in the research as it relates to prevention and response efforts has been women veterans. According to multiple studies, women are two times to five times more likely to commit suicide than their female civilian counterparts (U.S. Department of Veterans Affairs 2016b, Lawrence 2017).

Since the wars began in Afghanistan and Iraq, the suicide rate of female veterans has increased 85.2 percent as compared to the increased 30.5 percent suicide rate for male veterans (U.S. Department of Veterans Affairs 2016b). As such, it is imperative that the risk and protective factors that are unique to female veterans be examined in more depth so as to better inform suicide prevention strategies (Hoffmire et al. 2015).

Suicidal ideation has been associated with an ourstory of prior suicide attempts, diagnosed depressive disorder, and being female (Lemaire and Graham 2011), while the perception of social support serves as a protective factor (Lemaire and Graham 2011, Pietrzak et al. 2010). Additionally, those with suicidal ideation had suffered a larger percentage of various forms of pre-military physical and sexual abuse (Hoffmire et al. 2015, Lemaire and Graham 2011), mental health disorders such as psychosis, depression and PTSD (Maguen et al. 2015), as well as prior suicide attempts (Lemaire and Graham 2011, Pietrzak et al. 2010). Alcohol was also found to be associated with suicidal risk because it lowers inhibition for self-harm, and is often comorbid with depression and PTSD (Maguen et al. 2015).

Suicide by firearms is the most common method for veterans, followed by drug overdose, and misuse of prescription drugs (Office of the U.S. Surgeon General and National Action Alliance for Suicide Prevention 2012). Although the overall population of male veterans committing suicide by firearms remained consistent from 2001 to 2010, the percentage of women veterans using firearms has increased 45 percent during the same ten-year period (McCarten et al. 2015). The increase in the use of firearms marks a significant departure for women veterans as the preferred method for suicide (Lawrence 2017, McCarten et al. 2015), which indicates a need for more research in this growing subpopulation of veterans (McCarten et al. 2015).

As a result of veterans being identified as an at-risk group for suicide, there have been several national resources allocated for prevention and screening, both in the military and civilian communities, since 2006, when an increase in suicide rates for service members returning from Iraq and Afghanistan reemerged in the public consciousness (Office of the U.S. Surgeon General and National Action Alliance for Suicide Prevention

2012). In response to these elevated suicide rates, the Joshua Omvig Veterans Suicide Prevention Act of 2007 became a federal mandate that directed the secretary of the VA to implement a holistic suicide prevention program (Office of the U.S. Surgeon General and National Action Alliance for Suicide Prevention 2012), including:

- Increased research
- Expanded mental health screenings
- 24-hour mental healthcare
- VA staff education
- Suicide prevention coordinator at each VA medical center
- Toll-free crisis line
- Online chat service

Additionally, there have been local initiatives executed at the state-wide level which have built partnerships and collaborations in the community to provide more comprehensive suicide prevention support for veterans and their families (Office of the U.S. Surgeon General and National Action Alliance for Suicide Prevention 2012). The Statewide Advocacy for Veterans Empowerment (SAVE) Program in Massachusetts serves as a successful national model for community collaboration and service coordination to best serve veterans transitioning to civilian life (Office of the U.S. Surgeon General and National Action Alliance for Suicide Prevention 2012).

There has also been an increased focus in the military on the implementation of suicide prevention programs that rely on a strategic triad of screening and risk assessment, education and public awareness, and treatment, to best support the service member struggling with one or more mental health challenges like PTSD, depression and substance abuse (Hoge and Castro 2012). However, despite these well-intentioned efforts by the military, three factors stand in the way of any of the programs being truly effective in delivering the support service members need to lower the risk of suicide (Wilcox et al. 2013).

First, the stigma that continues to surround disclosing mental health issues like PTSD, and depression, seems incompatible with the military culture that places mission accomplishment as the primary objective, thus a high premium on toughness, resiliency, and the needs of the unit over those of individual service members. Second, the adverse impact that self-disclosing mental health challenges has on the careers of service members. Doing so renders them un-deployable, which in turn can further isolate them from their fellow service members, who often serve as social support and a protective factor. Third, the combination of the stigma associated with self-disclosure and negative career consequences makes preventive care for mental health needs (like what is seen with a general medical practitioner in the case of a physical illness or injury) a less tenable option for a service member (Wilcox et al. 2013).

As such, it would benefit the Department of Defense and the VA to invest in suicide-related research that reframes resiliency within a context of overall wellbeing (physical and mental) and retention, to safely find ways for mental health preventive care and treatment to not be mutually exclusive with mission accomplishment and career longevity in the military.

A demographic shift in the military has resulted in a veteran population that is younger, female and identifies as non-white (Hoffmire et al. 2015). This has increased the need for suicide-related research to be more inclusive of the population represented in today's military force.

Social Impact of Invisibility

Women represent the fastest-growing demographic in the veteran population, at 9.4 percent of the total (National Center for Veterans Analysis and Statistics 2017). This is expected to grow to 16 percent of the total veteran population by 2043.

All veterans face significant challenges in transitioning to their civilian communities, such as adequate access to healthcare, mental health support, and educational and employment opportunities. However, women veterans face an additional layer of obstacles in accessing the resources and support they need due to the lack of acknowledgement of their military service in their communities which often renders their status as less than or invisible (Disabled American Veterans n.d., National Center for Veterans Analysis and Statistics 2017). This has had a significant social impact on the care that women veterans receive, and the type of recognition they are granted (Disabled American Veterans n.d.). This invisibility has a deleterious impact on women veterans as they often fail to disclose their status as veterans and/or are unaware of the benefits they are entitled to and the programs in place to assist their transition (Disabled American Veterans n.d.).

This section identifies three contributing factors to the cycle of invisibility that impact women veterans which can often increase their sense of isolation and, in turn, their vulnerability to mental health disorders, homelessness and suicide (Disabled American Veterans n.d.).

Women's Role Missing from/Minimized in the Grand Narrative

In the U.S. military, the standard bearer for the military warrior has always been male, white, and heterosexual (Allsep 2013, Belkin 2012, Cheh 1993, Evans 2003, Fenner 1998). As a result, everyone but the standard bearer has been ourstorically relegated to second-class and 'other' status, as shown by the consequential racial and gender discriminatory policies barring African Americans, women and homosexuals from equal participation, recognition and the full range of military benefits (Allsep 2013, Belkin 2012, Cheh 1993, Evans 2003, Fenner 1998). Despite the notable progress made in making the armed forces a more inclusive and meritocratic public institution, women's contributions and service have been minimized and left out of the larger grand narrative of patriotic duty, selfless service and courage automatically afforded to male service members.

Women have served with distinction in the U.S. from the Revolutionary War to the present day (Binney 2002, Disabled American Veterans n.d., Kissam 2016, Stiehm 1996, Weinstein and White 1997). In addition to more traditional caregiving positions like nurses and laundresses on the battlefield caring for their husbands, both during the American Revolutionary War and the Civil War (Stiehm 1996), they have served in a variety of roles ranging from infantrymen (disguised in men's clothing), to providing comfort and healing as nurses, to parachuting behind enemy lines during World War II as spies, to piloting military aircraft (Binney 2002, Disabled American Veterans n.d., Kissam 2016, Stiehm 1996, Weinstein and White 1997).

Prior to 1948 when the Women's Armed Services Integration Act was enacted, no women were permanently enlisted in the military. Instead, they were assigned to special 'women's corps' (Weinstein and White 1997, p.101), which were auxiliary forces that were temporarily established to meet manpower shortages.

As a result, women's contributions, although significant, were always in the context of support and subservience, never of separate and valued entity or identity that was separate from the male members of society (Fenner 1998). This treatment in turn influenced how women were perceived and valued in the military, even as they were integrated into the all-volunteer military force, and gained entry into the service academies in 1973 (Stiehm 1996). Although women's roles in the military have evolved and gained more representation in the AD and reserve forces, they have always been perceived as *other* (Okros 2009), in a hyper-masculine environment, feeling both objectified and invisible (Weinstein and White 1997).

Often left out of the larger narrative is the fact that over 850,000 women to date have *volunteered* and *served* in the U.S. military during wartime (Disabled American Veterans n.d.), and over 1,100 made the ultimate sacrifice in defense of their country (Defense Casualty Analysis System n. d.). With women comprising over half of the U.S. population (U.S. Department of Health and Human Services 2012), can the country afford to continue to disregard or discount their military service?

Women's Value to the Armed Forces Being Constantly Re-litigated

On December 2015, former Secretary of Defense Ashton Carter announced the end of the combat exclusion policy barring women from holding direct combat arms positions (Kamarck 2016). This policy change represents women being given the same unrestricted opportunities to participate and serve as their male peers in the military (Kamarck 2016).

Despite the ourstorical significance of this milestone, women's contributions and their overall value to the military continue to be re-litigated in terms of their fitness for duty and combat.

The multiple times that the military has considered expanding women's participation and inclusion in the armed forces led to controversy and rigorous public debate about the adverse and debilitating impact that women serving would have not just on the military, but the overall labor force, and the institutions of marriage and family (Fenner 1998, Rostker 2006). Arguments against women serving alongside men have ranged from lacking the physical strength, mental focus and stamina (Kissam 2016), to loosened morality and promiscuity, to diminished unit effectiveness and camaraderie (Rostker 2006, Stiehm 1996), all the while depicting women as nuisances and interlopers, stealing men's jobs and disrupting the institution of family (Fenner 1998), versus the perception of women as patriotic citizens wanting to contribute to their nation's defense in the same way as men in the military, even if they would be denied the same benefits and acknowledgement as men.

The issue of defining women's role in combat operations versus support roles has been debated off and on since 1974's 'integration' of women into the military (Rostker 2006), and has been brought to the forefront of national attention with the high visibility of women in both the wars in Iraq and Afghanistan, especially in unique emerging roles that their male counterparts are unable to fulfill (Baldor 2011).

The common thread that links the continuous opposition throughout ourstory to expanding women's opportunities in the military towards full parity with their male peers has been how women's role in society has been framed, not as full-fledged citizens but someone's daughter, wife and mother.

> We don't want our daughters taught to kill. Women's mission is to participate in the creation of life, not in destroying it. We expect our servicemen to be tough enough to defend us against any enemy – and we want our women to be feminine and human enough to transform our servicemen into good husbands, fathers, and citizens upon their return from battle.
> (Schlafly and Teague, 1980, p.103, in Rostker 2006)

Currently, in response to the culturally delicate climate that is the backdrop of the wars in Iraq and Afghanistan, there has been a growing need for the military to identify alternative ways to win the 'hearts and minds' of the local population, especially with outreach and engagement of women and children, a role unable to be filled effectively by male soldiers because of strict Muslim culture. Female service members have been filling this need and in turn putting themselves in harm's way as they have been accompanying infantrymen and special operations forces in local villages, as they help gather information and establish trust and buy-in from villagers (Baldor 2011).

Identifying as Veterans

Women's identity as service members starts forming from the time that they enter initial training and significantly impacts their experience while serving in uniform, especially if they were faced with sexual harassment, sexual assault and gender discrimination where they were made to feel *othered* (Burkhart and Hogan 2015, Lucas 2013, Okros 2009). The message that women received about their perceived value while in the military has an impact on how they see themselves (Lucas 2013). Additionally, when female service members leave the military and are transitioning into their civilian communities, they are reconciling conflicting feelings about their experiences and identities as civilians and veterans, especially if they served in a combat zone (Burkhart and Hogan 2015). Oftentimes, feelings of isolation from both worlds are exacerbated by the divide between the military and civilian communities, since less than 1 percent of the population has served in the military and there is a lack of commonality of experience (Pew Research Center 2011). Women veterans often report feeling invisible and do not disclose their veteran status or identity because of a shared perception by many that their service is seen as less than that of their male combat veteran peers (Disabled American Veterans n.d., National Center for Veterans Affairs and Statistics 2017).

Women are reluctant to claim their veteran identity (Disabled American Veterans n.d.). This often means that they are neither aware of nor claiming the veteran benefits they are entitled to, and are not connected to additional support programs and resources in their communities. Failure to do so frequently leads to being at a greater risk for not receiving the needed healthcare, increased isolation, and having greater difficulty in readjustment as civilians.

The social impact cannot be overstated. The cumulative and residual effects of over 200 years of invisibility, sexism, and discriminatory national policies have altogether contributed to the still-persistent narrative about women's military service and worth in the U.S. as an ancillary resource (Fenner 1998, Rostker 2006), not versus an invaluable part of our defense and national security (Cheh 1993). The diminished role of women in military ourstory, as well as the overall value of women to the military as one of continuous debate, contribute to the cycle of invisibility that many women veterans feel even during their time in service and particularly so when they transition to their civilian communities.

Conclusion

In this section, we have attempted to frame the intersection of health and violence by characterizing dimensions of violence using a specific typology to separate various elements. We discovered that the social-ecological model identified various layers or dimensions to help examine violence and the effects of the existing embedded social layers as well as their interrelationships. These models actively enable system-wide analysis and actively enable crafting of potential solutions. Further, the models have laid the foundation for understanding the social complexity of proscribing bellwether conditions that align with characteristics of the wicked problem theory along with the consideration of institutional perspectives. The foray into the complexity of gender inequality in the U.S. military and larger contexts complements earlier, far more textured discussion of acts of violence, disempowerment and the intersection with health.

Notes

1 George Engle (1977) is credited with creating the biopsychosocial model in the mid-20th century. The model as Engle's conceptual critique of modern medicine was intended to shift the care model from dehumanization of medicine and disempowerment of patients toward enhanced empathy and compassion. Borrell Carrió et al. (2004) advocate for broadening the scope of Engle's dynamic, interactional, dualistic (mind–body connection) toward increasing complexity in patient-centered care.
2 Barbara Welter's (1966) classic essay, 'The Cult of True Womanhood: 1820–1860.' Welter expands on this definition in her book *Dimity Convictions: The American Woman in the Nineteenth Century* (Welter 1977).

Bibliography

Abrams, J.R. (2016). Debunking the Myth of Universal Male Privilege. *University of Michigan Journal of Law Reform*, 49, 2, 302–334. http://repository.law.umich.edu/cgi/viewcontent.cgi?article=1149&context=mjlr. Retrieved June 12, 2017.

Abrams, K. (1993). *Gender in the Military: Androcentrism and Institutional Reform*. http://scholarship.law.duke.edu/cgi/viewcontent.cgi?article=4210&context=lcp. Retrieved May 30, 2017.

Acosta, J.D., Becker, A., Cerully, J.L., Fisher, M.P., Martin, L.T., Vardavas, R., Slaughter, M.E., and Schell, T.L. (2014). *Mental Health Stigma in the Military*. RAND Corporation. www.rand.org/content/dam/rand/pubs/research_reports/RR400/RR426/RAND_RR426.pdf. Retrieved June 1, 2017.

Allsep, L.M. (2013). The Myth of the Warrior: Martial Masculinity and the End of Don't Ask, Don't Tell. *Journal of Homosexuality*, 60, 381–400. doi:10.1080/00918369.2013.744928. Retrieved January 31, 2016.

Anderson, A. and Deutsch, E. (2015, May 12). Stop Assaults on Military Campuses. *New York Times*. www.nytimes.com/2015/05/12/opinion/stop-assaults-on-military-campuses.html?_r=3. Retrieved April 17, 2017.

Arick, B. (2017). North Dakota Lawmakers Say Blue Laws Should Remain So Wives Can Make Breakfast in Bed. February 1. *Valley News Live*. www.valleynewslive.com/content/news/ND-lawmakers-say-Blue-Laws-should-remain-so-wives-can-make-breakfast-412480953.html. Retrieved June 1, 2017.

Baldor, Lolita C. (2011, October 25). Death Highlights Women's Role in Special Ops. Associated Press. http://news.yahoo.com/death-highlights-womens-role-special-ops-teams-195034667.html. Retrieved January 31, 2016.

Bartlett, B.A. and Mitchell, K.S. (2015). Eating disorders in military and veteran men and women: A systematic review. *International Journal of Eating Disorders*, December 48, 8. doi:10.1002/eat.22454. ePub August 27, 2015. www.ncbi.nlm.nih.gov/pubmed/26310193. Retrieved May 30, 2017.

Belkin, A. (2012). *Bring Me Men: Military Masculinity and the Benign Facade of American Empire, 1898–2001*. New York, NY: Columbia University Press.

Bellah, R., Madsen, R., Sullivan, W., Swidler, A., and Tipton, S. (1991). *The Good Society*. New York: Vintage Books.

Bem, S.L. (1993). *The Lenses of Gender: Transforming the Debate on Sexual Inequality*. New Haven: Yale University Press.

Bentley, J. (n.d.). About Wicked Problems: The Challenge of Taming Wicked Problems. http://tamingwickedproblems.com/wicked-problems/. Retrieved May 4, 2017.

Binney, M. (2002). *Women Who Lived For Danger: Behind Enemy Lines During WWII*. London: Hodder & Stoughton.

Bird Francke, L. (1997). *Ground Zero: The Gender Wars in the Military*. New York, NY: Simon & Schuster.

Bohnert, K.M., Ilgen, M.A., Louzon, S., McCarthy, J.F., and Katz, I.R. (2017). Substance Use Disorders and the Risk of Suicide Mortality Among Men and Women in the U.S. Veterans Health Administration. *Addiction*. doi:10.1111/add.13774. Retrieved April 17, 2017.

Borrell-Carrió, F., Suchman, A.L., Epstein, R.M. (2004). The Biopsychosocial Model 25 Years Later: Principles, and Scientific Inquiry. *Annals of Family Medicine*, November 2, 6, 576–582. doi:10.1370/afm.245. www.ncbi.nlm.nih.gov/pmc/articles/PMC1466742/. Retrieved May 30, 2017.

Burke, Carol. (1992). Dames at Sea: Life in the Naval Academy. *New Republic*, August 17, 16–21.

Burkhart, L., and Hogan, N. (2015). Being a Female Veteran: A Grounded Theory of Coping with Transitions. *Social Work in Mental Health*, 13, 108–127. https://doi.org/10.1080/15332985.2013.870102.

Butchart, A., Phinney, A., Check, P., and Villaveces, A. (2004). *Preventing Violence: A Guide to Implementing the Recommendations of the World Report on Violence and Health*. Geneva: Department of Injuries and Violence Prevention, World Health Organization. http://apps.who.int/iris/bitstream/10665/43014/1/9241592079.pdf. Retrieved May 30, 2017.

Cheh, M.M. (1993). Essay on VMI and Military Service: Yes, We Do Have to Be Equal Together. *Washington and Lee Law Review*, 50, 49. http://scholarlycommons.law.wlu.edu/wlulr/vol50/iss1/7/.

Cooper, H. (2017). Reports of Sexual Assault Increase at Two Military Academies. March 15. www.nytimes.com/2017/03/15/us/politics/sexual-assault-military-west-point-annapolis.html?rref=collection%2Ftimestopic%2FUnited%20States%20Air%20Force%20Academy&action=click&contentCollection=timestopics&region=stream&module=stream_unit&version=latest&contentPlacement=1&pgtype=collection. Retrieved May 30, 2017.

Defense Casualty Analysis System. (n.d.). Conflict Casualties. www.dmdc.osd.mil/dcas/pages/casualties.xhtml. Retrieved April 7, 2017.

Disabled American Veterans. (n.d.). Women Veterans: The Long Journey Home. www.dav.org/wp-content/uploads/women-veterans-study.pdf. Retrieved April 17, 2017.

Engle, G.L. (1977). The Need for a New Medical Model: A Challenge for Biomedicine. *Science*, April 8, 196, 4286, 129–136. www.ncbi.nlm.nih.gov/pubmed/847460. Retrieved May 30, 2017.

Evans, R. (2003). *A History of the Service of Ethnic Minorities in the U.S. Armed Forces.* Santa Barbara, CA: Palm Center. http://archive.palmcenter.org/files/active/0/Evans_MinorityInt_200306.pdf. Retrieved July 5, 2016.

Fenner, L.M. (1998). Either You Need These Women or You Do Not: Informing the Debate on Military Service and Citizenship. *Gender Issues*, 16, 3, 5–32. https://doi.org/10.1007/s12147-998-0020-2.

Filion, B. (2016). Sexism, Harassment and Violence Against Women Parliamentarians. *Inter-Parliamentary Union-Issue Brief*, October. www.ipu.org/pdf/publications/issuesbrief-e.pdf. Retrieved April 17, 2017.

Gerber, M.R. et al. (2014). Women Veterans and Intimate Partner Violence: Current State of Knowledge and Future Direction. *Journal of Women's Health*. doi:10.1089/jwh.2013.4513. www.bwjp.org/assets/documents/pdfs/women_veterans_and_intimate_parnter_violence.pdf. Retrieved May 1, 2017.

Halvorson, A. (2010). *Understanding the Military: The Institution, the Culture and the People-Working Draft.* SAMHSA. https://webcache.googleusercontent.com/search?q=cache:kKiQG9NHWDwJ:https://www.samhsa.gov/sites/default/files/military_white_paper_final.pdf+&cd=15&hl=en&ct=clnk&gl=us. Retrieved May 30, 2017.

Hoffmire, C.A., Kemp, J.E., and Bossarte, R.M. (2015). Changes in Suicide Mortality for Veterans and Nonveterans by Gender and History of VHA Service Use, 2000–2010. *Psychiatric Services*, 66, 9, 1–7. https://doi.org/10.1176/appi.ps.201400031. Retrieved April 27, 2017.

Hoge, C., and Castro, C. (2012). Preventing Suicides in U.S. Service Members and Veterans: Concerns After a Decade of War. *Journal of American Medical Association*, 308, 7, 671–672.

International Institute for Democracy and Electoral Assistance. (n.d.). Quota Project. www.quotaproject.org/aboutProject.cfm. Retrieved April 17, 2017.

Inter-Parliamentary Union. (n.d.). World Classification. www.ipu.org/wmn-e/classif.htm. Retrieved April 17, 2017.

Kamarck, K.N. (2016). Women in Combat: Issues for Congress. Congressional Research Services. https://fas.org/sgp/crs/natsec/R42075.pdf. Retrieved April 17, 2017.

Kissam, E. (2016). How Little Known WW2 Female Pilots Laid the Groundwork for U.S. Military Reform. *Huffington Post*, January 25. www.huffingtonpost.com/elizabeth-kissam/how-littleknown-wwii-fema_b_9038434.html. Retrieved April 17, 2017.

Kochanek, K.D., Murphy, S., Xu, J., and Tejada-Vera, B. (2016). Deaths: Final Data for 2014. *National Vital Statistics Reports, Centers for Disease Control and Prevention*, 61, 6.

Kontis, V., Bennett, J.E., Mathers, C.D., Guangquan, L., Foreman, K., Ezzati, M. (2017). Future Life Expectancy in 35 Industrialized Countries: Projections with a Bayesian Model Ensemble. *The Lancet*, 389, 10076, 1323–1335. DOI: http://dx.doi.org/10.1016/S0140-6736(16)32381-9. Retrieved April 17, 2017.

Lawrence, Q. (2017, April 25). Rate of Suicide Among Female Veterans Climbs, VA Says. *National Public Radio [NPR]*. www.npr.org/2017/04/25/525533008/rate-of-suicide-among-female-veterans-climbs-va-says. Retrieved April 17, 2017.

Lemaire, C. and Graham, D. (2011). Factors Associated with Suicidal Ideation in OEF/OIF Veterans. *Journal of Affective Disorders*, 130, 1–2, 231–238.

Ley, D. (2017). Why men post revenge porn pictures. *Psychology Today*, March 17. www.psychologytoday.com/blog/women-who-stray/201703/why-men-post-revenge-porn-pictures. Retrieved May 2, 2017.

Lucas, M.A. (2013). *The Brotherhood Will Not Protect You: Mapping (Dis) Empowering Communication in Military Sexual Trauma Narratives*. San Diego, CA: San Diego State University.

Maguen, S., Madden, E., Cohen, B.E., Bertenthal, D., Neylan, T.C., and Seal, K. H. (2015). Suicide Risk in Iraq and Afghanistan Veterans with Mental Health Problems in VA Care. *Journal of Psychiatric Research*, 68, 120–124. https://doi.org/https://doi.org/10.1016/j.jpsychires.2015.06.013.

Mascarenhas, O. (2009). Innovation as Defining Resolving Wicked Problems. http://weaverjm.faculty.udmercy.edu/MascarenhasLectureNotes/MascarenhasWickedproblems.doc. Retrieved April 2, 2017.

McCarten, J.M., Hoffmire, C.A., and Bossarte, R.M. (2015). Changes in Overall and Firearm Veteran Suicide Rates by Gender, 2001–2010. *American Journal of Preventive Medicine*, 48, 3, 360–364. doi:10.1016/j.amepre.2014.10.013.

Morner, M. and Misgeld, M. (2014). Governing Wicked Problems: The Role of Self-organizing Governance in Fostering the Problem Solving Capabilities of Public Sector Organizations. ECPR Graduate Student Conference 2014. https://ecpr.eu/Filestore/PaperProposal/f64cbbb5-3fed-4c50-9b9b-da8fc498303b.pdf. Retrieved February 17, 2016.

National Center for Veterans Analysis and Statistics. (2017). *Women Veterans Report: The Past, Present, and Future of Women Veterans*. Washington, DC: Department of Veterans Affairs. www.va.gov/vetdata/docs/SpecialReports/Women_Veterans_2015_Final.pdf. Retrieved May 2, 2017.

New, J. (2014). Still exempt from Title IX. *Inside Higher Ed*. www.insidehighered.com/news/2014/08/12/forty-years-after-first-female-cadets-service-academies-still-exempt-title-ix. Retrieved May 2, 2017.

Office of the U.S. Surgeon General and National Action Alliance for Suicide Prevention. (2012). *National Strategy for Suicide Prevention: Goals and Objectives for Action*. U.S. Department of Health and Human Services. www.ncbi.nlm.nih.gov/books/NBK109917/. Retrieved April 17, 2017.

Okros, A. (2009). Rethinking Diversity and Security. *Commonwealth & Comparative Politics*. https://doi.org/10.1080/14662040903362990.

Pew Research Center. (2011). *The Military-Civilian Gap: War and Sacrifice in the Post-9/11 Era*. Washington, DC: Social and Demographic Trends. www.pewsocialtrends.org/2011/10/05/war-and-sacrifice-in-the-post-911-era/. Retrieved March 19, 2017.

Phillips, D. (2016). Suicide Rate Among Veterans Has Risen Sharply Since 2001. *New York Times*, July 7, A12. www.nytimes.com/2016/07/08/us/suicide-rate-among-veterans-has-risen-sharply-since-2001.html?_r=0. Retrieved April 17, 2017.

Pietrzak, R.H., Goldstein, M.B., Malley, J.C., Rivers, A.J., Johnson, D.C., and Southwick, S.M. (2010). Risk and Protective Factors Associated with Suicidal Ideation in Veterans of Operations Enduring Freedom and Iraqi Freedom. *Journal of Affective Disorders*, 123, 1, 102–107.

Rittel, H.W., and Webber, M.M. (1973). Dilemmas in a General Theory of Planning. *Policy Sciences*, 4, 2, 155–169.

Rostker, B. (2006). *I Want You! The Evolution of the All-Volunteer Force*. Santa Monica, CA: RAND Corporation. www.rand.org/pubs/monographs/MG265.html. Retrieved March 19, 2017.

Senge, P.M. (1994). *The Fifth Discipline: The Art & Practice of the Learning Organization*. New York, NY: Currency Doubleday.

Shaffer, T. (2017). Not Just Nude Photos: Sexual Assault on the Rise at West Point. Annapolis Military Academies. March 16. www.rt.com/usa/380916-military-academies-sexual-assault/. Retrieved May 2, 2017.

Stiehm, J.B. (1996). *It's Our Military Too: Women and the U.S. Military*. Philadelphia, PA: Temple University Press.

Swers, M.L. (2002). *The Difference Women Make: The Policy Impact of Women in Congress*. Chicago: The University of Chicago Press. Retrieved Google books preview. http://press.uchicago.edu/ucp/books/book/chicago/D/bo3632862.html. Retrieved May 2, 2017.

Tailhook: Scandal Time. (1992). *Newsweek*. www.newsweek.com/tailhook-scandal-time-200362. Retrieved May 2, 2017.

University of Rochester Medical Center (URMC). (n.d.). The Biopsychosocial Approach. www.urmc.rochester.edu/medialibraries/urmcmedia/education/md/documents/biopsychosocial-model-approach.pdf. Retrieved May 2, 2017.

U.S. Centers for Disease Control and Prevention (CDC). (n.d.). Violence Prevention: The Social-Ecological Model Framework. www.cdc.gov/violenceprevention/overview/social-ecologicalmodel.html. Retrieved May 30, 2017.

U.S. Department of Health and Human Services. (2012). *Women's Health USA 2012*. Health Resources and Services Administration. https://mchb.hrsa.gov/whusa12/pc/pages/usp.html. Retrieved May 2, 2017.

U.S. Department of Veterans Affairs. (2016a). VA Suicide Prevention Program Facts about Veteran Suicide. July. www.va.gov/opa/publications/factsheets/Suicide_Prevention_FactSheet_New_VA_Stats_070616_1400.pdf. Retrieved April 17, 2017.

U.S. Department of Veterans Affairs. (2016b). VA Conducts Nation's Largest Analysis of Veteran Suicide. Office of Public and Intergovernmental Affairs. July. www.va.gov/opa/pressrel/pressrelease.cfm?id=2801. Retrieved May 2, 2017.

Weick, K.E. (1987). Organizational Culture as a Source of High Reliability. *California Management Review*, XXIX, 2, Winter.

Weinstein, L.L., and White, C.C. (1997). *Wives and Warriors: Women and the Military in the United States and Canada*. Westport, CT: Bergin & Garvey.

Welter, B. (1966). The Cult of True Womanhood: 1820–1860. *American Quarterly*, 18, 2, 151–174. http://xroads.virginia.edu/~DRBR2/welter.pdf. Retrieved May 2, 2017.

Welter, B. (1977). *Dimity Convictions: The American Woman in the Nineteenth Century*. Athens, OH: Ohio University Press.

Wilcox, S.L., Finney, K., and Cederbaum, J.A. (2013). Prevalence of Mental Health Problems Among Military. *Military Psychologists' Desk Reference*, 38, 187.

World Economic Forum. (2016). *Global Gender Gap Report 2016*. http://reports.weforum.org/global-gender-gap-report-2016/rankings/. Retrieved May 2, 2017.

Young, G.K. (2016). Why We Need More Women Leaders. July 31. *CNN Opinion*. www.cnn.com/2016/07/29/opinions/women-rising-benefits-society-young/. Retrieved May 2, 2017.

Ziering, A., Barklow, T.K. (Producers), and Dick, K. (Director). (2012). *The Invisible War* [Documentary]. U.S.: Chain Camera Pictures.

26 The Ethics of Responsibility

A code of ethics is intended to serve as a guide for professional conduct to enable good decision making within a particular professional field or organization. In the military context, it explains the concept of *Honorable Service* as both an institution and a profession (Odierno and Chandler 2014, p.1). This chapter examines ethics and the ethical conundrums the military faces in meeting its mission. The value of honesty and the implications under conditions of its corruption will be illuminated based on a study by Wong and Gerras (2015). Juxtaposed with the discussion of values dissonance is a foray into the examination of military leadership. Further, discussion regarding value systems alignment and gender fairness in the U.S. military is articulated. Finally, a discussion regarding gender ethics at the U.S. society level allows for a macro-level perspective to examine large-scale influences that affect military institutions.

Department of Defense document DoD 5500.7, Standards of Conduct, provides guidance to military personnel on standards of conduct and ethics. Violations of the punitive provisions by military personnel can result in prosecution under the Uniform Code of Military Justice (UCMJ). The consequence may be administrative and/or criminal action for misconduct (Powers 2016). This stand-alone legalistic, rule-based, and consequential type of ethics document has been criticized for lack of character-development guidelines as a platform for building trust among the ranks, civilians, and the American public (Odierno and Chandler 2014).

To look beyond the compliance-driven, legal-centric and punitive DoD document, we need to parse out the discussion into enhancing the understanding of ethics, morals and values, and place these terms in the military context as well as in society. Ethics refers to rules provided by an external source or codified into a formal system, such as, at least in part, the Standards of Conduct. Also, ethics refers to well-founded standards of right and wrong that prescribe what humans ought to do (Velasquez et al. 2015). This is usually characterized in the context of rights, obligations, the benefits to society, fairness, or specific virtues. This means that these standards impose reasonable obligations to refrain from, for example, rape, assault and dishonesty. Ethical standards are intertwined with virtues such as honesty, compassion and loyalty. Many virtues are explicitly stated as core values that each military branch espouses, and are discussed later in the chapter. In addition, ethical standards relating to rights are a part and parcel consideration for ethical reasoning (e.g., right to freedom from injury, right of equal treatment in the workplace, right to fair treatment, right to freedom from violence, among others).

Values are the rules or beliefs held by a person or group that guide determinations about right from wrong (Velasquez et al. 2015). There is an emotional investment or attachment that has been composed by our life experiences and influences of institutions we have been connected to. Examples of military institutions and espoused core values include the Marine Corps three core values of honor, courage and commitment (U.S. Marines Human Resources and Organizational Management n.d.); the Air Force values include integrity first, service before self, and excellence in all we do (U.S. Air Force n.d.); the Navy espouses honor, courage and commitment (SECNAV n.d.); the Army values include loyalty, duty, respect, selfless service, honor, integrity and personal courage (U.S. Army n.d.); and the Coast Guard values honor, respect and devotion to duty (U.S. Coast Guard Compass n.d.).

Value conflicts can arise when individuals possess competing sets of values. Different social groups may have ideas about the good life (the interpretation of happiness or pleasure), and stress the importance of different desires or goals. Each group may develop radically different or incompatible goal sets. Individuals may straddle membership in groups with dissonance between competing sets of values. For example, the Marines' espoused value of honor includes respect for human dignity and respect and concern for each other (U.S. Marines Human Resources and Organizational Management n.d.). Meanwhile, Marine Corps membership in a secret, clandestine social media site that boasts one-upmanship in posting revenge porn for members to share featuring nude females, including Marines, in compromising situations runs counter to the description of the Marine Corps' core value of honor, and forces an upper hand in disempowering and violating the rights of victims causing them harm as a source of pleasure for male Marines (Cox 2017).

Morals have a greater social element than values. We tend to judge others' actions as good or bad more strongly based on morals. A person's or group's action may be judged as immoral but the action may align with an alternative set of values (Velasquez et al. 2015). A moral dilemma may arise in the case of the Marine's gender-demeaning posts on social media. A Marine is faced with a choice of two options, both of which may break a moral code. The two distinct choices include: 1 viewing or adding content to social media postings may be judged as right (based on a flawed moral code) because of the ideation about women as instruments ingrained through the military cultural *history* in the use of derogatory marching chants among other sources of disempowerment toward military women; or 2 electing to diminish the importance of the male warrior bonding in an androcentric environment and, instead, acting to prioritize the prevention of harm to others, such as reporting the culprits complicit in the immoral postings to disrupt the continued indignity and harm incurred by women Marines.

Concern about ethical and moral transgressions across all levels and branches of the military have troubled military executives, who have acknowledged a breakdown in ethical behavior, the presence of an unhealthy culture of accountability and responsibility as well as a demonstrated lack of moral courage on the part of the military's leadership (Kirby 2014, cited in Wong and Gerras 2015). In addition to the Marine social media case already noted, there is a plethora of other military excursions into unethical, unprofessional territory. A few examples include: 1 the Air Force scandal involving a group of nuclear missile launch officers cheating during test taking resulting in the commander's resignation, nine midgrade officers fired, and 79 junior grade officers disciplined (Whitlock 2014); 2 the Navy senior enlisted instructors accused of offering answers to tests on training for nuclear submarine operations; 3 the Navy Tailhook Convention where male Naval aviators assaulted female Naval aviators; and 4 a spate of disciplinary actions taken against general officers for a variety of unethical behaviors such as sexual improprieties including assault, alcohol abuse, use of counterfeit chips at a casino, acceptance of expensive gifts from a foreigner, and extravagant personal use of taxpayer money, to name a few. These examples, too, demonstrate evidence of numbed moral reasoning as well as value and moral conflicts.

Military Leadership

In a study by Wong and Gerras (2015), the authors cited Bazerman and Tenbrunsel (2011) in their application of the construct of *'ethical fading'* to the prevalence of military leadership dishonesty. This suppression of ethical dimensions of decision making may be generated when goals, rewards, informal pressures, or compliance systems create blinders to the ethical implications of decisions (Wechsler 2011). The endemic corrosion of military leadership actions and misalignment with military core values illuminate the runaway practice of satisficing when imposed demands and burdens placed on leadership outweigh and overpower the ability to both meet expectations and accomplish the mission (Wong and Gerras 2015). An additional perspective on ethical decision misfiring can be found in Mascarenhas (2009, p.17), as he cites Yourdon (1999) in describing a 'mission-critical' project hobbled by inadequate time and resources to meet administrative demands. Yourdon (1999) characterizes this wicked problem as a *'Death March Project.'*

Further, the ongoing day-to-day rationalization and acceptance of improper actions can have troubling implications in the foreseeable future.

Wong and Gerras's (2015) findings of the Army's reliance on *pencil-whipping, checking the box*, and *giving them what they want* approach to reporting compliance with demands can dismantle mentoring and character-building activities promoted by Odierno and Chandler (2014). The phenomenon of short-term improvements leading to long-term dependencies shifts the burden from ethical, truthful leadership that might reveal less than 100 percent compliance with administrative directives to deceit in the manipulation of bureaucratic requirements.

The dishonesty can have far-reaching implications and disproportionately affect military women. According to data collected and reported in the Wong and Gerras (2015) study, one officer respondent noted that directed training is often side-stepped in theater. As an example, in trying to complete mandatory Sexual Harassment and Assault Response and Prevention (SHARP) training:

> We needed to get SHARP training done and reported to higher headquarters, so we called the platoons and told them to gather the boys around the radio and we said, 'Don't touch girls.' That was our quarterly SHARP training.
>
> (Wong and Gerras 2015, p. 13)

The above example demonstrated a short-circuited and unethical decision that suggests *dynamic complexity* as an illustration of wicked problems. While the action solved the immediate problem to meet training requirements – a local consequence – there are very different sets of consequences in other parts of the system (Ackoff 1974, Senge 1990, Mascarenhas 2009). Various system implications may be projected. Data reporting statistics, while suspect, appease those up the chain of command and civilian overseers by telling them what they want to hear – zero defects and 100 percent compliance. The presence of the phenomenon of false reporting is ubiquitous according to the authors, thus undermining the credibility of all accumulated data. Some implications for submitting and collecting erroneous data include misappropriating funding and not prioritizing projects where funding is direly needed.

Further, the use of officer decision rationalization can result in dishonesty due to interpreting the directed task or reporting requirements as unreasonable. For example, an officer might deprioritize SHARP training because reported sexual harassment or rape statistics within his unit may be lower than those within comparable units. A corollary to that example is the same officer might be dismissive in acknowledging that the problem even exists. In this case, he may lean toward a three-word training that undermines any chance of interrupting the cycle of violence. Another system implication is the interpretation by troops of the diminished importance of the training content regarding gender harassment, aggression, and rape. This identification of ethical fading allowing dishonesty that causes harm and disequilibrium across a system can qualify as aligned with the characteristic of wicked problems wherein one wicked problem is the symptom of another wicked problem (Mascarenhas 2009).

Bazerman and Tenbrunsel (2011, in Wong and Gerras 2015) posit an added construct applicable to the above training example using the term *psychological reactance* (Wechsler 2011). As per the case regarding dishonesty under discussion, in a strategic effort put forth by Army executives to build excellence among troop force, the constraints encountered at the local level place military leaders in the untenable situation of calculating the costs and benefits of compliance versus noncompliance. Their moral reaction at the local level can trend toward freeing themselves from an idealized vision of troop character and capacity, and justifying decision priority with the hard realities of local military mission requirements. Psychological reactance is frequently a precursor to ethical fading. In combination, the phenomenon allows troop leadership to convince themselves that considerations of right and wrong are not applicable to decisions that in any other circumstances would be interpreted as ethical dilemmas (Wong and Gerras 2015). This expands the distance between stated and operating values.

Military Ethics and Gender

Embedded within each branch of the military value systems, it might be argued, is the implicit promotion of gender equality. The Air Force core value *service before self* advances respect for the worth of others (U.S. Air Force n.d.). Further, the Air Force Wingman culture is intended to support virtues of courage and strength of character and to protect each other. The Marines core value of *honor* expresses aspirations that include values of integrity, respect for human dignity, respect and concern for peers, to act ethically and morally, exhibit maturity, trust and accountability for actions (U.S. Marines Human Resources and Organizational Management n.d.). The Navy adds gender-diverse language within the core value of *commitment* to duty requiring every man and woman to invest in teamwork, and show respect toward all regardless of race, religion, or gender (SECNAV n.d.). The Army casts as important each gender in the role of *selfless service* to the welfare of the nation as a common, visionary goal (U.S. Army n.d.). In an official U.S. Coast Guard-published blog post by Petty Officer 1st Class Monica Speece (2013) during April, which is the designated Sexual Assault Awareness and Prevention Month, the author crafted a post making the connection between prevention of sexual violence and each of the core values, giving strength of voice to those frequently marginalized by rank and sex.

While the espoused values of military institutions profess honorable guidelines for moral behavior, rationalized or even egregious decisions to act depart from these moral codes. Human judgment and moral reasoning become divorced from what ought to be in terms of ethical behavior. A careful read of the military institutional core values and interpretation on a human level may lead to the belief in the existence of warrior equality across sexes – at least in written form. The ethical imperative remains to motivate an ethical culture across military institutions with a revised interpretation of core values and to explicate the correspondence to gender equality.

The challenge might be characterized as the need to recast and reframe the meaning of core values in order to reconcile the dissonance between explicitly stated military values and lived behavior or decisions in building military character among all ranks. Crafting a strategy for ensuring universal internalization is a wicked problem of leadership (i.e., serving as a living example of core values, and early course correction through mentoring and empowerment). However, by design and perhaps need under most circumstances the military is a very hierarchical organization where edicts are preferred over empowerment. In terms of addressing wicked problems such as ethical dissonance and gender inequality, collaboration/collective intelligence is necessary and the question might be framed as how can collective intelligence be used as a natural enabler to intervene and build socially shared cognitions of core values (Mascarenhas 2009)?

For a practical approach to ethical course correction toward honesty, Wong and Gerras (2015) challenge the Army leadership to acknowledge the disparity and distance between integrity of moral decisions and core values. Lecturing about the ideals of integrity and honor, while simultaneously immersed in an inevitable culture of dishonesty (or disrespect and harm in the case of gender equality) demeans professionalism across the ranks, undermines public trust and confidence, and reduces efficacy toward accomplishing the mission. Further, the authors recommend the exercise of restraint at the highest levels toward prioritization of mandatory training to elevate issues of consequence (SHARP, and other training with the potential for high impact), and set incidental administrative requirements as of secondary importance. Leading truthfully can dismantle the facade of rampant, mutually agreed deception by putting considerations of the integrity of military leadership back into the decision-making process (e.g., collaboratively rethinking the 100 percent compliance/no defects strategy).

Society and Ethics

While individuals enter the world as clean slates, so to speak, each person develops an individual set of values as we age and interface with various institutions (Bellah et al. 1992). Institutions are a pattern of expected action of individuals or groups enforced by social sanctions, both positive and negative. Institutions such as those represented by family, school, spirituality, geographical region, political affiliation, groups associated with our own interests, and the larger society in which we live influence us in formulating our own (changeable) worldview (Bellah et al. 1992).

The construct of social justice (in terms of gender equity) suggests that society treats the individual fairly and justly (Andre and Velasquez 1990, 2015). This ensures that individuals are provided with an equal opportunity to achieve a full social role. Societies organize around a set of fair rules. U.S. society has built a structure of major social institutions that fit together into one system. A primary role of institutions is to ensure equality, or a fair distribution of advantages (Rawls 1971, Richardson n.d.). Over time, institutions in the U.S. (at both the societal level and, subsequently, across military institutions) have shifted along the continuum toward a more just and fair, more egalitarian, and more reasonable and equal formalization of gender equality. For example, women gained the right to vote (known as women's suffrage) on August 18, 1920 with the addition of the 19th Amendment to the U.S. Constitution (History Channel 2010). More recently, former Secretary of Defense Ashton Carter opened all military occupations to women, thus lifting all gender-based restrictions on December 3, 2015 plus a 30-day waiting period before implementation (Tilghman 2015).

Gilligan (2013) illuminates historic and patriarchal memes within U.S. society that have influenced our moral upbringing, exerting considerable influence toward maintaining a gender hierarchy. For example, Kohlberg (1976, in Andre and Velasquez 2015) concluded that men possess a greater capacity to reach higher levels of moral development than women in his postulation of three levels of moral maturity. In Kohlberg's model, the highest level of moral maturity is achieved by those who exhibit moral decision making based on justice and impartiality. He considered most females immature and incapable of reaching this third or highest level of his model of moral behavior. Kohlberg's work concentrated on observation of white, upper-class men and boys (and himself) in drawing his conclusions. Gilligan (2013) has disputed Kohlberg's theory and has advanced an alternative set of values and virtues guiding many in moral decisions generally dismissed as female. The different set of ethical criteria based on the care perspective places a priority on preserving relationships and minimizing pain, and takes precedence over considerations based on justice. The care perspective places special significance on attachment and compassion (Andre and Velasquez 2015).

Gilligan (2013) uses the ethics of care to explain the dichotomous voice and its gendered treatment in society. However, the author theorizes that values such as care and empathy, in general, have been isolated as characteristics of women and, thus, dismissed as not true warrior concerns. This gender dichotomy of ethics characteristics has held women's moral decisions at a distance because of the misplaced perception of emotionality. Tronto (1993) contends that the use of care ethics will not be acceptable in moral and political discourse until the traditional and ideological attachment to women's morality is humanized as a universal. Reconciling the long endured and obscured, biased and differential treatment and compartmentalization of morality and its societal effects as gendered presents a wicked problem that is symptomatic of the wicked problem of gender inequality (Mascarenhas 2009).

Williams (n.d.) provides an illuminating (exposing our pathetic condition) interpretation from the body of work by Thomas Hobbes (1588–1679) and his view of human nature. He describes our decisions to act as being based on our human nature of neediness and vulnerability, thus we are easily influenced in our efforts to understand the world around us. Further, humans' capacity to understand and reason is fragile, reliant on language, and prone to error and manipulation. This interpretation also corresponds with Abrams's (2016) advocacy for adding the lens of *masculinities* for understanding behavior by broadening the feminist perspective from gendered power struggles to considering our frailties as humans. Another expressive framing of power is differentiating gender inequality as a subjugation of one group by another group versus means of spreading insecurity that engulf the lives of many, the seemingly dominant group as well. The latter description seems to correspond with Hobbes's view of human nature, as interpreted by Williams (n.d.) and Abrams (2016).

The recent scholarly work in developing the construct of emotional intelligence and its connection to great leadership has upended the societal dismissal that exhibiting the virtues of empathy, care, interpersonal relations, and social skills such as nurturing are women-centric values that are incompatible with the warrior ethic. Daniel Goleman (2012) has advanced research into the construct of an *emotional intelligence* composed of dimensions of self-awareness, emotional self-management, empathy and social skills. While Goleman notes that, in general, there are gendered differences in the manifestation of the four broad characteristics, when he examined the upper 10 percent of high-performing and respected leaders, these gendered differences become nonexistent. These leaders have developed a holistic sense of self manifested in leadership qualities that include the integration of the four dimensions. The findings by Goleman (2012) suggest a positive trending toward Tronto's (1993) theorization that in order to build characteristics dismissed as feminine into our policies and institutions, there must be a dissociation of specific values and moralities from gender. Thus, Goleman's findings suggest the opening of a window toward holistic and full human agency in moral reasoning, and portray men and women on parallel and complementary tracks rather than arranged hierarchically (Gilligan 2013). This revelation could have significant implications for mitigating wicked problems such as ethical decision making and gender inequality at both the societal level and across military institutions.

Conclusion

Part of the definition of ethics is the study and development of ethical standards. This includes the constant self-reflection by individuals and groups, examining practices to ensure that actions are ethically reasonable and grounded in well-founded moral principles (Velasquez et al. 2015). The U.S. system of institutions is, by and large, the critical social structure that guides moral or ethical decisions and sanctions immoral or unethical ones. However, the interface of our social complexity and human vulnerabilities creates conditions ripe for the development of wicked problems at all levels of society. This was made evident in the discussion and analysis of disconnected espoused and operating values leading to military dishonesty and the legacy of gender inequality. In working toward alleviating the adversity from immersion into the chaos of wicked problems, creative, mutually agreed upon, socially composed remedies including continuous vigilance (Mascarenhas 2009), in tandem and guided by well-articulated, holistic ethical principles, value statements and aspiring virtues, could support a positive path forward for both the U.S. military and its larger social context.

Bibliography

Abrams, J.R. (2016). Debunking the Myth of Universal Male Privilege. University of Michigan. *Journal of Law Reform*, 49, 2, 303–333. http://repository.law.umich.edu/cgi/viewcontent.cgi?article=1149&context=mjlr. Retrieved July 15, 2017.

Ackoff, R. (1974). *Re-designing the Future: A Systems Approach to Societal Problems.* New York: John Wiley & Sons.

Andre, C. and Velasquez, M. (2015 [1990]). *Men & Women: Justice & Compassion.* Markkula Center for Applied Ethics. Santa Clara University. www.scu.edu/ethics/ethics-resources/ethical-decision-making/men-women-justice-compassion/. Retrieved July 15, 2017.

Bellah, R.N., Madsen, R., Sullivan, W.M., Swindler, A., and Tipton, S.M. (1992). *The Good Society.* New York: Vintage Books.

Cox, M. (2017). After Marine Photo Scandal, Services Issue Social Media Guidelines. *Military.com.* www.military.com/daily-news/2017/03/20/marine-photo-scandal-services-issue-social-media-guidelines.html. Retrieved July 14, 2017.

Gilligan, C. (2013a). Reframing the Conversation About Difference: The Contribution of Feminist Care Ethics Lecture. https://ethicsofcare.org/lectures-by-carol-gilligan-on-feminist-ethics-of-care/. Retrieved July 15, 2017.

Gilligan, C. (2013b). Resisting injustice: a feminist ethics of care lecture. https://ethicsofcare.org/lectures-by-carol-gilligan-on-feminist-ethics-of-care/. Retrieved July 15, 2017.

Goleman, D. (2012). Emotional Intelligence. www.youtube.com/watch?v=Y7m9eNoB3NU. Retrieved July 16, 2017.

History Channel. (2010). 19th Amendment. A&E Networks. www.history.com/topics/womens-history/19th-amendment. Retrieved July 17, 2017.

Mascarenhas, O. (2009). Innovation as Defining and Resolving Wicked Problems. http://weaverjm.faculty.udmercy.edu/MascarenhasLectureNotes/MascarenhasWickedproblems.doc. Retrieved March 20, 2017.

National Defense University. (n.d.). Values and Ethics. In *Strategic Leadership and Decision Making.* www.au.af.mil/au/awc/awcgate/ndu/strat-ldr-dm/pt4ch15.html. Retrieved July 15, 2017.

Odierno, R.T., and Chandler, R.F. (2014). *The Army Ethic White Paper.* www.army.mil/e2/c/downloads/356486.pdf. Retrieved July 10, 2017.

Powers, R. (2016). Military Ethics and Conflicts of Interest: Standards of Ethical Conduct. www.thebalance.com/military-ethics-and-conflicts-of-interest-3332000. Retrieved July 16, 2017.

Rawls, J. (1971). *A Theory of Justice.* Cambridge, MA: Harvard University Press.

Richardson, H.S. (n.d.). John Rawls (1921–2002). In *Internet Encyclopedia of Philosophy.* www.iep.utm.edu/rawls/. Retrieved July 20, 2017.

Secretary of the Navy (SECNAV). (n.d.). Department of the Navy Core Values Charter. www.secnav.navy.mil/Ethics/Pages/corevaluescharter.aspx. Retrieved July 17, 2017.

Senge, P.M. (1990). *The Fifth Discipline: The Art and Practice of Learning Organizations.* New York: Currency Doubleday.

Speece, M. (2013). These are My Core Values. Official Blog of the U.S. Coast Guard. http://coastguard.dodlive.mil/2013/04/these-are-my-core-values/. Retrieved July 17, 2017.

Tilghman, A. (2015). All Combat Jobs Open to Women in the Military. *Military Times* online. www.militarytimes.com/story/military/pentagon/2015/12/03/carter-telling-military-open-all-combat-jobs-women/76720656/ Retrieved July 20, 2017.

Tronto, J. (1993). *Moral Boundaries: A Political Argument for an Ethic of Care.* New York: Routledge, Chapman and Hall, Inc.

U.S. Air Force. (n.d.). It's Our Promise to Protect. www.airforce.com/mission/vision. Retrieved July 17, 2017.

U.S. Army. (n.d.). The Army Values. www.army.mil/values/. Retrieved July 17, 2017.

U.S. Coast Guard Compass. (n.d.). Official Blog of the U.S. Coast Guard. http://coastguard.dodlive.mil/2013/04/these-are-my-core-values/. Retrieved July 17, 2017.

U.S. Marines Human Resources and Organizational Management. (n.d.). www.hqmc.marines.mil/hrom/New-Employees/About-the-Marine-Corps/Values/. Retrieved July 17, 2017.

Velasquez, M., Andre, C., Shanks, T., and Meyer, M.J. (2015). What Is Ethics? Markkula Center for Applied Ethics, Santa Clara University. www.scu.edu/ethics/ethics-resources/ethical-decision-making/what-is-ethics/. Retrieved July 18, 2017.

Wechsler, R. (2011). Blind Spots III – Ethics Training, Ethics Fading, and Ethical Reasoning. CityEthics.org: Making Local Government More Ethical blog. www.cityethics.org/content/blind-spots-iii-%E2%80%94-ethics-training-ethics-fading-and-ethical-reasoning. Retrieved July 20, 2017.

Whitlock, C. (2014). Military Brass, Behaving Badly: Files Detail a Spate of Misconduct Dogging Armed Forces. *The Washington Post.* www.washingtonpost.com/world/national-security/military-brass-behaving-badly-files-detail-a-spate-of-misconduct-dogging-armed-forces/2014/01/26/4d06c770-843d-11e3-bbe5 6a2a3141e3a9_story.html?utm_term=.c563a255602c. Retrieved July 20, 2017.

Williams, G. (n.d.). Thomas Hobbes: Moral and Political Philosophy. In *Internet Encyclopedia of Philosophy.* www.iep.utm.edu/hobmoral/. Retrieved July 20, 2017.

Wong, L. and Gerras, S.J. (2015). *Lying to Ourselves: Dishonesty in the Army Profession.* Carlisle Barracks, PA: U.S. Army War College Press. http://ssi.armywarcollege.edu/pdffiles/pub1250.pdf. Retrieved July 10, 2017.

Part VIII
Conclusion

In recent years, the plight of women veterans has been garnering a bevy of overdue research into the unique challenges that they experience. Perhaps more so than ever before and due to the cumulative and adverse effects of Operations Enduring and Iraqi Freedom, two long and simultaneous wars over time, the resultant effects for all veterans, and especially so for female veterans, are now being illuminated. It was dubbed 'the mommy war' by the media (Holm 1992), given the perceived disproportionate effects that the mobilization of particularly single parents manifested. Although it was single fathers, not single mothers, who were overwhelmingly the source of the fallout, it was the few single mothers who were spurned and blamed for the ensuing problems. Operation Desert Storm was the first glimpse into the ramifications of what a large-scale deployment of military personnel overseas post-Vietnam Conflict can bring. It was also the first such mobilization since the advent of the all-volunteer military.

What was brought to light during these two most recent wars though was far more sinister in kind, yet, not unlike the guerrilla warfare of Vietnam, and especially so in Iraq, the U.S. military was caught off guard. Overconfidence as a consequence of overreliance on technology in waging an air campaign, the desire and uncanny ability to blow things up (Gray 1999, 2006), and the ignorance of the U.S. military of the local culture made for a recipe, at least initially, for not winning the hearts and minds of the local population whom the military was purported to be liberating and protecting from their oppressive regime. Nevertheless, the military recovered its footing on the fly with, as one of its many strategies, the insertion of all-female engagement teams to address the strict cultural mores in dealing with certain segments of the local population and in combatting the sources of wanton violence against American troops (McLagan and Sommers 2010, *Lioness Report* 2012). Yet, beyond this unforeseen level of violence, military women encountered an additional hurdle, an unlikely but familiar enemy – that of fellow male military peers and of civilian contractors employed by the military who as predators were lying in wait to sexually assault their prey with some deliberately masking their crimes by murdering the female victims (Monahan and Neidel-Greenlee 2010, Solaro 2006). This not to mention their illegal placement as noncombatants into positions for which, unlike their combatant male peers, military women were devoid of the necessary training, equipment and protection which rendered them even more vulnerable to the risk to losing life (Harris 2015, Solaro 2006). The above are just a few of the multiple afflictions that overwhelmingly affected military women in the most recent warzones. As they transition from active military service into the civilian sector, these women undoubtedly continue to carry these untreated burdens of war with them as veterans.

This book then represents a Herculean attempt on our part to unravel and identify the many forces at play that have engulfed women veterans, including those from past campaigns, and in which, like Operations Enduring and Iraqi Freedom, the military was equally ill prepared to tackle the unintended consequences of war. Framed as inherently wicked problems, we have delved into the roots of what makes these problems so wicked in the first place, particularly with regard to such tragic effects as post-traumatic stress disorder (PTSD) and specifically military sexual trauma (MST), homelessness, violence and suicide. At the outset, our rationale for writing this monograph becomes all the more evident for as active military and women veterans, given our own lived experiences, we are keenly aware of at least some of the ever-present and layered challenges. Owing to these experiences, we were thereby motivated, even compelled, to give voice to the female veteran. At center stage, the premise of this book is in highlighting the associated invisibility that comes with being a female veteran. Foremost, this takes shape by dispelling the accepted myth that is often invoked of the white male as the only true conception of the ideal and consummate warrior (Seifert 1994, Bird Francke 1997, Herbert 1998). This is indisputably not the case. Women are warriors and have been since the beginning of time (Grant DePauw 1998, Goldstein 2003, Jones 1997, Harris 2015). In fact, Grant DePauw (1998) goes as far as to say that women and war are inextricably linked. The treasure trove of women warriors of yesteryear, including those of ancient and modern-day heads of state, to some of today's living legends are only but a small portion of the full panoply of women's innate warrior spirit. Regrettably, as mentioned in Part V, beginning with the First Crusade and the ascent of Christianity, a 400-year span of calibrated and systematic intolerance, long enough to do irreparable damage, has resulted in the cumulative devolution of the status of women as a collective (Grant DePauw 1998), which still wreaks havoc today in how women are treated. It remains unsettled, though, as to how and why this phenomenon came to be.

During contemporary times and in the larger society, women have been reduced to much 'othering' as deviants who are considered out of the norm (Ellefson 1998, Law 1999), unlike the mainstream American connotation for the white male (DeMello Patterson 2000, Frankenberg 1993), with even the white female as so designated given gender. Consequently, women have been relegated to subordinate roles in the military as supporters, caregivers, and more insidiously labelled as sex objects or sex fiends (Harris 2009a). Given the various levels of intersectionality, women have been essentially marginalized, and women of color and black women in particular, are held even further at the margins of American society.

The early framers of the U.S. Constitution deliberately excluded women and other groups such as African Americans, then as slaves, as aspirants for citizenship. Only white males were worthy of this honor. As a consequence, both groups over time have resorted to mounting legal challenges to remediate past wrongs including ways to move them ever closer to the ideal of what constitutes a citizen, with especially African American men choosing military service as the primary vehicle (Harris and Lewis, forthcoming). Specifically for women, while the 19th Amendment brought about some redress, it was their obligation for military service that remained the most contentious and remote, increasingly putting their agency and thus status as citizens at odds and on a collision course. Says Kerber (1993), women's obligation for military service 'profoundly disturb [s] the sexual order' (p.109). Two landmark cases and rulings by the U.S. Supreme Court are of significance: the first *United States v. Schwimmer, 1928*; and the second, *Rostker v. Goldberg, 1980*.

In the former case, *United States v. Schwimmer, 1928*, while on one hand its ruling held fast to the original framers of the U.S. Constitution's notion of citizenship that women were not citizens, on the other hand, the ruling held that a woman seeking naturalization to the U.S. but who refuses to bear arms in defense of the country for which she seeks naturalization is not worthy of naturalization and thus citizenship even though at the time Schwimmer, the applicant and a woman, was already 50 years old (Kerber 1993). The latter case, or *Rostker v. Goldberg, 1980*, contested the Selective Service Act and by extension the Selective Service System, an all-male draft registration system, as unconstitutional and in violation of the Due Process Clause of the Fifth Amendment. As previously stated in Part VI, it is worth noting that Justice Thurgood Marshall, then the only African American on the High Court, scolded the institution for what he considered a hypocritical ruling in that the Court abdicated its responsibility to uphold the tenets of the Constitution by rendering such a verdict.

The drafters of the Equal Rights Amendment (ERA) sought to close these loopholes in an effort to inch ever closer to the ideal of citizenship, with one of its many mechanisms being the Selective Service System by way of the Selective Service Act that has remained an all-male draft registration system since its inception for a conscripted U.S. military. Advocates of the ERA sought to utilize the Selective Service System as a conduit for improving the economic status of women, especially with regard to pay, training and education, and financial security. Even President Jimmy Carter was an ardent supporter of women's inclusion into the Selective Service System, noting that the changing times had warranted this move (Kerber 1993). Further, he argued, since organizations within the civilian sector were assimilating women into the workplace, the military should be no exception. As well, few knew that President Carter was also of the mindset that organizations, including the military, should not be gendered, and despite Congress's insistence on women's exemption from the Selective Service System, notably from combat duty, the president compromised by agreeing that this discussion could take place at a later time while still insisting on women's inclusion into the Selective Service System. According to President Carter, '[e]qual obligations deserve equal rights' (Kerber 1993, p.117).

However, Congress balked, choosing to succumb to the instinctual visceral attitudes of their constituents, including their own feelings as politicians about the issue. Even then, an unevolved but self-described feminist like Congresswoman Patricia Schroder (D-CO) was for women's exemption from the Selective Service System and specifically from combat duty. Ironically, it was the religious heft by way of Judeo-Christian ethos that the anti-ERA and anti-women in the Selective Service System used to advance their argument. They successfully appealed by injecting into the debate the alleged alliance between an unholy tripartite of the ERA, homosexuality and abortion. The combat exclusion policy then became the pretext for women's continued and legal use by the military as a convenient resource, with exemption from the Selective Service System and with the expressed exclusion from combat duty for it was never the intent of Congress to include women in the military to begin with, much less in combat.

The combat exclusion policy and its attendant practices functioned as an effective tool to solidify as well as to regularly reinforce through acculturation white male privilege and entitlement; a military culture of domination; and the effeminization of the enemy, the latter of which is believed to be a proxy for women. Together, they all serve as a calculated backlash against women, so much so that Faludi (2006) describes the move as an undeclared war against American women. In the same vein, Hunter (2007) views the hypermasculinity and the need to pair violence with sex and thus the diminution of women as misogyny that signals an intrinsic fragility of men. Moreover, he counsels, military men are most threatened by three things: competent women, lesbian women and gay men (p.43). The common thread, as we have observed, is that all three denote elements of femininity and symbolize women. Brown (2012) explains that this fragility has been a flaw in men characterized by a lashing out, whereas Kimmel (1996) argues that American masculinity has always been in crisis during times of political, economic and social upheavals. We believe that the repeal of the combat exclusion policy in 2013, together with the accelerated move by then Secretary of Defense Ashton Carter to open up formerly closed positions to women as opposed to a phased-in approach, not to mention the 2011 repeal of the Don't Ask, Don't Tell and Don't Pursue policy (Rosenberg and Phillipps 2015), were all overdue. More recently, the military's repeal of its ban of transgender members (Reuters 2016) was a major tipping point for military men. The Marines United scandal where male Marines shared unauthorized and salacious nude photographs of fellow female Marines was a sign of this lashing out because for these miscreants this change in military policy was their tipping point. In fact, the spokesman for Marines United confirmed this speculation when he said that the scandal represented the reason why women should not be in the military (Grasso 2017). According to Kimmel (1996), 'American men try to control themselves; they project their fears onto others; and when feeling too pressured, they attempt to escape' (p.10). Similarly, '[w]ar was a potential way to reinvigorate a population that had grown "effeminate" through peace, office and factory work, and city life' (Kimmel 1996, p.111–112). Kimmel (2005) continued in more recent research that:

> To some men, masculinity became a relentless test, demanding that it be proved to increasingly physical demonstration. From 19th-century health reformers to contemporary bodybuilders, some men have pumped up to regain lost confidence. Others have actively resisted women's equality; from 19th-century anti-suffragists to VMI cadets and promoters of 'men's rights' ... And, finally, others have simply run away, escaping to some pristine homosocial world, whether mythic or real, as an all-male solace against encroaching dissolution. When the going's been tough, the tough have run away.
>
> (p.xi)

Far from today's uneasiness with women and power and women in power, as if the terms 'women' and 'power' are not synonyms but mutually exclusive, we find a complacency in women, who themselves, owing to entrenched acculturation, question their own specie's ability to leverage power while taking other women to task for challenging these unfounded myths. Women in ancient times as warriors and heads of state were unrivalled in their prowess for power and the adroitness that they exercised to control it in amassing more power and outmaneuvering their male competition. However, the modern woman, if elevated, wields power under such scrutiny that her selection to correctly steer the ship, so to speak, is motivated more for her selectors by her ability to do so successfully through a crisis by navigating through turbulent waters than it is for her ability to maintain the ship afloat and through calmer seas. As a consequence, women are reputed to be crisis leaders (Ryan et al. 2011, Ryan et al. 2007). Contrast men's inordinate selection to assume the helm once the entity has regained its footing and is on the stable path to success. Men are therefore known as success leaders. Sadly, despite many women's successes in achieving even what male colleagues cannot, they are not given credit for the success and are vilified when situations beyond their control go awry. This double bind (and for the few women of color, triple bind), either serves as a deterrent for women to aspire to positions of leadership or renders them impotent as a catalyst for change.

Women are relegated to such roles as tokens (Kanter 1977), or as proxies for men since they themselves cannot be sponsors (Elliott and Smith 2004). For these reasons and more, in an attempt to level an uneven and unfair playing field, women turn to such proven equalizers as securing an advanced education as the gateway to commanding greater economic security. Yet, even when women shrewdly choose these pathways, as seen in the unprecedented number of doctorates that women have achieved as compared to men (West and Curtis 2006), in both the public and private sectors and in every industry in the private sector, the wage disparities between white men and women, and more so for women of color, are stark (Catalyst.org 2017). More woeful is the fact that women in the new Trump Administration, for instance, and thus at the highest levels of the federal government, are less prone to seek either the limelight or the accompanying repercussions given the prominence of these positions, and earn substantially less than their male colleagues (Ingraham 2017). Here, the women staffers have been referred to as workhorses while the male staffers are called showhorses (Karni 2017). Does this sound familiar?

On average and at a time in their lives when they are least able to salvage the diminishing return of their incomes, women earn 70 percent of the lifetime earnings of the average white male (U.S. General Accountability Office (GAO) 2007). The outcome of this reduced lifetime income becomes dire for women in terms of a compromised standard of living at retirement age. Women veterans, despite their propensity for achieving higher levels of education as compared to male veterans (Walker and Borbely 2014), are similarly plagued.

The all-volunteer military in many respects has created an unforeseen and unintended consequence. At no time since the end of the Vietnam Conflict has there existed such a gulf between those who have served in the military and those within the general civilian population who have never served in the military. For example, only 0.05 percent of Americans have ever served on active duty (Pew Research 2011a). Further, as the military draws down from active campaigns in both Afghanistan and Iraq, the evidence becomes increasingly clear that the connections between those who have served in the military and those within the general civilian population who have not served, have become more tenuous. This divide is even more apparent for those within the general civilian population who are over the age of 50 and who have had a relative who served in the military at one time or another, versus those below the age of 50, although as Pew Research admits, this disconnect might be generational. Veterans are also more likely to have come from families with a tradition of military service.

If Congress is a microcosm of this civil–military divide, then the divide has only widened with the passing of time. Take 1981, when veterans comprised majorities in Congress (House 72 percent, and Senate 78 percent) (Wellford 2014). Today, only 18 percent of both houses of Congress have legislators with any military experience (Armed Forces Benefit Association (AFBA) 2016). Besides, as Ukman (2011) reports, members of the military themselves have become increasingly frustrated with this disconnect, given the response to a study conducted by Pew Research where 84 percent of respondents believe that Americans are clueless about the hardships that they endure and 83 percent said that their families have had to make unexpected sacrifices. Says Pew Research (2011b), 44 percent of respondents admit to experiencing readjustment challenges in the civilian sector and almost 50 percent cited deployments as having strained their family relationships. According to Mike Haynie, director of Syracuse University's Institute for Veterans and Military Families, the consequences of war have been disconnected from the general civilian population (Zucchino and Cloud 2015). Further, the general public has not been directly impacted by these wars.

The increasing civil–military divide also speaks, even as fundamentally an undemocratic institution in both its structure and policies, of the need for the military to be representative of the population from which it recruits. Likewise, the military has its origins in a democratic society and the institution is therefore beholden to Congress for its very existence and survival. This is especially relevant with an all-volunteer force and in light of a robust economy and civilian sector with which the military must compete for the best and brightest from American society (Population Report 2015). While some traditionally marginalized groups have turned to the military in the past because the institution is perceived as 'more racially fair' (Segal and Wechsler Segal 2004, p.19), it is no reason to assume, and particularly in a strong economy, that these groups will continue to do so. Therefore, how these groups are treated while they are in the military becomes a reliable predictor as to whether or not they will continue to view the military as a viable career option (Harris 2009a), or as Nixon (1993) retorts, as 'an employer of last resort' (p.59).

Harris (2009a) analyzed unpublished data from Moskos (2005, correspondence via email) to discover that white enlisted women are more likely than any other segment of the military's population to prematurely separate from the military. However, Harris hypothesizes that the women do so as a result of multiple factors, one of which includes sexually related offenses committed against them. Hosek et al. (2001) found a similar pattern among white female commissioned officers. However, Harris (2009a) does not necessarily see these premature attrition patterns as negative. She argues that these patterns are likely signs of the white female's struggle for full agency and that the military should take heed in not alienating them. Patten and Parker (2011), Parker et al. (2017), and the military (Population Report 2015) see a growing trend of women into the military, with an increasing and disproportionate representation by women of color. However, at this juncture a word of caution must be infused, for as explicated throughout Part VI of this book, these positive signs with respect to an increasing female workforce should not be taken for granted by the military. While it does appear that some components of the military are moving in the direction of fulfilling the criteria as called for by the repeal of the combat exclusion policy, others, namely the Marine Corps, remain staunchly opposed by employing traditional go-to delay tactics to register their displeasure at the repeal (Cahn 2017). This at a time when the Marine Corps is aggressively courting women to join its ranks (Associated Press 2016) and in the midst of a still unresolved sex scandal involving Marines United and its illegal sharing of nude photographs of female Marines via the Internet (Associated Press 2017). If the conditions for the repeal of the combat exclusion policy remain unfulfilled, these overtures by the Marine Corps, as expected, will prove futile, damaging even further the reputation of the Marine Corps and dragging down that of the military in the process. Harris (2015) hopes, though, that doing as the law requires will go far in facilitating women's full agency and correspondingly their full citizenship. We therefore remain cautiously optimistic that in being forced to change its behavior, the actions taken by the military as required by law will also translate into markedly reducing the invisibility of women in the military and as veterans once they transition into the civilian sector.

With respect to the legal systems of the military under the Uniform Code of Military Justice (UCMJ) and that of civil society, we recognize that they are worlds apart even as the two systems essentially emanated from the U.S. Constitution. Still, the civilian courts have never shied away from inserting themselves, when necessary, to protect the rights of military personnel as citizens when those rights have been abridged by the military. Another two precedent cases and rulings – one by the U.S. Supreme Court, the other by the federal district court – come to mind, and Harris (2015) was in the inimitable position of interviewing both main litigants. While the third case was never litigated in the civilian courts, the matter nonetheless became the direct precursor for dismantling the military's archaic and misplaced Don't Ask, Don't Tell and Don't Pursue policy. Had it not been for the direct intervention of the High Court in *Frontierro v. Richardson, 1973* and *Owens v. Brown, 1978*, and in doing so inserting itself into the direct affairs of the military, women's stature in the military would not have been advanced to become the foundation and impetus for current policymaking for all women in the military.

The first case, *Frontierro v. Richardson, 1973*, involved Air Force officer Sharron Frontierro, whose husband, a civilian, was being denied benefits as a dependent of then Second Lieutenant Frontierro simply because the roles, owing to misconstrued tradition that became policy and practice, had been reversed. Lieutenant Frontierro, the female officer, and her husband, the male dependent, were denied benefits solely based on the gender of the female officer. The U.S. Supreme Court found the policy and practice to be unconstitutional. Said Frontierro Cohen of her lawsuit, she challenged the policy because it was a matter of economics (Harris 2015). Further, she was 'pissed off' that such a draconian policy was in place (Harris 2015, p.171). In *Owens v. Brown, 1978*, Yona Owens, one of the first cohorts of female communications electricians in the Navy, was deliberately barred from shipboard duty, again, due to the problem that nature made her a woman, not a man (Harris 2015). With the help of the American Civil Liberties Union (ACLU) Women's Rights Project, then headed by its little-known founder Ruth Bader Ginsburg, now U.S. Supreme Court Justice, the federal district court ruled that the Navy's policy was unconstitutional. This was a slam dunk given that the lowest federal court ruled in favor of the litigants. Yet, the case demonstrates how Congress and the military can deliberately flout the rule of law when it is convenient or when no one takes notice by challenging the illegal practice. Said Owens, it was not until 1992, a full 13 years later, that Congress repealed the law and the Navy ceased its illegal practice (Harris 2015).

The third case involving Commander Zoe Dunning almost resulted in her discharge after the Navy's discovery of Commander Dunning's sexual orientation (Harris 2015). The first administrative hearing by the Navy resulted in the unanimous recommendation that she be discharged from the military. However, during the interim period, President Bill Clinton struck a compromise with Congress in the form of the Don't Ask, Don't Tell and Don't Pursue policy not to discharge any personnel from the military who openly self-identified as homosexual. The civilian attorneys for Commander Dunning prevailed in their request for the Navy to refrain from discharging the commander until the policy could be clarified. Consequently, Commander Dunning became the first person to openly serve in the military as a homosexual until the Navy secured clarification on the policy. In the Navy's second administrative hearing, it reversed itself thus freeing Commander Dunning to continue her military career but with the caveat that she not seek further redress in the civilian courts by suing the Navy or Department of Defense.

Cases like these then call into question the military's ability to represent the interests of its own population, given its undue punitive nature. Where the UCMJ then falls woefully short is not only in its failure to prosecute perpetrators of sexual assault and related offenses but in the questionable role that commanders play in the adjudicatory process. Commanders themselves may not be legally trained but they also represent the military and are themselves subject to the military's rules of law, yet function in the three-tiered role as judge, jury and executioner. Hence, for the accused, there is no impartiality in the process whatsoever under the UCMJ. Even after the bipartisan move spearheaded by Senator Kirsten Gillibrand (D-NY) to not only hold commanders accountable for fostering this unsafe climate but to remove them from the adjudication process altogether, the gallant effort failed (Tilghman 2013, Whitlock 2012). This is when the civilian court system should have intervened because of the military's failure to protect its personnel. Almost 50 years ago, even Sherman (1973) recommended that, given the shortsightedness of the UCMJ, like the military legal systems in other Western democracies that have since come under civilian rule, the UCMJ warrants reform as it has shown itself to be ineffective in protecting the rights of its own.

Unfortunately, yet unsurprisingly, the failure of the Department of Defense, the military and the U.S. Department of Veterans Affairs to address the outcomes of these maladies such as rampant sexual assault in the military, together represent wicked problems that manifest themselves in even greater problems once active military personnel transition as veterans into their respective civilian communities. The layered problems for women veterans are especially acute. These problems are so wicked that some of the afflicted resort to suicide as the only outlet for relief from the overwhelming pain. This vicious biological, psychological, and social cycle in the way of homelessness, PTSD, MST, substance abuse and suicide, has severe, incalculable implications for the rates of violence, both perpetrated by others and self-inflicted; the compromising and declining health of the afflicted, exacerbated by the ignorance of health professionals; the economic fallout with those affected unable to regain their footing and pursue stable lives; and the social and human costs to society. Such is the nature of wicked problems. It is their complexity, multidimensionality and conundrum in makeup in locating targeted solutions that make them so wicked (Head and Alford 2015). Hence, these problems are most resistant to identification with a consensus for solutions, thus making them all the more biting as public policy nightmares (Rittel and Webber 1973).

So, where do we go from here? Unlike tame problems, though overwhelming, wicked problems demand mitigation so that over time, with deliberate, concentrated and consistent effort, although never completely resolved, they, too, might become tame problems.

The aforementioned are not just problems of the military but by extension are also problems of American society. After all, while the primary defense of the nation rests with the military, the military does so on behalf of the society in which it has its roots. As such, both entities have the moral and ethical obligation to come to the assistance of these wounded warriors who have volunteered by putting their lives at risk, many losing their lives in the process of defending the country. Each military branch has a unique yet shared set of core values, or a code of ethics, if you will, which it espouses and uses as a guide in its decision making or as a moral compass for each person from the lowest to the highest ranking in the chain of command. In the case of the Army and Navy, both have recast their values in recognition of the importance of the roles that each gender plays in fulfilling the services' missions (U.S. Army n.d., SECNAV n.d.), but more unlikely than not, may depart from prescribed behaviors that are not in keeping with professed core values, even rationalizing the violations of them. The wicked problem of sexual assault, especially with the knowledge, direct or indirect, of leadership, is a primary example. One alternative solution, at least for the Army, say Wong and Gerras (2015), is for its leadership to acknowledge the dissonance and proceed in kind by working towards closing the gap between the professed core values and the actual practices that are reflected in the behaviors that clearly go against the desired culture.

At the societal level, democracies like the U.S. have moved towards more egalitarian practices, but even in a democracy, say Riccucci and Saidel (1997), the concerns of the citizenry are assiduously concentrated whereby the concerns of other constituents, such as women and people of color, are not part of the discourse and this is especially the case when these groups are absent from the top echelons of government or in positions of leadership to give voice to their unique interests, trepidations and lived experiences. Gilligan's (2013) desire is to have a society where care and empathy function as the overriding values in society to trump gendered considerations. Moreover, these preconceived female ways of thinking have been rejected outright as not in keeping with normative views. Helgesen (2005, 2017) views the ideal organizations in society that are less hierarchical and uses the web of inclusion and the female advantage where organizations led by women do so from the center outwards. Using emotional intelligence, Goleman (2005) envisions both the feminine and masculine ways of thinking and doing as complementary and analogous parts of a larger whole.

The military, however, is an inherently hierarchical institution. Again, with an all-volunteer force, it must balance the needs of its various constituencies, one of which includes women, while reacting nimbly to the vicissitudes of the times. This notwithstanding the ominous forewarning by the Military Leadership Diversity Commission (MLDC 2011) and that of the Defense Advisory Committee on Women in the Services (DACOWITS 2012) that in drawing down its forces, the military must be ever mindful that in light of the dearth of women and minorities at the senior levels of both the enlisted and commissioned corps, the institution must be strategic in how it moves forward. The Air Force's recent moves on two fronts are worth noting. First, the Air Force is engaging the national commercial airlines to explore partnership with them to stave off the premature attrition of pilots (Maucione 2017). Second, due to high year tenure but with the potential loss of institutional memory, critical skillsets and shortages in certain career fields, the Air Force is offering a two-year extension to those within the enlisted corps from 106 Air Force Specialty Codes (Keller 2017).

In 2003, the U.S. Supreme Court ruled in *Grutter v. Bollinger et al.* that it is of compelling government interest that the University of Michigan use race as one of multiple criteria for admission to its law school (Harris 2009b). The justification, said the institution's attorneys, was that race was deliberately invoked not only to increase the diversity of the law school's student body but to expose its students to the reality of their clientele once they become bona fide lawyers. It is also worth noting the presence of a number of military leaders together with the leaders of other organizations in court that filed 200 amicus briefs supporting the law school's decision (Karabel 2003). According to the military leaders present, '[c]ompelling considerations of national security and military mission justify consideration of race in selecting military officers' (Karabel 2003, p.1). We believe that the same rationale for the military applies with regard to gender and the need for the military to uphold the conditions of the repeal of the combat exclusion policy that call for the full integration of women throughout the military in all occupations, positions and critical assignments. It is of compelling government interest for the sake of national security that the military fulfill the requirements of the law.

While the above move is far from ideal in that it is short of passing the ERA and women's inclusion into the Selective Service System, it nevertheless, if fully implemented, will serve as a catalyst to bring women ever closer to the ideal of full citizenship, on par treatment with men as partners in possessing full agency, the elimination of the novelty effect (Mazur 1998) and the associated invisibility that is often experienced by military women and women veterans as a consequence. We are encouraged by the uptick in research on women veterans, yet we are concerned that women veterans do not simply become the new population *du jour* for study without the accompanying models and solutions via public policies given the overwhelming challenges that beset them. We therefore see this time as a call to action on behalf of women veterans through research with the explicit goal of realizing this research into practice, and hope that our work as active military service members and women veterans ourselves represents another endeavor in the calculated effort to combat the wicked problems and invisibility experienced by women veterans.

Bibliography

Armed Forces Benefit Association (AFBA). (2016). Number of Veterans in Congress Expected to Drop in 2017. November 1. www.afba.com/newsroom/articles/article/article/number-of-veterans-in-congress-expected-to-drop-in-2017. Retrieved August 5, 2017.

Associated Press. (2016). To Recruit More Women, Marines Turn to High School Sports Teams. August 13. *The New York Times*. www.nytimes.com/2016/08/14/us/to-recruit-more-women-marines-turn-to-high-school-sports-teams.html. Retrieved August 5, 2017.

Associated Press. (2017). Investigators Struggle with Marine Nude Photo-Sharing Scandal. May 6. Associated Press. https://finance.yahoo.com/news/investigators-struggle-marine-nude-photo-155309357.html. Retrieved August 6, 2017.

Bailey, M.J., and Dynarski, S.M. (2011). *Gains and Gaps: Changing Inequality in U.S. College Entry and Completion*. National Bureau of Economic Research

(NBER). http://users.nber.org/~dynarski/Bailey_Dynarski_Final.pdf. Retrieved March 18, 2017.

Bird Francke, L. (1997). *Ground Zero: The Gender Wars in the Military.* New York, NY: Simon and Schuster.

Brown, M.T. (2012). *Enlisting Masculinity. The Construction of Gender in U.S. Military Recruiting Advertising During the All-Volunteer Force.* New York: Oxford University Press.

Cahn, D. (2017). Groups Say Marines Slow in Integrating Women in to Combat Arms Jobs. April 5. *Stars and Stripes.* www.stripes.com/groups-say-marines-slow-in-integrating-women-into-combat-arms-jobs-1.462143#.WYgtFlWGPIU Retrieved August 4, 2017.

Catalyst.org. (2017). Women's Earnings and Income. Knowledge Center. June 21. www.catalyst.org/knowledge/womens-earnings-and-income. Retrieved August 4, 2017.

Defense Advisory Committee on Women in the Services (DACOWITS). (2009). *Status Report.* http://dacowits.defense.gov/Portals/48/Documents/Reports/2011/Documents/DACOWITS%20September%202011%20Committee%20Meeting/16%20USMC%20WISR%20DACOWITS%20Brief.pdf.

Defense Advisory Committee on Women in the Services (DACOWITS). (2012). *Status Report.* http://dacowits.defense.gov/Portals/48/Documents/Reports/2012/Annual%20Report/dacowits2012report.pdf. Retrieved August 3, 2017.

DeMello Patterson, M.B. (2000). America's Racial Unconscious: The Invisibility of Whiteness. In J.L. Kincheloe, S.R. Steinberg, N.M. Rodriguez, and R.E. Chennault (Eds.), *White Reign: Deploying Whiteness in America* (p.103–121). New York, NY: St. Martin's Press.

Ellefson, K.G. (1998). *Advancing Army Women as Senior Leaders – Understanding the Obstacles.* Carlisle Barracks, PA: U.S. Army War College. AD A344984.

Elliott, J.R., and Smith, R.A. (2004). Race, Gender, and Workplace Power. *American Sociological Review,* 69, 365–386.

Faludi, S. (2006). *Backlash. The Undeclared War Against American Women.* Revised Edition. New York, NY: Three Rivers Press.

Frankenberg, R. (1993). *The Social Construction of Whiteness: White Women, Race Matters.* Minneapolis: University of Minnesota Press.

Gilligan, C. (2013). *Reframing the Conversation about Difference: The Contribution of Feminist Care Ethics Lecture.* https://ethicsofcare.org/lectures-by-carol-gilligan-on-feminist-ethics-of-care/. Retrieved August 4, 2017.

Goldstein, J.S. (2003). *War and Gender. How Gender Shapes the War System and Vice Versa.* New York: Cambridge University Press.

Goleman, E. (2005). *Emotional Intelligence: Why It Can Matter More than IQ.* New York, NY: Bantam Books.

Grant DePauw, L. (1998). *Battle Cries and Lullabies. Women in War from Prehistory to the Present.* Norman: University of Oklahoma Press.

Grasso, S. (2017). Marines United Spokesman Blames Nude Photo Scandal on Women being in the Military. March 17. *The Daily Dot.* www.dailydot.com/irl/marines-united-nude-photo-scandal-marshall-chiles/. Retrieved August 8, 2017.

Gray, C.S. (1999). Why Strategy Is Difficult. *Joint Force Quarterly,* 22, 6–12.

Gray, C.S. (2006). Irregular Enemies and the Essence of Strategy: Can the American Way of War Adapt? www.StrategicStudiesInstitute.army.mil/. Retrieved August 4, 2017.

Harris, G.L.A. (2009a). The Multifaceted Nature of White Female Attrition in the Military. *Journal of Public Management and Social Policy*, 15, 1, 71–93.

Harris, G.L.A. (2009b). Recruiting, Retention and Race in the Military. *International Journal of Public Administration*, 32, 10, 803–828.

Harris, G.L.A. (2015). *Living Legends and Full Agency: Implications of Repealing the Combat Exclusion Policy*. New York, NY: Taylor & Francis Group, a division of CRC Press.

Harris, G.L.A., and Lewis, E.L. (n.d., forthcoming). *Blacks in the Military and Beyond*. Lanham, MD: Lexington Books/Rowman and Littlefield Publishers.

Head, B.W., and Alford, J. (2015). Wicked Problems: Implications for Public Policy and Management. *Administration and Society*, 47, 6, 711–739.

Helgesen, S. (2005). *The Web of Inclusion: Architecture for Building Great Organizations*. Frederick, MD: Beard Books.

Helgesen, S. (2017). *The Web of Inclusion: A New Architecture for Building Great Organizations*. Frederick, MD: Beard Books.

Herbert, M.S. (1998). *Camouflage Isn't Only for Combat. Gender, Sexuality, and Women in the Military*. New York, NY: New York University Press.

Holm, J. (1992). *Women in the Military. An Unfinished Revolution*. Revised Edition. Novato, CA: Presidio Press.

Hosek, S.D., Tiemeyer, P., Kilburn, R., Strong, D.A., Ducksworth, S., and Ray, R. (2001). *Minority and Gender Differences in Officer Career Progression*. Santa Monica, CA: RAND Publications.

Hunter, M. (2007). *Honor Betrayed. Sexual Abuse in America's Military*. Fort Lee, NJ: Barricade Press.

Ingraham, C. (2017). White House Pay Gap More Than Triples Under Trump. July 5. *Washington Post*. www.washingtonpost.com/news/wonk/wp/2017/07/05/white-house-gender-pay-gap-more-than-triples-under-trump/. Retrieved August 5, 2017.

Jones, D.E. (1997). *Women Warriors. A History*. Washington, DC: Potomac Books, Inc.

Kanter, R.M. (1977). *Men and Women of the Corporation*. New York, NY: Basic Books.

Karabel, J. (2003). Race and National Security. March 28. *Christian Science Monitor*. www.csmonitor.com/2003/0328/p11S01-coop.html. Retrieved August 4, 2017.

Karni, A. (2017). In Trump's White House, the Women Are the Survivors. August 2. *Politico*. www.politico.com/story/2017/08/02/trump-female-advisers-conway-powell-sanders-241231. Retrieved August 5, 2017.

Keller, M.B. (2017). Air Force Grants Potential Reprieve to Some Airmen Facing Separation. July 31. *Stars and Stripes*. www.stripes.com/news/air-force-grants-potential-reprieve-to-some-airmen-facing-separation-1.480775#.WYg5AFWGPIU. Retrieved August 6, 2017.

Kerber, L.K. (1993). 'A Constitutional Right to be Treated Like … Ladies': Women, Civic Obligation and Military Service. *The University of Chicago Law School Roundtable*, 1, 1, Article 15, 95–128.

Kimmel, M.S. (1996). *Manhood in America: A Cultural History*. New York, NY: Free Press.

Kimmel, M.S. (2005). *The History of Men: Essays in the History of American and British Masculinities*. Albany, NY: State University of New York Press.

Law, S.A. (1999). White Privilege and Affirmative Action. *Akron Law Review*, 32, 603–621.
Lee, W.Y., and Freeman, K. (2012). *From Diplomas to Doctorates: The Success of Black Women in Higher Education and Its Implications for Equal Educational Opportunities for All.* Sterling, VA: Stylus Publishing.
Lioness Report. (2012). *Cultivating Change: Lioness Impact Report. Based on Lioness, a feature documentary* directed by M. McLagan and D. Sommers. U.S.: Room 11 Productions.
Maucione, S. (2017). UPDATED: Air Force Meeting with Airlines on Pilot Shortage in May. March 27. *Federal News Radio*. https://federalnewsradio.com/air-force/2017/03/air-force-meeting-airlines-pilot-shortage-may/. Retrieved August 6, 2017.
Mazur, D.H. (1998). Women, Responsibility and the Military. *Notre Dame Law Review*, 74, 1, 1–45.
McLagan, M., and Sommers, D. (2010). Introductions: How We Came to Make 'Lioness.' July. www.pbs.org/pov/regardingwar/conversations/women-at-war/introductions-how-we-came-to-make-lioness.php. Retrieved August 2017.
Military Leadership Diversity Commission (MLDC). (2011). From Representation to Inclusion: Diversity Leadership for the 21st-Century. March 15. www.hsdl.org/?view&did=715693. Retrieved August 4, 2017.
Monahan, E.M., and Neidel-Greenlee, R. (2010). *A Few Good Women. America's Military Women from World War I to the Wars in Iraq and Afghanistan.* New York: Anchor Books.
Nixon, R.L. (1993). *Defense Downsizing and Blacks in the Military.* Monterey, CA: Naval Postgraduate School.
Parker, K., Cilluffo, A., and Stepler, R. (2017). 6 Facts About the U.S. Military and Its Changing Demographics. April 13. Pew Research Center, Fact Tank. www.pewresearch.org/fact-tank/2017/04/13/6-facts-about-the-u-s-military-and-its-changing-demographics/. Retrieved August 4, 2017.
Patten, E., and Parker, K. (2011). Women in the U.S. Military: Growing Share, Distinctive Profile. *Pew Social Trends.* December 22. www.pewsocialtrends.org/2011/12/22/women-in-the-u-s-military-growingshare-disctinctive-profile. Retrieved August 2017.
Pew Research Center. (2011a). The Military-Civilian Gap: Fewer Family Connections. November 23. www.pewsocialtrends.org/2011/11/23/the-military-civilian-gap-fewer-family-connections/. Retrieved August 5, 2017.
Pew Research Center. (2011b). War and Sacrifice in the Post-9/11 Era. Executive Summary. October 5. www.pewsocialtrends.org/2011/10/05/war-and-sacrifice-in-the-post-911-era/. Retrieved August 5, 2017.
Pew Research Center. (2013). In Educational Attainment, Millennial Women Outpace Men. December 10. www.pewsocialtrends.org/2013/12/11/on-pay-gap-millennial-women-near-parity-for-now/sdt-gender-and-work-12-2013-0-04/. Retrieved February 23, 2017.
Population Report. (2015). Population Representation in the Military Services. Center for Naval Analyses. www.cna.org/pop-rep/2015/links/links.html. Retrieved August 3, 2015.
Reuters. (2016). U.S. Military Repeals Ban on Transgender Service Members. June 30. www.reuters.com/article/us-usa-lgbt-pentagon-idUSKCN0ZG2MM. Retrieved August 9, 2017.

Riccucci, N., and Saidel, J.R. (1997). The Representativeness of State-Level Bureaucratic Leaders: A Missing Piece of the Representative Bureaucracy Puzzle. *Public Administration Review*, 57, 5, 423–430.

Rittel, H.W., and Webber, M.M. (1973). Dilemmas in a General Theory of Planning. *Policy Sciences*, 4, 155–169.

Rosenberg, M., and Phillips, D. (2015). All Combat Roles Now Open to Women, Defense Secretary Says. *The New York Times*. www.nytimes.com/2015/12/04/us/politics/combat-military-women-ash-carter.html. Retrieved August 9, 2017.

Ryan, M.K., Haslam, S.A., Hensby, M.D., and Bongiorno, R. (2011). Think Crisis – Think Female: The Glass Cliff and Contextual Variation in the Think Manager–Think Male Stereotype. *Journal of Applied Psychology*, 96, 470–489.

Ryan, M.K., Haslam, S.A., and Postmes, T. (2007). Reactions to the Glass Cliff: Gender Differences in the Explanations for the Precariousness of Women's Leadership Positions. *Journal of Organizational Change Management*, 20, 182–197.

Secretary of the Navy (SECNAV). (n.d.). *Department of the Navy Core Values Charter*. www.secnav.navy.mil/Ethics/Pages/corevaluescharter.aspx. Retrieved July 17, 2017.

Segal, D.R., and Wechsler Segal, M.W. (2004). America's Military Population. *Population Bulletin*, 59, 1, 1–42.

Sherman, E.F. (1973). Military Justice Without Military Control. *Indiana University Maurer School of Law*, 1398–1425. Paper 2265.

Seifert, R. (1994). War and Rape: A Preliminary Analysis. In *Mass Rape: the War Against Women in Bosnia-Herzegovina*. Lincoln and London: University of Nebraska Press.

Solaro, E. (2006). *Women in the Line of Fire. What You Should Know About Women in the Military*. Emeryville, CA: Seal Press.

Tilghman, A. (2013). Pentagon Advisory Panel: Strip Commanders' Ability to Prosecute Sexual Assaults. September 30. www.armytimes.com/article/20130930/NEWS06/309300029/Pentagon-advisory-panel-Strip-commanders-ability-prosecute-sexual-assaults. Retrieved August 4, 2017.

Ukman, J. (2011). The American Military and Civilians: Worlds Apart. October 5. *Washington Post*. www.washingtonpost.com/blogs/checkpoint-washington/post/the-american-military-and-civilians-worlds-apart/2011/10/04/gIQAhIDgLL_blog.html?utm_term=.e65ae151cb79. Retrieved August 5, 2017.

U.S. Army. (n.d.). *The Army Values*. www.army.mil/values/. Retrieved July 17, 2017.

U.S. General Accountability Office (GAO). (2007). Retirement Security. Women Face Challenges in Ensuring Financial Security in Retirement. GAO-08-105. October.

Walker, J.A., and Borbely, J.M. (2014). *Women Veterans in the Labor Force: Spotlight on Statistics*. U.S. Bureau of Labor Statistics, U.S. Department of Labor. www.bls.gov/spotlight/2014/women-vets/. Retrieved August 4, 2017.

Wellford, R. (2014). By the Numbers: Veterans in Congress. November 11. *PBS*. www.pbs.org/newshour/rundown/by-the-numbers-veterans-in-congress/. Retrieved August 4, 2017.

West, M.S., and Curtis, J.W. (2006). *AAUP Faculty Gender Equity Indicators 2006*. Washington, DC: American Association of University Professors.

Whitlock, C. (2012). Female Service Members Sue over U.S. Combat Exclusion Policy. *The Independent*. www.independent.co.uk/news/world/americas/female-

service-members-sue-over-us-combat-exclusion-policy-8363339.html. Retrieved August 4, 2017.
Wong, L., and Gerras, S.J. (2015). *Lying to Ourselves: Dishonesty in the Army Profession.* Carlisle, PA: U.S. Army War College Press.
Zucchino, D., and Cloud, D.S. (2015). U.S. Military and Civilians Are Increasingly Divided. May 24. *Los Angeles Times.* www.latimes.com/nation/la-na-warrior-main-20150524-story.html. Retrieved August 5, 2017.

Index

Note: Page numbers in *italic* type refer to *figures*
Page numbers in **bold** type refer to **tables**
Page numbers followed by 'n' refer to notes

Aberdeen Proving Ground (APG) scandal (1996) 99, 202, 351, 355n19, 362
Abramovitz, M. 149, 172 208
Abrams, J.R. 382, 385, 407
Abrams, K. 383–384
absent without leave (AWOL) 122
Abu Ghraib 192, 215
abuse: sex(ual) 15, 267, 355n19, 362, 366, 367, 370n1, 389; substance 109, 323, 331–332, 347, 370, 388, 390, 420
Abzug, B. 231
Acker, J. 234–235, 237
active duty(AD) 13, 14, 109, 119, 127, 173, 255, 268, 271–272, 287, 314, 346, 354n1, 354n12,355n17, 355n20, 355n24, 371n2, 416; biopsychosocial outcomes 376; health 305, 307–311, 318–321, 323–324, 327, 334; military selection 279; military sexual trauma (MST) 346, 351–353; veteran selection 103–106
active guard reserve (AGR) 103–104
Adams, D.B. 20–21
Administrative Procedure Act (APA, 1946) 105
advertisements 68–69
Advisory Committee on National Health Promotion and Disease Prevention (USHHS) 307
Aethelflaed 26, 225
affirmative action 175, 208, 235–237, 263–264

Afghanistan: wars in 278, 280, 322, 325–326, 328–329, 352, 389, 393, 416
Africa: as "Mother of all Nations" 22, 223
African American(s): discrimination 11, 16, 391, 403; enslavement 93, 97–98; integration 162; lynching 157; marginalization 65, 176, 231–232, 235, 278; pay 210, 261; recruitment 286, 288; rights 134–135. 13–14, 80, 109, 126, 134–135, 185, 371n6, 391, 413; *see also* Blacks, Black Women, Black Men 11–13, 15–16, 23, 25, 30, 34, 60, 65, 74–75, 93–94, 97, 107, 133–134, 137, 209, 215, 224, 231–232, 245, 248, 261, 265–267, 269, 271, 286, 371n6, 413
Agadya, King 29
age, 2, 56, 58, 66, 107–109, 112, 119, 121–122, 210, 221, 261, 265, unemployed: 266–267, 268–269, 271, 287, social determinants: 306, 311, 314–315, 321, MST: 344, 346–348, 387, effects of invisibility:416, society and ethics: 405
agency theory 91–93; women's agency 2, 6, 31, 70, 84, 89; agency and second-class status: 91–92, 93; citizenship and struggle for agency: 97, 100, 130,172, 176, 186, 193, 205; power and agency: 228–229, 256–257, 260, 281, 288–289, 413, 417–418, 422; determinants of health and agency: 311, 376; ethics and

agency: 425; *see also* collective agency 144, 289
Agent Orange 325–326, 329–330, 334n5
Agent Orange Act (1991) 325, 329
aggression 20–21, 202, 323, 381, 403
Ahmedse Nofretori 223
Ain't I a Woman? (Truth) 11–12, 74
Airborne Hazards and Open Burn Pit Registry 328
Aishah 28
Alexander the Great 23, 224
Alexander II, Pope 26
Alfred the Great, King of Wessex 26
Alice Paul Institute 139, 134–138, 140
All-Volunteer Force (AVF) 15, 56–57, 118–119, 129, 174, 199, 214, 254, 280–281, 417, 421; evolution 119–127
Allen, J., and Marmot, M. 306, 311
Allen, T.B. 22
Alpern, S.B. 20
Alviar, A., and Foster, G. 330
Amanirenas or Amenirenas, Queen 23, 224
Amazon Guards 24
Amazons 22–25, 27, 29, 94,143, 223, 226; African 23–24; Dahomey 29; Greek 22–24; Scythian 22–23, 223
American Association of University Women (AAUW) 210, 261
American Civil Liberties Union (ACLU) 29, 100, 135, 186–187, 228, 239, 300, 316, 368; ACLU-Connecticut 316; Women's Rights Project 135, 368, 419
American Civil War (1861–1865) 30, 33–34, 157, 248, 256, 279, 303, 392
American Community Survey (ACS) 261, 266, 314
Native Americans 345
American Judges Association (AJA) 293–294
American Revolution 55, 157, 248, 255
American Revolutionary War (1775–1783) 279, 332, 392
Anamishakhete 224
Apache Attack helicopter 156
Aquino, C. 227
Arlington National Cemetery 30, 33
armed forces, women's value 123, 127–129, 155, 179, 278, 281, 294, 314, 316, 332, 355n17, 392–393, 417

Armed Services Committee 128, 281; *see also* Congressional Armed Services Committees 118, 128–129, 299; Senate Armed Services Committee 67, 128, 295, 351; House Armed Services Committee 128, 281
Arnanatu, Queen 224
Ashby, J. *et al.* 247
Ashotep 223
assault *see* sexual assault
assimilated diversity 176
Atalanta 24, 224
attrition 8, 80, 65, 84, 92–93, 100, 205, 212, 216, 238, 252, 256; attraction selection 178; premature 214, 287–288, 417, 421
Aurelian 25–26, 225
Ayala, R. 213

Badr, Battle of 28
Baker, G. (Lucy Brewer) 30, 33, 255
Baker, C.N. 68
Baldor, L.C. 280, 393
Barrow, R. 54, 145, 194
Barton, C. 30, 33
Bazerman, M., and Tenbrunsel, A. 402, 404
Beale Air Force Base (AFB), Ninth Strategic Reconnaissance Wing (9 RW) 54, 155
Becker, G.S. 38
Beckman, T. 181
Bellah, R. *et al.* 385, 405, 406
Belsen concentration camp 192
Bem, S.L. 94, 379, 383, 386–387
benefits 233–237, 254, 256, 312, 400, 404; veterans' i, 3, 5, 53, 57–58, 98, 104–105, 110–111, 119, 121–123, 124, 128–129, 148, 159, 248–249, 252, 255, 268–269, 281, 314–316, 322–323, 325, 328, 331, 335n6, 368–369, 381, 391, 393–394, 418; other benefits 233–237, 254, 256, 312, 400, 404
benevolent sexism 366
Bensahel, N. *et al.* 114
Berdahl, J.L. 42–43, 78–80
Berkovitch, N. 81
Bernstein, K., and Williams, I. 347, 370
Bevans, M. 96
Bhagwati, A. 14
Bhutto, B. 226–227
biblical patriarchy 386
Bielby, D.D., and Furia, S.R. 69–71

Bill of Rights (1791) 292
Billing, Y.D. 80
biological argument 49, 51, 54
biopsychosocial: approach 377; dimension 376; lens 303; model, 307, 395n1; health outcomes, 388; construct: 307
Bird Francke, L. 36, 55–58, 60, 65, 77, 154–156, 160–164, 178, 185, 189–191, 195, 198–201, 203, 205, 228, 239, 386, 412
birth defects 326, 330
Black Hawk helicopter 156
Blalock, H.M. 7, 75–76, 211, 232
Blau, F.D.: *et al.* 261–262; and Kahn, L.M. 262
Blinde, E.M., and Taube, D.E. 37–39
Blosnich, J. *et al.* 310
Blotnick, S. 171–172, 208
Blue Laws 138, 387
Boards for Correction of Military Records 105
bonding breaks 214
Book of Deeds of Arms and of Chivalry, The (de Pisan) 28; *see also* de Pisan's *Feats of Arms and Chivalry* 27, 226 and *Treasure of the City of Ladies* 27
Booth, B. 272; *et al.* 272
Borbely, J.M., and Walker, J.A. 13, 58, 106, 107, 108, 265, *266–267*, 268–269, *270*, 416
Borgida, E., and Burgess, D. 36–37
Borginis, S. 30, 33, 255–256
Bosnia-Herzegovina Conflict (1992–1995) 40
Bourdieu, P. 173, 189
Boxer, B. 187
Bradford, S. 30, 248
Brah, A. 11–12
Branscombe, N.R., and Bruckmiller, S. 246
Braun, V., and Farrid, P. 68
Bray, L. 83–84, 92, 149, 176–177
Brennan, T. 151–152, 351, 361
Breuer, W.B. 56, 161
Brewer, L. (George Baker) 30, 33, 255
Brown, E.R. *et al.* 246
Brown, M.T. 174–175, 180, 185, 194–195, 414
Brown, R.P. *et al.* 237
Brownmiller, S. 39–40, 144, 190, 201
Bruckmiller, S., and Branscombe, N.R. 246

Brunner, E., and Marmot, M. 317
Buchanan and DiPrete 58
Buchanan, A. 264
Buchanan, N.T. *et al.* 93–94
built environment 313, 324–331, 334n1
Bull Run, First Battle (1861) 30, 33
Bureau of Labor Statistics (BLS) 106, 107, 210, 261, 265, *266*–267, 270, 313–314
bureaucracy, representative i, 7, 76, 277, 284–285; representative democracy 388
Burgess, D., and Borgida, E. 36–37
Burke, C. 178, 383–384
burn pits 325–326, 328
Burns *et al.* 343
Burns, U. 228
Burr, R. 246
Burrelli, D.D. 53
Burrelli, D.F. 320

cadets 66, 76–77, 119, 188, 201–203, 309, 316, 355n17, 370n1, 379, 415
Caesar, Julius 224
Camel, Battle of (657) 28
camel, female 26, 225
Candace, Queen of Ethiopia 23, 224
capable women 179, 194, 198, 414; *see also* competent women 75, 80, 164, 192, 209, 234, 414
care ethics 406
Carey, J. 154
Carlucci, F. 151
Carranza, E., and Prentice, D. 36–38
Carreiras, H. 143–144
Carter, A. (fmr. Secretary of Defense) 147, 186, 287, 392, 414, 406
Carter, J. (President) 122–123, 125, 413–414
Cassata, D. 147
Catalyst.org 137, 210, 264, 272, 416
Center for Military Readiness (CMR) 92, 118, 128, 158
Center for Women Veterans 14, 323
Centers for Disease Control and Prevention (CDC) 306, 377, 379, *380*
Central All-Volunteer Task Force 121
Central Intelligence Agency (CIA) 53
Chamorro, V. 227
Chandler, R. 212; and Odierno, R. 400, 403
Chang, I. 40, 188
character of service 105
Charles VII, King of France 29

Index 431

Chavez, L. 215
Cheng, C. 80
Chinook helicopter 156
Chisholm, S. 135
Chodrow, N. 35, 66
Christensen, D. 384
Christensen, S. 186
Christianity 26, 28, 33, 221, 227, 412
Cioca v. Rumsfeld et al. (2013) 66–67, 298–299, 369
citizenship 6, 81, 403; barriers to full citizen participation 127; full 31, 89, 97–100, 123, 130, 134, 229, 278, 281, 288–289, 418, 412; good/bad citizens 99; subordinate 99; citizenship, second-class 2, 3, 125, 379, 386; path to citizenship 16, 286; citizenship status 31, 124; U.S. citizenship 119–120; obligation for citizenship 129, 134, 191; women and citizenship 133, 413; white men and citizenship 175; African Americans/ Blacks and citizenship 413
Citizenship Clause (Fourteenth Amendment) 97–98–100, 136, 139, 300
civic responsibility 119–127
Civil Rights Act (1964) 97, 100; Title VII 134
Civil Service (British) 284; civil service (U.S.) 122
civilian law 293, 299
civil–military divide i, 7, 277, 281, 416–417
Clark, A.P. 203
Clarke, L. 366
Clarke, M. 149–150
Claudius 225
Clausewitz, K. von 21
Clausewitz, M. von 21
Cleopatra, Queen 25–26, 29, 224–225
Clinical Administered PTSD Scale (CAPS) 347, 354n14
Clinton, H. 97, 228–229, 245
Clinton, W. (Bill) 409
CMW (combat, masculine warrior) paradigm (Traditionalists) 312
Coast Guard *see* U.S. Coast Guard (USCG) 103, 106, 119, 154, 248, 255, 279, 287, 297, 345, 354n1, 354n16, 354n17, 354n20, 362–363, 371n2, 401, 404
Cochran, S.T. 277

Code of Federal Regulations (CFR): Title 10 103; Title 38 103
Cohen, B.E. *et al.* 112
Cohen, D.S. 35–36
Cohen, S. 81
Cohen, W. 144–145, 191, 213
cohesiveness 159, 305
Cold War (1947–1991) 92
collective violence 379
Combahee River Collective 12
combat areas of interest (CAI) 352–353
combat exclusion: policy 3, 6–8, 31, 34, 36, 50, 52–53, 71, 76, 83, 89, 91–92, 97–100, 111–112, 122, 127, 144–165, 171–173, 203–204, 211, 300, 369–370, 386–387, 404; repeal 129–130, 134,147–148, 153–154, 158, 162, 164–165, 171, 186–187, 191, 193, 204, 215–216, 228–229, 239, 255–257, 281, 285, 287–289, 387, 392, 418, 422
Commission on Social Determinants of Health (CSDH) 306
commitment 29, 51, 69, 76, 79, 140, 152, 202, 221, 233, 238, 256, 299, 311, 320, 334, 401, 404
Conaster, R. 156
conceptual men 37, 209
Concerned Women for America (CWA) 118
Confederate Army 30
confidence gap 113–114
Congressional Armed Services Committee 118, 128–129, 299
Congressional Office 41
congruency theory 94, 127
conscription 56, 81, 118–121, 127, 129, 163, 174, 252, 254, 299
Constitution 31, 89, 97–100, 120–126, 133–137, 408; Article I 292; Article II 292; Article III 292; Bill of Rights (1791) 292; Equal Rights Amendment (ERA) 6, 8, 31, 89, 97, 98–100, 120, 122–126, 133–140, 403–404, 412; First Amendment 292; Second Amendment 120; Fourth Amendment 292–293; Fifth Amendment 124–126, 403; Fourteenth (14th) Amendment 97–100, 136, 139, 300; Fifteenth (15th) Amendment 99–100, 134; Nineteenth Amendment 97, 134, 137, 139, 413, 418, 406; Section V 137

Consumer Financial Protection Bureau (CFPB) 245
containment, strategy 38, 76, 175
containment strategy 175
Continental Army 30, 248
continuum of harm 345, 353, 365, 370
Contras 53
Cooney, R.T. et al. 265
Corbin, M. 29, 248, 255
Cornum, R. 181
Correll, S.J., and Ridgeway, C.L. 37, 75, 208–209
Coser, L., and Laub Coser, R. 77, 209–210
Coughlin, S. 329
Coulter, A. 215
Court of Military Appeals 292, 294
Cox Commission 298–299
creature comforts 55, 60, 158, 173
Crenshaw, K. 11–12, 75
critical mass 1, 7, 34, 75–76, 175, 231–232, 234, 238–239, 271, 281
Crusades: First (1095–1099) 28, 33, 227, 402; Second (1147–1150) 28–29; Third (1189–1192) 28–29
Cruz, T. 187
Culp Hobby, O. 94, 249–250
Cult of Domesticity 386
cultural amnesia 4, 13, 52, 59, 144, 158, 228; *see also* collective amnesia 13, 285
Cultural Support Teams 280
culture of domination 6, 185, 414
Current Population Survey (CPS) 261
Currie, J. et al. 209

Dahia, Queen of Carthage 24, 224
Dahomey Amazons 29
Dall'Ara, E., and Maass, A. 78–79
Dames at Sea (Burke) 383
Damiano, C.M. 15, 37–38
Dansby, M., and Landis, D. 34, 234
Davis, A.Y. 93
Davis, S. 69
DD Form 214 53, 111
de Pisan, C. 27–28, 226
Death March Project 402
Declaration of Independence (1776) 133
Defense Advisory Committee on Women in the Services (DACOWITS) 51, 53, 147, 150, 154, 156, 164–165, 187, 199, 215–216, 228, 239, 249, 251, 288, 317, 411

Defense Manpower Data Center (DMDC) 280, 309, 351; Active Duty Personnel File 309, 355n20, 362, 345, 350, 353
Defense Sexual Assault Incident Database (DSAID) 350
democracy 7, 97, 99, 133, 228, 277, 284–285, 288–289, 388, 421
demographic15, 34, 93, 127, 133, 228, 255, 261, 264, 268–269, 284, 286, 299, 318, 322, 324, 328, 346, 366, 391
demographics: balance 81; gender binary 366; overview 278–279; victims and perpetrators 350
Department of Health and Human Services (DHHS), *Healthy People 2020* (HP, 2020) 305–306, 308, 310–311, 313
depression 68, 109, 160, 321–323, 347, 370, 389–390
descriptive stereotypes 36–37, 43
Devine, T. 54, 155, 161
Diantonio, N. 308–309
Dignified Burial and Other Veterans' Benefits Improvement Act (2012) 328
dioxin 325, 327–328, 334n5
direct combat probability coding (DCPC) 156
Disabled American Veterans (DAV) 2, 14, 391–392, 394
discrimination: African Americans 11, 16, 35, 60, 234, 391, 403; gender i, 5,11, 35, 67, 78, 97, 124–126, 136, 138–140, 231, 234, 237, 262, 264,316–318, 344–345, 355n18, 370, 386, 391, 394; race/racial 11, 60, 126, 134, 136, 140, 237, 264, 391; sex i, 5, 35–36, 67, 78, 97, 124–126, 136, 138–140, 231, 234, 237, 262, 264, 316–318, 344–345, 355n18, 370, 386, 394; outgroups 175; reverse discrimination 235
dishonor 66, 105, 323
distancing, psychological 188, 204–205; social and moral distancing 204–205
District Court (federal): 125–126, 192, 292, 298, 300, 418–419
diversity 76, 80, 165, 175, 234, 237–238, 263, 310, 312, 370, 421; Military Leadership Diversity Commission (MLDC) 165, 187, 215, 239, 286, 288, 421; assimilation 176

Doan, A., and Portillo, S. 312–313, 318
Dobbin, F., and Kelly, E. 237
Doerksen, T., and Trasler, J. 330
"doing gender" 95, 122, 181, 189
Dolsen, J. 14
dominance theory 191
domination: culture of i, 6, 185, 414; masculine 39, 49, 171–172, 189–190, 192, 194–195; military socialization 188, 193, 414
Donnell, J. 96
Donnelly, E. 158, 215
Don't Ask, Don't Tell and Don't Pursue (DADT) 285, 300, 369; repeal 15, 31, 66, 95, 165, 181, 187, 195, 212, 255, 285, 414, 418–419
double marginality 81; theory of multiple marginality 38, 76, 175, 178, 238; marginality 38, 76, 81, 175, 178, 238; marginalization 7, 11–13, 38, 77–78, 80–81, 93, 175, 178, 189, 204–205, 238, 272
Dreyer, G. 199–200
Due Process Clause (Fifth Amendment) 125–126, 413
Duffy, B. 322–323, 326, 330
Dunivin, K.O. 311–312, 334
Dunlap, T. 181
Dunning, Z. 419
Dunwoody, A. 185
Dutra, L. *et al.* 112
dynamic complexity 403

Eagle Forum 135
Eagly, A.H. *et al.* 80
Earhart, A. 214
eating disorders (EDs) 347, 378
ecological model 379, *380*, 381–382, 387; social–ecological model 385, 394
economic stability 313–315 334n1
education 7, 35, 58, 82, 124, 136, 177, 210–211, 221, 233, 236, 260, 264–266, 268–269, 271, 278, 287, 311, 313, 315–317, 323–324, 330–331, 334n1, 346, 379, 382, 387, 390–391, 413; higher 106–108, 110, 262, 268–269, 272, 314–317, 379, 416; co-educational training 50, 150, 194, 200,
egalitarianism 81, social egalitarian paradigm (Evolutionists) 312
Eisenhower, D. 121; *U.S.S. Dwight Eisenhower* 54

Eleanor of Aquitaine, Queen 27–29, 226
Eleanor Roosevelt, First Lady 251
11th Brigade 204
Ellefson, K.G. 13, 34, 37, 52, 175, 189, 204, 211, 232, 412
Ellemers, N. *et al.* 246–247
Elliott, G.C. *et al.* 39
Elshtain, J.B. 21, 149, 157, 202
Ely, R.J., and Meyerson, D.E. 237–238
Ember, C., and Ember, M. 20
emotional intelligence 382, 421, 407
employment 35, 69,108, 110–111, 114, 119, 125, 144, 216, 234, 260, 266–267, 269, *270,* 271–272, 278, 313–316, 391; Council on Veterans Employment Women Veterans Initiative 106, 271; women veterans employment 108, 266–267, 269, 271; civilian employment 110, 114, 260, 315–316; homeless veterans 332–333; employment and MST 344; U.S. Equal Employment Opportunity Commission 134; comparable employment rates for men and women 136; military employment of women 151, 229; other employment 152, 272 (i.e., military spouses); diversity in employment 237; *see also* unemployment
Endeavor Space Shuttle 67
Engineering Field Clerks 105
England, P. 75
England, Henry II 27, 226
England (country) 29, 226, 246
Engle, George 395n1
enlistment 95, 128; enlistment, fraudulent 57; enlistment contracts 56–57, 163, 252; enlistment and homosexuals 95–96; re–enlistments 163; women and enlistments 252; pre-enlistment 307
Enloe, C. 43–44, 81, 201, 272
Enos, B. 202–203
Environmental Protection Agency (EPA) 329
Equal Protection Clause (Fifth Amendment) 125; Equal Protection Clause (Fourteenth Amendment) 97–99, 136, 139, 300
Equal Rights Amendment (ERA) 6, 8, 31, 89, 97, 99, 120, 122–125, 133–140, 413–414, 422; anti- 125, 138, 413–414

434 Index

equality, gender 127, 133–134, 253, 256, 261, 265, 303–304, 308–310, 334, 376, 382–386, 395, 415, 404–408; Women's Equality Gender Gap Index 387; wages 136; under the law 137; inequality regimes 234–235, 237; inequality in the military 303–304, 312, 318; determinants of health 306, 308, 311, 320, 334; income 315, 317; disparity in benefits for women veterans 331; inequality and MST 349, 370; biological, psychological and sociological outcomes 382
Ervin, S. 124
ethical fading and military leadership 402–404
ethics: care 329, 406–409; code of 420, 400; and gender 329, 404–405; and society 405–407; of responsibility 8; MST 378; wicked problems 382
Etzkowitz, H. et al. 76, 175–176, 232
Eurocentrism 175, 232
Evolutionists (social egalitarian paradigm) 312
exceptionalism 97, 180
exclusion: 80, 97, 126, 285; ERA 133–134; the combat exclusion policy and repeal 3, 6–8, 31, 34–36, 50, 52–53. 66, 71, 76, 83, 89, 91–92, 97–100, 111–112, 122, 127–129, 143–165, 171–173, 181, 186–187, 191, 193, 195, 203–204, 211, 215–216, 228–229, 239, 255–257, 281, 285, 287–289, 300, 386–387, 392, 414, 418, 422; as a wicked problem 312; race and gender (Black women) 11, inclusive 70; social 317–318; determinants of health 321; MST 369–370

Faludi, S. 149, 171–174, 208, 414
Family Research Council (FRC) 118, 128
Farrell, W. 69
Farrid, P., and Braun, V. 68
Federal Bureau of Investigation (FBI) 111, 250
Federal Tort Claims Act (FTCA, 1946) 296–297
Female Engagement Teams (FETs) 52–53, 55, 146, 157, 280, 411
Feminine Mystique, The (Friedan) 135

femininity 76–78, 80, 94, 181, 189, 198, 414; personalities 79
feminist or feminism 12, 33, 51, 68, 70, 74–75, 124, 135, 162, 171, 173, 194, 208, 231, 253, 329, 382, 385, 414, 407
Fenner, L.M. 55–56, 58, 60, 118, 127, 161–164, 278–279, 281, 369, 391–394
Feres Doctrine 8, 296–299
Feres v. United States (1950) 297–298
Fifteenth Amendment (15th) 99–100, 134
Fifth Amendment (5th) 124–126, 403; Due Process Clause 126, 403; Equal Protection Clause 125
Finkel, S.K., and Olswang, S.G. 78, 211
Force 10 (1978) 70
Fort Brown 30, 33, 256
Fort Jackson 213
Fort Washington, Battle of (1776) 29, 248
Fortune 500 137, 211, 228
Foster, G., and Alviar, A. 324, 330
Foster, J. (Captain) 155
Fourteenth Amendment (14th) 97–100, 125, 136, 139, 300; Citizenship Clause, 300; Equal Protection Clause, 136, 139, 300
Fourth Amendment (4th) 292–293
Frankenberg, R. 13, 34, 93, 175, 204, 232, 412
Franklin, C. 294–295
fraudulent enlistment 57
Fredrickson, B., and Roberts, T. 68
Freedom of Information Act (FOIA, 1966) 368
Freud, S. 66
Friedan, B. 135, 231
Frontierro, S. 98, 300, 418–419
Frontierro v. Richardson (1973) 98, 300, 418–419
Furia, S.R., and Bielby, D.D. 69–71

Gadhafi, M. 24
Galbreath, N. 381, 384
Gandhi, I. 226
gang rape 40, 113, 188, 190, 204
Gardam, J. 1
Gartzia, L. et al. 246
gay men 179, 198, 414
gender: discrimination 11, 139–140, 264, 345, 355n18, 370, 386, 391, 394;

"doing gender" 95, 122, 181, 189; equality and inequality 265, 304, 308, 312, 334, 370, 376, 382–387, 395, 405, 407–408; and ethics 404–405; harassment 78, 93–94, 385, 403; identity continuum 366; inequality 304, 308, 310–312, 315–316, 329, 334, *368*, 376, 382–387, 395, 405, 407–408; oblivion 313; stereotypes 36, 94, 313, 366
gender-neutral standards 77, 100, 165, 209, 318, 321
General Accountability Office (GAO) 82, 135, 155, 159, 199, 210–211, 252, 260, 263, 333, 416
Geneva Convention (1949) 1
Gereben Schaefer, A. *et al.* 58–59
Germano, K. 148, 152–153
Gerras, S., and Wong, L. 411, 418, 402–403
Get Over It! We Are Not All Created Equal (Petronio) 50
Gherardi, S. 80
GI Bill (Serviceman's Readjustment Act, 1944) 58, 105, 268–269, 271, 315–316; GI Bill Improvements Act (1977) 104; Montgomery GI Bill (MGIB) 268; Post-9/11 GI Bill 105, 268, 271
Gibson, J.W. 180
Gildersleeve, V. 249
Gillard, T.S. 227
Gillibrand, K. 147, 187, 202, 294, 361, 363–364, 367, 381, 419
Gilligan, C. 406–407, 421
Ginsburg, R.B. 134–136, 140, 419
glass ceiling 97, 158, 237, 263
Glass Ceiling Act (1991) 97
Global Gender Gap Report (2016) 136, 381, 387
Goffman, E. 39, 94
Goldberg, R. 125, 281, 413
Goldberg v. Rostker et al. 1980 125, 281, 413
Goldin, C. 7, 36, 58, 75, 146–147, 209, 262
Goldsmith, J. 124–125
Goldstein, J.S. 6–7, 20, 22–24, 28–30, 33, 52, 55, 60–61, 145, 149, 157, 223–224, 226–227, 248–251, 254, 412
Goldstein, N. 66
Goleman, D. 411, 407

Gonzales v. Carhart (2007) 135
good order and discipline 343, 367, 369
Gottschalck, A.O., and Holder, K.A. 267
Gould, O., and Obicheta, O. 4, 14, 263
Gow, R.V., and Hibbeln, J.R. 323
grand narrative, women's role missing from/minimized in 391–392
Grant DePauw, L. 6–7, 20, 22–30, 33, 55, 60, 121, 149, 157, 223–228, 247–248, 250–253, 255, 402
Grant and Per Diem (GPD) Program 333
Gray, A. 151
Gray, C. 401
Great Depression 252
Greek Amazons 24
Green Berets (1978) 70
Green Berets (Special Forces) 186, 312, 318
Greene, L.S. 231–232
Grese, I. 192
Griggs v. United States (1950) 297
Grimes, D.S. 175
Ground Command Element Integrated Task Force 153
Grutter v. Bollinger et al. (2003) 411
Gulf War I (1990–1991) 13, 60, 106, *107*, 109, 265, *266*, 314–315, 320, 322
Gulf War II (Iraq War, 2003–2011) 1, 3, 13, 83, 92, 106, *107*, 109, 159, 176, 192, *266*, 314–315, 318–319, 322, 326, 347, 354n15, 388, 411, 412, 416; wicked problems 314, 315; biopsychosocial outcomes 389–395; determinants of health 313–314, 322, 325–326, 328–329; military selection 278, 280, 291–294; military sexual trauma (MST) 352; role of equalizers 7, 221, 260–271, 416; *see also* Operation Iraqi Freedom 318, 319, 322
Gunderson, J.R. 97
Gunter, R., and Stambach, A. 77–78
Gutman, S. 61, 99, 213–215, 362, 366

Hacker, B.C. 143
Hagel, C. 105, 203, 363
Hague, The 191
Hall, R. 30, 248
Hall, D.M. and Stevenson, H. 176
Haloran, L. 349, 361

harassment: gender 4, 15, 42, 49, 65, 78–80, 82, 93–94, 385, 403; *see also* sexual harassment
Hardwick, L. 143
Hareven, G. 81
Haring, E.L. 317–318
harm, continuum of 345, 353, 365, 370
Harpalyce, Queen of Thrace 24, 224
Harrell, M.: *et al.* 52, 59–60, 150, 156, 158–159; and Miller, L. 52, 59–60, 158–159, 204
Harris, G.L.A. 1–3, 5–6, 16, 20–21, 29–31, 34, 36–37, 50, 52–54, 58, 60, 65–67, 71, 76–77, 80, 83–84, 92–93, 95–100, 104, 110–112, 121, 133, 135, 144, 146–147, 149, 157–165, 175–176, 178, 187, 191–194, 200, 202, 205–206, 209–212, 223–225, 227–229, 233, 235–239, 253–256, 261–262, 264–265, 286, 295, 300, 412–413, 417–419, 421; agency and second-class status 91–93, 95–100; backlash against women 77, 147, 177, 209, 211–212; combat exclusion policy 3, 53, 71, 76, 83, 91, 98–100, 111, 144–146, 149, 157–162, 164–165; culture of domination 187, 191–193, 414; effeminization of enemy 205–206; legal frameworks 295, 300; and Lewis, E. 34; marginalization 76–77, 80, 83–84; multiple marginality 38, 74, 76, 178, 238; representative bureaucracy 286; role of equalizers 261–262, 264; veteran selection 110; white male privilege 175–176, 178; women as other 36–38, 44; women in power 223–225, 228–229; women as proxies for men 253–257; women as sex objects 65–67, 71; women as supporters and caregivers 50, 52–54, 58, 60; women as tokens 233, 235–239; women as warriors 20–21
Harris, G.L.A. and Lewis, E.L.L. 16, 34, 286
Harris, I.T. 14
Harris, K. 245–246
Harris, M. 54, 58, 162
Hartmann, H. *et al.* 263
Hartmann, S.M. 121
Haslam, S.A., and Ryan, M.K. 246
Hatshepsut, Queen of Egypt 22, 223
Hausa people 23, 224
Haynie, M. 417

Hays, J. 29, 247
health: disparity 305, 310, 320, 331; and healthcare 320–324; mental 109, 112, 148, 152, 319, 322–323, 331–332, 348, 369, 388–391; and violence 1, 8, 40, 194, 201, 376–377; wicked problems 312,329, 376–385, 388–391, *see also* social determinants of health (SDOH) 305–308, 311, 313, 334n1
Healthy People 2020 (HP 2020) 306, 310–311, 313, 334n1
Healthy People (1979) 311
hegemonic masculinity 35, 66, 70, 91, 175, 178; *see also* masculine hegemony/hegemony 49, 189, 238
Heilman, M.E.: *et al.* 114; and Okimoto, T.G. 114
Heilman *et al.* 114
Heilman and Blader 236
Helgesen, S. 411
helicopters 156, 279; Apache Attack 156; Chinook 156; Black Hawk 156
Helms, S. 67, 295
Hemmings, S. 133
Henry II, King of England 27–29, 226
Herbert, M.S. 55, 60, 94–96, 160, 180–181, 185, 191–193, 195, 198, 412
Heritage Action 128
Herodotus 22–23, 223
Herrmann, J. 98–99
Hester, L.A. 1, 83, 176–177
Hibbeln, J.R., and Gow, R.V. 323
Hickey, T. 156–157
Hicks Stiehm, J. 49
higher education 106, 108, 110, 262, 268, 314–316, 379
highly unsaturated fatty acids (HUFAs) 323
Higonnet, L.R., and Higonnet, M.R. 144
Himmelfarb, N. *et al.* 307
Hindal-Hinud 28
Hirsch, B.T., and Mehay, S.L. 265
Hispanics 13, 107, 137, 210, 215, 231–232, 261, 271, 278, 286; pay 210, 261
Hite, S. 171–172, 208
Hobbes, T. 425
Hoff, J. 97
Hoffmire *et al.* 2, 388–389, 391
Holcomb, T. 251
Holder, K.A., and Gottschalck, A.O. 267

Holm, J.: myths about military women 54–61; women as sex objects 65; agency, second-class status and citizenship 94–95, 100 106; equal rights amendment (ERA) 144–146, 149–151 backlash against women 212; combat exclusion policy 144–146, 149, 151, 154–164; military culture 180, 212; culture of domination 192, 194; Selective Service Act 121–122; white male privilege 180; effeminization of the enemy 201; women as proxies for men 247–254; women and power 255; women as supporters and caregivers 55, 57, 60–61; women as warriors 29–30, 33
Homeless Veterans' Reintegration Program (HVRP) 333
Homeless Women Veterans' Listening Sessions (2009) 331
homelessness: veterans 108–109, 308, 319, 323, 331–333, 348
Homelessness Prevention and Rapid Re–Housing Program (HPRP) 333
homosexuality 66, 95–96, 127, 138, 160, 179, 194, 198, 255, 278, 285, 300, 303, 391, 414, 419; gay men 179, 198, 414; lesbian baiting 15, 37–39; lesbians 15, 37–39, 96, 160, 179–181, 198, 310, 343, 365, 388, 414; LGBTQ community 343, 345, 365–366, 388
homosocial reproduction 177, 233; *see also* homosocial world 415
honor 21, 30, 33, 42, 43, 103–105, 152, 176–177, 179, 188, 201–203, 248, 303, 368, 413, 400–404
Honorable Service 400
hookup culture 295
Hopkins-Chadwick, D.L. 305, 310
Horrigan, C. 97–98
Hosek, S.D. *et al.* 51–52, 286, 417
hostile terrain 96
House of Representatives 135, 281, 296–297, *368,* 382
households, income of 108, 174, 268, 314, 334n4; head of household 209; household names 231; women veterans' households 315
HUD-VASH 333
Huey, M. 150
Hultgreen, K. 180–181

Hundley, B.S., and Lederer, F.I. 293–294
Hunter, M. 43–44, 65–67, 178–180, 185, 188–195, 198–199, 201–204, 228, 298, 343, 348, 369, 414
Hunter, D. (Congressman) 128
Hunter-gatherer 21
Hussein, S. 146
hypermasculinity 52, 160, 178–180, 189–191, 193–195, 199, 204–205, 216, 392, 414

identifying as veterans 394
Imade ad-Din 28
'incident to service test' 298–299
inclusive exclusion 70
income of households 334n4
individual duty training (IDT) 103–104
individual ready reserve (IRR) 104
indoctrination 40, 153, 178–179, 187–189, 198–199, 201, 248
inequality: gender 303–304, 308, 310–312, 315–316, 329, 334, *368,* 376, 382–387, 395, 405, 407–408; regimes 234–235, 237, 318; income 315, 317
Institute of Medicine 323, 325–327, 334n5; Committee on Nutrition, Trauma, and the Brain 323, 326–327
institutional betrayal 348, 367, 380–381
institutions 1, 4–5, 34, 37, 76–78, 83, 96, 138, 180, 193, 209, 231, 268, 305–306, 308, 311, 314, 316, 334, 348, 361, 369, 379–381, 385–387, 393, 400–401, 404–408
Inter-Parliamentary Union (IPU) 381
intercontinental ballistic missiles (ICBMs) 92, 145, 156
International Criminal Tribunal for the former Yugoslavia (ICTY) 191
International Society for Traumatic Stress Studies (ISTSS) 152
Internet 68–69, 171, 418
interpersonal violence 378
intersectionality 6, 11–13, 16, 1, 75, 234, 308, 413
invisibility 1–6, 8, 11–13, 16, 110–111, 113, 143, 237, 289, 388, 412, 418, 422; social impact 391, 394
Invisible War, The (2012) 187, 370
Iraq War *see* Gulf War II (Iraq War, 2003–2011) 13, 106, *107,* 109, *266,* 314–315, 322
Iskra, D. 15, 53, 185, 192, 229

Islam 28, 199
Islamophobia 227
Israeli Defense Forces (IDF) 34, 81, 205, 215, 234
Izraeli, D. 81

Jackson, R.M. 263
Jackson, D.M., and Vanden Brook, T. 349
Jacob, G. 153
Jebl Sahaba 223
Jefferson, T. 133–134
Jefferson v. United States (1950) 297
Jeffreys, S. 39–40, 42, 44, 49, 201, 204
Jim Crow laws 232
Joan of Arc 29
Johnson, LaVena 41, 370
Johnson, L.B. 253
Johnson, A.E., and Rivera, J.C. 13
Johnson, D.V., and Putko, M.M. 53, 59
Johnson, M. 185, 203
Jones, D.E. 20, 23–24, 223
Jones, K. 42
Jones, J., and Roth-Douquet, K. 286–287
Jorgenson, J. 37, 209
Joshua Omvig Veterans' Suicide Prevention Act (2007) 390
Judge Advocate General (JAG) 293–294
Judge, E. 246
Judith, Queen of the Falashes 24, 224

Kahn, L.M., and Blau, F.D. 262
Kang, H.K. *et al.* 324, 326
Kanter, R.M. 1, 7, 34, 75, 175–177, 211, 231–234, 406
Kaplan, F. 163
Kaplan, M. *et al.* 8, 14
Kassenbaum, N. 123
Katz, E. 66
Katz, L.S. *et al.* 346–348
Kay, K., and Simpson, C. 113–114
KBR (Kellogg, Brown and Root) 326, 329
Kelly, E., and Dobbin, F. 237
Kelly, L. 40, 201
Kennedy, A. 135
Kennedy, C. 42, 214
Kennedy, E. 135
Kennedy, M. 362
Kennedy-Pipe, C. 49, 52
Kerber, L.K. 31, 51, 89, 97, 120–126, 134–135, 413–414

Kevalah 28
Kimmel, M.S. 180, 195, 414–415
King, C.S. 245
Kintzle, S. *et al.* 307
Kirk, I. 143
Klay and Hellmer v. Panetta et al. (2013) 66–67
Klemke, L.W., and Tiedman, G.H. 38
Kleykamp, M.A. 34, 114, 266, 268–269, 286
Koeszegi, S.T. *et al.* 204–205, 234
Kohlberg, L. 406
Kohn, R.H. 277
Konrad, A.M. *et al.* 35, 232
Korean Conflict (1950–1953) 13, 106, 109, 161, 188, 204, 251–253, 256, 265, 326
Kravec-Kelly, T. 111
Krislov, S., and Rosenbloom, D. 284
Kumartunga, C.B. 227

labor market areas (LMAs) 272
Landis, D., and Dansby, M. 34, 234
Laning, V. 138
LaPorte, J. 152
Las Colinas Detention Facility 320
latent class analysis (LCA) 109
Laub Coser, R., and Coser, L. 77, 209–210
law: civilian 35, 75, 79, 119, 126, 137–138, 140, 146, 150, 175, 186, 208, 231, 234–235, 237, 245, 293, 299, 385, 421; sexual assault, sexual harassment and other military lawsuits 66–67, 78, 316; military 81, 83, 91, 97–99, 105, 126, 152, 154–155, 157, 252, 255, 291–293, 295, 296–299, 315, 325, 328, 350–351, 354n1, 355n17, 355n20, 355n22, 361, 418–419; tort 296, 299; lawlessness 204, 294; lawmakers 281; lawyers 294, 412; blue laws 387
Law, S.A. 13, 34, 175, 189, 204, 211, 232, 235, 412
Lawrence, Q., and Penaloza, M. 147
Lawrence, Q. 147, 389
Leavitt, J. 185
Ledbetter v. Goodyear Tire and Rubber Co. (2007) 134–136
Lederer, F.I., and Hundley, B.S. 293–294
Legal Information Institute (LII) 296–297
LeMay, C. 212

lesbians 15, 37–39, 96, 160, 179–181, 198, 310, 404; baiting 15, 38
Levin, M. 173–174
Levine, M.P. *et al.* 68
Levin, S., and van Laar, C. 237
Lewis, E., and Harris, G.L.A. 16, 34, 65, 286, 413
Lewis, M. 303
Ley, D. 382
LGBTQ community 343, 345, 365–366, 388
liberal considerations 105
Lily Ledbetter Fair Pay Act (2009) 134, 136
Lioness (2008) 5, 14, 34, 50–53, 55, 110, 157, 159, 280, 411
Lioness Report (2012) 5, 14, 53, 55, 157, 159, 401
Louis VI, King of France 27, 226
Lowe, N.K., and Ryan-Wenger, N.A. 324, 330
Lycungus of Thrace, King 24
Lynch, J. 92
Lynching (of African Americans) 157

Maass, A.: and Dall'Ara, E. 78–79; *et al.* 78–79
Mabus, R. 187
McAfee, M. 246, 250
McCain, J. 246, 294
McCaskill, C. 67, 295
McCauley, M.L.H. (Molly Pitcher) 29–30, 33–34, 55, 157, 247–248, 255
McClintock, M. 15, 38
McCracken, P. 71
McElrath, K. 2, 78, 157
McGrath, R. 211
Machmer, J. 42
Macke, R. 43
McPeak, M. 144–145, 191
Madison, J. 292
Mae Enge people 20
Malcolm X 74
Male Civilian Ferry Pilots 105
Malegereabar 224
males: privilege 385–386; white male culture 55, 93; white male privilege 172–181, 237, 414
Maloney, C. 135
manhood 35, 77, 94, 179–180
Maninger, S. 49, 51–52, 61, 157
manliness 189, 201
Mansbridge, J.J. 138

Manual for Courts Martial (MCM, 2008) 291
marginality 76, 175, 178; double 81; multiple 38, 74, 76, 175, 178, 238
marginalization 7, 11–13, 38, 77–78, 80–81, 83, 93, 175, 178, 189, 204–205, 238, 272; African Americans 11, 16, 65, 97–98, 134, 157, 176, 231–232, 235, 278, 391, 413
Marier, R. 201
Marine Corps *see* U.S. Marine Corps (USMC) 30, 50, 53–55, 58–59, 82, 103, 106, 113, 121, 145–146, 148, 151–154, 155–156, 158, 165, 171, 174, 179–180, 186–187, 189, 194–195, 198–199, 215, 239, 250–251, 255, 279–280, 294, 309, 317–318, 321, 345–346, 351, 355n17, 363, 378, 381–382, 384, 388, 418, 401, 404
Mark Antony 25, 224–225
Marmot, M.: and Allen, J. 306–307, 311; *et al.* 307–308, 317–318; and Siegrist, J. 307–308
Marquet and Kendzior v. Gates et al. (2012) 66
Marshall, G. 251–252
Marshall, T. 126, 413
Marshall scholars 201
Maryet-Nit 223
Mascarenhas, O. 308, 310, 312, 384, 387, 402–403, 407–408
masculinities lens 385, 407
masculinity 25, 35, 40, 44, 49, 80–81, 94, 160, 174, 181, 189, 193, 252; domination 39, 172, 189, 192–193, 195; hegemonic 35, 66, 70, 91, 175, 178; hypermasculinity 49, 52, 160, 178–180, 189–191, 193–195, 199, 204–205, 216, 392, 414; personalities 78–79; masculinity in crisis 195, 414–415
Massachusetts Institute of Technology (MIT) 80
Matilda 26, 225–226
Mattis, J. 148
Mazur, D.H. 20, 84, 91–93, 144–145, 257, 288, 422
Mbandi, Z. 24, 224
Mead, M. 239
Meggitt, B. 20
Mehay, S.L., and Hirsch, B.T. 265
Meier, K., and Nicholson-Crotty, J. 285

Meier, K., and Bohte, J. 284
Meir, G. 226
mental health: 8, 109, 112, 148, 152, 319, 322, 331 disorders 109, 332; outcomes 112; healthcare/services 322–323; issues 331, 388–391; professionals 8, 348, treatment 369; PTSD 319, 322–323; homelessness 331–332; MST 348, 369; suicide 388–391
Meulders, D. et al. 75
Mexican-American War (1846–1848) 30, 33, 256
Meyerson, D.E., and Ely, R.J. 237–238
military: evolution of women's role 31, 60, 70–71, 279–280, 392; justice system 296–300, 308, 361, 363–366, 370; law 291–293, 295, 298–299, 351; overview of demographics 15, 34, 81, 93, 127, 133, 255, 278–279, 286, 299, 318, 322, 324, 328, 366; MST and sexual assault 346, 350; unmasking friction 311–313; and women warriors 21, 29–31, 221, 303, 313, 331, 412; women's integration (1974) 49, 121, 146–147, 154, 229
Military Justice Improvement Act (MJIA, 2013) 367, 370
Military Leadership Diversity Commission (MLDC) 165, 187, 215–216, 239, 286, 288, 411
military sexual assault (MSA) 344–346, 350–352, 354n10, 361–362, 365, 369–370, 370n1; measuring and reporting 351, *352*, 353
military sexual harassment (MSH) 344–345, 350, 355n19, 361, 369, 370n1; measuring and reporting 353, 354n6–9
military sexual trauma (MST) i. 3, 14–15, 106, 109, 113, 148, 303, 307, 320, 322–323, 331–332, 343–350, 352–354, 361–362, 364–370, *368*, 378, 412, 420; definition 344–345; effects 347–348; gender disparity *368*; impact 345–346; measuring and reporting 349–351; military justice system 361, 363–364, 366, 370; opportunities for improvement and research 364–369; prevalence 349–353; prevention and response training 349–350, 361–363, 365–366, 369–370; significance to general public 348–349; threat to recruitment and retention 349; victim services and support 364
Miller, L. 204, 343; and Harrell, M. 52, 59–60, 158–159
Miller, M. and Weinstein-Matthews, G.L. 343
Miller, K., and Rosenthal, L. 349–350
Miller, T.C. 364
Millett, S. 179, 198
Minkowitz, D. 79
minority groups 13, 34, 76, 99, 210–211, 215, 231–232, 234, 236–237, 260–261, 265, 267, 279, 287,288, 305, 308, 310–312; underrepresented minority (URM) 13, 232, 235, 260–261, 263
minority proportion discrimination hypothesis 35, 234
mission–critical project 288, 420; mission critical 271, 288
Mitchell, B. 61, 144, 157, 378
Mitchell, K.S., and Bartlett, B.A. 378
mobilization 128–129, 143–144, 411; mobilize 57, 143; demobilization 59, 121, 144
Mohammed 28
mommy war 401
Monahan, E., and Neidel-Greenlee, R. 41, 55–56, 60–61, 112, 146, 149, 157–158, 160–161, 163, 192, 229, 249–251, 411
Monk v. Mabus (2014) 105
Monkiewicz, A.F. 71, 104, 255
Monmouth, Battle of (1778) 29, 33–34, 247
Montgomery GI Bill (MGIB) 268; *see also* GI Bill 58, 105, 271, 315–316
Montgomery, N. 361, 364
Moon, K. 43–44
Moore, B.L. 13, 65, 268, 286, 288
Moore, M. 151
Morner, M. and Misgeld, M. 361, 365, 383
Morris, R.B. 97
Morse Code 250
Moskos, C. 58, 93, 160, 286, 407
Mota, N.P. *et al.* 323
motherhood 37, 75, 81, 208–209; penalty 263; parenthood 164
Muller v. Oregon (1908) 386
multidimensionality 16, 114, 410
multiple marginality: theory of 38, 76, 178, 238

Munford, J. 187
myths 52, 55–56, 58–61, 149–150, 157–164, 235, 251, 412; mythologize (d) 24–25, 33; mythical 22; mythology 310; mythic 415

National Academy of Sciences (NAS) 325, 329
National Center for Veterans Analysis and Statistics (NCVAS) 13, 106–108, 268, 314–316, 391
National Commission on Military, National and Public Service 128
National Defense Authorization: Act (NDAA, 1961) 118, 128, 154, 281, 317, 351, 353
National Guard 13–14, 103–106, 109, 120, 255, 268–269, 279, 287, 308, 318–319, 323, 346, 351, 353, 354n13, 355n17; Army National Guard 388
National Guard Bureau (NGB) 353
National Honor Society (NHS) 201
National Institute of Mental Health (NIMH) 152
National Institutes of Health (NIH), Revitalization Act (1993) 321
National Organization for Women (NOW) 124, 139, 200
national security 8, 100, 171, 216, 229, 253, 286, 349, 353, 369–370, 384, 394, 422
National Service (Program) 118, 129, 281, 299
National Women's Conference (1977) 231
National Women's Law Center (NWLC) 186–187
Native Americans 107, 109, 137, 157, 210, 232, 261, 278, 345, 354n4; murdering 157; pay 210, 261
natural rights 98, 292
naturalization 120, 403
Naval Criminal Investigative Service (NCIS) 152, 378
Navy 15, 43, 53, 57, 82, 96–98, 103, 105–106, 150, 152, 154–156, 164, 180–181, 185–187, 189–190, 192, 202, 213–214, 229, 248–250, 255–256, 279, 293–294, 300, 309, 345–346, 351, 355n17, 363, 378, 419–420, 401–402, 404; *see also* U.S. Navy (USN); U.S. Naval Academy (USNA) 15, 82–83, 178, 185, 191, 199–200, 383

Navy Times 214
Nefraso-bak 223
Neidel-Greenlee, R., and Monahan, E. 41, 55–56, 60, 112, 146, 149, 157–158, 160–161, 163, 192, 229, 249–251, 411
neighborhood and built environment 313, 324–331, 334n1
Nettleman, M. 327
New Jersey Turnpike (NJTP) 29, 248
Newark, T. 20, 25–27, 225–226
Newidemek 224
Nicholson-Crotty, J., and Meier, K. 285
Nike Hercules Battery Missile Unit 92
Nineteenth Amendment 97, 134, 137, 139, 413, 406
Ninth Strategic Reconnaissance Wing (9 RW) 54, 155
Nixon, Richard 126
Nixon, R.L. 286, 407
Nkomo, S. 76, 176, 232, 237
normalization 39, 318
North Atlantic Treaty Organization (NATO) 155

Obama, B. 15, 30, 136, 153, 248
Obicheta, O., and Gould, O. 4, 14
Objectives for 2020 (Advisory Committee) 307
Occupational Safety and Health Administration (OSHA) 324; OSH Act (1970) 324
Ochberg, F. 152
Octavia (n) 25, 224–225
Odierno, R., and Chandler, R. 400, 403
Oedipus complex 66
Office of the Deputy Assistant Secretary of Defense 118, 278–279, 346
U.S. Office of Economic Opportunity (OEO) 314
U.S. Office of Emergency Management (OEM) 95
U.S. Department of Veterans Affairs, Office of Health Equity (OHE) 311, 324
U.S. Department of Veterans Affairs, Office of the Inspector General (OIG) 333
U.S. Office of Special Investigation (OSI) 202
O'Grady, L. 67
Okimoto, T.G., and Heilman, M.E. 114

Olswang, S.G., and Finkel, S.K. 78, 211
On War (Clausewitz) 21
O'Neal Greenhow, R. 30, 33
Operation Allied Force (1999) 256
Operation Desert Shield (1990–1991) 13, 106, 109, 256, 265, 286; *see also* Gulf War I 13, 315; and Persian Gulf War I 320
Operation Desert Storm (1991) 13, 56–58, 60, 145, 158, 161, 163–164, 179, 181, 198, 214, 411; *see also* Gulf War I 13, 314–315; Persian Gulf War 320
Operation Enduring Freedom (2001–2014) 8, 13, 158, 160, 199, 318–319, 326, 347, 354n15, 388, 411–412; *see also* Gulf War II 13, 314–315; Persian Gulf War; also known as Post 9/11 era 106, 109, 322
Operation Gridiron (2011) 202
Operation Iraqi Freedom (2003–2011) 1, 3, 8, 13, 83, 92, 159, 176, 192, 318–319, 326, 347, 354n15, 388, 411–412; *see also* Gulf War II 13, 314–315; Persian Gulf War; also known as Post 9/11 era 106, 109, 322
Operation Just Cause (1989–1990) 83, 92, 149, 156, 176, 256
Operation New Dawn (2010–2011) 31, 164, 216, 256, 288, 326
Operation Ranch Hand (1962–1971) 325
Operation Urgent Fury (1983) 256
Oregon Supreme Court (OSC) 386
organizational performance 237
organizational trauma 348, 367
Oron, I., and Pazy, A. 34, 205, 211, 234
Ortega, M. 53
OSH Act (1970) 324
other, women as: 13, 16, 33–44, 76, 127, 188–189, 201, 204, 232, 238, 366, 369, 379, 383, 386, 391–392, 394, 402; status 369
Owens, G.P. *et al.* 112
Owens v. Brown (1978) 98, 300, 418–419
Owens, Y. 419

Padavic, I., and Prokos, A. 265
Pakistani Army 39
Pakistan People's Party (PPP) 227
Pakistan 223, 226–227
Panetta, L. 66–67, 187, 321

Park Chung-hee 244
Park Geun-hye 244–246
Parker, K. *et al.* 287, 417
Parker, A. 187
Parrish, N. 67
particulate matter (PM) 328
Pateman, C. 120
Patten, E. 264
Patten, E., and Parker, K. 287, 417
patriarchy 15, 25, 33, 35, 44, 66, 81, 138, 195, 366, 386, 424; biblical 386
patrilocal residency 20
Patriot Battle Missile Unit 92
Paul, A. 135, 137; Institute 134–136, 138–140
Paul, R. 187
pay gap 136–137, 139, 210, 261–264, 268–269, 271–272
Pazy, A., and Oron, I. 34, 205, 211, 234
Peele, R.B. 318–319, 323
Pence, M. 147
Pentagon 15, 57, 67, 92, 164, 253–254, 364, 366–367
People's Party of Pakistan (PPP) 227
Pershing, J.L. 82–83, 205
Petronio, K. 50, 55, 158
Petronius 23, 224
Pew Research Center 58, 118, 210, 261, 264, 268, 278, 394, 416–417
Phipps, A. 248
Pierce, J.L. 235
Piestawa, L. 92
Pitcher, M. (Mary Ludwig Hays McCauley) 29–30, 33–34, 55, 157, 247–248, 255
Plato 92
Pollard, M.S. *et al.* 111–112
pollution theory 36, 146, 262
Polochek, S.W. 262–263
Polychlorinated Dibenzo-furans (PCDFs) 328
Polychlorinated Dibenzo-p-dioxins (PCDDs) 328, 334n5
polycyclic aromatic hydrocarbons (PAHs) 328
pornography 39–40, 79, 190, 200–201; revenge; 382; *see also* slut shaming
Portillo, S., and Doan, A. 312–313, 318
Post-9/11 GI Bill 105, 268, 271
Post-traumatic stress disorder (PTSD) 3, 50, 105, 109, 152, 307, 319–323, 331–332, 347–348, 354n14, 368, 378, 389–390, 402, 410; CAPS 347, 354n14

poverty 108–109, 125, 137, 271, 313
power 6–7, 15–16, 22, 24–27, 35, 38, 40, 52, 76, 78, 94, 119, 137, 144–145, 149, 161, 175, 178–179, 190, 192, 209, 213, 221, 223–228, 233–234, 236, 238, 239, 244, 260, 262, 268, 272, 277, 292, 312, 318, 343, 348, 363, 377, 385–386, 415, 407; powerless (ness) 67–68; powerful 125, 215, 223, 226, 233, 281, 312
Powers, R. 418
Pratkanis, A.R., and Turner, M.E. 133, 236
predominantly white institutions (PWIs) 76, 231–232
pregnancy 21, 52, 54–55, 57, 59–60, 155, 158, 192, 249–250, 252, 321–322, 330–331
Prentice, D., and Carranza, E. 36–37, 78
prescriptive stereotypes 36–37, 42
Presidential Commission 194
prevention and response training 349–350, 361–363, 365–366, 369–370; dominant narratives 365–366
Price Waterhouse v. Hopkins (1989) 78
Priest, T. 41–42
print advertisements 68
prisoner(s) of war (POWs) 55–56, 160–161, 179, 192, 198, 214–215, 249
privilege: male 6, 34, 38, 121, 129, 202, 385–386; white male 133, 172–173–181, 237, 404
Project Diane (Doan and Portillo) 312, 318
Prokos, A., and Padavic, I. 265
Proskos, A., and Cabage, L.N. 267
prostitution 39, 43–44, 201, 250–251; prostitute (s) 43–44, 70, 194, 250–251, 303
Protect Our Defenders (POD) 67, 349, 351, 361, 363–364, 367, 370, 384
psychological reactance 404
psychosocial environment 307–308, 317
public safety 349, 353

Quinn, K.A. *et al.* 236
Quinn, S. 135

racial discrimination 11–13, 16, 30, 34, 60, 65, 70, 74–75, 93–94, 126, 133–134, 136, 140, 176, 231–232, 234, 245, 260–261, 264, 272, 285, 346, 354n4, 412, 391
racism 190, 232, 236–237, 245, 286
Ramses II 22
RAND Corporation 58, 264, 346, 350–351
RAND Military Workplace Study (RMWS) 351–353, 370
Randal, M. 160; and Yanz, L. 160
rape 8, 24, 39–43, 66–67, 79, 93, 113, 163, 188, 190–191, 193–194, 201–202, 204, 294, 298, 331, 345–346, 351–352, 354n4, 363, 368, 400, 403; gang 40, 113, 188, 190, 204, 294
Rape of Nanking, The (Chang) 39–40, 188, 204
Rape Treatment Center (RTC, Santa Monica Hospital) 190
Rathbun-Nealy, M. 179, 198
Reagan, R. 150, 172
Reed, F. 57, 164
REFORGER 77 (REFWAC) Women's Army Corps 150
reorganization week (re-orgy week) 66, 201
Report to the President of the United States on SAPR (2014) 352
representative bureaucracy 7, 76, 277, 284–285
representative democracy 388
Republic (Plato) 92
republic, American 33, 129, 133–134, 139, 157, 178, 279; Democratic Republic of Congo 23, 224; Union of Soviet Social Republics (U.S.S.R.) 143, 248; other republics 81
requisite variety 384
Reserve Officers Training Corps (ROTC) 76–77
reservists 106, 318–319, 346
Reskin, B.F. *et al.* 38, 75, 94, 175, 232
Reskin, B., and Harper, S. 237
Resnick, E.M. *et al.* 111–112, 322
responsibility: civic 119–127, 277; social 349, 353; ethics 8; obligation for military service 89, 191, 206, 362; women's responsibility 91–92, 163, 174, 211, 260; government and military responsibility 138, 249, 296, 402; affirmative action 236; diversity

238; bureaucrat 284; individual 385; the courts 413
revenge porn 382, 401
Revitalization Act (1993) (National Institutes of Health (NIH) 321
Riccucci, N. M. 235, 237; and Saidel, J. 285, 411
Richard the Lionheart 29
Richards, A. 231
Richardson, H.S. 406
Ridgeway, C.L. 37, 75, 208–209, 263; and Correll, S.J. 37, 75, 208–209
rights: African Americans 134–135, 215; Equal Rights Amendment (ERA) 6, 8, 11, 31, 61, 79, 89, 97–100, 120, 122–125, 133–140, 146–147, 204, 216, 288, 379, 413–414, 419, 422; natural 98, 292; civil rights 70, 100, 231, 253, 292, 298; citizenship 89, 98, 100, 123–124, 139 288–289, 292, 300; voting rights 100; states' rights 138; prisoners' rights 215; constitutional rights 292–293, 300, 400–401, 418, 420; veterans 297, 299; MST 345, 348, 367–368, 419; men's rights 415
Rittel, H.W., and Webber, M.M. 7, 235, 263, 312, 343, 381, 383–384, 388, 420
Roberts, T., and Fredrickson, B. 68
Robinson, M.N. 112
Rodriguez, P. 110
Roe v. Wade (1973) 138, 147
Rogers, E.N. 249
Rogers, K. 246
Roosevelt, E. 251
Rosen, L.N. *et al.* 35, 59, 159–160, 205, 211, 234
Rosenberg, A. 251
Rosenthal, L., and Miller, K. 349–350
Rosenbloom, D., and Krislov, S. 284
Rosenberg, M. 366, 370
Rosenstein, R. 245–246
Rostker, B. 118–119, 121, 125–129
Rostker v. Goldberg (1980) 125, 281, 413
Roth-Douquet, K., and Jones, J. 286–287
Rousseff, D. 245
Routon, W. 266
Royal Marines (UK) 152
Ryan, M.K.: *et al.* 246–247; and Haslam, S.A. 246–247
Ryan-Wenger, N.A., and Lowe, N.K. 324, 330

sacred grove 6, 155, 203
safety, public 349, 353
Saidel, J., and Riccucci, N.M. 285, 411
Salayan Bint Malhan 28
Sammuramutar 223
Sanchez, R. 41
Sanchez v. City of Miami Beach (1989) 78
Sandinista National Liberation Front (FSLN) 53
Santa Monica Hospital, Rape Treatment Center (RTC) 190
Sarmatians 223
Sasson-Levy, O. 81–82
Satrom, B. 138, 387
Saywell, S. 56, 161
Scalia, A. 294
scandals: Aberdeen Proving Ground (APG, 1996) 99, 202, 351, 355n19, 362; Marine Corps 152–153, 171, 174, 180, 195, 198–199, 251, 381–382, 384, 405, 408; sexual abuse (MST) 152, 361–362, 366, 370n1; Tailhook Association (1991) 190, 202, 351, 355n18, 362, 378, 383, 402; WWII 250–251; Air Force missile launch officers cheating 320
Schafly, P. 135, 138
Schroeder, P. 51, 124, 414
Schulz, V. 79–80
Schwarzenbach, S.A. 97
Schwimmer, R. 120, 413
science, technology, engineering and mathematics (STEM) 264, 271
Scott, J.W. 175
Scythian Amazons 22–23, 223
Second Amendment 120
second-class status 134, 146, 155, 193,
security, national 8, 100, 171, 216, 229, 253, 286, 349, 353, 369–370, 384, 394, 422; economic security 22, 58, 272, 416; financial security 69, 413
Segal, D., and Wechsler Segal, M. 4, 13, 31, 51–52, 59, 77, 144, 158, 185, 209, 228, 255, 265, 285–286, 417
segregation, sex 35, 66, 75, 94, 231; racial 127, 190; job 237, 249, 262; self-segregation 38–39; economic 75; groups 231
Seifert, R. 40, 44, 66–67, 193–194, 201, 412
Selden, S.C., and Sowa, J.E. 284–285
Sekaquaptewa, D., and Thompson, M. 59

Selective Service Act (1917) 8, 118–121, 123–130, 134, 253, 413–414
Selective Service System 6, 31, 51, 89, 118–121, 123–130, 134, 252, 281, 287, 299, 413–414, 422
self-directed violence 377–378, 388, 420
self-objectification 68
self-segregation 38–39
selfless service 392, 419, 404
Senate Armed Services Committee 67, 128, 295, 351
Senior Executive Service (SES) 263–264
sensing sessions 214
sensitivity training 366
September 11 attacks (2001): post- 4, 105–6, 109, 127–128, 266, 280, 322, 354n15; GI Bill 105, 268, 271
service: before self 419, 422; character of 105; period of *107*, 199, *266*, 314–315; military campaigns 70
Service Women's Action Network (SWAN) 14–15, 147–148, 153, 186–187, 228, 239, 300, 315–316, 349, 351, 361, 364, 367–368, 370
Serviceman's Readjustment Act (GI Bill, 1944) 58, 105, 268–269, 271, 315–316
Sessions, J. 245–246
7th Pennsylvania Regiment 29, 247
sex: discrimination 3, 36, 67, 78, 94–95, 344; fiends 16, 193, 403; military personnel 104–105, 193, 216, 309–310; population data 308–309; segregation 35, 66
sexism 3, 76, 100, 138, 191, 200, 205–206, 232, 237, 246–247, 286, 366, 369, 394; benevolent 366
sex/sexual abuse scandal 15, 355n19, 361–362, 366–367, 370n1, 389
sexual assault 14, 34, 40–44, 60, 65–67, 71, 77, 99, 125, 147–148, 152–153, 165, 178–179, 187–190, 202–204, 294–295, 298–299, 307, 320, 322, 343–354, *352,* 354n4, 355n18, 355n19, 355n21, 355n22, 355n23, 361–370, *368,* 370n1, 379, 381, 384–385, 394, 404, 419–421; adverse treatment of victims 346, 364–366–369; definition 344–345, 385; military sexual assault (MSA) 148, 344–346, 350–353, *352,* 361–362, 365, 369–370, 370n1; reporting 14–15, 67, 82, 147, 152, 202, 295, 307, 349–350, 352–353, 355n21, 355n22, 365, 384, 403; unwanted sexual contact (USC) 352
Sexual Assault Awareness and Prevention Month 404
Sexual Assault Prevention and Response Office (SAPRO) 362, 371n2, 381, 384
sexual assault prevention and response (SAPR) 350, 362–364, 366, 381; training 361
sexual harassment 15, 36, 42, 49, 65, 78–80, 82, 93–94, 148, 202, 298–299, 316, 343–346, 348, 350–351, 353–354, 358n18, 358n19, 361–362, 365–370, *368*, 370n1, 381, 385, 394, 403; definition 344; military sexual harassment (MSH) 344–345, 350, 353, 354n6, 354n7, 354n8, 354n9, 355n19, 361, 369, 370n1; Sexual Harassment and Assault Response and Prevention (SHARP) 362–363, 403, 405
sexual trauma 3, 14, 106, 148, 303, 307, 322, 333, 343–344, 347, 361, 378, 412; *see also* military sexual trauma (MST)
Shammuramat, Queen of Assyria 22
Sheba, Queen of 24, 224
Shenakdah Kite 224
Sherman, E.F. 291–292, 295–296, 299–300, 420
Shinseki, E. 332
Siegrist, J., and Marmot, M. 307–308
Signal Corps Female Telephone Operators Unit 104–105
Silent Truth, The (2010) 370
Silva, J.M. 76–77
Simpson, C., and Kay, K. 113–114
Simpson, R. 87
Simpson, O.J. 51
Sirleaf, E.J. 227
Skelton, I. 351
slut-shaming 382
Smail, J. 204
Smith, L.G. 42
Smith, Senator Margaret Chase 251
Smith, R.A., and Elliott, J.R. 233, 416
Smith, C., and Keneally, M. 148
Smith, N. 244
Smith, C.P., and Freyd, J.J. 348, 367
Smith, S.E. 307
Smith, W. 253
Smith-Rosenberg, C. 97
Smith-Spark, L., and Sanchez, R. 186

Snitow, A. 37, 209
Snyder, R.C. 39, 52, 65, 77, 82, 100, 198–199, 201, 204–206
social cohesion 308, 317
social and community context 313, 317–320, 334n1
social determinants of health (SDOH) 305–308, 311, 313, 334n1; dimensions 303, 306–307, 313–331, 334; downstream factors 306–307; economic stability 313–315, 334n1; education 311, 313–317; health and healthcare 8, 313, 320–324, 334n1; importance 306, 308–311, 320; neighborhood and built environment 313, 324–331, 334n1; social and community context 313, 317–320, 334n1; upstream factors 306–307, 310, 334
social egalitarian paradigm (Evolutionists) 312, 334
social exclusion 317–318
social impact of invisibility 391
social responsibility 349, 353
social-ecological model 304, 379–382, *380*, 385, 394–395; community level 379, *380*, 382; individual level 379, *380*, 381–382; relationship level 379, *380*, 382; societal level 379, *380*, 381, 421
society, and ethics 423–425
Solaro, E. 55, 60, 146, 156, 158–162, 185, 229, 254, 279, 348, 351–352, 411–412
Solomon, King 24, 224
South Korean International Tourism Association 43
Sowa, J.E., and Selden, S.C. 284–285
Special Forces (Green Berets) 111, 214, 280, 312, 318
Speece, M. 404
Speier, J. 281
sponsorship 177, 233
Stambach, A., and Gunter, R. 77–78
Standard & Poor's 500 (S&P 500) 211
state self-objectification 68
Statewide Advocacy for Veterans' Empowerment (SAVE) 390
status: other 35, 83, 89, 127, 137, 174, 246, 369, 376, 391; second-class 2, 4–5, 12–13, 15, 31, 33, 37, 39, 42, 52, 74–76, 78, 91–100, 126, 134, 137, 146, 155, 189, 191, 193, 208, 211, 221, 232, 234, 237, 246, 249, 253,
260, 278, 288, 300, 308, 311–312, 334, 365–366, 369, 386, 391, 402, 403; socioeconomic 7, 262, 381, 413; financial 59, 210; employment 314; military and veteran status 105, 113, 124, 268, 305, 314–315, 320, 323, 346, 354n13, 376, 391, 394; marital 163, 261; motherhood 208–210
Steele, C.S. 113, 177, 233, 236
Steele, J. 320
Steele, S. 235
Stegner, B.L. 254
Steinem, G. 135, 231
stereotypes 36, 39, 65, 69–71, 80–81, 93–94, 96, 113, 177, 209, 211, 233, 236–237, 312, 365–366; descriptive 36–37, 43; gender 36, 94, 247, 313, 366; prescriptive 36–37, 42; traditional 69–70, 312–313
Stewart, L.P. *et al.* 94
stigmatization 38–39, 235, 367
Stipes, B. 92
Stockholm Syndrome 200
Stoltenberg, J. 190
Stop Taking Our Privileges (STOP) 135
strength, upper-body 51–52
Strite Murnane, L. 67
subordinate citizenship 99
subordination 11, 13, 16, 81, 99, 175, 189, 191, 194, 204–205, 232; *see also* insubordination 42, 153
substance abuse 109, 308, 319, 323, 331–332, 347, 370, 388, 390, 420
suffrage: universal 97, 99, 134, 137, 139, 144; women 134, 137–139, 406
suicide 2–3, 8, 25–26, 41–42, 112–113, 225, 308, 323, 347, 377–378, 412, 420; rates 388–391
Supplemental Nutrition Assistance Program (SNAP) 315
Supportive Services for Veteran Families Program (SSVF) 333
U.S. Supreme Court 97–98, 120, 126, 135, 138, 281, 292–294, 296–297, 386, 403, 418–419, 421; *see also* High Court 97–98, 120, 126, 135–136, 292, 300, 413, 418
survival, escape, resistance and evasion training (SERE) 56, 161
Survivor Experience Survey (SES) 350
SWAN, ACLU and ACLU-Connecticut v. DoD (2015) 316
Swers, M.L. 382
Szelwach, C.R. *et al.* 267

Taft, C.T. et al. 112
Tailhook Association scandal (1991) 190, 202, 351, 355n18, 362, 378, 383, 402
Taliban 199
Taube, D.E., and Blinde, E.M. 37–39
Taylor, C. 227
Taylor, Z. 30, 256
Teague, K. 125, 135, 393
Team Lioness 5, 14, 34, 50–53, 55, 110, 157, 159, 280, 411
television 68
temptresses 100, 193
Tenbrunsel, A., and Bazerman, M. 402, 404
Tet Offensive (1968) 55–56, 161, 254
Thatcher, M. 226
"think crisis – think female" rationale 247
Thomas, E. 202–203
Thomas, M.D., and Thomas, P.J. 57, 164
Thomas, R.R. 176
Thompson, D., and Sekaquaptewa, D. 59
Thompson, M. 213
Thompson, T. 52–53, 111
Thornberry, M. 281
Tiedman, G.H., and Klemke, L.W. 38
Title 10 (CFR) 103
Title 38 (CFR) 103
Title IX (1972) 379
Titunik, R.F. 52, 65, 83, 92, 99, 176, 199, 215–216
tokenism 34, 59, 75–76, 176–177, 211, 221, 231–234, 238–239, 253, 416
tort law 296–297, 299
toxin exposure 327, 335n7
training: sexual assault (MST/SHARP/SAPR) prevention and response 349–350, 361–363, 365–366, 369–370, 381, 385, 389, 403–405; sensitivity 71, 313, 322, 366; SERE 56, 161; training 42–43, 110, 124–125; co–educational 50, 58; military 50, 52, 60, 103–104, 106, 153, 155, 180, 253, 317, 330; combat/infantry 51, 112, 151, 157–158, 253, 317–318, 321, 412; basic 65, 77, 95–96, 153, 178, 188–189, 199, 204–205, 213, 355n19, 394; occupational/job 165, 256, 278, 286, 293, 333, 402; Reserve Officer Training Corps (ROTC) 76; education and training 236, 268, 413; diversity 237; providers (health/healthcare) 330
trait self-objectification 68
Trasler, J., and Doerksen, T. 330
trauma: organizational 194, 348, 367; sexual 307, 322, 333, 343, 347, 378; invisibility 2; psychological/emotional 160, 317, 324, 382; see also military sexual trauma (MST) 3, 14, 50, 106, 148, 303, 307, 320, 323, 343–347, 361–371, 378; PTSD 50, 105, 152, 307, 320, 323, 347, 354n14, 378, 412; post traumatic slave syndrome (PTSS) 237; wicked problems and health/healthcare 308, 320, 326–327; gender informed 319
traumatic brain injuries (TBI) 323, 331
Treasure of the City of Ladies, The (de Pisan) 27
tribalism 312
Tronto, J. 406–407
true women 386
Trump, D. 90, 147–148, 158, 165, 228, 416
Truth, S. 11–12, 15, 74–75
Tubman, H. 30, 34, 157, 248, 256
Turner, H., and Westwood, J. 83, 211
Turner, M.E., and Pratkanis, A.R. 133, 236

Ukman, J. 417
Underground Railroad 30, 34, 248
underrepresented minority (URM) 13, 210, 232, 235, 260–261, 263, 284, 365
unemployment 108, 261, 265–268, *266–267*, 271, 313**–315, 319, 331**
Uniform Code of Military Justice (UCMJ) 291–296, 298–300, 351, 355n17, 361, 363–365, 400, 418–420; Article 15 291–292; Article 120 351, 363
Union Army 30, 34, 157, 248, 256
United States v. Schwimmer (1928) 120, 413
University of Michigan 421
unwanted sexual contact (USC) 352, 352, 355n23
Urban II, Pope 227
U.S. Air Force Academy (USAFA) i, 3, 36, 54, 56, 58, 67, 92, 98, 103, 105–106, 144–145, 154–157, 161, 162, 185–186, 189–191, 200, 202–203, 212, 214, 249, 254, 256,

279, 291, 294–295, 300, 309, 328, 345, 346, 351, 355n17, 362–363, 370n1, 401, 402, 404, 418, 421; Honor Code 203
U.S. Air Force (USAF) 3, 36, 54, 56, 58, 67, 92, 98, 103, 105–106, 144–145, 154–157, 161–162, 185–186, 189–191, 200, 202–203, 212, 214, 249, 254, 256, 279, 291, 294–295, 300, 309, 328, 345–346, 351, 355n17, 362–363, 370n1, 401–402, 404, 418, 421; Officer Qualifying Test (AFOQT) 58, 162; Preventive Medicine and Public Health unit 328; Space Command (AFSPC) 67; Specialty Codes (AFSC) 411; wingman culture 404
U.S. Army 15, 23, 29–31, 33–34, 39–44, 50–53, 55, 57–60, 66, 81, 84, 92, 94–95, 99, 103, 105–106, 113, 121, 143, 146, 149–150, 156–160, 162–163, 176, 179–180, 185–187, 200–205, 213–214, 224–225, 248–250, 254, 256, 279–280, 309, 315, 321, 325–327, 345–346, 351, 355n17, 355n19, 362–363, 366, 388, 401, 403–405, 420–421; Aberdeen Proving Ground (APG) 99, 202, 351, 355n19, 362; Army Air Force 249, 363; Center for Health Promotion & Preventive Medicine (ACHPPM) 326–328; 11th Brigade 204; U.S. (Army) Military Academy (West Point) 66, 180, 188, 200–201, 203; National Guard (ARNG) 388; Nurse Corps (ANC) 248, 315; Occupational Health Program for Soldiers (Fort Campbell) 325; Ranger School 186
U.S. Coast Guard (USCG) 103, 106, 119, 154, 248, 255, 279, 287, 297, 345, 354n1, 354n16, 355n17, 355n20, 362–363, 371n2, 401, 402; Academy (USCGA) 354n1, 362; Reserve 279
U.S. Department of Defense (DoD): personnel needs 128–129; workforce 162–165, 215–216, 309–311, 349–351, 363–364, 368–370, 419–420; Directive 1010.10 (Health Promotion and Disease Prevention) 311; Directive 5500.7 (Standards of Conduct) 400; Directive 6495.01 (Sexual Assault Prevention and Response) 362; Instruction 6055.1 (Occupational Safety Health Program) 324–325; Sexual Assault Task Force 362; Workplace and Gender Relations Survey (WGRS) 351, 353
U.S. Department of Education 379
U.S. Department of Homeland Security (DHS) 103, 255, 279, 287, 354n1–2
U.S. Department of Justice (DOJ) 319
U.S. Department of Labor (DOL) 210, 260, 265, 333; Women's Bureau (WB) 323, 331
U.S. Department of the Navy (DoN) 154
U.S. Department of Veterans' Affairs (VA) 4–5, 104–106, 110–111, 308–311, 321–330, 332–334, 368–369; Airborne Hazards and Open Burn Pit Registry 328; HUD–VASH 333; Office of Health Equity (OHE) 311, 324; Office of the Inspector General (OIG) 333; Veterans' Benefits Administration (VBA) 314; Veterans' Health Administration (VHA) 306, 311, 378–379
U.S. Department of War 121
U.S. Marine Corps (USMC) 30, 50, 53–55, 58–59, 82, 103, 106, 113, 121, 145–146, 148, 151–154, 156, 158, 165, 171, 174, 179–180, 186–187, 189, 194–195, 198–199, 215, 239, 250–251, 255, 279–280, 294, 309, 317–318, 321, 345–346, 351, 355n17, 363, 378, 381–382, 384, 388, 401, 418; Marine Corps Recruit Depot Parris Island (MCRD PI) 96, 153–154; Marine Corps Reserve (MCR) 250; scandal 151–153, 171, 174, 180, 195, 198–199, 381–382, 384, 415, 418
U.S. Naval Academy (USNA), also see Naval Academy 15, 82–83, 178, 185, 191, 199–200, 383; Human Relations Council 199; Women Midshipmen Study Group 200; Working Uniform Blue Alpha (WUBA) 191
U.S. Navy (USN) 15, 43, 53, 57, 82, 96–98, 103, 105–106, 150, 152, 154–156, 164, 180–181, 185–187, 189–190, 192, 202, 213–214, 229, 248–250, 255–256, 279, 293–294,

300, 309, 345–346, 351, 355n17, 363, 378, 401–402, 404, 419–420
U.S.S. *Constitution* 30
U.S.S. *Dwight D. Eisenhower* 54
U.S.S. *Hector* 53
U.S.S. *Lexington* 156

value: role conflicts for women, to the armed forces 37, 65, 100, 178, 191, 280, 349, 378, 386–387, 392–394, 401, 407–408; women's equality 265, 268, 284; greedy institutions 83; Selective Service System 128; affirmative action 236; determinants of health 311, 334; wicked problems 380–381; service core values 400–402, 404–406, 420–421
Van Crevald, M. 49–50, 61, 144, 157
Velasquez, L.J. 30, 303
Velesquez, M., and Andre, C. 329, 406
Velasquez *et al.* 418–419, 426
Vessey Jr, J. 180, 194
Veterans Access, Choice and Accountability Act (2014) 106
Veterans and Agent Orange (1996) 326
Veterans Benefits Administration (VBA) 314
Veterans Equal Rights Protection Advocacy (VERPA) 297–299
Veterans of Foreign Wars (VFW) 322–323, 326, 330
Veterans Health Administration (VHA) 306, 311, 378–379
Veterans Legal Services Clinic (Yale University) 316
victims: adverse treatment of sexual assault victims 66–67, 152, 187, 195, 202, 322, 343–348, 350, 352, 354n4, 354n6, 355n21, 361, 363–370; services and support 364, 370; women as victims 49, 66–68, 84, 91, 161, 247, 380, 382, 411
Viet Cong 254, 325
Vietnam Conflict (1955–1975) 13, 40, 55–57, 60, 70, 105–106, *107*, 109, 120–121, 158, 161, 163, 180, 188, 190, 204, 252–254, 256, 265, *266,* 325–326, 329, 332, 335n6, 388, 411, 416; biopsychosocial outcomes 388–389; combat exclusion policy 158, 163; culture of domination 188, 190; determinants of health 325–326, 329, 332; effeminization of enemy 204; post- 56, 180, 411; role of equalizers 265; and Selective Service Act 120–121; Tet Offensive (1968) 55–56, 161, 254; veteran selection 105–106; women as other 40; women as proxies for men 252–254, 256; women as sex objects 70; women as supporters and caregivers 55–57, 60
violence: against women (and sexual) 1, 40, 66, 178–179, 188, 190, 193–194, 201–202, 307, 316, 331, 343, 345, 351, 354n5, 366, 385, 404, 411–412, 414, 420; health 7–8, 178–179, 193–194, 201–202, 376–377, *380,* 381–383, 394–395, 403–404; collective 379; interpersonal 378; self-directed 377–378; typology 377–382; wicked problems 303, 307, 324, 366, 387–394, 420; ethics 401, 403–404
Vojdik, V.K. 1, 36
volatile organic compounds (VOCs) 328
Voting Rights Act (1965) 100

Wagner DeCrew, J. 4, 12, 16, 52, 228, 285
Walker, J.A., and Borbely, J.M. 13, 58, 106–108, *107*, 265, *266–267,* 268–269, *270,* 416
War of 1812 (1812–1815) 30, 33, 255
War Horse, The 152
warrant officers 52, 111, 291, 309, 362, 371n4
Warren, E. 181, 245
warriors: women 6–7, 16, 20–31,33, 52, 221, 223–224, 226, 303, 313–331, 334, 415, 402; CMW paradigm (Traditionalists) 36, 44, 65–67, 71, 77, 127, 143, 151, 174, 178–180, 189, 194, 201, 310–312, 334, 386, 391, 412, 406–407; and military 29–31; spirit 65, 77, 174, 178–179, 189, 201, 405, 412, 420
Webber, M.M., and Rittel, H.W. 7, 235, 263, 312, 343, 381–384, 388, 420
Wechsler Segal, M. 4, 13, 31, 51–52, 59, 77, 144, 158, 185, 209, 228, 255, 265, 285–286, 417; and Segal, D. 265, 286, 417
Weick, K.E. 310, 312, 384
Weinberger, C. 150
Weiss v. United States (1994) 294
Welsh, M. 295

Welsh military 26, 225
Westwood, J., and Turner, H. 83, 211
white male culture 55, 93
white male privilege 172–181, 237, 414
wicked problems 7–8, 108, 226, 235, 263, 303–334, 343–355, 361, 364–365, 376, *380,* 381–385, 388, 395, 403–405, 407–408, 412, 420–422; women/MST 8, 226, 235, 263, 343, 361, 420; ERA 8; homelessness 108; framing/framework 376, 383–385; in violence and health 303–334, 381–382, 388–391; ethics 403–405, 407–408
Wilkerson, J. 295
William of Malmesbury 26
Williams, G. 407
Williams, I. and Bernstein, K. 347, 370
Wilmot, M. 50–51, 110–111
Wilson, B.A. 51–52
Wilson, W. 121
Wilson, W.J. 231
Wolfenbarger, J. 185
Women Accepted for Volunteer Emergency Services (WAVES) 249–250
Women in the Air Force (WAF) 212, 254
Women Airforce Service Pilots (WASPs) 71, 104, 121, 250, 255
Women in the Army (WITA) 150, 248
Women Content in Units Force Development Test (MAXWAC) 150
Women in International Security (WIIS) 186–187
Women's Armed Services Integration Act (1948) 121, 146, 154, 229, 279, 392
Women's Army Auxiliary Corps (WAAC) 249–250
Women's Army Corps (WAC) 94, 150
Women's Bureau (WB) 58, 106–08, 260, 268–269, 323, 331
women's corps 279, 392
Women's Rights Convention (Ohio, 1851) 11
Women's Rights Project (ACLU) 135, 368, 419
Wong, L. and Gerras, S. 402–403, 405, 421
Wood, R. 312

Woods, D. 41
Working Uniform Blue Alpha (WUBA) 191
Workplace and Gender Relations Survey (WGRS) 351, 353
World Economic Forum (WEF), *Global Gender Gap Report* (2016) 381, 387
World Health Organization (WHO) 306, 327, 377; Commission on Social Determinants of Health (CSDH) 306; *World Report on Violence and Health* 377
World War I (1914–1918) 31, 34, 69, 104, 121, 143, 149, 180, 248, 256
World War II (1939–1945) 1, 7, 13, 31, 34, 55, 57, 83, 94, 105–106, *107,* 109, 121, 162, 176, 179 185, 188–189, 198, 203, 248, 256, 265, *266,* 278–279, 286, 316, 386, 392; agency and second-class status 91–99; biopsychosocial outcomes 386, 392; combat exclusion policy 162; culture of domination 185, 188–189; determinants of health 316; effeminization of enemy 203–204; marginalization 83; military selection 278–279; representative bureaucracy 286; role of equalizers 265; Selective Service Act 121; veteran selection 105–106; white male privilege 176; women as other 34; women as proxies for men 248, 250–253, 256; women as supporters and caregivers 55, 57; women as warriors 31

Yanz, L., and Randal, M. 160
Yeager, C. 189
Yermonks, Battle of 28
Yoder, J.D. 7, 75–76, 211, 232, 234
Yoruba people 23, 224
Young, G.K. 381–382
Young, I.M. 99
Yourdon, E. 412

Zazzau, Queen of 23
Zenobia, Queen 25–26, 225
Zero-tolerance: 187, 351; policy, 367
Zimmer, L. 76, 176, 232
Zoli, C. *et al.* 106, 109–112